# The Pearson Custom Program for CIS

In Business
Manzo
Excel

**Pearson Learning Solutions**

New York Boston San Francisco
London Toronto Sydney Tokyo Singapore Madrid
Mexico City Munich Paris Cape Town Hong Kong Montreal

***Senior Vice President, Editorial and Marketing:*** Patrick F. Boles
***Editor:*** Ana Díaz-Caneja
***Development Editor:*** Christina Martin
***Operations Manager:*** Eric M. Kenney
***Production Manager:*** Jennifer Berry
***Art Director:*** Renée Sartell
***Cover Designers:*** Blair Brown and Kristen Kiley

*Cover Art:* Jerry Driendl/Getty Images, Inc.; Steve Bloom/Getty Images, Inc.; "Cheetah" courtesy of Marvin Mattelson/Getty Images; "Tabs" courtesy of Andrey Prokhorov/iStockphoto; "Open Doors" courtesy of Spectral-Design/iStockphoto; "Compass" courtesy of Laurent Hamels/Getty Images; "Fortune Teller" courtesy of Ingvald Kaldhussaeter/iStockphoto; "Ladder of Success" courtesy of iStockphoto; "Global Communication in Blue" courtesy of iStockphoto.



This special edition published in cooperation with Pearson Learning Solutions.

Printed in the United States of America.

Please visit our web site at *www.pearsoncustom.com/custom-library/custom-phit.*

Attention bookstores: For permission to return any unsold stock, contact us at *pe-uscustomreturns@pearson.com.*

Pearson Learning Solutions, 501 Boylston Street, Suite 900, Boston, MA 02116
A Pearson Education Company
www.pearsoned.com

ISBN 10: 1-256-18874-3
ISBN 13: 978-1-256-18874-2

# Contents

# Introduction

## Chapter Goals

Few software programs have elevated the importance of desktop computers for business managers as much as Microsoft Excel. Similar to the way they use e-mail, business managers use Excel every day to accomplish their daily routines and objectives. This chapter provides a general overview of Excel and the reasons it is such a vital tool for business managers. It is important to note the basic terminology covered in this chapter.

## >> Excel Skill Sets

**What Is Excel?**

- Why Are We Here?
- A Decision-Making Tool
- An Overview of Excel
- Ribbons, Tabs, and Icons
- The File Menu
- Excel 97–2003 File Format
- Right Click and Control Keys
- Settings and Status Bar
- Excel Help

Pearson Education/PH College

# Excel in Practice | Anecdote

### Excel in Business

Over the course of my career, I have experienced how information systems have changed the ways in which business professionals manage data and make decisions. I am often amazed when I think back to the beginning of my career and remember the analytical projects I used to do on paper. Doing these same projects on paper today would be unthinkable. Excel played a significant role in this transformation. In fact, the ways in which I used Excel throughout my career seemed to grow every year. I initially used Excel once in a while to project the monthly sales of my department. However, it was not long before I was using Excel every day to complete objectives such as managing inventory, tracking orders, communicating production plans, or developing sales strategies.

I have used Excel to complete business objectives in industries such as fashion, grocery, food, toys, finance, and technology. These are all real business objectives and situations that actually happened in my career, and you may be faced with these same objectives at some point in your own career.

>> Continued in this Chapter

# What Is Excel?

The focus of this text will be to illustrate how you can use Excel to complete a variety of business objectives. However, it is important to understand why Excel was created and the need it fulfills for business managers. In addition, you will need a basic understanding of the ways commands and features are accessed and activated. This section provides a fundamental definition of Excel and illustrates its basic functionality.

## Why Are We Here?

In its most basic form, Excel is an electronic version of a paper ***spreadsheet***. The primary use of any spreadsheet is to record numeric and text ***data*** for the purposes of making calculations, analyzing results, or tracking and storing information. As mentioned in the anecdote, before the use of electronic spreadsheets such as Excel, spreadsheets were created by hand on paper. Figure 1 shows an example of a paper spreadsheet. Notice that it consists of numbered columns and rows. Each digit of a number is written in a separate rectangle on the spreadsheet. An Excel spreadsheet has a similar purpose and design.

Figure 1 | **Example of Paper Spreadsheet**

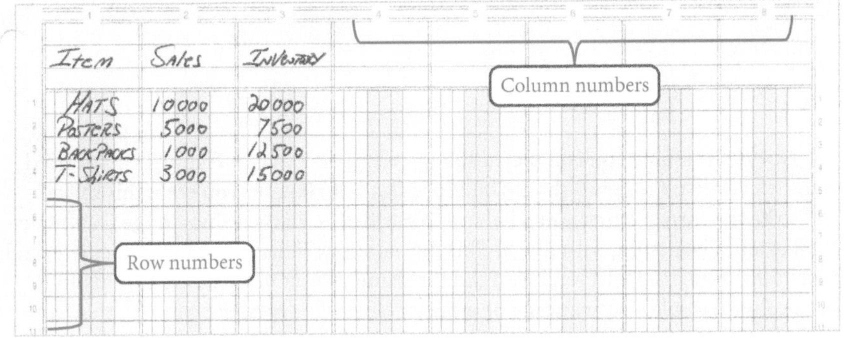


Figure 2 shows an example of a sales analysis project for 100 items sold in a small retail store. Because this project was done on a paper spreadsheet, the sales results for all 100 items are written by hand. In addition, a cumulative total is added in the second column to show the total after adding the sales results for each item. As a result, 100 calculations were performed using a calculator and added to the spreadsheet by hand. Just think how long it would take to write 100 numbers and make 100 calculations for this simple project.

Figure 2 | **Sales Project Done on Paper Spreadsheet**

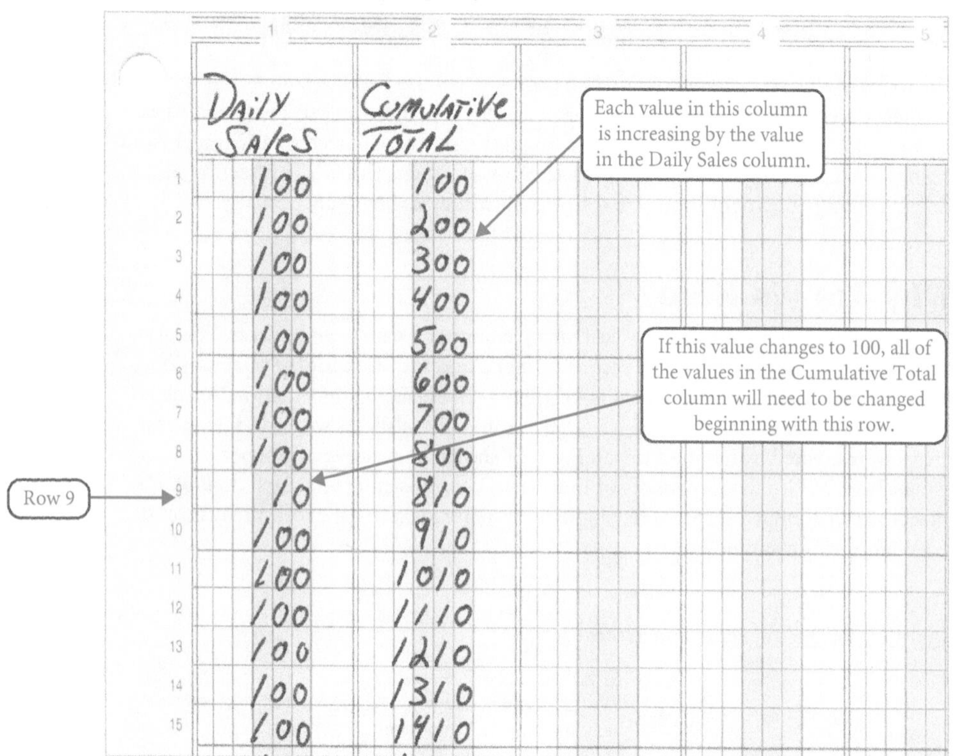


Now, let's assume you completed the spreadsheet shown in Figure 2 and noticed that the sales result in row 9 should be 100 instead of 10. After you erase this mistake and write the correct entry, you will have to recalculate all the values in the Cumulative Total column beginning with row 9. This means you will have to erase, recalculate, and rewrite 92 numbers. However, if you did this same project in Excel, the Cumulative Total column would automatically be adjusted after you typed the correct value into row 9. In fact, an Excel spreadsheet could be created such that if any of the numbers in your project are changed, all computations will automatically produce new outputs in a fraction of a second. This is what makes Excel extremely valuable for making business decisions and sets it apart from a paper spreadsheet.

Figure 3 shows how the project in Figure 2 appears in Excel. Notice that the column and row configuration are similar to the paper spreadsheet. However, letters are used to label each column instead of numbers.

Figure 3 | **Example of Project in an Excel Spreadsheet**

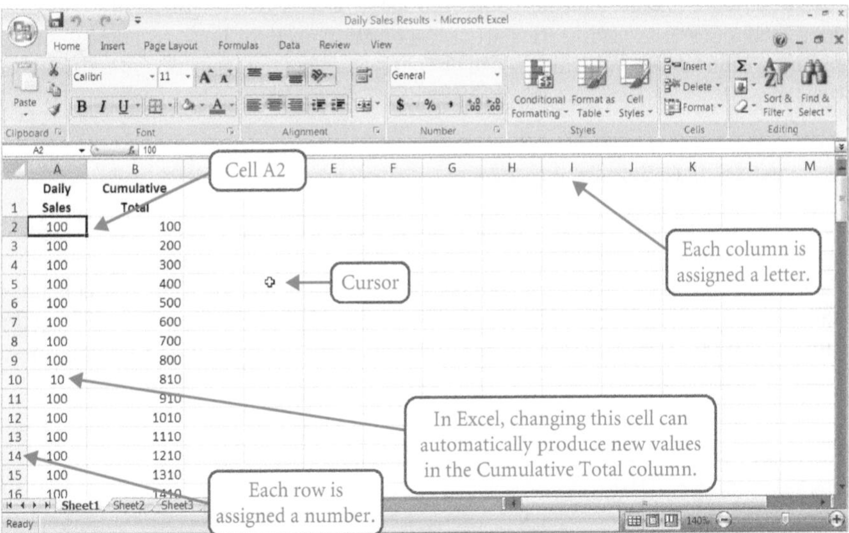


Another similarity between Figures 2 and 3 is that both spreadsheets are filled with small rectangles. In Excel, these rectangles are known as ***cells***, which is the intersection of a row and column. Data is typed into these cells as opposed to being handwritten, as shown in Figure 2. Each cell has a specific address called the ***cell location***, which is the column letter followed by the row number. In Figure 3, cell location A2 is activated. This is called cell *A2* because it is in column A and row 2.

Cell locations play a critical role when calculating data in Excel. If you were conducting mathematical computations using a calculator, you would enter numbers and mathematical operators to produce a result. With Excel, you will usually use cell locations, such as A2, instead of numbers when conducting the same mathematical computations. If the number in cell A2 is changed, Excel will automatically produce a new output. This is called ***cell referencing***, and it is this concept that gives Excel its power.

## A Decision-Making Tool

Business managers are often required to make numerous decisions in uncertain environments. These decisions can range from buying a publicly traded stock to calculating how many pairs of jeans to buy for a clothing store. In making these decisions, a business manager might ask questions such as "What if the stock market declines after buying a particular stock?" or "What if I don't buy enough jeans to satisfy the sales potential of a store?" These questions form the basis of ***what-if scenarios***. Business managers use what-if scenarios to understand how potential outcomes will impact the decisions they make. For example, a business manager who is buying a publicly traded stock might calculate how much he stands to lose if the stock declines 5%, 10%, or 20%. On the other hand, he could also calculate how much he could gain if the stock increases 5%, 10%, or 20%. Calculating these declines and increases equates to a total of six possible scenarios or outcomes to consider before making this decision. This manager could use Excel to calculate the results of each scenario by simply changing one number.

Most business executives would agree that information is power. Excel can be used to produce and evaluate far more information over a shorter period of time compared to paper spreadsheets. This fulfills a critical need for business managers to make informed decisions, which is usually a prerequisite for completing most business objectives.

## An Overview of Excel

When you first launch the Excel application, you will see a blank spreadsheet or worksheet, as shown in Figure 4. The term ***worksheet*** is used to describe one page of an Excel file or workbook. The term ***workbook*** refers to the entire Excel file that contains a collection of worksheets. You can switch from one worksheet to another by clicking the tabs at the bottom of the screen. Each worksheet has a capacity of over 1 million rows and over 16,000 columns.

Figure 4 | **Blank Excel Worksheet**

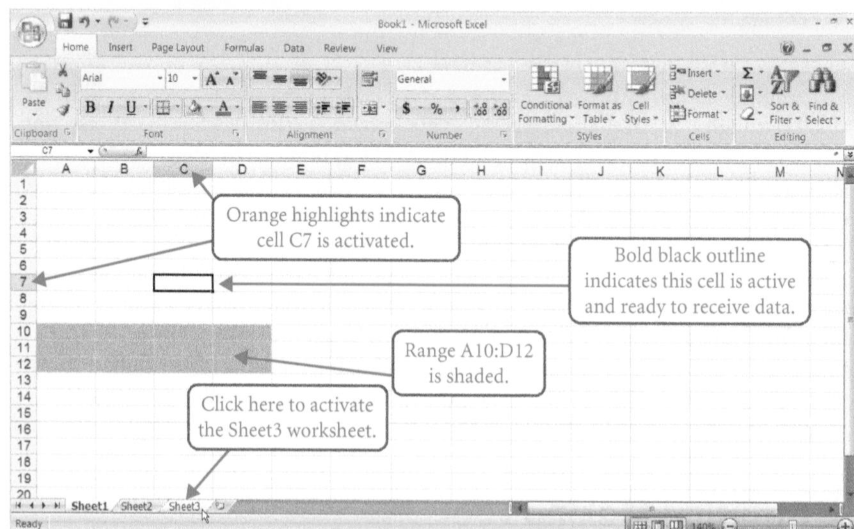


As shown in Figure 4, the highlighted column letter and row number indicate which cell is currently active. Notice that column letter C and row number 7 are highlighted in orange, indicating that cell C7 is active and ready to receive data. The cell is also outlined with a bold black line, which also indicates it is active. To activate other cells, use the arrow keys on your keyboard to move the black outline or move the cursor with the mouse and left click on a cell. You also can use your mouse to activate several cells or a range of cells at one time by left clicking and dragging. The term ***range*** refers to a group of cells on a worksheet and is noted by any two cell locations separated by a colon. For example, Figure 4 shows the range A10:D12 highlighted.

## Ribbon, Tabs, and Icons

Excel commands and features are contained in the area at the top of the screen called the ***Ribbon***. As shown in Figure 5, the Ribbon consists of several ***icons*** arranged in related groups that are used to activate any Excel command. For example, the **Number** group of icons is used to format any numbers that are typed into the cells of a worksheet. If you are familiar with Microsoft Word, you already know how to use many of these icons. For example, Excel icons such as **Save**, **Copy**, **Paste**, and **Bold** are identical to Word's icons.

Along the top of the Ribbon are several ***tabs***. Each tab opens a separate page of the Ribbon that contains a different set of icons. Additional tabs will automatically be added to the Ribbon if you are working with special objects such as charts or text boxes. You will learn how to use the commands in each tab of the Ribbon throughout this text. The following is a brief description for each of the tabs shown in Figure 5:

- **Home**: Contains fundamental commands that are most frequently used when working in Excel. Commonly used icons such as **Copy** and **Paste** as well as formatting icons such as **Bold** and **Italics** are found in this tab.
- **Insert**: Contains commands used when inserting objects such as charts, circles, or arrows onto a worksheet.
- **Page Layout**: Provides access to commands used to prepare a worksheet for printing.
- **Formulas**: Provides access to mathematical functions and formula auditing tools.
- **Data**: Provides access to sorting commands. In addition, this tab contains features used to import data from external sources such as Microsoft Access.
- **Review**: Provides access to commands such as Spell Check and Track Changes.
- **View**: Contains commands used for adjusting the visual appearance of your Excel screen. For example, this tab contains the **Zoom** icon, which is identical to the **Zoom** icon in Microsoft Word.

Figure 5 shows icons that are contained in the **Home** tab of the Ribbon. Notice that when the cursor is placed over the **Copy** icon, a description of the command appears on the worksheet.

Figure 5 | **The Home Tab of the Ribbon**

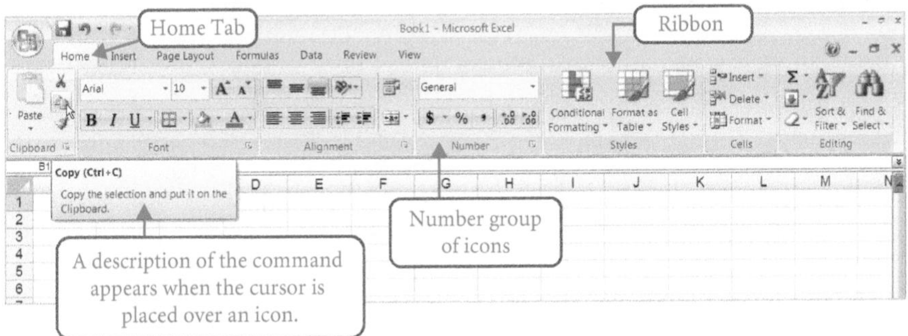


In addition to using the Ribbon, you can also access Excel commands through the ***Quick Access Toolbar***. The **Quick Access Toolbar** contains a few commonly used icons such as **Save** and **Undo**. As you can see in Figure 6, you can add additional icons by clicking the down arrow on the right side of the toolbar and selecting one of the commands listed in the menu or by clicking the **More Commands** option.

Figure 6 | **The Quick Access Toolbar**

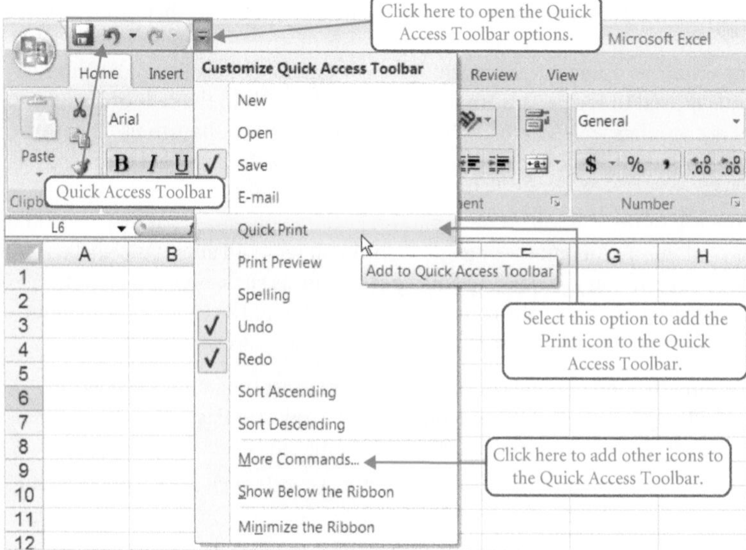


## The File Menu

If you have worked with previous versions of Microsoft Excel, such as Microsoft Excel 2003, you may have noticed that something was missing when you first looked at Figure 3. There are no drop-down menus. The drop-down menus have been replaced with the Ribbon system, which provides faster access to the commands you need. However, one drop-down menu does exist in this version of Excel: The **File** menu. The file menu is opened by clicking the **Office Button** as shown in Figure 7. Use the **File** menu for executing tasks such as opening existing Excel workbooks, creating new workbooks, or printing worksheets. Figure 7 shows the commands that are available in the **File** menu.

Figure 7 | **Commands in the File Menu**

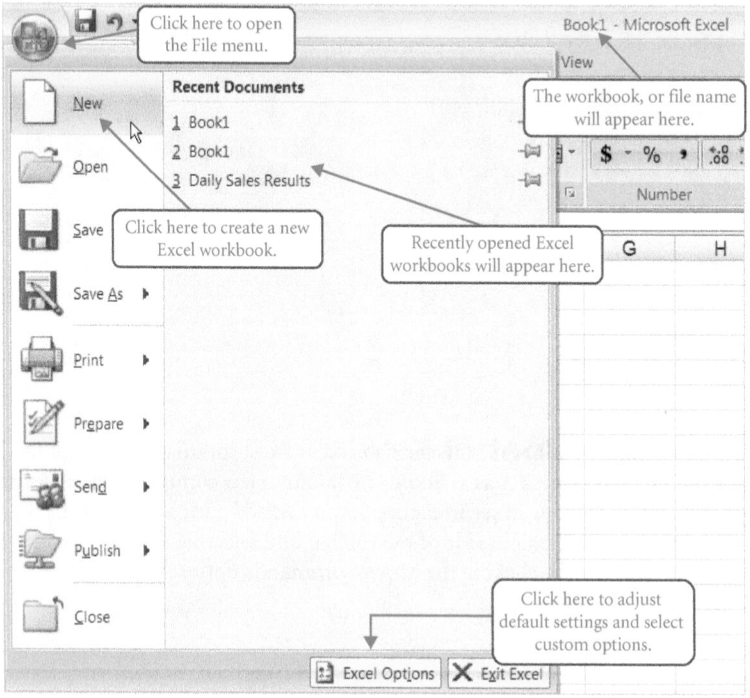

## Excel 97-2003 File Format

It is important to note that the **Save As** command is found in the **File** menu. If you are working with people who are using older versions of Microsoft Excel, you will need to save your workbooks in the Excel 97–2003 format. Someone who is using Microsoft Office 2003 will not be able to open workbooks saved in the 2007 format. You save files in this format as follows:

- Open an existing Excel workbook or create a new one (see Figure 7).
- Click the **Office Button.**
- Click the arrow pointing to the right next to the **Save As** option.
- Select the **Excel 97-2003 Workbook** option on the right side of the **File** menu (see Figure 8).

Figure 8 shows an Excel workbook that has been saved in the Excel 97–2003 format. Notice at the top of the Excel screen the words **[Compatibility Mode]** appear next to the workbook name. This naming convention indicates that the workbook is compatible with older versions of Excel. In addition, notice that the **Convert** option appears in the **File** menu list of options. Select this option to convert a workbook saved in an older version of Excel to the 2007 version.

Figure 8 | **Saving a Workbook in Excel 97–2003 Format**

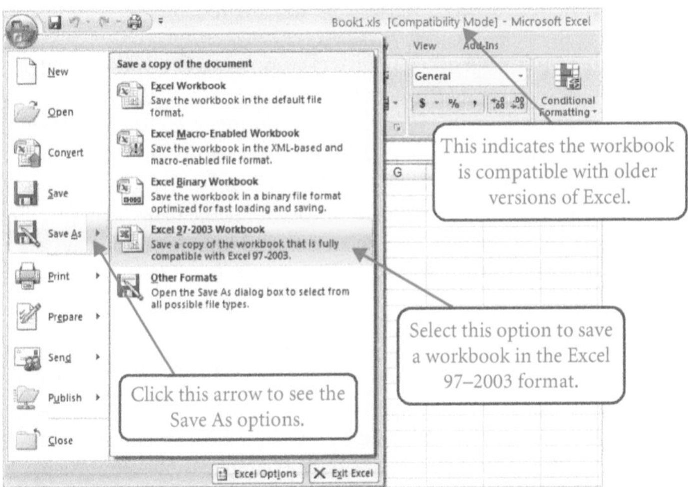


### COMMON MISTAKES | Opening Excel 2007 Workbooks

You will not be able to open an Excel 2007 workbook using Excel 2003 or other prior versions of Excel. Excel workbooks with the .xlsx file extension can be opened only in the 2007 version of Microsoft Office. You must convert or save these workbooks using the Excel 97–2003 format to open them using an older version of Excel.

>> **Quick Reference**

**Saving in Excel 97-2003 File Format**

1. Open an existing Excel workbook or create a new one.
2. Click the **Office Button**.
3. Click the arrow to the right of the **Save As** option.
4. Click the **Excel 97-2003 Workbook** option on the right side of the **File** menu.
5. Select a location and type a file name in the **Save As** dialog box.

## Right Click and Control Keys

If you have experience using older versions of Excel, you may be accustomed to accessing commands by right clicking or using Control keys. Both options are available in the 2007 version of Excel.

Right clicking provides you with the option of accessing a variety of commands without having to go to the Ribbon. As previously mentioned, older versions of Excel utilized a system of drop-down menus to access various Excel commands. Depending on the command you needed, you may have clicked through several drop-down menus to complete a task. However, the Ribbon system in the 2007 version of Excel considerably reduces the amount of clicking you need to do before activating a command. Therefore, you may or may not find right clicking useful. Figure 9 shows the Excel commands and icons that appear after the right mouse button is clicked on a worksheet. These options will change when you are working with other objects on a worksheet such as charts or text boxes.

Figure 9 | **Options When Right Clicking**

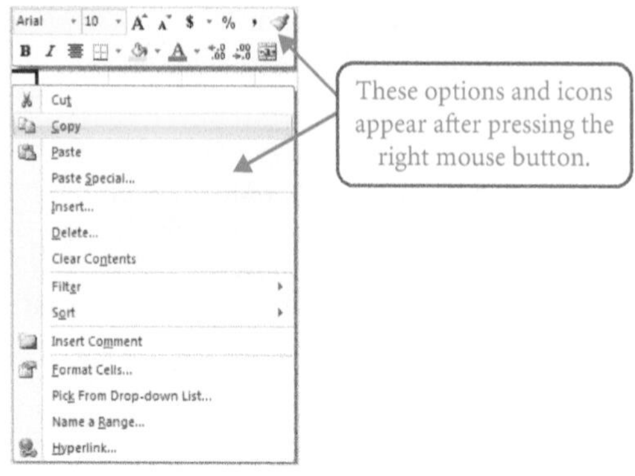


As mentioned, the other option for accessing Excel commands is through Control keys. In the earliest version of Microsoft Office, using Control keys was the primary method for accessing commands. That is, you activated a command by holding down the **Ctrl** key on your keyboard and pressing a letter or character. You can still use this system in Microsoft Office 2007. For several icons in the Ribbon, there is a corresponding **Ctrl** key combination. In fact, notice that the description for the **Copy** icon in Figure 5 shows that this command can also be activated by holding down the **Ctrl** key and pressing the letter C.

## Settings and Status Bar

You have the ability to customize the settings and ***Status Bar*** of the Excel screen. For example, when you first open Excel, all data typed into a worksheet will have a Calibri font style with an 11-point font size. However, you can change this to whatever font style and font size you wish. The following explains how to change these settings:

- Click the **Office Button.**
- Click the **Excel Options** button at the bottom of the menu (see Figure 7). This will open the **Excel Options** dialog box.
- Click the **Popular** option on the left side of the **Excel Options** dialog box.
- Click the down arrow next to the **Use this font** option. This option can be found under the section heading **When creating new workbooks.**
- Select a new font style.
- Click the **OK** button at the bottom of the dialog box. For some settings, you may have to close and reopen Excel for any change to take place.

Figure 10 shows the options in the **Popular** section of the **Excel Options** dialog box. Notice that there are several other options you can adjust to customize the settings of your Excel screen such as the font size and your user name.

Figure 10 | **Excel Options Dialog Box**

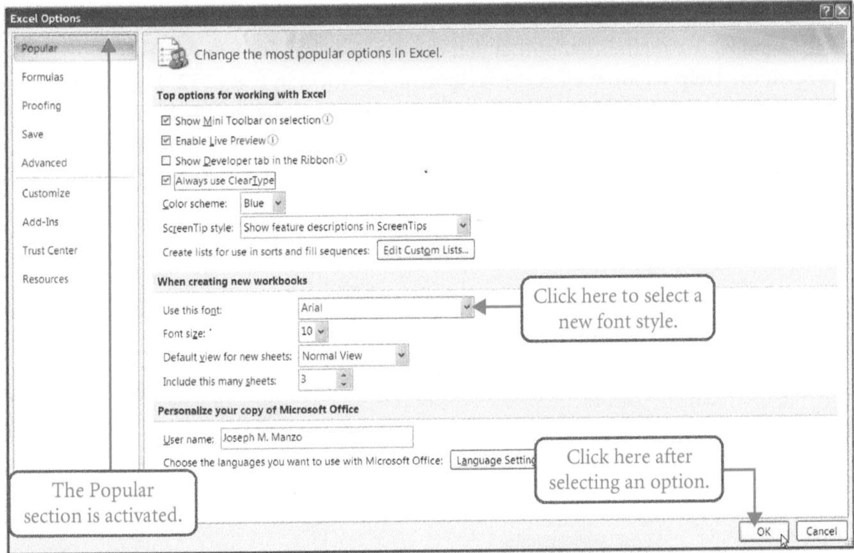


You can also customize the appearance of the Status bar at the bottom of the Excel screen. The Status bar in Figure 11 contains shortcuts for switching between various views as well as the Zoom Slider. To change what is displayed on the Status bar, place the cursor anywhere in the Status bar and right click. This will open the list of options shown in Figure 11.

Figure 11 | **Status Bar Options List**

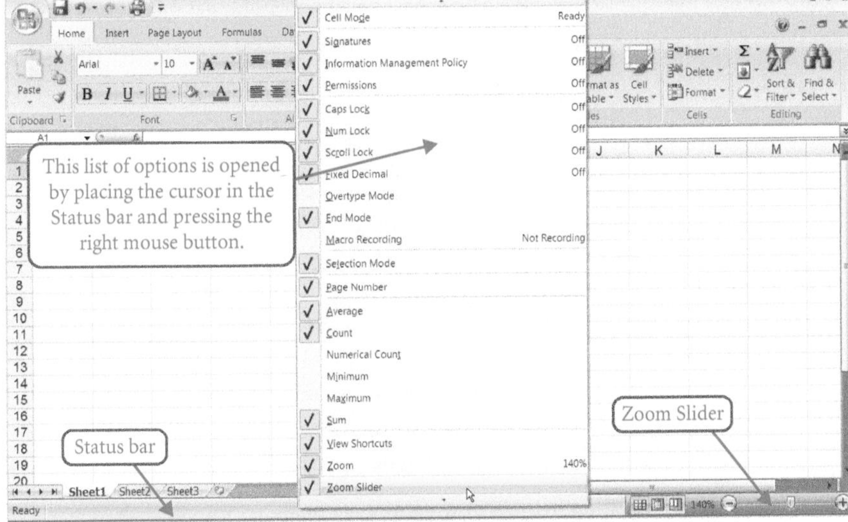


> **Quick Reference**
>
> **Changing the Font Setting for New Workbooks**
>
> 1. Open a blank Excel workbook.
> 2. Click the **Office Button**.
> 3. Click the **Excel Options** button.
> 4. Click the **Popular** section on the left side of the **Excel Options** dialog box.
> 5. Select a font style and size in the **When creating new workbooks** section of the **Excel Options** dialog box.
> 6. Click the **OK** button at the bottom of the dialog box.

## Excel Help

The last area that will be covered in this introduction to Excel is the **Help** window. The **Help** window is a reference tool that you can use to research various Excel commands. To open the **Help** window, click the **Help** icon, as shown in Figure 12. Then type a question or topic in the input box of the **Help** window and press the **Enter** key or click the **Search** button. You will then see a list of links that contain topics related to what you typed into the input box. Click a link to see instructions and information related to your topic.

Figure 12 | **The Help Window**

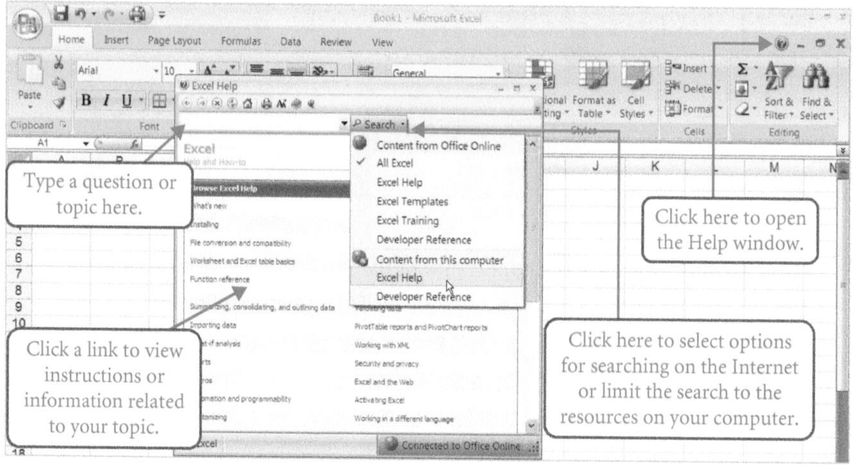
Type a question or topic here.
Click a link to view instructions or information related to your topic.
Click here to open the Help window.
Click here to select options for searching on the Internet or limit the search to the resources on your computer.

## >> Introduction to Excel

VIDEO WORKSHOP

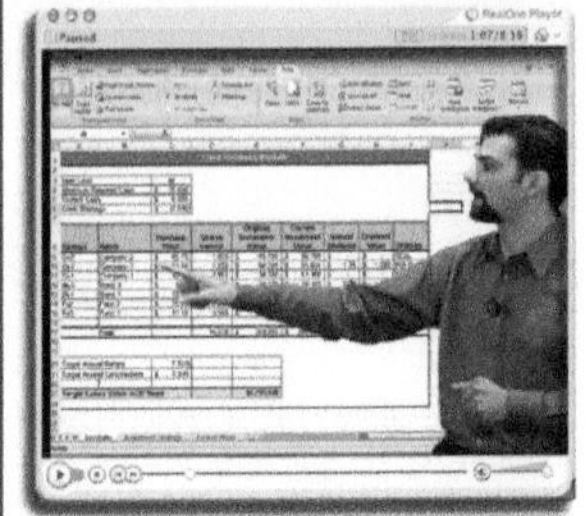

The purpose of this workshop is to open a blank Excel workbook and examine a few of the basic features that were described in this chapter. Try completing each task and then watch the video named **Introduction**.

1. **Open Excel (Video: Introduction)**
   a. Launch the Excel application.
   b. Use the up and down arrows to activate cell C7.
   c. Use the mouse to activate cell E3.
   d. Highlight the range B5:G10.
   e. Click each tab of the Ribbon and view the icons that are showing in each tab.
   f. Click the **Office Button** and save your workbook in Excel 97–2003 format. Save the workbook to any location on your computer and use any file name you wish.
   g. Activate **Sheet2** by clicking the worksheet tab.
   h. Use the Zoom Slider to increase the zoom to 140%.
   i. Open the **Help** window.
   j. Change the Search Option in the **Help** window to `Excel Help - Content from this computer`.
   k. Close the **Help** window.
   l. Close your workbook and then close Excel.

**EXERCISE**

**Why Do I Need This?**

## Cell Referencing

### Exercise

Cell referencing is Excel's most critical feature because it allows you to produce many mathematical outputs by changing just one or many inputs. The purpose of this exercise is to provide an introduction to Excel by looking at how cell referencing is used in the sales project example from the beginning of the chapter. You will need to open the file named ib_e01_dailysalesresults before completing the tasks in this exercise.

1. Activate cell A10. The number in this cell should be 10. Notice that the number in cell B10 is 810. This number is the result of a formula that takes the number in cell A10 and adds it to the value in cell B9. Each number in column B is calculated by similar formulas.

2. After activating cell A10, type the number **100**.

3. Press the **Enter** key. The number in cell B10 should change to 900, and every cell below B10 should also change. This is an example of how cell referencing is able to change many outputs by changing just one input.

4. Save and close your file.

Pearson Education/PH College

# Anecdote

Solution

Few tools changed my job performance and decision-making abilities like Excel. With Excel, I was able to evaluate large amounts of information in a fraction of the time it took using a calculator and paper spreadsheet. I was not only more productive, but also more confident about the recommendations and decisions I made. Although the amount of time I spent ensuring that my results were accurate remained the same, once I started using Excel, there was no way I could ever consider going back to paper.

## Questions for Discussion

1. Could a company gain a competitive advantage in its respective industry by having access to more information over its competitors? Why?
2. Does having more information automatically result in better business decisions?
3. The author mentioned that the amount of time ensuring the accuracy of results remained the same. Why wouldn't Excel automatically increase the accuracy of analytical projects?
4. The author mentions that after he started using electronic spreadsheets he could never consider going back to paper. Why do you think this is so?

# Review Questions

This section features questions that will help you review the key concepts and skills that were presented in the chapter. There will always be a mix of Fill in the Blank, True or False, or Short Answer questions. For the True or False questions, if you think an answer is false, provide a short explanation as to why you think the phrase or comment is false.

1. Multiple outcomes or potential results are also known as_________.
2. What methods can you use to activate a cell?
3. True or False: An Excel file is made up of multiple workbooks.
4. A _________ is two cell locations separated by a colon.
5. Excel's capability to automatically produce new mathematical outputs when one or more inputs are changed is possible because of ________________.
6. Commands used to prepare a worksheet for printing can be found in the _________ tab of the Ribbon.
7. True or False: The **Quick Access Toolbar** can contain only four icons, and it must always appear at the top of the Ribbon.
8. You must click the_________ to activate various worksheets in a workbook.
9. Explain how you would open an existing workbook that is saved on your computer.
10. What could you do if you need to send an Excel workbook to someone who is using the 2003 version of Excel?

# > Challenge Question

This section will follow the Skills Exam section and feature questions that require you to apply the skills you have learned to complete typical business objectives. There is usually no right or wrong method for completing the objectives presented in this section. However, the results you obtain must be accurate. This section might also include questions that ask you to identify how Excel or spreadsheets play a role in the success of a business or in the decision-making process of a business.

1. Identify three specific electronic devices or computer software programs that have changed the way you do things to such an extent that you cannot imagine living life without them? Explain the needs these devices or programs satisfy and the benefits they provide.

# Excel Basics

## Chapter Goals

This chapter covers the following basic Excel skills you need to begin creating an Excel spreadsheet: data entry, copy and paste, formatting, editing, and printing. It also features two common types of spreadsheets used in business: Financial Plans and Merchandise Sales Reports. It is important to note that business terms such as Gross Sales, Cost of Goods Sold, Gross Profit, and Unit Sales will be mentioned but not explained in detail. These terms are commonly used in the business world and will be covered in depth in your core business courses.

## >> Excel | Skill Sets

**Data Management**
- Data Entry
- Auto Fill
- Adjusting Columns and Rows
- Hiding Columns and Rows
- Copy and Paste
- Sorting Data (Single Level)
- Sorting Data (Multiple Levels)

**Formatting**
- Data Formats
- Data Alignment
- Number Formats
- Borders (Line Formats)
- Cell Color (Fill Color)

**Editing**
- Editing Data in a Cell
- Moving Data
- Deleting Columns and Rows
- Deleting Worksheets
- Inserting Columns and Rows
- Inserting, Moving, and Renaming Worksheet Tabs

**Printing**
- Page Setup
- Printing a Worksheet

iStockphoto.com

## Excel in Practice | Anecdote

### The Role of a Production Planning Manager

You may think that in business, information is processed and communicated electronically. This is the 21st century, after all. Imagine my surprise when not all that long ago I started working as a production planning manager for a large apparel manufacturing company that produced thousands of garments every year. My role was to manage all of the production plans sent to our offices in China—a seemingly straightforward task, except for the fact that the production plans were handwritten on 17" x 14" paper spreadsheets, reduced in a copy machine, and mailed overnight to China. Each garment had a separate production plan that documented every detail: buttons, color, fabric, labels, zippers, and packaging. And guess what happened if a designer decided to use corduroy instead of denim at the last minute? Out came the correction fluid, followed by a trip to the mailroom for another costly overnight delivery. Communicating information in this cumbersome way was simply part of the company's culture, which I inherited. However, after gallons of correction fluid (and lots of noxious fumes), I decided there had to be a better way to track and communicate this information.

>> Continued later in this Chapter

# Data Management

Skill Set

The different ways Excel spreadsheets are used in business are too numerous to count. However, using spreadsheets to track the sales results of retail merchandise or to create a financial plan are probably the most common. With regards to tracking and planning financial data, business managers typically use spreadsheets to evaluate whether a company is achieving its financial goals in a current year or to plan its financial goals for future years. This section illustrates how you can use Excel's data management skills to begin constructing these spreadsheets. In fact, data management skills such as entering data, adjusting the widths of columns and rows, copying and pasting, and sorting are typically needed in the early stages of developing any spreadsheet.

## Data Entry

***Data entry*** is the most basic and fundamental Excel skill. The term ***data*** refers to any numbers or text items that will be analyzed or displayed on a spreadsheet. In a financial plan, the text items usually typed into an Excel worksheet include a title and the financial category labels, such as Gross Sales, Net Sales, Cost of Goods Sold, and so on. To type a title into a worksheet, do the following:

- Open a blank workbook.
- Activate cell A1 by left clicking it with the mouse, or use the keyboard arrow key to move the black outline to cell A1. The black outline indicates an active cell.
- Type the words Financial Plan.
- Enter the title into cell A1 by performing one of the following actions:
  - Press the **Enter** key.
  - Press one of the arrow keys.
  - Left click another cell location.

Figure 1 shows the title entered into cell A1 as well as the financial category labels entered into cells A3 through A7.

Figure 1 | **Building a Worksheet for Financial Planning**

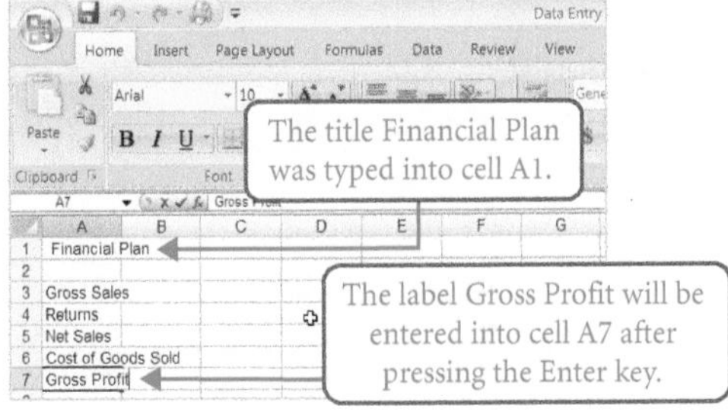


### COMMON MISTAKES | Data Entry

The most common data entry mistake is forgetting to press the **Enter** key after typing an entry. *Data will not be entered into a cell unless you press the **Enter** or arrow keys.* Other data entry mistakes typically occur from typing the wrong number or transposing numbers. For example, the number 253 could be ***transposed*** as 235. Always proofread your spreadsheet for any data entry errors.

When you are entering numeric data, it is good practice to omit any symbols, such as commas. Typing commas to separate thousands (for example, 10,000) for numbers used in functions will prevent the function from working or produce erroneous results. The next section of this chapter reviews how to add symbols, such as commas, dollar signs, percent signs, and so on, to numbers typed into a worksheet.

## Auto Fill

Commonly used in data entry tasks, ***Auto Fill*** automatically completes a set of data points that are in sequential order, such as numbers, years, months, or days of the week. With regards to the Financial Plan worksheet shown in Figure 1, the years 2008 through 2012 will be entered in cells B2 through F2. You can use the **Auto Fill** feature to complete this sequence of years by typing only the first two years in cells B2 and C2. The following points explain how this is accomplished.

- Type the year 2008 in cell B2 and 2009 in cell C2. Two sequential data points must be entered into two adjacent cells to use **Auto Fill**. For example, when completing a series of numbers in 100 unit increments, enter the number 100 into one cell and 200 in another. For creating a daily schedule, enter the word Monday in one cell and Tuesday in another.
- Highlight cells B2 and C2. To use the **Auto Fill** feature, you must have highlighted two cells containing sequential data.
- Place the cursor over the **Auto Fill Handle**. The **Auto Fill Handle** is the black square in the lower-right corner of a highlighted range.
- When you place the cursor over the **Auto Fill Handle**, it will change from a white plus sign to a black plus sign. When this occurs, left click and drag across to the right until the years increase to 2012 (see Figures 2 and 3).

### COMMON MISTAKES | Auto Fill

Remember that to complete a sequence of data using the **Auto Fill** feature, you must highlight two or more adjacent cell locations. If you click and drag the **Auto Fill Handle** when only one cell is activated, you will duplicate the contents of this one cell to other cells without completing any sequence.

Figure 2 | **Typing Years into the Financial Plan Worksheet**

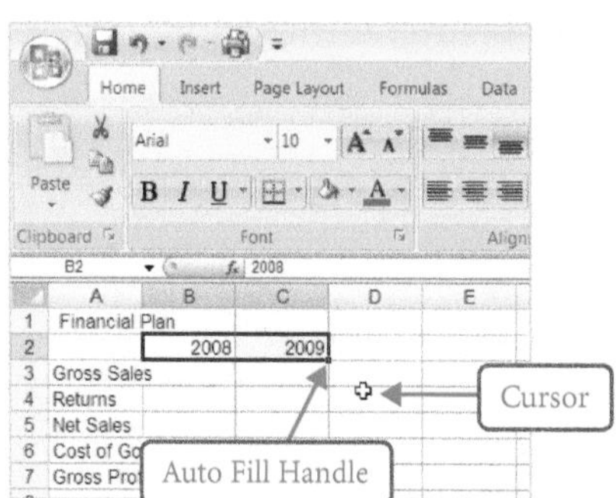


### Quick Reference

**Auto Fill**

1. Enter sequential data into at least 2 adjacent cell locations.
2. Highlight all cell locations containing sequential data.
3. Drag the cursor over the **Auto Fill Handle**.
4. When the cursor changes from a white to a black plus sign, click and drag across or down to continue the sequence of data.

Figure 3 | **Using Auto Fill to Complete the Sequence of Years**

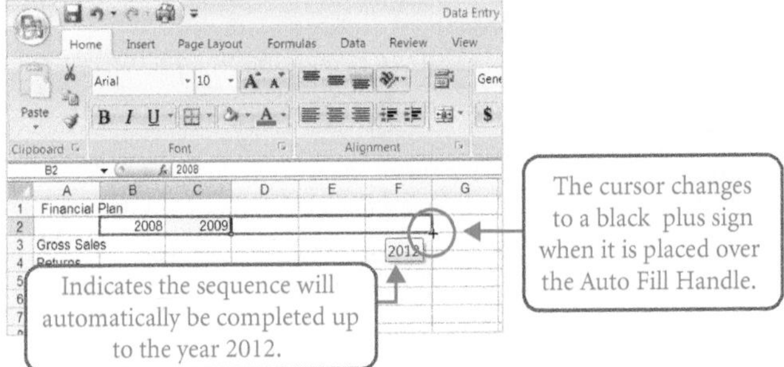

The cursor changes to a black plus sign when it is placed over the Auto Fill Handle.
Indicates the sequence will automatically be completed up to the year 2012.


## Adjusting Columns and Rows

When entering data into a spreadsheet, you may need to adjust the ***column width*** or ***row height,*** depending on the size of your entry. Entries too wide for a particular cell location may extend into one or more columns or appear truncated. For example, notice in Figure 1 that the Cost of Goods Sold entry in cell A6 extends into column B. However, when a number is typed into cell B6, the Cost of Goods Sold entry appears truncated, as shown in Figure 4.

Figure 4 | **Entries Too Long for a Cell Location Appear Truncated**

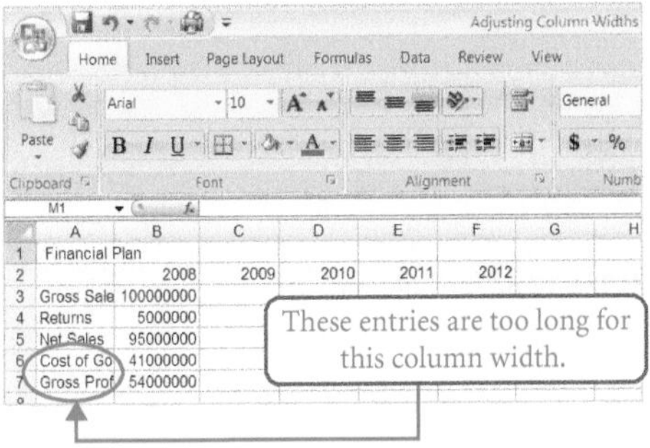


To prevent the entries shown in Figure 4 from being truncated, you will need to expand the width of column A. To accomplish this, do the following:

- Place the cursor between two columns.
- When the cursor changes from a white plus sign to a double black arrow, left click and drag to increase or decrease the column width (see Figure 5).
- Alternatively, when the cursor changes from a white plus sign to a double black arrow, double click with the left mouse button, and the column will automatically expand to fit the longest entry that has been typed. This method is especially helpful when you're working with large spreadsheets where you cannot see the largest entry on your screen.

Figure 5 | **Using the Cursor to Adjust Column Width**

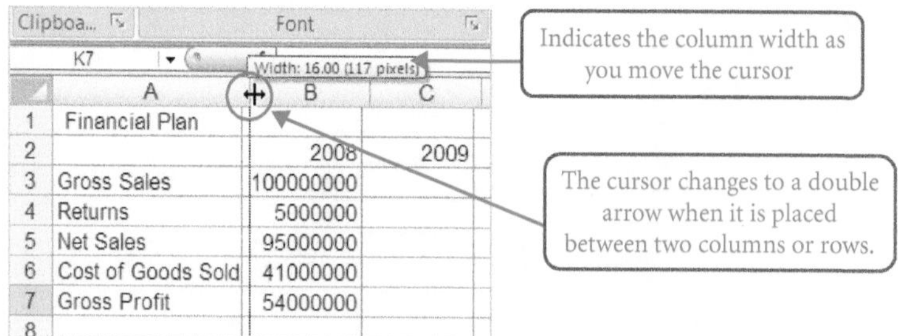


| | A | B | C |
|---|---|---|---|
| 1 | Financial Plan | | |
| 2 | | 2008 | 2009 |
| 3 | Gross Sales | 100000000 | |
| 4 | Returns | 5000000 | |
| 5 | Net Sales | 95000000 | |
| 6 | Cost of Goods Sold | 41000000 | |
| 7 | Gross Profit | 54000000 | |
| 8 | | | |

## COMMON MISTAKES | Columns Too Narrow for Numbers

When entering numbers into a worksheet that is too long for the width of a column, you may see the symbols shown in Figures 6 and 7.

People often think these symbols are errors. However, they simply mean the column is too narrow to fit the number entered into the cell. Excel will not truncate numbers if a column is too narrow because you could be misled into thinking the number is a smaller value than reality. Therefore, increase the width of a column to remove scientific notation or "######" signs.

Figure 6 | **Scientific Notation When Number Is Too Wide for Column**

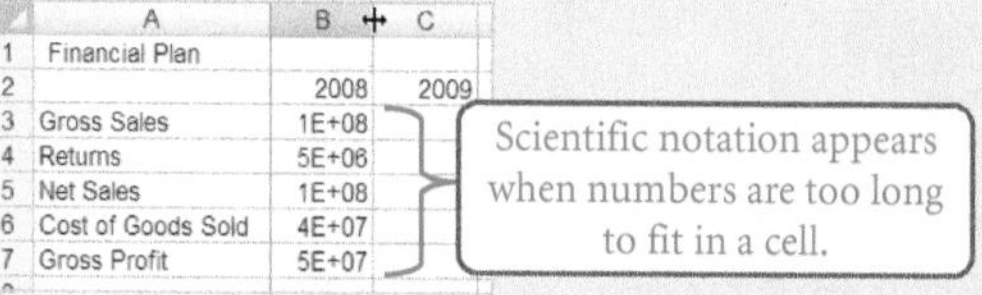


| | A | B | C |
|---|---|---|---|
| 1 | Financial Plan | | |
| 2 | | 2008 | 2009 |
| 3 | Gross Sales | 1E+08 | |
| 4 | Returns | 5E+06 | |
| 5 | Net Sales | 1E+08 | |
| 6 | Cost of Goods Sold | 4E+07 | |
| 7 | Gross Profit | 5E+07 | |

Figure 7 | **"#####" Signs When Number Is Too Wide for Column**

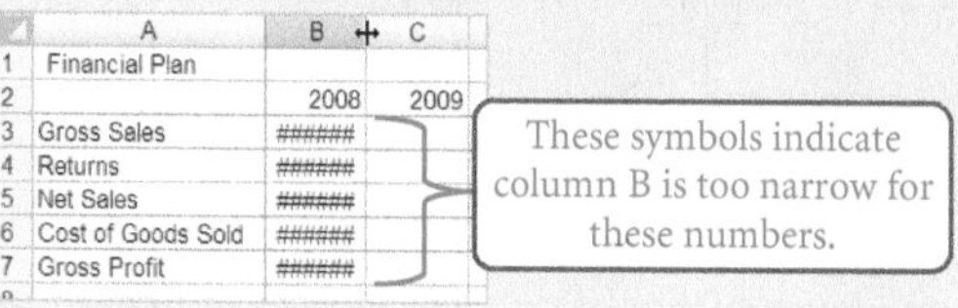


| | A | B | C |
|---|---|---|---|
| 1 | Financial Plan | | |
| 2 | | 2008 | 2009 |
| 3 | Gross Sales | ###### | |
| 4 | Returns | ###### | |
| 5 | Net Sales | ###### | |
| 6 | Cost of Goods Sold | ###### | |
| 7 | Gross Profit | ###### | |

Similar to adjusting the width of a column, you may need to adjust the height of a row to show that cell's content. However, you can also use row height to highlight important information on a worksheet. For example, with regards to our example of a Financial Plan, the Gross Profit is an important financial result that can be highlighted by increasing the height of a row. The method for adjusting the height of rows is almost identical to adjusting the width of columns:

- Place the cursor between two rows.
- When the cursor changes from a white plus sign to a double black arrow, left click and drag up or down to increase or decrease the height of a row.
- Alternatively, when the cursor changes from a white plus sign to a double black arrow, double click with the left mouse button, and the row will automatically expand to fit the largest entry.

Figure 8 shows the Financial Plan worksheet with an expanded row 7. Notice that all of the numbers as well as the words *Gross Profit* automatically stay at the bottom of the cells when the row height is increased. This creates space between the Cost of Goods Sold numbers and the Gross Profit numbers, which makes it easier for a business manager to evaluate the Gross Profit results of this plan. Adjusting the vertical position of data within a cell is covered in more detail in the next section.

Figure 8 | **Using the Cursor to Increase Row Height**

| | A | B | C | D | E | F |
|---|---|---|---|---|---|---|
| 1 | Financial Plan | | | | | |
| 2 | | 2008 | 2009 | 2010 | 2011 | 2012 |
| 3 | Gross Sales | 100000000 | 110000000 | 120000000 | [illegible] | [illegible] |
| 4 | Returns | 5000000 | 5500000 | 6000000 | [illegible] | [illegible] |
| 5 | Net Sales | 95000000 | 104500000 | 114000000 | 13 | [illegible] |
| 6 | Cost of Goods Sold | 41000000 | 45100000 | 49200000 | 57400000 | 65600000 |
| 7 | Gross Profit | 54000000 | 59400000 | 64800000 | 75600000 | 86400000 |

Height: 20.25 (27 pixels)

The increased height of this row accents the Gross Profit results.

Click and drag up or down to adjust the row height.

An alternative way of changing the width of columns or the height of rows is to use the **Format** icon in the **Home** tab of the Ribbon (see Figure 9). Clicking the **Format** icon will open the following options.

- **Row Height:** Use to set a specific height for a row or group of rows. You must highlight at least one cell location in every row you intend to change *before* selecting this option. After you select this option, a dialog box will appear, asking you to enter a specific height number (the higher the number, the greater the height).
- **Auto Fit Row Height:** This option is identical to double clicking the cursor when it is placed between two rows. The height of rows containing cell locations that have been highlighted will automatically adjust to fit any data entries.
- **Column Width:** Use to set a specific column width. You must highlight at least one cell in every column you intend to change before selecting this option. After you select this option, a dialog box will appear, asking you to enter a specific width number (the higher the number, the wider the column).
- ***Auto Fit Column Width:*** This option automatically changes the width of a column to fit the width of the longest entered data. You must highlight at least one cell in each column to apply this option.
- **Default Width:** Use to set a specific width for every column in a spreadsheet. Since every column is being formatted, you don't need to highlight any cells to apply this option.

Figure 9 | **Using the Ribbon to Change Column Width and Row Height**

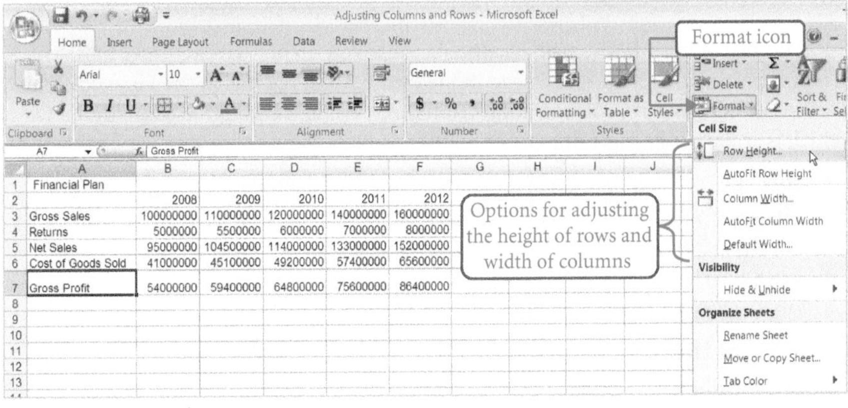


**Quick Reference**

**Adjusting Column Widths**

1. Place the cursor between 2 columns.
2. Click and drag to desired width or double click to automatically set to the widest data point.

Or

1. Highlight at least one cell in the columns you want to change.
2. Click the **Home** tab of the Ribbon.
3. Click the **Format** icon.
4. Select **Column Width**.
5. Enter a desired width number in the **Column Width** dialog box.
6. Click the **OK** button.

**Quick Reference**

**Adjusting Row Heights**

1. Place the cursor between 2 rows.
2. Click and drag to desired height or double click to automatically set to the largest data point.

Or

1. Highlight at least one cell in the rows you want to change.
2. Click the **Home** tab of the Ribbon.
3. Click the **Format** icon.
4. Select **Row Height**.
5. Enter a desired height number in the **Row Height** dialog box.
6. Click the **OK** button.

## Hiding Columns and Rows

In some situations you may want to hide a column or row in a worksheet. Hiding certain columns or rows might make a worksheet easier to read, depending on its use. For example, if someone was interested only in using the Financial Plan worksheet (see Figure 8) to compare the years 2008 and 2012, columns containing data for the years 2009 through 2011 can be hidden from view. The following points explain how to hide these columns:

- Highlight the range C1:E1. At least one cell in each column you wish to hide must be highlighted. It does not matter which row number is highlighted.
- Click the **Home** tab of the Ribbon.
- Click the **Format** icon.
- Click the **Hide & Unhide** option. This will open a submenu of options showing items that you can hide or unhide.
- Select the **Hide Columns** option.

Figure 10 shows the Financial Plan worksheet with columns C, D, and E hidden from view. Notice that the column letters at the top of the worksheet grid are out of sequence.

Figure 10 | **Hiding Columns**

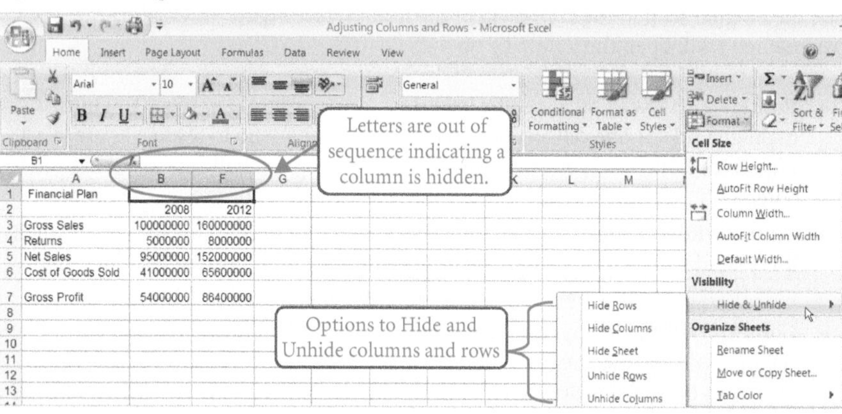


> **Quick Reference**
>
> **Hide Columns and Rows**
>
> 1. Highlight at least one cell in each column or row you want to hide.
> 2. Click the **Home** tab of the Ribbon.
> 3. Click the **Format** icon.
> 4. Select the **Hide & Unhide** option.
> 5. Select one of the **Hide** options from the submenu.

> **Quick Reference**
>
> **Unhide Columns and Rows**
>
> 1. Click and drag over to a cell on either side of the hidden column or row.
> 2. Click the **Home** tab of the Ribbon.
> 3. Click the **Format** icon.
> 4. Select the **Hide & Unhide** option.
> 5. Select one of the **Unhide** options from the submenu.

### COMMON MISTAKES | Checking for Hidden Columns and Rows

Always check for hidden columns and rows when you're working with an Excel file that was created by someone else. People often spend time re-creating or adding data to a worksheet because it appears to be missing when in fact it is contained in a hidden column or row. Remember that the column letters at the top of a worksheet or row numbers along the left side of a worksheet will be out of sequence if a column or row is hidden.

Hiding columns is a valuable feature because you do not have to move or delete data from a worksheet you may need in the future. With regards to the Financial Plan worksheet in Figure 10, you can always unhide columns C through E when needed, which is accomplished as follows:

- Highlight a cell on the left and right of the hidden column. Notice in Figure 10, cell locations B1 and F1 are highlighted. The reason is that both cell locations border the columns that are hidden.
- Click the **Home** tab of the Ribbon.
- Click the **Format** icon.
- Click the **Hide & Unhide** option.
- Select **Unhide Columns.**

## Copy and Paste

The ***Copy*** and ***Paste*** commands are perhaps the most convenient and commonly used Excel commands. This section demonstrates these commands using both a Merchandise Sales Report and the Financial Plan worksheet (created in Figures 1 through 10).

The purpose of the Merchandise Sales Report in this example is to show the sales results for products sold in an apparel retail store. The first few items in the report are from the Tops category. Here, we will use the **Copy** and **Paste** commands instead of typing the word "Tops" several times in the Category column:

- Activate cell A2 (see Figure 11). Before copying data, you must activate the cell or range of cells you need duplicated. In this example, the word *Tops* in cell A2 must be duplicated 4 times.
- Click the **Home** tab of the Ribbon.
- Click the **Copy** icon (see Figure 11).
- Highlight the range A3:A6. After clicking the **Copy** icon, highlight the cell, or range of cells, where the data needs to be duplicated.
- Click the **Paste** icon (see Figure 12). After you click the **Paste** icon, the word "Tops" will appear in cells A3 through A6.

Figure 11 | **Copying Data on the Merchandise Sales Report**

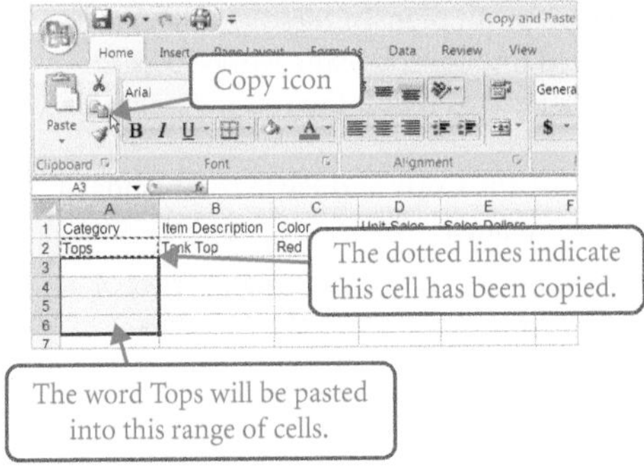


Figure 12 | **Pasting Data**

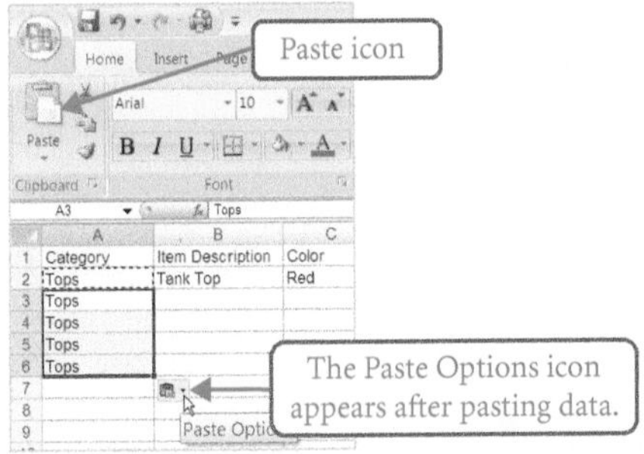


It is important to note that the **Paste** icon pastes all data and formats from the cell that was copied. However, you can choose various pasting options by clicking the smaller **Paste Options** icon, which appears on your worksheet each time you click the

**Paste** icon. These options are also referred to as **Paste Special** options and will be covered in the next chapter.

Data can also be duplicated using the **Auto Fill Handle**. As previously mentioned, **Auto Fill** is usually used to complete a sequence of data when two cells are highlighted. However, if you click and drag on the **Auto Fill Handle** when only one cell location is activated, the contents of that cell will be duplicated to other cell locations (see Figure 13).

Figure 13 | **Using Auto Fill to Duplicate Data**

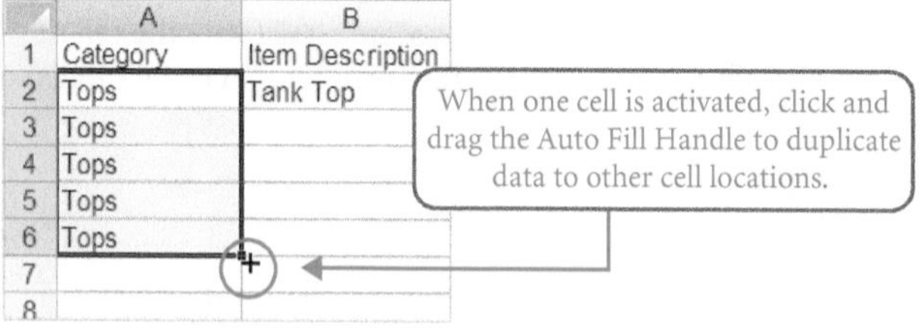


Another common use of the **Copy** and **Paste** commands is to create duplicate copies of an entire worksheet. Business managers can use this technique to create different scenarios for sales plans or business strategies. For example, a sales manager might need to develop three different scenarios showing the potential sales results for a region of retail stores. A financial planning manager might want to show a base case, worst case, or best case scenario for a company's profit plan. In these situations, a base worksheet is created and then copied and pasted into several blank worksheets. Once the worksheet is duplicated, the data can be changed to reflect the various scenarios for a particular business situation.

The following example explains how you use the **Copy** and **Paste** commands to create different versions for the example of the Financial Plan:

- Highlight the entire worksheet by clicking the box in the upper-left corner of Sheet1 (see Figure 14).

Figure 14 | **Copying an Entire Worksheet**

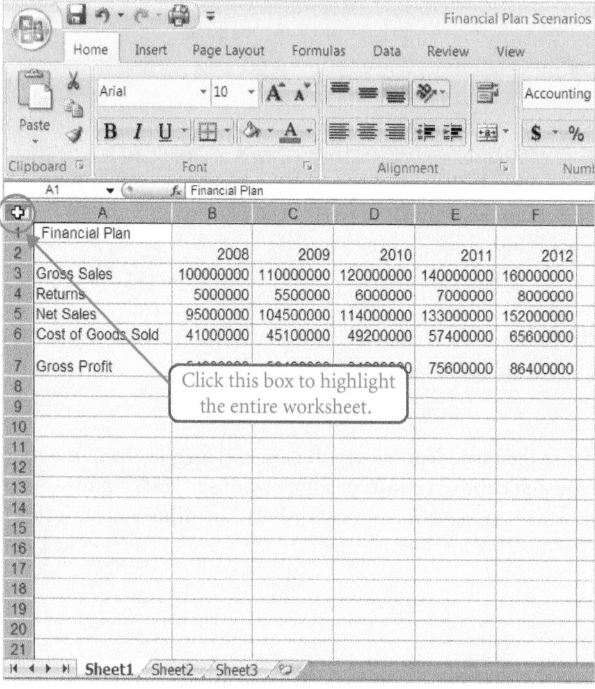

- Click the **Home** tab of the Ribbon.
- Click the **Copy** icon to copy the entire contents of the worksheet.
- Click the Sheet2 worksheet tab and activate cell A1. When pasting the contents of an entire worksheet, you must activate cell A1; otherwise, Excel will produce an error message.
- Click the **Paste** icon (see Figure 15).

Figure 15 | **Pasting an Entire Worksheet**

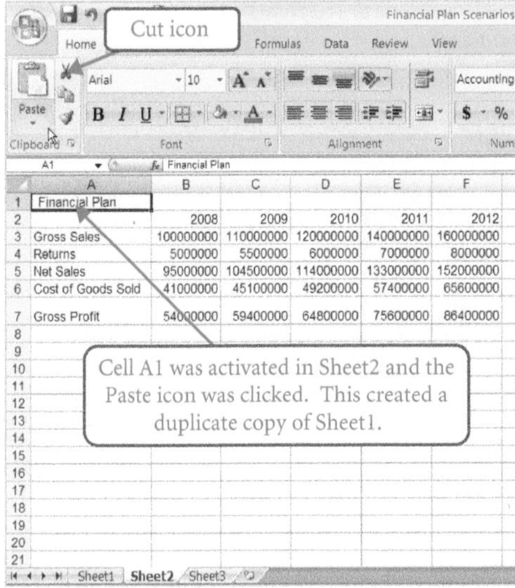


In some cases you may want to remove contents from one area of a worksheet and paste it to another. For these situations you can use the Cut command, which is activated by clicking the scissors icon in the **Home** tab of the Ribbon. After clicking the **Cut** icon, activate a cell or range of cells where the data should be replaced and click the **Paste** icon.

## Sorting Data (Single Level)

After you construct a spreadsheet, you may need to sort the data. ***Sorting*** is one of the most critical Excel commands because it can rearrange data in a specific sequence or rank that enables business managers to assess information efficiently and make key decisions. For example, retail managers use sorting to rank merchandise based on sales results. This allows them to identify top-selling items that should be reordered as well as low-selling items that should be discontinued. Finance managers may rank a list of public companies with the highest shareholder return. This could help them identify stocks that should either be purchased or sold. Sorting data in Excel can be broken down into two broad categories: single level and multiple level. This segment will focus on single-level sorting, and the following segment will focus on multiple-level sorting.

Figure 16 shows the completed Merchandise Sales worksheet originally started in Figure 11. As previously mentioned, a retail manager might sort the items in this worksheet based on the Unit Sales column. If the manager wanted to identify the best-selling items, this data could be sorted so items with the highest unit sales appear at the top of the worksheet (***descending order***). If the manager wanted to identify the lowest-selling items, this data could be sorted so items with the lowest unit sales appear at the top of the worksheet (***ascending order***). These sorting options are considered single level because one column of data is used as the basis for ranking the items. The following explains how you sort the worksheet in Figure 16 in descending order:

- Activate any cell location that contains a number in column D. Since the goal is to sort this worksheet in descending order based on data in the Unit Sales column,

> **Quick Reference**
>
> **Copy and Paste**
>
> 1. Highlight a cell or range of cells to be copied.
> 2. Click the **Copy** icon in the Ribbon.
> 3. Highlight a cell or range of cells where copied data should appear.
> 4. Click the **Paste** icon in the Ribbon.

one cell in this column must be activated. Note that the cell you activate cannot be blank; otherwise, you will get an error message.

- Click the **Data** tab at the top of the Ribbon.
- Click the **Z to A** icon in the **Sort & Filter** group of the Ribbon (see Figure 17). After you click this icon, the Unit Sales column as well as all adjacent columns will be sorted in descending order. It is important to note that only adjacent columns are sorted when you use either the **Z to A** or **A to Z** icons (see Common Mistakes for this section).

Figure 16 | **Merchandise Sales Report Before Sorting**

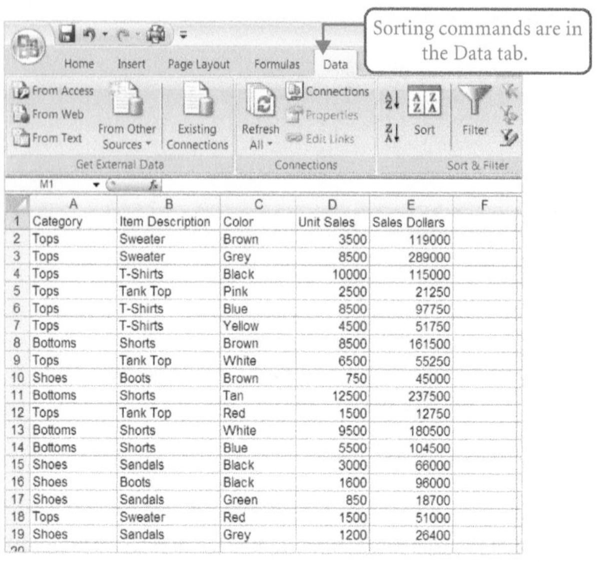


| | A | B | C | D | E |
|---|---|---|---|---|---|
| 1 | Category | Item Description | Color | Unit Sales | Sales Dollars |
| 2 | Tops | Sweater | Brown | 3500 | 119000 |
| 3 | Tops | Sweater | Grey | 8500 | 289000 |
| 4 | Tops | T-Shirts | Black | 10000 | 115000 |
| 5 | Tops | Tank Top | Pink | 2500 | 21250 |
| 6 | Tops | T-Shirts | Blue | 8500 | 97750 |
| 7 | Tops | T-Shirts | Yellow | 4500 | 51750 |
| 8 | Bottoms | Shorts | Brown | 8500 | 161500 |
| 9 | Tops | Tank Top | White | 6500 | 55250 |
| 10 | Shoes | Boots | Brown | 750 | 45000 |
| 11 | Bottoms | Shorts | Tan | 12500 | 237500 |
| 12 | Tops | Tank Top | Red | 1500 | 12750 |
| 13 | Bottoms | Shorts | White | 9500 | 180500 |
| 14 | Bottoms | Shorts | Blue | 5500 | 104500 |
| 15 | Shoes | Sandals | Black | 3000 | 66000 |
| 16 | Shoes | Boots | Black | 1600 | 96000 |
| 17 | Shoes | Sandals | Green | 850 | 18700 |
| 18 | Tops | Sweater | Red | 1500 | 51000 |
| 19 | Shoes | Sandals | Grey | 1200 | 26400 |

Figure 17 shows the Merchandise Sales Report after the items are sorted in descending order based on the Unit Sales column. The manager of this business can quickly glance at the top of this report and see that the Tan Shorts and the Black T-Shirts are the two highest-selling items based on unit sales.

> **Quick Reference**
>
> **Sorting Data (Single Level)**
>
> 1. Activate a cell in the column you wish to use as the basis for sorting your data. The cell you activate must not be blank.
> 2. Make sure there are no blank columns separating data you wish to sort and the column containing the cell you activated in step 1.
> 3. Click the **Data** tab at the top of the Ribbon.
> 4. Click the **Z to A** (descending order) or **A to Z** (ascending order) icon in the **Sort & Filter** section of the Ribbon.

Figure 17 | **Merchandise Sales Report Sorted Based on the Unit Sales Column**

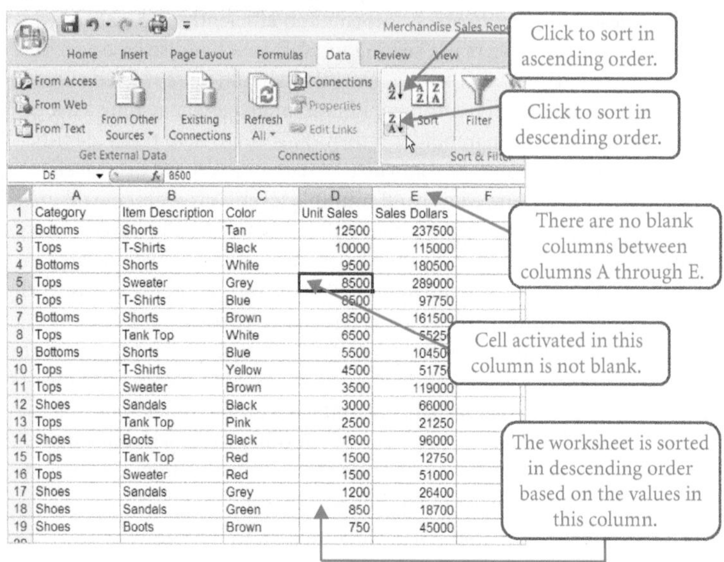


| | A | B | C | D | E |
|---|---|---|---|---|---|
| 1 | Category | Item Description | Color | Unit Sales | Sales Dollars |
| 2 | Bottoms | Shorts | Tan | 12500 | 237500 |
| 3 | Tops | T-Shirts | Black | 10000 | 115000 |
| 4 | Bottoms | Shorts | White | 9500 | 180500 |
| 5 | Tops | Sweater | Grey | 8500 | 289000 |
| 6 | Tops | T-Shirts | Blue | 8500 | 97750 |
| 7 | Bottoms | Shorts | Brown | 8500 | 161500 |
| 8 | Tops | Tank Top | White | 6500 | 5525 |
| 9 | Bottoms | Shorts | Blue | 5500 | 10450 |
| 10 | Tops | T-Shirts | Yellow | 4500 | 5175 |
| 11 | Tops | Sweater | Brown | 3500 | 119000 |
| 12 | Shoes | Sandals | Black | 3000 | 66000 |
| 13 | Tops | Tank Top | Pink | 2500 | 21250 |
| 14 | Shoes | Boots | Black | 1600 | 96000 |
| 15 | Tops | Tank Top | Red | 1500 | 12750 |
| 16 | Tops | Sweater | Red | 1500 | 51000 |
| 17 | Shoes | Sandals | Grey | 1200 | 26400 |
| 18 | Shoes | Sandals | Green | 850 | 18700 |
| 19 | Shoes | Boots | Brown | 750 | 45000 |

## COMMON MISTAKES | Using the Z to A or A to Z Icons

When using the **Z to A** (descending) or **A to Z** (ascending) icons, make sure there are no blank columns in the data range you are sorting. These icons will sort data only in columns that are adjacent or connected to the column that contains the activated cell. For example, in Figure 18, the **A to Z** icon was used to sort the worksheet based on the Unit Sales column. Only columns A through D are sorted. Since a blank column separates columns D and F, column F is not sorted. As a result, it appears that the Brown Boots generated over 237,500 in sales dollars when these sales are actually associated with the Tan Shorts.

Figure 18 | **Example of a Sorting Error When Using the Ascending Icon**

| | A | B | C | D | E | F |
|---|---|---|---|---|---|---|
| 1 | Category | Item Description | Color | Unit Sales | | Sales Dollars |
| 2 | Shoes | Boots | Brown | 750 | | 237500 |
| 3 | Shoes | Sandals | Green | 850 | | 115000 |
| 4 | Shoes | Sandals | Grey | 1200 | | 180500 |
| 5 | Tops | Tank Top | Red | 1500 | | 289000 |
| 6 | Tops | Sweater | Red | 1500 | | 97750 |
| 7 | Shoes | Boots | Black | 1600 | | 161500 |

This column is not sorted and does not align with the data on this worksheet.

## Sorting Data (Multiple Levels)

The focus of the preceding segment was single-level sorting. This segment will focus on multiple-level sorting. Use multiple-level sorting when duplicate values appear in the column that is used to sort the data in a worksheet. For example, notice in Figure 17 that 8500 units were sold for the Grey Sweater, Blue T-Shirt, and Brown Shorts. With multiple-level sorting, all items that sold 8500 units can be sorted by the values in the Sales Dollars column. This could help a manager prioritize the ordering of these items based on the number of sales dollars they generate for the business. The following explains how to accomplish this sort:

- Highlight the range A1:E19. Notice that this range includes the column headings in row 1. Also, when you are sorting data, it is important to note that all columns related to a single row of data must be highlighted. Leaving a column out of the highlighted range could distort the data, making it unusable.
- Click the **Data** tab on the Ribbon.
- Click the **Sort** icon in the Ribbon. This will open the **Sort** dialog box.
- Click the **Options** button and check to see that the **Sort top to bottom** option is selected. You can sort data from left to right in rows or top to bottom in columns. However, you will need to select the **Sort top to bottom** option when working with a list of items such as this example.
- Click the **OK** button in the **Sort Options** dialog box.
- Make sure a green check appears in the box next to the **My data has headers** option in the upper-right side of the **Sort** dialog box. Since column headings were included in the highlighted range before you opened the **Sort** dialog box, you must check this option.
- Click the drop-down arrow of the option box below the **Column** heading and select the Unit Sales column.
- Click the drop-down arrow of the option box below the **Sort On** heading and select the Values option. This drop-down box also contains options that allow you to sort data based on the font color or cell color in a column.
- Click the drop-down arrow of the option box below the **Order** heading and select **Largest to Smallest**. This box also contains an option called **Custom List**. This

option is helpful when you need to sort data by months of the year or days of the week.

- Click the **Add** button in the upper-left corner of the **Sort** window. This will add another set of option boxes to create a second sort level. You can add as many sort levels as needed.
- Make the following settings in the second sort level:
  - Column: **Sales Dollars**
  - Sort On: **Values**
  - Order: **Largest to Smallest**
- Click the **OK** button at the bottom of the **Sort** dialog box.

Figure 19 shows the final settings entered into the **Sort** dialog box. The data in a worksheet will be sorted in the order of the levels listed. Therefore, the Merchandise Sales Report will be sorted by the values in the Unit Sales column first. If duplicate values appear in the Unit Sales column, the data will be sorted by the values in the Sales Dollars column. You can change the order in which the sort levels are listed by clicking a level and then clicking one of the arrow buttons at the top of the **Sort** dialog box.

Figure 19 | **Settings in the Sort Dialog Box for the Merchandise Sales Report**

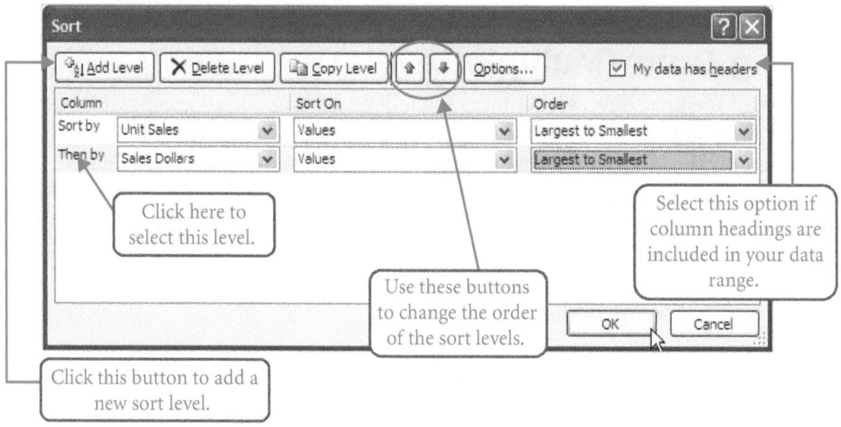


Figure 20 shows the final results of sorting the Merchandise Sales Report by the Unit Sales column and then by the Sales Dollars column. Notice that three items which sold 8500 units are now sorted in descending order based on the values in the Sales Dollars column.

> **Quick Reference**
>
> **Sorting Data (Multiple Levels)**
>
> 1. Highlight *all* the data on your worksheet that will be sorted.
> 2. Click the **Data** tab of the Ribbon.
> 3. Click the **Sort** icon in the Ribbon.
> 4. Click the **Options** button in the **Sort** dialog box and select the **Sort top to bottom** option if you are sorting a list of items.
> 5. Click the **OK** button in the **Sort Options** dialog box.
> 6. Select the **My data has headers** option if column headings are included in the range you highlighted for step 1.
> 7. Set the **Column**, **Sort On**, and **Order** options for the first sort level.
> 8. Add other sort levels as needed by clicking the **Add Level** button.
> 9. Click the **OK** button.

## COMMON MISTAKES | Missing Column Headings in the Sort Dialog Box

The column headings in your worksheet should appear in the drop-down box below the **Column** heading in the **Sort** dialog box. If you do not see the column heading names in these drop-down boxes, check to make sure you included them when you highlighted the range of cells to be sorted. If the column headings are included in your highlighted range but still do not appear in the drop-down boxes, check to see that the **My data has headers** option is selected in the upper-right corner of the **Sort** dialog box.

Figure 20 | **Merchandise Sales Report Sorted Based on Unit Sales and Sales Dollars**

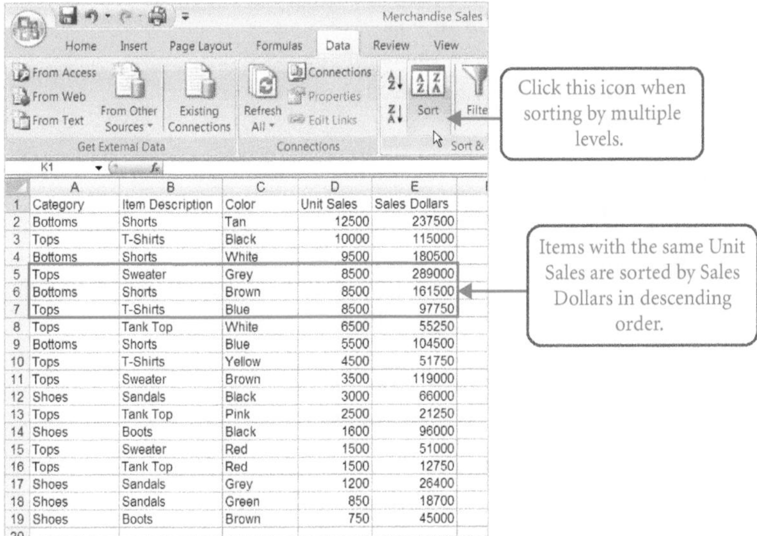


| | A | B | C | D | E |
|---|---|---|---|---|---|
| 1 | Category | Item Description | Color | Unit Sales | Sales Dollars |
| 2 | Bottoms | Shorts | Tan | 12500 | 237500 |
| 3 | Tops | T-Shirts | Black | 10000 | 115000 |
| 4 | Bottoms | Shorts | White | 9500 | 180500 |
| 5 | Tops | Sweater | Grey | 8500 | 289000 |
| 6 | Bottoms | Shorts | Brown | 8500 | 161500 |
| 7 | Tops | T-Shirts | Blue | 8500 | 97750 |
| 8 | Tops | Tank Top | White | 6500 | 55250 |
| 9 | Bottoms | Shorts | Blue | 5500 | 104500 |
| 10 | Tops | T-Shirts | Yellow | 4500 | 51750 |
| 11 | Tops | Sweater | Brown | 3500 | 119000 |
| 12 | Shoes | Sandals | Black | 3000 | 66000 |
| 13 | Tops | Tank Top | Pink | 2500 | 21250 |
| 14 | Shoes | Boots | Black | 1600 | 96000 |
| 15 | Tops | Sweater | Red | 1500 | 51000 |
| 16 | Tops | Tank Top | Red | 1500 | 12750 |
| 17 | Shoes | Sandals | Grey | 1200 | 26400 |
| 18 | Shoes | Sandals | Green | 850 | 18700 |
| 19 | Shoes | Boots | Brown | 750 | 45000 |

### COMMON MISTAKES | Multiple-Level Sorting

When you are defining multiple levels to sort the data in a worksheet, it is important to highlight all data that is to be sorted first. *Any data that is not highlighted will not be sorted.* For example, if you forget to highlight a column that is related to your dataset, Excel will sort the highlighted columns creating an alignment problem with the column that was not highlighted. This will distort your data, and it may not be possible to correct this error. This problem is similar to the Common Mistake illustrated for the **Z to A** and **A to Z** icons in the previous segment.

# >> Data Management Skills

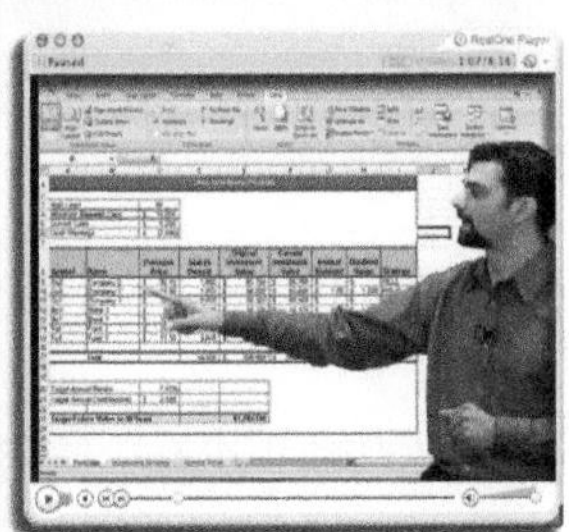

The purpose of this workshop is to demonstrate the data management skills presented in this section of the chapter. We will be creating a spreadsheet that tracks the sales results of a product line that could be sold at a university bookstore. I will be demonstrating the tasks in this workshop in the following four videos: **Data Entry**, **Adjusting Rows and Columns**, **Copy and Paste**, and **Sorting Data**. After completing each section of tasks, watch the related video in parentheses. Remember to try the tasks on your own first before watching the video.

1. **Open and Save a Workbook (Video: Data Entry)**
   - **a.** Open a blank Excel workbook.
   - **b.** Save the workbook as **`ib_e02_videoworkshop`**.
   - **c.** Remember where you save this file. You will need this file to complete the three remaining video workshops in this chapter.

2. **Data Entry (Video: Data Entry continued)**
   a. Activate Sheet1 by clicking the worksheet tab.
   b. Type the following data into the cell locations listed:
      Cell A1: **University Bookstore Sales Report**
      Cell A2: **Season**
      Cell A3: **Fall**
      Cell A4: **Spring**
      Cell A5: **Spring**
      Cell A6: **Fall**
      Cell A7: **Spring**
      Cell A8: **Fall**
      Cell A9: **Spring**
      Cell A10: **Fall**
      Cell A11: **Fall**
      Cell A12: **Spring**
      Cell B2: **Item Description**
      Cell B3: **Sweatshirt**
      Cell B4: **T-Shirts**
      Cell B5: **Baseballs**
      Cell B6: **Scarves**
      Cell B7: **Sunglasses**
      Cell B8: **Sweaters**
      Cell B9: **Sandals**
      Cell B10: **Blankets**
      Cell B11: **Footballs**
      Cell B12: **Sunscreen**
      Cell D2: **Unit Sales**
      Cell D3: **5000**
      Cell D4: **8500**
      Cell D5: **1200**
      Cell D6: **2200**
      Cell D7: **1800**
      Cell D8: **3200**
      Cell D9: **2200**
      Cell D10: **900**
      Cell D11: **500**
      Cell D12: **1800**
      Cell E2: **Average Price**
      Cell E3: **49.99**
      Cell E4: **18.99**
      Cell E5: **12.99**
      Cell E6: **9.99**
      Cell E7: **22.99**
      Cell E8: **69.99**
      Cell E9: **29.99**
      Cell E10: **32.99**
      Cell E11: **59.99**
      Cell E12: **5.99**
      Cell F2: **Sales Dollars**
      Cell F3: **249950**
      Cell F4: **161415**
      Cell F5: **15588**
      Cell F6: **21978**
      Cell F7: **41382**
      Cell F8: **223968**
      Cell F9: **65978**

Cell F10: **29691**
Cell F11: **29995**
Cell F12: **10782**

c. In cell C2, type **Item Number**.
d. In cell C3, type the number **70500**.
e. In cell C4, type the number **70501**.
f. Use **Auto Fill** to extend the series to cell C12. The number in Cell 12 should be 70509.

**3. Adjusting Rows and Columns (Video: Adjusting Rows and Columns)**

a. Expand the height of row 1 to 27 points.
b. Expand the height of row 2 to 31.5 points.
c. Expand the width of column B to 12 points.

**4. Copy and Paste (Video: Copy and Paste)**

a. Select all contents in Sheet1 by clicking the square in the upper-left corner next to column A.
b. Click the **Copy** icon in the **Home** tab of the Ribbon to copy Sheet1.
c. Activate Sheet2 by clicking the worksheet tab.
d. Activate cell A1.
e. Click the **Paste** icon in the **Home** tab of the Ribbon to paste Sheet1 into Sheet2.
f. Activate Sheet3.
g. Activate cell A1.
h. Paste Sheet1 into Sheet3 by using the **Paste** icon.

**5. Sort (Video: Sorting Data)**

a. Sort the data in Sheet1 as follows:
   i. Season: **A to Z**
   ii. Sales Dollars: **Largest to Smallest**

b. Sort the data in Sheet2 as follows:
   i. Unit Sales: **Largest to Smallest**
   ii. Sales Dollars: **Largest to Smallest**

c. Sort the data in Sheet3 as follows:
   i. Average Price: **Smallest to Largest**
   ii. Item Description: **A to Z**

**6. Save (Video: Sorting Data continued)**

a. Save and close your workbook. Remember where you save this file as you will need it to do the next video workshop on formatting skills.

**EXERCISE**

**Why Do I Need This?**

## >> Creating Merchandise Sales Reports

Knowing the skills covered in this section is essential for creating spreadsheets in Excel. For example, if you don't know how to adjust the width of columns, you may not be able to see the data that was entered onto a spreadsheet. Or, if you don't know how to use the copy and paste commands, you would always have to retype data when you wanted to create an identical or similar spreadsheet. Finally, knowing how to use a basic skill such as sorting can be critical in making business decisions.

### Exercise

The purpose of this exercise is to create Merchandise Sales Reports for three different business managers. Each business manager will need a different arrangement of the merchandise report based on the decisions they are required to make. As a result, the spreadsheets you will create in this exercise will highlight information that is most important to the reader. Open the file named ib_e02_merchandise performancereport and complete the following tasks:

1. Copy the data in Sheet1 and paste it into Sheet2 and Sheet3.
2. Use Sheet1 to create a sales report for a buyer. The buyer will need to evaluate the sales performance of merchandise within each category. Sort the data in Sheet1 based on the columns listed below to show the buyer what item is generating the most sales dollars within each category:
   a. Category: Ascending order
   b. Total Sales Dollars: Descending order
3. Use Sheet2 to create a report for an inventory manager. An inventory manager will typically focus on the unit inventory and weeks of supply for each item. This information will be used to decide which orders to rush into the warehouse and which orders to postpone. Sort the data based on the columns listed below:
   a. Weeks of Supply: Ascending order
   b. Inventory Units: Descending order
4. Since the inventory manager is focusing only on the Weeks of Supply and Inventory Units column, hide the Units Sales, Price, and Total Sales Dollar columns.
5. Use Sheet3 to create a report for a pricing manager. The pricing manager will need to manage how items are priced and determine how many price tickets should be printed for each price point. Sort Sheet3 based on the columns listed below:
   a. Price: Ascending order
   b. Color: Ascending order
6. Since the pricing manager is focusing on the price for each item, hide the Unit Sales, Total Sales Dollars, Inventory Units, and Weeks of Supply columns.
7. Which item generates the most dollars for each category?
8. How many $19 price tickets will the pricing manager need to print?

PROBLEM & EXERCISE

## >> What's Wrong with This Spreadsheet?

### Problem

You are approached by a coworker who is having some difficulty with an Excel project. He sends you an Excel file with two spreadsheets in it. Sheet1 is the original spreadsheet that was given to him by an assistant buyer. Sheet2 is the spreadsheet he has been working on and is causing him trouble. The following is a list of problems the coworker has sent to you:

1. I don't know why these "####" errors appear on the spreadsheet. I was only entering numbers for the sales report, and these "####" errors keep popping up.
2. The data in Sheet1 was given to me by an assistant buyer. She told me that this worksheet would include the cost for each item. I don't see it! She keeps insisting the cost information is in there; however, I have a feeling I am going to have to enter this data myself.
3. I copied the data in Sheet1, pasted it into Sheet2, and sorted it by Sales Dollars. I had no problem sorting it except I did not see the name of each column in the Column drop-down boxes. I read somewhere that you should see the column names in those boxes, but I just saw Column A, Column B, and so on. I showed the report to one of the buyers in my department, and she said the department numbers don't seem to match the department name. I wonder if the assistant buyer did something wrong?

### Exercise

The file this coworker sent you is named ib_e02_salesreporthelp. What's wrong with this spreadsheet? Consider the following points:

1. What would cause the "####" signs to appear on a spreadsheet? Is this really an error? How can this be fixed?
2. In point 2 of the Problem, the cost information is indeed in the spreadsheet. How can you tell if data exists on a spreadsheet if it cannot be seen?
3. Assume that the data in Sheet1 is accurate. What can you do to check the accuracy of the data your coworker sorted in Sheet2? Why is the coworker not seeing the column names in the Column drop-down boxes?

Write a short answer for each of these questions and fix the data in Sheet2. If a problem cannot be fixed, explain why.

## >> Formatting

Skill Set

The previous section demonstrated how you can use Excel to construct a Financial Plan and a Merchandise Sales Report. This section will demonstrate how Excel's ***formatting*** commands can enhance the visual appearance of these spreadsheets. Excel's formatting features can transform the appearance of a basic spreadsheet into a professional-looking document. However, formatting also serves a more functional purpose in that it guides the reader's attention to the most critical information. This allows a business manager to scan a spreadsheet efficiently and identify the most important information required to make key decisions.

Excel's primary formatting features are found in the **Font**, **Alignment**, and **Number** groups of the **Home** tab in the Ribbon (shown in Figure 21). This section will

Figure 21 | **Formatting Features Are Found in the Home Tab of the Ribbon**

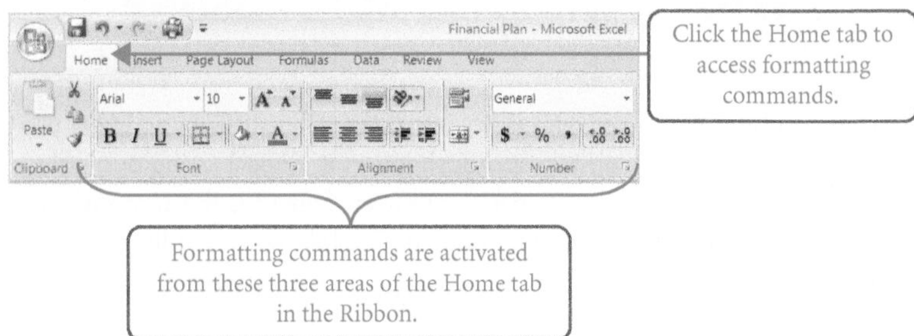
Click the Home tab to access formatting commands.
Formatting commands are activated from these three areas of the Home tab in the Ribbon.

illustrate the formatting commands that are available in each of these three groups and demonstrate how you apply them to the Financial Plan or Merchandise Sales Report spreadsheets, which were introduced previously in this chapter.

## Data Formats

Commands you use to format the appearance of data are found in the Font group, as shown in Figure 22. Frequently used icons in this Group are the **Font Size**, **Font Color**, **Bold**, **Italic**, and **Underline**.

Figure 22 | **Format Icons in the Font Group**

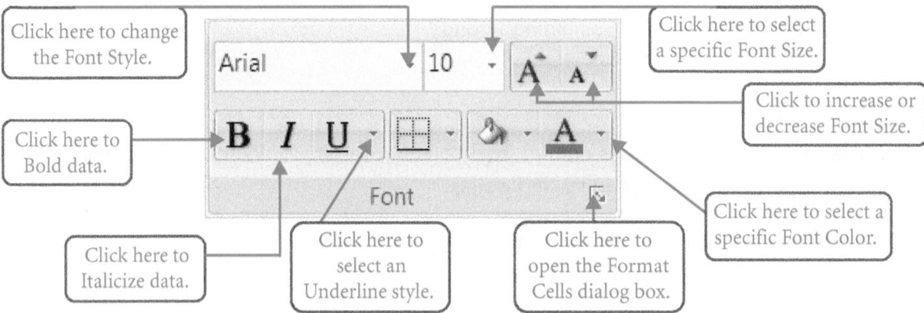
Click here to change the Font Style.
Click here to select a specific Font Size.
Click to increase or decrease Font Size.
Click here to Bold data.
Click here to select a specific Font Color.
Click here to Italicize data.
Click here to select an Underline style.
Click here to open the Format Cells dialog box.

The icons highlighted in Figure 22 are valuable when you're making data stand out on a worksheet. For example, you can use them to enlarge the title of a worksheet, bold a critical row of data, or enhance the appearance of column headings. Formatting column headings can be particularly important because it separates the heading from the actual data, making it easier for the reader to locate specific types of data. The following points explain how to format the column headings for the Merchandise Sales Report shown in Figure 20:

- Highlight the range A1:E1. Before using any of the formatting icons in the **Home** tab of the Ribbon, you must first highlight a cell or range of cells that will be formatted.
- Click the **Home** tab of the Ribbon.
- Click the **Bold** icon.
- Click the **Italic** icon.
- Click the down arrow next to the **Font Color** icon and click the Dark Red square. When using icons such as the **Font Color**, **Font Size**, or **Font Style**, you will see the data in your highlighted range change as you move the cursor over the various options. This allows you to preview what your data will look like when it is formatted before making a choice (see Figure 23).

Figure 23 shows the Merchandise Sales Report with the column headings formatted. This simple enhancement makes it easy for the reader to separate the column headings from the actual data and identify what each column of data represents.

# INDIANA UNIVERSITY SOUTH BEND

## *Section 24345 Evaluation*

## valuation Responses Have Been Recorded.

the "PRINT" method of evaluation completion verification. Please print this page and turn it into your instructor.

**time to submit your evaluation. Your feedback is important to this institution and its faculty.**

Be assured that your responses are completely anonymous.

Submit another Evaluation

INDIANA UNIVERSITY
SOUTH BEND

1700 Mishawaka Ave. P.O. Box 7111
South Bend, IN 46634
Phone: (574) 520-IUSB
(574) 520-4872



Each semester students are asked to evaluate the teaching of all faculty members. Numerical results will be tabulated by an electronic evaluation program called IU-EVAL. Upon completion of each course evaluation, the department secretary will process the information and hold it until after grades have been submitted. The instructor will receive copies of the typed comments and tabulated results. The overall assessment of a faculty member's teaching effectiveness includes information from a variety of sources. Student evaluations of teaching are one important component of this assessment. Student evaluations and comments can also provide valuable information to help improve the course or reshape the department's curriculum. Transcribed comments and tabulated results will be read by the instructor's supervisor and will become part of the instructor's record. It is important that you give thoughtful consideration to your answers.

**eval.iusb.edu**

BUS-K 201
THE COMPUTER IN BUSINESS
Instructor: Mark Paul Schroeder
Section: 24345
Must be completed by midnight on December 10, 2011

Password: **FPVVNXSS4X**

Figure 23 | **Formatted Column Headings for the Merchandise Sales Report**

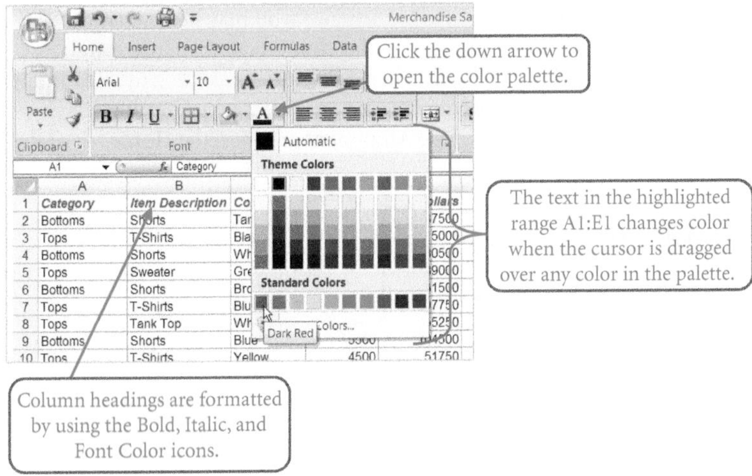


The icons shown in Figure 22 should satisfy almost all of your data format needs. However, you can find additional formatting options by opening the **Format Cells** dialog box. The **Format Cells** dialog box contains almost every available formatting option in Excel. You can open it by clicking the button in the lower-right corner of the **Font, Alignment**, and **Number** groups in the **Home** tab of the Ribbon (see Figure 22). Figure 24 shows the **Format Cells** dialog box and highlights options where an icon is not available in the Ribbon.

Figure 24 | **The Format Cells Dialog Box**

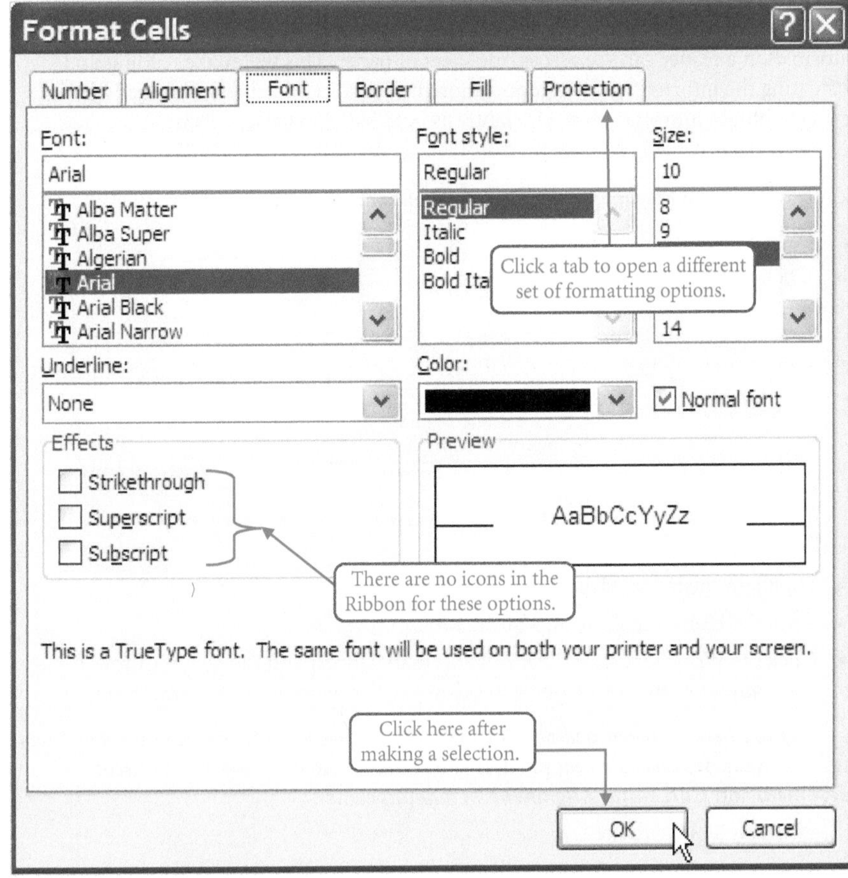


> **Quick Reference**
>
> **Formatting Data**
>
> 1. Highlight a range of cells to be formatted.
> 2. Click the **Home** tab of the Ribbon.
> 3. Click one of the icons in the **Font** group of the Ribbon or open the **Format Cells** dialog box by clicking the button in the lower-right corner of the **Font** group.
> 4. If using the **Format Cells** dialog box, click the **OK** button after making a selection.

## Data Alignment

After applying data formatting techniques to a worksheet, you may need to adjust the ***alignment*** of data in a cell. For example, you may need to use the **Horizontal Alignment** icons to center or right justify data in a cell. If you are setting up accounting statements, you will need to use the **Indent** icons for certain financial headings. Figure 25 highlights the icons available in the **Alignment** group in the **Home** tab of the Ribbon.

Figure 25 | **Alignment Icons**

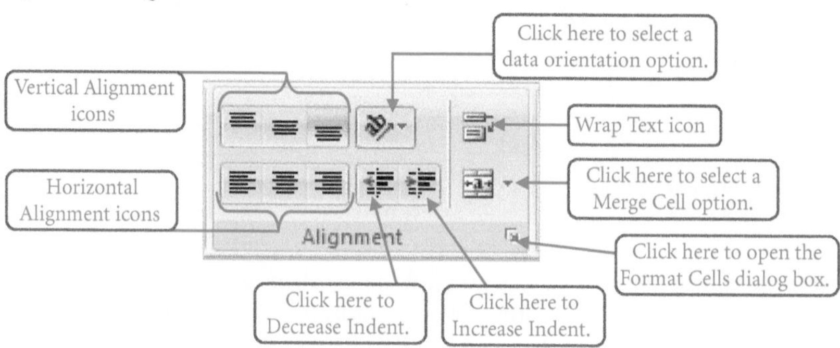


The ***Wrap Text*** icon is a commonly used feature because it will automatically expand the row height and create a second line to fit long entries. This reduces the need to expand the width of columns, which decreases the amount of information that can be seen on one screen or one page. For example, in Figure 26, the font size of the column headings in the Merchandise Sales Report was increased. These headings are now too large to fit in the space allocated for each column. You could resolve this problem by expanding the width of each column; however, doing so may reduce the amount of information a reader can see across one sheet of paper. This will make reading and evaluating the information on a report more difficult for a business manager who is trying to obtain information as efficiently as possible to make key decisions.

Figure 26 | **Column Headings Are Truncated When Font Size Is Increased**

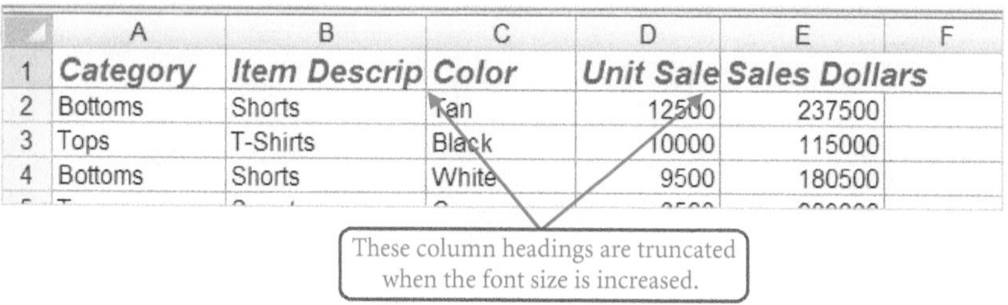


The following explains how to use the **Wrap Text** feature to correct the column headings in the range A1:E1 in Figure 26:

- Highlight the range A1:E1.
- Click the **Home** tab at the top of the Ribbon.
- Click the **Wrap Text** icon. This will automatically expand the height of row 1 and place any word that was truncated below the first word in the column heading.

Figure 27 shows the appearance of the Merchandise Sales Report column headings after the **Wrap Text** feature is applied. In addition, notice that both the ***Vertical Alignment*** and ***Horizontal Alignment*** were set to center.

Figure 27 | **Columns Headings with Wrap Text Applied**

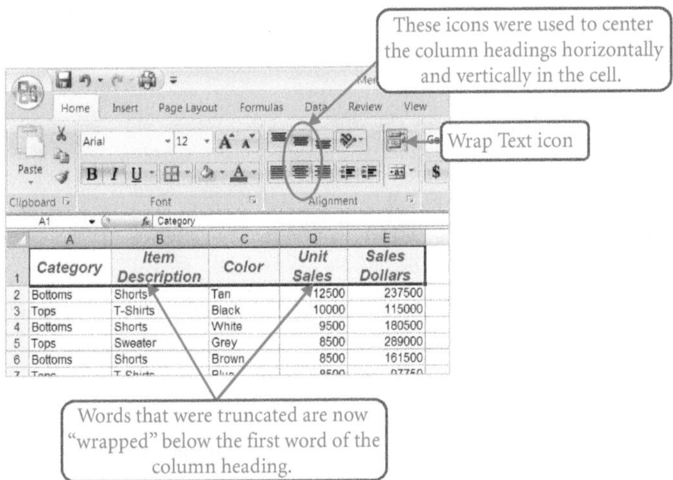


Another common feature used in the **Alignment** area is the **Merge & Center** icon. ***Merge & Center*** allows you to create one big cell out of several smaller cells and is commonly used to center a title at the top of a spreadsheet. For example, Figure 28 shows the Financial Plan spreadsheet. The **Merge & Center** icon will be used to center the title in cell A1 over the center of the worksheet. The following points explain how you accomplish this:

- Highlight the range A1:F1 (see Figure 28). When you are using the **Merge & Center** icon, cell locations within a highlighted range will be transformed into one cell.
- Click the **Home** tab of the Ribbon.
- Click the down arrow next to the **Merge & Center** icon and select the **Merge & Center** option. This will transform the cells in the range A1:F1 into one cell and horizontally center any data in the range. You could also use the **Merge Cells** option to just combine cells without centering the data.

Figure 28 | **Merge Cell Options**

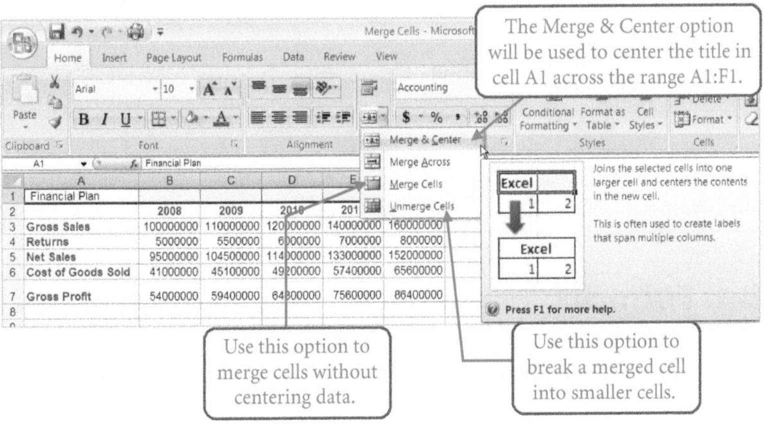

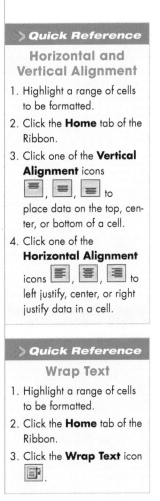

**Quick Reference**

**Horizontal and Vertical Alignment**

1. Highlight a range of cells to be formatted.
2. Click the **Home** tab of the Ribbon.
3. Click one of the **Vertical Alignment** icons , , to place data on the top, center, or bottom of a cell.
4. Click one of the **Horizontal Alignment** icons , , to left justify, center, or right justify data in a cell.

**Quick Reference**

**Wrap Text**

1. Highlight a range of cells to be formatted.
2. Click the **Home** tab of the Ribbon.
3. Click the **Wrap Text** icon .

Figure 29 shows the results of using the **Merge & Center** option to format the title of the Financial Plan. Notice that the font size was increased to 14 points, with bold and italic formats added.

Figure 29 | **Formatted Title in the Financial Plan Worksheet**

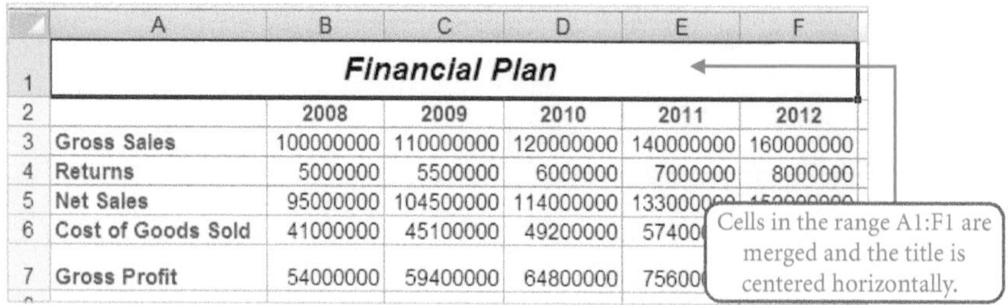


As mentioned in the previous section, in some situations you may need to access additional formatting features through the **Format Cells** dialog box. The **Format Cells** dialog box will be opened to the **Alignment** tab when you click the button in the lower-right corner of the **Alignment** section of the Ribbon (see Figure 25). Figure 30 highlights a few useful features such as the indent and ***orientation*** settings. These options provide you with more detail when making specific indent settings or orienting data on a specific angle within a cell.

Figure 30 | **Alignment Tab of the Format Cells Dialog Box**

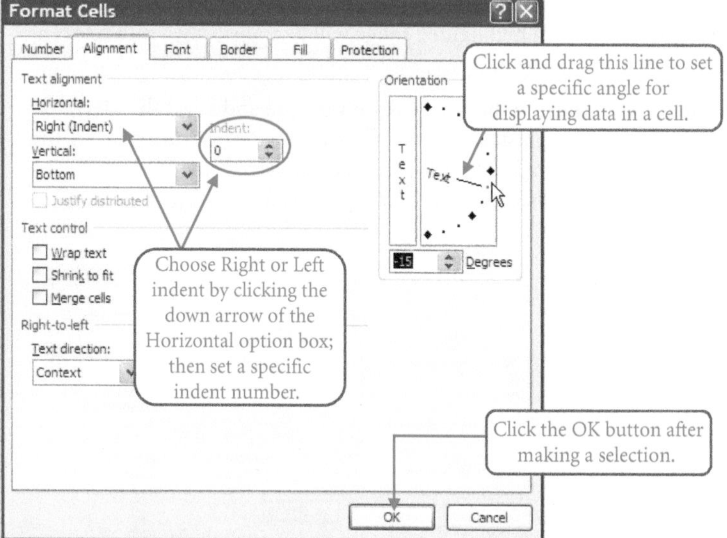


> **Quick Reference**
>
> **Merge Cells**
>
> 1. Highlight a range of cells to be merged.
> 2. Click the **Home** tab of the Ribbon.
> 3. Click the down arrow of the **Merge & Center** icon and select an option.

## Number Formats

Commands used to format the appearance of numbers are found in the **Number** group, as shown in Figure 31. These options allow you to format numeric data such as currency, percentages, dates, or fractions.

Figure 31 | **Icons for Number Formats**

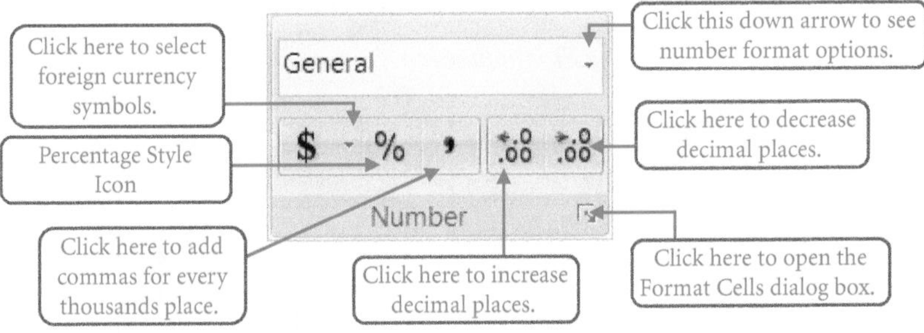


Figure 32 shows the options that are available when clicking the down arrow of the **Number Format** icon.

Figure 32 | **Number Format Icons Drop-Down Box**

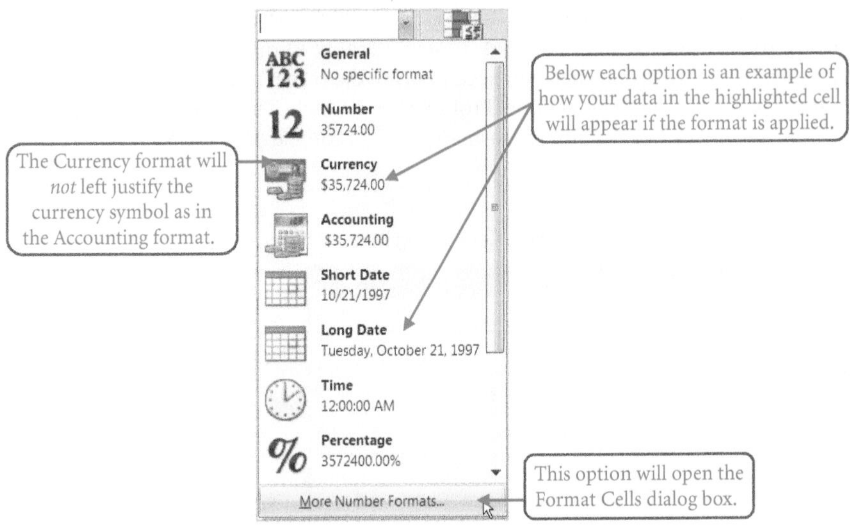


The following steps explain how you apply the Accounting format to the numbers in the Financial Plan worksheet. The Accounting format will left justify the currency symbol, add a comma for every thousands place, add two decimal places, and place negative numbers in parentheses.

- Highlight the range B3:F7. As with other formatting commands, you must highlight a range of cells first before selecting a number format.
- Click the **Home** tab on the Ribbon.
- Click the **Accounting Number Format** icon. If you are working with foreign currency, you can select a different currency symbol such as Euros or English Pounds by clicking the down arrow of this icon.
- Click the **Decrease Decimal** icon twice. As with most financial plans, carrying financial projections to two decimal places is not necessary. Therefore, you remove the decimal places by clicking the **Decrease Decimal** icon twice.

> **Quick Reference**
>
> **Accounting Format**
>
> 1. Highlight a range of cells to be formatted.
> 2. Click the **Home** tab of the Ribbon.
> 3. Click the **Accounting Number Format** icon [$ ▾]. Click the down arrow next to this icon to change the currency symbol.
> 4. Click the **Increase** or **Decrease Decimal** icons [.00] and [.0] as needed.

Figure 33 | **Accounting Format Applied to the Financial Plan Worksheet**

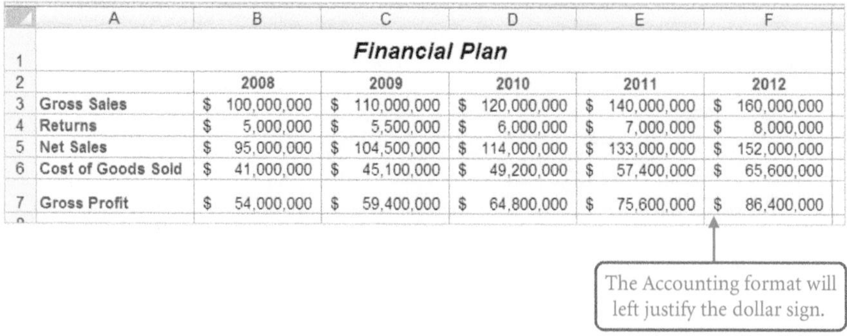

| | A | B | C | D | E | F |
|---|---|---|---|---|---|---|
| 1 | **Financial Plan** | | | | | |
| 2 | | 2008 | 2009 | 2010 | 2011 | 2012 |
| 3 | Gross Sales | $ 100,000,000 | $ 110,000,000 | $ 120,000,000 | $ 140,000,000 | $ 160,000,000 |
| 4 | Returns | $ 5,000,000 | $ 5,500,000 | $ 6,000,000 | $ 7,000,000 | $ 8,000,000 |
| 5 | Net Sales | $ 95,000,000 | $ 104,500,000 | $ 114,000,000 | $ 133,000,000 | $ 152,000,000 |
| 6 | Cost of Goods Sold | $ 41,000,000 | $ 45,100,000 | $ 49,200,000 | $ 57,400,000 | $ 65,600,000 |
| 7 | Gross Profit | $ 54,000,000 | $ 59,400,000 | $ 64,800,000 | $ 75,600,000 | $ 86,400,000 |

The Accounting format will left justify the dollar sign.

As you can see in Figure 32, you can open the **Format Cells** dialog box by selecting the **More Number Formats** option in the **Number Format** drop-down box. When you are applying number formats, the **Format Cells** dialog box provides several options that are not available in the Ribbon. For example, when applying the Currency format, you can choose an option that converts negative numbers to a red font color. This color is most helpful when you need to bring the reader's attention to negative results that are critical, such as Gross Profit or Net Income. The **Format Cells** dialog box also provides more options for formatting dates compared to the **Number Format** icon. These options are highlighted in Figure 34.

Figure 34 | **Number Tab of the Format Cells Dialog Box**

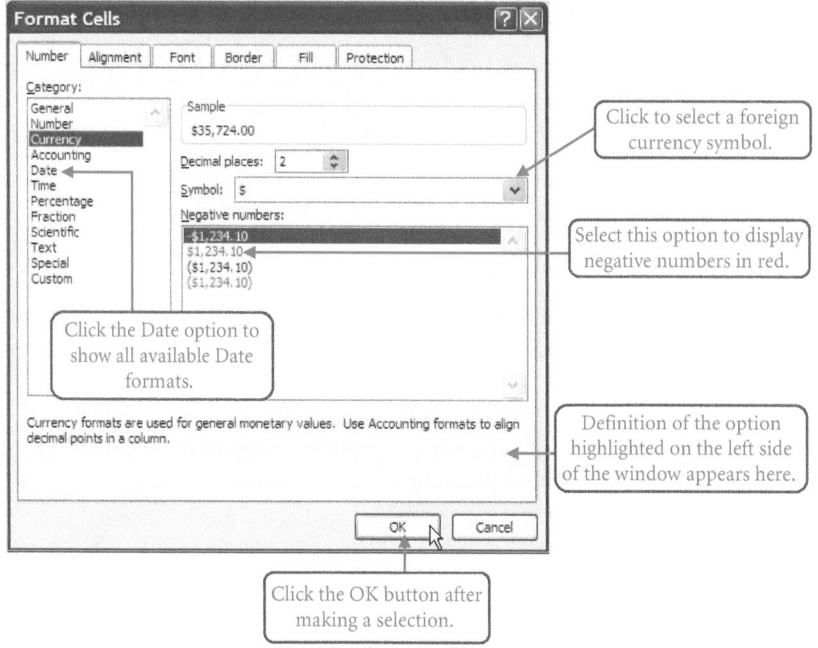
Format Cells
Number
Alignment
Font
Border
Fill
Protection
Category:
General
Number
Currency
Accounting
Date
Time
Percentage
Fraction
Scientific
Text
Special
Custom
Sample
$35,724.00
Decimal places: 2
Symbol: $
Negative numbers:
-$1,234.10
$1,234.10
($1,234.10)
($1,234.10)
Currency formats are used for general monetary values. Use Accounting formats to align decimal points in a column.
OK
Cancel
Click to select a foreign currency symbol.
Select this option to display negative numbers in red.
Click the Date option to show all available Date formats.
Definition of the option highlighted on the left side of the window appears here.
Click the OK button after making a selection.

> **Quick Reference**
> **Formatting Numbers**
> 1. Highlight a range of cells containing numbers to be formatted.
> 2. Click the **Home** tab of the Ribbon.
> 3. Click one of the icons in the **Number** group of the Ribbon or open the **Format Cells** dialog box by clicking the button in the lower-right corner of the **Number** group.
> 4. If using the **Format Cells** dialog box, click the **OK** button after making a selection.

## COMMON MISTAKES | Using the Currency Format

When selecting the Currency format from the **Format Cells** dialog box, check the **Symbol** setting. Occasionally, this box may be set to **none**. Also, if you are working on an accounting assignment and would like to left justify the dollar signs, use the Accounting format. Dollar signs will be placed in front of the value and will not align when using the Currency format.

## Borders (Line Formats)

Use the ***Border*** command to place lines on an Excel worksheet. As previously mentioned, a key purpose for enhancing the appearance of a worksheet is to make it easy for a reader to find and analyze needed information. Adding lines to a worksheet advances this purpose because it helps the reader keep track of data associated with each row and also helps distinguish labels from data.

The **Borders** icon is found in the **Font** group in the **Home tab** of the Ribbon. Figure 35 illustrates the options that are available when you click the down arrow of the **Borders** icon. You add borders to a worksheet by first highlighting a range of cells and then selecting one of the line styles and placement options shown in the figure.

Figure 35 | **Line and Placement Options in the Borders Icon**

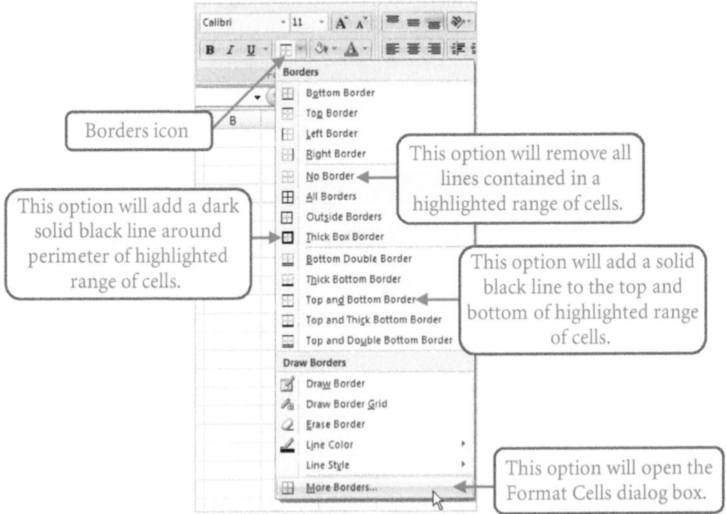


As illustrated in Figure 35, the **Borders** icon provides several options for adding lines to a worksheet. However, you may find these options limiting. For example, the options in the **Borders** icon will only provide black lines and contain only a few line styles. As a result, you may need to use the **Format Cells** dialog box when adding lines to a worksheet. The following steps explain how you use both the **Borders** icon and the **Format Cells** dialog box to add lines to the Merchandise Sales Report:

- Highlight the range A1:E19.
- Click the **Home** tab of the Ribbon.
- Click the down arrow in the **Borders** icon.
- Select the **Thick Box Border** option. A dark black line will appear around the perimeter of the highlighted range.
- Highlight the range A2:E19.
- Click the down arrow in the **Borders** icon and select the **More Borders** option. This will open the **Format Cells** dialog box to the **Border** tab. You can also click the button in the lower-right corner of the **Font** section in the Ribbon and click the **Border** tab when the **Format Cells** dialog box opens.
- Click the down arrow of the **Color** box and select the black square.
- Click the regular solid line style on the left side of the dialog box.
- Click the **Inside** icon at the upper-right side of the dialog box. You will see vertical and horizontal lines appear in the locator box. This option of placing lines only on

the inside of a range of cells and not the perimeter is not available in the **Borders** icon. This is why the **Format Cells** dialog box is needed in this case.

- Click the down arrow of the **Color** box and select the Dark Red square in the lower-left corner of the color palette.
- Click the dark solid line style on the left side of the dialog box.
- Click the top of the locator box on the right side of the dialog box. This will place a dark solid red line at the top of the highlighted range. Different line colors are not available in the **Borders** icon options. Therefore, you must use the **Format Cells** dialog box in these situations.

Figure 36 shows the final settings that were made in the **Border** tab of the **Format Cells** dialog box. Notice the red line that appears at the top of the locator box. This indicates that the line will be placed at the top of the highlighted range cells. If the middle of the locator box were selected, a red line would appear between every row in the middle of the highlighted range.

Figure 36 | **The Border Tab of the Format Cells Dialog Box**

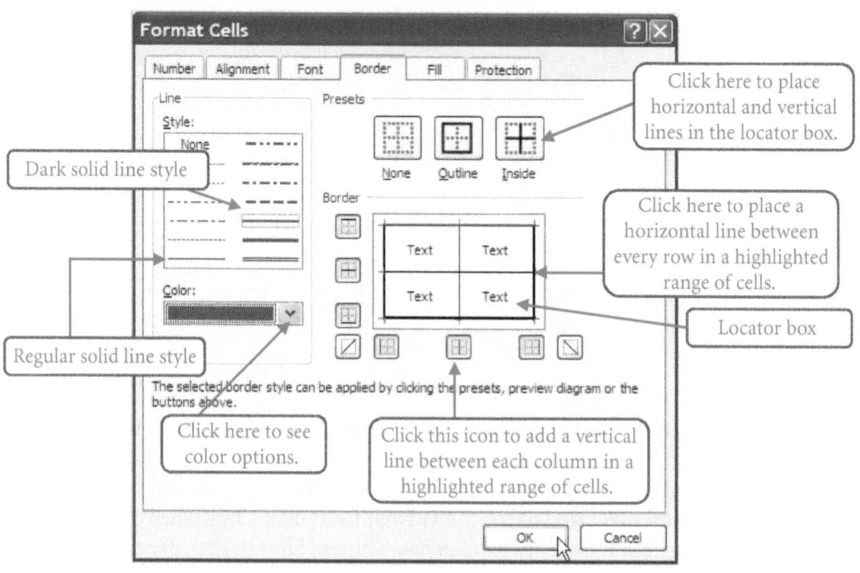


## COMMON MISTAKES | Borders

Forgetting to select the color and line styles first are the most common mistakes people make when using the **Format Cells** dialog box to add borders to a worksheet. You must select the line color and style first before selecting a placement in the locator box.

Figure 37 shows the results of adding lines to the Merchandise Sales Report. The lines make it easier to read all the data pertaining to each row and also help to separate each column. Notice that the numbers in columns D and E are formatted.

>> **Quick Reference**

### Borders

1. Highlight a range of cells where lines should appear.
2. Click the **Home** tab of the Ribbon.
3. Click the down arrow in the **Borders** icon .
4. Select a line style and placement option.

Or

1. Highlight a range of cells where lines should appear.
2. Click the **Home** tab of the Ribbon.
3. Click the down arrow in the **Borders** icon and select the **More Borders** option.
4. Select a color and line style on the right side of the window.
5. Select the placement of the line using the locator box or placement icons.
6. Click the **OK** button.

Figure 37 | **Results of Adding Lines to the Merchandise Sales Report**

|  | A | B | C | D | E |
|---|---|---|---|---|---|
| 1 | ***Category*** | ***Item Description*** | ***Color*** | ***Unit Sales*** | ***Sales Dollars*** |
| 2 | Bottoms | Shorts | Tan | 12,500 | $237,500 |
| 3 | Tops | T-Shirts | Black | 10,000 | $1[illegible] |
| 4 | Bottoms | Shorts | White | 9,500 | $1[illegible] |
| 5 | Tops | Sweater | Grey | 8,500 | $2[illegible] |
| 6 | Bottoms | Shorts | Brown | 8,500 | $16[illegible] |
| 7 | Tops | T-Shirts | Blue | 8,500 | $97,750 |
| 8 | Tops | Tank Top | White | 6,500 | $55,250 |
| 9 | Bottoms | Shorts | Blue | 5,500 | $104,500 |
| 10 | Tops | T-Shirts | Yellow | 4,500 | $51,750 |
| 11 | Tops | Sweater | Brown | 3,500 | $119,000 |
| 12 | Shoes | Sandals | Black | 3,000 | $66,000 |
| 13 | Tops | Tank Top | Pink | 2,500 | $21,250 |
| 14 | Shoes | Boots | Black | 1,600 | $96,000 |
| 15 | Tops | Sweater | Red | 1,500 | $51,000 |
| 16 | Tops | Tank Top | Red | 1,500 | $12,750 |
| 17 | Shoes | Sandals | Grey | 1,200 | $26,4[illegible] |
| 18 | Shoes | Sandals | Green | 850 | $18,7[illegible] |
| 19 | Shoes | Boots | Brown | 750 | $45,0[illegible] |

Vertical lines were added to the range A1:E1 using the Format Cells dialog box.

Numbers in these columns are formatted.

## Cell Color (Fill Color)

Changing the color of the cells in a worksheet is another formatting technique that makes titles and column headings stand out. You change the cell colors in a worksheet by using the ***Fill Color*** icon shown in Figure 38.

Figure 38 | **Fill Color Icon**

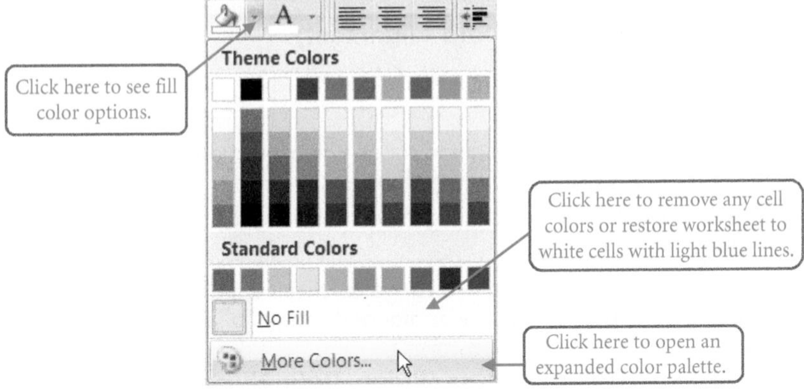
Theme Colors
Standard Colors
No Fill
More Colors...
Click here to see fill color options.
Click here to remove any cell colors or restore worksheet to white cells with light blue lines.
Click here to open an expanded color palette.

The following explains how you change the cell colors in the Financial Plan worksheet to make the title stand out:

- Highlight the range A1:F1.
- Click the **Home** tab of the Ribbon.
- Click the down arrow in the **Fill Color** icon.
- Click the Dark Blue box at the bottom of the color palette. You will notice the highlighted range changes as you move the cursor over the color palette. This allows you to see how your worksheet will appear before making a selection.
- Click the down arrow in the **Font Color** icon and select the white square. Since a dark cell color is being used, changing the color of the text to white will make the text stand out.

Figure 39 shows the results of the Financial Plan worksheet with cell colors added. In addition to the title, cells in the range B2:F2 and A3:A7 were changed to orange.

>> ***Quick Reference***

**Cell Color**

1. Highlight range of cells to be colored.
2. Click the **Home** tab of the Ribbon.
3. Click the down arrow of the **Fill Color** icon.
4. Select a color from the palette.

Figure 39 | **Results of Adding Cell Color to the Financial Plan**

| | A | B | C | D | E | F |
|---|---|---|---|---|---|---|
| 1 | **Financial Plan** | | | | | |
| 2 | | 2008 | 2009 | 2010 | 2011 | 2012 |
| 3 | Gross Sales | $ 100,000,000 | $ 110,000,000 | $ 120,000,000 | $ 140,000,000 | $ 160,000,000 |
| 4 | Returns | $ 5,000,000 | $ 5,500,000 | $ 6,000,000 | $ 7,000,000 | $ 8,000,000 |
| 5 | Net Sales | $ 95,000,000 | $ 104,500,000 | $ 114,000,000 | $ 133,000,000 | $ 152,000,000 |
| 6 | Cost of Goods Sold | $ 41,000,000 | $ 45,100,000 | $ 49,200,000 | $ 57,400,000 | $ 65,600,000 |
| 7 | Gross Profit | $ 54,000,000 | $ 59,400,000 | $ 64,800,000 | $ 75,600,000 | $ 86,400,000 |
| 8 | | | | | | |

**VIDEO WORKSHOP**

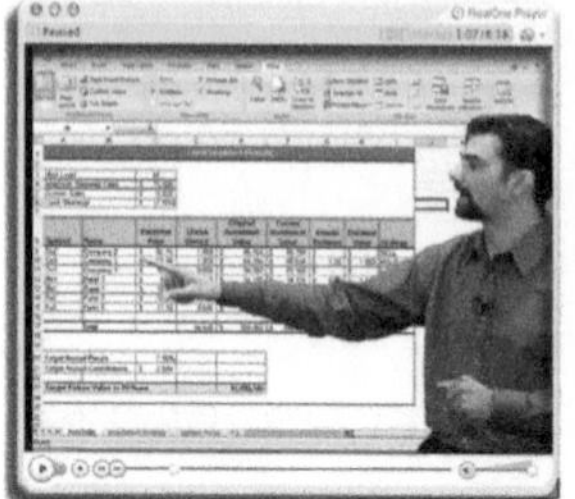

## >> Formatting

The purpose of this workshop is to demonstrate the formatting skills presented in this section of the chapter. We will continue to build the spreadsheet that was started in the Data Management Video Workshop. I will be demonstrating the tasks in this workshop in the following four videos: **Data Alignment**, **Number and Font Formats**, **Cell Color**, and **Borders**. After completing each section of tasks, watch the related video in parentheses. Remember to try the tasks on your own first before watching the video.

1. **Open File**
   a. Open the file named ib_e02_videoworkshop, which you completed for the Data Management Video Workshop previously in this chapter.
2. **Data Alignment (Video: Data Alignment)**
   a. Activate Sheet1 by clicking the worksheet tab.
   b. Highlight the range A1:F1.
   c. Merge the cells in the highlighted range without centering the text using the **Merge & Center** icon in the Ribbon.
   d. Set the horizontal and vertical alignment for the highlighted range to center.
   e. Highlight the range A2:F2.
   f. Wrap the text in the highlighted range by clicking the **Wrap Text** icon in the Ribbon. Then set the horizontal and vertical alignment to center.
3. **Adjusting Columns and Rows (Video: Data Alignment continued)**
   a. Change the width of column D to 7 points.
   b. Change the width of column F to 12 points.
   c. Change the height of row 8 to 23 points. Use the **Height** option in the **Format** icon, which is in the **Home** tab of the Ribbon.
   d. Repeat steps a and b for Sheet2 and Sheet3.
4. **Numbers and Fonts (Video: Number and Font Formats)**
   a. Activate Sheet1.
   b. For cell A1, make the following font settings: Type: Garamond; Style: Bold and Italic; Size: 14 points.
   c. Bold the text in the range A2:F3 and A8:F8
   d. Format the range D3:D12 with commas and 0 decimal places.
   e. Format the range E3:E12 to U.S. currency and 2 decimal places.

f. Format the range F3:F12 to U.S. currency and 0 decimal places.
g. Repeat steps d, e, and f for Sheet2 and Sheet3.

5. **Cell Color (Fill Color) (Video: Cell Color)**
   a. Activate Sheet1.
   b. For cell A1, change the cell color to brown and change the text color to white.
   c. Change the cell color to yellow for the range A2:F2.
   d. Change the text color to blue for the range A3:F3 and A8:F8.

6. **Borders (Video: Borders)**
   a. Highlight the range A1:F12 and add a thick bold black line around the perimeter of the range. Use the **Format Cells** dialog box to add this border.
   b. Highlight the range A1:F2 and add a horizontal bold black line in the middle and bottom of the range. Use the **Format Cells** dialog box to add these borders.
   c. Highlight the range A2:F2 and add a vertical regular black line to the middle of the range. Use the **Format Cells** dialog box to add this border.
   d. Highlight the range A3:F12 and add horizontal and vertical regular black lines to the middle of the range. Use the **Format Cells** dialog box to add these borders.
   e. Highlight the range A7:F7 and add a red double line to the bottom of the range. Use the **Format Cells** dialog box to add this border.
   f. Save and close your file. Remember where you saved this file because it will be used in the Editing Video Workshop.

## >> Creating a Store Performance Report

**EXERCISE**
**Why Do I Need This?**

Formatting techniques are used to direct the reader to the most critical information on a spreadsheet and are often the difference between a mediocre and professional spreadsheet. It is important for you to be aware of the formatting commands available in Excel and how they can be applied to create an effective spreadsheet.

### Exercise

Open the file named ib_e02_storeperformancereport. You will see a worksheet without any formatting techniques applied. Your goal will be to format this spreadsheet for the distribution manager of a retail store chain. Follow the directions and remember to save your work periodically.

1. Copy Sheet1 and paste it into Sheet2.
2. Make the title of the report stand out so that it can be easily distinguished from other reports this manager will be evaluating. Highlight the range A1:N1 in Sheet2 and apply the following formats:
   a. Merge the cells.
   b. Set the horizontal and vertical alignment to center.
   c. Change the font size to 14, the font style to bold, and change the font color to white.
   d. Change the cell color to green.

3. Your next task is to fix the column headings of the report. You will notice that in some instances you cannot see the entire column heading because it is too long to fit in a cell. Adjust the headings as follows:
   a. Highlight the range I2:N2. Merge the cells, set the horizontal alignment to center, and then bold and italicize the text.
   b. Highlight the range A3:N3. Instead of increasing the width of these columns to show the column headings, format the cells to wrap text, set the horizontal alignment to center, bold the text, and change the color of the cells to yellow.
   c. Since this spreadsheet has several columns, keep the width as narrow as possible. Make the following column width adjustments:
      i. Column A: **7.5**
      ii. Column B: **12**
      iii. Column C: **6**
      iv. Column E: **10**
      v. Column H: **10**
      vi. Column J: **9**
4. Format the numbers on the spreadsheet as follows:
   a. D4:E28: Number format with commas, 0 decimal places.
   b. F4:G28: U.S. Currency format, 0 decimal places. You may need to readjust the column widths.
   c. H4:H28: Number format with 0 decimal places.
   d. I4:N28: U.S. Currency format, 0 decimal places. You may need to readjust the column widths.
5. The information the distribution manager is most concerned about is the estimated annual truck deliveries. The distribution manager will need this information to calculate the shipping costs by store and for the entire retail chain. To make this column of data stand out, add the following format settings to the range H4:H28:
   a. Set the horizontal alignment to center.
   b. Bold and italicize the text.
   c. Italicize the text in cell H3.
   d. Change the color of the text in the range H3:H28 to dark blue.
6. The distribution manager will use the right side of this spreadsheet as a reference to get an idea of how the volume of deliveries might change from month to month. This section needs to be visually separated form the rest of the worksheet. Change the cell color to light green for the range I4:N28.
7. The last step in this formatting exercise is to add lines to the spreadsheet. Without lines, it will be very difficult to follow the data for each store across the spreadsheet. Add the following lines to the spreadsheet:
   a. Add regular black lines to the inside of the range A3:N28. Every cell in this range should have a regular black outline.
   b. Add a heavy dark bold line around the perimeter of the range A3:N28.
   c. Add a regular bold line around the perimeter of the range A3:N3.
   d. Add a regular bold line to the bottom of cell A1.
   e. Add a bold line to the left of range I2:I28.
8. Sort the worksheet based on the Estimated Annual Truck Deliveries column in descending order.

9. Compare Sheet1 and Sheet2. What formatting techniques make the biggest impact?

10. What stores are expected to receive 37 annual truck deliveries, and what is the size of these stores in square feet?

11. What information was necessary before adding format techniques to this spreadsheet?

12. Save and close your file.

## >> What's Wrong with This Spreadsheet?

**PROBLEM & EXERCISE**

### Problem

You are approached by a coworker who works in the price change division of a jewelry store. The company is having a sale and reducing the prices on several pieces of jewelry. Your coworker was asked to prepare a spreadsheet that lists all the items that will be included in the sale, the original price, and the new reduced price. She attaches an Excel file in an e-mail and asks for your help. Her e-mail includes the following points:

1. I set up a spreadsheet that shows all the sale items for this weekend. I listed each item with the current price, and I am trying to add a column to show the new reduced price. For some reason, no matter what I type into this column, nothing appears. Try it! I entered the first price which is $90. But nothing shows up in the cell. When I activate the cell (D3), I can see it says $90 in the formula bar, but I can't see it in the cell. I can't understand why this is happening. I didn't do anything but type in the price. Oh wait. . . I did try something. I tried to change the color of the cells by clicking on one of those icons at the top, but it didn't work. That still doesn't explain why nothing shows up in the cell.

2. The other problem I am having is with the border around the worksheet. I am simply trying to add a bold outline around the worksheet. I opened the Format Cells dialog box to the Border tab and clicked on all four sides of the locator box on the left. Then I clicked the dark bold line on the right and clicked the OK button. However, the regular thin line keeps appearing instead of the bold line. I must have clicked that bold line a hundred times, but I keep getting this stupid thin black line. At this point, I am beginning to think there is something seriously wrong with my computer! However, I heard you were really good with this stuff. Can you help?

### Exercise

Open the file named ib_e02_pricechangeproblems. What's wrong with this spreadsheet? Consider the following points:

1. Try typing a number in any of the cells in the range D3:D12. Why can't you see the number?

2. Why is this coworker having trouble getting the bold line to appear on the worksheet? Follow the steps she explained in point 2 carefully. Is this right?

Write a short answer for each of these points and fix the spreadsheet for this coworker.

Skill Set

# Editing

After creating a spreadsheet, you may need to make edits. Editing a spreadsheet may involve changing the data in a cell location, adding a new column of data, or deleting an existing column of data. The editing commands covered in this section can be found in the **Home** tab of the Ribbon. As in previous sections, we will again use the Financial Plan and Merchandise Sales Report spreadsheets to demonstrate the editing commands.

## Editing Data in a Cell

After typing data into a cell location, you can change it by using the ***formula bar*** or by double clicking the cell. The formula bar, as shown in Figure 40, will always show the contents of an active cell. To change the data in an active cell, click the formula bar, type any adjustments, and press the **Enter** key. Figure 40 shows how the word "Description" was added to cell A1 using the formula bar. This edit can also be accomplished by double clicking cell A1.

Figure 40 | **Editing Data Using the Formula Bar**

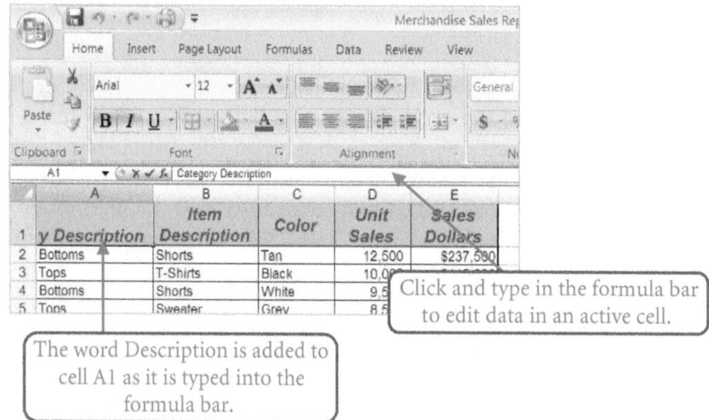
Click and type in the formula bar to edit data in an active cell.
The word Description is added to cell A1 as it is typed into the formula bar.

> **Quick Reference**
>
> **Editing Data**
>
> 1. Activate cell containing data.
> 2. Click in the formula bar.
> 3. Type edits in the formula bar.
> 4. Press the **Enter** key.
>
> Or
>
> 1. Double click a cell with data.
> 2. Type edits.
> 3. Press the **Enter** key.

### COMMON MISTAKES | Editing Data

Even though you are editing data, as opposed to entering data, you must still press the **Enter** key after completing your edits. Edits will not be finalized unless you press the **Enter** key, or you left click another cell. If you are using the formula bar to edit data in a cell, you can enter the change by clicking the check mark that appears on the left of the formula bar.

## Moving Data

You can move data in Excel by clicking and dragging the edge of an active cell or a range of cells. Move the cursor to the edge of the active cell or range cells. When the cursor changes from a white plus sign to crossed arrows, click and drag the data to a new location on a spreadsheet (see Figure 41).

> **Quick Reference**
>
> **Moving Data**
>
> 1. Activate a cell or highlight a range of cells to be moved.
> 2. Move the cursor to the edge of the cell or range.
> 3. When the cursor changes to crossed arrows, click and drag.

Figure 41 | **Moving Data**

| | A | B | C | D | E |
|---|---|---|---|---|---|
| 1 | Category | Item Description | Color | Unit Sales | Sales Dollars |
| 2 | Bottoms | Shorts | Tan | 12,500 | $237,500 |
| 3 | Tops | T-Shirts | Black | 10,000 | $115,000 |
| 4 | Bottoms | Shorts | White | 9,500 | $180,500 |
| 5 | Tops | Sweater | Grey | 8,500 | $289,000 |
| 6 | Bottoms | Shorts | Brown | 8,500 | $161,500 |
| 7 | Tops | T-Shirts | Blue | 8,500 | $97,750 |
| 8 | Tops | Tank Top | White | 6,500 | $55,250 |
| 9 | Bottoms | Shorts | Blue | 5,500 | $104,500 |
| 10 | Tops | T-Shirts | Yellow | 4,500 | $51,750 |
| 11 | Tops | Sweater | Brown | 3,500 | $119,00 |
| 12 | Shoes | Sandals | Black | 3,000 | $66,0 |
| 13 | Tops | Tank Top | Pink | 2,500 | $21,2 |
| 14 | Shoes | Boots | Black | 1,600 | $96,0 |
| 15 | Tops | Sweater | Red | 1,500 | $51,0 |
| 16 | Tops | Tank Top | Red | 1,500 | $12,7 |
| 17 | Shoes | Sandals | Grey | 1,200 | $26,400 |
| 18 | Shoes | Sandals | Green | 850 | $18,700 |
| 19 | Shoes | Boots | Brown | 750 | $45,000 |

This range of cells can be moved by clicking and dragging to a new location when the cursor changes to crossed arrows.

## Deleting Columns and Rows

A common Excel editing feature is deleting columns and rows, which is especially helpful when you are using a subset of data from a larger spreadsheet. For example, you may have received a large dataset from a classmate or coworker and want to reduce the spreadsheet to only the data you need. Or, you may need to remove rows of data that are no longer relevant to the purpose of a spreadsheet. The command to delete columns and rows is found in the **Cells** group of the **Home** tab in the Ribbon, as shown in Figure 42.

Figure 42 | **Icons in the Cells Group of the Ribbon**

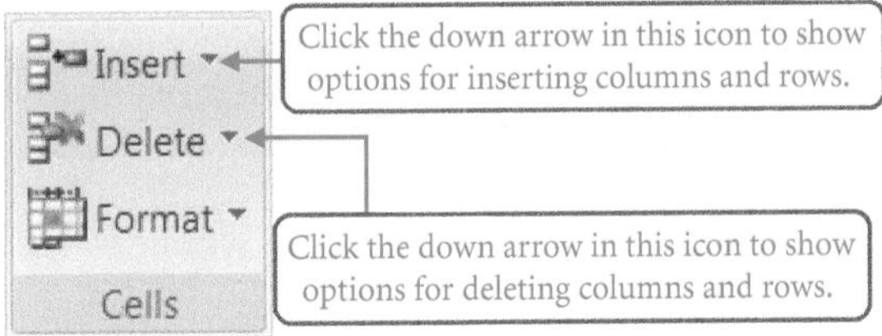
Insert
Delete
Format
Cells
Click the down arrow in this icon to show options for inserting columns and rows.
Click the down arrow in this icon to show options for deleting columns and rows.

The following steps explain how you delete a row from the Merchandise Sales Report. This example assumes that the Green Sandals are being returned to the manufacturer and will no longer be sold in the store. Therefore, this row is being deleted from the sales report.

- Activate any cell in row 18. Since the Green Sandals are in row 18, you can activate any cell in this row to delete the entire row.
- Click the **Home** tab in the Ribbon.
- Click the drop-down arrow in the **Delete** icon in the **Cells** group.
- Select the **Delete Sheet Rows** option. This will remove row 18 and shift the data in row 19 up to row 18.

Figure 43 illustrates how row 18 is deleted from the Merchandise Sales Report. Note that the steps for deleting a column are identical to deleting a row; however, you need to activate one cell in the column that is being deleted. For example, notice that cell F18 in Figure 43 is activated. When the **Delete Sheet Rows** option is selected from the **Delete** icon, this row will be deleted. However, if the **Delete Sheet Columns** option is selected, *column* F will be deleted.

> **Quick Reference**
>
> **Deleting Columns or Rows**
>
> 1. Activate one cell in the row or column you want to delete.
> 2. Click the **Home** tab in the Ribbon.
> 3. Click the down arrow in the **Delete** icon in the **Cells** group.
> 4. Select the **Delete Sheet Columns** or **Delete Sheet Rows** options.

Figure 43 | **Deleting a Row from the Merchandise Sales Report**

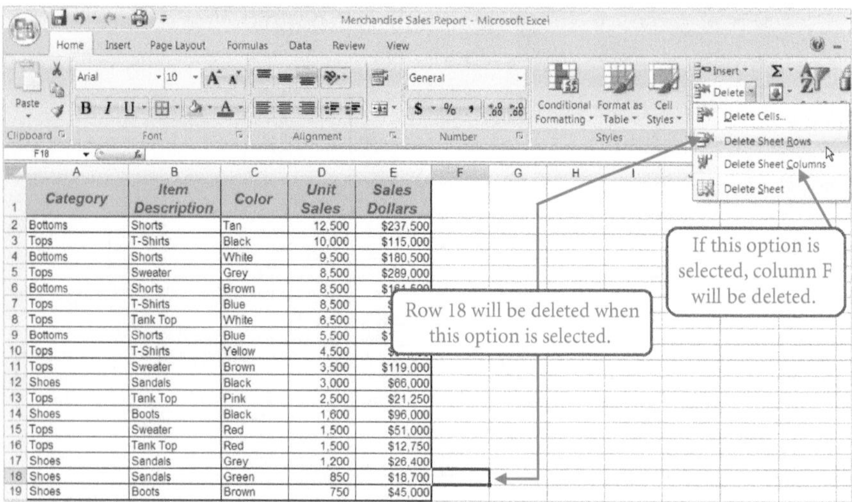


| | Category | Item Description | Color | Unit Sales | Sales Dollars |
|---|---|---|---|---|---|
| 2 | Bottoms | Shorts | Tan | 12,500 | $237,500 |
| 3 | Tops | T-Shirts | Black | 10,000 | $115,000 |
| 4 | Bottoms | Shorts | White | 9,500 | $180,500 |
| 5 | Tops | Sweater | Grey | 8,500 | $289,000 |
| 6 | Bottoms | Shorts | Brown | 8,500 | [illegible] |
| 7 | Tops | T-Shirts | Blue | 8,500 | [illegible] |
| 8 | Tops | Tank Top | White | 6,500 | [illegible] |
| 9 | Bottoms | Shorts | Blue | 5,500 | [illegible] |
| 10 | Tops | T-Shirts | Yellow | 4,500 | [illegible] |
| 11 | Tops | Sweater | Brown | 3,500 | $119,000 |
| 12 | Shoes | Sandals | Black | 3,000 | $66,000 |
| 13 | Tops | Tank Top | Pink | 2,500 | $21,250 |
| 14 | Shoes | Boots | Black | 1,600 | $96,000 |
| 15 | Tops | Sweater | Red | 1,500 | $51,000 |
| 16 | Tops | Tank Top | Red | 1,500 | $12,750 |
| 17 | Shoes | Sandals | Grey | 1,200 | $26,400 |
| 18 | Shoes | Sandals | Green | 850 | $18,700 |
| 19 | Shoes | Boots | Brown | 750 | $45,000 |

## COMMON MISTAKES | Deleting Columns and Rows

You cannot delete a column or row by highlighting cells and pressing the **Delete** key. When you delete a column, the remaining columns should shift to the left. When you delete a row, the remaining rows should shift up.

## Deleting Worksheets

Included in the **Delete** icon in the **Cells** group of the Ribbon is an option for deleting entire worksheets from a workbook. The reasons you may need to delete an entire worksheet are similar to the reasons explained for deleting columns and rows. The following steps explain how you delete a worksheet from a workbook:

- Activate a worksheet that will be deleted by clicking the worksheet tab.
- Click the **Home** tab of the Ribbon.
- Click the down arrow in the **Delete** icon in the **Cells** group.
- Select the **Delete Sheet** option (see Figure 44). When the **Delete Sheet** option is selected, a warning box will appear if there is data in the worksheet you are trying to delete.
- Click the **Delete** button on the warning box to delete the active worksheet (see Figure 45).

> **Quick Reference**
>
> **Deleting Worksheets**
>
> 1. Activate the worksheet you want to delete by clicking the worksheet tab.
> 2. Click the **Home** tab of the Ribbon.
> 3. Click the down arrow in the **Delete** icon in the **Cells** group.
> 4. Click the **Delete Sheet** option.
> 5. Check the worksheet carefully to make sure it is okay to delete.
> 6. Click the **Delete** button at the bottom of the warning box.

Figure 44 | **Deleting Worksheets**

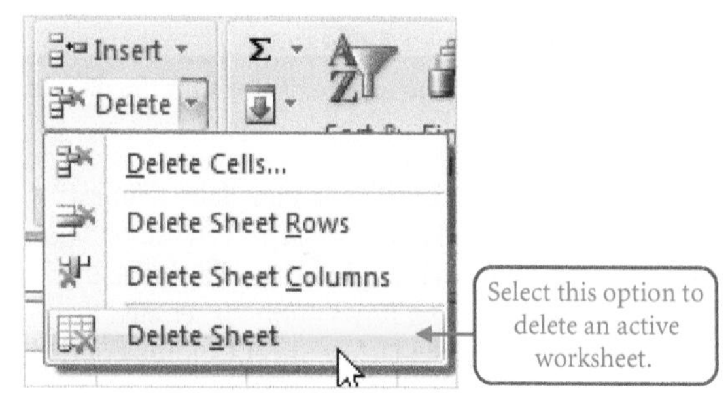

Figure 45 | **Warning Message When Deleting Worksheets**

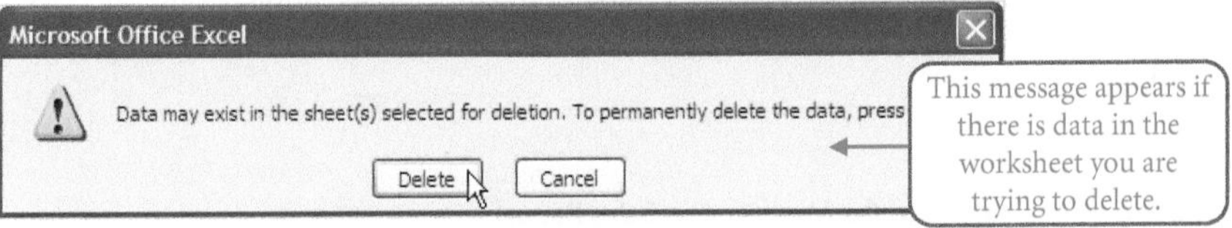

Microsoft Office Excel
Data may exist in the sheet(s) selected for deletion. To permanently delete the data, press
Delete
Cancel
This message appears if there is data in the worksheet you are trying to delete.


## COMMON MISTAKES | Deleting Worksheets

You cannot use the **Undo** icon after a worksheet is deleted. Therefore, check the worksheet carefully before clicking the **Delete** button on the warning box shown in Figure 45. There is no way to retrieve a worksheet after it is deleted.

# Inserting Columns and Rows

Another common Excel editing feature is inserting columns and rows. Often, you may need to add additional rows or columns of data to your own or other people's spreadsheets. For example, a noticeable omission in the Merchandise Sales Report (see Figure 43) is a title. If the report is without a title, it is impossible to know if the data in the Unit Sales column represents a week of sales, annual sales, or monthly sales. Therefore, a new row above the first row must be inserted for a title.

Similar to deleting columns and rows, the icon for inserting columns and rows also resides in the **Cells** group in the **Home** tab of the Ribbon (see Figure 42). The following steps explain how you add a row to the Merchandise Sales Report for the purpose of adding a title:

- Activate cell A1. Rows are always inserted above an active cell or range of cells. In this example, a row needs to be added above the first row in the worksheet. Therefore, cell A1 is activated.
- Click the **Home** tab in the Ribbon.
- Click the down arrow in the **Insert** icon in the **Cells** group.
- Click the **Insert Sheet Rows** option. After you select this option, a blank row will appear above row 1.

Figure 46 illustrates a row being inserted in the Merchandise Sales Report worksheet. Note the steps for inserting a column are identical to inserting a row; however, a column will always be inserted to the left of an active cell after you select the **Insert Sheet Columns** option from the **Insert** icon.

Figure 46 | **Inserting a Row in the Merchandise Sales Report**

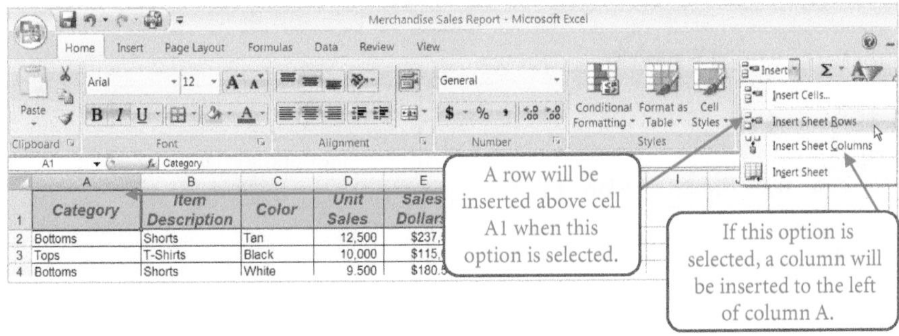

Figure 47 shows the results of adding a title to the Merchandise Sales Report. This figure reflects formatting enhancements that were added to make the title stand out. A reader can now see that the sales data shown in this worksheet are for the month of June.

Figure 47 | **Title Added to the Merchandise Sales Report**

| | A | B | C | D | E |
|---|---|---|---|---|---|
| 1 | ***Sales for the Month of June*** | | | | |
| 2 | ***Category Description*** | ***Item Description*** | ***Color*** | ***Unit Sales*** | ***Sales Dollars*** |
| 3 | Bottoms | Shorts | Tan | 12,500 | $237,500 |
| 4 | Tops | T-Shirts | Black | 10,000 | $115,000 |
| 5 | Bottoms | Shorts | White | 9,500 | $180,500 |
| 6 | Tops | Sweater | Grey | 8,500 | $289,000 |
| 7 | Bottoms | Shorts | Brown | 8,500 | $161,500 |
| 8 | Tops | T-Shirts | Blue | 8,500 | $97,750 |

## Inserting, Moving, and Renaming Worksheet Tabs

As mentioned earlier in this chapter, business managers will often create multiple versions or scenarios of a plan by copying an existing worksheet and pasting it into other worksheets in a workbook. This scenario was illustrated in Figure 14 for the Financial Plan spreadsheet. As a result, you may need to add additional worksheets to a workbook, arrange the order of those worksheets, and rename each worksheet tab. The following points explain how to accomplish each of these tasks:

- Click the **Insert Worksheet** tab at the bottom of a worksheet to add additional worksheets to a workbook (see Figure 48).
- Click and drag a worksheet tab to adjust the order it appears among the other worksheet tabs (see Figure 49).
- Double click a worksheet tab and type a new name. Press the **Enter** key after you type a desired name into the worksheet tab (see Figure 50).

Figure 48 | **Inserting New Worksheets**

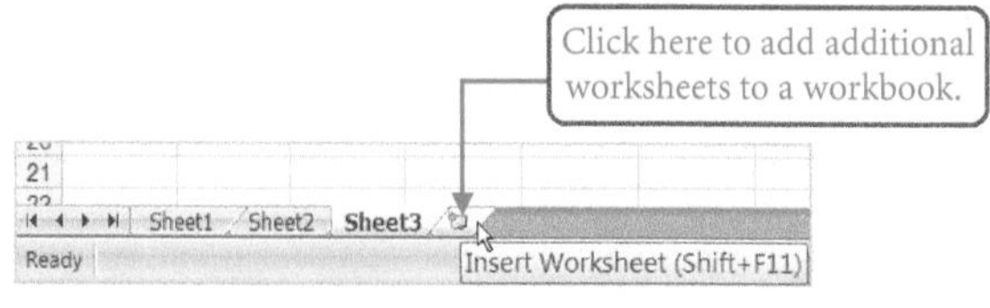


Figure 49 | **Moving Worksheets**

19
20
Sheet2 Sheet1 Sheet3 Sheet4
Ready

Sheet1 was moved to the right of Sheet2 by clicking and dragging the worksheet tab.

> **Quick Reference**
>
> **Insert Columns or Rows**
>
> 1. Activate a cell depending on where a blank column or row should be inserted. Rows are inserted above an active cell; columns are inserted to the left of an active cell.
> 2. Click the **Home** tab.
> 3. Click the down arrow in the **Insert** icon in the **Cells** group of the Ribbon.
> 4. Select **Insert Sheet Rows** or **Insert Sheet Columns**.

Figure 50 | **Renaming Worksheets**

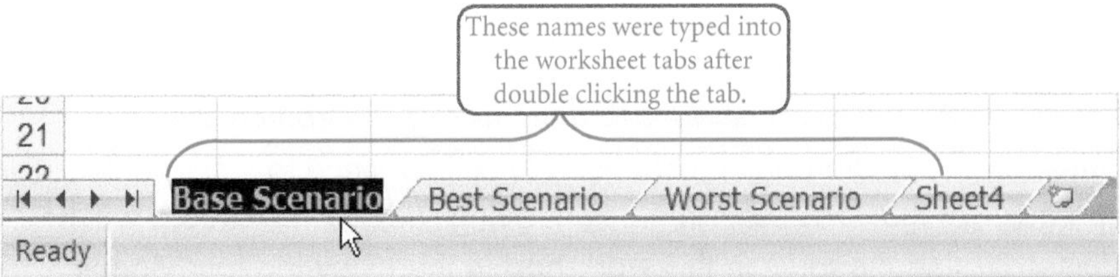


You can also rename worksheets by placing the cursor over a worksheet tab and clicking the right mouse button. This will open the set of worksheet commands shown in Figure 51. These commands are also contained in the **Format** icon in the **Cells** section of the Ribbon. The benefit of using this method is that it provides other options such as changing the color of the worksheet tab.

Figure 51 | **Changing the Worksheet Tab Color**

| | A | B | C | D | E | F |
|---|---|---|---|---|---|---|
| 1 | Financial Plan | | | | | |
| 2 | | 2008 | 2009 | 2010 | 2011 | 2012 |
| 3 | Gross Sales | $ 100,000,000 | $ 110,000,000 | $ 120,000,000 | $ 140,000,000 | $ 160,000,000 |
| 4 | Returns | $ 5,000,000 | $ 5,500,000 | $ 6,000,000 | $ 7,000,000 | $ 8,000,000 |
| 5 | Net Sales | $ 95,000,000 | $ 104,500,000 | $ 114,000,000 | $ 133,000,000 | $ 152,000,000 |
| 6 | Cost of Goods Sold | $ 41,000,000 | $ 45,100,000 | $ 49,200,000 | $ 57,400,000 | $ 65,600,000 |
| 7 | Gross Profit | | 59,400,000 | $ 64,800,000 | $ 75,600,000 | $ 86,400,000 |



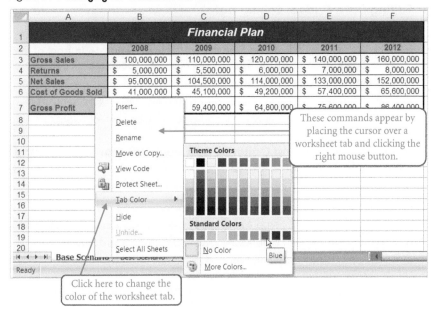

## COMMON MISTAKES | Naming Worksheet Tabs

Excel will not let you use the same name for multiple worksheet tabs. Each tab must have a unique name. If you are getting a duplicate worksheet name error but do not see another worksheet with the same name, check to see whether any worksheets are hidden by selecting the **Unhide Sheet** option in the **Hide & Unhide** submenu of the **Format** icon.

> **Quick Reference**
>
> **Inserting Worksheets**
>
> 1. Click the **Insert Worksheet** tab at the bottom of the Excel screen.

> **Quick Reference**
>
> **Moving Worksheets**
>
> 1. Click and drag the worksheet tab.

> **Quick Reference**
>
> **Renaming a Worksheet Tab**
>
> 1. Double click the worksheet tab you wish to rename.
> 2. Type the new name.
> 3. Press the **Enter** key.

> **Quick Reference**
>
> **Worksheet Tab Color**
>
> 1. Click the worksheet tab where the color is to be changed.
> 2. Place the cursor over the worksheet tab.
> 3. Right click.
> 4. Select **Tab Color**.
> 5. Select a color from the color palette.

**VIDEO WORKSHOP**

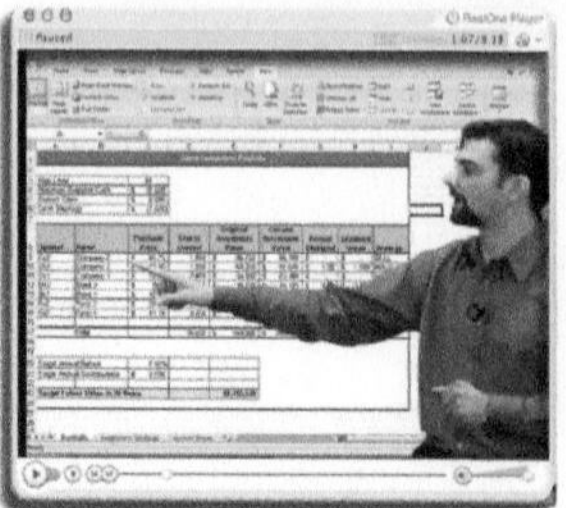

# >> Editing

The purpose of this workshop is to demonstrate the editing skills presented in this section of the chapter. We will continue to work on the spreadsheet that was used in the Formatting Video Workshop. I will be demonstrating the tasks in this workshop in the following four videos: **Editing Data**, **Inserting and Deleting Columns and Rows**, **Moving Data**, and **Renaming Worksheet Tabs**. After completing each section of tasks, watch the related video in parentheses. Remember to try the tasks on your own first before watching the video.

1. **Open File**
   a. Open the file named ib_e02_videoworkshop, which you completed for the Formatting Video Workshop.

2. **Editing Data (Video: Editing Data)**
   a. Activate cell A1 in Sheet1.
   b. Click in the formula bar and type the word **Merchandise** in front of the word *Sales*. Then press the **Enter** key. In Sheet1, double click cell F2.
   c. Add the word **Total** in front of the word *Sales* and press the **Enter** key.
   d. Copy the range A1:F2 in Sheet1 and paste into cell A1 of Sheet2.
   e. Copy the range A1:F2 in Sheet1 and paste into cell A1 of Sheet3.

3. **Inserting and Deleting Columns and Rows (Video: Inserting and Deleting Columns and Rows)**
   a. Insert a row above row 1 in all three worksheets.
   b. Delete row 1 in Sheet1.
   c. For Sheet2 in cell A1, type **Arranged for Distribution Center**.
   d. For Sheet3 in cell A1, type **Arranged for Merchandisers**.
   e. For Sheet3, insert a column between columns A and B.

4. **Moving Data and Adjusting Formats (Video: Moving Data)**
   a. In Sheet3, move the range D3:D13 to column B beginning in cell B3.
   b. Move the range G3:G13 to column D beginning in cell D3.
   c. Adjust the width of column D to 12 points.
   d. Delete column G.
   e. For cell D3, convert the bold line on the right side of the cell to a regular line.
   f. Highlight the range A2:F13 and add a heavy bold line on the left, right, and bottom of the range.
   g. Highlight the range A4:F13 and add regular horizontal and vertical lines inside the range.
   h. Activate Sheet2.
   i. Highlight the range A4:F13 and add a heavy bold line to the left, right, and bottom of the range and add regular horizontal and vertical lines inside the range.

5. **Worksheet Tabs (Video: Renaming Worksheet Tabs)**
   a. Change the tab name for Sheet1 to **`Standard`**.
   b. Change the tab name for Sheet2 to **`DC Format`**.
   c. Change the tab name for Sheet3 to **`Merchant Format`**.
   d. Save and close the file. Remember where this file is saved because you will use it in the next Video Workshop on Printing.

## >> Editing Store Sales Reports

**EXERCISE**

**Why Do I Need This?**

In business, you will always need to adjust and format spreadsheets based on your reader's requirements. The editing skills covered in this section provide you with more tools to accomplish this task. Business managers are often very demanding when it comes to seeing information and reports that address their needs. This often results in your creating several spreadsheets that are different in appearance but display the same or similar data.

### Exercise

Open the spreadsheet named ib_e02_monthlystoresalesreport. The goal of this exercise will be to edit this report for the manager of store 6214. We will assume that the primary concern of this manager is the change in sales year to date this year over last year. In addition, the manager would like to compare how his store is performing against other stores in his district. Make the following adjustments to create this report:

1. Copy the spreadsheet in the **Original Data** tab and paste it into Sheet2.
2. In Sheet2, sort the data based on the values in the District column in ascending order and the values in the Change in Sales to Date column in descending order.
3. Since this store manager wants to focus only on his store and the other stores in his district, delete any rows pertaining to districts 1 and 3.
4. Since the primary concern of this manager is the sales information for his store and other stores in his district, delete the following columns:
   a. Current Inventory Value
   b. Inventory pr Sqr Foot
   c. Total Deliveries
   d. Week 1
   e. Week 2
   f. Week 3
   g. Week 4
5. To place the Change in Sales to Date column next to the Size in Sqr Feet column, first insert a column between column C and D. Then move the Change in Sales to Date column next to the Size in Sqr Feet column.
6. Unmerge the range A1:G1 by clicking the **Merge & Center** and **Center Cells** icons and merge the cells in the range A1:F1.
7. Add a heavy bold border around the range A1:F13 and remove the line at the top of cell G1.

8. Change the name of the worksheet tab for Sheet2 to **`Store Manager Report`**.

9. Hide the Original Data worksheet.

10. Delete Sheet3.

11. How is store 6214 performing relative to other stores in this district?

12. What stores are experiencing a decrease in sales compared to last year?

13. Overall, how does the district appear to be performing? Are most stores seeing an increase in sales over last year, decrease, no change?

14. Save and close your file.

**PROBLEM & EXERCISE**

## >> What's Wrong with This Spreadsheet?

### Problem

You are the manager of an audio electronics store and have a meeting scheduled with your district manager. You have asked your assistant to make some changes to the annual Merchandise Sales Report since your conversation with the district manager will be focused on the change in sales this year verses last year. You have given your assistant the following instructions:

1. Copy the spreadsheet in the Original Report tab and paste it into Sheet2.

2. Rename the tab for Sheet2 as **`Sales Change`**.

3. Delete the following columns: Receipt Date, Next Order Date, and Inventory.

4. Sort the spreadsheet by the Sales Change column in descending order.

Your assistant completes everything except he keeps getting an error when trying to rename the tab for Sheet2 to Sales Change. He explains that everything else you requested has been done.

### Exercise

Open the file named ib_e02_audiobreakdown and look at what the assistant completed on Sheet2. Are you comfortable presenting this spreadsheet to your district manager? Consider the following questions:

1. Did the assistant delete the columns you asked for? If not, what did he do? How could you fix this?

2. Why is your assistant getting an error when he tries to rename the tab for Sheet2 to Sales Change?

3. Do you have any other concerns with this spreadsheet?

Write a short answer to each of the following questions. Correct any problems you see on the spreadsheet. If you cannot correct a problem explain why.

# Printing

Skill Set

After completing formatting and editing adjustments to a worksheet, you may want to print a hard copy or bring several copies to a business meeting. This section covers the features and commands used for printing Excel worksheets.

## Page Setup

Before printing a worksheet, you will need to apply settings that manage how a document will appear when it is printed. These settings can be found in the **Page Layout** tab of the Ribbon. Commands related to printing a worksheet are found in the **Page Setup**, **Scale to Fit**, and **Sheet Options** groups, as shown in Figure 52.

Figure 52 | **Commands Used to Prepare a Worksheet for Printing**

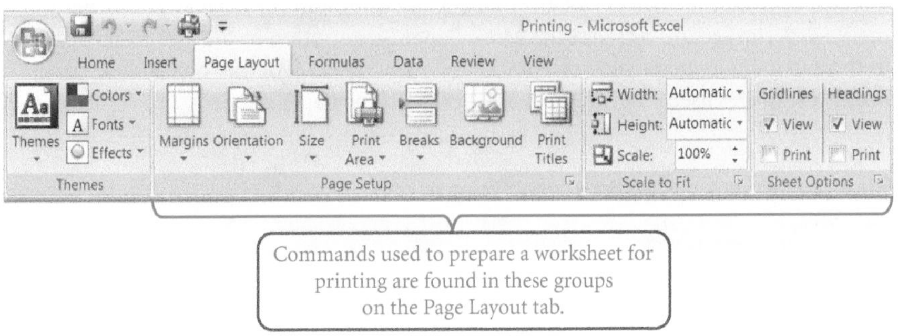


The commands needed to prepare a worksheet for printing will vary from project to project. If you are printing a small worksheet for your own reference, you may be able to print without using any of the commands shown in Figure 52. However, most worksheets will require some type of preparation. The following commands from the **Page Layout** tab are commonly used:

- ***Margins***: Click this icon to select one of three preset margin settings for a document. The **Custom Margins** option will open the **Page Setup** dialog box. Here, you can make your own settings for the margins of a document. The **Page Setup** dialog box is covered later in this section.
- **Orientation**: Click this icon to select either a ***Portrait*** or ***Landscape*** orientation for a document.
- **Size**: Click this icon to select from a list of different paper sizes. The **More Paper Sizes** option will open the **Page Setup** dialog box.
- ***Print Area***: Use this icon if you wish to print only a portion of a worksheet. Highlight the range of cells you wish to print, click this icon, and select the **Set Print Area** option.
- ***Print Titles***: This feature duplicates the column headings or row headings of a worksheet on each page that is printed. Clicking this icon opens the **Page Setup** dialog box, which is covered later in this section.
- **Width**: This icon allows you to determine how many pages are used to print the width of a worksheet. If you wish to print all the data contained in a worksheet on one piece of paper, you would set both the **Width** and **Height** icons to 1 page. The **More** option in this icon will open the **Page Setup** dialog box.
- **Height**: This icon is similar to the **Width** icon, but it allows you to determine how many pages are used to print the length of a worksheet.

- ***Scale***: Click this icon to manually reduce or enlarge the printed appearance of a worksheet.
- **Gridlines**: Click the box next to the **Print** option if you wish to print the ***gridlines*** that appear on the worksheet. Gridlines that appear on a worksheet when the Fill Color is set to No Fill will not appear in print unless this option is selected.
- **Headings**: Click the box next to the **Print** option if you wish to print the column letters and row numbers.

Similar to Excel's formatting commands, several of the features used to prepare a worksheet for printing are not available through the icons in the Ribbon. For these features, you will need to use the **Page Setup** dialog box. The descriptions of the icons in Figure 52 provided earlier indicate how you can open the **Page Setup** dialog box. In addition, you can open the **Page Setup** dialog box by clicking any of the buttons in the lower-right corner of the **Page Setup**, **Scale to Fit**, and **Sheet Options groups** sections of the Ribbon.

Figure 53 shows the **Page** tab of the **Page Setup** dialog box. The **Page Setup** dialog box will open to the **Page** tab when you click the button in the lower-right corner of the **Page Setup** section or select the **More Paper Sizes** option in the **Size** icon. Options in this tab include the printed orientation of a worksheet (Portrait or Landscape), the number of pages used to print the worksheet, and the paper size.

Figure 53 | **Page Tab of the Page Setup Dialog Box**

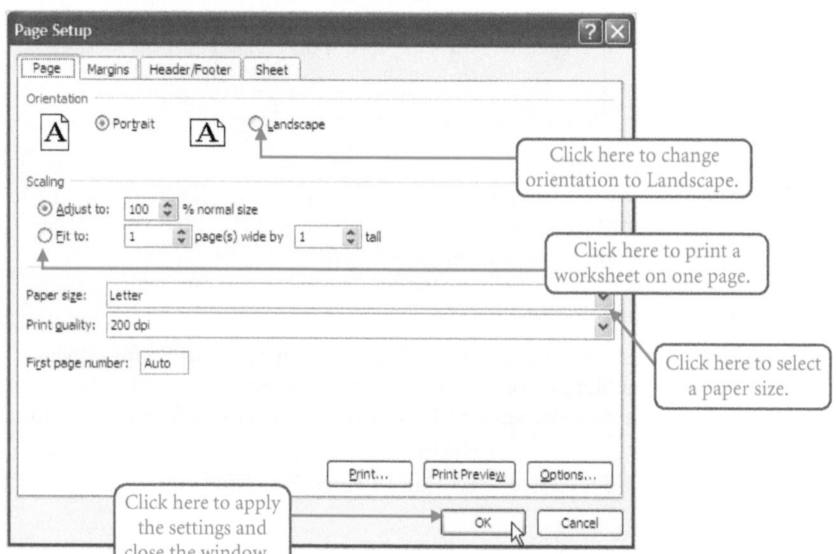


Figure 54 shows the **Margins** tab of the **Page Setup** dialog box. This tab allows you to make specific settings for the printed margins of a worksheet.

Figure 54 | **Margins Tab of the Page Setup Dialog Box**

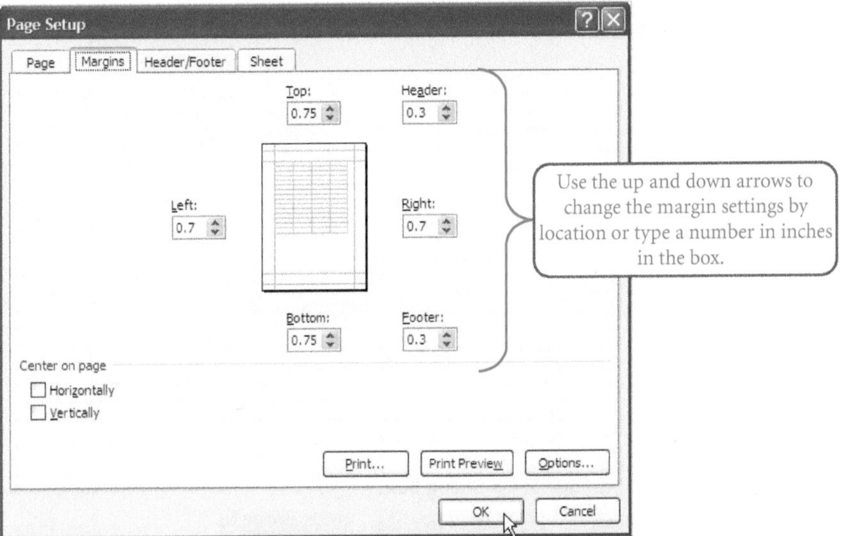


Figure 55 shows the **Header/Footer** tab of the **Page Setup** dialog box. This tab provides preset header and footer options that you can use to display items such as the page number, file name, or worksheet tab name at the top or bottom of a printed document. In addition, you can create your own header of footer by clicking either the **Custom Header** or **Custom Footer** buttons. Figure 56 shows the **Custom Header** dialog box, which opens after you click the **Custom Header** button. This is one of two options for creating custom ***headers*** and ***footers***. The second option is to type a header or footer directly on the worksheet when the workbook is in **Page Layout** view.

Figure 57 shows the **Sheet** tab of the **Page Setup** dialog box. Options in this tab allow you to set a specific print range, designate columns or rows to be printed on each page, or show gridlines in the printed output.

Figure 55 | **Header/Footer Tab of the Page Setup Dialog Box**

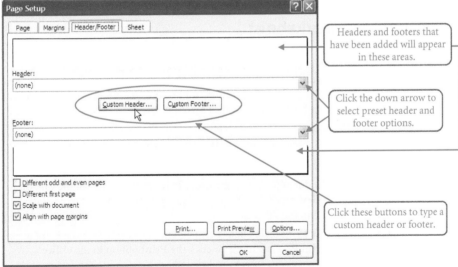

Page Setup

Page | Margins | Header/Footer | Sheet

Header: (none)

Custom Header... | Custom Footer...

Footer: (none)

Different odd and even pages

Different first page

Scale with document

Align with page margins

Print... | Print Preview | Options...

OK | Cancel

Headers and footers that have been added will appear in these areas.

Click the down arrow to select preset header and footer options.

Click these buttons to type a custom header or footer.

Figure 56 | **The Custom Header Dialog Box**

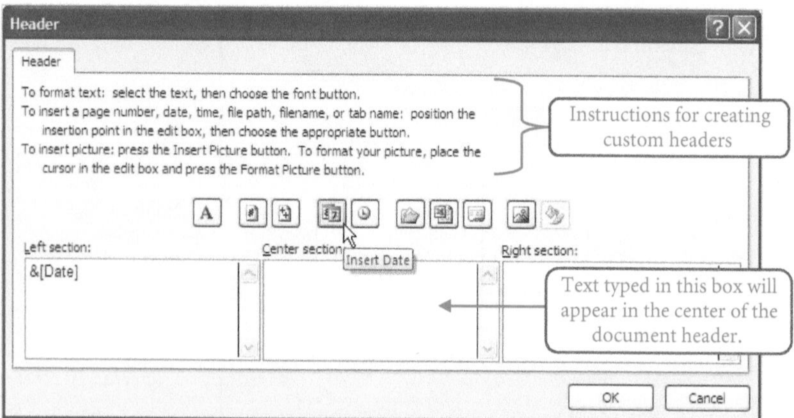


Figure 57 | **Sheet Tab of the Page Setup Dialog Box**

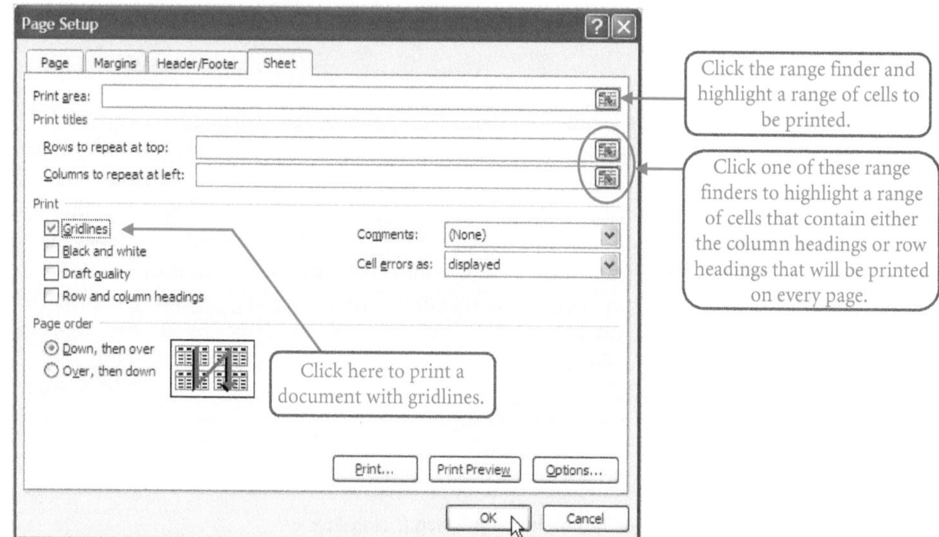


> **Quick Reference**
>
> **Printing Worksheets**
>
> 1. Activate a worksheet to be printed.
> 2. Click the **Page Layout** tab of the Ribbon.
> 3. Make any necessary Page Setup adjustments by using the icons in the Ribbon or by opening the **Page Setup** dialog box.
> 4. Click the **Office Button**.
> 5. Click the side arrow next to the **Print** option and select **Print Preview** to view the document.
> 6. Click the **Print** icon in the **Print Preview** mode Ribbon.
> 7. Make any necessary settings in the **Print** dialog box.
> 8. Click the **OK** button in the **Print** dialog box.

## Printing a Worksheet

When you have finished setting any **Page Setup** options for a worksheet, you should ***preview*** the worksheet in **Print Preview** mode before printing. Viewing a worksheet before printing will reveal any additional changes that need to be made and could save you wasted paper if the document is distorted from setting an option improperly. The following points explain how you accomplish this:

- Click the **Office Button** in the upper-left corner of the Excel screen.
- Place the cursor over the side arrow of the **Print** option.
- Select the **Print Preview** option from the submenu.
- After reviewing the document, click the **Close Print Preview** icon in the Ribbon to exit the **Print Preview** mode. Or, if you want to send the worksheet to a printer, click the **Print** icon in the Ribbon.

Figure 58 shows the **Print** dialog box. This will open after you click the **Print** icon in the Ribbon of the **Print Preview** mode or click the **Print** option in the **Office Button**. Make any necessary adjustments and click the **OK** button to send your worksheet to a printer.

Figure 58 | **The Print Dialog Box**

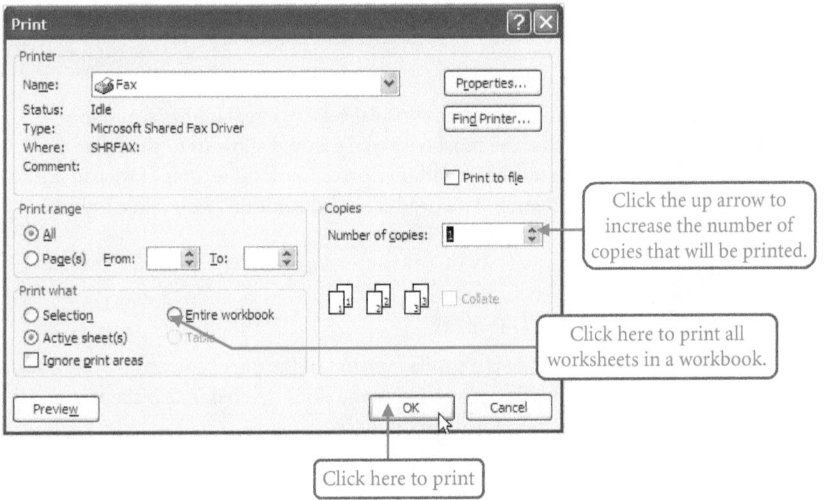


## » Printing

**VIDEO WORKSHOP**

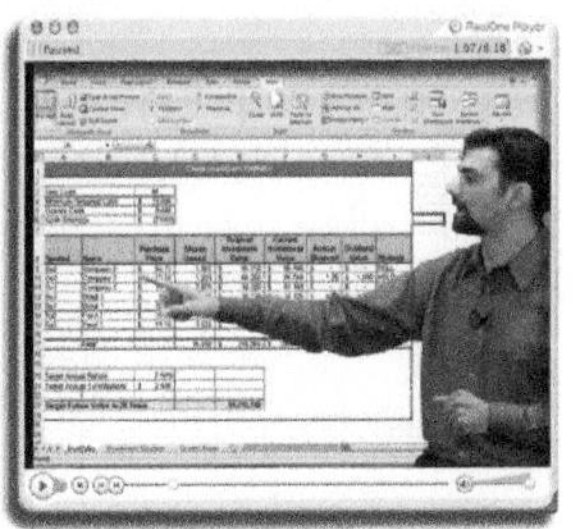

The purpose of this workshop is to demonstrate the printing features and commands reviewed in this section. We will be printing the spreadsheet that was completed in the Editing Video Workshop. I will be demonstrating the tasks in this workshop in the video named **Printing**. Remember to try the tasks on your own first before watching the video.

1. **Open the File**
   a. Open the file named, ib_e02_videoworkshop, which you completed for the Editing Video Workshop.

2. **Page Setup (Video: Printing)**
   a. Make the following Page Setup adjustments for the Standard worksheet:
      i. Set the orientation to Landscape.
      ii. Set the scaling to fit on 1 page wide by 1 page tall.
      iii. Increase the left and right margins to 1 inch.
      iv. Add a header with the date left justified and the following title in the center: `Standard Report Format`. Format this title to a 12-point font and italicize.
      v. Click the drop-down arrow to show the list of preset footers. Select the option that shows the file name of your Excel workbook and the page number.

   b. Make the same Page Setup adjustments for the DC Format worksheet and add the following title in the header: `Unit Volume Performance Report`.
   c. Make the same Page Setup adjustments for the Merchant Format worksheet and add the following title in the header: `Sales Revenue by Item`.

3. **Print (Video: Printing)**
   a. Preview each spreadsheet before printing.
   b. Print the three spreadsheets in this workbook.
   c. Save and close your file.

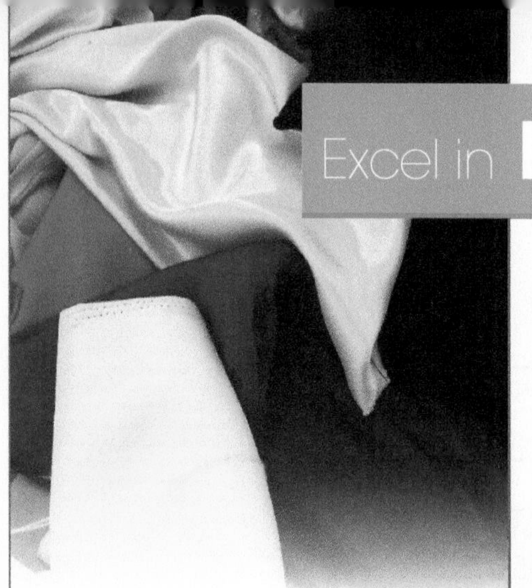

iStockphoto.com

# Excel in **Practice** | Anecdote

**Solution**

I was using electronic spreadsheets on a regular basis, and it seemed that the most basic skills would allow us to get rid of the paper spreadsheets and the correction fluid forever. If we had all our production data produced electronically, we could eliminate all paper and mailing charges.

## Assignment

The following is a similar version of the paper spreadsheet used for our production plans. Using the skills covered in this chapter, create the same spreadsheet in Excel.

| Production Spreadsheet | | | | | | | |
|---|---|---|---|---|---|---|---|
| Plan Number: | S143W | Season: | Fall 07 | | Division: | Men's Sportswear | |
| Style Number: | K44435 | | Description: | | 3 Button Rugby Long Sleeve Knit | | |
| Packaging code: | | PB | | Button Style Code: | SRB.WT | | |
| **Production Details** | | | | | | | |
| | Size | | | | | | |
| Color | S | M | L | XL | XXL | Dozens | Ship Date |
| Solid Blue | 10% | 25% | 30% | 25% | 10% | 5,000 | 7/15/07 |
| Solid Ivory | 10% | 25% | 30% | 25% | 10% | 2,500 | 7/15/07 |
| Solid Green | 10% | 25% | 30% | 25% | 10% | 5,000 | 7/15/07 |
| Navy / Ivory Stripe | 10% | 25% | 30% | 25% | 10% | 5,000 | 8/30/07 |
| Green / Gold Stripe | 10% | 25% | 30% | 25% | 10% | 2,500 | 8/30/07 |
| Green / Ivory Stripe | 10% | 25% | 30% | 25% | 10% | 2,500 | 8/30/07 |

## Questions for Discussion

1. What other benefits, beyond those described in the anecdote, can you think of by converting the paper production plans into Excel spreadsheets?
2. What are some of the things that could go wrong with this project?
3. Identify solutions that could prevent any potential problems from occurring.

# Review Questions

The following questions are related to the concepts addressed in this chapter. There are three types of questions: Short Answer, True or False, and Fill in the Blank. If your answer to a True or False question is False, write a short explanation as to why you think the statement is not true.

1. The following number was entered exactly as shown into a cell: 2,000. Is there anything wrong with this entry?
2. Besides pressing the **Enter** key, what else can you do to ensure data is entered into a cell?
3. What could typically go wrong with data entry tasks?
4. The following months were entered into two consecutive cells: January, June. Can **Auto Fill** be used to complete the rest of the months of the year? Why or why not?
5. What causes these symbols to appear in a cell: ####?
6. When using the **Format** icon to increase the height or width of a row or column, you must _________ in either the row or column you are adjusting.
7. The row numbers on the left side of a spreadsheet read 1,2,4,5,6,8,9,11. What does this mean?
8. What icon in the Ribbon can you use to hide a column?
9. In what Ribbon tab will you find the **Sort** command?
10. When you are using the **Sort** command, any column that is _________ will not be sorted.
11. True or False: Column headings should never be highlighted when sorting data.
12. True or False: If a column letter is missing at the top of a spreadsheet, it means that the column was deleted.
13. To center data over several cells, you would use the _________ command.
14. True or False: Selecting the **Currency** option when formatting numbers will always add a $ in front of the number.
15. True or False: There is no special accounting format for projects that require dollar signs and decimals to align.
16. True or False: Numbers and text entries will always be truncated if they are too large to fit into a cell. This is why you need the wrap text command.
17. You must select a _________ first when using the **Border** tab of the **Format Cells** dialog box.
18. The difference between a mediocre and professional-looking spreadsheet is often the result of _________ techniques.
19. List two options for changing data that has already been entered into a cell.

20. The cursor must change from a _________ sign to _________ before data can be dragged to a new location on a spreadsheet.

21. True or False: When you delete a column, the data disappears and an empty column remains.

22. Columns are inserted to the _________ of an active cell, and rows are inserted _________ an active cell.

23. Which icon in the Ribbon can you use to change the color of a worksheet tab?

24. True or False: To change the name of a worksheet tab, you can simply double click on the tab and type the new name.

25. How can you find out if there are any hidden spreadsheets in a workbook?

26. How can you change the order in which worksheet tabs are displayed in a workbook?

27. True or False: You cannot print all the spreadsheets in a workbook at one time. You have to activate each spreadsheet and print them one at a time.

28. True or False: Grid lines, besides the ones you may have added to a spreadsheet, will always appear on paper when a worksheet is printed.

29. How can you get column headings or row headings to print on every page when printing long or wide spreadsheets?

# Skills Exam

The following exam is designed to test your ability to recognize and execute the Excel skills presented in this chapter. Read each question carefully and answer the questions in the order they are listed. You should be able to complete this exam in 60 minutes or less.

1. Open the ib_e02_skillsexam.
2. Copy the worksheet named "Original" and paste it into Sheet2.
3. For Sheet2, insert 2 rows above row 1.
4. Enter the title **Cost Analysis Report** in cell A1.
5. Merge the cells in the range A1:H1. Then color the cells Blue, change the color of the text to white, change the font size to 16, bold and italicize the text, and set both the horizontal and vertical alignment to center.
6. Increase the height of row 1 to 25 points.
7. For the range A3:H3, wrap the text, color the cells light yellow, bold the text, and set the horizontal alignment to center.
8. Adjust the column widths as follows:
   a. Column B: **11.5**
   b. Column C: **8**
   c. Column D: **8**
   d. Column E: **11**
   e. Column F: **9.5**
   f. Column G: **13**
   g. Column H: **14**
9. In Sheet2, use Auto Fill to add 18 more cost components to the list in column A. There should be a total of 20 cost components beginning in cell A4 and ending in cell A23.
10. Copy the range B4:B23 and paste it into column G beginning with cell G4.
11. Enter data into the following cells: H4: 5000, H5: 2500, H6: 8500, H7: -2000, H8: 3100, H9: 10000, H10: 1000, H11: -5000, H12: 4050, H13: 2925, H14: -150, H15: 1800, H16: -200, H17: 3800, H18: 5500, H19: -3000, H20: 250, H21: 16500, H22: 2000, H23: 35000.
12. Delete row 2.
13. Add a heavy bold border around the perimeter of the range A1:H24.
14. Add horizontal and vertical regular solid black lines to the range A1:H22.
15. Add a bold black line to the bottom of the range A2:H2.
16. Add a bold black line to the bottom of cells D22 and F22.
17. Bold and italicize the text in cells A24, D24, and F24.
18. Format the following ranges to a number with commas and 0 decimal places: B3:B22, E3:E22, and G3:G22.
19. Format the range C3:C22 to U.S. currency 2 decimal places.
20. Format the range D3:D22 and F3:F22 to U.S. currency 0 decimal places.
21. Format cells D24 and F24 to U.S. currency 2 decimal places.
22. Format the range H3:H22 as a number with commas, 0 decimal places, and show any negative numbers in parentheses and in red.
23. Eliminate any #### errors that may have appeared on the spreadsheet.
24. Rename the tab for Sheet2 to **All Cost Data**.
25. Make a copy of the All Cost Data spreadsheet and paste it into Sheet3.
26. Rename the tab for Sheet3 as **Total Cost Analysis**.

27. Add two new worksheets to the workbook. Paste a copy of the All Cost Data spreadsheet into these two worksheets.

28. Change the tab name for one of the two new worksheets to **Inventory Cost Analysis**. Change the tab name of the remaining worksheet to **Purchasing Analysis**.

29. Arrange the worksheet tabs in the following order and change the color of each tab as indicated:
    a. Original: Blue
    b. All Cost Data: Green
    c. Total Cost Analysis: Red
    d. Inventory Cost Analysis: Yellow
    e. Purchasing Analysis: Purple

30. Make the following adjustments to the Total Cost Analysis worksheet:
    a. Delete the following columns: Current Inventory Units, Inventory Cost, Future Consumption, and Current Inventory Less Future Consumption.
    b. Sort the spreadsheet based on the Total Cost column in descending order and for any duplicate entries sort by the Unit Cost column in descending order. Note: The Totals row (row 24) must remain at the bottom of the spreadsheet.
    c. Add a heavy bold line to the right side of the range D1:D24.
    d. Change the text in cell A1 to read **Total Cost Analysis**.

31. Make the following adjustment to the Inventory Cost Analysis spreadsheet:
    a. Delete the following columns: Total Cost, Future Consumption, and Current Inventory Less Future Consumption.
    b. Sort the spreadsheet based on the Inventory Cost column in descending order and for any duplicate entries sort by the Current Inventory Units column in ascending order. Note: The Totals row (row 24) must remain at the bottom of the spreadsheet.
    c. Add a heavy bold line to the right side of the range E1:E24.
    d. Change the text in cell A1 to read **Inventory Cost Analysis**.

32. Make the following adjustments to the Purchasing Analysis spreadsheet:
    a. Delete the following columns: Current Inventory Units, Unit Cost, Total Cost, and Inventory Cost.
    b. Sort the spreadsheet based on the Current Inventory Less Future Consumption column in ascending order and for any duplicate entries sort by the Item column in ascending order. Note: The Totals row (row 24) must remain at the bottom of the spreadsheet.
    c. Add a dark bold line to the right side of the range D1:D24.
    d. Change the text in cell A1 to read **Purchasing Analysis**.

33. What two components have both the highest Total cost and the highest Inventory cost?

34. If this company has a standard of not going below 1000 units when considering current inventory less future consumption, what components would have to be purchased?

35. Make the following adjustments so each worksheet will print as follows:
    a. Landscape
    b. Fits onto one page
    c. 1 inch margin for top, bottom, left, and right
    d. The date on the left side of the header and the worksheet name in center of the header
    e. The page number in the right side of the footer
    f. Print grid lines

36. Save and close your file.

# Challenge Questions

The following questions are designed to test your ability to apply the Excel skills you have learned to complete a business objective. Use your knowledge of Excel as well as your creativity to answer these questions. For most questions, there are several possible ways to complete the objective.

1. What information will you need before starting an Excel project?
2. You are evaluating a long-term project for building several retail stores. The project will start on March 20 of this year and will take 35 months before the stores will be open for business. The months of January through April are very slow business periods. Historical sales suggest that it is best to open stores in May or August. Given the start date and the 35-month duration, are the stores opening at a good time? Using the skills in this chapter, how can you use Excel to help answer this question?
3. Open the file named ib_e02_purchasingmanagerdata. This file needs to be formatted and adjusted for the purchasing manager of a sports equipment store who is responsible for assessing the current unit inventory for each item and the weeks of supply for each item. From this information, the manager will determine which items need to be purchased or which items should be returned to the manufacturer. The purchasing manager will make this decision based on the weeks of supply data. Any item with a weeks of supply less than 4 will be purchased. Any item with a weeks of supply greater than 20 will be returned to the manufacturer. Use the skills covered in this chapter to format the spreadsheet based on the needs of this purchasing manager.
4. Open the file named ib_e02_furniturefiasco. How many mistakes can you find in this spreadsheet? Make a copy of the spreadsheet and correct as many mistakes as you can. If you cannot correct a mistake, explain why.
5. Open the file named ib_e02_merchandisedataforpresentation. Look at this spreadsheet carefully. Would you be comfortable presenting this information for a class project or to the executive managers of a company? Why or why not?

# Calculating Data

## Formulas and Functions

## Chapter Goals

This chapter introduces the calculating power of Excel through two main objectives. The first is to present the fundamental techniques of creating formulas and functions, which are the primary tools used to calculate data. The second is to show how cell referencing is used within formulas and functions to maximize the dynamic abilities of Excel. In other words, formulas and functions will automatically produce new outputs when the data in one or more cell locations is changed. In business, these dynamic abilities are critical when evaluating what-if scenarios. This chapter demonstrates how to perform common business calculations and analyses using formulas and functions.

## >> Excel | Skill Sets

**Formulas**

- Basic Formulas
- Copying and Pasting Formulas (Relative Reference and Paste Special)
- Complex Formulas
- Auditing Formulas.

**Basic Functions**

- Basic Statistical Functions
- AutoSum
- Absolute References (Turning Off Relative References)

**Financial Functions**

- The Future Value Function
- The Payment Function
- The Function Library

iStockphoto.com

## Excel in Practice | Anecdote

### My Role as a Merchandise Analyst

If asked, could you predict how well printed skirts will sell this summer or say with certainty whether hip huggers are going out of style? Posing such what-if scenarios was my livelihood when I worked as a merchandise analyst for a women's fashion retail company where I projected the sales and profit for my department. Our goal each season was to sell all the clothes in the casual sportswear line with nothing left over. For example, every year we might purchase 25,000 pairs of shorts, which sold from the end of March to the end of July. If shorts still hung from the racks by the end of July, we were stuck with inventory, costing the department thousands of dollars in profit. To make matters worse, no one wanted last season's shorts, so reselling a previous season's inventory rarely worked.

Using a paper spreadsheet, I evaluated the sales of every item in my department, trying to determine what was hot and what was in danger of hitting the markdown table. While markdowns often increased the sales of an item, they also decreased our profits. Fortunately, sales in my department were booming, so I found myself working until midnight almost every day, recalculating sales and inventory data on my spreadsheets. While being part of a fast-growing business was a great experience, I had to find a better way of managing the sales and profit of my department; otherwise, I would burn out from exhaustion.

>> Continued later in this Chapter

# Formulas

Skill Set

The most basic method of calculating mathematical outputs in Excel is through formulas. Formulas not only reduce the risk of data-entry errors by producing values electronically, but they also provide the ability to evaluate what-if scenarios. This section will highlight the analytical benefits of formulas and demonstrate the construction of several formulas typically used in business.

## Basic Formulas

For the purposes of this text, ***basic formulas*** are defined as any equations that consist of two variables separated by a ***mathematical operator*** such as + (addition), – (subtraction), etc. Business managers use a variety of basic formulas to calculate key metrics such as Gross Profit, Net Sales, or Inventory Turn. The types of formulas used by business managers depend on their areas of responsibility. Typical basic formulas used in business include

- **Gross Profit**: Net Sales − Cost of Goods Sold
- **Net Sales**: Gross Sales − Returns
- **Average Price**: Sales Dollars ÷ Unit Sales
- **Inventory Turn:** Net Sales ÷ Average Inventory Value
- **Sales Dollars**: Price × Sales Units

It is important to note that the math operators you see on a calculator are not always the same in Excel. For example, the "×" symbol on a calculator is usually used for the multiplication operation. However, in Excel you would use the asterisk (*) for multiplication. Figure 1 shows a list of symbols used for constructing formulas in Excel.

Figure 1 | **Mathematical Operator Symbols Used in Excel**

| Symbol | Operation |
|---|---|
| + | Addition |
| – | Subtraction |
| / | Division |
| * | Multiplication |
| ^ | Power/Exponent |

As previously mentioned, you can use a basic formula to calculate the Net Sales for a Financial Plan such as the one shown in Figure 2. This formula is added to the worksheet as follows:

- Activate cell B5. This cell represents the Net Sales for the year 2008 (see Figure 2).
- Type an equal sign. An equal sign signifies that Excel will be calculating data instead of displaying what is typed into a cell.
- Type the cell location B3. As illustrated earlier, the formula for Net Sales is Gross Sales – Returns. Since cell B3 contains the Gross Sales for 2008, this cell is added to the formula first. You can also add this cell to the formula by clicking the cell location after typing the equal sign.
- Type a subtraction sign.

- Type cell location B4. The value in cell B4 represents the Returns for the year 2008. Since this cell location comes after the subtraction sign, it will be subtracted from the value that is contained in cell B3.
- Press the **Enter** key.

Figure 2 shows the setup of the formula calculating Net Sales in the Financial Plan worksheet. It is important to note that this formula is composed of ***cell references***. As a result, any value typed into cell B4 will be subtracted from any value typed into cell B3. If the value in either cell B3 or B4 is changed, the output of the formula will also change.

Figure 2 | **Basic Formula Calculating Net Sales**

SUM =B3-B4

| | A | B | C | D |
|---|---|---|---|---|
| 1 | | | Financial Plan | |
| 2 | | 2008 | 2009 | 2010 |
| 3 | Gross Sales | $ 100,000,000 | $ 110,000,000 | $ 120,000,0 |
| 4 | Returns | $ 5,000,000 | $ 5,500,000 | $ 6,000,0 |
| 5 | Net Sales | =B3-B4 | | |
| 6 | Cost of Goods Sold | $ 41,000,000 | $ 45,100,000 | |
| 7 | Gross Profit | | | |

Formula appears in the formula bar as you type.

Cell references used in the formula are outlined in color.

The equal sign must precede the formula to produce an output.

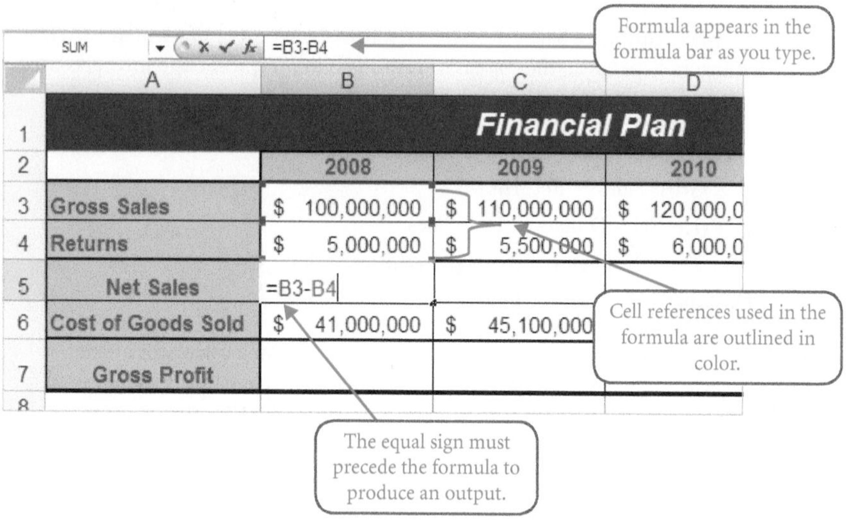

Figure 3 shows the result of the Net Sales formula in cell B5. Notice that when B5 is activated, you can see the formula `=B3 - B4` in the formula bar. This indicates that the value $95,000,000 is a formula output and that the number itself has not been entered into the cell. Excel is calculating this output because an equal sign precedes the formula. If the equal sign was omitted, you would see B3-B4 displayed in the cell.

Figure 3 | **Results of the Net Sales Formula**

B5 =B3-B4

| | A | B | C | D |
|---|---|---|---|---|
| 1 | | | Financial Plan | |
| 2 | | 2008 | 2009 | 2010 |
| 3 | Gross Sales | $ 100,000,000 | $ 110,000,000 | $ 120,000 |
| 4 | Returns | $ 5,000,000 | $ 5,500,000 | $ 6,000 |
| 5 | Net Sales | $ 95,000,000 | | |
| 6 | Cost of Goods Sold | $ 41,000,000 | $ 45,100,000 | $ 49,200 |
| 7 | Gross Profit | | | |

Formula appears in the formula bar when the cell is activated.

Formula output

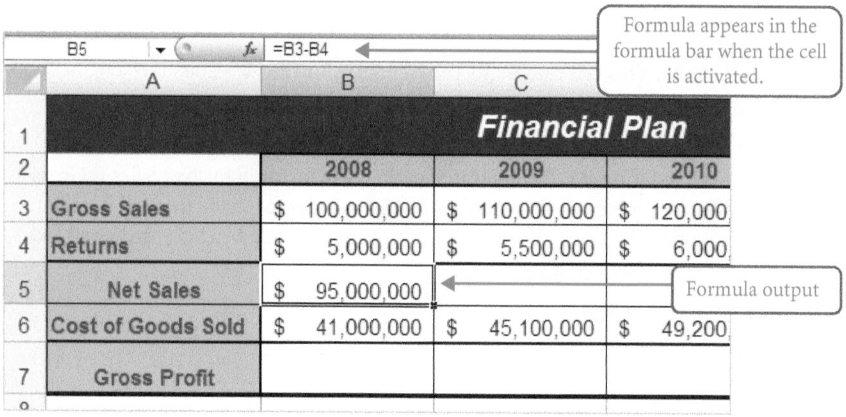

## COMMON MISTAKES | Formulas

When doing calculations in Excel, never use a calculator and type the result into a spreadsheet. Typing computed results into a spreadsheet completely eliminates Excel's cell referencing capabilities. Formulas created with cell references will automatically recalculate outputs when data is changed in any of the referenced cell locations. In addition, creating formulas with cell references provides a record of how outputs are being calculated.

As previously mentioned, the formula shown in Figure 2 utilizes cell references. If the values in cells B3 or B4 are changed, the formula will produce a new output. Therefore, what will happen to Net Sales if returns are $10 million higher than planned for the year 2008? Type 15000000 in cell B4, and the formula automatically calculates a new value, as shown in Figure 4.

Figure 4 | **Changing the Returns Value in Cell B4 Produces a New Value for Net Sales**

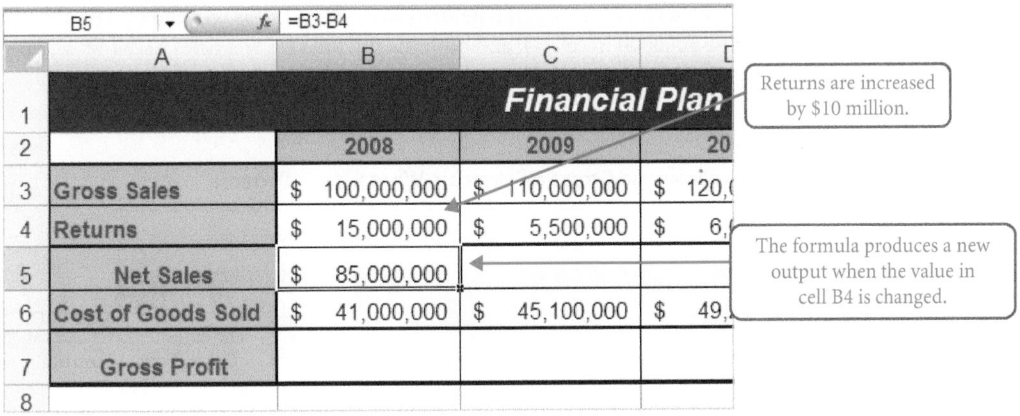

B5 =B3-B4

| | A | B | C | D |
|---|---|---|---|---|
| 1 | | | Financial Plan | |
| 2 | | 2008 | 2009 | 20 |
| 3 | Gross Sales | $ 100,000,000 | $ 110,000,000 | $ 120,( |
| 4 | Returns | $ 15,000,000 | $ 5,500,000 | $ 6,( |
| 5 | Net Sales | $ 85,000,000 | | |
| 6 | Cost of Goods Sold | $ 41,000,000 | $ 45,100,000 | $ 49, |
| 7 | Gross Profit | | | |
| 8 | | | | |

Returns are increased by $10 million.

The formula produces a new output when the value in cell B4 is changed.

Figures 5 and 6 show the setup and result of a basic formula calculating the Gross Profit in the Financial Plan worksheet. Notice that this formula references cell B5, which contains the formula for Net Sales. Therefore, if the output of the Net Sales formula is changed, the output of the Gross Profit formula will also change.

Figure 5 | **Basic Formula Calculating Gross Profit**

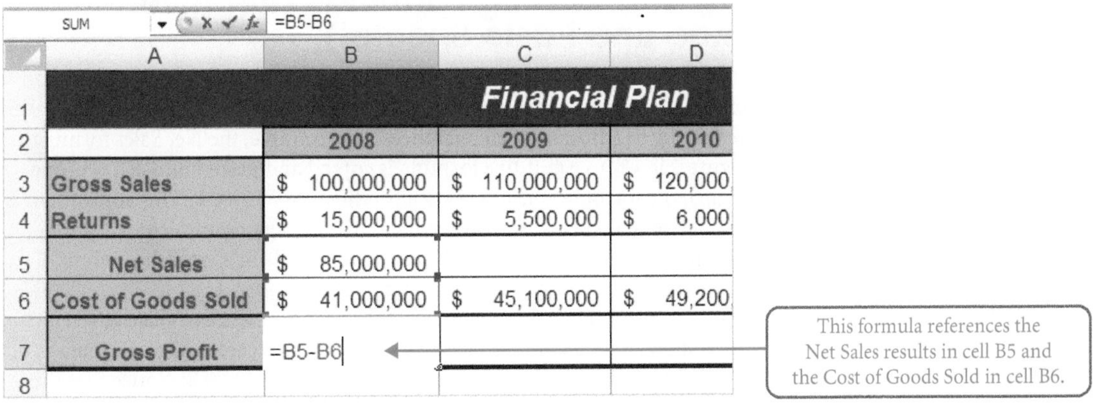

SUM =B5-B6

| | A | B | C | D |
|---|---|---|---|---|
| 1 | | | Financial Plan | |
| 2 | | 2008 | 2009 | 2010 |
| 3 | Gross Sales | $ 100,000,000 | $ 110,000,000 | $ 120,000 |
| 4 | Returns | $ 15,000,000 | $ 5,500,000 | $ 6,000 |
| 5 | Net Sales | $ 85,000,000 | | |
| 6 | Cost of Goods Sold | $ 41,000,000 | $ 45,100,000 | $ 49,200 |
| 7 | Gross Profit | =B5-B6 | | |
| 8 | | | | |

This formula references the Net Sales results in cell B5 and the Cost of Goods Sold in cell B6.

Figure 6 | **Results of the Gross Profit Formula**

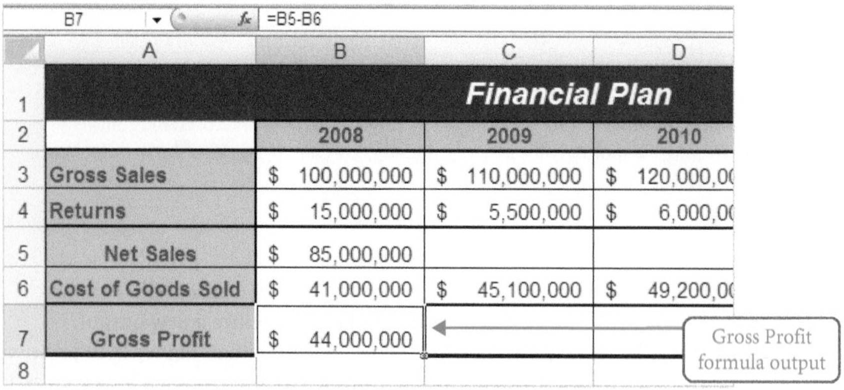

B7 =B5-B6

| | A | B | C | D |
|---|---|---|---|---|
| 1 | | | Financial Plan | |
| 2 | | 2008 | 2009 | 2010 |
| 3 | Gross Sales | $ 100,000,000 | $ 110,000,000 | $ 120,000,0( |
| 4 | Returns | $ 15,000,000 | $ 5,500,000 | $ 6,000,0( |
| 5 | Net Sales | $ 85,000,000 | | |
| 6 | Cost of Goods Sold | $ 41,000,000 | $ 45,100,000 | $ 49,200,0( |
| 7 | Gross Profit | $ 44,000,000 | | |
| 8 | | | | |

Gross Profit formula output

As mentioned, the formula calculating Gross Profit in the Financial Plan worksheet is referencing cell B5, which contains the formula for Net Sales. As a result, what will happen to the Gross Profit if the Returns value in cell B4 is reduced by $10 million? Type the value 5000000 in cell B4, and both the formula for Net Sales in cell B5 and the formula for Gross Profit in cell B7 produce new outputs, as shown in Figure 7.

Figure 7 | **Net Sales and Gross Profit Increase When Returns Decrease**

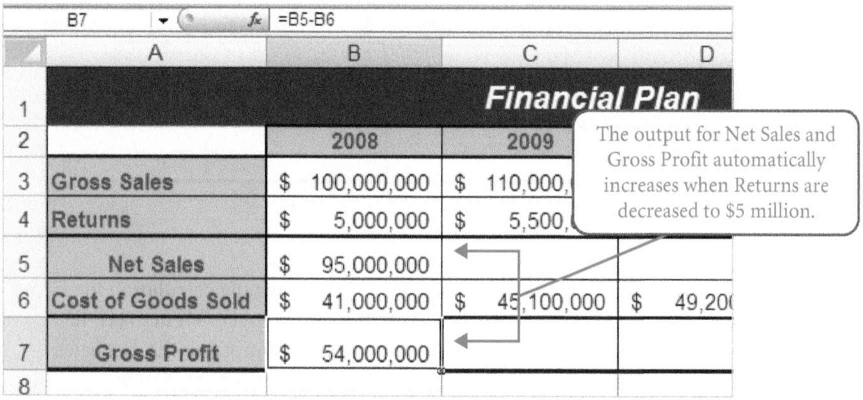

B7 =B5-B6

| | A | B | C | D |
|---|---|---|---|---|
| 1 | | | Financial Plan | |
| 2 | | 2008 | 2009 | |
| 3 | Gross Sales | $ 100,000,000 | $ 110,000,( | |
| 4 | Returns | $ 5,000,000 | $ 5,500,( | |
| 5 | Net Sales | $ 95,000,000 | | |
| 6 | Cost of Goods Sold | $ 41,000,000 | $ 45,100,000 | $ 49,20( |
| 7 | Gross Profit | $ 54,000,000 | | |
| 8 | | | | |

The output for Net Sales and Gross Profit automatically increases when Returns are decreased to $5 million.

> **Quick Reference**
>
> **Basic Formulas**
>
> 1. Activate the cell where formula output should appear.
> 2. Type an equal sign.
> 3. Type or click a cell location that contains a value that will be used to compute the formula output.
> 4. Type a math operator (see Figure 1).
> 5. Type or click a second cell location that contains a value that will be used to compute the formula output.
> 6. Press the **Enter** key.

## Copying and Pasting Formulas (Relative Reference and Paste Special)

After constructing a formula in Excel, you can copy and paste it to other locations on a worksheet. When you paste a formula to a new location, Excel utilizes a process called ***relative referencing*** to adjust any cell references. For example, the Net Sales formula shown in Figure 2 is `=B3-B4`. If this formula is copied and pasted into cell C5 (one cell to the right), the formula will automatically adjust to `=C3-C4`. This adjustment is the result of relative referencing. Relative referencing is a very convenient feature because, without it, you would have to retype every formula in a worksheet even though it may be performing the same mathematical function.

The following example further demonstrates the convenience of relative references. Figure 8 shows a merchandise sales worksheet. In this case, a basic formula is created in cell D2 to calculate the average price for the item in row 2. Notice that the forward slash symbol is used for division.

Figure 8 | **Average Price Formula**

SUM =B2/C2

| | A | B | C | D |
|---|---|---|---|---|
| 1 | Item | Sales Dollars | Unit Sales | Average Price |
| 2 | T-Shirts | $ 150,000 | 12,000 | =B2/C2 |
| 3 | Notebooks | $ 85,000 | 32,500 | |
| 4 | Sweatshirts | $ 225,000 | 5,000 | |
| 5 | Hats | $ 125,000 | 8,200 | |
| 6 | Scarves | $ 9,000 | 750 | |
| 7 | Sweaters | $ 120,000 | 2,500 | |
| 8 | Diploma Frames | $ 187,500 | 1,500 | |

Forward slash is used for division.

Figure 9 shows the results of copying and pasting the formula in cell D2 to cells D3 through D5. Notice that the formula in cell D5 reads `=B5/C5`, which accurately calculates the average price for the Hats in row 5. However, the formula that was typed into cell D2, as shown in Figure 8, was `=B2/C2`. Relative referencing increased the row numbers of the cell references by 3 because the formula was pasted 3 rows below its original location. Without relative referencing, this formula would calculate the average price of the T-Shirts in row 2 for every item in the worksheet.

Figure 9 | **Relative Referencing Adjusts Cell References in the Average Price Formula**

SUM =B5/C5

| | A | B | C | D |
|---|---|---|---|---|
| 1 | Item | Sales Dollars | Unit Sales | Average Price |
| 2 | T-Shirts | $ 150,000 | 12,000 | $12.50 |
| 3 | Notebooks | $ 85,000 | 32,500 | $2.62 |
| 4 | Sweatshirts | $ 225,000 | 5,000 | $45.00 |
| 5 | Hats | $ 125,000 | 8,200 | =B5/C5 |
| 6 | Scarves | $ 9,000 | 750 | |
| 7 | Sweaters | $ 120,000 | 2,500 | |
| 8 | Diploma Frames | $ 187,500 | 1,500 | |

Row numbers in the cell references increase by 3 because the formula is pasted 3 rows below the original location.

While relative references provide a convenient way to copy and paste formulas, in some situations you may need to paste only the value of a formula and not the formula itself. For example, Figure 10 shows a worksheet used to calculate the sales plans for six retail stores. Column D contains basic formulas to add the Planned Growth values to the Last Year Sales values for each store.

Figure 10 | **Retail Store Sales Plans**

SUM =B2+C2

| | A | B | C | D |
|---|---|---|---|---|
| 1 | Store Number | Last Year Sales | Planned Growth | Total Sales Plan |
| 2 | 1 | $5,750,000 | $125,000 | =B2+C2 |
| 3 | 2 | $4,250,000 | $400,000 | $4,650,000 |
| 4 | 3 | $6,500,000 | $250,000 | $6,750,000 |
| 5 | 4 | $3,250,000 | $750,000 | $4,000,000 |
| 6 | 5 | $5,250,000 | $500,000 | $5,750,000 |
| 7 | 6 | $2,750,000 | $1,000,000 | $3,750,000 |
| 8 | | | | |

This formula is calculating the Total Sales Plan by adding the Last Year Sales values to the Planned Growth values.

Figure 11 shows a new worksheet that will be used by a manager to monitor the Actual Sales for each store to see if the store is achieving its Total Sales Plan. Therefore, the Total Sales Plan numbers calculated in Figure 10 need to be pasted into this new worksheet.

Figure 11 | **Plan versus Actual Sales Worksheet**

| | A | B | C | D |
|---|---|---|---|---|
| 1 | Store Number | Total Sales Plan | Actual Sales | Difference |
| 2 | 1 | | | |
| 3 | 2 | | | |
| 4 | 3 | | | |
| 5 | 4 | | | |
| 6 | 5 | | | |
| 7 | 6 | | | |
| 8 | | | | |

The values from the formulas created in column D from Figure 10 will be placed in this column.

As mentioned, the Total Sales Plan numbers calculated in Figure 10 need to be pasted into the Plan versus Actual Sales worksheet in Figure 11. However, using the **Copy** and **Paste** icons in this situation will paste the formula that is used to calculate the Total Sales Plan values, not the result. To paste only the result of this formula, you will need to use a command called **Paste Values**. You accomplish this by doing the following:

- Highlight the range D2:D7 in the worksheet shown in Figure 10. This is the range of cells that contain the formulas which calculate the Total Sales Plan values.
- Click the **Copy** icon.
- Activate cell B2 in the worksheet shown in Figure 11.
- Click the down arrow below the **Paste** icon to open a list of paste options (see Figure 12). The paste options list allows you to access a few commonly used commands from the ***Paste Special*** dialog box.

Figure 12 | **Paste Options List**

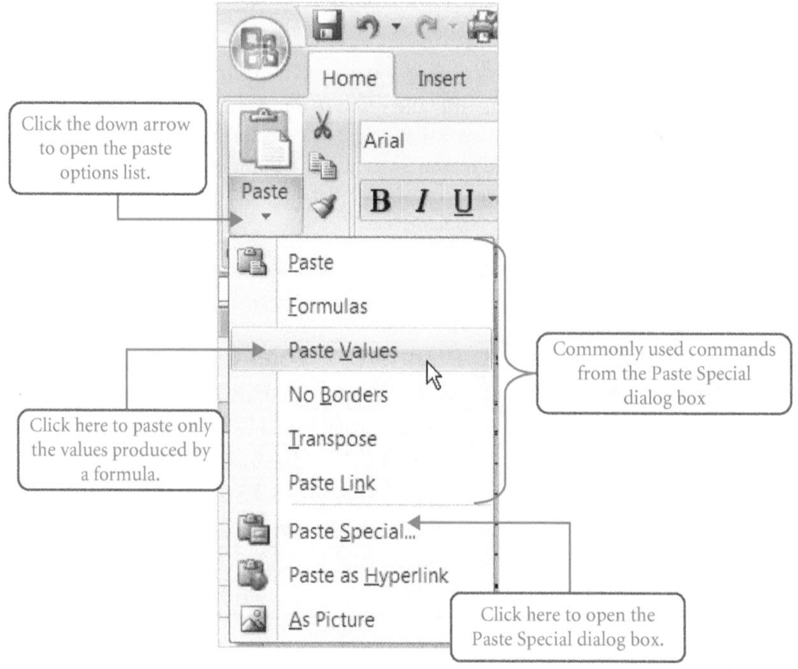
Home
Insert
Arial
Paste
B I U
Click the down arrow to open the paste options list.
Paste
Formulas
Paste Values
No Borders
Transpose
Paste Link
Paste Special...
Paste as Hyperlink
As Picture
Commonly used commands from the Paste Special dialog box
Click here to paste only the values produced by a formula.
Click here to open the Paste Special dialog box.

- Select the **Paste Values** option from the paste options list. This will paste only the values created by the Total Sales Plan formulas and not the formulas themselves (see Figure 13).

Figure 13 shows the results of pasting the values of the Total Sales Plan formulas from Figure 10. When cell B2 is activated, the formula bar shows that the content of the cell is a number. In addition, notice the **Paste Options** icon, which appears on the worksheet after selecting a paste command. You can use this icon to select a different paste option if the one you originally selected does not provide desirable results.

Figure 13 | **Pasting Formulas as Values**

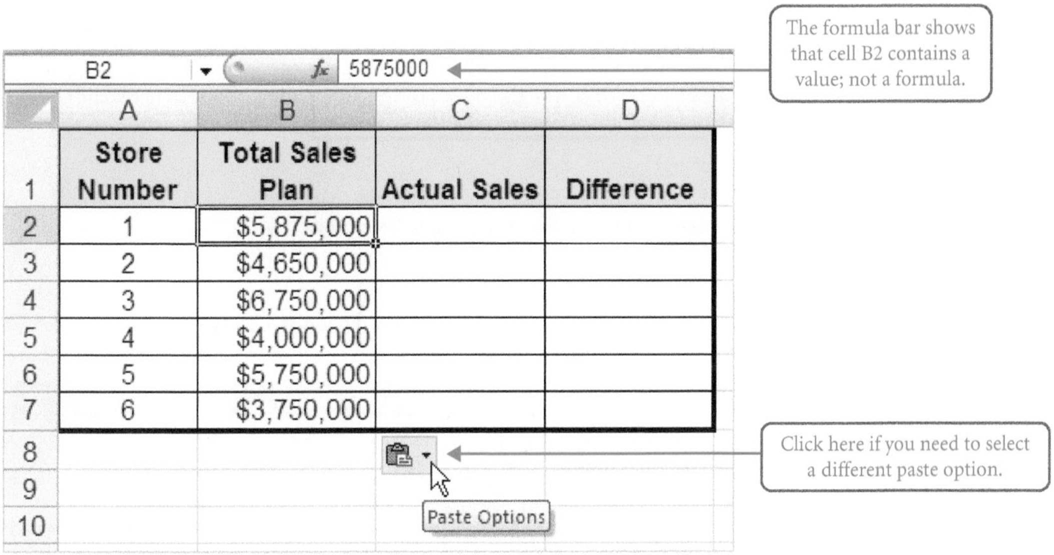

B2 fx 5875000

| | A | B | C | D |
|---|---|---|---|---|
| 1 | Store Number | Total Sales Plan | Actual Sales | Difference |
| 2 | 1 | $5,875,000 | | |
| 3 | 2 | $4,650,000 | | |
| 4 | 3 | $6,750,000 | | |
| 5 | 4 | $4,000,000 | | |
| 6 | 5 | $5,750,000 | | |
| 7 | 6 | $3,750,000 | | |
| 8 | | | | |
| 9 | | | | |
| 10 | | | | |

Paste Options

The formula bar shows that cell B2 contains a value; not a formula.

Click here if you need to select a different paste option.

The paste options list contains a few commonly used commands from the **Paste Special** dialog box shown in Figure 14. To open the **Paste Special** dialog box and view all the available commands, click the **Paste Special** option, as shown in Figure 12. The following are a few key options:

- **Formats**: This option allows you to paste only the formats from a range of cells that has been copied. As a result, you can paste a specific arrangement of borders, number formats, or cell colors from one area of a worksheet to another.
- **All except borders**: This option appears as **No Borders** in the paste options list. Use it in situations in which you need to paste all content and formats from a range of copied cells except for the borders.
- **Formulas**: Use this option when you want to paste only the formulas from a range of copied cells without any of the format settings.
- **Transpose**: This option, found at the bottom of the **Paste Special** dialog box, can be used in situations in which a range of cells copied in a column needs to be transposed to a row or vice versa. Figure 15 illustrates an example of this option.

**>> Quick Reference**

**Paste Special**

1. Copy a cell or range of cells.
2. Activate the cell where data is to be pasted.
3. Click the down arrow below the **Paste** icon to open the paste options list.
4. Select one of the paste options or select the **Paste Special** option to open the **Paste Special** dialog box.
5. If you are using the **Paste Special** dialog box, select an option and click the **OK** button.

Figure 14 | **Paste Special Dialog Box**

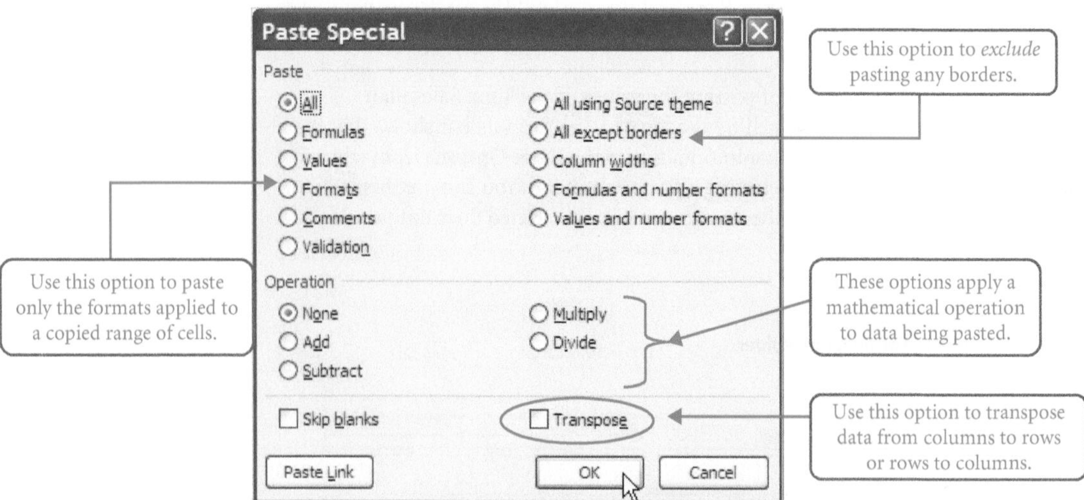


Figure 15 | **Transpose Option in the Paste Special Dialog Box**

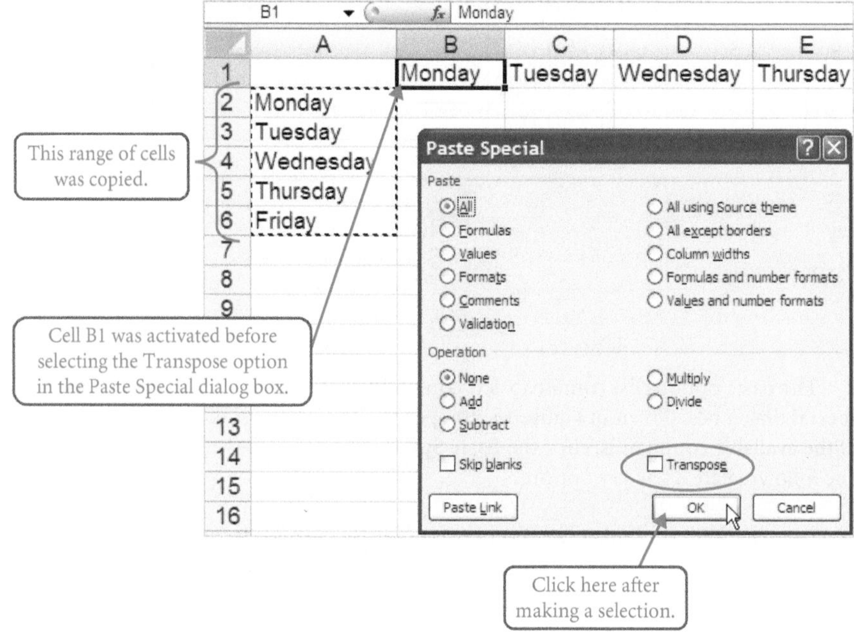


## Complex Formulas

For the purposes of this text, ***complex formulas*** are defined as any equations that consist of more than two variables and require two or more mathematical operators. As previously illustrated, basic formulas are used to conduct several key calculations in business. However, business computations often require the use of formulas that consist of more than two variables. For example, you may need to add several components together to calculate the cost of a product. Or, you may need to estimate daily sales from weekly sales to calculate an annual inventory turn. These situations require more than two variables and may also require the use of constants or numeric values. In addition, parentheses may be necessary to change the standard order of mathematical operations.

Since a complex formula contains at least two or more mathematical operations, it is important to note the order in which Excel will execute each mathematical operation when calculating an output. Figure 16 lists the order in which Excel executes mathematical operations in a formula that does not contain parentheses. Note that the symbols shown in this figure were previously defined in Figure 1.

Figure 16 | **Order of Math Operations**

| Symbol | Operation Order |
|---|---|
| ^ | First: Excel executes all exponential calculations. |
| * or / | Second: Excel executes multiplication and division after exponents. If both symbols are used in a formula, they are executed in order from left to right. |
| + or - | Third: Excel executes addition and subtraction after multiplication and division. If both symbols are used in a formula, they are executed in order from left to right. |

The complexity of formulas created in Excel is virtually limitless. As mentioned, when you are creating complex formulas involving several cell locations with several mathematical operators, Excel calculates the order of each operation as shown in Figure 16. However, in many situations you will need to change the order that each math operation is executed by adding parentheses. Math operations enclosed in parentheses are always executed first and override the order of operations shown in Figure 16. When several parentheses are used in a formula, Excel executes math operations by starting with the innermost parentheses and ends with the outermost parentheses.

Figure 17 illustrates an example in which parentheses are required in a complex formula. This worksheet shows an item from a merchandise worksheet similar to the example shown in Figure 9. The purpose of the formula in cell D2 is to estimate the inventory days on hand, which is calculated by dividing the inventory units by the number of units sold per day. However, notice that the sales results shown in column B are for last week. Therefore, assuming this store sells merchandise 7 days a week, the unit sales must first be divided by 7, and then the inventory units must be divided by this result to calculate the inventory days on hand.

Figure 17 | **Calculating Inventory Days on Hand**

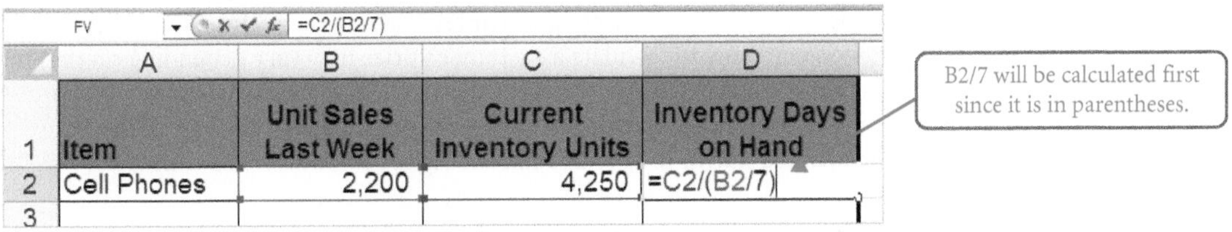

FV =C2/(B2/7)

| | A | B | C | D |
|---|---|---|---|---|
| 1 | Item | Unit Sales Last Week | Current Inventory Units | Inventory Days on Hand |
| 2 | Cell Phones | 2,200 | 4,250 | =C2/(B2/7) |
| 3 | | | | |

B2/7 will be calculated first since it is in parentheses.

Figure 18 shows the results of the Inventory Days on Hand formula, which is 13.52. Thus, if no additional inventory is received, this company will sell out of cell phones in approximately two weeks. Retail buyers often use this type of calculation to determine when products should be reordered from suppliers.

Figure 18 | **Results of Calculating Days on Hand Inventory**

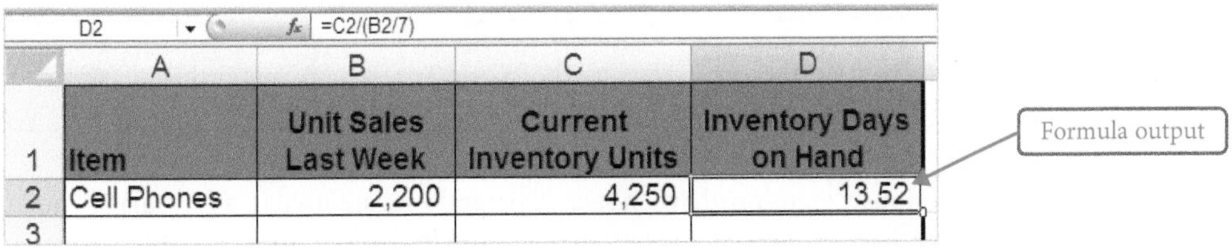

D2 =C2/(B2/7)

| | A | B | C | D |
|---|---|---|---|---|
| 1 | Item | Unit Sales Last Week | Current Inventory Units | Inventory Days on Hand |
| 2 | Cell Phones | 2,200 | 4,250 | 13.52 |
| 3 | | | | |

Formula output

Figure 19 illustrates the importance of using parentheses when creating the Inventory Days on Hand formula from Figure 17. Notice that no parentheses are used in this formula (see formula bar). As a result, Excel will execute each division operation in the order it appears in the formula from left to right. Therefore, Excel will first divide B2 into C2, and this result will be divided by 7. This produces an erroneous result of .28.

Figure 19 | **Invalid Result When Removing Parentheses**

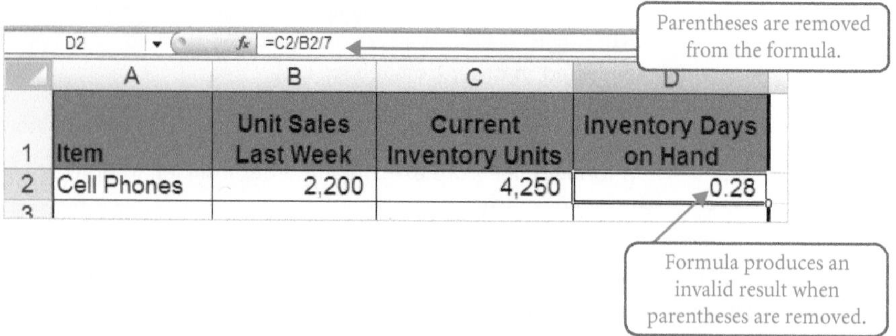


## COMMON MISTAKES | Using Numeric Values in Formulas

Be careful when using numeric values in formulas, as shown in Figure 17. You should use numeric values when dealing with constant values that do not change, such as days of the week, months of the year, minutes in an hour, and so on. Do not type numeric values that exist in cell locations into a formula. Typing the numeric value instead of using the cell reference eliminates the ability to recalculate an output when data is changed in the referenced cell or cells. Whenever possible, always use cell references when creating formulas.

Figure 20 illustrates a second example requiring the use of parentheses to control the order of mathematical operations. The manager of a transportation company might use this worksheet to determine how much a customer should be charged for delivering merchandise to a warehouse or retail store. The method used by a transportation company to calculate a customer's price may vary depending on the company and the merchandise that is being delivered. This example assumes that a customer will be charged the company's total cost per mile plus a 25% markup for profit. The formula shown in cell F2 is calculating the price for a 750-mile trip.

Figure 20 | **Calculating the Price of a Merchandise Delivery**

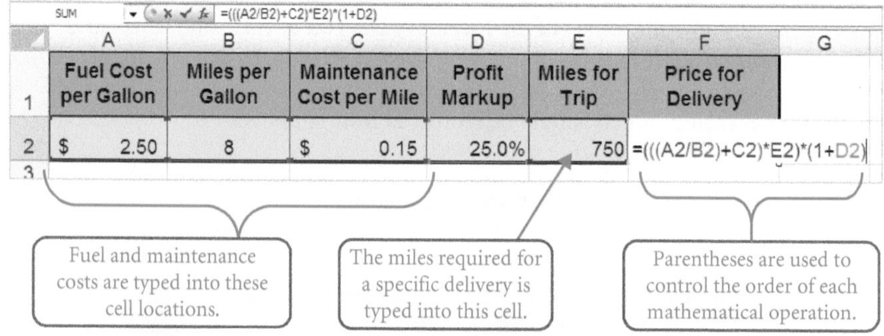


As previously mentioned, when several parentheses are used in a formula as shown in Figure 20, Excel will execute the math operation in the innermost parentheses first and continue toward the outermost parentheses. The order of each calculation for this example is as follows:

1. `(A2 / B2)`: This is the innermost set of parentheses, which is why this operation is being calculated first. This part of the formula is calculating the fuel cost per mile by dividing the Fuel Cost per Gallon in cell A2 by the Miles per Gallon in cell B2.
2. `((A2 / B2) + C2)`: After the fuel cost per mile is calculated, the Maintenance Cost per Mile is added. At this point, Excel has calculated one number that represents the fuel and maintenance cost per mile.
3. `(((A2 / B2) + C2) * E2)`: After Excel has calculated one number representing the transportation manager's cost per mile, it is multiplied by the number of miles typed into cell E2. The customer for this particular example has a delivery that requires a distance of 750 miles. At this point, Excel has calculated the total cost for a 750-mile trip.
4. `(((A2 / B2) + C2) * E2) * (1 + D2)`: This is the complete formula shown in Figure 20. The last operation to be performed is multiplying the cost of the trip by the markup. As previously mentioned, it is assumed that this company establishes a price based on a 25% profit markup. Excel will first add 1 to the markup percent typed into cell D2 because this operation is in its own set of parentheses. Then, this result is multiplied by the total cost of the trip established in step 3. Since .25 is typed into cell D2, the total cost of this trip will be increased by 1.25 or 25%.

## COMMON MISTAKES | Unequal Number of Parentheses

When constructing formulas, remember that each opening parenthesis must always have a closing parenthesis. This mistake occurs mostly in situations in which you are creating a formula that contains multiple sets of parentheses. If you have an unequal number of parentheses, the Formula Error dialog box will appear, as shown in Figure 21. The good news is that Excel will offer to fix the error for you if you click the **Yes** button.

Figure 21 | **Formula Error Dialog Box for Unequal Parentheses**

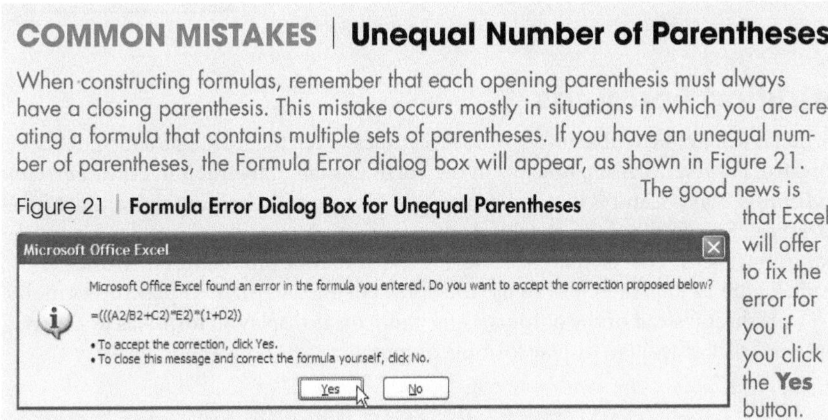


Figure 22 shows the final result of the formula calculating the price of a 750-mile trip. Because cell references were used in the construction of this formula, a new output can be calculated when any of the values in the yellow cells is changed. In fact, the cells in the range A2:E2 were intentionally colored yellow to indicate that these values can and should be changed when calculating a price for a new customer.

Figure 22 | **Results of Calculating the Price of a Merchandise Delivery**

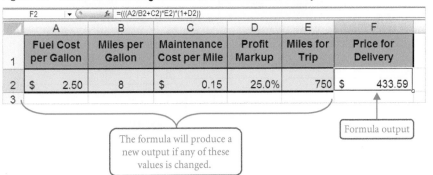

F2 =(((A2/B2+C2)*E2)*(1+D2))

| | A | B | C | D | E | F |
|---|---|---|---|---|---|---|
| 1 | Fuel Cost per Gallon | Miles per Gallon | Maintenance Cost per Mile | Profit Markup | Miles for Trip | Price for Delivery |
| 2 | $ 2.50 | 8 | $ 0.15 | 25.0% | 750 | $ 433.59 |
| 3 | | | | | | |

The formula will produce a new output if any of these values is changed.

Formula output

Because cell references are used in the formula shown in Figure 20, Excel calculates a new output when any of the values are changed in the range A2:E2. In fact, a transportation manager will most likely be changing these values on a daily basis. For example, the price of fuel might change, a new customer may request a price for a trip that is only 250 miles, or the company may need to lower its profit targets because of increased competition. How much will the company charge for the 750-mile trip shown in Figure 22 if the price of fuel increases to 2.75, and the profit markup is reduced to 20%? The answer is shown in Figure 23.

Figure 23 | **Formula Calculates a New Output When Data is Changed**

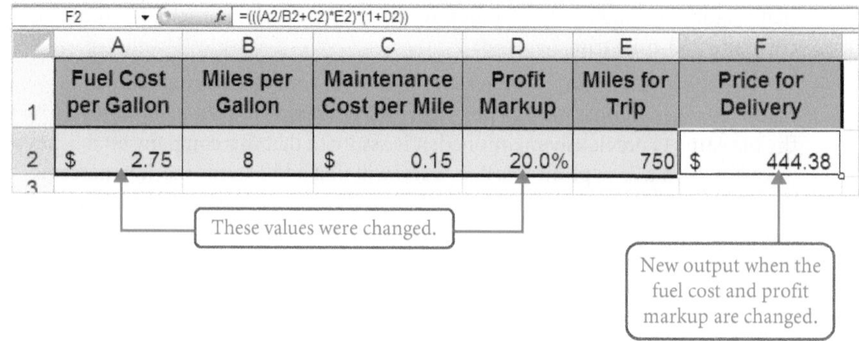


## Auditing Formulas

Formulas will not be visible on a spreadsheet unless a cell that contains a formula is activated. However, a group of icons in the **Formulas** tab of the Ribbon called ***Formula Auditing*** contains features that can be used for viewing and checking all formulas in a worksheet. This feature is most helpful when you are proofreading formulas for accuracy or tracing the cell references of a formula that may be producing an erroneous result. Figure 24 illustrates how to use the **Show Formulas** icon to display the formulas in a worksheet instead of the outputs. Click this icon to display all formulas in a worksheet and click it again to display formula outputs.

> **Quick Reference**
>
> **Complex Formulas**
>
> 1. Activate the cell where formula output should appear.
> 2. Type an equal sign.
> 3. Type or click cell locations or type numeric values if necessary.
> 4. Use parentheses and math operators where necessary.
> 5. Check that each opening parenthesis has a closing parenthesis.
> 6. Press the **Enter** key.

Figure 24 | **Show Formulas Instead of Outputs on a Worksheet**

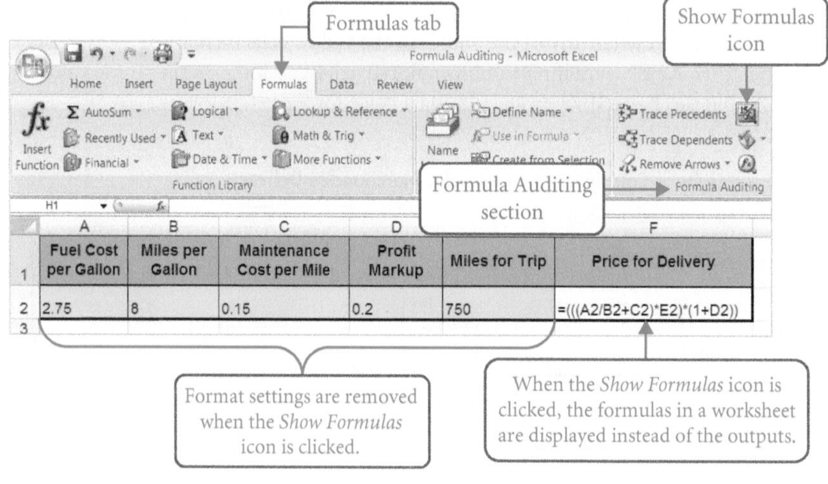

Another helpful proofreading option in the **Formula Auditing** section is the **Trace Precedents** icon. This feature will trace all cell references that are used in a formula. Activate a cell location that contains a formula and click the **Trace Precedents** icon. A blue arrow will appear on the worksheet indicating which cell locations are used in a formula, as shown in Figure 25. To remove the blue arrow, click the **Remove Arrows** icon, or click the down arrow next to this icon and select **Remove Precedent Arrows.**

Figure 25 | **Trace Precedents Arrow**

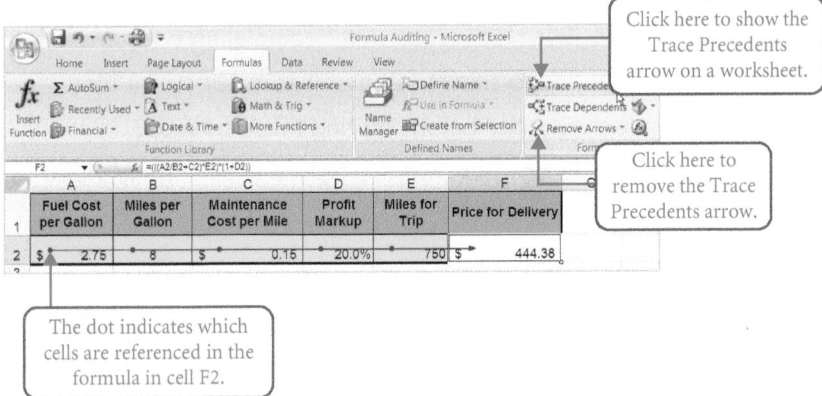


Use the **Trace Dependents** icon when you need to see where a particular cell is referenced in a formula. This capability is helpful if a cell has been improperly referenced in several formulas and you need to identify which formulas need to be edited. Activate a cell location and click the **Trace Dependents** icon. A blue arrow will point to the cell location that contains a formula where the cell is referenced, as shown in Figure 26. To remove the arrow, click the **Remove Arrows** icon, or click the down arrow next to this icon and select **Remove Dependent Arrows.**

Figure 26 | **Trace Dependents Arrow**

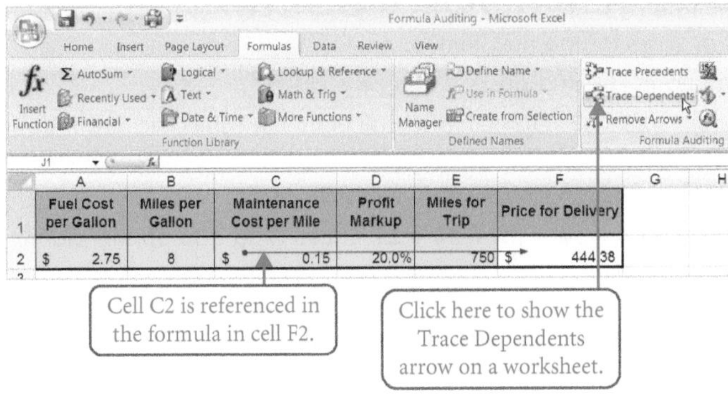


**>> Quick Reference**

**Show Formulas**

1. Click the **Formulas** tab of the Ribbon.
2. Click the **Show Formulas** icon.
3. Click the **Show Formulas** icon again to display the formula outputs.

**>> Quick Reference**

**Trace Precedents**

1. Activate a cell location that contains a formula.
2. Click the **Formulas** tab on the Ribbon.
3. Click the **Trace Precedents** icon.
4. Use the **Remove Arrows** icon to remove the **Trace Precedents** arrow.

**>> Quick Reference**

**Trace Dependents**

1. Activate a cell location that is referenced in a formula on a worksheet.
2. Click the **Formulas** tab on the Ribbon.
3. Click the **Trace Dependents** icon.
4. Use the **Remove Arrows** icon to remove the **Trace Dependents** arrow.

VIDEO WORKSHOP

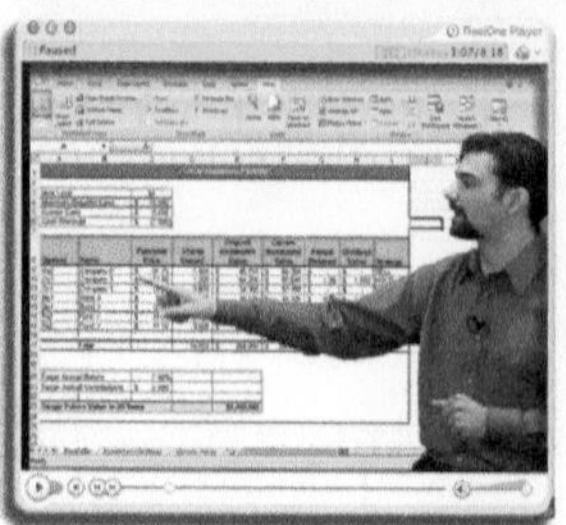

# >> Formulas

The purpose of this workshop is to demonstrate the use of basic and complex formulas presented in this section of the chapter. We will be using formulas to develop sales projections for items sold in a retail clothing store. I will be demonstrating the tasks in this workshop in the **Formulas** and **Paste Special** videos. After completing each section of tasks, watch the related video shown in parentheses. Open the file named ib_e03_salesprojections before starting this workshop. Remember to try the tasks on your own first before watching the video.

1. **Data Entry (Video: Formulas)**
   a. Type the following data into the Sheet1 worksheet for the cell locations listed:
      Cell C3: **10**
      Cell C4: **−15**
      Cell C5: **−50**
      Cell C6: **20**
      Cell C7: **0**
   b. Type the formula **=B3+(B3*C3)** into cell D3 to calculate the Plan Unit Sales This Year.
   c. Copy the formula in cell D3 and paste it into cells D4:D7.
   d. Type the formula **=F3*D3** into cell G3 to calculate the Plan Sales Dollars for the first item.
   e. Copy the formula in cell G3 and paste it into cells G4:G7.
   f. Type the formula **=(G3−(D3*E3))/G3** into cell H3 to calculate the profit as a percent of sales for the first item.
   g. Copy the formula in H3 and paste it into cells H4:H7.
   h. Type the formula **=H3*G3** into cell I3 to calculate the estimated profit dollars for the first item.
   i. Copy the formula in cell I3 and paste it into cells I4:I7.
   j. Type the formula **=I3 + I4 + I5 + I6 + I7** in cell I9 to add up the plan profit dollars for all items.

2. **Creating a New Scenario (Video: Formulas)**
   a. Rename the Sheet1 worksheet tab to **Profit Scenario 1**.
   b. Insert a new worksheet.
   c. Change the name of this new worksheet tab to **Profit Scenario 2**.
   d. Copy the entire Profit Scenario 1 worksheet.
   e. Activate cell A1 in the Profit Scenario 2 worksheet and click the **Paste** icon.

f. In the Profit Scenario 2 worksheet, type the following values in the cell locations listed:

   C4: **0**
   C5: **0**

3. **Paste Special (Video: Paste Special)**
   a. Copy the range D3:D7 in the Profit Scenario 2 spreadsheet.
   b. Activate cell C3 in the Sales Report spreadsheet.
   c. Click the down arrow below the **Paste** icon and select the **Paste Values** option.
   d. Click the **Paste Options** icon, which appears in cell D8 after completing step c.
   e. Select the **Values and Number Formatting** option.
   f. Save and close your workbook.

## >> Startup Costs for a New Business

**EXERCISE**

**Why Do I Need This?**

Have you ever thought about starting your own business? One of the most significant challenges in starting a new business is determining how much sales are needed to pay for startup costs. Startup costs usually involve purchases such as machines, office equipment, or permanent marketing materials such as signs. In addition, certain statistics will either be fixed or inflexible. For example, the market price that customers are willing to pay for certain products and services may be fairly rigid. In these cases, raising the price of your product or service to cover startup costs will usually result in a losing proposition.

### Exercise

The purpose of this exercise is to use Excel to determine how much sales are required to pay the startup costs of a landscaping business. Open the file named ib_e03_landscapingstartup and complete each of the following tasks:

1. Type the number **25** in cell B3 and change the color of the cell to yellow. You change the cell color to yellow to indicate where values need to be typed into the worksheet. The number 25 is simply a place holder for the number of customers this business might service in a year. This number will be adjusted in later steps of the exercise.

2. Indent the range A9:A11 by clicking the **Increase Indent** icon twice. Indenting will make the spreadsheet easier to read and is a common practice on most accounting and financial documents.

3. Indent cell A16 twice and then indent the range A21:A23 twice.

4. Type a formula in cell C12 that adds the values in cells C9, C10, and C11. This type of calculation is typically done with a function, which will be covered in the next section of this chapter. For now, use a formula to add these three values. This amount represents the total startup costs for this business. The primary focus of this business will be lawn care. Therefore, this exercise assumes that a lawnmower, trimmer, and blower are necessary startup purchases.

5. Type a formula that calculates the total cost of supplies in cell C16. The formula should multiply the value in cell B16 by the value in cell B3. This exercise assumes that supplies will cost $10 for every customer serviced. Costs such as fuel, garbage bags, and oil are usually consumed on every job. Therefore, the purpose of the formula is to multiply the cost per customer by the total number of customers planned for the business.

6. Type a formula in cell C18 that adds the value in cell C12 and C16. The output of this formula represents the total costs of the business.

7. Type a formula in cell B23 that calculates the Average Sales Revenue per Customer, which is Price per Acre multiplied by the Average Number of Acres per Lawn. This exercise assumes that the customer is willing to pay only $30 to service 1 acre of land. In addition, this case assumes that the average amount of land a customer will own in neighborhoods you service is 1.5 acres.

8. Type a formula in cell C25 that multiplies the Average Sales Revenue per Customer by the Number of Customers Serviced This Year.

9. Type a formula in cell B5 that takes the Total Sales in cell C25 and subtracts the Total Costs in cell C18. This is the Net Profit of the business. Is this business making any money if it services only 25 customers per year?

10. Change the value in cell B3 to **100**. Will this business be profitable if 100 customers are serviced per year?

11. How many customers must be serviced for the Net Profit to be approximately 0? How many customers for the profit to be approximately $5,000?

12. What if the price customers were willing to pay per acre dropped to $25, but the average number of acres per lawn increased to 1.75? How many customers will it take to achieve approximately $5,000 in Net Profit?

13. Save and close your file.

**PROBLEM & EXERCISE**

## >> What's Wrong with This Spreadsheet?

### Problem

You are directing a division of a major department store company. Your division is made up of four departments. At the beginning of each year, the directors from every division meet with the president of the company to discuss sales and profit targets. A colleague in another division gave you a spreadsheet with an assurance that it included all necessary formulas and that the only thing you had to do was enter numbers in the yellow cells that relate to your sales and profit targets.

### Exercise

The spreadsheet that was given to you is named ib_e03_departmentstoreplanningmeeting. Open this file and examine the Sheet1 worksheet carefully. Would you be comfortable using this worksheet to plan the sales and profit targets for your division? Consider the following:

1. Look at the totals in cells B8, C8, and F8. Do the numbers add up?
2. Give the spreadsheet a test drive by changing the value in cell D4 to **.10**. The sales results in column C are calculated by multiplying the Sales Last Year in column B by the Sales Growth percentages in column D. Do you see a new sales plan number in cell C4 that makes sense?
3. Change the value in cell B4 to **8000000**. Do you see a new sales plan number in cell C4 when the value in cell B4 was changed?
4. The Profit Dollars in column F are calculated by multiplying the Profit Percent values in column E by the Sales values in column C. Change the value in cell E4 to **.20**. Does this change produce a new profit dollar value in cell F4?
5. Look at the totals in cells B8, C8, and F8. Do the numbers still add up?
6. What could you use to see and check all the formulas in this worksheet? What clues would tell you that something might be wrong with a formula?

What's wrong with this spreadsheet? Write a short answer for each of the points listed in the preceding problem. Then, fix any errors, adjust, or add formulas that you believe would make this spreadsheet more reliable.

# Basic Functions

Skill Set

As previously mentioned, the two primary tools for conducting mathematical computations in Excel are formulas and functions. ***Functions*** are slightly different from formulas in that you do not have to define mathematical operators to produce an output. The mathematical operations are predefined depending on the function that is used. For example, the **AVERAGE** function can be used to calculate the average for a range of ten cells in a worksheet. Functions can produce exactly the same output as formulas. However, when a mathematical output requires the use of many cell locations, it is easier and faster to add a function to a worksheet as opposed to a formula. This section will review the use of basic statistical functions and illustrate why it is more efficient to use them for certain calculations instead of formulas.

## Basic Statistical Functions

Using basic statistical methods to analyze data is a common practice in business. For example, a business manager may sum the sales results for a group of stores in a district, calculate the average trips per week for a fleet of trucks, or evaluate the most common number of items purchased when customers visit a store. In Excel, basic statistical functions can provide a convenient way to accomplish these computations, as opposed to using formulas. For example, the Merchandise Sales Report worksheet in Figure 28 contains sales information for 18 items. If you wanted to calculate the sum of the Unit Sales for all items in column D, you could add all 18 cell locations from D2 to D19 individually to a formula. Or, you could just add the range D2:D19 to the **SUM** function to produce the same result.

All Excel functions can be created using the following method:

- Type an equal sign. Similar to formulas, all functions begin with an equal sign in a cell location. The equal sign signifies that Excel will be performing some type of computation instead of displaying what is typed in a cell.
- Type the function name. After you type the first letter of a function, a list of possible function names beginning with the letter you typed will appear (see Figure 27). This feature is especially helpful if you forgot how to spell a particular function name. After you find the name of the function you would like to use, you can double click the name from the list or continue typing the function name manually.
- Type an open parenthesis. If you double click a function name from the function list as shown in Figure 27, Excel will insert the open parenthesis for you automatically.
- Type a cell range or define arguments. The information you type after the open parenthesis will depend on the type of function you are using. For the basic statistical functions covered in this section, you will need to type a cell range (two cell locations separated by a colon) after the open parenthesis. You can also type specific cell locations separated by commas if you are applying the function to cells that are not contained in a continuous range (for example, B2,H5,D10). Note that functions containing arguments are covered in the next section.
- Type a close parenthesis and press the **Enter** key. After you press the **Enter** key, the function output will be displayed in the cell.

As mentioned, when you begin typing the name of a function, a list of possible function names beginning with the first letter you typed will appear on the worksheet. For example, Figure 27 shows the function list after typing an equal sign and the letter S. In addition, if you click a function name one time, a definition of the function will appear.

Figure 27 | **The Function List**

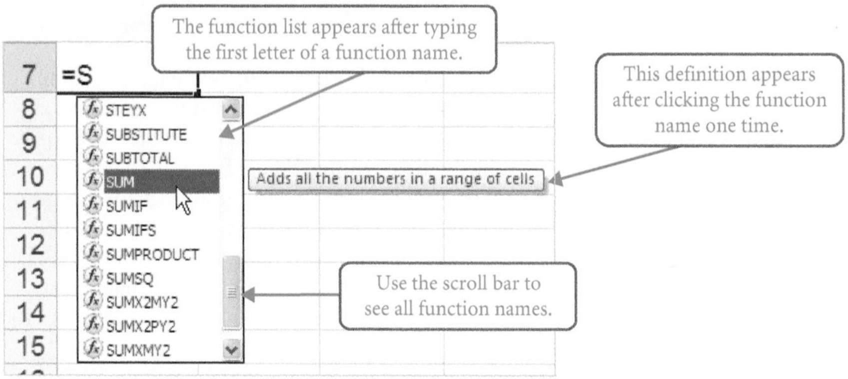

The function list appears after typing the first letter of a function name.

This definition appears after clicking the function name one time.

Adds all the numbers in a range of cells

Use the scroll bar to see all function names.

Figures 28 and 29 show the setup and results of adding a **SUM** function to the Merchandise Sales Report worksheet. Here, the **SUM** function was added to calculate the total number of units sold for all items in the worksheet. As mentioned, it is more convenient to use the **SUM** function in this situation because a total is being computed from 18 cell locations. The following explains how to add this function to the worksheet:

- Activate cell D20. This is the last cell at the bottom of the Unit Sales column.
- Type an equal sign.
- Type the function name SUM. You can also double click the word **SUM** from the function list.
- Type an open parenthesis. If you double clicked the function name from the function list, the open parenthesis will already be added.

- Type the range D2:D19. You can also add this range to the function by clicking and dragging over cells D2 through D19.
- Type a close parenthesis.
- Press the **Enter** key.

Figure 28 | **Adding the SUM Function to the Merchandise Sales Report**

SUM =SUM(D2:D19)

The function appears in the formula bar when cell D20 is activated.

| | A | B | C | D | E |
|---|---|---|---|---|---|
| 1 | *Category Description* | *Item Description* | *Color* | *Unit Sales* | *Sales Dollars* |
| 2 | Bottoms | Shorts | Tan | 12,500 | $237,500 |
| 3 | Tops | T-Shirts | Black | 10,000 | $115,000 |
| 4 | Bottoms | Shorts | White | 9,500 | $180,500 |
| 5 | Tops | Sweater | Grey | 8,500 | $289,000 |
| 6 | Bottoms | Shorts | Brown | 8,500 | $161,500 |
| 7 | Tops | T-Shirts | Blue | 8,500 | $97,750 |
| 8 | Tops | Tank Top | White | 6,500 | $55,250 |
| 9 | Bottoms | Shorts | Blue | 5,500 | $104,500 |
| 10 | Tops | T-Shirts | Yellow | 4,500 | $51,750 |
| 11 | Tops | Sweater | Brown | 3,500 | $119,000 |
| 12 | Shoes | Sandals | Black | 3,000 | $66,000 |
| 13 | Tops | Tank Top | Pink | 2,500 | $21,250 |
| 14 | Shoes | Boots | Black | 1,600 | $96,000 |
| 15 | Tops | Sweater | Red | 1,500 | $51,000 |
| 16 | Tops | Tank Top | Red | 1,500 | $12,750 |
| 17 | Shoes | Sandals | Grey | 1,200 | $26,400 |
| 18 | Shoes | Sandals | Green | 850 | $18,700 |
| 19 | Shoes | Boots | Brown | 750 | $45,000 |
| 20 | ***Total*** | | | =SUM(D2:D19) | |

This range can be added to the function by clicking and dragging over cells D2 through D19 after typing =SUM(.

Figure 29 | **Results of the SUM Function in the Merchandise Sales Report**

J1

| | A | B | C | D | E |
|---|---|---|---|---|---|
| 1 | *Category Description* | *Item Description* | *Color* | *Unit Sales* | *Sales Dollars* |
| 2 | Bottoms | Shorts | Tan | 12,500 | $237,500 |
| 3 | Tops | T-Shirts | Black | 10,000 | $115,000 |
| 4 | Bottoms | Shorts | White | 9,500 | $180,500 |
| 5 | Tops | Sweater | Grey | 8,500 | $289,000 |
| 6 | Bottoms | Shorts | Brown | 8,500 | $161,500 |
| 7 | Tops | T-Shirts | Blue | 8,500 | $97,750 |
| 8 | Tops | Tank Top | White | 6,500 | $55,250 |
| 9 | Bottoms | Shorts | Blue | 5,500 | $104,500 |
| 10 | Tops | T-Shirts | Yellow | 4,500 | $51,750 |
| 11 | Tops | Sweater | Brown | 3,500 | $119,000 |
| 12 | Shoes | Sandals | Black | 3,000 | $66,000 |
| 13 | Tops | Tank Top | Pink | 2,500 | $21,250 |
| 14 | Shoes | Boots | Black | 1,600 | $96,000 |
| 15 | Tops | Sweater | Red | 1,500 | $51,000 |
| 16 | Tops | Tank Top | Red | 1,500 | $12,750 |
| 17 | Shoes | Sandals | Grey | 1,200 | $26,400 |
| 18 | Shoes | Sandals | Green | 850 | $18,700 |
| 19 | Shoes | Boots | Brown | 750 | $45,000 |
| 20 | ***Total*** | | | 90,400 | |

Output produced by the SUM function.

The example in Figure 30 illustrates the **AVERAGE** function. This worksheet contains the sales and profit results for six stores in a district of a retail company. The **AVERAGE** function is used to calculate the average sales results that are achieved for each store in the district. Notice that the range in the **AVERAGE** function includes cell C7, which does not contain a numeric value. Statistical functions will ignore cells that are blank or do not contain numeric data. Therefore, the **AVERAGE** function will ignore this cell until a numeric value is typed into it.

Figure 30 | **The AVERAGE Function**

SUM =AVERAGE(C2:C7)

| | A | B | C | D |
|---|---|---|---|---|
| 1 | District | Store Number | Annual Sales | Net Profit |
| 2 | 5 | 505 | $ 3,007,782 | $ |
| 3 | 5 | 522 | $ 5,738,273 | $ |
| 4 | 5 | 560 | $ 7,144,261 | $ |
| 5 | 5 | 575 | $ 3,058,901 | $ |
| 6 | 5 | 580 | $ 5,646,718 | $ 656,467 |
| 7 | 5 | 590 | New Store | N/A |
| 8 | | Averages | =AVERAGE(C2:C7) | |

The AVERAGE function will ignore this cell because it does not contain a numeric value.

Relative referencing (explained previously in the "Formulas" section) also applies to functions. Figure 31 shows the **AVERAGE** function after it was pasted into cell D8, which is one cell to the right of the cell location shown in Figure 30. Notice that the column letters of the range in the function changed from C to D. This function will show the average of the Net Profit results in column D and will ignore cell D7 because it does not contain a numeric value.

Figure 31 | **Relative Referencing Adjusts the Range in the AVERAGE Function**

SUM =AVERAGE(D2:D7)

| | A | B | C | D | E |
|---|---|---|---|---|---|
| 1 | District | Store Number | Annual Sales | Net Profit | |
| 2 | 5 | 505 | $ 3,007,782 | $ 320,311 | |
| 3 | 5 | 522 | $ 5,738,273 | $ 716,445 | |
| 4 | 5 | 560 | $ 7,144,261 | $ (142,885) | |
| 5 | 5 | 575 | $ 3,058,901 | $ 467,068 | |
| 6 | 5 | 580 | $ 5,646,718 | $ 656,467 | |
| 7 | 5 | 590 | New Store | N/A | |
| 8 | | Averages | $ 4,919,187 | =AVERAGE(D2:D7) | |

The column letters in this range automatically adjusted when the function was pasted into cell D8 from C8.

Figure 32 shows how the **AVERAGE** function produces a new output when numeric data is typed into C7 and D7. As mentioned, these cells were previously ignored by the function because they did not contain numeric values. However, because of cell referencing, the functions automatically produce a new output when numeric values are typed into these cells.

Figure 32 | **The AVERAGE Function Produces a New Output When Data Is Changed**

| | A | B | C | D |
|---|---|---|---|---|
| 1 | District | Store Number | Annual Sales | Net Profit |
| 2 | 5 | 505 | $ 3,007,782 | $ 320,311 |
| 3 | 5 | 522 | $ 5,738,273 | $ 716,445 |
| 4 | 5 | 560 | $ 7,144,261 | $ (142,885) |
| 5 | 5 | 575 | $ 3,058,901 | $ 467,068 |
| 6 | 5 | 580 | $ 5,646,718 | $ 656,467 |
| 7 | 5 | 590 | $ 8,534,000 | $ 775,640 |
| 8 | | *Averages* | *$ 5,521,656* | *$ 465,508* |

Values are typed into cells C7 and D7.

This output changed when a value was typed into cell C7.

## COMMON MISTAKES | Cell Ranges versus Specific Cells in Functions

Be careful when using a range of cells versus selected cells in basic statistical functions. If you want to apply a statistical function to a group of consecutive cells, you must use a range. A range is any two cells separated by a colon, NOT a comma. For example, the **SUM** function shown in Figure 33 will add only cells A2 and A6, providing an output of 3000. The reason is that a *comma* is separating the two cell locations. For this **SUM** function to add all of the values in cells A2 through A6, the range **A2:A6** must be typed between the parentheses of the function. Therefore, always check the outputs of all functions used in a worksheet. If you were expecting the **SUM** function to add all the values in column A in Figure 33 and saw an output of 3000, you would know something is wrong because one of the values in this column is 5000 (cell A4).

Figure 33 | **SUM Function Adding Values in Only Two Cell Locations**

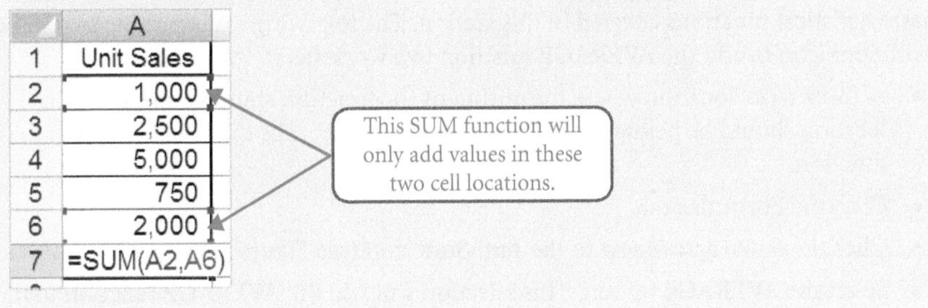

| | A |
|---|---|
| 1 | Unit Sales |
| 2 | 1,000 |
| 3 | 2,500 |
| 4 | 5,000 |
| 5 | 750 |
| 6 | 2,000 |
| 7 | =SUM(A2,A6) |

This SUM function will only add values in these two cell locations.

The **SUM** function and the **AVERAGE** function were used to demonstrate basic statistical functions in this section. However, this usage just scratches the surface of the 300+ functions in Excel. Figure 34 shows other commonly used statistical functions. The details of what these functions do and how they are applied in business situations will likely be covered in your business statistics or economics courses.

**>> Quick Reference**

**Basic Functions**

1. Activate a cell where the output of the function should appear.
2. Type an equal sign.
3. Type the name of the function or double click a function name from the function list.
4. Type an open parenthesis if you typed the function name manually.
5. Type a range or click and drag a range of cells (if you are using specific cells not in a continuous range, type or click each cell and separate with a comma).
6. Type a closing parenthesis.
7. Press the **Enter** key.

Figure 34 | **Table of Common Statistical Functions**

| Function Name | Purpose |
|---|---|
| SUM | Calculates the total for numeric values in a range of cells or selected cells. |
| AVERAGE | Calculates the average for a series of numeric values. |
| MEDIAN | Returns the value that is in the middle of a *sorted* numeric series (the range of cells used with this function must be sorted in order for the function to produce an accurate result). |
| MODE | Identifies the value that occurs the most in a numeric series. |
| STDEV | Calculates the standard deviation for a range of cells. |
| VAR | Calculates the variance for a range of cells. |
| MIN | Returns the lowest value in a numeric series. |
| MAX | Returns the highest value in a numeric series. |
| COUNT | Counts the number of cells that contain a numeric value. |
| COUNTA | Counts the number of cells that contain either a numeric value or text value. |
| PRODUCT | Calculates the product of the values contained in a range of cells or selected cells. |
| SQRT | Returns the square root of a number. |
| ABS | Returns the absolute value of a number. |

## AutoSum

The **AutoSum** icon in the **Formulas** tab of the Ribbon provides quick access to a few basic statistical functions covered in this section. The following explains how to use the **AutoSum** icon to add the **AVERAGE** function to a worksheet:

- Activate a cell location where the output of the function should appear. This cell location should be below or to the right of a range of cells that will be used in the function.
- Click the **Formulas** tab.
- Click the down arrow next to the **AutoSum** icon (see Figure 35).
- Select the **AVERAGE** option. This selection will add the **AVERAGE** function to the worksheet and automatically select a range of cells immediately above the activated cell location (see Figure 36).
- Press the **Enter** key.

**Quick Reference**

**AutoSum**

1. Activate the cell where the output of the function should appear. The cell location should be below or to the right of a range of cells that will be used in the function.
2. Click the **Formulas** tab in the Ribbon.
3. Click the down arrow next to the **AutoSum** icon.
4. Select a function.
5. Press the **Enter** key.

Figure 35 | **Options in the AutoSum Icon**

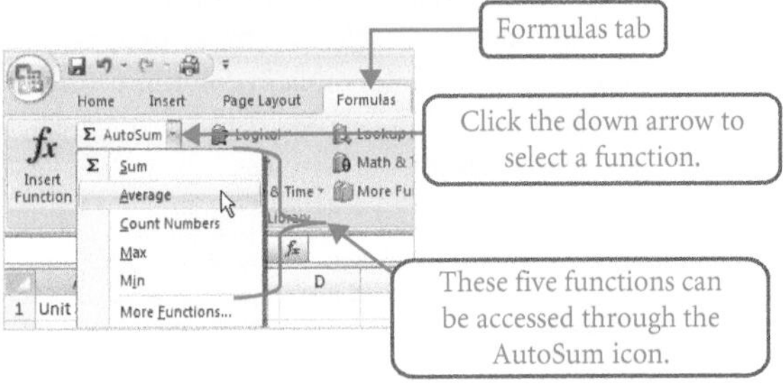


Figure 36 | **The Range Is Added to the AVERAGE Function Automatically**

SUM =AVERAGE(A2:A6)

| | A | B | C |
|---|---|---|---|
| 1 | Unit Sales | | |
| 2 | 1,000 | | |
| 3 | 2,500 | | |
| 4 | 5,000 | | |
| 5 | 750 | | |
| 6 | 2,000 | | |
| 7 | =AVERAGE(A2:A6) | | |

When creating a function with the AutoSum icon, this range is automatically defined.

## Absolute References (Turning Off Relative References)

As previously mentioned, because of relative referencing, Excel will automatically adjust the cell references used in formulas and functions when they are pasted into new cell locations. However, certain circumstances may require you to turn off this relative reference feature. In other words, you may need to paste a formula or function to a new cell location but do not want Excel to adjust the cell references. In these situations you will need to apply an ***absolute reference*** or a ***mixed reference*** to the cell references in a formula.

To place an absolute reference on a cell location, type a dollar sign in front of the column letter and row number. Placing the dollar sign here prevents relative referencing from adjusting the cell location when the formula is pasted to a new cell location. You can also create mixed references which is when a dollar sign is typed in front of the column letter *or* the row number. For example, if a dollar sign is typed only in front of the row number, the row number becomes an absolute reference, but the column letter remains a relative reference. If this cell was referenced in a formula, the column letter will change, but the row number will not when the formula is pasted into a new cell location. The following are examples of absolute and mixed references.

- `$C$10`: This is an absolute reference. This cell reference will not change when it is pasted to another cell location on a worksheet.
- `C$10`: This is a mixed reference. The row number will not change when this cell is pasted to a new location on a worksheet.
- `$C10`: This is another example of a mixed reference. The column letter will not change when this cell is pasted to a new location on a worksheet.

The example in Figure 37 illustrates when an absolute reference is used in a business situation. This worksheet shows a list of annual expenses for a hypothetical company. A **SUM** function was created in cell B8 to total the Cost Values for all expense items in column B. The goal for this example is to create a formula in column C that divides the Cost Value for each expense item by the total in cell B8. This will show what percentage each item contributes to the total expenses for the business.

Figure 37 | **Annual Expense Information for a Hypothetical Business**

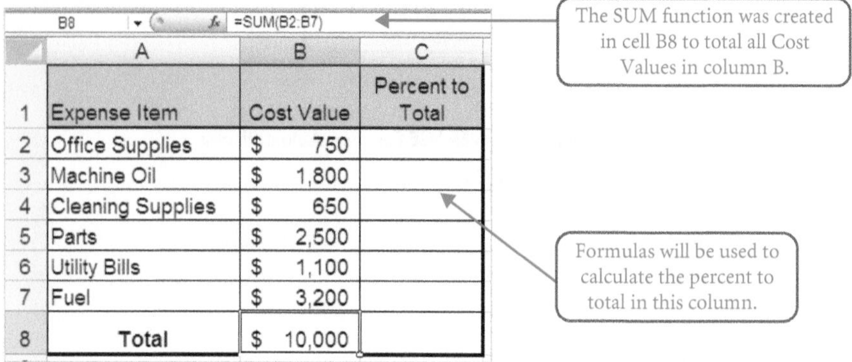

B8 =SUM(B2:B7)

| | A | B | C |
|---|---|---|---|
| 1 | Expense Item | Cost Value | Percent to Total |
| 2 | Office Supplies | $ 750 | |
| 3 | Machine Oil | $ 1,800 | |
| 4 | Cleaning Supplies | $ 650 | |
| 5 | Parts | $ 2,500 | |
| 6 | Utility Bills | $ 1,100 | |
| 7 | Fuel | $ 3,200 | |
| 8 | Total | $ 10,000 | |



Figure 38 shows the formula that was created in cell C2 to compute the Percent to Total for Office Supplies. The result shows that Office Supplies makes up 7.5% of the total annual expenses for this business. This formula will be copied and pasted to cells C3 through C7 to calculate the Percent to Total for the rest of the Expense Items in column A.

Figure 38 | **Formula Used to Compute the Percent to Total**

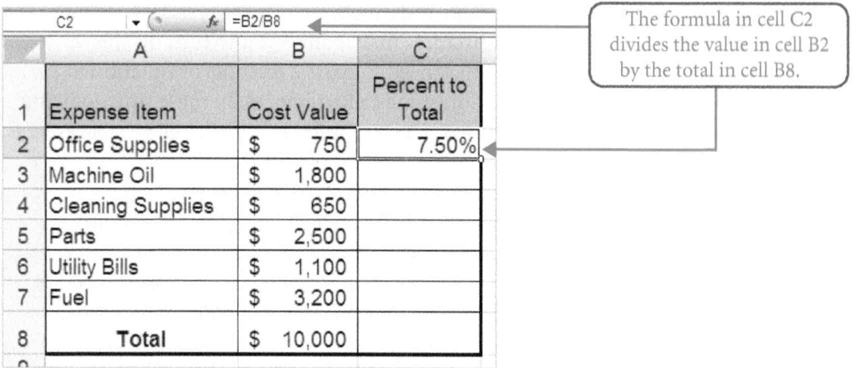

C2 =B2/B8

| | A | B | C |
|---|---|---|---|
| 1 | Expense Item | Cost Value | Percent to Total |
| 2 | Office Supplies | $ 750 | 7.50% |
| 3 | Machine Oil | $ 1,800 | |
| 4 | Cleaning Supplies | $ 650 | |
| 5 | Parts | $ 2,500 | |
| 6 | Utility Bills | $ 1,100 | |
| 7 | Fuel | $ 3,200 | |
| 8 | Total | $ 10,000 | |



Figure 39 shows that a divide by zero error (#DIV/0!) occurs when the formula created in cell C2 is pasted into cells C3 through C7. This error occurred because relative referencing is adjusting the cell that is being divided into the Cost Value for each Expense item.

Figure 39 | **Divide by Zero Error**

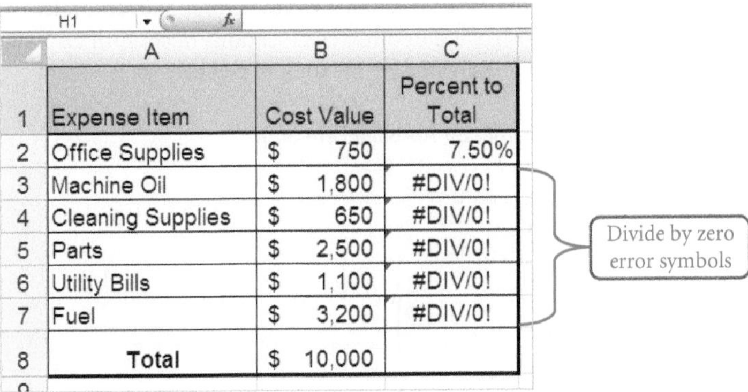

| | A | B | C |
|---|---|---|---|
| 1 | Expense Item | Cost Value | Percent to Total |
| 2 | Office Supplies | $ 750 | 7.50% |
| 3 | Machine Oil | $ 1,800 | #DIV/0! |
| 4 | Cleaning Supplies | $ 650 | #DIV/0! |
| 5 | Parts | $ 2,500 | #DIV/0! |
| 6 | Utility Bills | $ 1,100 | #DIV/0! |
| 7 | Fuel | $ 3,200 | #DIV/0! |
| 8 | Total | $ 10,000 | |

H1
Divide by zero error symbols

Figure 40 shows why the divide by zero error occurred in Figure 39. The goal of the formula created in cell C2 is to divide the Cost Value for the Office Supplies expense by the total annual expenses for the business. Therefore, the value in cell B2 is divided by the total in cell B8. However, notice how relative referencing adjusted the cell references in this formula when it was pasted into cell C3. The value in cell B3 is being divided by the value in cell B9. Since there is nothing in cell B9, the divide by zero error appears. Therefore, we need to prevent relative referencing from changing cell B8 when it is copied from cell C2 to other cell locations in the column. This is done by adding an absolute reference to cell B8 in the formula that was created in cell C2 (see Figure 38).

Figure 40 | **How Relative Referencing Causes the Divide by Zero Error**

SUM =B3/B9

| | A | B | C |
|---|---|---|---|
| 1 | Expense Item | Cost Value | Percent to Total |
| 2 | Office Supplies | $ 750 | 7.50% |
| 3 | Machine Oil | $ 1,800 | =B3/B9 |
| 4 | Cleaning Supplies | $ 650 | #DIV/0! |
| 5 | Parts | $ 2,500 | #DIV/0! |
| 6 | Utility Bills | $ 1,100 | #DIV/0! |
| 7 | Fuel | $ 3,200 | #DIV/0! |
| 8 | Total | $ 10,000 | |
| 9 | | | |

Because of *relative* referencing, the second part of this formula is being divided by an empty cell.

As mentioned, to prevent relative referencing from adjusting cell B8 in the formula shown in Figure 38, we must use an absolute reference. This is accomplished by typing a dollar sign in front of the column letter and row number of cell B8, as shown in Figure 41.

Figure 41 | **Adding an Absolute Reference to Cell B8**

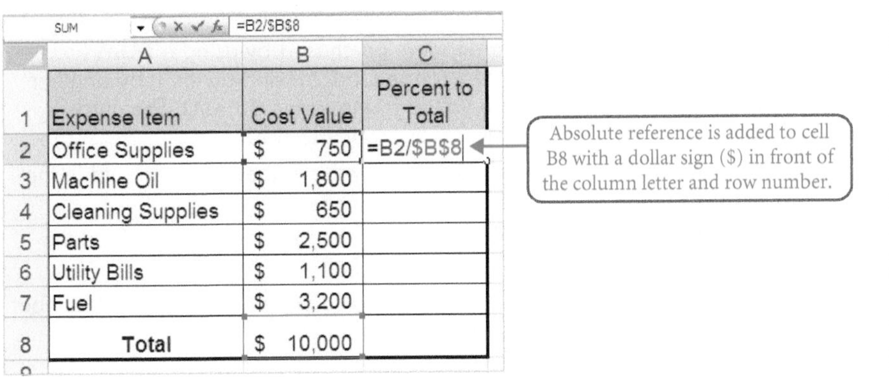

| | A | B | C |
|---|---|---|---|
| 1 | Expense Item | Cost Value | Percent to Total |
| 2 | Office Supplies | $ 750 | =B2/$B$8 |
| 3 | Machine Oil | $ 1,800 | |
| 4 | Cleaning Supplies | $ 650 | |
| 5 | Parts | $ 2,500 | |
| 6 | Utility Bills | $ 1,100 | |
| 7 | Fuel | $ 3,200 | |
| 8 | Total | $ 10,000 | |

SUM
=B2/$B$8
Absolute reference is added to cell B8 with a dollar sign ($) in front of the column letter and row number.

> **Quick Reference**
>
> **Absolute Reference**
>
> 1. Identify a cell reference within a formula or function that requires an absolute reference or mixed reference.
> 2. Type a dollar sign in front of the column letter and row number of a cell reference to apply an absolute reference.
> 3. Type a dollar sign in front of the column letter or row number to apply a mixed reference.

Figure 42 shows the results of pasting the formula in Figure 41 to cell locations C3 through C7. As shown in the figure, there are no divide by zero errors. The reason is that cell B8 did not change when it was pasted to other cell locations in column C. Now all the Cost Values in column B are being divided by the total in cell B8.

Figure 42 | **Results of Pasting a Formula with an Absolute Reference**

SUM =B4/$B$8

| | A | B | C |
|---|---|---|---|
| 1 | Expense Item | Cost Value | Percent to Total |
| 2 | Office Supplies | $ 750 | 7.50% |
| 3 | Machine Oil | $ 1,800 | 18.00% |
| 4 | Cleaning Supplies | $ 650 | =B4/$B$8 |
| 5 | Parts | $ 2,500 | 25.00% |
| 6 | Utility Bills | $ 1,100 | 11.00% |
| 7 | Fuel | $ 3,200 | 32.00% |
| 8 | Total | $ 10,000 | |

Cell B8 does not change when the formula is pasted to a new cell location.

**VIDEO WORKSHOP**

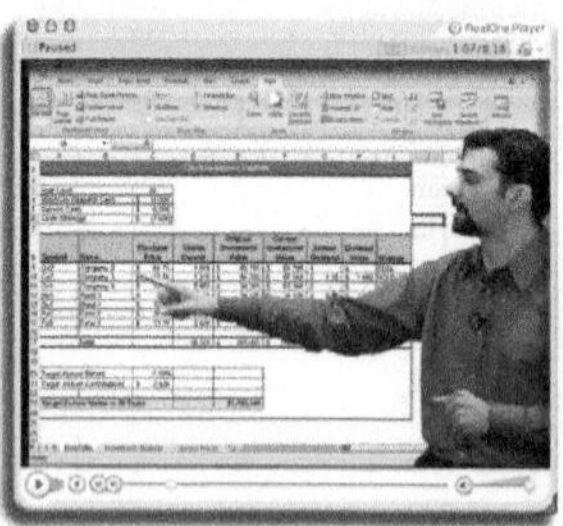

## >> Statistical Functions

The purpose of this workshop is to demonstrate the use of statistical functions when conducting mathematical computations. We will be using statistical functions to summarize transaction data for a typical retail business. I will be demonstrating the tasks in this workshop in the **Statistical Functions** video. Open the file named ib_e03_retailtransactions before starting the following tasks:

1. **Statistical Functions (Video: Statistical Functions)**
   a. Type the **COUNT** function in cell G3 to count all the Transaction Numbers in the range A3:A50.
   b. Type a **SUM** function in cell G4 to add up the Amount Paid in the range C3:C50.
   c. Type an **AVERAGE** function in cell G5 to calculate the average Number of Items in the range B3:B50.
   d. Type an **AVERAGE** function in cell G6 to calculate the average of the range C3:C50.
   e. Calculate the average price per item purchased by using a **SUM** function to add up the values in the range C3:C50 and divide it by another **SUM** function adding up the values in the range B3:B50. The entry should be as follows: =Sum(C3:C50)/Sum(B3:B50).
   f. Type a **MAX** function in cell G8 to show the highest amount paid in the range C3:C50.
   g. Type a **MIN** function in cell G9 to show the lowest amount paid in the range C3:C50.
   h. Type a **MODE** function in cell G10 to calculate the most frequent number of items purchased in the range B3:B50.
   i. Save and close your file.

## >> Absolute References

**VIDEO WORKSHOP**

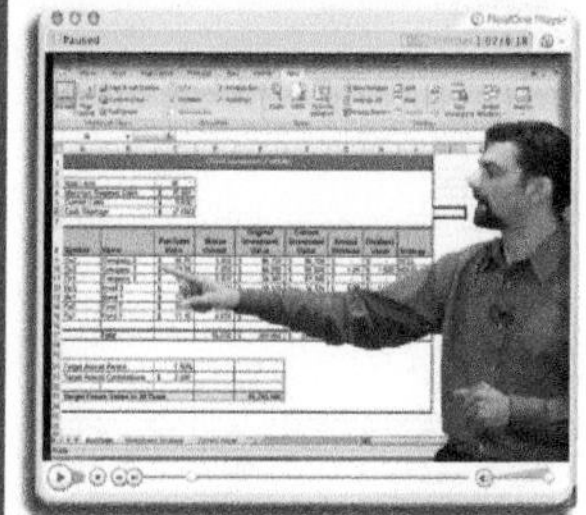

The purpose of this workshop is to demonstrate how and why absolute references are used in business situations. We will be using an absolute reference to calculate the percent to total for items on a merchandise sales spreadsheet. I will be demonstrating the tasks in this workshop in the **Absolute Reference** video. Open the file named ib_e03_merchandisesales before starting the following tasks:

1. **Functions (Video: Absolute Reference)**
   a. Create a **SUM** function in cell E12 to add up the profit dollars in column E.
2. **Formulas (Video: Absolute Reference)**
   a. Type a formula in cell F3 that divides the profit dollars in cell E3 by the total profit dollars in cell E12.
   b. Format the output of the formula in cell F3 to a percentage with 2 decimal places.
3. **Absolute References (Video: Absolute Reference)**
   a. Edit the formula in cell F3 by placing an absolute reference on cell E12.
   b. Copy cell F3 and paste it into cells F4:F11.
   c. Save and close your file.

## >> Evaluating a Transportation Business

**EXERCISE**

**Why Do I Need This?**

Summarizing data plays a critical role in making business decisions. The amount of data businesses store and analyze can be massive, especially in large corporations. Most business managers face the constant challenge of quickly summarizing large sets of data to assess business results. Knowing how to summarize data using the statistics functions covered in this section will enable you to quickly summarize and assess large sets of data relating to almost any business situation.

### Exercise

The purpose of this exercise is to use statistical functions to evaluate the performance of a transportation company. Open the file named ib_e03_transportationperformance and complete the following tasks:

1. Using the **COUNT** function in cell C3, calculate the number of trips in the range A13:A52.
2. Use the **AVERAGE** function in cell G3 to calculate the average miles per trip in the range C13:C52.
3. Find the highest miles driven for a single trip in the range C13:C52 by using the **MAX** function in cell C4.

4. Find the lowest miles driven for a single trip in the range C13:C52 by using the **MIN** function in cell G4.
5. Using the **MODE** function in cell C6, determine which trailer size was used the most from the range B13:B52.
6. Calculate the average capacity per trip by typing an **AVERAGE** function in cell G6. The capacity for each trip is in the range D13:D52.
7. Use the **MAX** function in cell C7 to determine the highest capacity for a single trip in the range D13:D52.
8. Use the **MIN** function in cell G7 to determine the lowest capacity for a single trip in the range D13:D52.
9. Type the value `2.50` in cell G9 and `.25` in cell G10.
10. Calculate the total fuel cost in cell C9 by using a **SUM** function to add up all the fuel consumed in the range E13:E52 and multiplying it by the fuel cost in cell G9.
11. Calculate the dollars billed in cell C10 by using a **SUM** function to add up all the miles driven in the range C13:C52 and multiplying it by the current charge per mile in cell G10.
12. Compare the output of the formulas you created in cells C9 and C10. Is this company making enough money to cover its fuel cost?
13. If fuel prices are increased to $3.05 per gallon, how much will this company have to increase its charge per mile to cover the cost of fuel plus make approximately $1,000 in profit?
14. This company has a goal of maintaining an average capacity per trip of 90%. Is this company achieving its goal?
15. What could this company do to get closer to its capacity target of 90%? How else could you analyze the Trip Detail statistics in the range A12:E52 to answer this question? HINT: What size trailers are reaching the highest capacity levels on a consistent basis?
16. Save and close your file.

**PROBLEM & EXERCISE**

## >> What's Wrong with This Spreadsheet?

### Problem

Your classmate is having trouble with a project and has come to you for help. He is using Excel for an industry analysis project that is due for one of his business classes. He completed the spreadsheet but explains that for some reason a lot of the numbers do not look right. He e-mails the Excel file to you with the following explanation:

1. I am trying to calculate the market share for each company on the spreadsheet, which is nothing more than a percent to total. I used an absolute reference on one of the cell locations in the formula (you know, that dollar sign thing), but I still keep getting this error.
2. I'm wondering if my market share error in column C has something to do with the **SUM** function I used in cell B8. It worked fine, but before I e-mailed the file to you, I noticed that the number looked a little low.

3. The other thing that looks weird is the average I calculated in cell B9. The result is $43,750,000, but every company is below this number except for Company A. I used the **AVERAGE** function, so it must be right. I don't know; it just seems weird.

4. Finally, I used the **COUNT** function in cell C11 to count the number of companies in the spreadsheet, but it keeps giving me a result of 0. At this point I am wondering if this file got corrupted somehow. Can you take a look at this and let me know if I should just make another spreadsheet on a different computer?

### Exercise

The file this classmate has sent to you is named ib_e03_industryanalysistrouble. Open the file and review each of the concerns listed in the Problem section. Is it the computer that's causing these problems? What's wrong with this spreadsheet? Write a short answer explaining what mistakes were made for each of the points your classmate listed. Then, correct any errors you find.

## >> Financial Functions

Skill Set

The statistical functions demonstrated in the previous section were constructed by typing a range of cells or specific cell locations separated by commas between parentheses. However, other functions may require the definition of several inputs or ***arguments*** to produce an output. The purpose and number of arguments will vary depending on the function. This section reviews two such functions: Future Value and Payment. Both are related to the financial aspects of business with regard to evaluating investments and loans. This section will demonstrate how these functions are constructed and highlight how they can be used for making both professional and personal business decisions.

### The Future Value Function

The ***Future Value***, or ***FV*** function, is used to calculate the value of investments over a specific period of time. To better understand how the **Future Value** function calculates the value of an investment, it is helpful to review an example relating to the time value of money.

Figure 43 illustrates the principles of the time value of money by showing how a bank account grows over three years. This example assumes that a bank is very generous and offers an interest rate of 8% for a traditional savings account. In reality, the interest rate that is usually offered for a traditional savings account is much less. The first row of the table, labeled Year 1, shows that an account is opened with $10. Assuming the interest rate does not change, the value of the account after one year will be $10.80 as shown in the End Balance column. The reason is that $.80 was paid in interest (see the Interest Earned column). The second row, labeled Year 2, assumes that another $10 is deposited into the account as shown in the Deposit column. Notice that the Interest Earned column increases from $.80 in Year 1 to $1.66 in Year 2. The value of the account at the end of Year 2 is $22.46, as shown in the End Balance column. At the end of the third year, the ending balance of the account is $35.06. However, if you add the values in the Deposits column, only $30 was added to this account. The additional money is the total amount of interest paid over the three-year period, which is $5.06. This is the sum of the values in the Interest Paid column.

Figure 43 | **Time Value of Money Example**

| | Begin Balance | Deposit | Interest Rate | Interest Paid | End Balance |
|---|---|---|---|---|---|
| Year 1 | 0 | $10.00 | 8% × $10.00 | $ .80 | $10.80 |
| Year 2 | $10.80 | $10.00 | 8% × $20.80 | $1.66 | $22.46 |
| Year 3 | $22.46 | $10.00 | 8% × $32.46 | $2.60 | $35.06 |

The Future Value function will be used to calculate this result.

The **Future Value** function can be used to calculate the End Balance value, which is circled in Figure 43. You add the function to a worksheet by typing an equal sign (=), the function name FV, and an open parenthesis. You can also double click the function name FV from the function list after typing the equal sign and the letter F. To complete the function, you will need to define at least three of the five arguments shown in Figure 44. The arguments will appear in a hint box after you type an open parenthesis or double click the function name from the function list. The following is a definition for each of these arguments:

- **rate**: The interest rate applied to an investment.
- **nper**: The number of periods an investment is added to an account or the amount of time an investment is being measured. This argument must correspond to the interest rate entered in the **rate** argument. For example, if an annual interest rate is entered in the **rate** argument, the **nper** argument must be the number of years. If a monthly interest rate is entered in the **rate** argument, the **nper** argument must be the number of months. If a daily interest rate is used in the **rate** argument, the **nper** argument must be the number of days.
- **pmt**: The value of the payments that are added to an account. This argument is used when money is being added to an account over a period of time (such as $100 per month or $2,000 per year). The period of time will be the value that is entered in the **nper** argument. A negative sign must be placed in front of values or cell locations used to define this argument.
- ***[pv]: Present Value***: The argument used when a one-time investment is made to an account. It can be used with or without the **pmt** argument. You must place a negative sign in front of values or cell locations used to define this argument.
- **[type]**: The argument used to define when payments are made to an account; it can either be a 1 or 0. If this argument is not defined, Excel will assume the value is 0.
  - 1: Used for payments made at the beginning of a period (i.e., at the beginning of a month, year, etc.).
  - 0: Used for payments made at the end of a period.

Figure 44 | **Arguments of the Future Value Function**

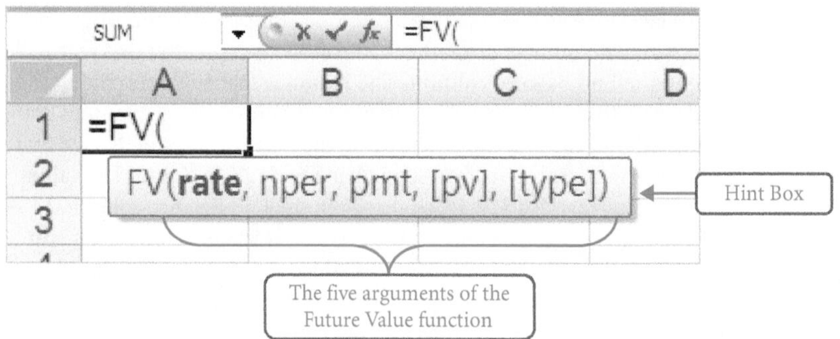

As mentioned, the **Future Value** function can be used to calculate the End Balance value circled in Figure 43. The following illustrates how each argument of the function would be defined based on the Time Value of Money Example (Figure 43). Remember, you must use a comma to separate each value that is used to define the arguments of the function.

- **rate**: `.08` This represents the annual interest rate shown in the Interest Rate column in Figure 43. When you are entering numbers into this function, it is best *not* to use any symbols except for decimal points. This is why the 8% interest rate is typed into the function as .08. If you are not sure how to convert a percentage to a decimal, simply divide the percent by 100 (i.e., `8 ÷ 100 = .08`).
- **nper**: `3` The Time Value of Money Example in Figure 43 shows that $10 is deposited into a bank account every year for three years. Therefore, the number 3 (representing 3 years) is entered for this argument. It is important to note that since an annual interest rate was entered in the **rate** argument, the time period entered for this argument must be in years.
- **pmt**: `-10` Since $10 is being deposited into a bank account over a three-year period, the number -10 is entered for this argument. *You must put a negative sign in front of any number or cell location used for this argument.*
- **[pv]**: This argument is used to evaluate a one-time lump sum investment. However, this example assumes that deposits are being made to the account annually. Therefore, this argument will be skipped by adding a comma with no spaces.
- **[type]**: For this example, we will assume that the $10 is being deposited into the account at the beginning of each year. Therefore, a value of 1 is entered for this argument.

Figure 45 shows how the arguments of the **Future Value** function are defined based on the Time Value of Money Example in Figure 43. Notice that each argument is separated with a comma. In addition, since the **[pv]** argument was skipped, a comma was typed with no spaces.

Figure 45 | **Setup of the Future Value Function Based on the Time Value of Money Example**

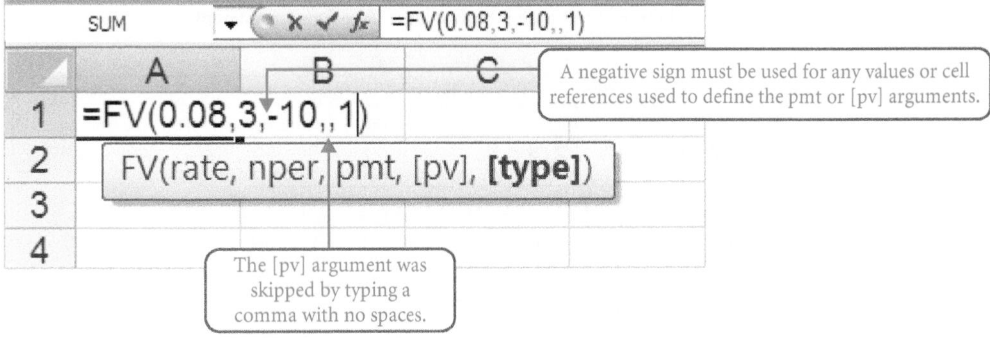


Figure 46 shows the results of the **Future Value** function after the **Enter** key was pressed. Notice that this output is identical to the End Balance number in Year 3 from the Time Value of Money Example in Figure 43.

Figure 46 | **Results of the Future Value Function**

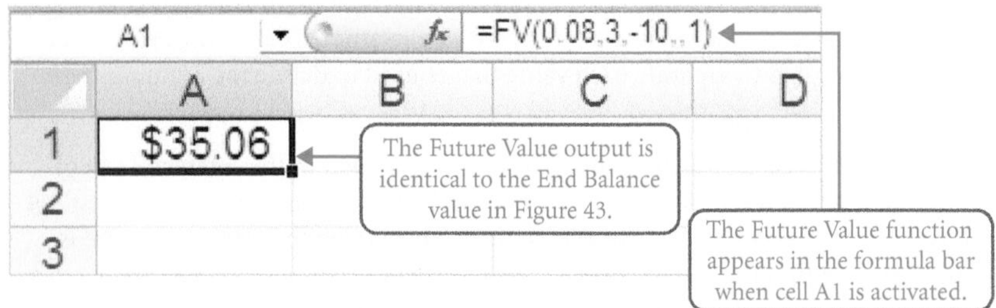


## COMMON MISTAKES | Separate Arguments with Commas

You must type a comma after each argument of the **Future Value** function. If you are skipping an argument, as in Figure 45, type a comma with no spaces. If you are skipping both the **[pv]** and **[type]** arguments, you can type a closing parenthesis after the **pmt** argument. This is the reason these arguments are displayed in brackets [ ]. The function will produce an output if these arguments are not defined. Note that Excel assumes payments are made at the *end* of the year if the **[type]** argument is skipped.

As previously mentioned, the **Future Value** function can also evaluate an investment made in one lump sum. This would require the **[pv]** argument to be defined instead of the **pmt** argument. When using the **[pv]** argument, you must use a negative sign for all values or cell locations as in the **pmt** argument. Figure 47 shows how the arguments of the **Future Value** function are defined if $30 is deposited into a bank account at the beginning of Year 1 as opposed to making $10 deposits over a three-year period as shown in the Time Value of Money Example in Figure 43. It is assumed that the annual interest rate is 8% and that it will not change over the three-year period.

Figure 47 | **Setup of the Future Value Function for a One-Time Investment**

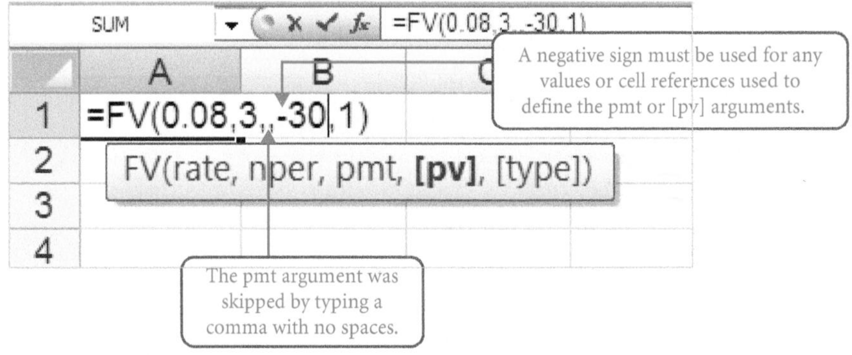


Figure 48 shows the output of the **Future Value** function which was set up in Figure 47. Notice that this output is higher than the output shown in Figure 46. The reason is that more interest is being paid into the account since $30 is deposited into the bank account on day 1 as opposed to being deposited over three years.

Figure 48 | **Results of the Future Value Function for a One-Time Investment**

A1 | $f_x$ =FV(0.08,3,,-30,1)

| | A | B | C |
|---|---|---|---|
| 1 | $37.79 | | |
| 2 | | | |

Figure 49 shows another example of the **Future Value** function. In this example, the information from the Time Value of Money Example (Figure 43) has been typed into a worksheet. Notice that the arguments of the function are defined using cell references (see the formula bar). As a result, the **Future Value** function will calculate a new output when any of the values are changed in the range B2:B5. Also, you will see that the output of the function is identical to the output shown in Figure 46. The reason is that the values that are typed into the cell references used to define the arguments of the function are identical to the values that were used to set up the **Future Value** function in Figure 45.

Figure 49 | **Future Value Function Using Cell References Instead of Numeric Values**

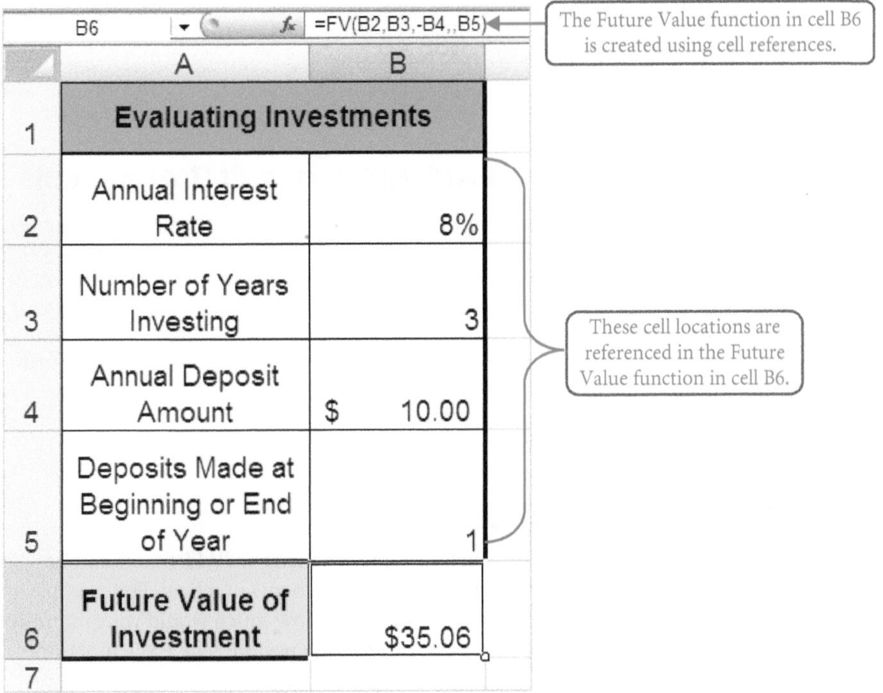


The benefit of using cell references to define the arguments of the **Future Value** function is that it allows you to conduct what-if scenarios with investments you may be evaluating professionally or personally. For example, what if you increased the Annual Deposit Amount in Figure 49 from $10 to $12, and what if you invested this money over a four-year period instead of a three-year period? Figure 50 shows how the output of the **Future Value** function changes when these values are changed in the worksheet.

Figure 50 | **Values in Cells Referenced by the Future Value Function Are Changed**

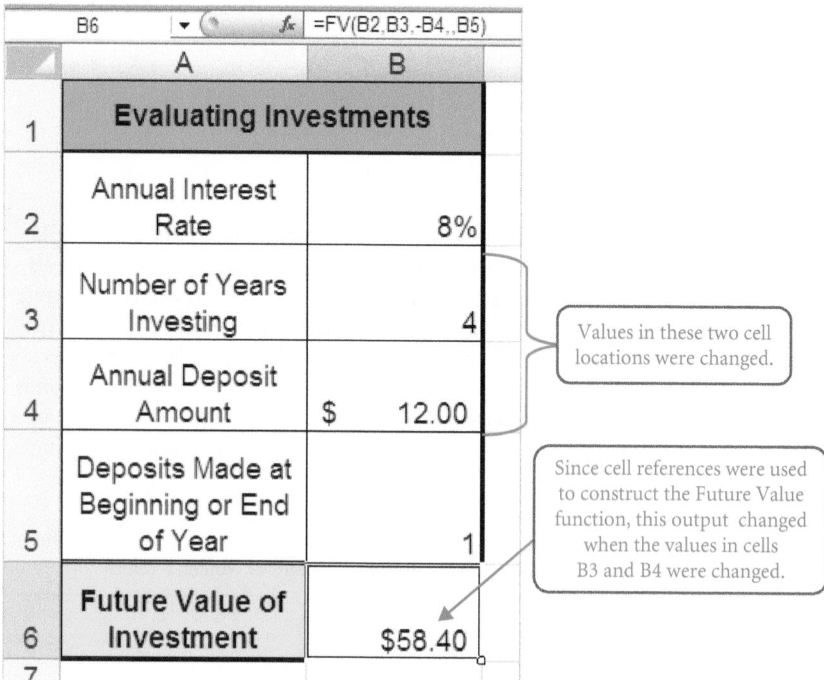


### COMMON MISTAKES | RATE, NPER, and PMT Arguments

Always check that the **rate**, **nper**, and **pmt** arguments of the **Future Value** function are expressed in equal terms. For example, investments might be made on a monthly basis, but the interest or return rate quoted by a bank or financial institution is expressed on an annual basis. In this case, you would have to define the **rate** argument by dividing the annual interest rate by 12 if the number of months is used to define the **nper** argument and the monthly investment value is used to define the **pmt** argument. The key is to make sure the **rate**, **nper**, and **pmt** arguments are all defined using equivalent terms.

**>> Quick Reference**

**Future Value Function**

1. Activate the cell where output should appear.
2. Type an equal sign.
3. Type the function name FV or double click **FV** from the function list.
4. Type an open parenthesis (if you double clicked the function from the function list, this will already be added).
5. Define the following arguments:

   **rate**: Interest Rate

   **nper**: Number of Periods or Amount of time

   **pmt**: Payments (must use a negative sign)

   **[pv]**: Present Value

   **[type]**: When payments are made (1 = beginning of year; 0 = end of year)
6. Close the parenthesis.
7. Press the **Enter** key.

## The Payment Function

A close relative of the **Future Value** function is the ***Payment*** or ***PMT*** function. The **PMT** function is most helpful when calculating the payments of a loan. For example, if you were buying a home and had to borrow $225,000, how much would your monthly payment be if a bank charged 6% interest over a 30-year period? The **PMT** function can be used to answer this question.

Similar to the **Future Value** function, at least three of five arguments must be defined for the **Payment** function to produce an output. Figure 51 shows the five arguments of the **Payment** function, which are very similar to the arguments of the **Future Value** function. The following defines each of these arguments:

- **rate**: The interest charged by a lender.
- **nper**: The number of payments or, as in the **Future Value** function, a period of time (i.e., years, months, weeks, etc.).
- **pv**: Present Value; the argument used to define the amount of money being borrowed or the principal of the loan. As in the **Future Value** function, *you must use a negative sign for any values or cell references used for this argument.*
- **[fv]**: Future Value; the argument used when part of a loan is paid off with periodic payments and the balance of the loan is paid off in one lump sum at a future point

in time. This argument is especially helpful when evaluating the lease payments of a car. However, if a loan is structured such that there is no lump sum payoff at a future point in time, you can skip this argument by adding a comma with no spaces.

- **[type]**: A value that determines if payments are made at the beginning or end of a period and can either be a 1 or 0. If this argument is not defined, Excel will assume the value is 0.
  - 1: Used for payments made at the beginning of a period (i.e., at the beginning of a month, year, etc.).
  - 0: Used for payments made at the end of a period.

Figure 51 | **Arguments of the Payment Function**

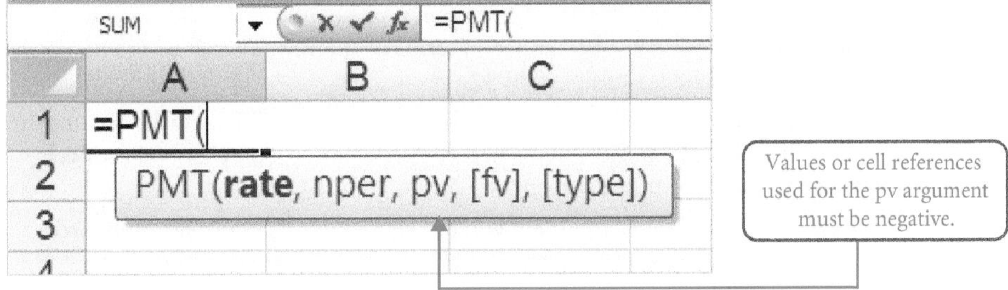


Figure 52 shows a worksheet that contains loan information for the purchase of a $250,000 home. The **Payment** function will be used in cell B6 to calculate the monthly mortgage payments for this loan. This example assumes that the bank will charge an interest rate of 6.5%, which is shown in cell B2. In addition, the repayment period for the loan is 30 years, as shown in cell B3. The amount of money that will be borrowed from the bank is $225,000. This example assumes a down payment of $25,000. Therefore, the remaining balance to pay for the house is $225,000, which is shown in cell B4. Finally, the number 1 is shown in cell B5, indicating that payments will be made at the beginning of each month.

Figure 52 | **Using the Payment Function to Determine the Monthly Payments of a Loan**

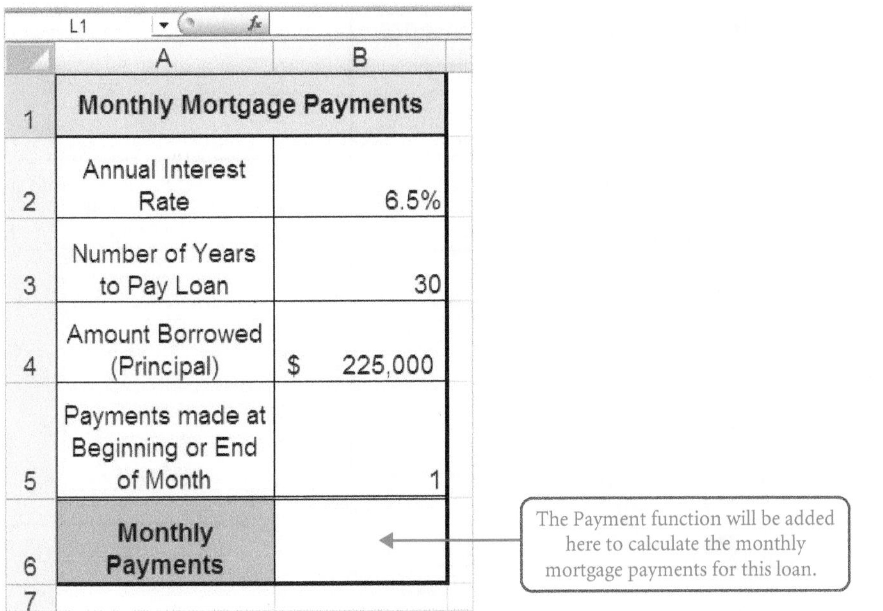

As mentioned, the **Payment** function will be constructed in cell B6 of Figure 52 to determine the monthly mortgage payments for this loan. The following explains the setup of this function:

- Activate cell B6.
- Type an equal sign, the function name PMT, and an open parenthesis. This will open the hint box showing the arguments of the function (see Figure 51).
- Define the arguments of the **Payment** function as follows:
  - **rate**: `B2/12` The formula `B2/12` is used to define the **rate** argument of the function. The goal of this example is to calculate the monthly payments of the loan. However, cell B2 contains an annual interest rate. Therefore, this annual interest rate must be converted to a monthly interest rate so the payments can be expressed in terms of months instead of years.
  - **nper**: `B3*12` The formula `B3*12` is used to define the **nper** argument. Since the goal of this exercise is to calculate the monthly payments, the repayment period of the loan must be defined in terms of months. Therefore, the number of years in cell B3 is multiplied by 12.
  - **pv**: `-B4` The present value argument is defined using cell B4 which contains the principal of the loan. However, a negative sign must precede any value or cell reference used for this argument.
  - **[fv]**: , The future value argument will be skipped in this example. Therefore, a comma is typed with no spaces.
  - **[type]**: `B5` Cell B5 contains a value that indicates if payments are made at the beginning or end of the month. Therefore, it is referenced for this argument of the function.
- Type a closing parenthesis.
- Press the **Enter** key.

Figure 53 shows the results of the **Payment** function. Cell B6 is activated so you can see the setup of the function in the formula bar. Notice how formulas were used to define the **rate** and **nper** arguments. Similar to the **Future Value** function, the **rate**,

Figure 53 | **Results of the Payment Function**

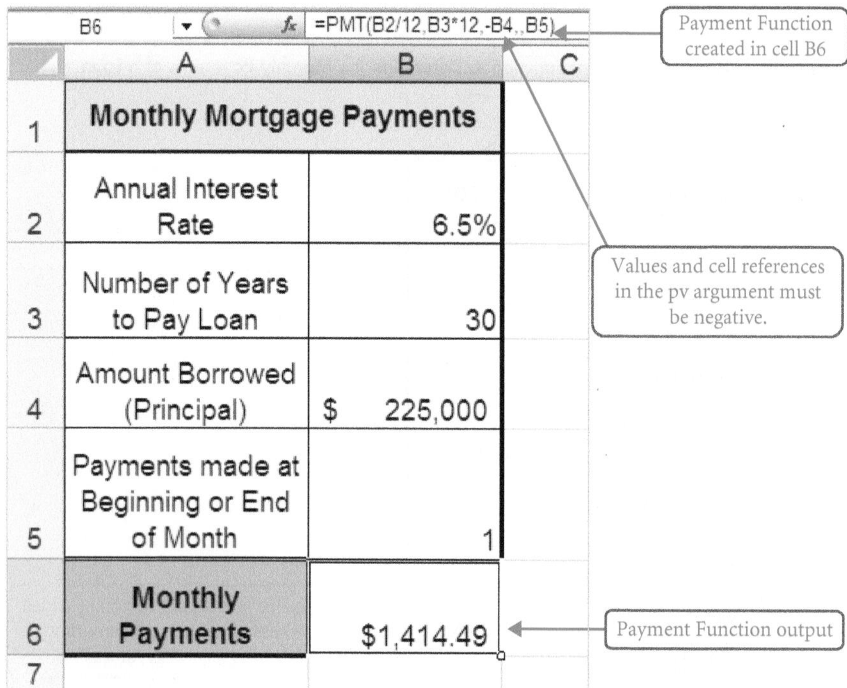

nper, and [pv] arguments of the **Payment** function must be expressed in equivalent terms. The formulas in the **rate** and **nper** arguments are converting the interest rate and repayment period to months. The results in this figure show that the monthly mortgage payment for this loan is $1,414.49.

### COMMON MISTAKES | Negative Output for the FV or PMT Functions

If the output of a **Future Value** function or **Payment** function is negative, check the **pmt** and **[pv]** arguments of the **Future Value** function or the **pv** argument of the **Payment** function. Values and cell references used to define these arguments must be negative. If the negative sign is omitted for these arguments, the function will produce a negative number.

It is important to note that the **Payment** function constructed in Figure 53 uses cell references to define each of the arguments. As a result, if the values in cells B2 through B5 are changed, the function will produce a new output. Therefore, what if you decided that the loan payments shown in Figure 53 are too expensive for your budget? You can lower the principal in cell B4 and lower the interest rate in cell B2. Lowering these values will decrease the monthly mortgage payments. Figure 54 shows the results of the **Payment** function if the value in cell B4 is lowered to $205,000 and the interest rate in cell B2 is lowered to 6%.

Figure 54 | **New Output When Data Is Changed**

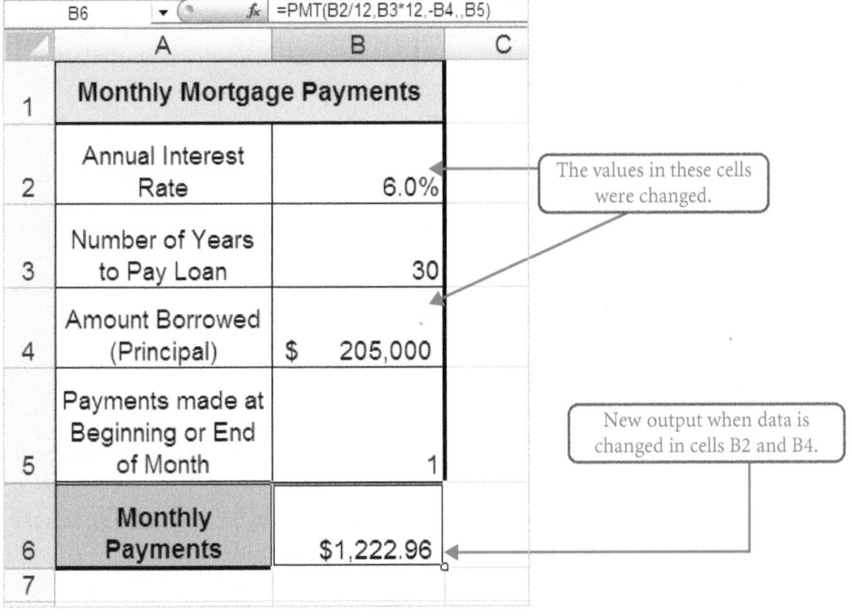


As previously mentioned, you can also use the **Payment** function to calculate the lease payments of a car. Leasing cars is often used as an alternative to buying. When leasing a car, a person pays only the value of the car that is used during a set period of time. The car dealer usually charges an interest rate for allowing the buyer to pay off the lease over several years.

The worksheet in Figure 55 contains data that will be used to calculate the monthly lease payments for a $23,000 car. The interest rate charged on the lease is 5% as shown in cell B2, and the car will be leased over a four-year period, as shown in cell B3. The residual value, or the future value, of the car is assumed to be $9,500 in four years (see cell B5). Therefore, if the car is worth $9,500 in four years, and the price of the car is $23,000, then the value of the car used during the four-year lease period is $13,500 ($23,000 – $9,500). The **Payment** function will automatically calculate this difference, factor in the interest rate, and determine the monthly payments.

Figure 55 | **Data Used to Calculate the Lease Payments of a Car**

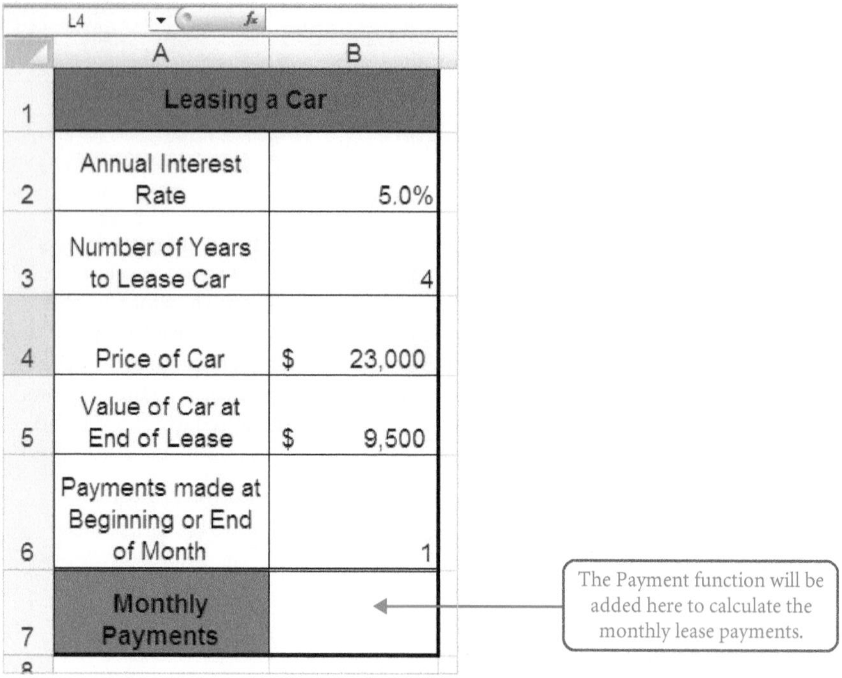

| | A | B |
|---|---|---|
| 1 | Leasing a Car | |
| 2 | Annual Interest Rate | 5.0% |
| 3 | Number of Years to Lease Car | 4 |
| 4 | Price of Car | $ 23,000 |
| 5 | Value of Car at End of Lease | $ 9,500 |
| 6 | Payments made at Beginning or End of Month | 1 |
| 7 | Monthly Payments | |

The Payment function will be added here to calculate the monthly lease payments.

> **Quick Reference**
>
> **Payment Function**
>
> 1. Activate a cell where output should appear.
> 2. Type an equal sign.
> 3. Type the function name PMT or double click **PMT** from the function list.
> 4. Type an open parenthesis (if you double clicked the function from the function list, this will already be added).
> 5. Define the following arguments:
>
>    **rate**: Interest rate
>
>    **nper**: Number of payments or period of time
>
>    **pv**: Present value
>
>    **[fv]**: Future value
>
>    **[type]**: When payments are made (1 = beginning of year, 0 = end of year)
> 6. Close the parenthesis.
> 7. Press the **Enter** key.

The following explains how the **Payment** function is constructed in cell B7 in the worksheet shown in Figure 55 to calculate the lease payments of the car:

- Activate cell B7.
- Type an equal sign, the function name PMT, and an open parenthesis.
- Define the arguments of the **Payment** function as follows:
  - **rate:** `B2/12` This formula converts the annual interest rate to a monthly interest rate.
  - **nper:** `B3*12` This formula converts the number of years to lease the car to months. As a result, both the **rate** and **nper** arguments are expressed in terms of months.
  - **pv:** `-B4` The present value argument is defined using cell B4, which contains the price of the car. This cell reference is preceded by a negative sign.
  - **[fv]:** `B5` The future value argument is defined by referencing cell B5, which contains the value of the car at the end of the lease.
  - **[type]:** `B6` Cell B6 contains a value indicating if payments are made at the beginning or end of the month.
- Type a closing parenthesis.
- Press the **Enter** key. The results of the function are shown in Figure 56.

Figure 56 | **Results Showing the Monthly Lease Payments**

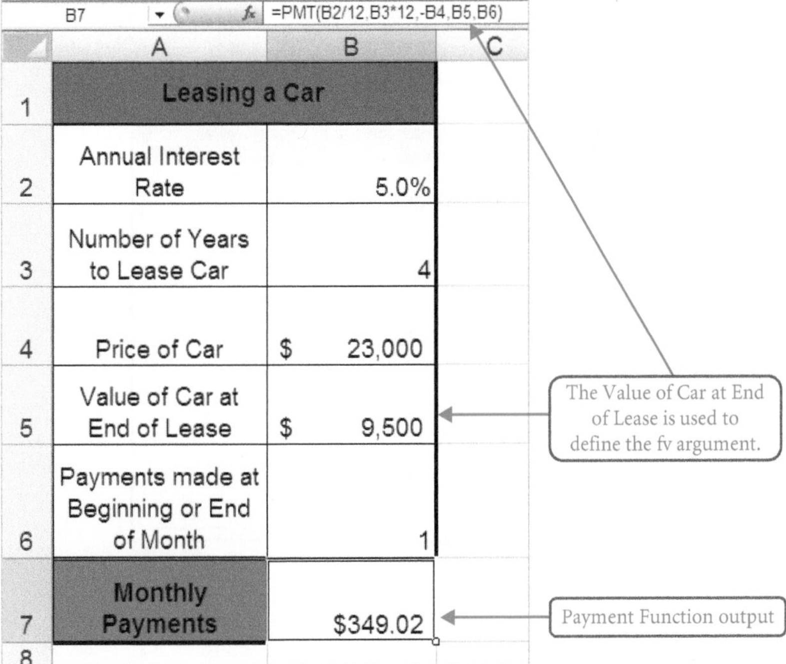


## The Function Library

The Function Library is a resource that can be used to research and build any of the functions available in Excel. As shown in Figure 57, the Function Library is a group in the **Formulas** tab of the Ribbon. The icons in Function Library categorize all the functions in Excel by topic. For example, to see a list of all financial functions, click the **Financial** icon.

Figure 57 | **The Function Library**

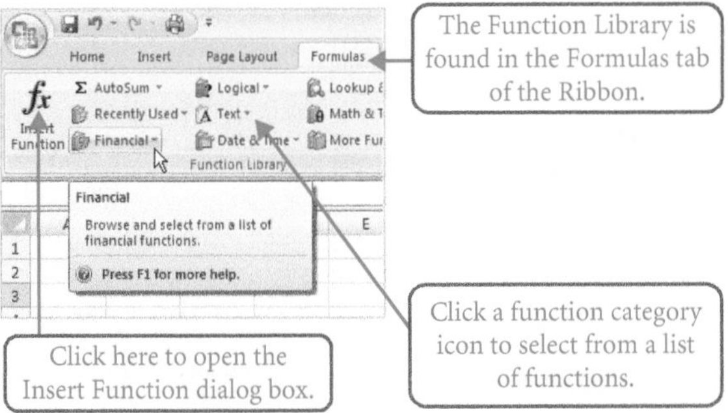


Use the Function Library to research detailed information regarding the purpose and arguments for all Excel functions. In addition, the Function Library can serve as an alternative way of building functions. After activating a cell location, select a function from one of the category icons in the Function Library. This will open the **Function Arguments** dialog box, which provides input boxes for each argument as well as a link to get detailed help in building the function. Figure 58 shows the **Function Arguments** dialog box for the **Future Value** function.

> **Quick Reference**
>
> **Insert Function**
>
> 1. Activate a cell where the output of a function should appear.
> 2. Click the **Formulas** tab in the Ribbon.
> 3. Select a function from one of the function category icons in the Function Library or click the **Insert Function** icon.
> 4. If using the **Insert Function** icon, select a function from the **Insert Function** dialog box and click the **OK** button.
> 5. Use the input boxes or range finders to define the arguments of the function in the **Function Arguments** dialog box.
> 6. Click **Help on this function** to see an expanded definition and instructions for building the function.
> 7. Click the **OK** button at the bottom of the **Function Arguments** dialog box.

Figure 58 | **The Function Arguments Dialog Box for the Future Value Function**

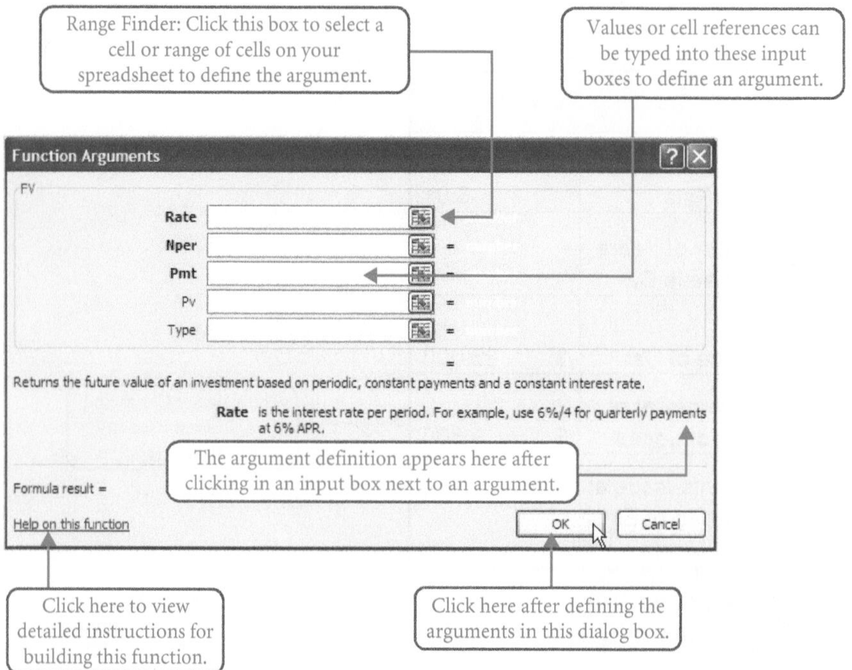


Excel functions can also be researched and built from the **Insert Function** icon. After activating a cell location where the output of the function should appear, click the **Insert Function** icon. This will open the **Insert Function** dialog box, as shown in Figure 59. Select a function from the middle of the dialog box and click the **OK** button. This will open the **Function Argument**s dialog box, as shown in Figure 58. Note that you can also open the **Insert Function** dialog box by clicking the **fx** symbol next to the formula bar.

Figure 59 | **The Insert Function Dialog Box**

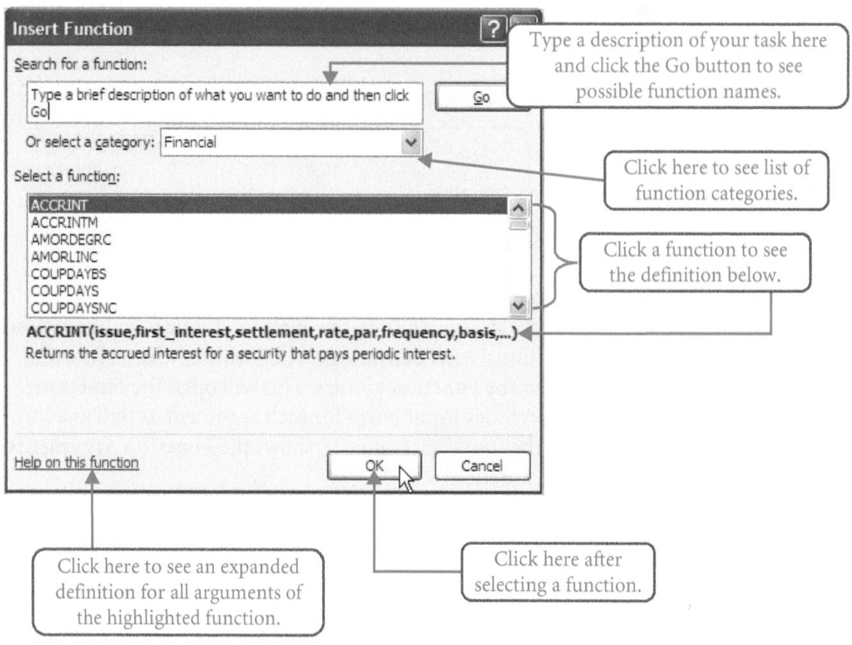

# » Future Value Function

VIDEO WORKSHOP

The purpose of this workshop is to review the use and construction of the **Future Value** function. I will be demonstrating the tasks in this workshop in the **Future Value Function** video. Open the file named ib_e03_thetimevalueofmoney before starting the following tasks.

1. **Data Entry (Video: Future Value Function)**
   a. Activate the Periodic Investment worksheet.
   b. Type the following values into the cell locations listed:
      Cell B2: **.08**
      Cell B3: **3**
      Cell B4: **10**
      Cell B5: **1**
   c. Format cell B2 to a percent with 1 decimal place and then format cell B4 to U.S. currency with 2 decimal places.

2. **Calculating the Future Value of a Periodic Investment (Video: Future Value Function)**
   a. Type an equal sign in cell B6, followed by the function name **FV** and an open parenthesis.
   b. Click cell B2 and type a comma.
   c. Click cell B3 and type a comma.
   d. Type a negative sign.
   e. Click cell B4 and type a comma.
   f. Type another comma.
   g. Click cell B5 and type a closing parenthesis.
   h. Press the **Enter** key.

3. **Calculating the Future Value of a One-Time Investment (Video: Future Value Function)**
   a. Activate the One Time Investment worksheet.
   b. Type an equal sign in cell B6, followed by the function name **FV** and an open parenthesis.
   c. Click cell B2 and type a comma.
   d. Click cell B3 and type a comma.
   e. Type another comma.
   f. Type a negative sign.
   g. Click cell B4 and type a comma.
   h. Click cell B5 and type a closing parenthesis.
   i. Press the **Enter** key.
   j. Save and close your file.

VIDEO WORKSHOP

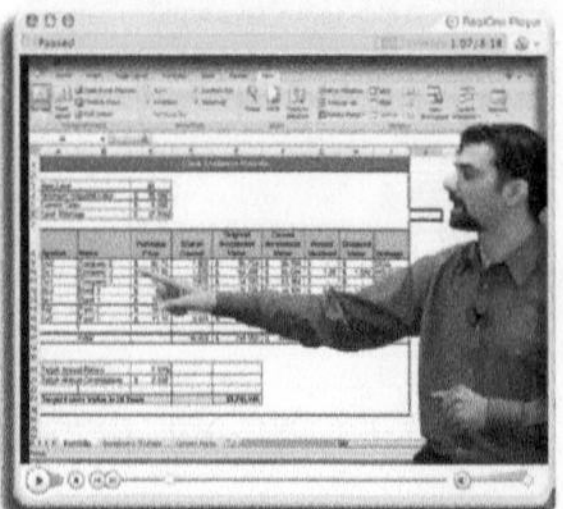

# >> Payment Function

This purpose of this workshop is to demonstrate how the **Payment** function is used to determine the mortgage payments for buying a home and the lease payments for a car. I will be demonstrating the tasks in this workshop on the video named **Payment Function**. Open the file named ib_e03_buyingahomeleasingacar before starting this workshop:

1. **Data Entry (Video: Payment Function)**
   a. Activate the Buying a Home worksheet.
   b. Type the following values into the cell locations listed:
      Cell B2: **.065**
      Cell B3: **30**
      Cell B4: **225000**
      Cell B5: **1**
   c. Format cell B2 to a percent with 1 decimal places and then format cell B4 to U.S. currency with 0 decimal places.

2. **Calculating the Monthly Payments for a Loan (Video: Payment Function)**
   a. Type an equal sign in cell B6, followed by the function name **PMT** and an open parenthesis.
   b. Click cell B2, type a forward slash (for division), type the number **12**, and type a comma.
   c. Click cell B3, type an asterisk (for multiplication), type the number **12**, and type a comma.
   d. Type a negative sign.
   e. Click cell B4 and type a comma.
   f. Type another comma.
   g. Click cell B5 and type a closing parenthesis.
   h. Press the **Enter** key.

3. **Data Entry (Video: Payment Function)**
   a. Activate the Leasing a Car worksheet.
   b. Type the following values into the cell locations listed:
      Cell B2: **.05**
      Cell B3: **4**
      Cell B4: **23000**
      Cell B5: **9500**
      Cell B6: **1**
   c. Format cell B2 to a percent with 1 decimal place and then format cells B4 and B5 to U.S. currency with 0 decimal places.

4. **Calculating the Lease Payment of a Car (Video: Payment Function)**
   a. Type an equal sign in cell B7, followed by the function name **PMT** and an open parenthesis.

b. Click cell B2, type a forward slash (for division), type the number **12**, and type a comma.
c. Click cell B3, type an asterisk (for multiplication), type the number **12**, and type a comma.
d. Type a negative sign.
e. Click cell B4 and type a comma.
f. Click cell B5 and type a comma.
g. Click cell B6 and type a closing parenthesis.
h. Press the **Enter** key.
i. Save and close your file.

## >> The Function Library

**VIDEO WORKSHOP**

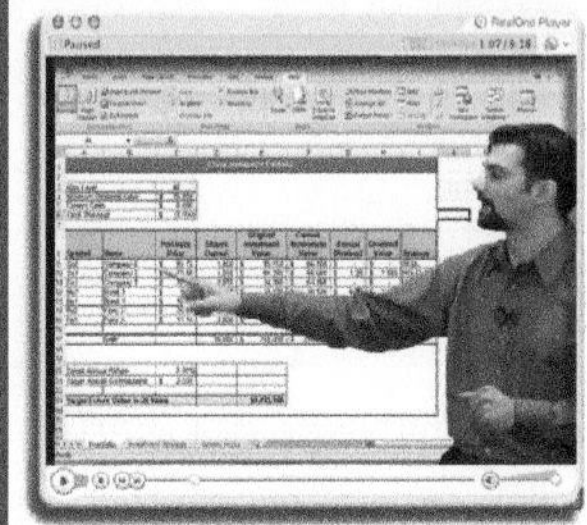

The purpose of this workshop is to demonstrate the Function Library. I will be demonstrating the tasks in this workshop on the video named **Function Library**. Open the file named ib_e03_propertyvalue before starting this workshop:

1. **Selecting a Function (Video: Function Library)**
   a. Activate cell D5 in the Commercial Property worksheet.
   b. Click the **Formulas** tab on the Ribbon.
   c. Click the **Financial** icon in the Function Library.
   d. Click the **FV** function.
   e. Click **Help on this function** in the lower left of the **Function Arguments** dialog box.
   f. Close the help window by clicking the X in the upper-right corner.

2. **Defining Arguments for the Future Value Function (Video: Function Library)**
   a. Click the range finder (box with the red arrow) to the right of the Rate argument.
   b. Click cell D2 on the worksheet and press the **Enter** key.
   c. Click the range finder next to the **nper** argument.
   d. Click cell D3 on the worksheet and press the **Enter** key.
   e. Type a negative sign in the box next to the **pv** argument.
   f. Click the range finder next to the **pv** argument.
   g. Click cell D4 on the worksheet and press the **Enter** key.
   h. Type the number 1 in the box next to the Type argument.
   i. Click the **OK** button at the bottom of the window.
   j. Save and close your file.

**EXERCISE**

**Why Do I Need This?**

# Financial Planning for Retirement

A potential career goal for a person studying finance might be to work as a financial planner. One of the responsibilities a financial planner might have is to help people plan for retirement. This involves estimating how many years a person will work before they retire and how much money they can contribute to a retirement account. The financial planner's job is to evaluate various scenarios to see how clients can maximize the growth of a retirement account so they can live comfortably when they stop working. In this situation, the **Future Value** function can become a critical tool.

## Exercise

Whether you have aspirations of being a financial planner or not, retirement is something everyone will eventually face. The purpose of this exercise is to construct a spreadsheet for a person who is planning to open a retirement account. Your job is to evaluate what interest rate and amount of contribution this person needs to achieve to make the account grow to $2 million. In addition, this person is age 25 and, for now, would like to plan on retiring at age 65. To do the tasks listed here, you will need to open the file named ib_e03_retirementplanning.

1. Type the value **.04** in cell B6 and type the word **Low** in cell C6. In this scenario, the money for this person's retirement will be invested in a conservative fashion. Therefore, the risk of losing money is low, but the potential growth is also low.
2. Type the value **.08** in cell B7 and the word **Medium** in cell C7. In this scenario, the risk is increased to Medium, but the potential return is increased to 8%.
3. For the final scenario, type the value **.15** in cell B8 and the word **High** in cell C8. In this scenario, both the risk and the potential return are high.
4. Type the number **40** in cell E2. Since this person is now 25 and is planning to retire at 65, she will be working and making contributions to her retirement account for 40 years.
5. Type the number **75** in cell E3. This person was thinking of putting $75 a month into this account but is not sure if this will get her to the goal of $2 million.
6. Calculate the future value of the conservative scenario. Use the **Future Value** function in cell D6 and define each argument of the function as follows:
   a. Use cell B6 to define the rate. This represents the Annual Potential Growth of the retirement investments.
   b. Use cell E2 to define the **nper** argument. Add an absolute reference to this cell reference. This function will be pasted into cells D7 and D8 to calculate the future value for the other two scenarios. Therefore, an absolute reference is used for cell E2 to prevent it from changing when the function is pasted.
   c. Type the formula **-E3 * 12** for the **pmt** argument and add an absolute reference to cell E3. This formula is used to convert the monthly payments to annual payments since both the **rate** and **nper** arguments are annual numbers. The absolute reference is used on cell E3 for the same reason explained in letter b.
   d. Type a closing parenthesis and press the **Enter** key. This person will not be making any lump sum investments to this account, and deposits will be made at the end of the month. Therefore, it is not necessary to define the **[pv]** or **[type]** arguments.

7. Copy the function created in cell D6 and use the **Paste Special** command to paste only the function into cells D7 and D8.

8. Given the current contribution of $75 per month, will this person reach her target through any of the scenarios?

9. How much money will she have to deposit in her account per month (approximately) to reach $2 million taking the Aggressive investment scenario?

10. How much money will she have to deposit in her account per month (approximately) to reach $2 million taking the Conservative investment scenario?

11. Save and close your file.

## >> What's Wrong with This Spreadsheet?

PROBLEM & EXERCISE

### Problem

You are the director of a real estate investment firm. An intern has just completed a project for you evaluating a potential investment. You are about to present the results to the president of the firm showing the potential return on property near a growing U.S. city. A recent assessment has shown that similar commercial properties in this area have been increasing in value 15% every six months. You will propose that the firm buy 10 acres of land at a total price of $1,750,000. You will recommend that the land be held for three years and then sold to developers.

You have asked the intern to

1. Evaluate the future value of the investment in three years given the 15% growth rate stated in the problem. The property will be purchased in one lump sum investment at the beginning of the first year.

2. Calculate the monthly payments of this loan considering the following: The company may opt to finance the price of the property through a bank instead of paying for the land in cash. A bank has offered a 15-year loan at a 3.5% interest rate if the company makes a $500,000 down payment. Payments will be made at the end of the month.

Open the file the intern has completed, named ib_e03_realestateresults. Look at the file carefully. Are you comfortable presenting these numbers to the president of the company? Consider the following:

1. Look at the results calculated on the spreadsheet. Do they make sense? What estimates can you quickly do to see if the results are in the "ballpark."

2. Were the arguments in the **PMT** and **FV** functions properly defined?

3. Are the statistics of the investment properly considered in the analysis?

### Exercise

Write a short answer for each of the points in the Problem section. Then, make any adjustments or corrections that will improve the reliability of the spreadsheet.

# Excel in **Practice** | Anecdote

Solution

I finally found relief after creating a spreadsheet that maintained and tracked all the items we were selling in the department. Projections that used to take 12 hours I could now do in minutes. I made the spreadsheet as flexible as possible so that if anyone asked "what if. . ." I would be able to give an answer in a few minutes. The only thing that took a lot of time was the preparation of the spreadsheet. At that time, our sales data was printed on paper, so I had to key the weekly sales results for every item. However, working late one night a week was better than working five nights.

iStockphoto.com

## Assignment

Open the file named ib_e03_casualappareldepartment. This file includes data for several items that are typically sold in a women's specialty retail store. Create a flexible spreadsheet that will evaluate the sales performance of each item and project the sales and profit for the department. You will have to add formulas, functions, and formatting to this spreadsheet. Following are formulas and information that will help in completing this assignment:

1. Current Weeks of Supply = Current Inventory Units ÷ Last Week Unit Sales
2. New Price = Current Price – (Markdown Percent x Current Price)
3. Projected Sales Dollars = Sales Dollars YTD + (Current Inventory x New Price)
4. Total Cost = Total Units Purchased x Item Cost
5. Projected Profit = Projected Sales Dollars – Total Cost
6. The price of any product that has a Current Weeks of Supply greater than 8 should be reduced through a markdown.
7. When the price of an item is reduced, unit sales for next week will generally increase as follows: a 50% price reduction will double sales; a 25% price reduction will increase unit sales by 50%; a 10% price reduction will increase sales by 25%.
8. If the price of an item is not reduced, assume unit sales remain constant.
9. Come up with a plan that reduces the overall weeks of supply for the department to 8.5, while maintaining at least 34% profit (Projected Profit ÷Projected Sales Dollars).

## Questions for Discussion

1. When creating spreadsheets for business, why is it important to make them as flexible as possible?
2. What are some of the things that could go wrong with the spreadsheet solution described in the case?
3. Besides saving time, what other benefits could the spreadsheet solution described in the anecdote bring to the business?

# Review Questions

The following questions are related to the concepts addressed in this chapter. There are three types of questions: Short Answer, True or False, and Fill in the Blank. If your answer to a True or False question is False, write a short explanation as to why you think the statement is not true.

1. The _______________ is used when creating formulas in Excel that require multiplication.

2. Hold the Shift key and press the number _______________ key when using exponents or raising a number to a certain power when creating formulas in Excel.

3. Explain why you should never do computations on a calculator and type the result into an Excel spreadsheet.

4. True or False: In cell referencing, the cell locations in a formula automatically change when you paste them to a new location.

5. When should you use numbers in Excel formulas?

6. True or False: You cannot use both numbers and cell locations in an Excel formula.

7. The_______________ _______________ command can be used to paste the value of a formula instead of the formula itself.

8. Why would you need to use parentheses in a formula?

9. True or False: Even if a formula contains only two cell references and one mathematical operator, you must still use parentheses.

10. In the following formula, what will be calculated second? `=((A4+B8)/C10)+A9+E6`.

11. True or False: This is a formula that will add the values in ten cell locations: `=SUM(A2:A10)`.

12. All functions start with an _______________, an ________________________, and a _______________.

13. What function could you use to count the names of people listed on a spreadsheet?

14. How would you type an **AVERAGE** function in a spreadsheet if you wanted to take the average of five cells in column C starting with cell location C1?

15. True or False: The following function will find the minimum value in cell locations B3 through and including B15: `=MIN(B3,B15)`.

16. A _________________ _________________ is used to apply an absolute reference to a cell location.

17. True or False: You cannot add two functions together like a formula; for example, `=SUM(C3:C10)+SUM(A4:A9)`.

18. True or False: Cell referencing will work with formulas but not with functions. Therefore, you must always retype functions and cannot copy and paste them to new cell locations.

19. True or False: If the following cell reference is used in a formula, the row number will change, but the column letter will remain the same when the formula is pasted to a new location: `C$10`.

20. What is the purpose of the **pmt** argument in the **Future Value** function?

21. What is the purpose of the **fv** argument in the **Payment** Function?

22. If you use the **Future Value** function to evaluate the growth of an investment over a 16-month period at a growth rate of 12% per year, what number would you enter in the **rate** argument?

23. When you use the **Future Value** function, you use the ______________ argument if you are making a one-time lump sum investment.

24. True or False: You cannot define both the **pmt** argument and the **pv** argument of the **Future Value** function. You must define one or the other; otherwise, Excel will give you an error message.

25. True or False: The following **Payment** function will return the monthly payments of a loan that charges a 6% annual interest rate over ten years with a principal of $25,000 and a down payment of $5,000. The payments will be made at the beginning of each month. `=PMT(.06,10,-25000,5000,1)`.

26. What should you do if you are skipping an argument in either the **PMT** or **FV** function?

27. What does Excel assume if you skip the **type** argument of either the **PMT** or **FV** function?

28. You must use a negative sign for numbers or cell locations entered for the ______________ argument and the ______________ argument when using the **Future Value** function.

29. True or False: You must always use a negative sign for both the **fv** and **pv** arguments of the **Payment** function.

30. What tab in the Ribbon would you click to find the Function Library?

# Skills Exam

The following exam is designed to test your ability to recognize and execute the Excel skills presented in this chapter. Read each question carefully and answer the questions in the order they are listed. You should be able to complete this exam in 60 minutes or less.

1. Open the file named ib_e03_skillsexam.
2. Type a **SUM** function in cell B9 that adds the values in cells B3 through B8. Correct any #### signs if necessary.
3. Copy the **SUM** function in cell B9 and paste it into cell C9. Correct any #### signs if necessary.
4. Type a formula in cell D3 to calculate the growth rate. Your formula should subtract the Value Last Year in cell B3 from the Present Value in cell C3 and divide that result by the Value Last Year in cell B3: `(Present Value - Value Last Year) ÷ Value Last Year`.
5. Format the result in cell D3 to a percentage with 1 decimal place.
6. Copy cell D3 and paste it into cells D4:D9.
7. Type an **AVERAGE** function in cell B10 that calculates the average of cells B3 through B8.
8. Copy cell B10 and paste it into C10.
9. Calculate the average growth rate in cell D10 using the **SUM** and **COUNT** functions. Follow this example: `((Sum of Present Value C3:C8 ÷ Count of Present Value C3:C8)-(Sum of Value Last Year B3:B8 ÷ Count of Value Last Year B3:B8))/(Sum of Value Last Year B3:B8 ÷ Count of Value Last Year B3:B8)`.
10. Format the result in cell D10 to a percentage with 1 decimal place. The result in D10 should match the value in cell D9.
11. Type a formula in cell E3 that divides the present value in cell C3 by the total of the present values in cell C9. Place an absolute reference on cell C9.
12. Format the result in cell E3 to a percent with 2 decimals. Then, copy cell E3 and paste it to cells E4 through E8.
13. Use the **Payment** function in cell D14 to calculate the monthly mortgage payments. Your function should use cell A14 for the rate, B14 for the periods, and C14 for the present value. Assume that payments are made at the end of the month.
14. Use the **Payment** function in cell E18 to calculate the monthly lease payments. Your function should use cell A18 for the rate, B18 for the periods, C18 for the present value, and D18 for the future value. Assume payments made at the end of the month.
15. Use the **Future Value** function in cell E21 to calculate the future value of all the investments in two years. Your function should use cell D9 for the rate and the number 2 for the periods. The total present value for all investments in cell C9 should be treated as a one-time lump sum investment. Assume that this investment is made at the beginning of the year. Format the result to U.S. currency with 0 decimal places. Correct any #### signs if necessary.
16. Type a formula in cell E22 that subtracts the total present value of all investments in cell C9 from the future value of all investments in cell E21.
17. Type a formula in cell E23 that multiplies the monthly mortgage payments in cell D14 by 24. Format the result to U.S. currency with 0 decimal places.
18. Type a formula in cell E24 that multiplies the monthly lease payments in cell E18 by 24. Format the result to U.S. currency with 0 decimal places.
19. Type a formula in cell E25 that subtracts the result of adding cells E23 and E24 from cell E22. Format the result to U.S. currency with 0 decimal places. Fix any #### signs if necessary.
20. Sort the range A2:E8 in ascending order based on the values in the Present Value column.
21. Save and close your file.

# Challenge Questions

The following questions are designed to test your ability to apply the Excel skills you have learned to complete a business objective. Use your knowledge of Excel as well as your creativity to answer these questions. For most questions, there are several possible ways to complete the objective.

1. *Without* using the **Future Value** function, create a worksheet that determines the value of an investment if a person deposits $1,500 into a mutual fund at the beginning of every year for 20 years. Assume that the mutual fund achieves a 6% annual growth rate every year. Your worksheet should show the value of this investment at the end of every year for 20 years. In addition, your worksheet should be flexible to show what the value of the account would be at different deposit amounts or annual growth rates. For example, be able to show the value of the account in 20 years if a person decides to deposit only $1,200 per year but achieves an annual growth rate of 7%. Then, show the value of the account if a person deposits $1,000 per year but achieves an annual growth rate of 8%.
2. Complete question 1 again using the **Future Value** function. However, your worksheet should show only one number indicating the value of the investment in 20 years. Remember to keep your worksheet flexible so a new output will be produced if the annual deposit amount or annual growth rate values are changed.
3. A person asks you for help on an investment she is thinking of making. She wants to invest $5,000 into a medium-term bond that earns 4.5% interest per year. In addition, she wants to add $100 at the beginning of every month into the account. She wants to know what the value of her investment will be after five years. Create a worksheet showing her the value of this investment.
4. If you were going to lease a car, but could afford to pay only *$175 a month*, what would be the maximum price you could pay for a car? Assume the lease will run for four years, the annual interest rate is 3%, and that the car will retain 40% of its value after four years. Create a worksheet that shows the maximum price of the car you can lease.
5. You have an opportunity to invest in residential property that will cost $325,000. A real estate survey has shown that the value of property in this town has been increasing at a rate of 25% per year. However, you will have to take out a loan to be able to purchase the property. You can secure a 30-year loan at an annual interest rate of 6.5%. You will also be making a down payment of $75,000. Your plan is to sell this property after three years. After selling the property, you will pay off the loan. Create a spreadsheet that will calculate how much money you will make on this investment.

# Evaluating Data

## Chapter Goals

Business managers are responsible for making numerous decisions every day based on various measures and statistics. For example, a retail buyer may decide to place orders, cancel future orders, issue returns, or do nothing depending on the ratio of current sales to current inventory. A finance manager may decide to sell, buy, or hold a particular stock based on a client's unrealized gain or loss. The challenge for these business managers is usually not the decision itself, but rather the volume of decisions they are required to make. For example, a retail buyer might be responsible for purchasing thousands of items. A finance manager might be managing portfolios for hundreds of clients. This chapter will review how business managers use Excel's logical and lookup functions to evaluate large volumes of data and produce decision outputs. As you will soon discover, logical and lookup functions can dramatically increase a business manager's decision-making power through Excel.

## >> Excel | Skill Sets

**Logical Functions (The IF Function)**
- IF Function
- Nested IF Functions

**Logical Functions (AND OR)**
- AND Function
- OR Function
- Combining AND, OR, and IF Functions

**Lookup Functions**
- VLookup Function
- HLookup Function

# Excel in Practice | Anecdote

iStockphoto.com

## Managing Retail Store Expansion

Location is everything, especially in the retail industry. I learned this quickly while working on a consulting project for a major retail corporation. One of our biggest challenges was deciding where the company should build new stores as part of a growth strategy plan. Constructing a new store costs several million dollars and requires significant sales revenue to justify the investment. To support our recommendations, my team analyzed enormous amounts of data to determine the best locations for potential new stores. Our analysis began with a spreadsheet containing over 20,000 United States ZIP codes and associated population, population growth, number of households, household income, population by gender, and, most important, competitors. We finally limited the number of potential locations to 400 ZIP codes and set a meeting with the company's president to discuss our findings. However, at 7:00 PM the night before our meeting, my partner and I made a startling discovery. The real estate analyst who originally sent us the data did not include the state or city names in his file. We had no idea what state or city belonged to each ZIP code. To make matters worse, not only had the real estate analyst gone home for the day, but he was going to be on vacation for the next week. Needless to say, we were not thrilled with the idea of looking up 400 ZIP codes and manually typing the state and city names into our spreadsheet.

>> Continued later in this chapter

# Logical Functions (The IF Function)

Skill Set

Functions are used to conduct statistical and financial calculations in business. However, functions can also be used to evaluate data and provide an output based on the results of a test. These are known as ***logical functions***. The most commonly used logical function in Excel is the **IF** function. The **IF** function can produce an output that you define based on the results of a ***logical test***. As with all logical functions, the results of a logical test will either be true or false. This section will demonstrate how business managers use **IF** functions to evaluate and highlight key statistics that require their attention for the purposes of making decisions.

## IF Function

The **IF** function is used to evaluate data and provide an output based on the results of a logical test. Business managers often use the **IF** function to highlight key statistics related to their area of responsibility. For example, the inventory control manager of a candy company might be required to maintain at least 10,000 pounds of each ingredient used to produce a line of chocolate bars. Maintaining a specific inventory target is a common practice for companies that continually use the same components to produce a product, such as a candy manufacturer. Figure 1 shows a worksheet that contains ingredients that might be used to produce chocolate bars. An inventory control manager could use the **IF** function in the Status column (column C) to identify items in which the inventory in column B is less than 10,000 pounds.

Figure 1 | **Inventory Data for Chocolate Bar Production**

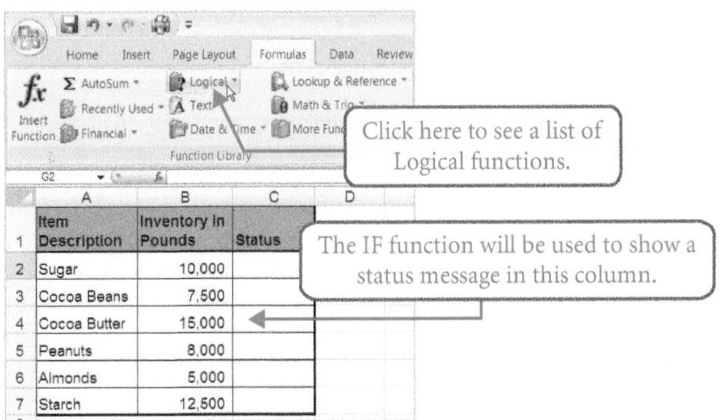


| | A | B | C | D |
|---|---|---|---|---|
| 1 | Item Description | Inventory in Pounds | Status | |
| 2 | Sugar | 10,000 | | |
| 3 | Cocoa Beans | 7,500 | | |
| 4 | Cocoa Butter | 15,000 | | |
| 5 | Peanuts | 8,000 | | |
| 6 | Almonds | 5,000 | | |
| 7 | Starch | 12,500 | | |

To use the **IF** function, you will need to define three arguments, as shown in Figure 2. The definition for each of these arguments is as follows:

- **logical_test**: Used for evaluating the data in a cell location based on a test that you define. The results of this test will be either true or false. A basic logical test usually starts with a cell reference followed by a comparison operator (see Figure 3 for a list of comparison operators used in logical tests). The second part of the test can be a multitude of possibilities. For example, you may need to compare the value in a cell to a number, another cell location, a formula, a function, or a word. If you are using words, or text data, you must put them in quotation marks. Examples of logical tests are

  - B9 > 25
  - H7 < D12
  - L8 = "Car"
  - D17 < (A9 - 12) * 10

- **[value_if_true]**: Used for defining the output of the **IF** function if the results of the logical test are true. This argument can be defined with a cell reference, formula, function, number, or words. As in the **logical_test** argument, if you are going to use words, you must put them in quotation marks.
- **[value_if_false]**: Used to define the output of the function if the results of the logical test are false. The options for defining this argument are identical to the **[value_if_true]** argument.

Figure 2 | **Arguments of the IF Function**

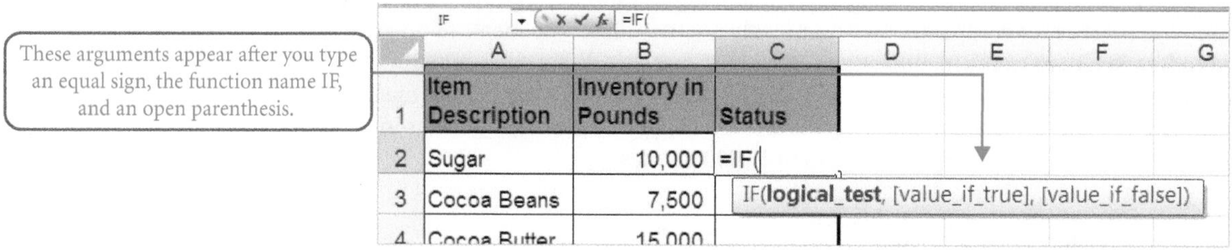

These arguments appear after you type an equal sign, the function name IF, and an open parenthesis.

IF =IF(

| | A | B | C | D | E | F | G |
|---|---|---|---|---|---|---|---|
| 1 | Item Description | Inventory in Pounds | Status | | | | |
| 2 | Sugar | 10,000 | =IF( | | | | |
| 3 | Cocoa Beans | 7,500 | IF(**logical_test**, [value_if_true], [value_if_false]) | | | | |
| 4 | Cocoa Butter | 15,000 | | | | | |

Figure 3 | **Comparison Operators Used in Logical Tests**

| Symbol | Definition |
|---|---|
| = | Equal To |
| > | Greater Than |
| < | Less Than |
| <> | Not Equal To |
| >= | Greater Than or Equal To |
| <= | Less Than or Equal To |

An inventory control manager could use the **IF** function in the worksheet shown in Figure 1 to identify items in which the inventory is less than 10,000 pounds. The following points explain how you add this to the worksheet:

- Activate cell C2.
- Type an equal sign, the function name IF, and an open parenthesis.
- Type B2<10000 to define the **logical_test** argument. This will test if the value in cell B2 is less than 10000. As noted previously, this example assumes that the inventory control manager is maintaining at least 10,000 pounds of inventory for each item. Type a comma after this argument.
- Type "LOW INV" to define the **[value_if_true]** argument. If the value in cell B2 is less than 10000, the message LOW INV will be displayed in cell C2. Notice that since this is a text message, it is put in quotation marks. Type a comma after this argument.

- Type "OK" to define the **[value_if_false]** argument. If the value in cell B2 is not less than 10000, the message OK will be displayed in cell C2. Again, notice that since this a text message, it is enclosed in quotation marks.
- Type a closing parenthesis and press the **Enter** key.
- Copy cell C2, which now contains the completed **IF** function, and paste it to cells C3 through C7. Since the cell reference B2 was used in the **logical_test** argument, it will automatically adjust to the appropriate row number because of relative referencing.

Figure 4 shows the arguments of the **IF** function that were typed into cell C2 of the worksheet shown in Figure 1. Notice that the text messages used to define the **[value_if_true]** and **[value_if_false]** arguments are enclosed in quotation marks. Also, notice that no commas were used in the value 10000 in the **logical_test** argument.

Figure 4 | **Setup of the IF Function to Evaluate Inventory Values in Column B**

IF =IF(B2<10000,"LOW INV","OK")

| | A | B | C | D | E | F | G |
|---|---|---|---|---|---|---|---|
| 1 | Item Description | Inventory in Pounds | Status | | | | |
| 2 | Sugar | 10,000 | =IF(B2<10000,"LOW INV","OK") | | | | |
| 3 | Cocoa Beans | 7,500 | IF(logical_test, [value_if_true], **[value_if_false]**) | | | | |
| 4 | Cocoa Butter | 15,000 | | | | | |
| 5 | Peanuts | 8,000 | | | | | |
| 6 | Almonds | 5,000 | | | | | |

Words or text messages are enclosed in quotations.

Figure 5 shows the output of the **IF** functions in the range C2:C7. By glancing at the worksheet, the inventory control manager can easily see that three items—Cocoa Beans, Peanuts, and Almonds—are below the target of 10,000 pounds.

Figure 5 | **IF Function Outputs Based on the Values in Column B**

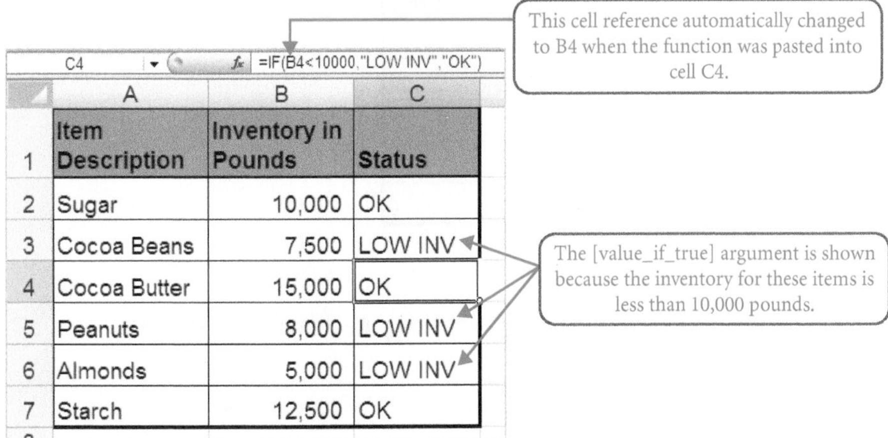

C4 =IF(B4<10000,"LOW INV","OK")

| | A | B | C |
|---|---|---|---|
| 1 | Item Description | Inventory in Pounds | Status |
| 2 | Sugar | 10,000 | OK |
| 3 | Cocoa Beans | 7,500 | LOW INV |
| 4 | Cocoa Butter | 15,000 | OK |
| 5 | Peanuts | 8,000 | LOW INV |
| 6 | Almonds | 5,000 | LOW INV |
| 7 | Starch | 12,500 | OK |

This cell reference automatically changed to B4 when the function was pasted into cell C4.
The [value_if_true] argument is shown because the inventory for these items is less than 10,000 pounds.

Figure 6 shows another way the **IF** function can be used to help an inventory control manager maintain a target of at least 10,000 pounds for each item shown in Figure 1. In this example, the **IF** function is used to calculate how much inventory needs to be purchased if an item is below the 10,000 pound target. As a result, notice that a formula is used to define the **[value_if_true]** argument. Each argument of the function is defined as follows:

- **logical_test:** `B2 < 10000` This is the same test that was used for the example shown in Figure 4.

- **[value_if_true]**: `10000 - B2` If the value in cell B2 is less than 10000, the function will calculate how many pounds need to be purchased to reach the 10,000 pound target.
- **[value_if_false]**: `0` If the value in cell B2 is at or above 10000, the function will display a value of 0, indicating there is no need to purchase additional inventory.

Figure 6 | **Using the IF Function to Calculate Order Quantities**

If the logical_test is true, the function will display the results of this formula.

IF =IF(B2<10000,10000-B2,0)

| | A | B | C | D | E | F | G |
|---|---|---|---|---|---|---|---|
| 1 | Item Description | Inventory in Pounds | Order Quantity | | | | |
| 2 | Sugar | 10,000 | =IF(B2<10000,10000-B2,0) | | | | |
| 3 | Cocoa Beans | 7,500 | IF(logical_test, [value_if_true], **[value_if_false]**) | | | | |
| 4 | Cocoa Butter | 15,000 | | | | | |

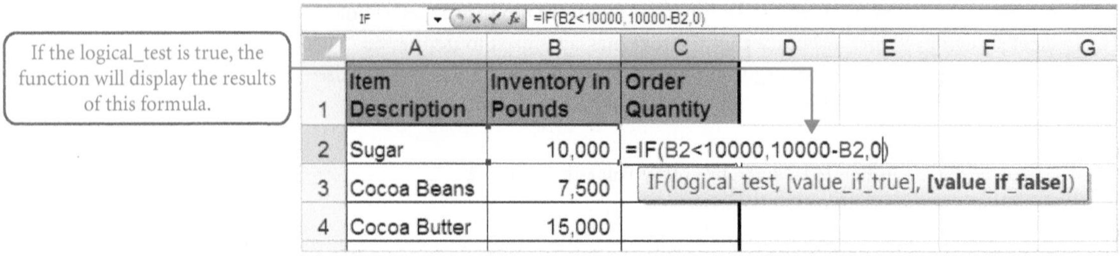

Figure 7 shows the output of the **IF** function created in Figure 6. Similar to the example shown in Figure 5, this function was created in cell C2 and then copied to cells C3 through C7. In addition, the worksheet was sorted in descending order based on the order quantities produced by the **IF** function. As a result, the **IF** function not only identifies items that need to be ordered, but automatically calculates how much inventory needs to be purchased by item.

Figure 7 | **Results of Using the IF Function to Calculate Order Quantities**

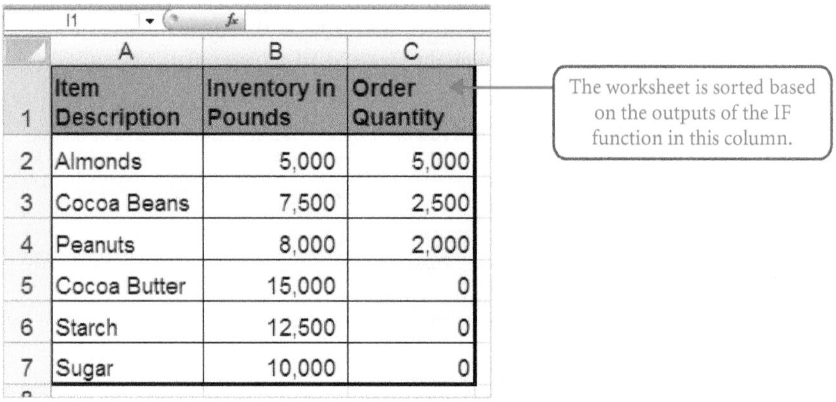

| | A | B | C |
|---|---|---|---|
| 1 | Item Description | Inventory in Pounds | Order Quantity |
| 2 | Almonds | 5,000 | 5,000 |
| 3 | Cocoa Beans | 7,500 | 2,500 |
| 4 | Peanuts | 8,000 | 2,000 |
| 5 | Cocoa Butter | 15,000 | 0 |
| 6 | Starch | 12,500 | 0 |
| 7 | Sugar | 10,000 | 0 |

The worksheet is sorted based on the outputs of the IF function in this column.

## COMMON MISTAKES | Defining Arguments of the IF Function

People often make the mistake of using commas in values typed into the **logical_test** argument of the **IF** function. For example:

```
=IF(C2 < 10,000,"Low","High")
```

Excel will read the logical test for this function as C2 < 10, not C2 < 10000. The reason is that a comma signals the end of one argument and the start of another. For this example, Excel will display a warning stating too many arguments were entered because it assumes you are trying to define four arguments instead of three.

## Nested IF Functions

By itself, the **IF** function provides the entry of one logical test and one output (value if true or value if false). However, a business project may require the function to display one of many possible outputs. For example, the items shown in Figure 1 may require a status rating based on five potential options: Very Low, Low, Good, High, or Very High. To produce one output from these five possibilities, you would need to create an **IF** function with four logical tests. You can accomplish this by using a nested **IF** function.

A nested **IF** function will be used to evaluate the inventory data shown in Figure 8, which contains revised data from Figure 1. For this example, we will assume the target inventory remains at 10,000 pounds. However, if the inventory level is too high for any item, it may spoil. On the other hand, if the inventory is significantly below 10,000 pounds, the company may fall short of its production goals. This example will use a nested **IF** function to display one of the following four outputs:

- Less than 5,000 pounds: Display the message "Prod Risk."
- Greater than 5,000 pounds but less than 10,000 pounds: Display the message "Low."
- Greater than 14,000 pounds: Display the message "Spoil Risk."
- Between 10,000 and 14,000 pounds: Display the message "OK."

Figure 8 | **Revised Inventory Data for Chocolate Bar Production**

| | A | B | C |
|---|---|---|---|
| 1 | Item Description | Inventory in Pounds | Status |
| 2 | Sugar | 10,000 | |
| 3 | Cocoa Beans | 7,500 | |
| 4 | Cocoa Butter | 22,000 | |
| 5 | Peanuts | 5,200 | |
| 6 | Almonds | 1,200 | |
| 7 | Starch | 12,500 | |

A nested IF function will be created in column C to categorize each inventory value in column B as Prod Risk, Low, Spoil Risk, or OK.

The following points explain how to create a nested **IF** function in cell C2 of Figure 8 to display one of four outputs:

- Activate cell C2.
- Type an equal sign, the function name IF, and an open parenthesis.
- Type B2<5000 to define the **logical_test** argument. This will be the first of three logical tests that will be created in this function. Type a comma after this argument.
- Type "Prod Risk" to define the [**value_if_true**] argument. If the first logical test is true, the function will display this message. Type a comma after this argument.
- Type the function name **IF** followed by an open parenthesis to define the [**value_if_false**] argument. If the logical test is false, you will need to conduct a second logical test. You do this by starting a second **IF** function.
- Type B2 < 10000 to define the **logical_test** argument of the second **IF** function. If the first logical test, which is B2 < 5000, is false, then this logical test will evaluate if the value in cell B2 is less than 10000. Note that if the first logical test failed, and this logical test is true, then you can conclude that the value in cell B2 is greater

than 5,000 pounds but less than 10,000 pounds. Type a comma after this argument.

- Type "Low" to define the [**value_if_true**] argument of the second **IF** function. As previously mentioned, if the inventory quantity is greater than 5,000 pounds but less than 10,000 pounds, the status message should read "Low." Type a comma after this argument.
- Type the function name **IF** followed by an open parenthesis to define the [**value_if_false**] argument of the second **IF** function. As previously mentioned, to show one of four potential outputs, you will need to conduct three logical tests. To conduct a third logical test, you start a third **IF** function.
- Type B2 > 14000 to define the **logical_test** argument of the third **IF** function. If the previous two logical tests are false, then you can conclude that the value in cell B2 is greater than or equal to 10,000. Therefore, the third and final logical test will evaluate if the value in B2 is greater than 14,000 pounds. As mentioned, if any item has an inventory greater than 14,000 pounds, it will be at risk of spoiling. Type a comma after this argument.
- Type "Spoil Risk" to define the [**value_if_true**] argument of the third **IF** function. Type a comma after this argument.
- Type "OK" to define the [**value_if_false**] argument of the third **IF** function. If all logical tests are false, then you can conclude that the value in cell B2 is between 10,000 and 14,000 pounds.
- Type three closing parentheses. It is important to note that a closing parenthesis is required for every **IF** function you started. In this example, you started a total of three **IF** functions for the purpose of conducting three logical tests. Therefore, you must type three closing parentheses at the end of the function.
- Press the **Enter** key.
- Copy the cell C2, which now contains the nested **IF** function, and paste it into cells C3 through C7.

Figure 9 shows the setup of the nested **IF** function that was created in cell C2. In this example, a new **IF** function is started in the [**value_if_false**] argument for the purpose of conducting multiple logical tests. However, both the [**value_if_true**] and [**value_if_false**] arguments could be used to add multiple logical tests.

Figure 9 | **Setup of the Nested IF Function**

| | A | B | C |
|---|---|---|---|
| 1 | Item Description | Inventory in Pounds | Status |
| 2 | Sugar | 10,000 | =IF(B2<5000,"Prod Risk",IF(B2<10000,"Low",IF(B2>14000,"Spoil Risk","OK"))) |
| 3 | Cocoa Beans | 7,500 | |
| 4 | Cocoa Butter | 22,000 | |
| 5 | Peanuts | 5,200 | |

Three closing parentheses

The logical tests are in a sequence from lowest to highest.

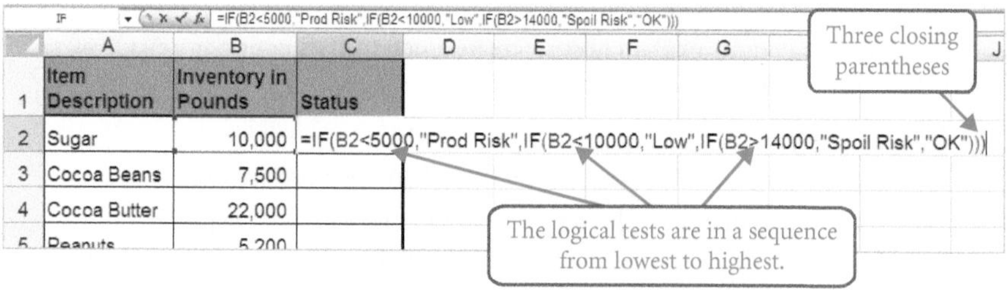

Figure 10 shows the outputs of the nested **IF** functions in column C. The inventory control manager can use this information to decide which items need to be purchased or which items may need to be monitored and tested for spoilage. In this case, the manager can easily see that purchasing additional inventory for Almonds is critical to support the production goals of the business. On the other hand, the Cocoa Butter needs to be monitored for possible spoilage. The inventory control manager might also inform the production manager to use containers of Cocoa Butter with the oldest receipt date first to reduce potential waste.

Figure 10 | **Outputs Produced by the Nested IF Function**

| | A | B | C |
|---|---|---|---|
| 1 | Item Description | Inventory in Pounds | Status |
| 2 | Sugar | 10,000 | OK |
| 3 | Cocoa Beans | 7,500 | Low |
| 4 | Cocoa Butter | 22,000 | Spoil Risk |
| 5 | Peanuts | 5,200 | Low |
| 6 | Almonds | 1,200 | Prod Risk |
| 7 | Starch | 12,500 | OK |

This nested IF function displays one of four potential outputs for each item.

## COMMON MISTAKES | Nested IF Functions

You *cannot* enter a logical test directly into the **[value_if_false]** or **[value_if_true]** argument without typing the function name IF followed by an open parenthesis. For example, the following nested **IF** function will not work:

```
=IF(B2 < 5000,"Very Low",B2 < 10000,"Low","OK")
```

The logical test B2 < 10000 was entered directly into the **[value_if_false]** argument. This will produce an error stating too many arguments were defined. The following is the corrected version of this example:

```
=IF(B2 < 5000,"Very Low",IF(B2 < 10000,"Low","OK"))
```

It is important to note that Excel will execute the logical tests of a nested **IF** function from left to right. Therefore, the sequence of each logical test shown in Figure 9 makes the nested **IF** function work. Notice that each logical test is in a sequence that tests for the lowest possible value in cell B2 to the largest possible value. For example, the first logical test looks for the lowest possible values (B2 < 5000). The second test looks for any values below 10,000 (B2 < 10000), and the third test looks for the highest values (B2 > 14000). What would happen if the first logical test in this example was B2 < 10000 instead of B2 < 5000? It would be impossible to test if B2 contains a value less than 5000 because these values would immediately test true for B2 < 10000. Therefore, you must carefully plan the sequence of each logical test in a nested **IF** function so that a value cannot test true for two tests.

## COMMON MISTAKES | Logical Test Sequence in a Nested IF Function

Excel will execute the logical tests in a nested **IF** function from left to right. If you are using the **[value_if_false]** argument only to add additional logical tests to a nested **IF** function, the function will immediately end when the results of a logical test are true. Therefore, you must check the sequence of each logical test to make sure a value cannot test true for two tests. The following points can help you create a valid logical test sequence:

1. Identify the lowest and highest values you are testing in your worksheet. The logical tests should be sequenced to look for the lowest values to highest values, or highest values to lowest values. This will prevent a value from testing true for two logical tests.
2. Talk through each logical test in sequence for a few data points on your spreadsheet and write down the result. In addition, try to consider various hypothetical data points that would trigger a true output for each test.

**Quick Reference**

**IF Functions and Nested IF Functions**

1. Activate a cell where the output of the function should appear.
2. Type an equal sign, the function name **IF**, and an open parenthesis.
3. Create a test for the **logical_test** argument.
4. Define an output for the **[value_if_true]** argument (text outputs must be in quotation marks).
5. Define an output for the **[value_if_false]** argument or enter another **IF** function by typing the function name **IF** and an open parenthesis.
6. Type a closing parenthesis. If creating a nested **IF** function, type a closing parenthesis for each **IF** function that you started.
7. Press the **Enter** key.

**VIDEO WORKSHOP**

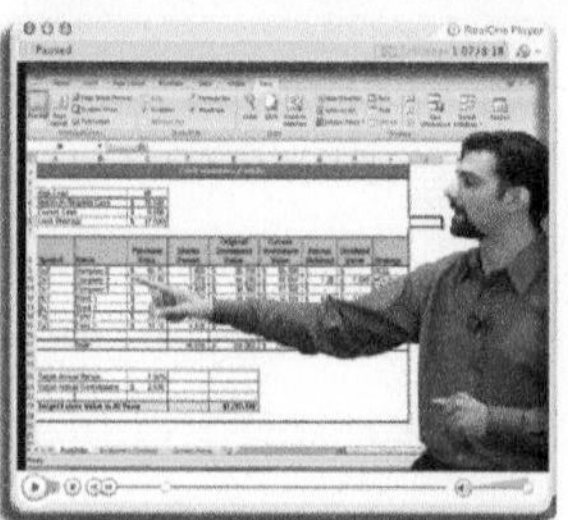

# >> IF Functions

The purpose of this workshop is to demonstrate the use of the **IF** and nested **IF** functions. I will be demonstrating the tasks in this workshop in the **IF Functions** and **Nested IF Functions** videos. After completing each section of tasks, watch the related video shown in parentheses. Open the file named ib_e04_markdownanalysis. Remember to try the tasks on your own first before watching the videos.

1. **Basic IF Function (Video: IF Functions)**
   a. Activate cell G3.
   b. Type an equal sign, the function name `IF`, and an open parenthesis.
   c. Define the **logical_test** argument by typing `B3 = C3` and then type a comma.
   d. Define the **[value_if_true]** argument by typing the word `"Regular"`. Be sure to include the quotation marks. Then type a comma.
   e. Define the **[value_if_false]** argument by typing the word `"Markdown"`.
   f. Type a closing parenthesis and press the **Enter** key.
   g. Copy cell G3 and paste it into cells G4:G7 using the **Paste Formulas** option.

2. **Nested IF Function (Video: Nested IF Functions)**
   a. Activate cell H3.
   b. Type an equal sign, the function name `IF`, and an open parenthesis.
   c. Define the **logical_test** argument by typing `F3 <= 8` and then type a comma.
   d. Define the **[value_if_true]** argument by typing the number `0` and then type a comma.
   e. Define the **[value_if_false]** argument by starting a second **IF** function. Type the function name `IF` followed by an open parenthesis.
   f. Define the **logical_test** argument of the second **IF** function by typing `F3 <= 12` and then type a comma.
   g. Define the **[value_if_true]** argument of the second **IF** function by typing the number `.15` and then type a comma.
   h. Define the **[value_if_false]** argument of the second **IF** function by adding a third **IF** function. Type the function name `IF` followed by an open parenthesis.
   i. Define the **logical_test** argument of the third **IF** function by typing `F3 <= 16` and then type a comma.
   j. Define the **[value_if_true]** argument of the third **IF** function by typing the number `.25` and then type a comma.
   k. Define the **[value_if_false]** argument of the third **IF** function by typing the number `.50`.
   l. Finish the function by typing three closing parentheses and then press the **Enter** key.
   m. Copy cell H3 and paste it to cells H4:H7 using the **Paste Formulas** option.
   n. Save and close your file.

## >> Price Management

Price management is a common exercise for any business. As consumer demand changes, business managers must manage the price of their products and services to be able to maintain a company's sales goals and market share. Price management is especially critical for companies that need to sell large amounts of inventory. However, there are many questions to consider before changing the price of a product. For example, will sales increase for a given item if a price is decreased? If so, how much will sales increase? If the price of an item is decreased, its profitability will usually decrease. Therefore, how much can a price decrease before the company starts losing money on the item? A flexible spreadsheet that can evaluate product sales, inventory, and pricing is an extremely valuable tool in answering these questions.

**EXERCISE**

**Why Do I Need This?**

### Exercise

This exercise demonstrates how **IF** functions can dramatically increase the calculating flexibility of Excel. Your goal is to build a price management tool that will not only calculate price changes, but enable a pricing manager to override these calculations if needed. To begin this exercise, open the Excel file named ib_e04_pricemanagementreport.

1. Enter a **SUM** function in cell D8 that adds the values in the range D3:D7.
2. Copy the **SUM** function in cell D8 and paste it into cells E8 and F8.
3. Type a formula in cell G3 that divides the Current Unit Inventory (cell F3) by the Sales Units LW (cell D3). Then copy the formula and paste it into cells G4:G8. This formula calculates the current weeks of supply, which will give the pricing manager an idea of how much the current inventory supply will last if sales remain constant.
4. Type a nested **IF** function in cell H3 that will calculate the suggested markdown. This type of calculation could be used by a company that sets target weeks of supply for the items it sells. If the weeks of supply get too high, the company may reduce, or mark down, the price to increase sales. Use the following criteria when creating the function. Also, make sure each logical test is entered into the function in the order listed here:
   a. If the Current Weeks of Supply <= 8, the suggested markdown should be 0.
   b. If the Current Weeks of Supply <= 14, the suggested markdown should be .15.
   c. If the Current Weeks of Supply <= 18, the suggested markdown should be .25.
   d. If the Current Weeks of Supply is greater than 18 ( or not less than or equal to 18), the markdown should be .40.
5. Copy and paste the nested **IF** function in cell H3 to cells H4:H7.
6. Type a nested **IF** function into cell I3 to calculate the New Price. The goal of this worksheet is to allow the price change manager to override this calculation by entering a new price into one of the cells in column J. This **IF** function will see whether the price entered into column J is greater than 0. If it is, that number will become the new price. If the value in column J is less than or equal to 0, the nested **IF** function will calculate the new price based on the suggested markdown. The logical tests and outputs for this nested **IF** function are as follows. Be sure to enter each logical test in the sequence listed.
   a. If J3 > 0, the output of the function should be the value in cell J3. If J3 is greater than 0, the pricing manager has manually set a new price for this item.

b. If H3 = 0, the output of the function should be cell C3. If H3 is 0, then there is no suggested markdown. The output of the function should be whatever the current price is in cell C3.

c. If both logical tests ( J3 > 0 and H3 = 0) are false, then the function should calculate the new price using the formula C3 - (C3 * H3).

7. Copy the function in cell I3 and paste it to cells I4:I7.

8. Type a regular **IF** statement in cell K3 to calculate the markdown in dollars. If the New Price (cell I3) is equal to the Current Price (cell C3), then the markdown dollars are 0 because the price did not change. Otherwise, calculate the markdown dollars using the formula (C3 - I3) * F3.

9. Copy the function in cell K3 and paste it to cells K4:K7. Then enter a **SUM** function in cell K8 to add the markdown dollars in this column.

10. Type the formula **(D3 - E3) / E3** in cell L3 to calculate the change in sales. Copy this formula and paste it into cells L4:L8.

11. Even though the weeks of supply for T-shirts is below 8, the directors of the company are concerned that a major competitor will be having a T-shirt sale this weekend. Override the new price by typing **7.99** in cell J3.

12. Even though the weeks of supply for denim shirts is slightly higher than 8, sales are up compared to last year. Maintain the current price by typing **24.99** in cell J6.

13. The company did not want to go over 150,000 markdown dollars (cell K8). Is it achieving this goal? Override the price for the Polo and Twill shirts so the company does not go over its target.

14. Save and close your file.

**PROBLEM & EXERCISE**

## >> What's Wrong with This Spreadsheet?

### Problem

You just started a new job as a raw materials buyer for a manufacturing company. One of the analysts in your division has prepared a spreadsheet analyzing the firm's current inventory position. The goal of the spreadsheet is to help you decide which items need to be purchased because inventory is too low, or which items should be canceled or returned because inventory is too high. Your boss left a copy of the company's inventory policy on your desk. The inventory guidelines are as follows:

1. Weeks of Supply <= 4: Orders must be rushed in because the company may be at risk of losing production.

2. Weeks of Supply < 8: It's time to place new orders to keep up with the production schedule.

3. Weeks of Supply >10: Try to get suppliers to postpone the delivery date to keep inventory from accumulating too high.

4. Weeks of Supply > 15: Place a hold on all current and new orders. At this level the inventory is getting too high and will be at risk of spoiling.

5. Weeks of Supply > 20: Consumer demand must be declining for the product that uses this item for production. Return item to the supplier if possible.

6. The inventory status is normal for any item that does not fit into these categories.

The analyst e-mails the spreadsheet containing the inventory analysis to you. He states the following in his e-mail: "Sorry I could not discuss this with you in person. I have an Excel training seminar all morning. In any event, the inventory status for the department is in good shape. By looking at the Suggested Action column, you will see that a few items need to be purchased, and there are a few items for which we might need to push back the delivery date. Thankfully, there are no major things like rush orders or returns! I will stop by when I am finished with the training seminar."

### Exercise

The spreadsheet this analyst sent to you is named ib_e04_inventorystatus. Are you comfortable making decisions based on the Suggested Action column? Consider the following:

1. Do the suggested actions make sense given the inventory guidelines listed in the Problem section?

2. How is the data for the Suggested Action column being calculated?

3. Follow the calculation method used for the Suggested Action column for a few data points in the Weeks of Supply column. Does the method make sense?

4. What else could you do to make this spreadsheet easier to read?

What's wrong with this spreadsheet? Write a short answer for each of the points listed and fix any errors you see on the spreadsheet that the analyst sent to you.

# >> Logical Functions (AND OR)

Skill Set

The previous section identified how **IF** functions are used to evaluate data and produce various outputs based on a logical test. This section introduces two other logical functions that are also used to evaluate data based on logical tests. They are the **AND** and **OR** functions. These functions can be used independently but are often used in the logical test argument of an **IF** function. This section will first review how the **AND** and **OR** functions are used independently and then will demonstrate how they are used with the **IF** function to dramatically increase Excel's analytical capabilities.

## AND Function

In many situations, business managers must decide if a group of conditions apply to a specific aspect of their business. This is especially relevant for companies that make specialized products for a specific target customer. For example, Figure 11 shows customer demographic data from a company that is seeking to sell a new product to people who are female, have children, and are less than 45 years old. The marketing manager of this firm would probably find it challenging to identify these people from a list of 100,000 potential customers. However, the **AND** function can automatically evaluate and highlight customers that meet all of the characteristics targeted by this product.

Figure 11 | **Customer Data**

The AND function will be used in this column to identify the target customers.

This worksheet continues down to row 22.

| | A | B | C | D | E | F |
|---|---|---|---|---|---|---|
| 1 | Customer Detail Information | | | | | |
| 2 | Name | State of Residence | Gender | Age | Children | Target Customer |
| 3 | Customer 1 | CA | F | 22 | No | |
| 4 | Customer 2 | MO | M | 44 | Yes | |
| 5 | Customer 3 | TX | F | 65 | Yes | |
| 6 | Customer 4 | NJ | M | 73 | No | |
| 7 | Customer 5 | FLA | M | 29 | Yes | |
| 8 | Customer 6 | PA | F | 26 | Yes | |
| 9 | Customer 7 | GA | F | 34 | No | |
| 10 | Customer 8 | NH | F | 54 | Yes | |
| 11 | Customer 9 | NY | M | 36 | No | |
| 12 | Customer 10 | CO | F | 41 | Yes | |
| 13 | Customer 11 | NJ | M | 30 | Yes | |
| 14 | Customer 12 | NM | F | 24 | No | |
| 15 | Customer 13 | NY | F | 28 | Yes | |
| 16 | Customer 14 | VA | M | 44 | No | |
| 17 | Customer 15 | PA | M | 52 | Yes | |

The **AND** function evaluates data using the same logical test that was explained in the **IF** function section. However, with this function, you can enter up to 30 logical tests. Based on the results of all logical tests entered, the **AND** function will produce one of two possible outputs. If all logical tests are true, the function will display the word TRUE. If the results of any logical test are false, the function will display the word FALSE. The following points explain how to use the **AND** function to evaluate the customer data in Figure 11 to highlight any customers who are female, have children, and are younger than 45:

- Activate cell F3, which is the first cell location in the Target Customer column. Remember, the **AND** function will display either the word TRUE or FALSE based on the results of the logical tests. Therefore, the **AND** function will identify target customers by displaying the word TRUE.
- Type an equal sign, the function name AND, and an open parenthesis.
- Type C3 ="F" to define the first logical test. Since being female is one of the characteristics of the target customer, the first logical test will evaluate if the gender of the customer is female. Notice that since the logical test uses text data, it is placed in quotation marks. Just as in the logical test in the **IF** function, any words or text data must be placed in quotation marks. Type a comma after this argument.
- Type D3 < 45 to define the second logical test. This will evaluate if the age of the customer is less than 45. Type a comma after this argument.
- Type E3 ="Yes" to define the third logical test. This will evaluate if the customer has children. Similar to the first logical test, since text data is being used, it is enclosed in quotation marks.
- Type a closing parenthesis and press the **Enter** key.
- Copy the completed **AND** function in cell F3 and paste it into cells F4 through F22. Since cell references were used in each of the three logical tests, they will automatically adjust through relative referencing when the formula is pasted to the rest of the cells in this column.

**Quick Reference**

**AND Function**

1. Activate a cell location where the output of the function should appear.
2. Type an equal sign, the function name AND, and an open parenthesis.
3. Create at least one but no more than 30 logical tests. Separate each logical test with a comma. *All* tests must be true to produce a TRUE output.
4. Type a closing parenthesis.
5. Press the **Enter** key.

- Sort the worksheet based on the **AND** function outputs in the Target Customer column in descending order. This will place any customers showing a TRUE output in the Target Customer column at the top of the worksheet.

Figure 12 shows the setup of the **AND** function that will be used to identify target customers. Notice that each argument of the function is a complete logical test utilizing the comparison operators shown in Figure 3.

Figure 12 | **Setup of the AND Function**

AND | =AND(C3="F",D3<45,E3="Yes")

| | A | B | C | D | E | F |
|---|---|---|---|---|---|---|
| 1 | Customer Detail Information | | | | | |
| 2 | Name | State of Residence | Gender | Age | Children | Target Customer |
| 3 | Customer 1 | CA | F | 22 | No | =AND(C3="F",D3<45,E3="Yes") |
| 4 | Customer 2 | MO | M | 44 | Yes | AND(logical1, [logical2], **[logical3]**, [logical4], ...) |
| 5 | Customer 3 | TX | F | 65 | Yes | |
| 6 | Customer 4 | NJ | M | 73 | No | |

Each argument of this function is a complete logical test.

Figure 13 shows the results of the **AND** function. The word TRUE is displayed in the Target Customer column for any customer that meets all three logical tests that were typed into the function. The word FALSE is displayed if the results are false for any of the three logical tests. Notice how all target customers are grouped together in the first rows of the worksheet. The marketing manager using this worksheet can easily identify the target customers since the data is sorted based on the results of the **AND** function.

Figure 13 | **Results of the AND Function**

F10 | =AND(C10="F",D10<45,E10="Yes")

| | A | B | C | D | E | F |
|---|---|---|---|---|---|---|
| 1 | Customer Detail Information | | | | | |
| 2 | Name | State of Residence | Gender | Age | Children | Target Customer |
| 3 | Customer 6 | PA | F | 26 | Yes | TRUE |
| 4 | Customer 10 | CO | F | 41 | Yes | TRUE |
| 5 | Customer 13 | NY | F | 28 | Yes | TRUE |
| 6 | Customer 16 | MD | F | 20 | Yes | TRUE |
| 7 | Customer 18 | PA | F | 39 | Yes | TRUE |
| 8 | Customer 1 | CA | F | 22 | No | FALSE |
| 9 | Customer 2 | MO | M | 44 | Yes | FALSE |
| 10 | Customer 3 | TX | F | 65 | Yes | FALSE |
| 11 | Customer 4 | NJ | M | 73 | No | FALSE |
| 12 | Customer 5 | FLA | M | 29 | Yes | FALSE |
| 13 | Customer 7 | GA | F | 34 | No | FALSE |
| 14 | Customer 8 | NH | F | 54 | Yes | FALSE |
| 15 | Customer 9 | NY | M | 36 | No | FALSE |

Because of sorting, all TRUE outputs are grouped at the top of the worksheet.

The AND function produces a FALSE output here because one of the three logical tests is false (see formula bar).

## COMMON MISTAKES | Outputs for the AND Function

You cannot define the output for the **AND** function. People often try to define the output for the **AND** function similar to the **[value_if_true]** or **[value_if_false]** arguments of the **IF** function. The only arguments you can define for the **AND** function are logical tests. The only output that will be produced by the **AND** function is the word TRUE or FALSE. This is also true for the **OR** function, which is covered in the next section.

## OR Function

A close relative of the **AND** function is the **OR** function. The arguments of both functions are defined by logical tests. However, if *any* logical test is true, the **OR** function will display the word TRUE. The function displays the word FALSE if *all* logical tests are false. The **OR** function is used to evaluate data where the existence of just one criterion is required to trigger a decision or action. For example, a company may have a limited number of states where it can sell and distribute products. The **OR** function can be used to identify if a customer lives in one of the states within the company's territory. This information can then be used to distribute marketing information or promotional material relating to the company's product line.

The following demonstrates a variation for identifying target customers in Figure 11. In this example, a target customer is any person who lives in any of these three states: New York, Pennsylvania, or New Jersey. You use the **OR** function in this situation to produce a TRUE output if a person lives in *any* one of these three states. You add this function to the worksheet as follows:

- Activate cell F3.
- Type an equal sign, the function name OR, and an open parenthesis.
- Type B3="NJ" to define the first logical test. This will evaluate if the person lives in the state of New Jersey. Notice that quotation marks are placed around NJ because it is text data. Type a comma after this argument.
- Type B3="NY" to define the second logical test. This will evaluate if the customer lives in the state of New York. Type a comma after this argument.
- Type B3 ="PA" to define the third logical test. This will evaluate if the customer lives in the state of Pennsylvania.
- Type a closing parenthesis and press the **Enter** key.
- Copy the completed **OR** function in cell F3 and paste it into cells F4 through F22.

Figure 14 shows the setup of the **OR** function that is being used to evaluate if a customer lives in one of three states. Notice that each argument of the **OR** function, similar to the **AND** function, is a complete logical function.

Figure 14 | **Setup of the OR Function**

OR =OR(B3="NJ", B3="NY",B3="PA")

| | A | B | C | D | E | F |
|---|---|---|---|---|---|---|
| 1 | Customer Detail Information | | | | | |
| 2 | Name | State of Residence | Gender | Age | Children | Target Customer |
| 3 | Customer 1 | CA | F | 22 | No | =OR(B3="NJ", B3="NY",B3="PA") |
| 4 | Customer 2 | MO | M | 44 | Yes | OR(logical1, [logical2], **[logical3]**, [logical4], ...) |
| 5 | Customer 3 | TX | F | 65 | Yes | |
| 6 | Customer 4 | NJ | M | 73 | No | |

This function will display the word TRUE if *any* of these logical tests is true.

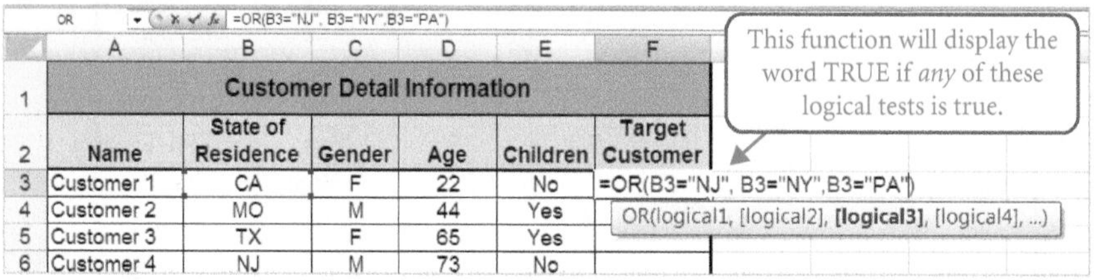

### COMMON MISTAKES | Arguments of the OR and AND Functions

You must type complete logical tests when defining the arguments of both the **AND** and **OR** functions. People often try to enter multiple results separated by commas to test multiple values for one cell location as shown in the following example. This **OR** function will produce a TRUE output regardless of what value is contained in cell D10:

```
=OR(D10 = 14,25,33,55)
```

The following example illustrates how you should create the **OR** function if you are evaluating if *one* of four values (14, 25, 33, 55) is contained in cell D10.

```
=OR(D10 = 14,D10 = 25,D10 = 33,D10 = 55)
```

Figure 15 shows the results of the **OR** function. Similar to the output of the **AND** function in Figure 13, this worksheet was also sorted based on the function outputs in the Target Customer column. Notice that if NY or NJ or PA is shown in the State of Residence column for a customer, the output of the **OR** function is TRUE. A marketing manager can use this information to initiate a direct mail marketing campaign to the target customers identified in this worksheet.

Figure 15 | **Results of the OR Function**

F6 =OR(B6="NJ", B6="NY",B6="PA")

| | A | B | C | D | E | F |
|---|---|---|---|---|---|---|
| 1 | Customer Detail Information | | | | | |
| 2 | Name | State of Residence | Gender | Age | Children | Target Customer |
| 3 | Customer 4 | NJ | M | 73 | No | TRUE |
| 4 | Customer 6 | PA | F | 26 | Yes | TRUE |
| 5 | Customer 9 | NY | M | 36 | No | TRUE |
| 6 | Customer 11 | NJ | M | 30 | Yes | TRUE |
| 7 | Customer 13 | NY | F | 28 | Yes | TRUE |
| 8 | Customer 15 | PA | M | 52 | Yes | TRUE |
| 9 | Customer 18 | PA | F | 39 | Yes | TRUE |
| 10 | Customer 20 | NJ | M | 41 | Yes | TRUE |
| 11 | Customer 1 | CA | F | 22 | No | FALSE |
| 12 | Customer 2 | MO | M | 44 | Yes | FALSE |
| 13 | Customer 3 | TX | F | 65 | Yes | FALSE |
| 14 | Customer 5 | FLA | M | 29 | Yes | FALSE |
| 15 | Customer 7 | GA | F | 34 | No | FALSE |
| 16 | Customer 8 | NH | F | 54 | Yes | FALSE |

The function produces a TRUE output in these cells because at least one of the three logical tests is true (see formula bar).

This worksheet continues down to row 22.

## Combining AND, OR, and IF Functions

The **OR** and **AND** functions can produce only one of two outputs: the word TRUE or the word FALSE. However, you can use these functions with the **IF** function to produce any output that is required for your project. This technique will be demonstrated using the worksheet shown in Figure 16, which contains customer buying data from a hypothetical retail company. Retailers typically offer a variety of reward promotions or discounts based on the buying history of their customers. For example, you may have signed up for a frequent shopper card at your favorite store or agreed to have a company contact you regarding future promotions when you purchased something online. These activities are usually indicative of a company that is running some type of customer loyalty program. A marketing manager will use the data collected from these programs to develop various discounts and promotional programs depending on a customer's buying history. The technique of combining the **AND**, **OR**, and **IF** functions can be used to tell the marketing manager what promotions should be sent to each customer.

The following points explain how you combine the **AND** and **IF** functions to show which promotion each customer should receive in Figure 16. This example assumes that a customer could receive one of two discount coupons. The first is a 50% off coupon for customers who have been purchasing products from the company for more than one year and have not made a purchase in the last 12 months. All other customers will receive a regular 10% off promotional coupon.

>> ***Quick Reference***

**OR Function**

1. Activate a cell location where the output of the function should appear.
2. Type an equal sign, the function name OR, and an open parenthesis.
3. Create at least one but no more than 30 logical tests.
4. Separate each logical test with a comma. Only one test needs to be true to produce a TRUE output.
5. Type a closing parenthesis.
6. Press the **Enter** key.

Figure 16 | **Customer Rewards Program**

| | A | B | C | D | E |
|---|---|---|---|---|---|
| 1 | Customer Rewards Program | | | | |
| 2 | Name | Years Purchasing | LY Spend | Months Since Last Purchase | Customer Reward |
| 3 | Customer 1 | 3 | $ 500 | 4 | |
| 4 | Customer 2 | 1 | $ 1,200 | 2 | |
| 5 | Customer 3 | 8 | $ 200 | 10 | |
| 6 | Customer 4 | 0.5 | $ - | 3 | |
| 7 | Customer 5 | 2 | $ 400 | 1 | |
| 8 | Customer 6 | 12 | $ 1,800 | 5 | |
| 9 | Customer 7 | 0.25 | $ - | 2 | |
| 10 | Customer 8 | 1 | $ 125 | 6 | |
| 11 | Customer 9 | 4 | $ 1,575 | 2 | |
| 12 | Customer 10 | 8 | $ 450 | 7 | |
| 13 | Customer 11 | 20 | $ 200 | 9 | |
| 14 | Customer 12 | 14 | $ - | 24 | |
| 15 | Customer 13 | 12 | $ 1,100 | 2 | |

The AND, OR, and IF functions will be used in this column to show what promotion or discounts should be sent to each customer.

This worksheet continues down to row 17.

- Activate cell E3, which is the first cell location in the Customer Reward column.
- Type an equal sign, the function name IF, and an open parenthesis.
- Type the function name AND followed by an open parenthesis. The **AND** function will be used in defining the **logical_test** argument of the **IF** function.
- Type B3>1 to define the first logical test of the **AND** function. This test will evaluate if the value in the Years Purchasing column is greater than 1. Type a comma after defining this argument.
- Type D3>=12 to define the second logical test of the **AND** function. This test will evaluate if the value in the Months Since Last Purchase column is greater than or equal to 12.
- Type a closing parenthesis to complete the **AND** function.
- Type =TRUE followed by a comma to complete the **logical_test** argument of the **IF** function. The logical test of the **IF** function will now evaluate if the output of the **AND** function is TRUE. Notice that quotation marks are *not* placed on the word TRUE. The reason is that the word TRUE is an output of the **AND** function and not a text message or word that has been typed into a cell.
- Type "Please Come Back 50% Off" to define the [**value_if_true**] argument of the **IF** function. If the logical test of the **IF** function is true, then the output of the **AND** function is true. This indicates a person has been buying products from the company for more than one year *and* has not made a purchase in 12 or more months. Therefore, this message tells the marketing manager to send this customer a 50% off coupon. Type a comma after this argument.
- Type "Customer Appreciation 10% Off" to define the [**value_if_false**] argument of the **IF** function. Any customer that does not qualify for the 50% off coupon will be sent a 10% off coupon.
- Type a closing parenthesis and press the **Enter** key to complete the function.
- Copy the function in cell E3 and paste it into cells E4 through E17.
- Sort the worksheet based on the Customer Reward column in descending order.

Figure 17 shows the setup of the functions. Notice that the **AND** function defines the left side of the logical test. Also, note that the messages defining the value_if_true and value_if_false arguments are placed in quotation marks.

Figure 17 | **Setup for Combining the IF and AND Functions**

=IF(AND(B3>1,D3>=12)=TRUE,"Please Come Back 50% Off","Customer Appreciation 10% Off")

| | B | C | D | E |
|---|---|---|---|---|
| 1 | Customer Rewards Program | | | |
| 2 | Years Purchasing | LY Spend | Months Since Last Purchase | Customer Reward |
| 3 | 3 | $ 500 | 4 | =IF(AND(B3>1,D3>=12)=TRUE,"Please Come Back 50% Off","Customer Appreciation 10% Off") |
| 4 | 1 | $ 1,200 | 2 | IF(**logical_test**, [value_if_true], [value_if_false]) |
| 5 | 8 | $ 200 | 10 | |
| 6 | 0.5 | $ - | 3 | |
| 7 | 2 | $ 400 | 1 | |

The AND function is used in the logical_test argument

Figure 18 shows the results of combing the **IF** function and **AND** function to determine the type of discount coupon that should be sent to each customer. Since the spreadsheet was sorted, the marketing manager can easily see that the first two customers listed on the worksheet should be sent the 50% off coupon.

Figure 18 | **Results of Combining the IF and AND Functions**

E4 =IF(AND(B4>1,D4>=12)=TRUE,"Please Come Back 50% Off","Customer Appreciation 10% Off")

| | A | B | C | D | E |
|---|---|---|---|---|---|
| 1 | Customer Rewards Program | | | | |
| 2 | Name | Years Purchasing | LY Spend | Months Since Last Purchase | Customer Reward |
| 3 | Customer 12 | 14 | $ - | 24 | Please Come Back 50% Off |
| 4 | Customer 15 | 6 | $ - | 14 | Please Come Back 50% Off |
| 5 | Customer 1 | 3 | $ 500 | 4 | Customer Appreciation 10% Off |
| 6 | Customer 2 | 1 | $ 1,200 | 2 | Customer Appreciation 10% Off |
| 7 | Customer 3 | 8 | $ 200 | 10 | Customer Appreciation 10% Off |
| 8 | Customer 4 | 0.5 | $ - | 3 | Customer Appreciation 10% Off |
| 9 | Customer 5 | 2 | $ 400 | 1 | Customer Appreciation 10% Off |
| 10 | Customer 6 | 12 | $ 1,800 | 5 | Customer Appreciation 10% Off |
| 11 | Customer 7 | 0.25 | $ - | 2 | Customer Appreciation 10% Off |
| 12 | Customer 8 | 1 | $ 125 | 6 | Customer Appreciation 10% Off |
| 13 | Customer 9 | 4 | $ 1,575 | 2 | Customer Appreciation 10% Off |
| 14 | Customer 10 | 8 | $ 450 | 7 | Customer Appreciation 10% Off |

Since both logical tests of the AND function are true, the IF function displays the value_if_true output for this customer.

Figure 19 shows the setup of combining the **IF** and **OR** functions. This example assumes that the marketing manager will send a 25% off discount coupon to customers who have either been making purchases for more than two years or have spent more than $1,000 in the past year. Since customers will qualify for this coupon if they satisfy either criteria, the **OR** function will be used in defining the logical test of the **IF** function. The following points explain how you create this function using the worksheet shown in Figure 16:

- Activate cell E3.
- Type an equal sign, the function name IF, and an open parenthesis.
- Type the function name OR followed by an open parenthesis.
- Type B3>2 to define the first logical test of the **OR** function. This test will evaluate if the value in the Years Purchasing column is greater than 2. Type a comma after defining this argument.
- Type C3>1000 to define the second logical test of the **OR** function. This test will evaluate if the value in the LY Spend column is greater than 1000.
- Type a closing parenthesis to complete the **OR** function.
- Type =TRUE followed by a comma to complete the **logical_test** argument of the **IF** function. The logical test of the IF function is now evaluating if the output of the **OR** function is TRUE. Notice that quotation marks are *not* placed on the word TRUE.
- Type "Thanks for being loyal 25% Off" to define the **[value_if_true]** argument of the **IF** function. If the logical test of the **IF** function is true, then the output of the **OR** function is true. This indicates a person has been purchasing products from the company for more than two years *or* has spent more than $1,000 in the past year. Type a comma after defining this argument.
- Type "Customer Appreciation 10% Off" to define the **[value_if_false]** argument. Any customer who does not satisfy either criteria specified in the **OR** function will be sent a 10% off coupon.

- Type a closing parenthesis and press the **Enter** key to complete the function.
- Copy the completed function in cell E3 and paste it to cells E4 through E17.
- Sort the worksheet based on the Customer Reward column in descending order.

Figure 19 | **Combining the IF and OR Functions**

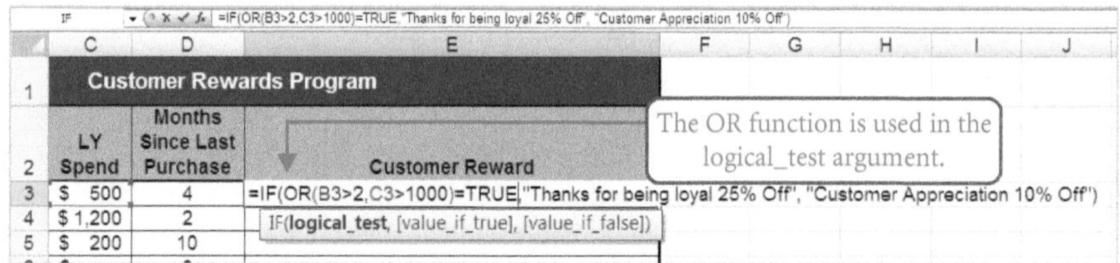


Figure 20 shows the results of combining the **IF** and **OR** functions. Similar to the results shown in Figure 18, the marketing manager can easily see which discount coupon goes to each customer because the worksheet was sorted based on the output in the Customer Reward column.

Figure 20 | **Results of Combining the IF and OR Functions**

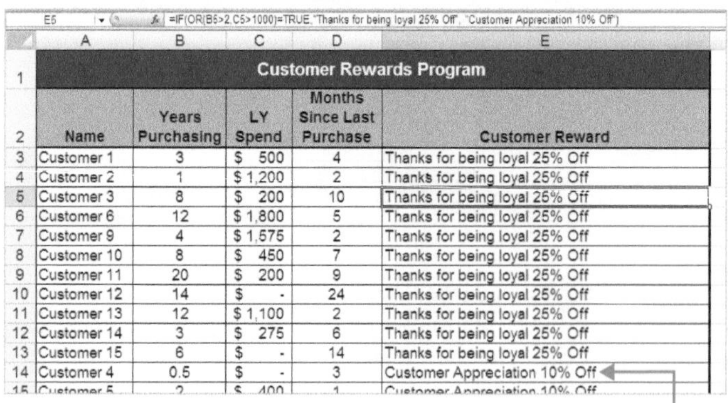

=IF(OR(B5>2,C5>1000)=TRUE,"Thanks for being loyal 25% Off","Customer Appreciation 10% Off")

Customer Rewards Program

| Name | Years Purchasing | LY Spend | Months Since Last Purchase | Customer Reward |
|---|---|---|---|---|
| Customer 1 | 3 | $ 500 | 4 | Thanks for being loyal 25% Off |
| Customer 2 | 1 | $ 1,200 | 2 | Thanks for being loyal 25% Off |
| Customer 3 | 8 | $ 200 | 10 | Thanks for being loyal 25% Off |
| Customer 6 | 12 | $ 1,800 | 5 | Thanks for being loyal 25% Off |
| Customer 9 | 4 | $ 1,575 | 2 | Thanks for being loyal 25% Off |
| Customer 10 | 8 | $ 450 | 7 | Thanks for being loyal 25% Off |
| Customer 11 | 20 | $ 200 | 9 | Thanks for being loyal 25% Off |
| Customer 12 | 14 | $ - | 24 | Thanks for being loyal 25% Off |
| Customer 13 | 12 | $ 1,100 | 2 | Thanks for being loyal 25% Off |
| Customer 14 | 3 | $ 275 | 6 | Thanks for being loyal 25% Off |
| Customer 15 | 6 | $ - | 14 | Thanks for being loyal 25% Off |
| Customer 4 | 0.5 | $ - | 3 | Customer Appreciation 10% Off |
| Customer 5 | 2 | $ 400 | 1 | Customer Appreciation 10% Off |

Both logical tests in the OR function were false for this customer.

## COMMON MISTAKES | Combining the AND, OR, and IF Functions

You cannot use the word **AND** or the word **OR** to combine multiple logical tests in an **IF** function. For example, the following **IF** function will produce an error:

```
=IF(B3 > 2 AND C3 > 500 AND D3 > 12,"Free Gift","Discount Coupon")
```

Based on the preceding example, if you wanted to show the words *Free Gift* in a cell if the value in cell B3 is greater than 2 *and* the value in C3 is greater than 500 *and* the value in D3 is greater than 12, then you need to use the **AND** function. The corrected **IF** function is as follows.

```
=IF(AND(B3 > 2,C3 > 500,D3 > 12) = TRUE, "Free Gift", "Discount Coupon")
```

Notice that the **AND** *function* is used in the **logical_test** argument of the **IF** function. If the **AND** function produces a TRUE output, the words *Free Gift* will appear in the cell. If the **AND** function produces a FALSE output, the function will show the words *Discount Coupon* in the cell.

# AND and OR Functions

VIDEO WORKSHOP

The purpose of this workshop is to demonstrate the use of the **AND** and **OR** functions. We will be using these functions to construct a merchandise allocation plan. I will be demonstrating the tasks in this workshop in the following three videos: **AND Function**; **OR Function**; and **Combining AND, OR, and IF Functions**. After completing each section of tasks, watch the related video shown in parentheses. Open the file named ib_e04_merchandiseallocations. Remember to try these tasks on your own first before watching the video.

1. **The AND Function (Video: AND Function)**
   a. Activate cell G3 in Sheet1.
   b. Type an equal sign, the function name `AND`, and an open parenthesis.
   c. Type `B3 = "Yes"` to define the first logical test and then type a comma.
   d. Type `F3 = "Yes"` to define a second logical test.
   e. Type a closing parenthesis and then press the **Enter** key.
   f. Copy cell G3 and paste it into cells G4:G13.

2. **The OR Function (Video: OR Function)**
   a. Activate cell H3.
   b. Type an equal sign, the function name `OR`, and an open parenthesis.
   c. Type `C3 = "Yes"` to define the first logical test and then type a comma.
   d. Type `D3 = "Yes"` to define a second logical test and then type a comma.
   e. Type `E3 >= 5000000` to define a third logical test.
   f. Type a closing parenthesis and press the **Enter** key.
   g. Copy cell H3 and paste it into cells H4:H13.

3. **OR, AND, and Nested IF Function (Video: Combining AND, OR, and IF Functions)**
   a. Activate cell I3.
   b. Type an equal sign, the function name `IF`, and an open parenthesis.
   c. Define the **logical_test** argument by typing the function name `AND` followed by an open parenthesis.
   d. Type the following logical tests for the **AND** function:
      `B3 = "Yes"`
      `F3 = "Yes"`
   e. Type a closing parenthesis to complete the **AND** function.
   f. Type an equal sign followed by the word `FALSE` and then type a comma to complete the **logical_test** argument of the **IF** function.
   g. Define the **[value_if_true]** argument by typing a `0` followed by a comma.
   h. Define the **[value_if_false]** argument by starting a new **IF** function. Type the function name `IF` followed by an open parenthesis.
   i. Define the **logical_test** argument of the second **IF** function by typing the function name `OR` followed by an open parenthesis.

j. Enter the following logical tests for the **OR** function:

```
C3 = "Yes"
D3 = "Yes"
E3 >= 5000000
```

k. Type a closing parenthesis to complete the **OR** function.

l. Type an equal sign followed by the word **TRUE** and then type a comma to complete the **logical_test** argument of the second **IF** function.

m. Define the **[value_if_true]** argument of the second **IF** function by typing the number 1 followed by a comma.

n. Define the **[value_if_false]** argument of the second **IF** function by typing 0. Then complete the function by typing two closing parentheses and press the **Enter** key.

o. Copy cell I3 and paste it into cell I4:I13.

p. Save and close your file.

**EXERCISE**

**Why Do I Need This?**

## >> Managing Product Shipments

When it comes to managing the process of shipping merchandise from a distribution center to a retail store, transportation managers often find themselves stuck between a rock and a hard place. On one hand they are under a lot of pressure to keep shipping costs as low as possible. To do this, transportation managers will try to maximize either the cubic capacity or weight capacity of every truck that leaves the distribution center. On the other hand, they need to ship products as frequently as possible so all stores have every item in stock all the time. As a result, if they wait too long to maximize the capacity of a truck, a store may run out of certain products, which could decrease sales.

### Exercise

The goal of this exercise is to evaluate the shipping status for a fleet of trucks servicing a chain of retail stores. You will use the **AND**, **OR**, and **IF** functions to determine which trucks should ship and which trucks should be held at the distribution center. You will need to open the file named ib_e04_transportationstatus before completing the following tasks:

1. A truck must have fuel and not require any maintenance before it can be released to ship products. Use the **AND** function in cell J3 to determine if the first truck can be cleared for shipping. The function should show the word TRUE if cell H3 in the Fuel column is Yes and cell I3 in the Maintenance Required column is No.

2. Copy the **AND** function in cell J3 and paste it into cells J4:J20.

3. Use the **OR** function in cell K3 to determine if the first truck achieved the company capacity goal. The capacity goal is achieved when either the Current Cube (cell F3) or the Current Weight (cell G3) is greater than or equal to 90% of capacity. The logical tests to evaluate the current weight and cubic capacity are as follows:

   a. Current Cubic Capacity: `F3 >= D3 * .90`

   b. Current Weight Capacity: `G3 >= E3 * .90`

4. Copy the **OR** function in cell K3 and paste it to cells K4:K20.

5. Enter a nested **IF** function in cell L3 to determine if a truck should be held or shipped. The following logical tests should be used in this function in the order listed.
   a. If the output of the **AND** function in cell J3 is FALSE, then the output of this **IF** function should be the word *HOLD*. If the truck does not have fuel or requires maintenance, the transportation manager cannot allow it to leave the distribution center.
   b. If the output of the **OR** function in cell K3 is TRUE, then the output of this function should be SHIP.
   c. If the output of the **OR** function in cell K3 is FALSE and the value in cell C3 (Days Since Last Delivery) is greater than or equal to 3, the function should display the word *SHIP*. As mentioned, in order for the transportation manager to control shipping costs, the capacity of each truck must be maximized before shipping. However, a store needs to receive frequent deliveries to prevent merchandise from going out of stock. Therefore, even if a truck has not reached its capacity goal, it must be shipped.
   d. If all logical tests in this function fail, you can assume that a truck has not reached its capacity goal and it has been less than three days since the store received a delivery. Therefore, the output should be HOLD.
6. Copy the function in cell L3 and paste it to cells L4:L20.
7. Sort the spreadsheet based on the Ship or Hold column (column L) in ascending order and then based on the Fuel & Maintenance Ready column (column J) in ascending order.
8. How many trucks are being held?
9. How many trucks are being held only because of fuel and maintenance issues?
10. How many trucks had to be shipped without reaching their capacity goals?
11. Save and close your file.

## >> What's Wrong with This Spreadsheet?

PROBLEM & EXERCISE

### Problem

Your friend is working on a project for her finance class. She is having trouble putting together a spreadsheet in Excel and asks for your help. She attaches an Excel workbook to an e-mail and includes the following message:

*Hi, I pulled together some data for a project I have to do for my finance class. I am trying to complete the Status column and the Investment Opportunity column. I thought these would be easy calculations; however, as you can see, something is going radically wrong here! Please help.*

1. *For the Status column I'm trying to show the words Market Leader if the market share is greater than 20% or the sales growth is greater than 10%. I figured the* ***OR*** *function would be perfect for this, but as you can see, I keep getting errors.*
2. *For the Investment Opportunity column, I am just trying to identify public companies that have a 5-year sales growth rate greater than 10%. I am trying to use the* ***AND*** *function for this one, but as you can see, this is not working either.*

### Exercise

The workbook your friend e-mailed to you is named ib_e04_companyanalysis. Take a look at the functions in the Status column and the Investment Opportunity column. What's wrong with this spreadsheet? Consider the following points:

1. Based on the criteria explained in your friend's e-mail, is she using the right functions to accomplish her goals?
2. Are the arguments for each function properly defined?

Write a short answer for each of the preceding points and fix the spreadsheet based on the facts stated from the message in the Problem section.

Skill Set

## Lookup Functions

The previous sections in this chapter addressed how logical functions are used to evaluate the data in a worksheet. This section will review functions that can be used for assembling data in a worksheet. The data required for business projects rarely comes in one neat convenient spreadsheet. In many instances, you will have to pull data from several sources or pick specific points from larger datasets. The anecdote at the beginning of this chapter is an excellent example of having to pull pieces of information from one data source and insert them into a worksheet. Theses tasks can be accomplished through ***Lookup functions***. Lookup functions are valuable assets when you are assembling data from several sources. The two lookup functions covered in this section are **VLookup** and **HLookup**.

### VLookup Function

***VLookup*** is a lookup function used mostly to display data from one worksheet or workbook into another. For example, you may have a worksheet filled with ZIP codes and need to insert the city and state, similar to the anecdote at the beginning of the chapter. Or, you may have a list of product codes and need to insert the product description. You can use the **VLookup** function to look for specific data values in a second worksheet or workbook and display the needed values in your primary worksheet.

The data in Figure 21 shows product sales and inventory data for a hypothetical retail store. The Sales Data worksheet contains several product numbers along with sales and inventory data. Notice that the Product Description column is blank. Therefore, we do not know which products are associated with each product number. However, the Product Data worksheet contains a list of the same product codes found on the Sales Data worksheet along with a variety of descriptive information.

Figure 21 | **Sales and Inventory Data by Product**

| | A | B | C | D |
|---|---|---|---|---|
| 1 | Product Description | Product Code | Sales Units | Inventory Units |
| 2 | | 89632 | 500 | 1,200 |
| 3 | | 55412 | 1,200 | 2,500 |
| 4 | | 67425 | 250 | 850 |
| 5 | | 55879 | 850 | 2,300 |
| 6 | | 22415 | 1,470 | 4,000 |

The Product Description for each Product Code is missing.

This worksheet contains descriptive information for each Product Code.

Sales Data / Product Data

Figure 22 shows the data contained in both worksheets from Figure 21 side by side. The goal of this example is to show how you can use the **VLookup** function to match the product codes in the Sales Data worksheet with the product codes in the Product Data worksheet. When a match is found, the function will show the Product Description from column C of the Product Data worksheet in column A of the Sales Data worksheet. There are two main reasons why you would want to accomplish this task using the **VLookup** function instead of typing these descriptions manually into the worksheet. The first is accuracy. Data entry errors are very common when information is manually typed into a worksheet. Using the **VLookup** function to bring data from one worksheet into another prevents data entry errors. The second reason is time. The data in Figure 22 represents a simplified example so it is easier for you to learn this function. However, imagine if you were faced with the situation that was described in the anecdote. It would probably take you a few hours to accurately type the state and city names for 400 ZIP codes into a worksheet. With the **VLookup** function, this task would take just a few minutes.

Figure 22 | **Sales Data and Product Data Worksheets Side by Side**

Sales Data worksheet

| | A | B | C | D |
|---|---|---|---|---|
| 1 | Product Description | Product Code | Sales Units | Inventory Units |
| 2 | | 89632 | 500 | 1,200 |
| 3 | | 55412 | 1,200 | 2,500 |
| 4 | | 67425 | 250 | 850 |
| 5 | | 55879 | 850 | 2,300 |
| 6 | | 22415 | 1,470 | 4,000 |

Product Data worksheet

| | A | B | C | D | E |
|---|---|---|---|---|---|
| 1 | Product Code | Product Color | Product Description | Status | Last Order Date |
| 2 | 89632 | Blue | Hats | Active | 3/15/05 |
| 3 | 55412 | Grey | Jackets | Active | 12/30/04 |
| 4 | 67425 | Red | Sweaters | Inactive | 9/30/04 |
| 5 | 55879 | Brown | Coffee Mugs | Active | 2/15/05 |
| 6 | 22415 | White | T-Shirts | Active | 4/15/05 |

The Product Codes in both worksheets are identical.

As shown in Figure 23, the **VLookup** function contains four arguments that must be defined in order to display data from one worksheet or workbook into another. Each of these arguments is defined as follows:

- **lookup_value**: The common data point that exists in two different worksheets or in two parts of the same worksheet. Based on the data shown in Figure 22, the lookup value would be defined using cell locations in the Product Code column because these values exists in both the Sales Data and Product Data worksheets.
- **table_array**: The range of cells where both the lookup value and the data that will be used for the output of the function exist. *The first column of this range must contain the lookup value.* The function will look vertically (hence the name **Vlookup**) down the first column of this range to find the lookup value. Based on the data in Figure 22, the table array would be the range A2:E6 in the Product Data worksheet. This range starts with cell A2 because column A contains the product codes that would be used to define the **lookup_value** argument.
- **col_index_num**: The column number, counting from left to right beginning with the first column in the table array range, which contains the data you wish to display as the output of the function. As mentioned, the function will look vertically down the first column of the table array range to find the lookup value. When the lookup value is found, the function will use the column index number to count the number of columns from left to right to find the data you wish to display. When determining the column index number, you must consider the first column in the table array range as 1. Based on the data shown in Figure 22, the column index number would be 3, because the Product Description column in the Product Data worksheet is the third column in the range A2:E6.
- [**range_lookup**]: This argument guides the function to look for values that are either a close match or an approximate match to the lookup value. In most situations you will want the function to look for an exact match to the lookup value. However, you might want to look for close matches in situations such as survey scores. For example, a survey score of 90 to 100 might be given a description of "Excellent." The actual value on your primary worksheet might be the number 97. However, the worksheet containing the description of each score might have only the number 90. In this situation, setting the **range_lookup** argument to find an approximate match would be necessary. This argument is defined with one of two possible options:
  - **True**: Type the word True (no quotation marks) if you want the function to look for approximate matches to the lookup value. You must consider the following if you are using this option:
    - The range of cells used to define the **table_array** range *must be sorted in ascending order*; otherwise, the function may produce erroneous results.
    - The function will look for the next highest value that is *less than* the lookup value. For example, if the table array range contains the number 90, and the lookup value is 97, the function will match to the number 90. If the number 90 was the lowest value in the table array range, and the lookup value was 89, the function will produce an error. There reason is that there is no number in the table array range that is less than 89.
  - **False**: Type the word False (no quotation marks) if you want the function to look for exact matches to the lookup value. *It is important to note that if you do not define the [**range_lookup**] argument, the function will assume the True option.*

Figure 23 | **Arguments of the VLookup Function**

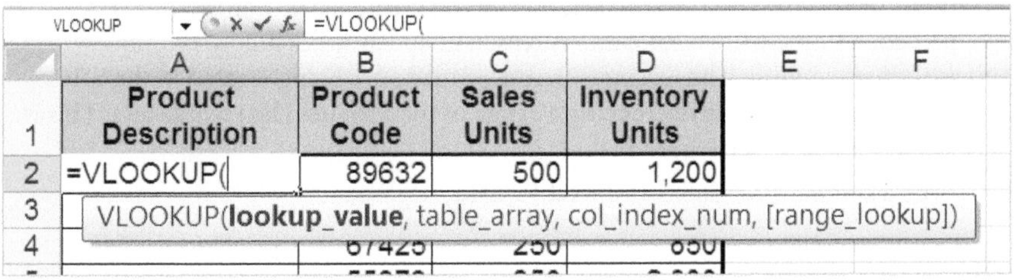

VLOOKUP =VLOOKUP(

| | A | B | C | D | E | F |
|---|---|---|---|---|---|---|
| 1 | Product Description | Product Code | Sales Units | Inventory Units | | |
| 2 | =VLOOKUP( | 89632 | 500 | 1,200 | | |
| 3 | VLOOKUP(**lookup_value**, table_array, col_index_num, [range_lookup]) | | | | | |
| 4 | | 67425 | 250 | 650 | | |

As mentioned, the **VLookup** function will be used to complete the Product Description column in the Sales Data worksheet shown in Figure 22. The following explains how you accomplish this:

- Activate cell A2 in the Sales Data worksheet shown in Figure 22.
- Type an equal sign, the function name VLOOKUP, and an open parenthesis.
- Type cell B2 to define the **lookup_value** argument. Cell B2 contains the product code for the first item in the Sales Data worksheet.
- Type a comma.
- Click the Product Data worksheet tab (see Figure 24).

Figure 24 | **Click the Product Data Worksheet Tab to Define the Table Array Range**

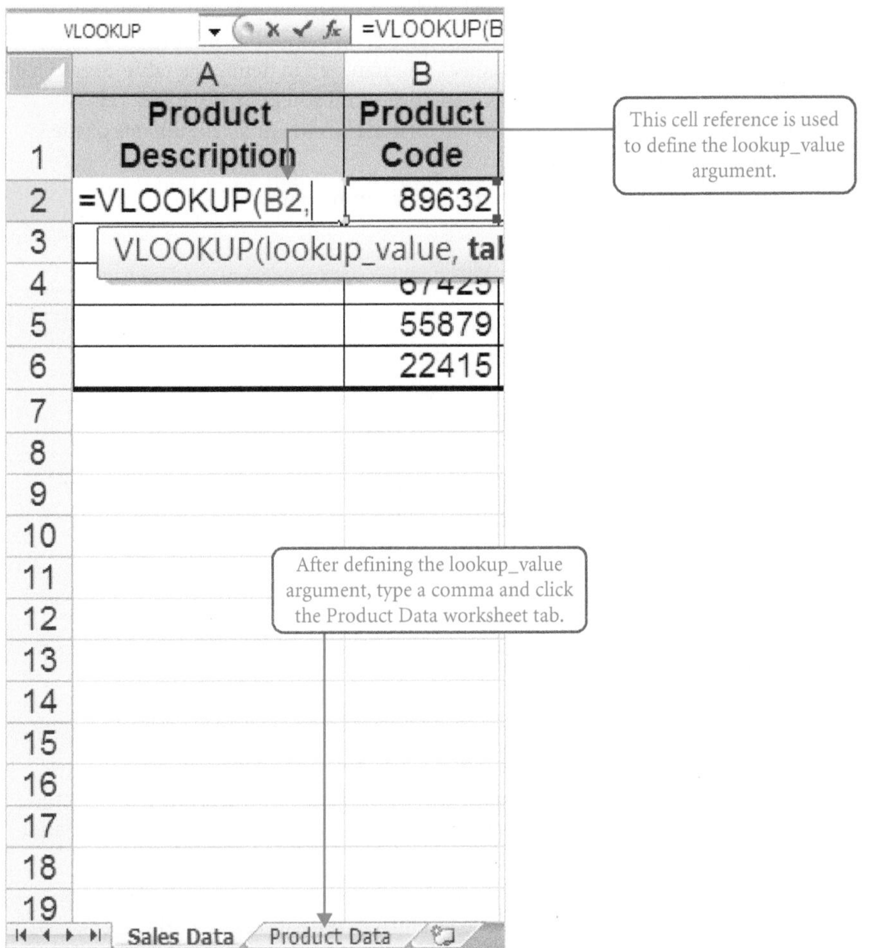

- Highlight the range A2:E6 in the Product Data worksheet to define the **table_array** argument. You may notice in the formula bar that this range is preceded by the worksheet name enclosed in apostrophes followed by an exclamation point. The reason is that the function is being created in the Sales Data worksheet but is referencing a range in the Product Data worksheet. This is known as a *link* (see Figure 25).
- Type a comma after defining the **table_array** argument.

Figure 25 | **Defining the Table Array Range in the Product Data Worksheet**

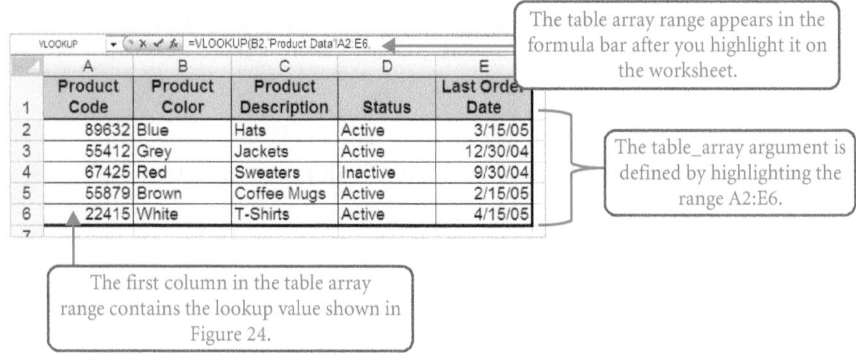

| | A | B | C | D | E |
|---|---|---|---|---|---|
| 1 | Product Code | Product Color | Product Description | Status | Last Order Date |
| 2 | 89632 | Blue | Hats | Active | 3/15/05 |
| 3 | 55412 | Grey | Jackets | Active | 12/30/04 |
| 4 | 67425 | Red | Sweaters | Inactive | 9/30/04 |
| 5 | 55879 | Brown | Coffee Mugs | Active | 2/15/05 |
| 6 | 22415 | White | T-Shirts | Active | 4/15/05 |

VLOOKUP
=VLOOKUP(B2,'Product Data'!A2:E6,
The table array range appears in the formula bar after you highlight it on the worksheet.
The table_array argument is defined by highlighting the range A2:E6.
The first column in the table array range contains the lookup value shown in Figure 24.

- Type the number 3 to define the **col_index_num** argument. The Product Description is the third column in the table array range. It is important to note that since the Product Data worksheet was activated to define the **table_array** argument, you will remain in this worksheet until you press the **Enter** key. Therefore, you will have to look in the formula bar to see the arguments of the function being defined (see Figure 26).
- Type a comma after defining the **col_index_num** argument.

Figure 26 | **Defining the Column Index Number**

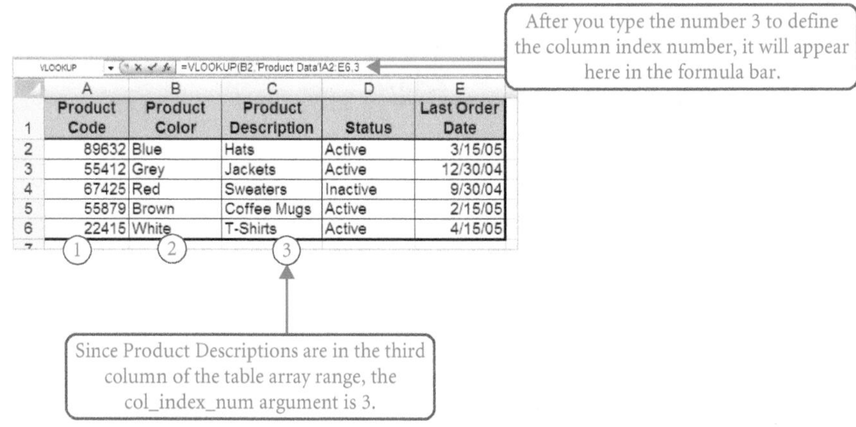

| | A | B | C | D | E |
|---|---|---|---|---|---|
| 1 | Product Code | Product Color | Product Description | Status | Last Order Date |
| 2 | 89632 | Blue | Hats | Active | 3/15/05 |
| 3 | 55412 | Grey | Jackets | Active | 12/30/04 |
| 4 | 67425 | Red | Sweaters | Inactive | 9/30/04 |
| 5 | 55879 | Brown | Coffee Mugs | Active | 2/15/05 |
| 6 | 22415 | White | T-Shirts | Active | 4/15/05 |

VLOOKUP
=VLOOKUP(B2,'Product Data'!A2:E6,3
After you type the number 3 to define the column index number, it will appear here in the formula bar.
1
2
3
Since Product Descriptions are in the third column of the table array range, the col_index_num argument is 3.

- Type the word False (no quotation marks) to define the **[range_lookup]** argument. You enter False into this argument so the function will look for an exact match for the lookup value. Remember to look in the formula bar to see this argument being defined as you type.
- Complete the function by typing a closing parenthesis and press the **Enter** key. After you press the **Enter** key, you will return to the Sales Data worksheet.
- Double click cell A2 in the Sales Data worksheet and add an absolute reference to both cell locations in the range used to define the **table_array** argument. You do

this so the range does not change from relative referencing when the function is pasted to the rest of the cell locations in column A. Remember that you add an absolute reference by typing a dollar sign in front of the column letter and row number of the cell reference.

- Copy the completed **VLookup** function in cell A2 and paste it into cells A3 through A6.

Figure 27 shows the final setup and results of the **VLookup** function. The function displays the word *Hats* in cell A2 of the Product Description column. The reason is that it found Product Code 89632 in the first column of the table array range, which is A2:E6 in the Product Data worksheet, and pulled the word *Hats* in the third column of this range (see Figure 26). In addition, notice that an absolute reference is placed on the range used to define the **table_array** argument.

Figure 27 | **Final Setup and Results of the VLookup Function**

A2 =VLOOKUP(B2,'Product Data'!$A$2:$E$6,3,FALSE)

| | A | B | C | D | E |
|---|---|---|---|---|---|
| 1 | Product Description | Product Code | Sales Units | Inventory Units | |
| 2 | Hats | 89632 | 500 | 1,200 | |
| 3 | Jackets | 55412 | 1,200 | 2,500 | |
| 4 | Sweaters | 67425 | 250 | 850 | |
| 5 | Coffee Mugs | 55879 | 850 | 2,300 | |
| 6 | T-Shirts | 22415 | 1,470 | 4,000 | |
| 7 | | | | | |

An absolute reference is placed on this range defining the table_array argument.

The VLookup function displays the product descriptions relating to all the product codes in column B.

## COMMON MISTAKES | VLookup

The following mistakes are often made when using the **VLookup** function:

1. After defining the range for the **table_array** argument, immediately type a comma. People often click the original worksheet tab before typing a comma after defining the range for the **table_array** argument. This will distort the **table_array** argument and prevent the function from working.
2. Before pasting the **VLookup** function to other cells, do not forget to add an absolute reference on the table array range. The **#N/A** error codes in the worksheet shown in Figure 28 happened because the table array range was added without an absolute reference.

Figure 28 | **#N/A Errors After Pasting the VLookup Function**

K15

| | A | B | C | D |
|---|---|---|---|---|
| 1 | Product Description | Product Code | Sales Units | Inventory Units |
| 2 | Hats | 89632 | 500 | 1,200 |
| 3 | Jackets | 55412 | 1,200 | 2,500 |
| 4 | #N/A | 67425 | 250 | 850 |
| 5 | #N/A | 55879 | 850 | 2,300 |
| 6 | T-Shirts | 22415 | 1,470 | 4,000 |

3. When defining the column index number **(col_index_num)**, count the first column in table array range as 1. You will get an output that is one column to the left of what is intended if you forget to count the first column.

**Quick Reference**

### VLookup

1. Activate the cell where the output should appear.
2. Type an equal sign, the function name VLookup, and an open parenthesis.
3. Define the following arguments:
   a) **lookup_value**: Cell location that contains the value to be searched and matched in a second worksheet.
   b) **table_array**: Range in a second worksheet or workbook that contains both the lookup value and data for the output of the function (first column in the range *must* contain the lookup value).
   c) **col_index_num**: Number of columns in the table array range counting from left to right that contains data for the output of the function (count the first column as 1).
   d) **range_lookup**: Type the word False to find an exact match to the lookup value. This argument will assume True and look for an approximate match for the lookup value if this argument is not defined.
4. Type a closing parenthesis and press the **Enter** key.
5. Use an absolute reference ($) on the range used to define the **table_array** argument if pasting the function to other cells.

## HLookup Function

The previous section demonstrated how you use the **VLookup** function to search for a lookup value vertically down the first column of a range of cells. However, your data might be organized such that you have to look across a row instead of down a column to search for a lookup value. In these situations you will need to use an ***HLookup*** function. The **HLookup** function is identical to the **VLookup** function; however, it looks horizontally across the first row of a range of cells to find a lookup value instead of vertically down a column. For example, Figure 29 contains a workbook that a strategic planning manager might use to compare financial statistics between his company and other competitors in the industry. There are two worksheets in this workbook: Comparison and Competitor Data. The Competitor Data worksheet contains the financial statistics that need to be displayed in column C of the Comparison worksheet. However, the competitor names, as shown in cell C2 in the Comparison worksheet, are listed across row 2 in the Competitor Data worksheet. Therefore, the **HLookup** function would be needed to display the competitor data in Column C of the Comparison worksheet.

Figure 29 | **Data for Competitor Analysis**

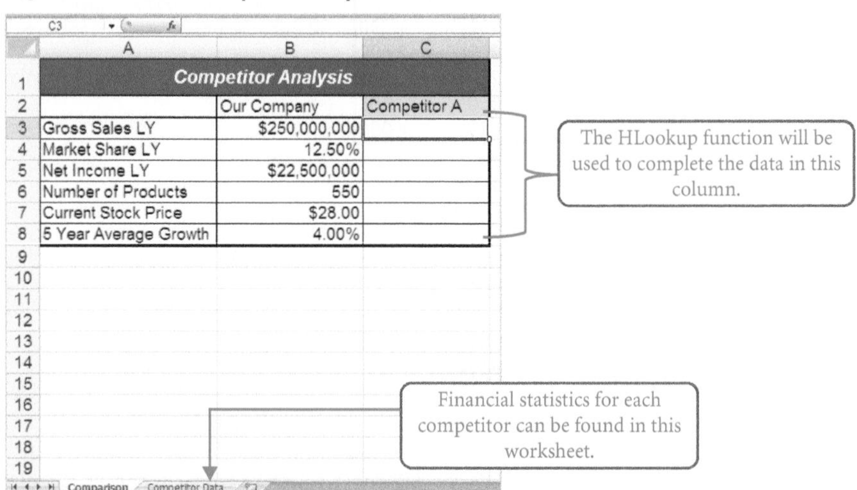

Competitor Analysis
Our Company
Competitor A
Gross Sales LY
$250,000,000
Market Share LY
12.50%
Net Income LY
$22,500,000
Number of Products
550
Current Stock Price
$28.00
5 Year Average Growth
4.00%
Comparison
Competitor Data
The HLookup function will be used to complete the data in this column.
Financial statistics for each competitor can be found in this worksheet.


Figure 30 shows the two worksheets from Figure 29 side by side. Notice that the competitor names are listed across row 2, and the financial statistics relating to each competitor are listed in the column below each competitor's name. The **HLookup** function will be used to look for the competitor name typed into cell C2 of the Comparison worksheet in row 2 of the Competitor Data worksheet. When a match is found, the function will show the relevant financial statistic in the Comparison worksheet.

Figure 30 | **Comparison and Competitor Data Worksheets**

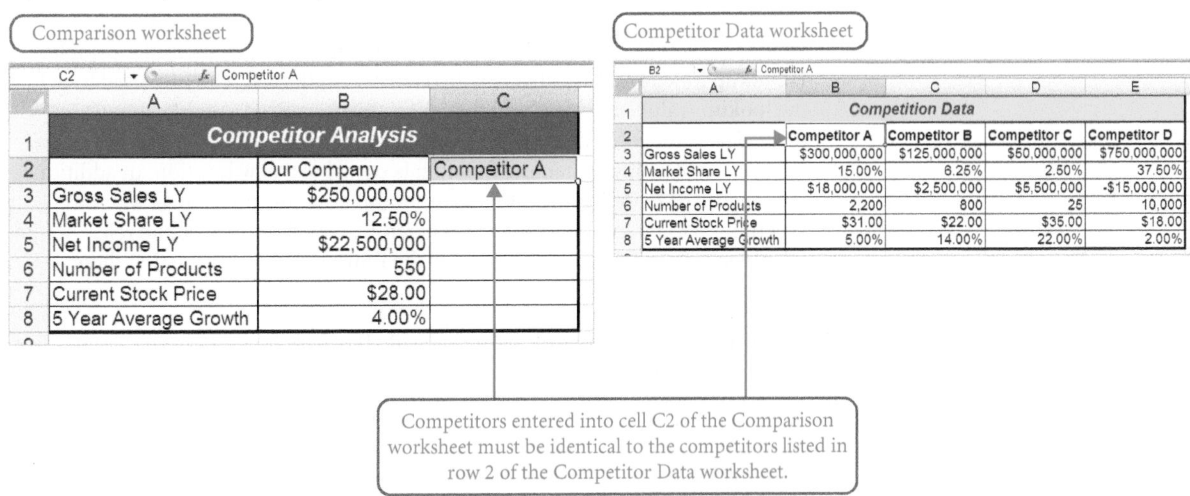


The arguments of the **HLookup** function are identical to the **VLookup** function with the exception of the **col_index_num** argument. Since the **HLookup** function looks horizontally across a row, it uses a row index number to count the number of rows from top to bottom in the range used to define the **table_array** argument. Similar to the column index number, the first row in the table array range must be counted as 1.

As mentioned, the **HLookup** function will be used to show the competitor information in column C of Figure 30. Here is how you accomplish this:

- Activate cell C3 in the Comparison worksheet. The **HLookup** function will be used to show the Gross Sales LY for the competitor typed into cell C2.
- Type an equal sign, the function name HLOOKUP, and an open parenthesis.
- Type cell C2 to define the **lookup_value** argument. The function will look for the competitor name that is typed into cell C2 of the Comparison worksheet.
- Type a comma.
- Click the Competitor Data worksheet tab.
- Highlight the range B2:B8 on the Competitor Data worksheet to define the **table_array** argument. When you are defining the **table_array** argument for the **HLookup** function, the first *row* in this range must contain the values used to define the **lookup_value** argument. This is similar to the **VLookup** function where the first *column* of the table array must contain the lookup values. The **HLookup** function will search horizontally (hence the name **HLookup**) across the first row in the range used to define the **table_array** range to find the lookup value.
- Type a comma.
- Type the number 2 to define the **row_index_num** argument. As previously mentioned, the purpose of this **HLookup** function is to show the Gross Sales LY for the competitor name typed into cell C2 of the Comparison worksheet. In the Competitor Data worksheet, the Gross Sales LY is in the second row of the range that was used to define the **table_array** argument (B2:E8). Remember to count the first row in the table array range as 1.
- Type a comma.
- Type the word False (no quotation marks) to define the [**range_lookup**] argument. For this example, you must search for an exact match to the lookup value. The rules applying to the **range_lookup** argument for the **HLookup** function are identical to the **VLookup** function. However, if you are using the **True** option for this function, the range used to define the **table_array** argument must be sorted in ascending order from left to right based on the values in the first row of the range.

- Type a closing parenthesis and press the **Enter** key to complete the function. This will bring you back to the Comparison worksheet.
- Double click cell C3 in the Comparison worksheet, which contains the complete **HLookup** function. Place an absolute reference on the cell reference used to define the **lookup_value** argument and the range used to define the **table_array** argument. The competitor name will always be entered into cell C2; therefore, this reference cannot change when the function is pasted to a new location. In addition, the range used to define the **table_array** argument must not change when the function is pasted to a new location. Therefore, you place an absolute reference on the range defining this argument. Press the **Enter** key after completing these adjustments.

Figure 31 shows the setup of the completed **HLookup** function in the Comparison worksheet. Notice that absolute references are used in the **lookup_value** and **table_array** arguments.

Figure 31 | **Setup for the HLookup Function in the Comparison Worksheet**

Absolute references are added to both the lookup value and the table array range.

HLOOKUP =HLOOKUP($C$2,'Competitor Data'!$B$2:$E$8,2,FALSE)

| | A | B | C |
|---|---|---|---|
| 1 | Competitor Analysis | | |
| 2 | | Our Company | Competitor A |
| 3 | Gross Sales LY | $250,000,000 | =HLOOKUP($C$2,'Competitor Data'!$B$2:$E$8,2,FALSE) |
| 4 | Market Share LY | 12.50% | HLOOKUP(lookup_value, table_array, row_index_num, [range_lookup]) |
| 5 | Net Income LY | $22,500,000 | |
| 6 | Number of Products | 550 | |

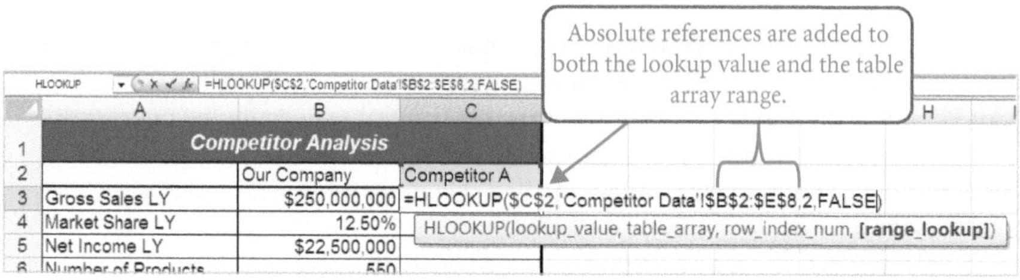

Figure 32 shows the output of the **HLookup** function. The function found Competitor A in the first row of the table array range in the Competitor Data worksheet, moved down two rows (counting the first row as 1), and displayed the value in this cell location. Following this path, you will find that two rows down from Competitor A (cell B2) in the Competitor Data worksheet is the number $300,000,000. Therefore, this number becomes the output of the function in cell C3 of the Comparison worksheet.

Figure 32 | **Results of the HLookup Function in the Comparison Worksheet**

Two rows below Competitor A in the Competitor Data spreadsheet is the value $300,000,000 (the first row is counted as 1).

C3 =HLOOKUP($C$2,'Competitor Data'!$B$2:$E$8,2,FALSE)

| | A | B | C |
|---|---|---|---|
| 1 | Competitor Analysis | | |
| 2 | | Our Company | Competitor A |
| 3 | Gross Sales LY | $250,000,000 | $300,000,000 |
| 4 | Market Share LY | 12.50% | |
| 5 | Net Income LY | $22,500,000 | |
| 6 | Number of Products | 550 | |
| 7 | Current Stock Price | $28.00 | |
| 8 | 5 Year Average Growth | 4.00% | |

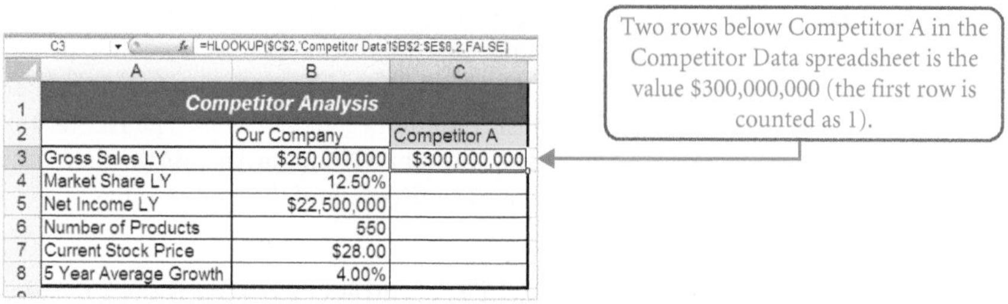

To complete the rest of the cell locations in column C of the Comparison spreadsheet, you cannot copy and paste the **HLookup** function without making additional adjustments. The reason is that each statistic in column C will require a different row index number. For example, cell location C5 in the Comparison worksheet is the Net Income LY statistic. This is four rows down from the first row in the table array range in the Competitor Data worksheet. The following points explain how to paste and adjust the **HLookup** function to complete cells C4 through C8 in Figure 32.

- Copy cell C3 in the Comparison worksheet, which contains the completed **HLookup** function.

- Highlight the range C4:C8 and select the **Formulas paste** option from the **Paste** icon.
- Double click cell C4, change the **row_index_num** to 3, and press the **Enter** key.
- Double click cell C5, change the **row_index_num** to 4, and press the **Enter** key.
- Double click cell C6, change the **row_index_num** to 5, and press the **Enter** key.
- Double click cell C7, change the **row_index_num** to 6, and press the **Enter** key.
- Double click cell C8, change the **row_index_num** to 7, and press the **Enter** key.

When the spreadsheet is complete, you can change the competitor name in cell C2 of the Comparison worksheet, and the data for column C will automatically change to reflect the financial statistics of the new competitor. Figure 33 shows a completed spreadsheet with the competitor changed to Competitor D.

Figure 33 | **Final Outputs of the HLookup Function**

C5 =HLOOKUP($C$2,'Competitor Data'!$B$2:$E$8,4,FALSE)

| | A | B | C |
|---|---|---|---|
| 1 | Competitor Analysis | | |
| 2 | | Our Company | Competitor D |
| 3 | Gross Sales LY | $250,000,000 | $750,000,000 |
| 4 | Market Share LY | 12.50% | 37.50% |
| 5 | Net Income LY | $22,500,000 | -$15,000,000 |
| 6 | Number of Products | 550 | 10,000 |
| 7 | Current Stock Price | $28.00 | $18.00 |
| 8 | 5 Year Average Growth | 4.00% | 2.00% |

The row index number for each of these cells was adjusted to pull the proper financial statistic from the Competitor Data spreadsheet.

## COMMON MISTAKES | Error Codes for HLookup and VLookup

The following two error codes are common when using either the **VLookup** or **HLookup** functions.

**#N/A**: The Not Available error signifies that the function cannot find the lookup value in the table array range. Typical reasons this error occurs include

1. The first column of the table array range does not contain the lookup value. Check the range in the **table_array** argument and make sure the first column of the range contains the lookup value.
2. The lookup value does not exist at all in the second spreadsheet. Check the spreadsheet you are using for the table array range and make sure the lookup value is there.
3. The table array range or the lookup value was changed when the function was pasted to a new cell location. If you are copying and pasting the function, check both the **lookup_value** and **table_array** arguments. In most cases, you will need to use an absolute reference for these arguments to prevent cell references from changing when the function is pasted to a new location.

**#REF!**: The Reference error occurs because either the column index number or row index number is too high given the range that was used to define the **table_array** argument. For example, if the table array range contains four rows for an **HLookup** function and the row index number is 8, the Reference error will appear.

### Quick Reference

### HLookup

1. Activate the cell where output should appear.
2. Type an equal sign, the function name HLookup, and an open parenthesis.
3. Define the following arguments:
   a) **lookup_value**: Cell location that contains the value to be searched in a second worksheet.
   b) **table_array**: Range in a second worksheet or workbook that contains both the lookup value and data for the output of the function (the first row in this range *must* contain the lookup value).
   c) **row_index_num**: Number of rows in the table array range counting from top to bottom that contains data for the output of the function (count the first row as 1).
   d) **range_lookup**: Type the word False to find the exact match to the lookup value. This argument will assume True and look for an approximate match for the lookup value if this argument is not defined.
4. Type a closing parenthesis and press the **Enter** key.
5. Use an absolute reference ($) on the range of the table array segment if copying and pasting the function to other cells. You may also need an absolute reference on the lookup value depending on your project.
6. Check the row index number after pasting to see if any adjustments are necessary.

VIDEO WORKSHOP

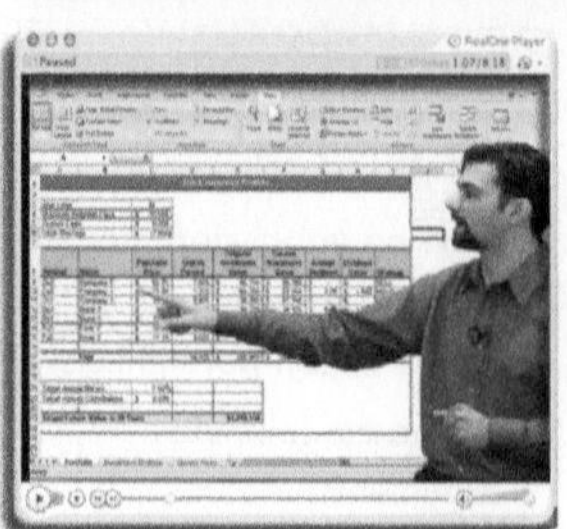

# >> The VLookup Function

The purpose of this workshop is to demonstrate the use of the **VLookup** function. We will be reviewing the same example that was presented earlier in this section. I will be demonstrating the tasks in this workshop in the video named **VLookup Function**. Watch this video after completing the tasks in this workshop. Open the file named ib_e04_vlookuppractice before starting the following tasks:

1. **Defining the VLookup Arguments (Video: VLookup Function)**
   a. Activate cell A2 on the Sales Data worksheet.
   b. Type an equal sign, the function name **VLOOKUP**, and an open parenthesis.
   c. Type **B2** or click on cell location B2 to define the **lookup_value** argument.
   d. Type a comma.
   e. Click the **Product Data** worksheet tab.
   f. Highlight the range A2:E6 to define the **table_array** argument.
   g. Type a comma.
   h. Counting column A as number 1, count the number of columns to go from column A to column C. Column C should be the third column, which is the Product Description column.
   i. Type the number **3** to define the **col_index_num** argument.
   j. Type a comma.
   k. Type the word **False** with no quotation marks.
   l. Type a closing parenthesis and press the **Enter** key.

2. **Absolute Reference (Video: VLookup Function)**
   a. Double click cell A2 on the Sales Data worksheet.
   b. Add an absolute reference to the range A2:E6 in the **table_array** argument.
   c. Press the **Enter** key.

3. **Copy and Paste Formulas (Video: VLookup Function)**
   a. Copy cell A2 on the Sales Data worksheet.
   b. Highlight the range A3:A6.
   c. Click the **Home** tab of the Ribbon.
   d. Click the down arrow on the **Paste** icon.
   e. Select the **Formulas** option.
   f. Save and close your file.

## >> The HLookup Function

**VIDEO WORKSHOP**

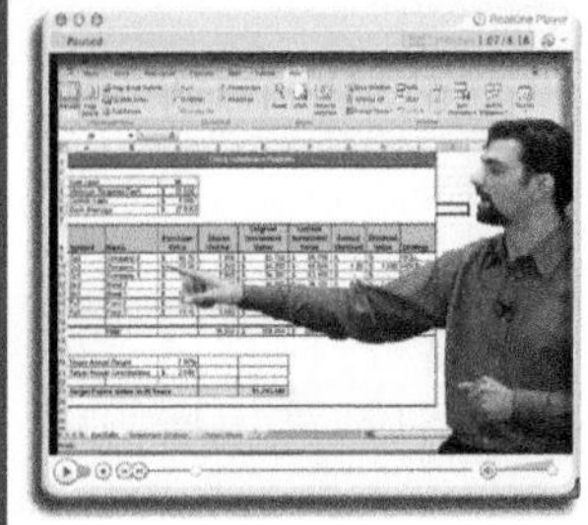

The purpose of this workshop is to demonstrate the use of the **HLookup** function. We will be reviewing the same example that was presented earlier in this section. I will be demonstrating the tasks in this workshop in the video named **HLookup Function**. Watch this video after completing the tasks in this workshop. Open the file named ib_e04_hlookuppractice before starting the following tasks:

1. **Defining the HLookup Arguments (Video: HLookup Function)**
   a. Activate cell C3 on the Comparison worksheet.
   b. Type an equal sign, the function name **HLOOKUP**, and an open parenthesis.
   c. Type **C2** or click cell location C2 to define the **lookup_value** argument.
   d. Type a comma.
   e. Click the **Competitor Data** worksheet tab.
   f. Highlight the range B2:E8 to define the **table_array** argument.
   g. Type a comma.
   h. Counting row 2 as number 1, count the number of rows to go from row 2 to row 3. This should be the second row, which is Gross Sales LY.
   i. Type the number **2** to define the **row_index_num** argument.
   j. Type a comma.
   k. Type the word **False** with no quotation marks.
   l. Type a closing parenthesis and press the **Enter** key.

2. **Absolute Reference (Video: HLookup Function)**
   a. Double click cell C3 on the Comparison worksheet.
   b. Add an absolute reference to cell location C2 in the **lookup_value** argument. Then add an absolute reference to the range B2:E8 in the **table_array** argument.
   c. Press the **Enter** key.

3. **Copy and Paste Formulas (Video: HLookup Function)**
   a. Copy cell C3 on the Comparison worksheet.
   b. Highlight the range C4:C8.
   c. Click the **Home** tab of the Ribbon.
   d. Click the down arrow on the **Paste** icon.
   e. Select the **Formulas** option.

4. **Editing the Row Index Numbers (Video: HLookup Function)**
   a. Double click cell C4 on the Comparison worksheet.
   b. Change the row index number from 2 to **3** and press the **Enter** key.
   c. Repeat step **b** for each cell in the range C5:C8 increasing the row index number from 2 to **4**, then 2 to **5**, then 2 to **6**, and 2 to **7** for the last cell.

**5. Evaluate the Competition (Video: HLookup Function)**

a. Change the competitor in cell C2 on the Comparison worksheet to read `Competitor D`.

b. Change the competitor again to `Competitor B`.

c. Save and close your file.

EXERCISE

Why Do I Need This?

# >>Personal Investment Strategies

A professional financial planner will develop investment strategies for people based on their risk preference. That is, some people prefer to make low risk investments, whereas others will take on higher risk strategies with the hopes of higher returns. The lookup functions covered in this chapter can provide significant value to a financial planner who is managing investments for several clients.

## Exercise

The purpose of this exercise is to develop a spreadsheet for a financial planner who is deciding how to invest money for several clients. Open the file named ib_e04_investmentstrategies before starting this exercise.

1. Use a **VLookup** function in cell C3 of the Investment Plan worksheet to find the Risk Preference of the customer showing in cell C2. You can find the data in the Customers worksheet. Define the arguments of the function as follows:
   a. **lookup_value**: Cell location C2. The function will look for the customer name that is typed into this cell in the Customers worksheet.
   b. **table_array**: The range A2:C11 in the Customers worksheet. Once the **lookup_value** argument is defined, you can click the Customers worksheet tab and highlight this range.
   c. **col_index_num**: The number 3. The reason is that the Risk Preference column is the third column in the range defined for the **table_array** argument.
   d. **range_lookup**: The word `False`.

2. Use a **VLookup** function in cell C4 of the Investment Plan worksheet to find the number of dollars being invested for the customer name showing in cell C2. Each argument will be defined identically to the **VLookup** function that was created in number 1. However, the **col_index_num** argument should be 2 instead of 3.

3. Use the **HLookup** function in cell C7 of the Investment Plan worksheet to calculate the customer's proposed investment for Bonds. Use the function to find the investment percentage for Bonds in the Risk Levels worksheet based on the customer's risk preference showing in cell C3 on the Investment Plan worksheet. The arguments of this function should be defined as follows:
   a. **lookup_value**: Cell location C3. The function will look for the risk preference that appears in cell C3 of the Investment Plan worksheet in the Risk Levels worksheet.
   b. **table_array**: The range B2:D5 in the Risk Levels worksheet. Once the **lookup_value** argument is defined, you can click the Risk Levels worksheet and then highlight this range.

c. **row_index_num**: The number 2. The reason is that the percentage for the Bonds category is in the second row of the range defined for the **table_array** argument.

d. **range_lookup**: The word `False`.

4. Edit the **HLookup** function you created in step 3 by typing an asterisk after the function and cell location C4. This will multiply the Dollars Investing in cell C4 of the Investment Plan worksheet by the percentage for Bonds in the Risk Levels worksheet.

5. Use the **HLookup** function in cell D8 of the Investment Plan worksheet to calculate the customer's investment plan for Mutual Funds. This function will be identical to the function created in steps 3 and 4. However, the row index number should be 3 instead of 2.

6. Use the **HLookup** function in cell D9 of the Investment Plan worksheet to calculate the customer's investment plan for Stocks. This function will be identical to the function created in steps 3 and 4. However, the row index number should be 4 instead of 2.

7. Change the customer name in cell C2 of the Investment Plan worksheet to Customer 2. Is this customer investing more money or less money compared to Customer 1?

8. How much money is Customer 8 planning to invest in Stocks?

9. On the Risk Levels worksheet, change the Moderate investment strategy to 30% Bonds, 30% Mutual Funds, and 40% Stocks.

10. How did the change you made to the Risk Levels worksheet in number 9 change the investment strategy for Customer 8?

11. Save and close your file.

## >> What's Wrong with This Spreadsheet?

PROBLEM & EXERCISE

### Problem

In one of your business classes, you are working on a project that involves researching historical data for Company D. You must compare the current stock price of Company D with other firms in the industry. One of your teammates volunteers to compile everyone's research and create a spreadsheet. He explains that by simply typing the year into a cell, you will be able to use the spreadsheet to pull the historical data for Company D. In addition, he explains that by typing a ticker symbol into another cell, you can compare Company D's current stock price with other firms in the industry. Impressed with his plan, the team agrees to let him build the spreadsheet to complete the analysis required for the project.

### Exercise

The spreadsheet your teammate created is named ib_e04_groupproject. Look at the data in this spreadsheet. Would you be comfortable submitting this file to your professor for your team grade? Consider the following points.

1. Look at the data on the Company D Analysis worksheet. Does the data appear to make sense?

2. Test-drive the spreadsheet. Your teammate explained that the Year in cell C3 and the Stock Symbol in cell C9 can be changed. In addition, you will see the values that are available to enter on the right of these cell locations. When you change the Year and Stock Symbol, does the data still make sense?

3. What method is your teammate using to show the data in cells C4:C6 and C10:C11? Do these methods appear to be entered correctly?

4. How many worksheets does this workbook contain? What will you need to do to check the accuracy of the data appearing in the Company D Analysis worksheet?

What's wrong with this spreadsheet? Write a short answer to each of the questions listed here. Then fix any errors you discover in the Company D Analysis worksheet.

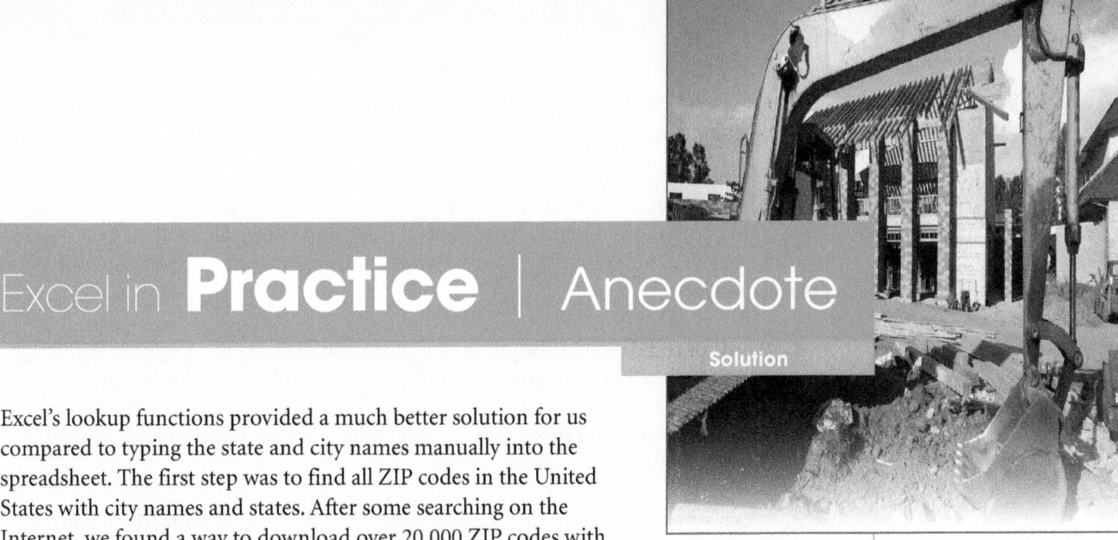


iStockphoto.com

Excel's lookup functions provided a much better solution for us compared to typing the state and city names manually into the spreadsheet. The first step was to find all ZIP codes in the United States with city names and states. After some searching on the Internet, we found a way to download over 20,000 ZIP codes with state and town names included. Once we had this data in a separate worksheet, our problem was essentially solved. A few seconds later we had the states and city names in our worksheet for every ZIP code.

## Assignment

1. Open the file named ib_e04_newstorestrategy. This is a small subset of data similar to what was described in the anecdote.
2. Use this data to create a spreadsheet that will evaluate potential locations for new stores. You will need to add formulas, functions, and formats.
3. Your spreadsheet should include the following:
   a. Add the city and state for each ZIP code listed on the Potential Locations worksheet. You can find a master list of several ZIP codes, states, and cities on the Zip Codes worksheet.
   b. Add a column that shows if a ZIP code has a high population of children and a low number of competitors. High child population is anything greater than or equal to 30% of children population over total population. Low competitors is if a ZIP code has less than or equal to two competitors.
   c. Add a column that shows what ZIP codes would qualify as being potential locations for a new store. A potential location is any ZIP code that has high children and low competition, or an average household income greater than $50,000. However, a ZIP code cannot be considered for a new store if it has more than five competitors.
4. Show ZIP codes that qualify as potential locations for new stores on a separate worksheet. Assume this will be presented to the president of the company. Create a way to summarize this data on another worksheet so you can start off the presentation with highlights of your analysis.

## Questions for Discussion

1. Why is it important to know alternative ways of calculating and manipulating data?
2. The anecdote mentioned that ZIP codes were downloaded from the Internet. What other sources are available on the Internet that could be used for the project described in the anecdote (i.e., population statistics, household income, number of household)?

# Review Questions

The following questions are related to the concepts addressed in this chapter. There are three types of questions: Short Answer, True or False, and Fill in the Blank. If your answer to a True or False question is False, write a short explanation as to why you think the statement is not true.

1. Words or text data must be put in _______ when defining the output of the _______ function as well as the logical tests of the _______ and _______ functions.
2. Explain why commas should not be used when entering numbers for the logical test argument of the **IF** function.
3. When you are using text data for either the **value_if_true** or **value_if_false** arguments of the **IF** function, the comma separating the arguments goes _______ the quotation marks.
4. What are the differences and similarities between financial functions and logical functions?
5. True or False: A spreadsheet cannot be sorted based on the output of an **IF** function.
6. True or False: The sequence of the logical tests in a nested **IF** function does not matter because the function will always evaluate all logical tests.
7. True or False: When you are creating a nested **IF** function, you can add logical tests without typing the function name **IF** and an open parenthesis.
8. Explain what you can do to make sure the logical tests of a nested **IF** function are in the appropriate sequence.
9. True or False: A nested **IF** function will not work if the logical tests are in the wrong sequence. An error code will appear telling you that something is wrong with the function.
10. What are the arguments of the **AND** function?
11. Briefly explain how the **AND** function works.
12. True or False: You do not need to use quotation marks when using text data with either an **OR** or **AND** function.
13. If only one of five logical tests in an **OR** function is False, the function will display the word ___________.
14. True or False: This function will test whether D7 is equal to the value in either C7, A7, or H7: =OR(D7 = C7,A7,H7).
15. What would you do to try to fix an #N/A error when using either the **VLookup** or **HLookup** functions?
16. What does the #REF! error mean?
17. When you are defining the column index number of the **VLookup** function, it is important to always count the first column as number _______.
18. Before pasting either a **VLookup** or an **HLookup** function, always check to see whether _______ are needed.

19. The range of cells used to define the table array of either a **VLookup** or an **HLookup** function must contain both the _______ and the _______ that is needed for the output.

20. True or False: You cannot use a **VLookup** function or an **HLookup** function to calculate data.

21. True or False: Lookup functions cannot be combined with logical functions.

22. True or False: When defining the **table_array** argument of either the **VLookup** or **HLookup** functions, you can just click another worksheet tab and highlight the range of cells needed.

23. True or False: Excel will always assume you need to find an exact match for the lookup value when using either a **VLookup** or an **HLookup** function.

24. What is the Range lookup argument used for in the either the **VLookup** or **HLookup** functions?

# Skills Exam

The following exam is designed to test your ability to recognize and execute the Excel skills presented in this chapter. Read each question carefully and answer the questions in the order they are listed. You should be able to complete this exam in 60 minutes or less.

1. Open the ib_e04_skillsexam file. All of the tasks listed in this exam should be executed in the Portfolio worksheet.
2. Use the **HLookup** function in cell C4 to display the minimum cash requirement. The function should look for the Risk Level code showing in cell C3 on the Portfolio worksheet in row 3 of the Investment Strategy worksheet. The minimum cash requirements are listed for each risk level in row 8.
3. Enter a formula in cell C6 that subtracts the minimum cash requirement in cell C4 from the current cash value in cell C5.
4. Use an **IF** function in cell A6 to determine if there is a shortage or surplus of cash. The function should display the message *Cash Surplus* if the value in cell C6 is greater than or equal to 0. Otherwise, the function should display the message *Cash Shortage.*
5. Enter a formula in cell E9 that calculates the value of the original investment. The formula should multiply the Shares Owned by the Purchase Price. Copy and paste this formula to cells E10:E15.
6. Use a **VLookup** function to calculate the Current Investment Value in cell F9. The function should look for the symbol in cell A9 of the Portfolio worksheet in column A of the Current Prices worksheet and determine what Current Price relates to that symbol. The result of the **VLookup** function should be multiplied by the Shares Owned in cell D9.
7. Copy the function in cell F9 and paste it into cells F10:F15.
8. Use an **IF** function to calculate the Dividend Value in cell H9. The function should check to see if cell G9 is greater than 0. If it is, then multiply cell G9 by D9. Otherwise, display the number 0.
9. Determine the Strategy in cell I9 by entering a nested **IF** function. The function should display the following outputs based on the criteria listed.

   If the dividend in cell G9 is greater than 0 *and* the Current Investment in cell F9 is greater than or equal to the Original Investment in cell E9, display the word *HOLD.*

   If the Current Investment in cell F9 is less than the Original Investment in cell E9 *or* the Current Investment is less than the Original Investment multiplied by 1.035, then display the word *SELL.*

   Otherwise, display the word *HOLD.*
10. Copy the function in cell I9 and paste it to cells I10:I15.
11. Enter a **SUM** function in cell D17 to add the values in the range D9:D15.
12. Copy the **SUM** function in cell D17 and paste it to cells E17 and F17.
13. Use the **Future Value** function in cell E23 to calculate the Target value of the portfolio in 20 years. This function should use cell C20 as the rate of return, C21 as the target payments to be made every year for the next 20 years, and F17 as the one-time lump sum payment. The function should calculate payments being made at the beginning of the period. Correct any ### signs if they appear.
14. Use your judgment in adding any formatting features that will enhance the visual appearance and readability of the spreadsheet.
15. Save and close your file.

# Challenge Questions

The following questions are designed to test your ability to apply the Excel skills you have learned to complete a business objective. Use your knowledge of Excel as well as your creativity to answer these questions. For most questions, there are several possible ways to complete the objective.

1. Open the spreadsheet named ib_e04_frequentshopper. Use a nested **IF** function to complete the Customer Reward column. The output and criteria of the function are listed below.

   - **Welcome & Thanks 30% Off**: This reward is given to customers who spent $0 last year and the number of years purchasing is less than one.
   - **Please Come Back 50% Off**: This reward is given to customers who have been purchasing from the store for more than one year but have not made a purchase in the past 12 months.
   - **Thanks for Being Loyal 25% Off**: This reward is given to customers who have been making purchases for more than two years or spent more than $1,000 last year.
   - **Customer Appreciation 10% Off**: This reward is given to any customer who does not meet the criteria of the other three rewards.

2. Open the spreadsheet named ib_e04_competitoranalysis. This is the same spreadsheet that was used for the video workshop. Edit this spreadsheet so that the **HLookup** function can be created in cell C3 and then copied and pasted to cells C4:C8. Your revised spreadsheet should have the same appearance as the original. Hint: Cell locations should be used for every argument of the function except for the range lookup.

3. Open the file named ib_e04_investmentstrategy. This file was used for the exercise in the **VLookup** function section. How would you modify this file such that the financial planner can override any of the proposed investments in cells C7:C9?

# Presenting Information with Charts

## Chapter Goals

Presenting data and information is a common and often critical routine for most business managers. Although Excel worksheets are useful for tracking, reporting, calculating, and analyzing data, they are typically ineffective for presenting business data and information to an audience. As a result, most business managers rely on charts when preparing and delivering presentations. This chapter illustrates a variety of charts available in Excel and demonstrates how business managers use them to study and communicate key information and trends.

## >> Excel | Skill Sets

| | |
|---|---|
| **Creating Charts** | Column Charts (Data Comparisons)<br>Stacked Column Charts (Percent to Total Over Time)<br>Line Charts (Trends Over Time)<br>Pie Charts (Percent to Total) |
| **Formatting Charts** | Titles and Legends<br>Plot Area and Data Series<br>X- and Y-Axes Labels<br>Adding Annotations and Objects |
| **Advanced Chart Options** | Defining the X- and Y-Axes Manually<br>The Scatter Plot Chart<br>Pasting Charts into PowerPoint and Word |

SuperStock, Inc

# Excel in Practice | Anecdote

## My Role as a Consultant

You may *think* that, after you've completed hours of intense research and analysis related to a project, the hard work is over. However, in reality, how you present your findings is just as critical as the quality of the information you present. I learned this lesson quickly when I first began working as a consultant. My primary responsibility was to analyze the performance of a client's business and compare it with other companies within that industry. My results then served as a basis for developing recommendations on ways my clients could improve or grow their business. Although I had piles of written documents to support my findings, my main forum for sharing this information was in front of an audience of business owners or head managers at meetings called progress reviews. These people had busy schedules and little time. The pressure to deliver an accurate, appropriate, and efficient presentation was always an intense challenge.

>> Continued later in this chapter

# Creating Charts

Skill Set

This section will illustrate one of two methods for creating charts in Excel. If you are working with data that is arranged in adjacent columns or rows, you can use Excel to automatically assign values to the X- and Y-axes of a chart. In these situations, you can simply highlight a range of cells before selecting the chart you wish to create. This section will use this method to illustrate four basic charts commonly used by business managers: column charts, stacked column charts, line charts, and pie charts.

## Column Charts (Data Comparisons)

The ***column chart*** is the most common chart type used to present business data and is most useful when making comparisons. For example, it can compare the earnings of companies within an industry, sales projections for a new business, or the sales growth of product categories. The column chart can compare data at a specific point in time or show how this comparison changes over a period of time. Figure 1 shows four years' worth of data for a hypothetical car manufacturer. The example demonstrates the construction of a column chart that compares the sales for each automobile class in the year 2006. Then a second column chart will show how the sales for each auto class changes over a four-year period.

Figure 1 | **Automobile Sales Data**

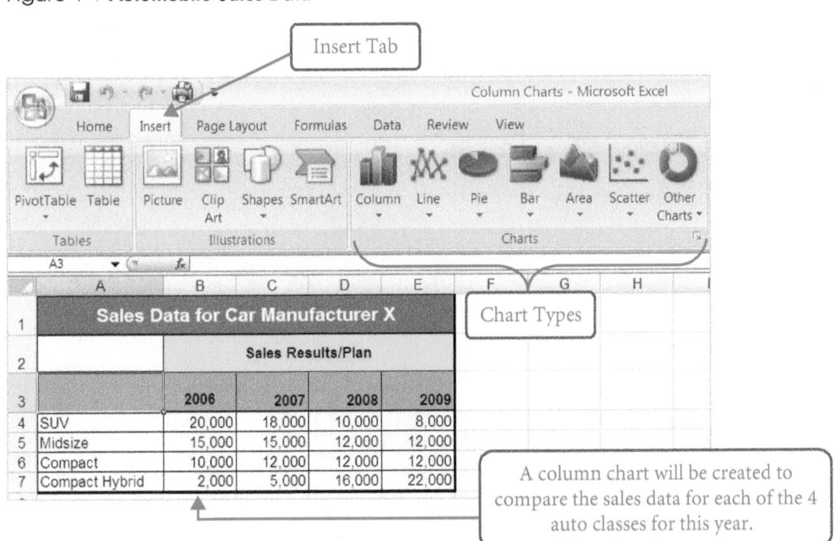


| Sales Data for Car Manufacturer X | | | | |
|---|---|---|---|---|
| | Sales Results/Plan | | | |
| | 2006 | 2007 | 2008 | 2009 |
| SUV | 20,000 | 18,000 | 10,000 | 8,000 |
| Midsize | 15,000 | 15,000 | 12,000 | 12,000 |
| Compact | 10,000 | 12,000 | 12,000 | 12,000 |
| Compact Hybrid | 2,000 | 5,000 | 16,000 | 22,000 |

Creating a chart in Excel typically involves the following five steps:

- *Identify the data that will be used to define the X- and Y-axes values.* This section will demonstrate examples in which the data used to define the X- and Y-axes are in a contiguous range. Therefore, you can highlight a range of cells before selecting a chart type.
- *Select a chart type.* Figure 1 shows the chart types available in the **Insert** tab on the Ribbon.
- *Select a chart format.* For each chart type, Excel provides a variety of format options. These options establish the arrangement of data and visual appearance of a chart.
- *Specify a location.* When a chart is initially created, it will be embedded in the worksheet that is currently activated. You can then move the chart to another

worksheet or create a new worksheet that is dedicated for the chart, which is known as a ***chart sheet.***

- *Add or adjust the chart and axis titles.* A chart will not contain proper titles for the X- and Y-axes when it is initially created. You must add or adjust them after creating the chart.

This example creates a column chart to compare the 2006 sales by automobile class from Figure 1. The following points explain how to create this chart:

- Highlight the range A3:B7 on the worksheet shown in Figure 1. The data in this range will define the values for the X- and Y-axes of the chart.
- Click the **Insert** tab on the Ribbon.
- Select a chart type by clicking the **Column** icon on the Ribbon (see Figure 2).
- Select a chart format by clicking the **Clustered Column** option under the **2-D Column** heading (see Figure 2). After you select this option, the column chart will appear in the worksheet that is currently active.

Figure 2 shows the selections that were made to create a two-dimensional column chart. Excel provides a variety of format options for creating a column chart. Some options give the chart a three-dimensional appearance, and others change the shape of the columns to cylinders, cones, or pyramids. In addition, selecting an option called **All Chart Types** at the bottom of the format list opens the **Create Chart** dialog box, which provides access to every chart type and format available in Excel. Use this as an alternative method for selecting a chart type and format. After you select the chart format from either the list shown in Figure 2 or the dialog box shown in Figure 3, the chart will appear in the worksheet that is currently active.

Figure 2 | **Selecting a Chart Type and Format**

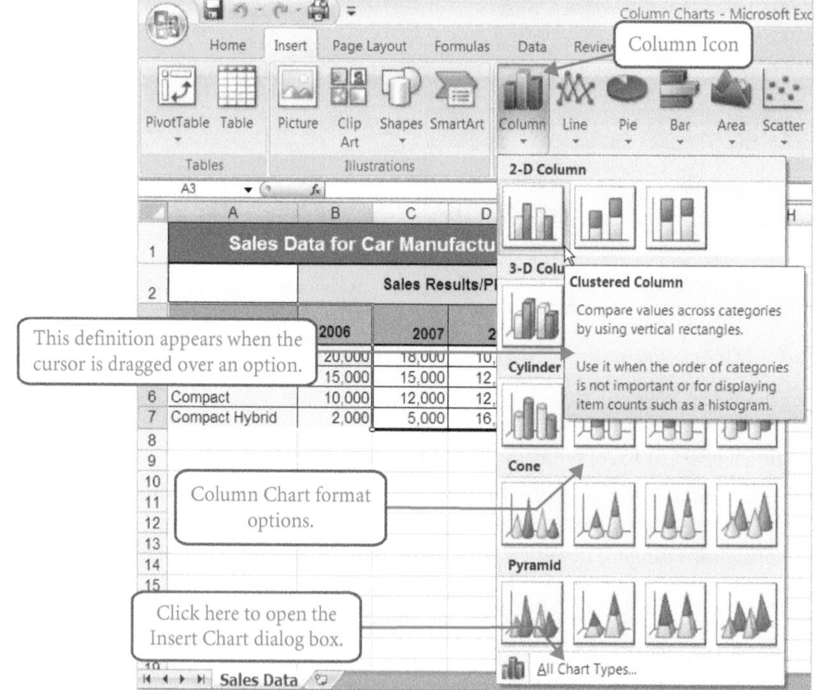

Figure 3 | **Create Chart Dialog Box**

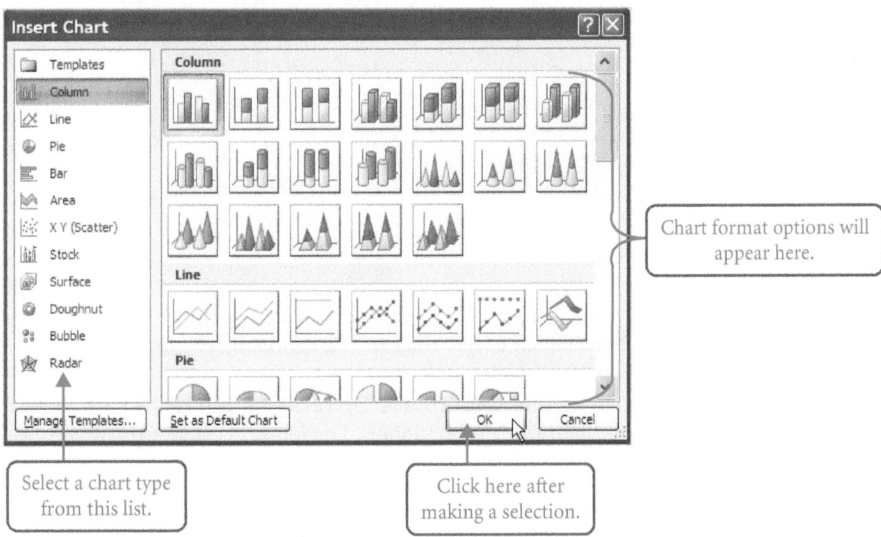


Figure 4 shows the column chart created to display the sales of each automobile class from Figure 1. This is known as an ***embedded chart*** because it appears within a worksheet that could also contain other data. After embedding the chart in a worksheet, you can move it on that worksheet by clicking and dragging the chart frame. You then can adjust the size of the chart by clicking and dragging on any of the dotted areas on the frame, which are also known as ***sizing handles***. Notice that a new set of tabs

Figure 4 | **Embedded Column Chart**

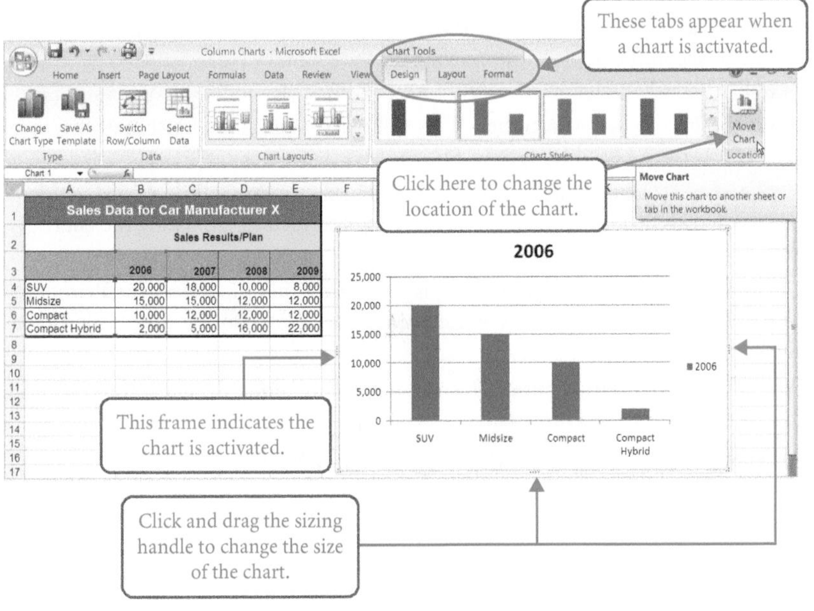

## COMMON MISTAKES | Activating a Chart to Use Chart Tools

You must activate a chart to be able to see the **Chart Tools** tabs on the Ribbon. People often make the mistake of going back to the **Insert** tab on the Ribbon to find the **Chart Tools** commands. However, the commands in the **Insert** tab are used only to create a chart. The **Chart Tools** tabs will appear on the upper-right side of the Ribbon only when a chart is active. To activate a chart, click anywhere inside its border. A frame will appear around the chart when it is active, as shown in Figure 4.

called ***Chart Tools*** has been added to the Ribbon. The commands contained in this new set of tabs will be used to complete this chart.

After creating charts, you can adjust them as necessary by using the **Chart Tools** tabs that are added to the right side of the Ribbon. The following steps explain how to change the location, change the chart title, and add the X- and Y-axes titles:

- Activate the chart by clicking it. A chart is activated when a frame appears around its perimeter, as shown in Figure 4.
- Click the **Move Chart** icon in the **Design** tab of the **Chart Tools** set of tabs on the Ribbon (see Figure 4). This will open the **Move Chart** dialog box.
- Click the **New Sheet** option in the **Move Chart** dialog box and type the name **`Auto Sales 2006`** in the box next to this option (see Figure 5). Then click the **OK** button at the bottom of the dialog box. This will place the chart in a dedicated worksheet called a chart sheet with the tab name Auto Sales 2006.
- Activate the chart title at the top of the chart by clicking it once. Then click a second time at the beginning of the title to place the cursor in front of the first number of the year 2006 (see Figure 6). This will allow you to change or type a new chart title. For this example, the title is changed to Unit Sales by Auto Class 2006.
- Click the **Layout** tab in the **Chart Tools** set of tabs on the Ribbon and click the **Axis Titles** icon. Then place the cursor over the **Primary Horizontal Axis Title** option. This will open a set of options for placing a title along the X-axis.
- Select the **Title Below Axis** option. This will place a box at the bottom of the ***X-axis*** that can be used for typing a title.
- Type **`Auto Class`** in the X-axis title box. The method for adding or adjusting the title in this box is identical to the method described for adjusting the chart title.
- Click the **Axis Titles** icon again, but this time, place the cursor over the **Primary Vertical Axis Title** option. This will show a list of options for placing a title along the Y-axis.
- Select the **Rotated Title** option. This will place a box along the left side of the ***Y-axis*** that can be used for typing a title.
- Type **`Sales in Units`** in the Y-axis title box. The method for adding or adjusting the title in this box is identical to the method described for the chart title.

Figure 5 | **Move Chart Dialog Box**

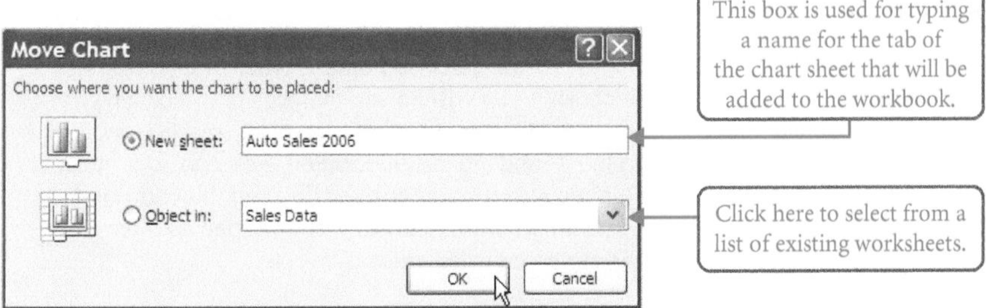


Figure 6 shows the adjustment that was made to the chart title. Notice the dots that appear on each corner of the chart title box. They indicate that the title box is activated. Also, notice that the cursor was placed in front of the year 2006 by clicking a second time. This method is also used for adjusting the X- and Y-axes titles.

Figure 6 | **Adjusting the Title of a Chart**

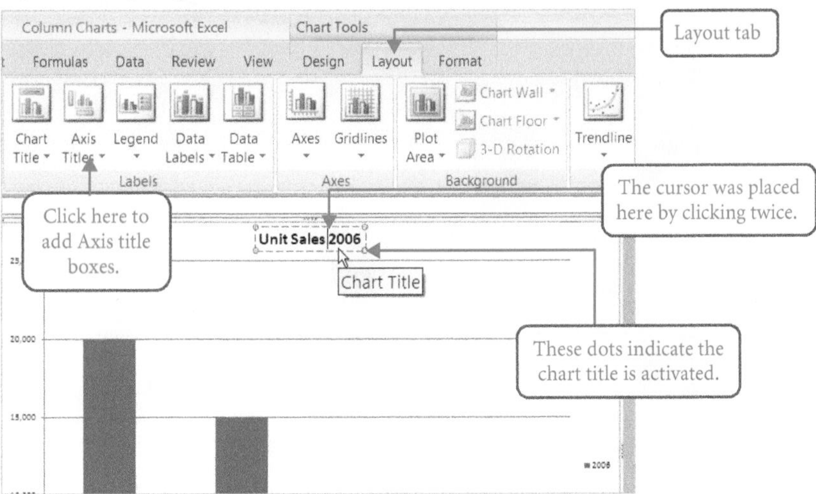


Figure 7 shows the completed column chart using the automobile sales data from Figure 1. The reader of this chart can immediately see that SUVs generated the most unit sales compared to the other three auto classes in the year 2006. Notice that the bars appear on the chart in order from tallest to shortest. The reason is that the values in column B of Figure 1 are sorted in descending order.

## COMMON MISTAKES | Sorting Data for a Column Chart

The order of the bars on a column chart will be based on the order of the values on the worksheet used to create the chart. If you wish to see the bars on a column chart in height sequence (tallest to shortest or shortest to tallest) you must sort the range of cells that contain values defining the X- and Y-axes. In addition, *you can sort this data after the chart is created.* People often make the mistake of deleting the chart and re-creating it if the bars are not in a desirable sequence. However, the sequence of the bars will change if the data is sorted after the chart is created.

Figure 7 | **Final Column Chart for the Car Manufacturer Sales Data**

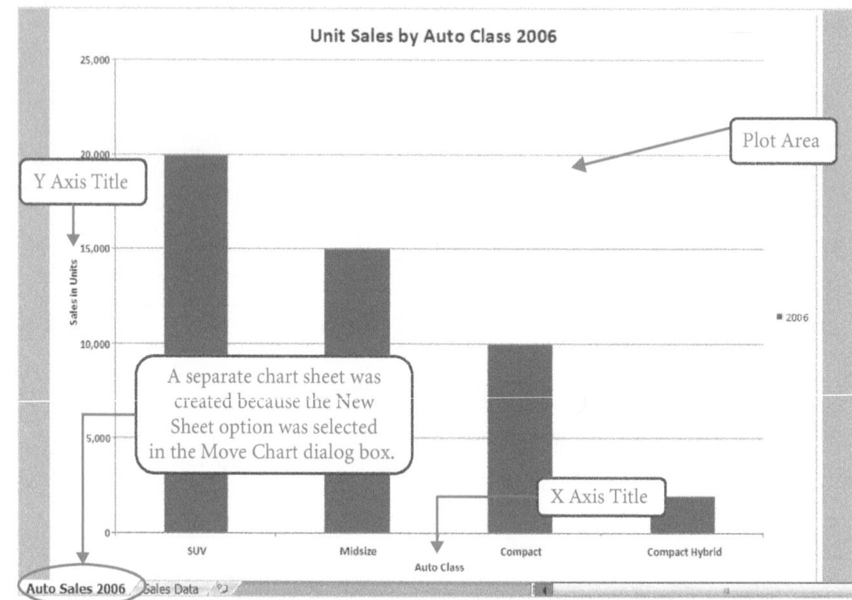


Figure 8 shows the second chart created using the worksheet shown in Figure 1. The purpose of this chart is to show how the sales comparison of each auto class changes over time. The method used to create this chart is identical to the first column chart shown in Figure 4. However, the range A3:E7 was highlighted before creating the chart. This range includes all the values for each auto class for the years 2006 through 2009. Notice how Excel automatically adjusted the X-axis and the ***chart legend***. Instead of placing each auto class on the X-axis (see Figure 7), Excel shows each year. As a result, each bar on the chart represents a different auto class. The legend shows which color corresponds to the appropriate auto class. In addition, an alternate chart style was selected from the **Design** tab on the Ribbon to enhance the colors of each bar in the chart. The next section covers some additional formatting features that can be used to enhance the appearance of a chart.

Figure 8 | **Second Column Chart Showing a Four-Year Sales Comparison**

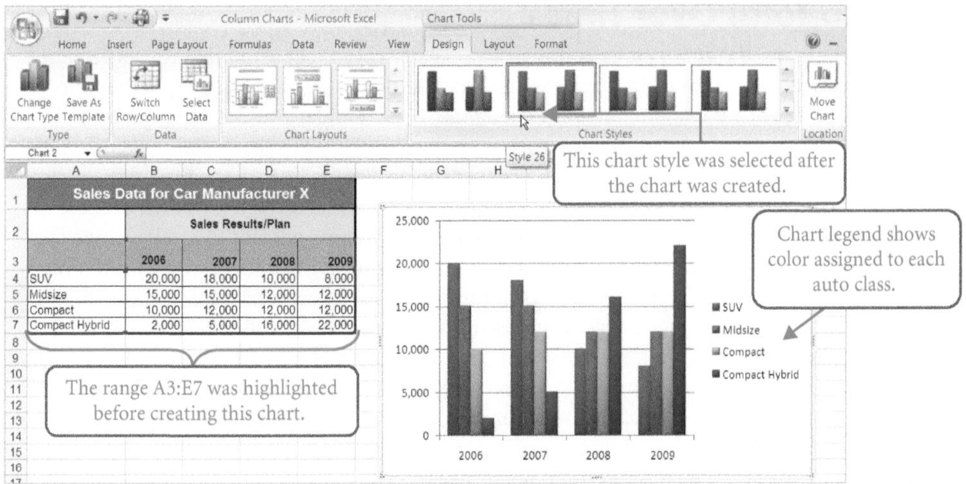


Figure 9 shows the final version of the second column chart. The method used to place this chart in a separate worksheet, or chart sheet, along with the addition of axis titles, is identical to that used for the first column chart shown in Figure 7. The chart title was added by selecting **Centered Overlay Title** from the **Chart Title** icon in the **Layout** tab of the **Chart Tools** section on the Ribbon. This places the title over the ***plot area*** of the chart. The reader of this chart can quickly see a shift in the projected sales of the car manufacturer's product line. In the year 2006, the SUV class dominates the other three auto classes in unit sales. However, by the year 2009 the Compact Hybrid is expected to become the dominant class in unit sales. The chart also shows a small decrease in the Midsize line of cars, while the Compact line of cars remains mostly consistent over the four-year period. A business manager can use this chart to visually show how the product sales of the company are expected to change over time.

Figure 9 | **Final Column Chart Showing Four-Year Automobile Sales Comparison**

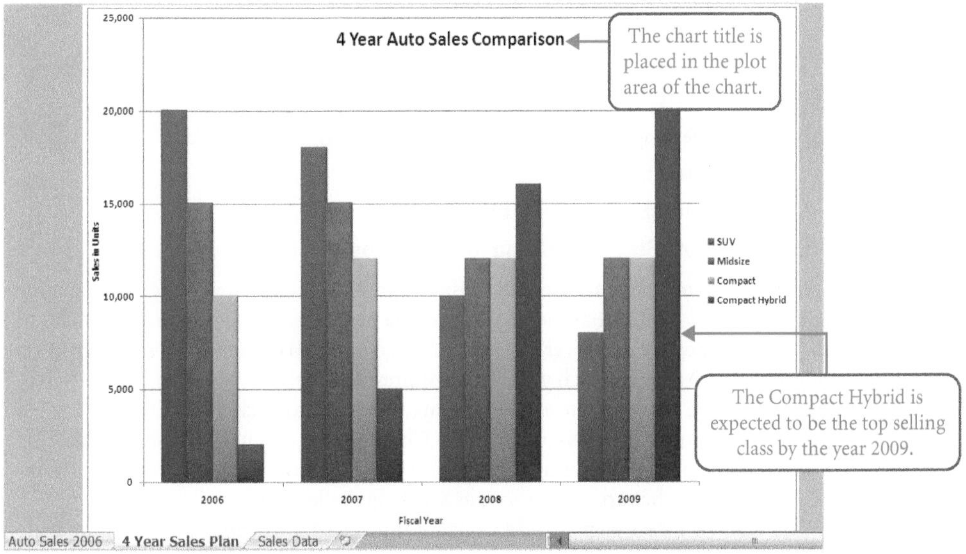

## Stacked Column Charts (Percent to Total Over Time)

The ***stacked column chart*** is similar to a regular column chart in that it uses vertical bars to display data. However, the stacked column chart shows the proportion or percentage each category contributes to a total. For example, a stacked column chart can be used to show the percentage each division contributes to the overall sales of a large corporation, the percentage each product category represents to the total sales of an industry, or the market share percent by company for an industry. In each of these cases, the stacked column chart can also show how these percent to totals change over time. Figure 10 shows hypothetical data for the Sporting Goods Industry for the years 1990 and 2000. The 100% Stacked Column format option is selected to show the percentage each product category represents to the total sales of the Sporting Goods industry between the years 1990 and 2000. Looking at the data in Figure 10, you will notice that sales have increased for each product category. However, this chart will show how the *rate* of sales growth for each product category has changed over time.

Figure 10 | **Hypothetical Sales Data for the Sporting Goods Industry**

Select this option to create a 100% Stacked Column chart.

| Sporting Goods Industry Sales (in Billions) | | |
|---|---|---|
| | 1990 | 2000 |
| Equipment | $14.2 | $26.3 |
| Footwear | $10.9 | $14.8 |
| Clothing | $10.1 | $11.2 |

Product categories for the Sporting Goods Industry

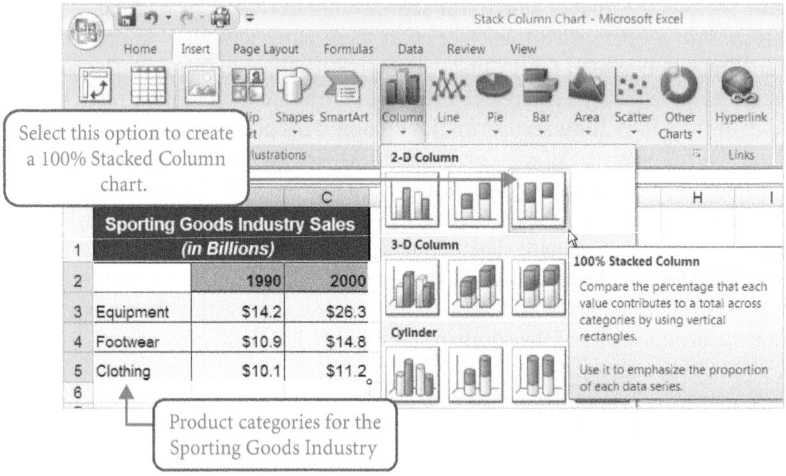

The following points explain how a 100% Stacked Column Chart is created using the data from Figure 10:

- Highlight the range A2:C5 in the worksheet shown in Figure 10.
- Click the **Insert** tab on the Ribbon.
- Click the **Column** chart type icon.
- Click the **100% Stacked Column** format option, as shown in Figure 10.

Figure 11 shows the initial result of the column chart, which was created using the data in Figure 10. Notice that each bar shows the percentage each year represents for each product category. However, the goal of this chart is to compare the sales percent of each product category for each year. This requires that the year is shown on the X-axis as opposed to the product category. Therefore, you need to click the **Switch Row/Column** icon in the **Design** tab of the **Chart Tools** area on the Ribbon. This places the years that are currently displayed in the legend on the X-axis and places the product categories that are shown on the X-axis in the legend.

The following steps explain additional options used to complete the column chart that was started in Figure 11:

- Click the **Layout** tab of the **Chart Tools** section on the Ribbon.
- Click the **Data Table** icon (see Figure 12) and select the **Show Data Table with Legend Keys** option. This will place a table at the bottom of the chart showing the

Figure 11 | **Initial Result of the 100% Stacked Column Chart**

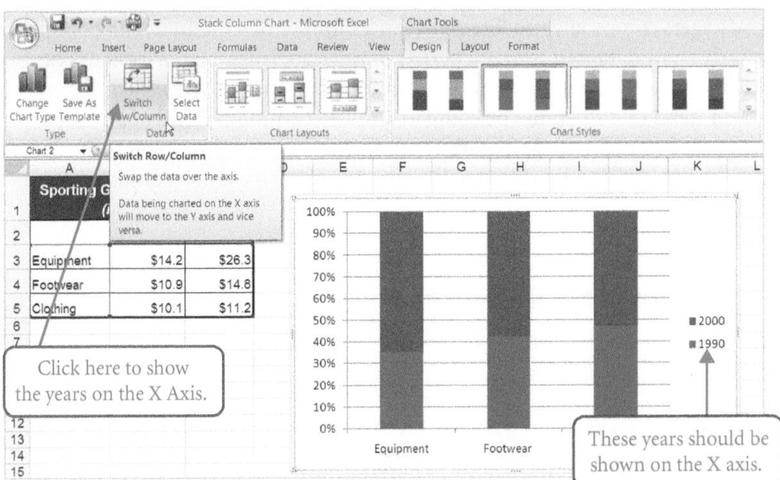


dollar values for each product category. In addition, the legend showing which color corresponds to each product category will be included in the table.

- Click the **Legend** icon.
- Select the **None** option. This will remove the legend that is shown on the right side of the chart in Figure 11. As shown in Figure 12, the data table that was added to the bottom of the chart shows which color corresponds to each product category. Therefore, the legend on the right side of the chart is not needed.

Figure 12 shows the final 100% Stacked Column chart. By looking at the Y-axis, you can see how the percentage each product represents to the total sales of the industry changes from 1990 to the year 2000. Notice that the "Equipment" category represents 40% of the industry's sales in 1990 and grows to 50% in the year 2000. The "Footwear" category is approximately the same at 30% in 1990 and 2000. However, the "Clothing" category declines from approximately 30% of the industry's sales in 1990 to 20% in 2000. Product and/or marketing managers typically conduct this type of analysis to identify what areas of an industry present the best opportunities for growth.

Figure 12 | **Final 100% Stacked Column Chart**

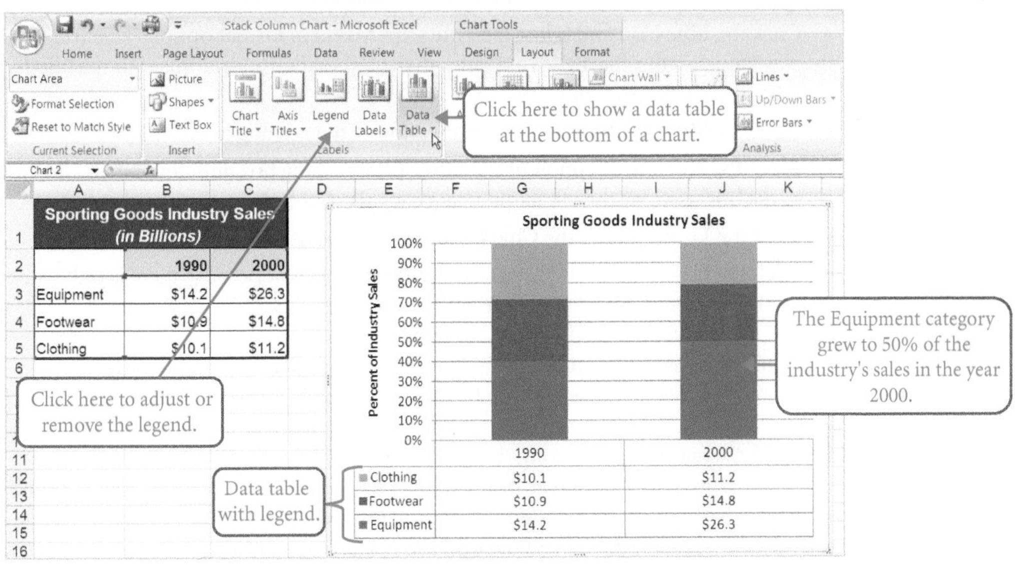

## Line Charts (Trends Over Time)

Business managers commonly use ***line charts*** in a number of situations. For example, they effectively show data trends over a period of time, such as changes in stocks or stock market averages. Line charts are also great tools to compare trends. For example, the 12-month trend of a stock can be compared to the 12-month trend of an index like the Dow Jones Industrial Average. Figure 13 shows data for the Dow Jones Industrial Average for the year 2004. A line chart will be used to show the adjusted closing price for each month.

Figure 13 | **2004 Adjusted Average Close of the Dow Jones**

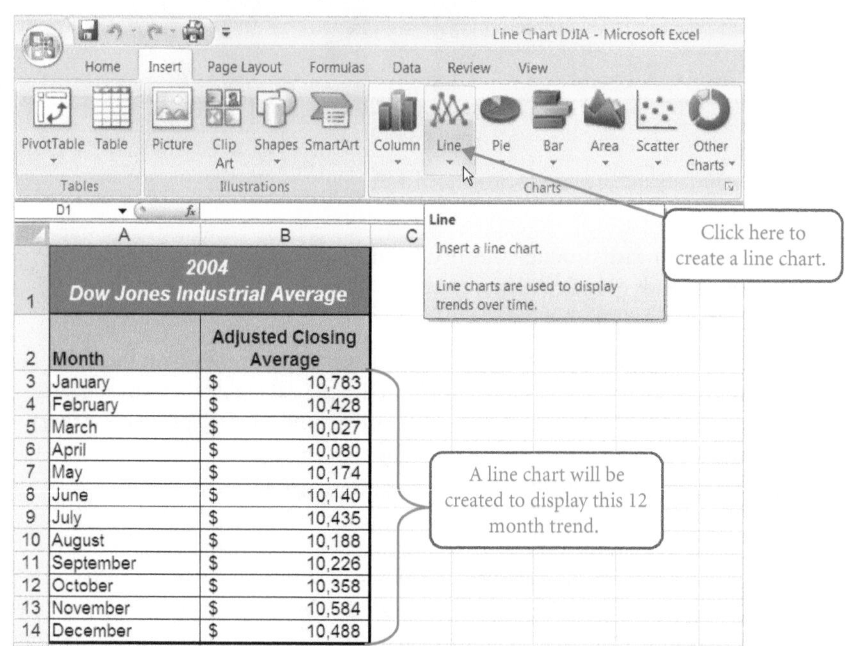


The following points explain how to create a line chart using the data in Figure 13:

- Highlight the range A2:B14. Then click the **Insert** tab on the Ribbon.
- Click the **Line** icon and select the **Line with Markers** format option. This will display a line on the chart with a diamond-shaped marker indicating each specific value from column B in Figure 13.
- Click the **Move Chart** icon to open the **Move Chart** dialog box.
- Select the **New sheet** option in the **Move Chart** dialog box and type **`DJIA 2004`** in the box used for the tab name. Then click the **OK** button.
- Click the **Layout** tab in the **Chart Tools** set of tabs on the Ribbon.
- Click the **Legend** icon and then select the **None** option. Because there is only one line of data on this chart, the legend is not needed.

Figure 14 shows the completed line chart, which displays the trend of the Dow Jones Industrial Average in 2004. The title for this chart was adjusted and a title for the Y-axis was added. The reader of this line chart can immediately see how the Dow Jones Industrial Average trended during the year 2004. The chart clearly shows a significant drop in the beginning of the year from January to March. With the exception of a spike in the month of July, there is a gradual increase for the remainder of the year. However, the chart shows that the Dow Jones ended the year a few hundred points lower than the beginning.

Figure 14 | **Line Chart Showing the Adjusted Average Close of the Dow Jones in 2004**

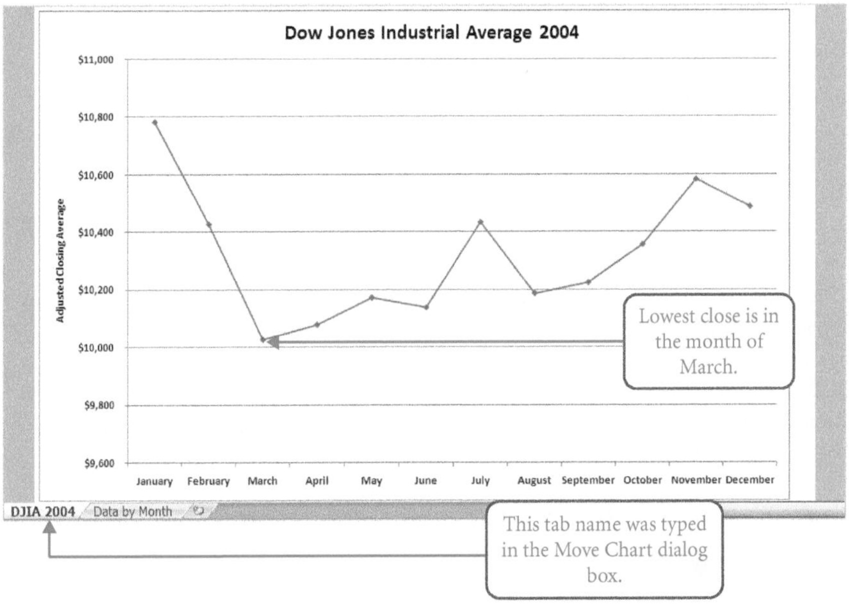

## Pie Charts (Percent to Total)

The ***pie chart*** is the last chart demonstrated in this section. Similar to the stacked column chart, the pie chart shows a percent to total comparison for various data categories. However, unlike the stacked column chart, the pie chart is not effective in showing a percent to total change over time. It is mostly used to show how several components make up a total for one specific point in time. For example, a business manager might use a pie chart to show the percentage each asset category contributes to the total startup costs for a business. Examples of asset categories are Land, Machines, Office Supplies, Automobiles, and so on. An example of this data is shown in Figure 15.

Figure 15 | **Startup Costs for a Business**

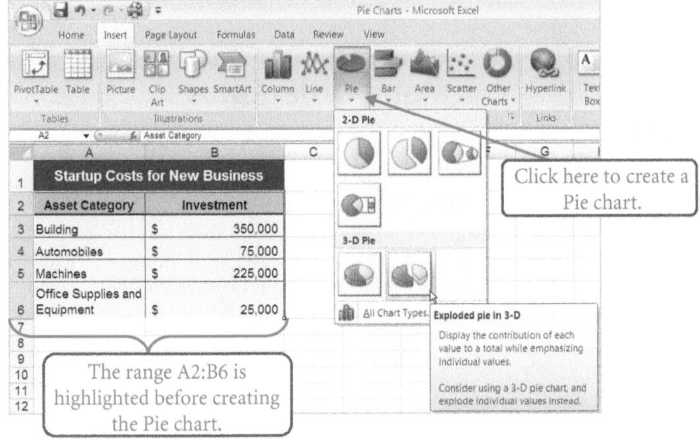

The following points explain how to create a pie chart to visually show the percentage each asset category in column A in Figure 15 represents to the total startup costs of the business:

- Highlight the range A2:B6 in the worksheet shown in Figure 15. Then click the **Insert** tab on the Ribbon.
- Click the **Pie** icon and then click the **Exploded pie in 3-D** format option, as shown in Figure 15. This will produce a three-dimensional view of the pie chart and slightly separate each section from the center of the chart. This view will enhance the visual display showing the amount each investment represents to the total.
- Click the chart title and change the title to Startup Costs.

Figure 16 shows the initial setup of the pie chart. Notice that a legend appears on the right side of the chart. Pie charts typically show the category name next to each wedge of the pie chart. A legend could be used in cases in which several categories are displayed in a pie chart. However, adding too many categories to a pie chart can make it difficult or impossible to see any relationships to the total. A pie chart is typically used to show a maximum of 10 to 12 categories.

Figure 16 | **Initial Setup of the Pie Chart**

| Startup Costs for New Business | |
|---|---|
| Asset Category | Investment |
| Building | $ 350,000 |
| Automobiles | $ 75,000 |
| Machines | $ 225,000 |
| Office Supplies and Equipment | $ 25,000 |

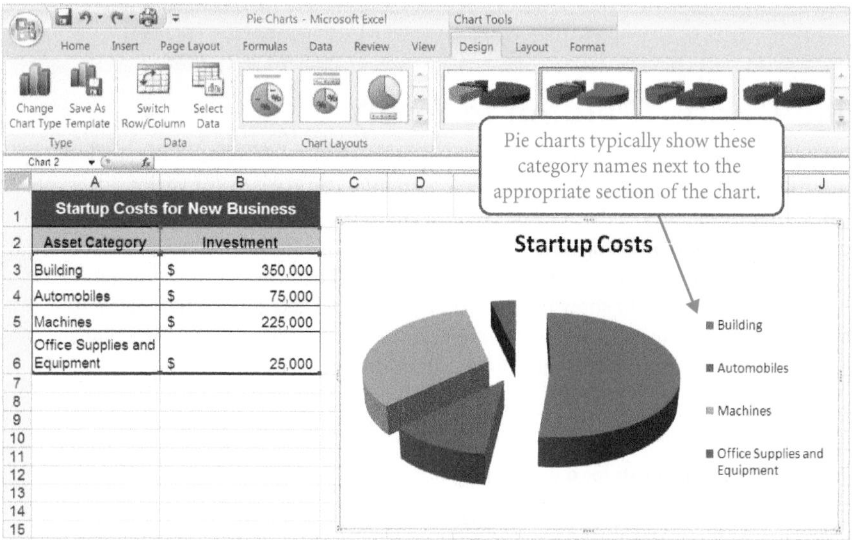

## COMMON MISTAKES | Too Many Categories for a Pie Chart

The most common mistake people make when creating pie charts is trying to add too many categories. A pie chart can typically show a maximum of 10 to 12 categories. As the number of categories added to a pie chart exceeds 12, it becomes increasingly difficult to determine what each category represents to the total. If you need to create a chart with more than 12 categories, consider using a column chart or create subgroups that represent multiple categories.

The following points explain how to show each Asset Category shown in the legend of Figure 16 next to each section of the pie chart:

- Click the **Layout** tab in the **Chart Tools** set of tabs on the Ribbon.
- Click the **Legend** icon and select the **None** option. Because the category name will be placed next to each section of the chart, the legend is not needed.
- Click the **Data Labels** icon and select the **More Data Label Options** (see Figure 17). This will open the **Format Data Labels** dialog box.

- In the **Format Data Labels** dialog box, click the box next to the **Value** option to remove the green check. Then click the box next to the **Category name** option to add a green check (see Figure 18).
- Click the **Outside End** option and then click the **Close** button at the bottom of the **Format Data Labels** dialog box. This will add the category labels next to each section of the pie chart. You can adjust the position of these labels by clicking and dragging.

Figures 17 and 18 show how to open the **Format Data Labels** dialog box. Notice the settings in the **Format Data Labels** dialog box in Figure 18.

Figure 17 | **Opening the Format Data Labels Dialog Box**

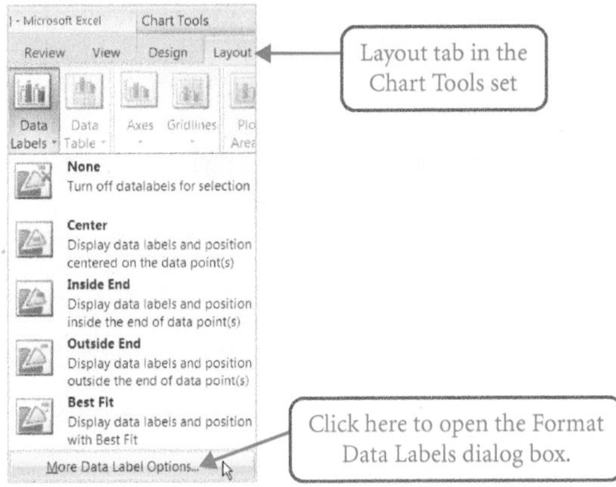


Figure 18 | **Settings in the Format Data Labels Dialog Box**

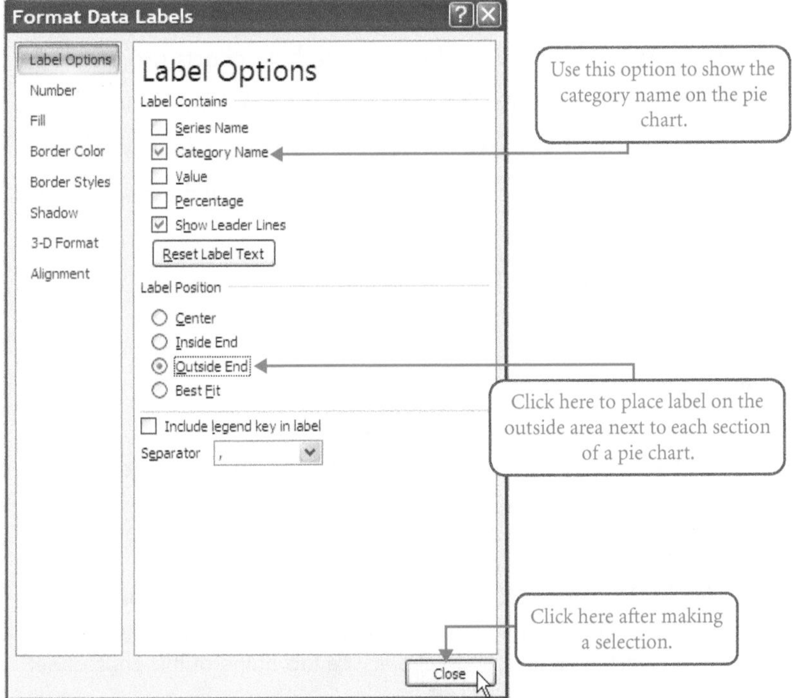


Figures 19 shows the final pie chart, which is embedded in a worksheet. A business manager can use this chart to demonstrate that most of the startup costs for this business will be dedicated to the Building and Machines asset categories. Notice how each section of the pie chart is separated or pulled away from the center. This makes it easier to see the proportion each section represents to the total. The reader of this chart can easily see that the cost of the Building represents a little over 50% of the total startup costs for this business.

>> **Quick Reference**

**Creating Charts**

1. Highlight a range of cells that contain values that will be used to define the X- and Y-axes of the chart.
2. Click the **Insert** tab on the Ribbon.
3. Click one of the **Chart Type** icons in the **Charts** group on the Ribbon.
4. Select a chart format option based on the needs of your project and the desired visual appearance.
5. Click the **Switch Row/Column** icon (in the **Design** tab) if the data on the X- and Y-axes needs to be reversed.
6. Click the **Move Chart** icon (in the **Design** tab) to move the chart to another existing worksheet or place the chart in a separate chart sheet.
7. Click the **Layout** tab in the **Chart Tools** section on the Ribbon and click the **Chart Title** and/or **Axis Titles** icons to add or adjust boxes for the chart title or axis titles.
8. After adding a title box to the chart, click it twice to type a new title or description.

Figure 19 | **Final Pie Chart**

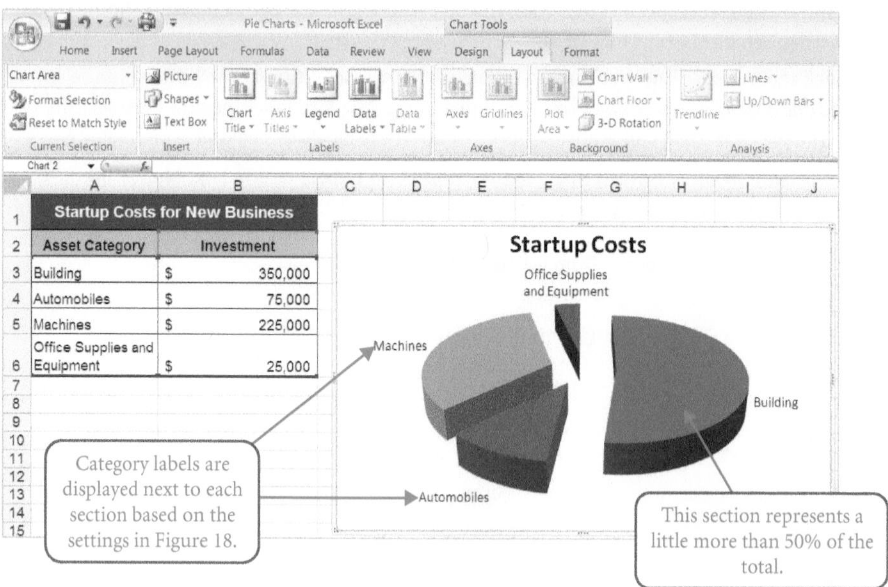


**VIDEO WORKSHOP**

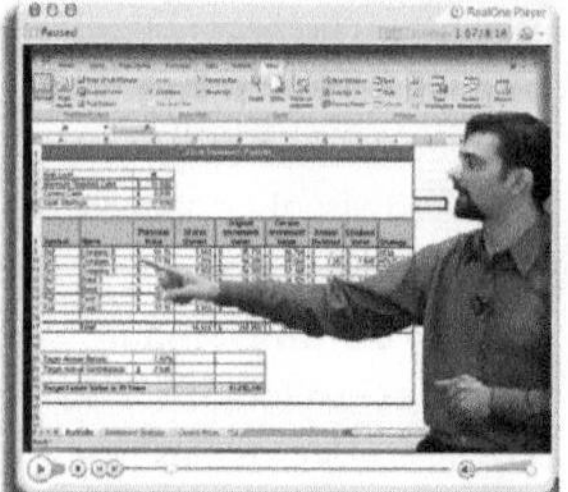

## >> Creating Charts

The purpose of this workshop is to demonstrate how charts are created in Excel. I will be demonstrating the tasks in this workshop in the following four videos: **Column Charts**, **Stacked Column Charts**, **Line Charts**, and **Pie Charts**. Each video name appears at the beginning of each section of tasks. Open the file named ib_e05_chartsforbusiness before starting this workshop. Try completing the tasks on your own and then watch the video.

1. **Column Charts (Video: Column Charts)**
   a. Activate the worksheet named Auto Sales Data.
   b. Highlight the range A3:E7 and then click the **Insert** tab on the Ribbon.
   c. Click the **Column** icon and select the two-dimensional **Clustered Column** format option.
   d. Select **Style 34** from the **Chart Style** options found in the **Design** tab.
   e. Use the **Move Chart** icon in the **Design** tab on the Ribbon to the move the column chart to its own chart sheet. The tab name of this chart sheet should be **`4 Year Sales Plan`**.
   f. Click the **Chart Title** icon in the **Layout** tab on the Ribbon to add a title box to the chart. Select the **Above Chart** option.
   g. Click the chart title box and change the title to **`4 Year Auto Sales Comparison`**.
   h. Using the **Axis Titles** icon, add a title box to the X- and Y-axes. For the Y-, or vertical, axis, select the **Rotated Title** option.

i. Click the X-axis title box twice and change the title to `Fiscal Year`.
j. Click the Y-axis title box twice and change the title to `Sales in Units`.

2. **Stacked Column Charts (Video: Stacked Column Charts)**
   a. Activate the worksheet named Industry Sales.
   b. Highlight the range A2:C5 and then click the **Insert** tab on the Ribbon.
   c. Click the **Column** icon and select the **100% Stacked Column** format option.
   d. Click the **Switch Row/Column** icon in the **Design** tab on the Ribbon to show the years on the X-axis instead of the product categories.
   e. Select **Style 10** from the **Chart Style** options found in the **Design** tab.
   f. Remove the legend on the chart by clicking the **Legend** icon in the **Layout** tab on the Ribbon and select the **None** option.
   g. Move the chart so the upper-left corner is in cell E2 by clicking and dragging the frame.
   h. Place a data table at the bottom of the chart by clicking the **Data Table** icon and selecting the **Show Data Table with Legend Keys** option.
   i. Increase the size of the chart by clicking and dragging the bottom sizing handle to the bottom of row 20. Then click and drag the right sizing handle to the right side of column N.
   j. Add a chart title `Sporting Goods Industry Sales`. Use the **Above Chart** option in the **Chart Title** icon.
   k. Add a title to the Y-axis `Percent of Industry Sales`. Use the **Rotated Title** option from the **Axis Title** icon.

3. **Line Charts (Video: Line Charts)**
   a. Activate the worksheet named Dow Jones Data.
   b. Highlight the range A2:B14 and click the **Insert** tab on the Ribbon.
   c. Click the **Line** icon and select the **Line with Markers** format option.
   d. Use the **Move Chart** icon in the **Design** tab on the Ribbon to move the line chart to its own chart sheet. The tab name of this chart sheet should be `DJIA 2004`.
   e. Use the **Legend** icon in the **Layout** tab to remove the legend.
   f. Change the chart title to `Dow Jones Industrial Average 2004`.
   g. Add a Y-axis title `Adjusted Closing Average`.

4. **Pie Charts (Video: Pie Charts)**
   a. Activate the worksheet named Startup Cost.
   b. Highlight the range A2:B6 and click the **Insert** tab on the Ribbon.
   c. Click the **Pie** icon and select the **Exploded pie in 3-D** format option.
   d. Select the **Style 26** chart style.
   e. Remove the legend.
   f. Change the title of the chart to `Startup Costs`.
   g. Open the **Format Data Labels** dialog box. Select the **More Data Label Options** in the **Data Labels** icon in the **Layout** tab on the Ribbon.

h. In the **Format Data Labels** dialog box, click the **Value** option to remove the green check. Then click the **Category Name** option to add a green check. Then click the **Outside End** option and click the **Close** button.

i. Save and close your file.

**EXERCISE**

**Why Do I Need This?**

## >> Analyzing Industry Statistics

Analyzing an industry is a critical exercise when developing business strategies. Understanding whether an industry is growing or declining and identifying the top-performing companies are critical when making strategic decisions. The outcome of this analysis could support decisions such as entering a market, exiting a market, or making an acquisition. The chart techniques covered in this section are valuable for presenting industry statistics, but they can also be used as analytical tools.

### Exercise

The purpose of this exercise is to construct two charts for the purpose of analyzing and presenting statistics that have been collected for a hypothetical industry. To begin the exercise, open the file named ib_e05_industryx.

1. Activate the worksheet named Sales Growth.
2. Highlight the range A3:H7 and create a line chart. Use a chart format that shows markers at each data point. The purpose of this chart is to show the seven-year sales trend for each of the companies listed in the Sales Growth worksheet. Notice that the averages located in row 7 are included in the highlighted range. This will enable the reader of the chart to compare the growth trends for each company with the overall average of the industry.
3. Select a chart style that assigns a different color for each of the lines on the chart. Select a style that keeps the plot area white or light grey.
4. Move the line chart to a separate chart sheet. The tab name for this chart sheet should be **`Industry Sales by Company`**.
5. Move the legend to the bottom of the chart.
6. Add the title **`Industry X Sales Analysis`** to the chart. The title should appear above the chart.
7. Add a title **`Change in Sales`** to the Y-axis. Use the **Vertical Title** option.
8. What company is showing a sales growth trend from the year 2000 to 2006 that is most similar the overall average of the industry?
9. Activate the worksheet named Competitors.
10. Highlight the range A2:B6 and create a pie chart. Use a chart format that will show each section of the chart separated from the center and have a three-dimensional appearance. The purpose of this chart is to show the total net sales for all the companies in Industry X. When placed in a pie chart, this data will show how much market share or percentage of sales

each company obtained in the industry last year. This chart will show if the industry is dominated by a few companies or if the sales are divided among several small firms.

11. Select a chart style that assigns a different color for each section of the pie chart. Select a style that keeps the plot area white or light grey.
12. Change the title of the chart to **`LY Market Share`**.
13. Remove the chart legend.
14. Add data labels outside each section in the chart. The data labels should show both the category name and the value. As a result, the chart should show the company name as well as the total net sales.
15. Which company has the highest market share in the industry?
16. Does the company with the highest market share also have the highest sales growth rate relative to the industry average?
17. Which company—A, B, or C—has the lowest market share?
18. Reports in this industry claim Company A is "stealing" market share away from Company C. Does this claim make sense when looking at the line chart you created? Why?
19. Save and close your file.

## >> What's Wrong with This Spreadsheet?

PROBLEM & EXERCISE

### Problem

You are a business analyst working in the product development division of a large products manufacturing company. Your boss, the director of product development, is preparing for a meeting with the president of the company to explain potential sales opportunities based on three years' worth of historical sales data. He is having difficulty creating a chart that visually displays the sales trends for five product categories and asks for your help. He explains his goal for this chart as follows:

1. I am trying to create a basic column chart that shows how the product sales mix of the company has changed over the past three years. Our sales are increasing every year; however, the sales of some product categories have increased dramatically, whereas others have actually declined. Therefore, I am trying to create a chart that shows the three years at the bottom of the chart with bars representing the sales for each of the five product categories. However, the column chart I created shows the exact opposite configuration. I was wondering if I should re-create my data so the column headings in row 2 show the product categories instead of the years.

2. If possible, I would like to show the bars for the year 2004 in order, starting with the tallest bar down to the shortest. I know the height of the bars will change for the following two years; however, it is so much easier to see these trends when the bars for the first year are in order.

3. Is there any way to create this chart without having all the bars green? It would be nice if each bar is a different color. Someone told me that there is a **Design** tab on the Ribbon that would allow me to select a new color scheme. However, I must have a different version of Excel because I don't see this tab.

### Exercise

The chart your boss created is in the Excel file named ib_e05_productmixpresentation. Open the file and consider the following points:

1. Your boss mentioned that he might have to re-create the data in his worksheet to display the years on the bottom of the chart. Is this necessary?
2. In the second point, your boss mentioned that he would like to change the order in which the bars are displayed for the year 2004. Is this possible? How?
3. With regards to the third point, why is your boss not seeing the **Design** tab?
4. Is anything missing from the chart your boss attempted to create in this file?
5. Read the first point carefully. Your boss mentioned that he would like to create a basic column chart. Would you recommend that your boss use another chart in this situation? Why?

Write a short answer for each of the points listed here. Then fix the chart based on the points your boss mentioned and add anything you think is missing. In addition, create an alternate version of this chart that might improve your boss's presentation to the president.

## Skill Set >> Formatting Charts

The previous section demonstrated how charts are created and used in a variety of business situations. However, formatting can significantly enhance the appearance of these charts. Appropriate formatting can often make the difference between a mediocre and professional-looking spreadsheet. The same rule applies to charts. Formatting can direct the reader to the most critical data points on a chart and bring the appearance of charts to a professional level. This section will demonstrate various formatting techniques using the charts created in the previous section.

### Titles and Legends

After creating a chart, you might need to make formatting adjustments to the legend and titles. For example, you may have noticed that the axis titles as well as the legend in the column chart shown in Figure 9 are hard to read because the font size is so small. Formatting adjustments can solve this problem.

There are many ways to apply formatting commands to any area of a chart. The best method to use ultimately depends on your preference and needs. The following points demonstrate these methods using the chart title from Figure 9:

- Activate the chart title and select one of the formatting icons on the **Home** tab on the Ribbon. When an area on the chart is activated, you can click the **Home** tab and use any of the formatting icons such as **Font Size**, **Bold**, **Italics**, and so on.
- Activate the chart title and right click on it. Right clicking will provide access to the formatting icons in the **Home** tab on the Ribbon as well as other commands. The benefit of using this method is that you can access icons on the **Home** tab while another tab on the Ribbon is active (see Figure 20).
- Activate the chart title and use the commands in the **Format** tab in the **Chart Tools** area on the Ribbon (see Figure 21).
- Activate the chart title and open the **Format Chart Title** dialog box (see Figure 22). A formatting dialog box can be opened for every area of a chart. For example, there is a **Format Plot Area** dialog box, **Format Axis** dialog box, **Format Legend** dialog box, and so on. You can open these format dialog boxes by clicking

the **Format Selection** icon in the **Format** tab after activating the area of the chart you wish to format (see Figure 21). The benefit of this method is that it provides access to more detailed formatting controls in addition to the commands found in the **Format** tab.

Figures 20 through 22 illustrate the various methods for accessing and implementing formatting commands for charts. As previously mentioned, the method you choose depends on your preference and project needs.

Figure 20 | **Right-Click Method to Access Formatting Commands**

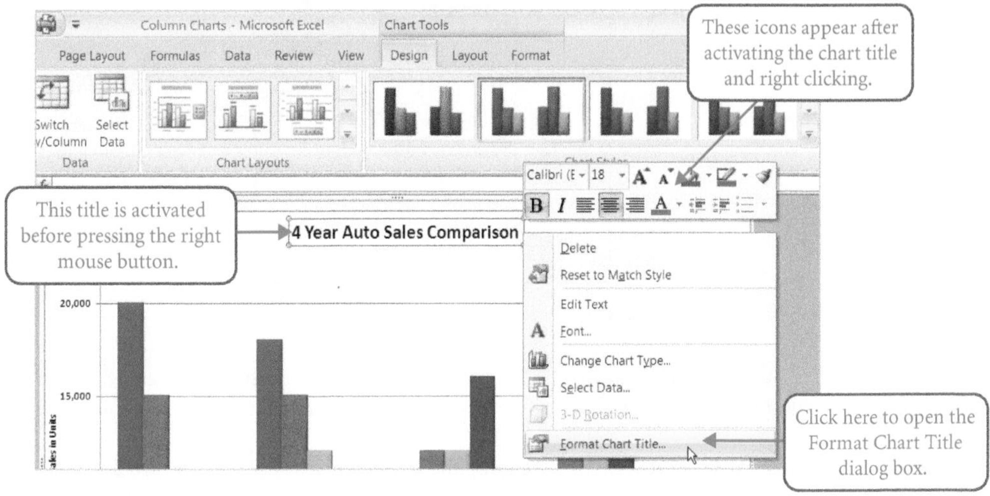


Figure 21 | **Chart Formatting Commands in the Format Tab**

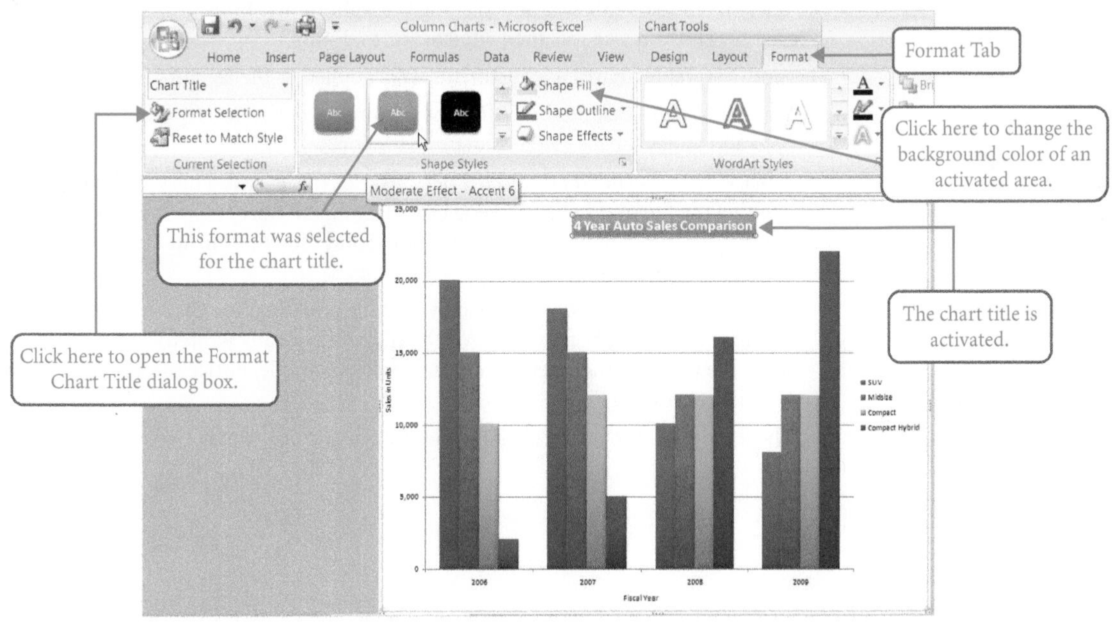

Figure 22 | **Format Chart Title Dialog Box**

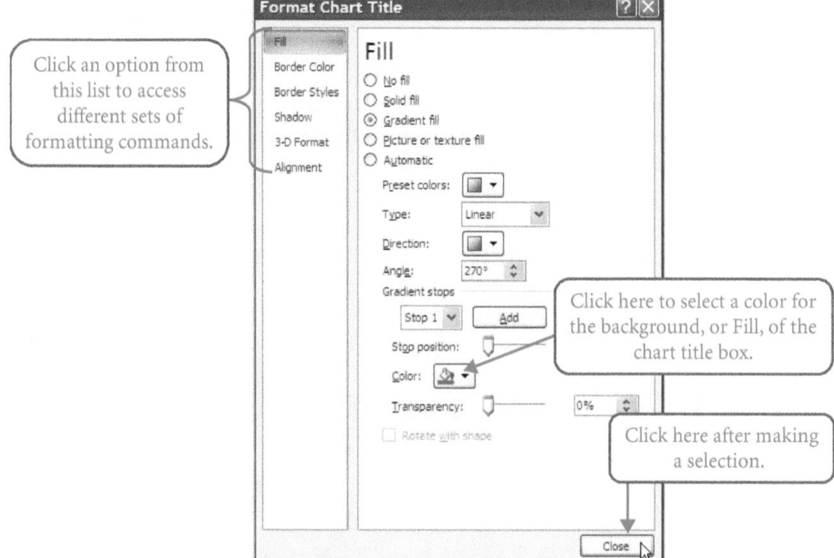


Figure 24 shows the results of the final formatting applied to the legend and titles on the column chart from Figure 9. The formatting changes made include the following:

- **Chart Title:** In addition to applying the style that was shown in Figure 21, the font size was increased to 20 points and italicized. The title was also repositioned above the chart by selecting the **Above Chart** option in the **Chart Title** icon of the **Layout** tab.
- **X- and Y-Axes Titles:** The font size was increased to 14 points. This was done by selecting the axis title box and clicking the right mouse button, as shown in Figure 20. The font size was then adjusted to 14 points.
- **Legend:** Several formatting adjustments were applied to the legend:
  - Using the right-click method, the font size was increased to 16 points, and the bold and italics formats were added.
  - A black line was added around the perimeter of the legend. This was done by opening the **Format Legend** dialog box, clicking the Border Color category on the left side of the dialog box, selecting the **Solid Line** option, and selecting the color black from the color palette (see Figure 23).
  - The size of the legend was changed by clicking and dragging the sizing handles that appear when it is activated. Words will automatically wrap to a second line when the width of the legend is decreased. For example, notice the Compact Hybrid category in Figure 24.
  - The legend was moved by clicking and dragging after it was activated.

>> **Quick Reference**

**Formatting Titles and Legends**

1. Activate the legend or title by clicking it once.
2. Select any of the format icons in the **Home** tab on the Ribbon and/or the icons in the **Format** tab of the **Chart Tools** area on the Ribbon.
3. To access more detailed formatting controls, click the **Format Selection** icon in the **Format** tab to open the **Format Legend** or **Format Title** dialog box.
4. To edit the wording of a title, click it twice and type any adjustments.
5. To move the legend or titles, click and drag it.
6. To change the size of the legend or titles, click and drag on one of the sizing handles.

Figure 23 | **Format Legend Dialog Box**

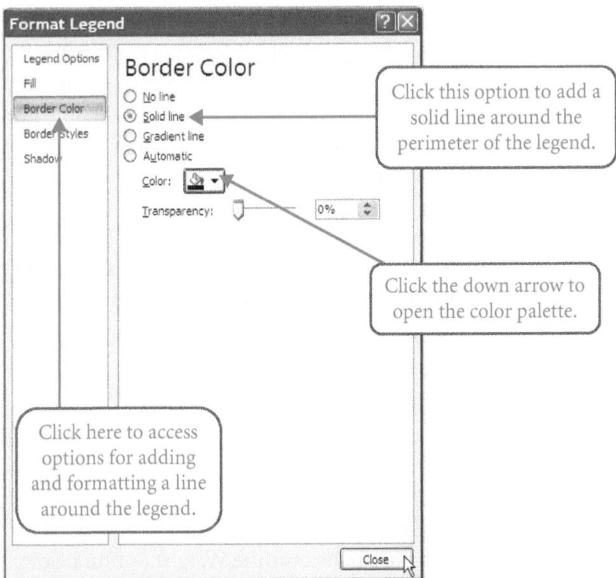


Figure 24 | **Formatting Changes Applied to the Legend and Titles**

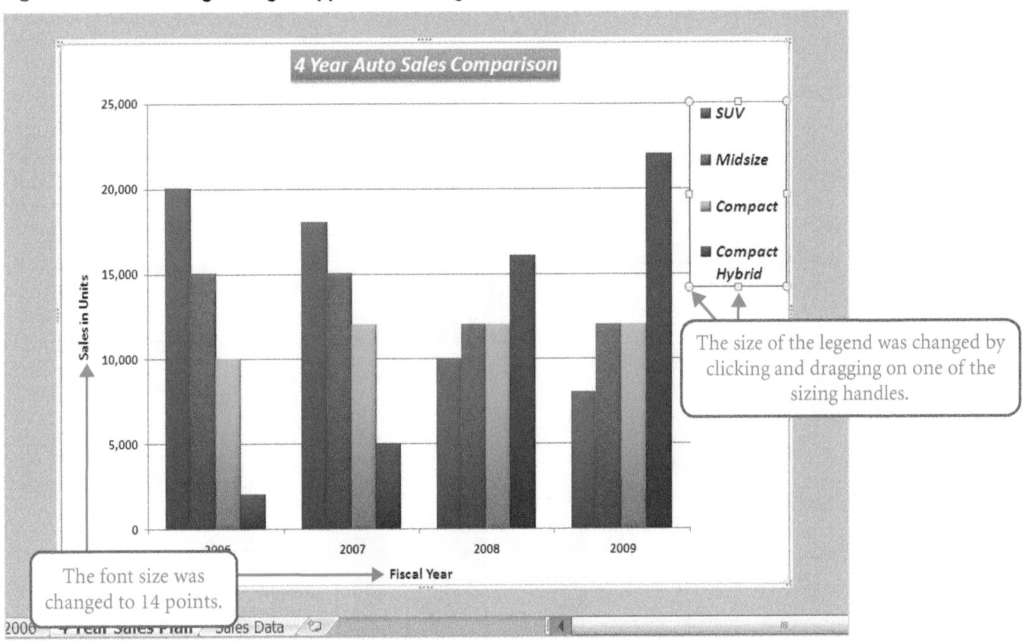

## Plot Area and Data Series

The plot area is an area of a chart that frequently requires formatting adjustments. The color of the plot area can make a significant difference in the appearance of the data that is being displayed. The color or background you choose for the plot area will depend on the colors and type of chart you are constructing. This section will illustrate how the plot area of the column chart in Figure 24 is formatted. In addition, this segment will also illustrate how you can apply formatting adjustments to the data series of a chart.

After activating the plot area of a chart, you usually format it using the **Shape Fill** and **Shape Outline** icons in the **Format** tab or by opening the **Format Plot Area** dialog box. The following steps explain how to format the plot area for the column chart in Figure 24 using the icons in the **Format** tab:

- Activate the plot area by clicking inside the X- and Y-axes but not on one of the grid lines.
- Click the **Format** tab.
- Click the **Shape Fill** icon and select the color light grey (darker 15%) from the palette. This will change the color of the plot area to light grey.
- Click the **Shape Outline** icon and place the cursor over the **Weight** option below the color palette (see Figure 25). Then select the **1½ pt** option. This will place a black outline around the perimeter of the plot area.

Figure 25 | **Adding a Black Outline around the Perimeter of the Plot Area**

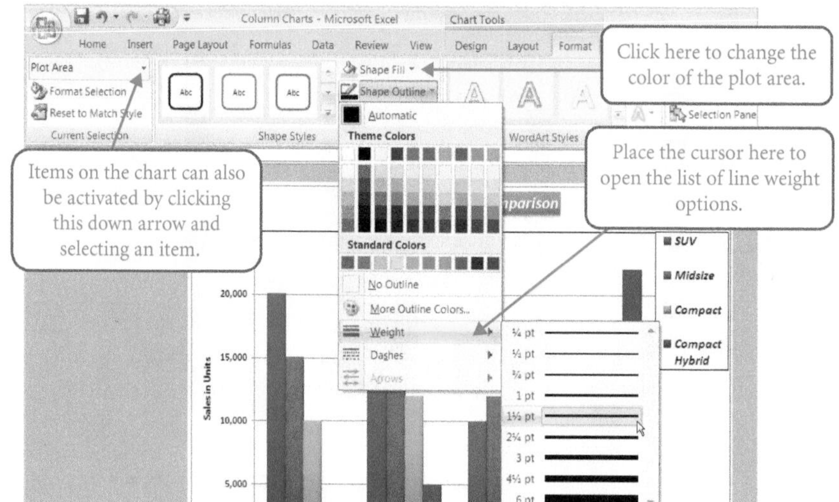


Figure 26 shows the results of the final formatting adjustments made to the plot area of the column chart. In addition, space was created on the bottom, left, and right sides of the plot area by clicking and dragging on the sizing handles, which appear when the plot area is activated. Notice how the axis labels and values appear more prominent when the color of the plot area is changed to light grey. This makes it easy for the reader to see the magnitude of the bars in the plot area.

Figure 26 | **Formatted Plot Area**

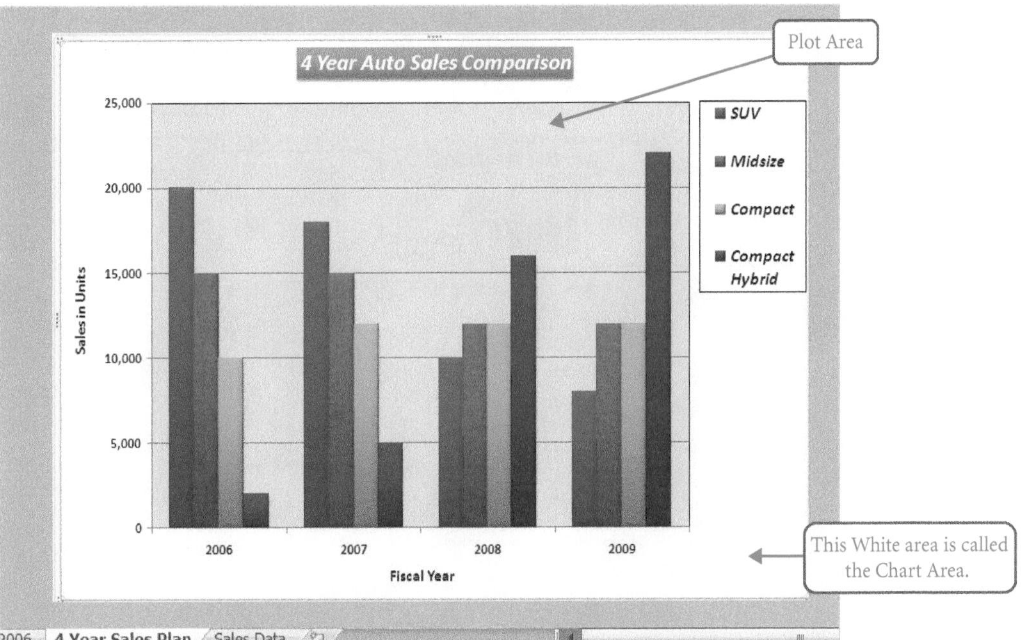


As previously mentioned, you can also format the data series displayed on a chart. A ***data series*** refers to the image that appears on the chart that is representing a category of values. For example, the blue bars in the column chart shown in Figure 26 represent the SUV data series. On a line chart, markers could be used to represent a data series. For this formatting example, the color of the bars representing the Compact and Compact Hybrid categories will be changed. You may recall that the color of these bars was determined by selecting one of the chart styles in the **Design** tab when the chart was initially created (see Figure 8). However, what if you wanted the bars for the Compact Hybrid category to be green because this car is environmentally friendly? You can change this color to green by applying formatting techniques to the data series.

The method used to format the data series of a chart is similar to formatting the plot area. When one element of a data series is clicked one time, images related to the data series will be activated. For example, when one of the bars representing the Compact Hybrid category is clicked, all the Compact Hybrid bars will be activated. If one of the bars representing the Compact Hybrid category is clicked a second time, that specific bar, or ***series point***, will be activated. This gives you the option of formatting all the bars or images related to a data series or just one. After activating a data series or series point, you can use the **Shape Fill** and **Shape Outline** icons in the **Format** tab to change the color and the line around its perimeter. The following points explain how to format both the Compact and Compact Hybrid data series:

- Click one of the green bars representing the Compact car category on the column chart shown in Figure 26. This will activate all the green bars on the chart.
- Click the **Format** tab and then click the **Shape Fill** icon. Select the color yellow at the bottom of the palette (see Figure 27). You should see the color of the bars change as you drag the cursor over a color in the palette. In addition, the **Shape Fill** icon also contains an option called **Picture**. This option enables you to import a digital picture you have saved on your computer into the area that is activated on the chart.
- Click one of the purple bars representing the Compact Hybrid car category on the column chart. This will activate all the purple bars on the chart.
- Click the **Format** tab and then click the **Shape Fill** icon. Select the color light green at the bottom of the palette.

>> **Quick Reference**

**Formatting the Plot Area**

1. Activate the plot area by clicking it once.
2. Click the **Format** tab in the **Chart Tools** set of tabs.
3. Click the **Shape Fill** icon and select a color from the palette to change the plot area color.
4. Click the **Shape Outline** icon and select a color from the palette, one of the **Weight** options, or one of the **Dashes** options.

Figure 27 | **Using the Shape Fill Icon to Format a Data Series**

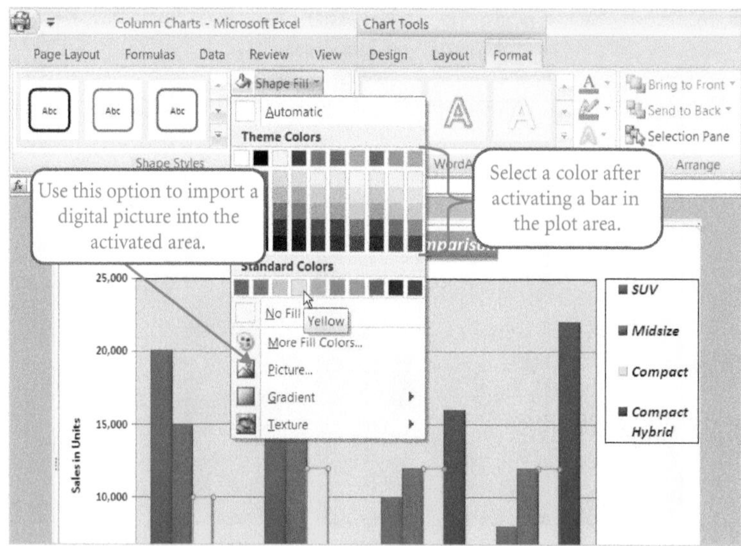


Figure 28 shows the final changes made to the Compact and Compact Hybrid data series. Notice that the legend adjusts automatically after the color of the data series is changed. Remember that you can access other formatting features by opening the **Format Data Series** dialog box using the **Format Selection** icon. For example, you can adjust the size of the gap between each set of bars. This capability is helpful when you want to show more or less space between each category on the X-axis of a column chart.

Figure 28 | **Completed Formatting Adjustments to the Data Series**

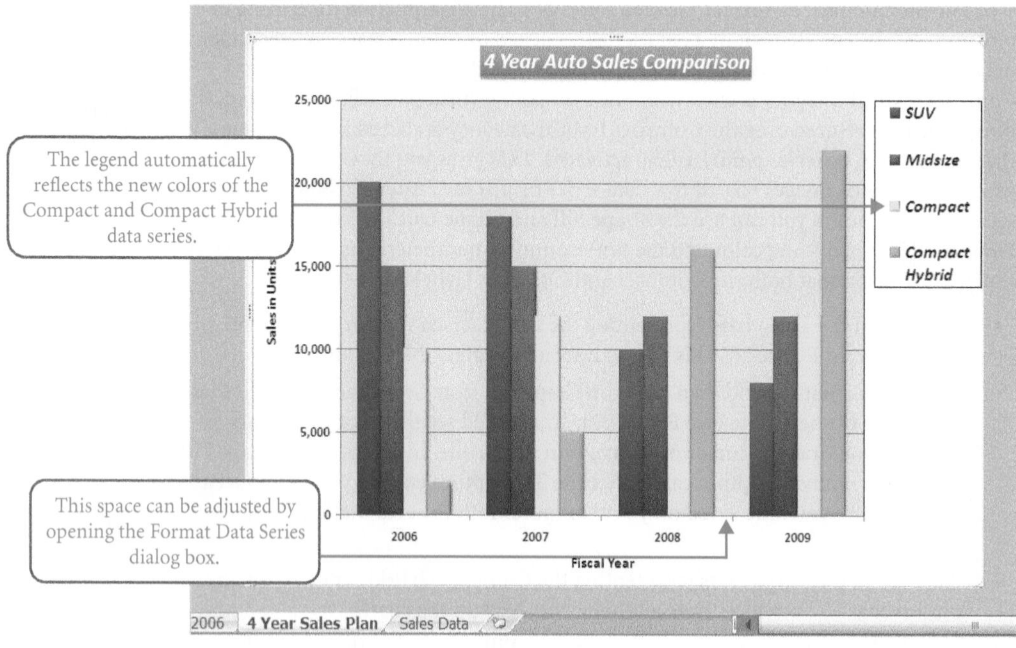

## X- and Y-Axes Labels

The last areas that will be formatted on the column chart shown in Figure 28 are the X- and Y-axes. Similar to the Axis titles, the values or labels along the X- and Y-axes frequently require formatting so they are easy to see and read.

As with other chart formatting features, you can change the appearance of either the X- or Y-axis by clicking it once and using the icons in the **Home** and **Format** tabs. However, you can access other important features such as controlling the scale of an axis, tick marks, position of the axis labels, or grid lines through the **Format Axis** dialog box. You open it by clicking the axis one time and selecting the **Format Selection** icon in the **Format** tab. Figure 29 shows the **Format Axis** dialog box for the Y-axis of the column chart in Figure 28.

Figure 29 | **Format Axis Dialog Box**

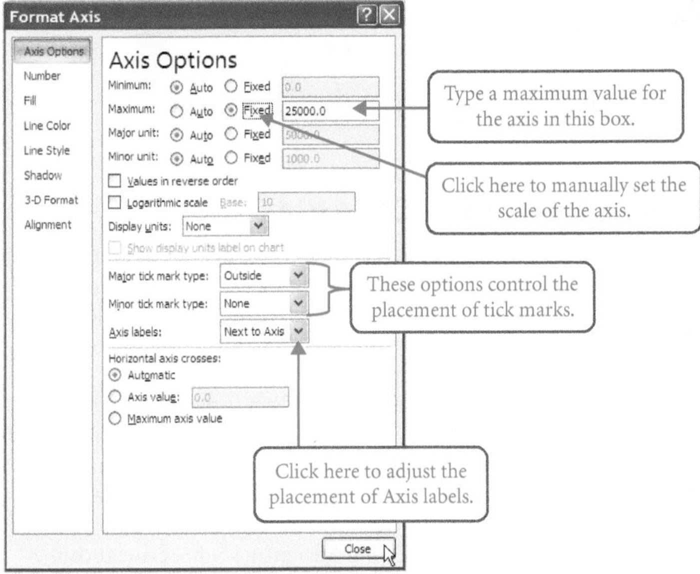


Figure 30 shows the final column chart that was started in Figure 9. The font size for the sales values and years along the X- and Y-axes was increased to 14 points. Notice how formatting features were used to make all the key elements of the chart easier to see and read such as the titles, legend, and bars.

>> **Quick Reference**

**Formatting a Data Series**

1. Activate a data series by clicking an image (i.e., bar, marker, pie section) one time. Or click an image a second time to activate a series point.
2. Click the **Format** tab in the **Chart Tools** set of tabs.
3. Click the **Shape Fill** icon and select a color from the palette to change the data series or series point color.
4. Click the **Shape Outline** icon and select a color from the palette, one of the **Weight** options, or one of the **Dashes** options.

Figure 30 | **Final Automobile Sales Chart with the X- and Y-Axes Formatted**

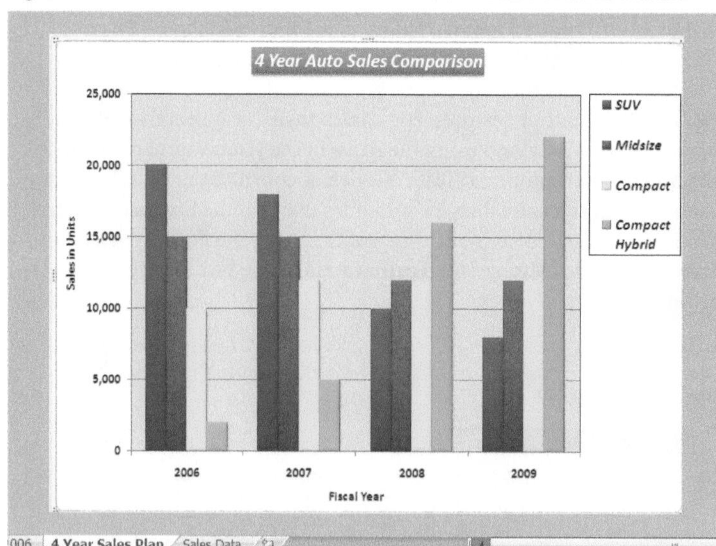


## Adding Annotations and Objects

Depending on your project, you may need to add annotations, callouts, or other shapes to a chart. These items can be especially helpful in guiding the attention of an audience during a presentation or for adding additional information that helps the reader identify key facts and trends. The next example demonstrates these formatting features using the 100% Stacked Column chart originally created in Figure 12.

As shown in Figure 31, the Sporting Goods Industry chart (previously shown in Figure 12) includes several formatting features, and it was moved to its own chart sheet. Two formatting enhancements are typically added to stacked column charts such as the one shown in this Figure 31. The first shows the total value for all the stacks in each bar. Because the Y-axis shows only the percent to total, it is difficult to see the total sales that were generated in the industry. The second formatting enhancement connects the top of each stack with a line. This feature will make it easier for the reader to see how the percent to total changes over time for each stack in the bar.

**Formatting X- and Y-Axes Labels**

1. Activate the X- or Y-axis by clicking once anywhere along the axis.
2. Select any of the format icons in the **Home** tab on the Ribbon and/or the icons in the **Format** tab of the **Chart Tools** area on the Ribbon.
3. To access more detailed formatting controls such the axis scale, tick marks, or label position, click the **Format Selection** icon in the **Format** tab to open the **Format Axis** dialog box.

Figure 31 | **Sports Industry 100% Stacked Chart with Formatting Enhancements**

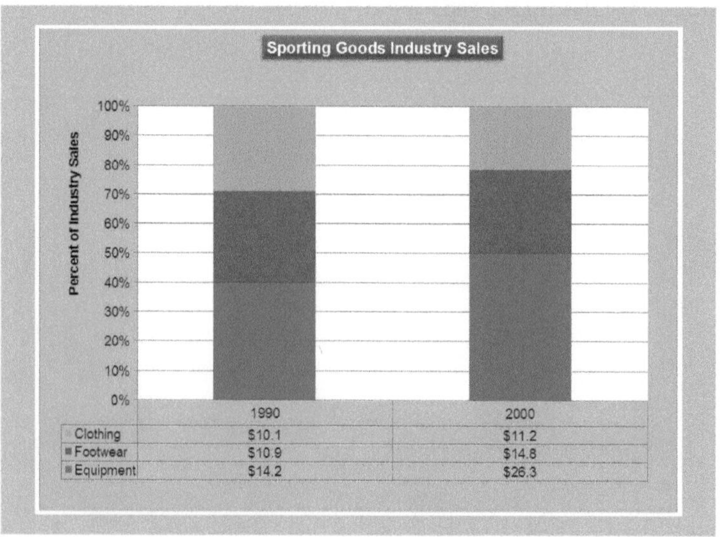

The following steps explain how to add annotations to the chart in Figure 31 to show the total industry sales at the top of each bar:

- Activate the chart.
- Click the **Layout** tab in the **Chart Tools** section on the Ribbon.
- Click the **Text Box** icon. Then click and drag a rectangle box over the top of the Y-axis, as shown in Figure 32. This text box can be used for typing annotations or information onto the chart.
- Place the cursor over one of the sizing handles of the text box and click the right mouse button. This will open a menu of options used for adding and formatting the data or message typed into the text box (see Figure 33). Select the **Edit Text** option and type **`100% of Sales =`**. This tells the reader that sales figures showing at the top of each bar represent the total sales results for the industry. Additional text boxes will be added to show these sales figures on the chart.
- Highlight the message you typed into the text box and click the right mouse button. Use the formatting icons as shown in Figure 33 to change the font size to 12 and then bold and italicize the text.
- Click and drag the right sizing handle to the right so the message does not wrap to two lines.

Figure 32 | **Adding a Text Box to a Chart**

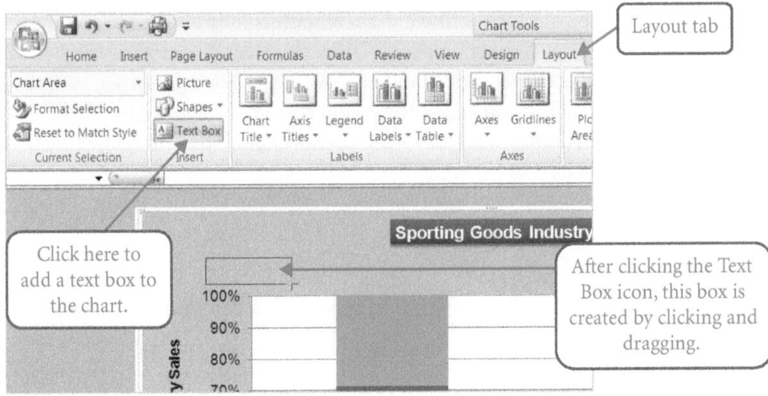


Figure 33 | **Right-Click Options for a Text Box**

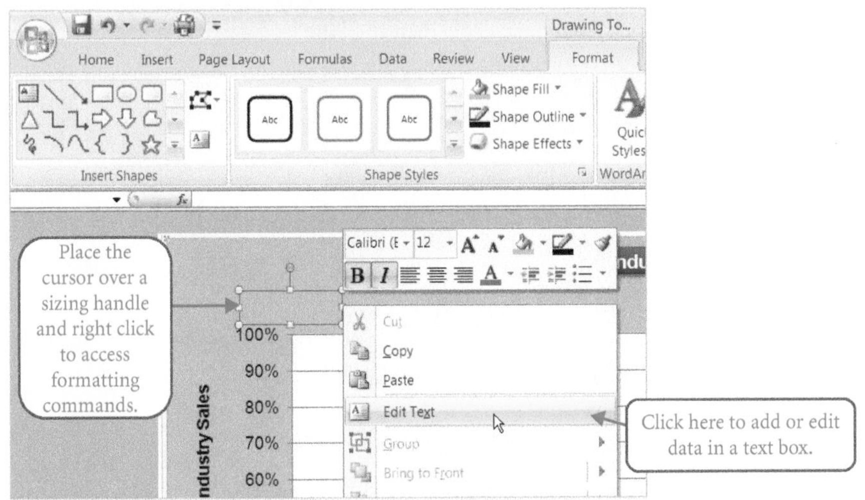

Figure 34 shows the completed text box. Notice that after the text box is added to the chart, a **Format** tab is added to the Ribbon under the heading **Drawing Tools**. The commands in this tab are used for applying formatting features to any added object that is activated on a chart or worksheet. Similar to the **Chart Tools Format** tab, the benefit of using icons in this tab is that you can see how a particular formatting command appears before selecting it.

Figure 34 | **Completed Text Box**

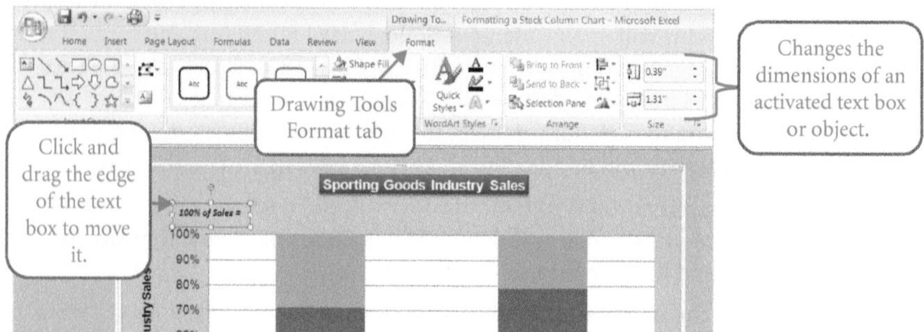


As mentioned earlier, the second formatting enhancement usually applied to a 100% Stacked Column chart is a line connecting the top of each stacked section of the bar. Besides text boxes, other objects can also be added to a chart, such as lines, arrows, circles, callout boxes, and so on. You can access these objects in the **Layout** tab of the **Chart Tools** section on the Ribbon. The following points explain how to add a line to the 100% Stacked Column chart in Figure 31:

- Activate the chart.
- Click the **Layout** tab in the **Chart Tools** section on the Ribbon.
- Click the **Shapes** icon. This will open a list of objects that can be added to the chart (see Figure 35).
- Click the **Line** option from the shapes list. Then move the cursor to the top of the blue stack of the bar for 1990 and click and drag over to the top of the blue stack for the year 2000 (see Figure 36).
- Click the **Shape Outline** icon in the **Format** tab of the **Drawing Tools** section on the Ribbon. The line must be activated to see the **Drawing Tools** section on the Ribbon. Select black from the palette; then click the icon again and select the **1 ½ pt** weight option.

Figure 35 | **Options for Adding Shapes to a Chart**

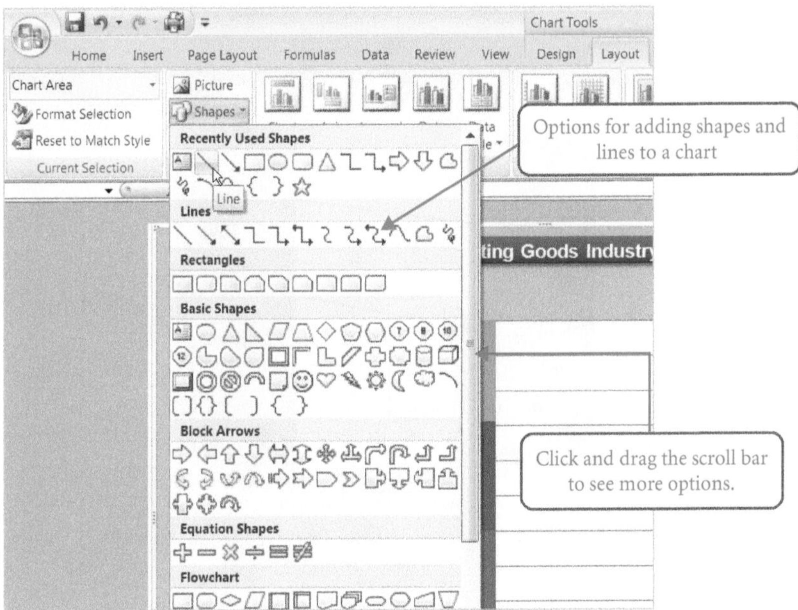


Figure 36 shows the line that was added to the 100% Stacked Column chart. Notice that because the line is moving in an upward direction, the reader can easily see that the percent to total sales for Equipment increased from 1990 to 2000.

Figure 36 | **Adding a Line to a 100% Stacked Column Chart**

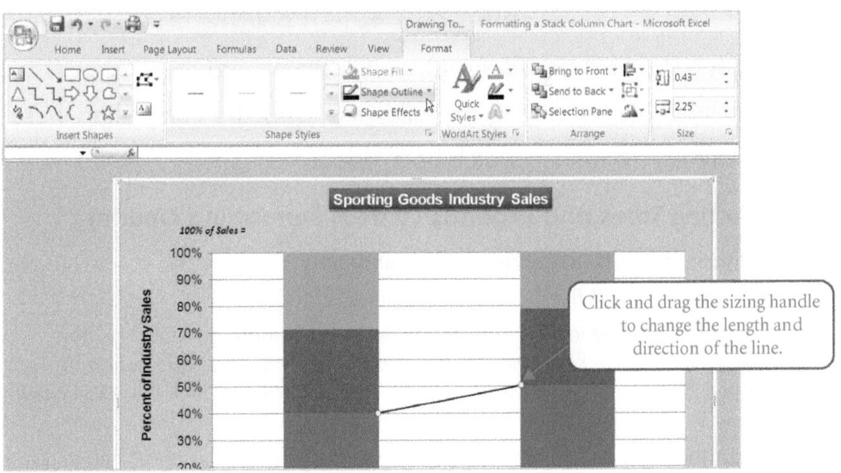


Figure 37 shows the final 100% Stacked Column chart showing the sales trend for the Sporting Goods Industry. Notice that text boxes were added to the top of each bar showing the total industry sales for the year. In addition, a second line was added connecting the "Footwear" category between the 1990 and 2000 bars.

**>> Quick Reference**

**Adding Annotations and Objects**

1. Activate the chart.
2. Click the **Layout** tab of the **Chart Tools** area on the Ribbon.
3. Click the **Text Box** icon to add an annotation or the **Shapes** icon to add an object. If adding an object, select an option after clicking the **Shapes** icon.
4. Click and drag on the chart to place and set the desired size of the text box or object.
5. Format the text box or object by activating it and right clicking, or using the icons in the **Format** tab of the **Drawing Tools** area on the Ribbon.

Figure 37 | **Final 100% Stacked Column with Lines and Annotations Added**

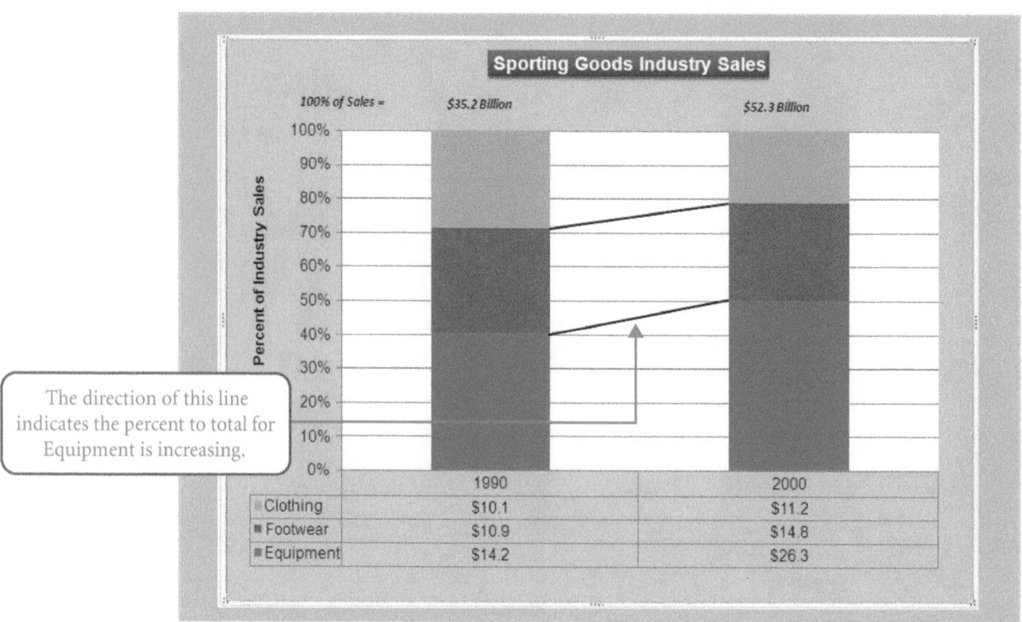

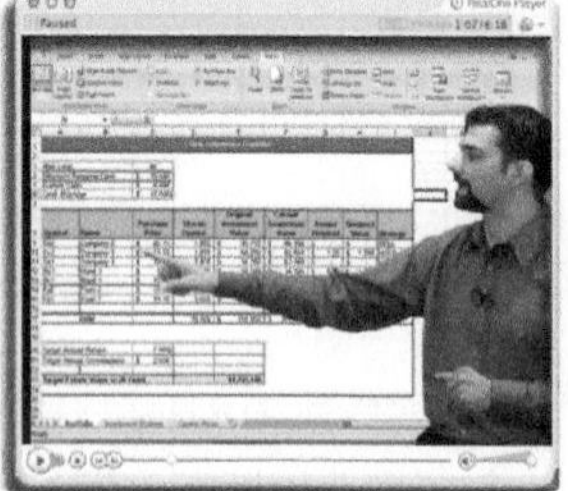

## » Formatting Charts

The purpose of this workshop is to review the techniques used to format the appearance of charts. I will be demonstrating the tasks in this workshop in the **Formatting Charts** and **Adding Annotations and Objects to Charts** videos. Open the file named ib_e05_formattingcharts before starting the following tasks. Try completing these tasks on your own and then watch both videos.

1. **Formatting Titles and Legends (Video: Formatting Charts)**
   a. Activate the worksheet named Column Chart.
   b. Activate the chart title by clicking it once.
   c. Click the **Format** tab in the **Chart Tools** section on the Ribbon. Then select the "Intense Effect-Accent 6" **Shape Styles** icon. This option has an orange background with white letters. You will have to click the scroll down arrow to find this option.
   d. Using the right-click method, change the font size of the chart title to 20 points and italicize the text.
   e. Activate the Legend. Using either the right-click method or the format icons in the **Home** tab on the Ribbon, increase the font size to 14 points; then bold and italicize the text.
   f. Click the **Shape Outline** icon in the **Format** tab on the Ribbon. Place the cursor over the **Weight** option and select the **1 pt** line weight. Then click the **Shape Outline** icon again and select the color black.
   g. Click the top edge of the legend and move it up so the top of the legend is aligned with the 35,000 grid line. Make sure you do not click and drag on a sizing handle to move the legend.

h. Click the X-axis title and increase the font size to 14 points.
i. Click the Y-axis title and increase the font size to 14 points.

**2. Formatting the Plot Area and Data Series (Video: Formatting Charts)**

a. Activate the plot area of the column chart.
b. Click the **Format** tab on the Ribbon.
c. Click the **Shape Fill** icon and select the white color in the upper-left side of the palette.
d. Click the **Shape Outline** icon, place the cursor over the **Weight** option, and click the **1 ½ pt** line weight. Then click the **Shape Outline** icon again and select the color black.
e. Activate the Compact data series by clicking one of the green bars.
f. Click the **Shape Fill** icon in the **Format** tab and select the color yellow.
g. Activate the Compact Hybrid data series by clicking one of the purple bars.
h. Click the **Shape Fill** icon in the **Format** tab and select the color light green.

**3. Formatting the X- and Y-Axes Labels (Video: Formatting Charts)**

a. Click any of the years on the X-axis.
b. Change the font size to 12 points.
c. Click any sales value on the Y-axis.
d. Change the font size to 12 points.

**4. Annotations and Objects (Video: Adding Annotations and Objects to Charts)**

a. Activate the worksheet named Stacked Column Chart.
b. Activate the chart.
c. Click the **Layout** tab and then click the **Text Box** icon.
d. Click and drag the shape of a rectangle above the Y-axis.
e. Place the cursor over one of the sizing handles on the text box and click the right mouse button. Then select the **Edit Text** option.
f. Type the description `100% of Sales =`. Then highlight this description, right click, and change the font size to 12. Then bold and italicize the text.
g. Click anywhere in the chart area to deactivate the text box.
h. Click the **Layout** tab and then click the **Text Box** icon to add a second text box.
i. Click and drag the shape of a rectangle above the 1990 bar.
j. Place the cursor over one of the sizing handles on the text box and click the right mouse button. Then select the **Edit Text** option.
k. Type the description `$35.2 Billion`. Then highlight this description, right click, and change the font size to 12. Then bold and italicize the text.
l. Click anywhere in the chart area to deactivate the text box.
m. Click the **Layout** tab and then click the **Text Box** icon.
n. Click and drag the shape of a rectangle above the year 2000 bar.
o. Place the cursor over one of the sizing handles on the text box and click the right mouse button. Then select the **Edit Text** option.

p. Type the description **`$52.3 Billion`**. Then highlight this description, right click, and change the font size to 12. Then bold and italicize the text.

q. Click anywhere in the chart area to deactivate the text box.

r. Click the **Layout** tab and then click the **Shapes** icon.

s. Click the first **Line** option in the Lines category of shapes.

t. Place the cursor at the top right of the blue stack of the 1990 bar. Then click and drag to the top left of the blue stack in the year 2000 bar.

u. Click the **Shape Outline** icon and select the color black. Then click the **Shape Outline** icon again and select the **1 ½ pt** line weight.

v. Click anywhere in the chart area to deactivate the line.

w. Click the **Layout** tab and then click the **Shapes** icon. Select the first **Line** option in the Lines category of shapes.

x. Place the cursor at the top right of the red stack of the 1990 bar. Then click and drag to the top left of the red stack in the year 2000 bar.

y. Click the **Shape Outline** icon and select the color black. Then click the **Shape Outline** icon again and select the **1 ½ pt** line weight.

z. Click anywhere in the chart area to deactivate the line.

aa. Save and close the file.

**EXERCISE**

**Why Do I Need This?**

## >> Charting Stocks versus the Dow Jones Industrial Average

Formatting enhancements are often needed when a chart is initially created. In fields such as consulting, adding formatting enhancements to charts can be a critical component to running a successful client meeting. In addition, the formatting enhancements made to a chart are often a sign of a consulting firm's professionalism and attention to detail.

### Exercise

The purpose of this exercise is to enhance the appearance of a chart that has been created for a business presentation. The purpose of the chart is to compare the change in a company's stock price to the change in the adjusted closing average of the Dow Jones Industrial Average. Open the file named ib_e05_stockpricecomparison. The following tasks will require you to add several formatting features to this chart:

1. Add the title **`Change in Market Value by Month`** to the chart. Add the following formatting enhancements:
   a. Font size should be 18 points, bold, and italic.
   b. Add a white fill by selecting the color white from the **Shape Fill** icon.
   c. Add a black line around the title with a 1-point weight.
   d. Add a shadow. You do this by clicking the **Shape Effects** icon, placing the cursor over the **Shadow** option, and selecting the **Offset Diagonal Bottom Right** option, which is the first option in the Outer set of options.
2. Add the title **`Change in Value Year to Date`** for the Y-axis. Apply the same formatting features that are listed in number 1 except make the font size 14 points instead of 18. Move the title to the left to create space between the title and the percentages along the Y-axis.

3. Format the Legend by applying the same formatting features listed in step 1. Then adjust the size of the legend so all the text is visible and move it so it is centered at the bottom of the chart.
4. Activate the Chart Area and change the color to light green by clicking the **Shape Fill** icon. Then click the **Shape Fill** icon again and place the cursor over the **Gradient** option. Select the **From Corner** option. This is the fourth option in the first row of the Dark Variations set of gradients.
5. Format the percentages along the Y-axis to a 12-point font size and change the color to white. Because this side of the chart is dark green, a white font will make the percentages easier to read.
6. Format the months along the X-axis to a 12-point font size.
7. Add a 2 ¼ point black line around the perimeter of the plot area.
8. Activate the "DJIA" data series. Change the color of the line to dark red and increase the weight of the line to 2 ¼ points. You can apply both formatting features by using the **Shape Outline** icon. This will make it easier to see the Dow Jones Industrial Average trend against the white background of the plot area.
9. Activate the "Our Company" data series. Change the color of the line to dark blue and increase the weight of the line to 2 ¼ points. This will make it easier to see the trend of the stock price for the managers of this company.
10. Add a text box named **`Fed Rate Increase in March`** to the plot area of the chart. Notice that the DJIA trend drops significantly from February to March. This text box will tell the reader that this was a key factor contributing to the decline in the market. Therefore, place this text box by the month of March at the 2% grid line and apply the following formats:
    a. The text should have a font size of 12 points, bold, and italic.
    b. The fill color should be orange.
    c. The perimeter should have a black line with a 1-point weight.
    d. Adjust the size of the text box so all the text is visible.
11. Add a second text box named **`Earnings Decrease Announced in Sept`** to the plot area of the chart. Notice that the trend for the company's stock drops significantly from September to December. This text box will explain why this decline occurred. Therefore, place this text box by the month of September at the 6% grid line and apply the same formats listed in step 10.
12. Save and close your file.

## >> What's Wrong with This Spreadsheet?

**PROBLEM & EXERCISE**

### Problem

You just finished creating a chart for a strategy meeting and have asked one of the interns in the department to make a few formatting enhancements to help highlight the product trends. After several hours, the intern comes to you in a panic asking for help. He explains that he tried to make several of the formatting enhancements you requested but is afraid he may have ruined the chart. He admits he was rushing to get this job done and thinks the entire chart will have to be deleted and re-created. The intern mentions the following points in his discussion with you:

1. I'm not sure what happened, but one of the bars seems to have disappeared. I was trying to change the color of the bars for the Casual Knits category to purple. I though this might look better. However, the bar for 2007 has mysteriously disappeared.

2. The other thing that happened was a bunch of the bars got cut off. I was using the dialog box to format the Y-axis, and then the phone rang. I went to pick up the phone and dropped it on my keyboard. I looked at the screen and a bunch of the bars were cut off.

3. Finally, I added the data labels to each bar like you asked, but they look terrible. A lot of the numbers are running into each other, and you really can't see them that well.

### Exercise

The chart the intern was working on is named ib_e05_chartchaos. Open this file and look at the Product Chart. Consider the following points:

1. Did the Casual Knits bar in the year 2007 really disappear? Can an individual bar be formatted on a column chart?
2. Why are some of the bars cut off at the top of the chart? Look at the worksheet named Sales Data. What is the highest unit sales value? Compare this to the highest sales value along the Y-axis. How could the values or scale for the Y-axis change?
3. In the years 2007 and 2008, several data labels merged together. Can an individual data label be formatted or moved?

What's wrong with this chart? Write a short answer for each of the points listed here. Then fix the formatting problems for the Product Chart. In addition, add any other formatting enhancements that you think will make the chart easier to read.

Skill Set

## >> Advanced Chart Options

This section will illustrate techniques that utilize Excel's dynamic capabilities. As long as you use cell locations to define the source data, a chart will adjust itself automatically when the source data changes. Therefore, charts are useful for visually studying data trends when certain inputs are changed. This capability is helpful in economic fields that study changes in consumer demand or market supplies. This section will also illustrate how charts are created when data is not contained in adjacent columns and rows. Finally, this section will close with an illustration on how you can paste Excel charts into Word documents when writing reports or PowerPoint slides for presentations.

### Defining the X- and Y-Axes Manually

Throughout this chapter so far, all the examples and exercises have utilized the method in which Excel automatically assigns values and labels to the X- and Y-axes. This method is used when the data you are displaying on a chart exists in a contiguous range of cells. However, in business, you will frequently be working with data that is not in a continuous range. For example, look at the column chart displayed in Figure 38. The purpose of this chart is to show the sales values in column C for each item listed in column A. However, notice that column B contains descriptive information that is not related to the sales of each item. When the range A2:C8 is highlighted to create the column chart, the data in column B distorts the labels along the X-axis.

Figure 38 | **Distorted Column Chart**

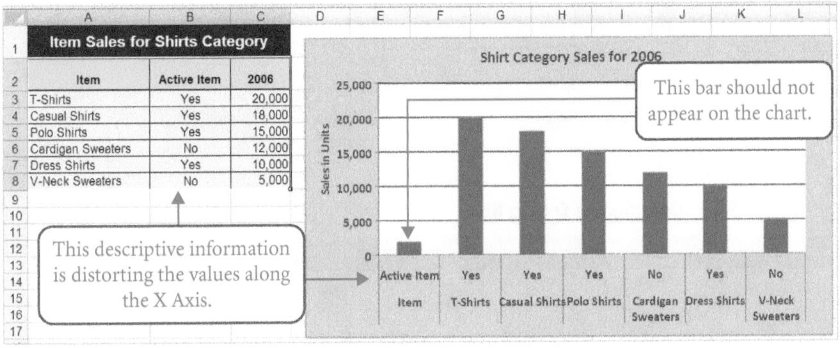
Item Sales for Shirts Category
Item
Active Item
2006
T-Shirts
Yes
20,000
Casual Shirts
Yes
18,000
Polo Shirts
Yes
15,000
Cardigan Sweaters
No
12,000
Dress Shirts
Yes
10,000
V-Neck Sweaters
No
5,000
This descriptive information is distorting the values along the X Axis.
Shirt Category Sales for 2006
This bar should not appear on the chart.
Sales in Units
25,000
20,000
15,000
10,000
5,000
0
Active Item
Item
Yes
T-Shirts
Yes
Casual Shirts
Yes
Polo Shirts
No
Cardigan Sweaters
Yes
Dress Shirts
No
V-Neck Sweaters

To create a basic column chart using the data in Figure 38, you will manually define the labels shown on the X-axis and the values shown on the Y-axis. As a result, instead of highlighting a range of cells and selecting a chart type in the **Insert** tab, you will activate a blank cell. This will produce a blank chart where the data series, as well as the values and labels assigned to the X- and Y-axes, can be defined manually. You accomplish this method as follows:

- Activate any blank cell that is at least two columns to the right or two rows below the data shown in Figure 38. You must leave at least one blank column or one blank row between the activated cell and the data on your worksheet. For this example, cell F2 is activated.
- Click the **Insert** tab, click the **Column** icon, and select the **Clustered Column** chart format. This will add a blank column chart to the worksheet, as shown in Figure 39.
- In the **Design** tab of the **Chart Tools** section on the Ribbon, click the **Select Data** icon. This will open the **Select Data Source** dialog box, as shown in Figure 40.

Figure 39 shows the appearance of a blank column chart and the **Select Data** icon, which is used to open the **Select Data Source** dialog box shown in Figure 40. Using the **Select Data Source** dialog box, you can define data series and the values and labels that are assigned to the X- and Y-axes. For a column chart, you use the left side of the **Select Data Source** dialog box to add data series or bars to the chart, which also adds values to the Y-axes and creates the legend. On the right side of the **Select Data Source** dialog box, you can define the range of cells that will be used to display the labels along the X-, or horizontal, axis.

Figure 39 | **Inserting a Blank Column Chart**

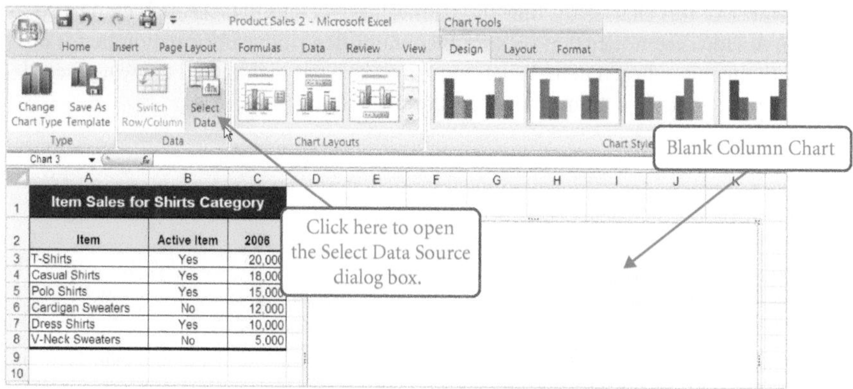


Figure 40 | **Select Data Source Dialog Box**

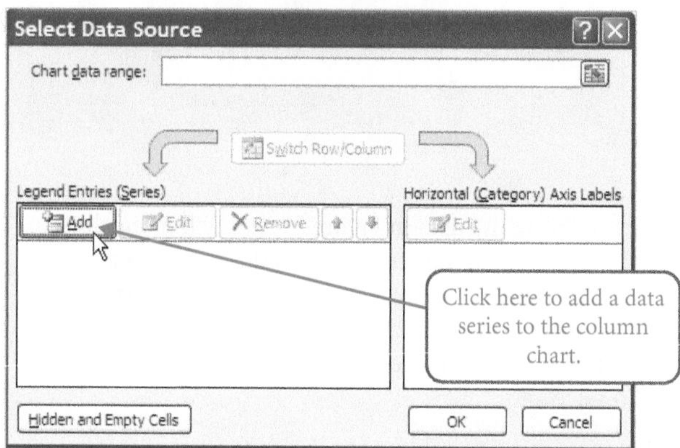


To complete the blank chart shown in Figure 39, you must define the data series and the labels for the X-, or horizontal, axis. You accomplish this as follows:

- Click the **Add** button on the left side of the **Select Data Source** dialog box under the **Legend Entries (Series)** heading. This will open the **Edit Series** dialog box (see Figure 41). For a column chart, a data series represents the bars that appear in the plot area of the chart. Therefore, the settings in the **Edit Series** dialog box will define how the bars are classified in the legend and assign values to the Y-, or vertical, axis.
- Click the range finder next to the **Series name** input box, highlight cell C2, and press the **Enter** key. This will add one data series to the column chart with the name "2006" in the legend.
- Click the range finder next to the **Series values** input box, highlight the range C3:C8, and press the **Enter** key. This will define the values for the 2006 data series. It is important to note that a bar will appear on the chart for every cell in the range C3:C8. As a result, six bars will appear on the column chart—one for each item in column A of the worksheet.
- Click the **OK** button at the bottom of the **Edit Series** dialog box after defining the Series values.
- Click the **Edit** button on the right side of the **Edit Data Source** dialog box. This will open the **Axis Labels** dialog box (see Figure 42).

- Click the range finder next to the **Axis Label Range** input box, highlight the range A3:A8, and press the **Enter** key. As previously mentioned, six bars will be added to the chart for each item in column A. Therefore, the X-, or horizontal, axis labels are defined using the descriptions in the range A3:A8.
- Click the **OK** button on the **Axis Labels** dialog box and then click the **OK** button on the **Select Data Source** dialog box.

Figure 41 shows the settings in the **Edit Series** dialog box. Notice that the description in the cell location used to define the Series name appears in the legend. Figure 42 shows the **Axis Labels** dialog box. The descriptions in the range of cells that appear in the input box will appear on the X-axis.

Figure 41 | **Edit Series Dialog Box**

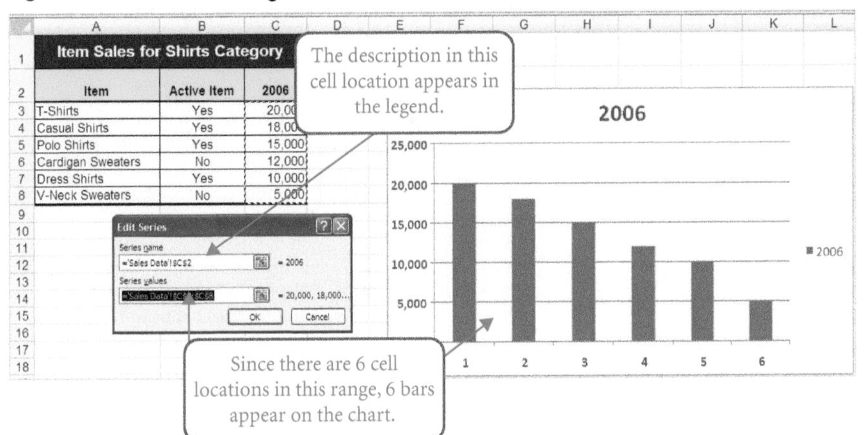


## COMMON MISTAKES | Defining a Series Name

When using the **Edit Series** dialog box to add a data series to a chart, be sure to use only one cell location for the **Series name** input box. Highlighting a range of cells for this input box will distort your chart. You can also define the Series name by typing a description; however, you must place your description in quotation marks.

Figure 42 | **Axis Labels Dialog Box**

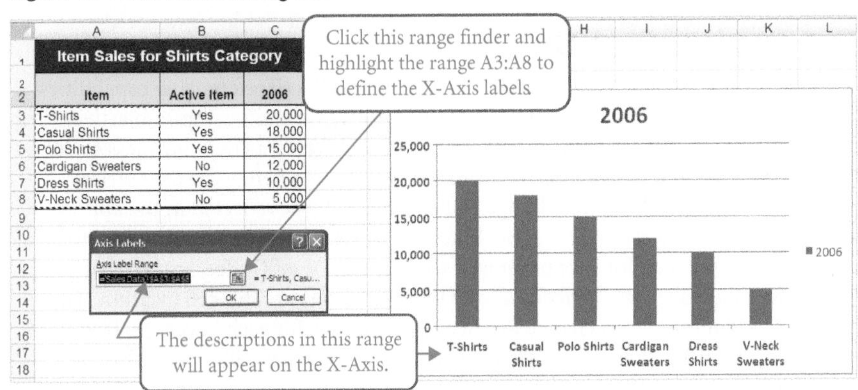

>> **Quick Reference**

### Manually Defining a Column Chart

1. Activate a blank cell on a worksheet. A blank column or a blank row must appear between the data on a worksheet and the blank cell that is activated.
2. Select a chart type from the **Insert** tab on the Ribbon.
3. Select a chart format.
4. With the blank chart activated, click the **Select Data** icon in the **Design** tab on the Ribbon.
5. Click the **Add** button on the left side of the **Select Data Source** dialog box to add a data series.
6. Define the Series name in the **Edit Series** dialog box with one cell location or type a name in quotation marks.
7. Define the Series values with a range of cells.
8. Click the **OK** button to close the **Edit Series** dialog box.
9. Repeat steps 5–8 to add additional data series if needed.
10. Click the **Edit** button on the right side of the **Select Data Source** dialog box.
11. Use a range of cells to define the Axis Label Range. The descriptions in this cell range will be used for the X-axis labels.
12. Click the **OK** button on the **Axis Labels** dialog box.
13. Click the **OK** button on the **Select Data Source** dialog box.

Figure 43 shows the final settings in the **Select Data Source** dialog box. Figure 44 shows the final column chart that was created by manually defining the data series, and the values and labels along the X- and Y-axes. In addition, several formatting enhancements were added to the chart. Notice that the legend was removed because the chart represents only one year's worth of data. If this chart displayed several years' worth of data, such as the chart shown in Figure 30, a data series would be added for each item in column A, and the years would be used as labels for the X-axis. This would require you to click the **Add** button in Figure 43 six times and set the **Edit Series** dialog box for each of the six items in column A in Figure 44.

Figure 43 | **Final Settings in the Select Data Source Dialog Box**

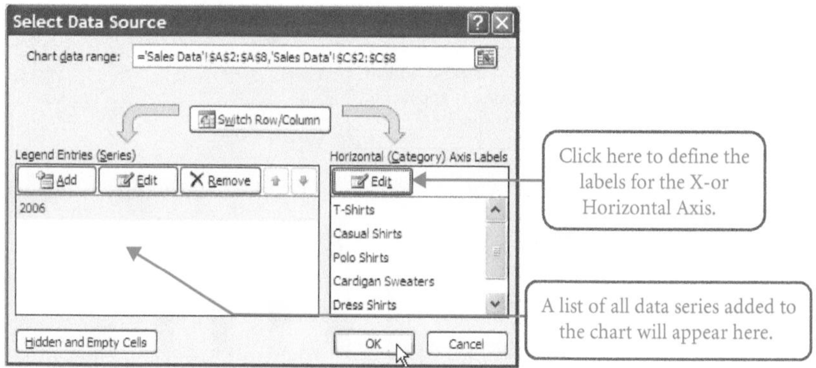


Figure 44 | **Final Column Chart Including Format Enhancements**

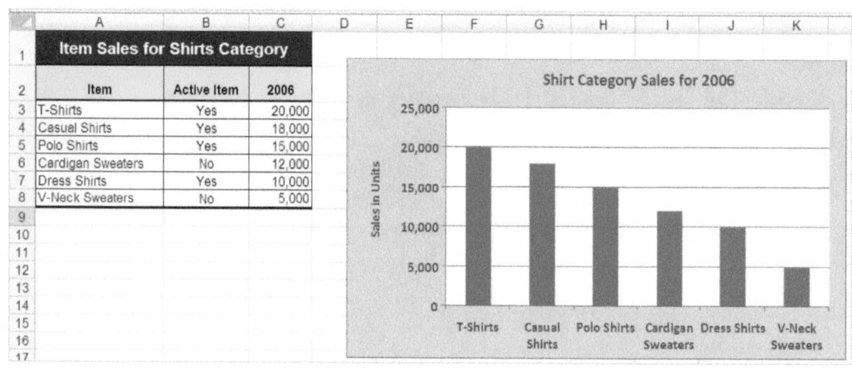


## The Scatter Plot Chart

Throughout this text you have seen the benefits of Excel's cell referencing capabilities through the use of formulas and functions to complete various business objectives. Cell referencing can also play a valuable role when using charts to analyze business or economic data. That is, if the values change in the cells used to define the data series, X-axis, or Y-axis of a chart, this change will automatically be reflected in the appearance of the chart. For example, the worksheet shown in Figure 45 contains hypothetical price and demand data for four beverages: Coffee, Tea, Decaf Coffee, and Herbal Tea. Notice the value called the "Price Change Driver" in cell D15. This cell location is used in formulas that calculate a change in price for each week for each beverage. Therefore, if the value in D15 is changed to 5%, the price of all beverages will increase by 5% every week for each of the 10 weeks listed on the worksheet (see Figure 46). If the value is changed to –5%, the price for each beverage will decrease 5% every week for the 10 weeks listed on the worksheet. As the price changes for each beverage in columns B through E, another set of formulas calculates the sales demand in columns F through I. As a result, when this data is used to create a chart, if the value is changed in cell D15, all the values in the worksheet will change, which will automatically be reflected in the appearance of the chart.

Figure 45 | **Beverage Demand Data Worksheet**

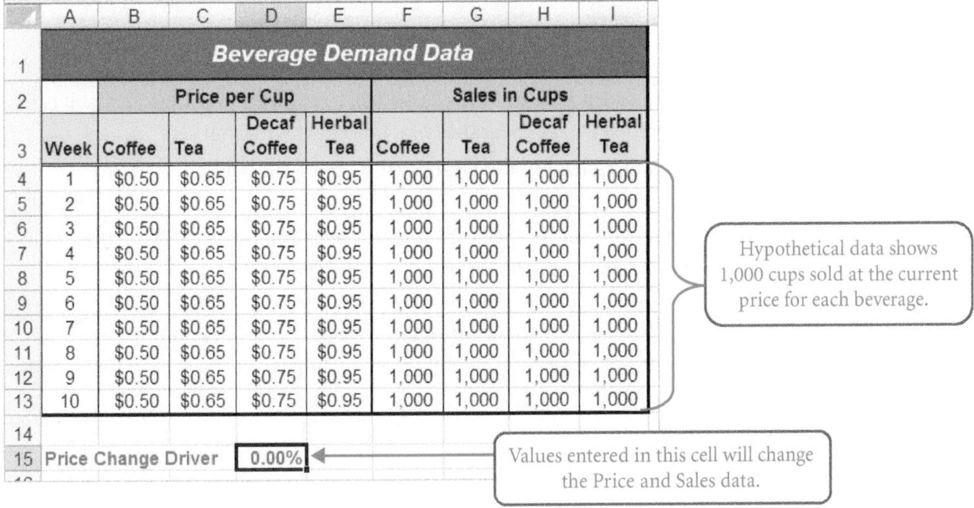

| | A | B | C | D | E | F | G | H | I |
|---|---|---|---|---|---|---|---|---|---|
| 1 | Beverage Demand Data | | | | | | | | |
| 2 | | Price per Cup | | | | Sales in Cups | | | |
| 3 | Week | Coffee | Tea | Decaf Coffee | Herbal Tea | Coffee | Tea | Decaf Coffee | Herbal Tea |
| 4 | 1 | $0.50 | $0.65 | $0.75 | $0.95 | 1,000 | 1,000 | 1,000 | 1,000 |
| 5 | 2 | $0.50 | $0.65 | $0.75 | $0.95 | 1,000 | 1,000 | 1,000 | 1,000 |
| 6 | 3 | $0.50 | $0.65 | $0.75 | $0.95 | 1,000 | 1,000 | 1,000 | 1,000 |
| 7 | 4 | $0.50 | $0.65 | $0.75 | $0.95 | 1,000 | 1,000 | 1,000 | 1,000 |
| 8 | 5 | $0.50 | $0.65 | $0.75 | $0.95 | 1,000 | 1,000 | 1,000 | 1,000 |
| 9 | 6 | $0.50 | $0.65 | $0.75 | $0.95 | 1,000 | 1,000 | 1,000 | 1,000 |
| 10 | 7 | $0.50 | $0.65 | $0.75 | $0.95 | 1,000 | 1,000 | 1,000 | 1,000 |
| 11 | 8 | $0.50 | $0.65 | $0.75 | $0.95 | 1,000 | 1,000 | 1,000 | 1,000 |
| 12 | 9 | $0.50 | $0.65 | $0.75 | $0.95 | 1,000 | 1,000 | 1,000 | 1,000 |
| 13 | 10 | $0.50 | $0.65 | $0.75 | $0.95 | 1,000 | 1,000 | 1,000 | 1,000 |
| 14 | | | | | | | | | |
| 15 | Price Change Driver | | | 0.00% | | | | | |

Hypothetical data shows 1,000 cups sold at the current price for each beverage.
Values entered in this cell will change the Price and Sales data.

Figure 46 | **Beverage Demand Data Worksheet with 5% Price Increase per Week**

| | A | B | C | D | E | F | G | H | I |
|---|---|---|---|---|---|---|---|---|---|
| 1 | Beverage Demand Data | | | | | | | | |
| 2 | | Price per Cup | | | | Sales in Cups | | | |
| 3 | Week | Coffee | Tea | Decaf Coffee | Herbal Tea | Coffee | Tea | Decaf Coffee | Herbal Tea |
| 4 | 1 | $0.50 | $0.65 | $0.75 | $0.95 | 1,000 | 1,000 | 1,000 | 1,000 |
| 5 | 2 | $0.53 | $0.68 | $0.79 | $1.00 | 988 | 975 | 950 | 900 |
| 6 | 3 | $0.55 | $0.72 | $0.83 | $1.05 | 975 | 951 | 903 | 810 |
| 7 | 4 | $0.58 | $0.75 | $0.87 | $1.10 | 963 | 927 | 857 | 729 |
| 8 | 5 | $0.61 | $0.79 | $0.91 | $1.15 | 951 | 904 | 815 | 656 |
| 9 | 6 | $0.64 | $0.83 | $0.96 | $1.21 | 939 | 881 | 774 | 590 |
| 10 | 7 | $0.67 | $0.87 | $1.01 | $1.27 | 927 | 859 | 735 | 531 |
| 11 | 8 | $0.70 | $0.91 | $1.06 | $1.34 | 916 | 838 | 698 | 478 |
| 12 | 9 | $0.74 | $0.96 | $1.11 | $1.40 | 904 | 817 | 663 | 430 |
| 13 | 10 | $0.78 | $1.01 | $1.16 | $1.47 | 893 | 796 | 630 | 387 |
| 14 | | | | | | | | | |
| 15 | Price Change Driver | | | 5.00% | | | | | |

The demand for each beverage is decreasing at different rates when the price is increased.

Entering the number 5 in this cell increased the price 5% each week in columns B, C, D, and E.

Looking at Figure 46, you can see that the formulas calculating the Sales in Cups for each beverage are based on fundamental economic principles. That is, as the Price per Cup for each beverage increases in columns B through E, the Sales in Cups, or quantity demanded, decrease in columns F through I. However, a key question that most business managers try to answer is how much will demand increase or decrease when the price of a product is changed? To help answer this question, the next example constructs a scatter plot chart using the data from Figure 45. A scatter plot chart will place a marker for each beverage in the plot area based on its price and quantity demanded. Therefore, for each data series, or each beverage, the value for both the Y-axis and X-axis must be defined. This example is different from the charts that were demonstrated in the first two sections of this chapter; in those examples, values were assigned only to the Y-axis and labels were assigned to the X-axis (i.e., months, product category). Furthermore, the values for the X- and Y-axes in Figure 45 are not in a continuous range. Therefore, you must use the method of manually defining the data series, X-axis and Y-axis, that was demonstrated in the preceding section. The following points explain how this is accomplished:

- Activate cell K5, which is a blank cell. This will create a blank chart on the worksheet.
- Click the **Scatter** icon in the **Insert** tab on the Ribbon.
- Select the **Scatter with Straight Lines and Markers** format option. This will create a chart that has the visual appearance of a line chart with markers.
- Click the **Select Data** icon in the **Design** tab to open the **Select Data Source** dialog box.
- Click the **Add** button in the **Select Data Source** dialog box to add the first data series, which is Coffee. Notice that when the **Edit Series** dialog box opens, it has input boxes for both the X-axis and Y-axis values (see Figure 47).
- Click the range finder next to **Series name**, highlight cell B3, and press the **Enter** key. Cell B3 contains the word *Coffee*, which will appear in the legend to describe this data series.
- Click the range finder next to **Series X values**, highlight the range F4:F13, and press the **Enter** key. As mentioned, the goal of this chart is to show the quantity demanded, or Sales in Cups on the X-axis and the Price per Cup on the Y-axis. The range F4:F13 contains the quantity demanded for Coffee.
- Click the range finder next to **Series Y values**, highlight the range B4:B13, and press the **Enter** key. This range contains the price of Coffee for each of the 10 weeks listed in column B.
- Click the **OK** button to close the **Edit Series** dialog box. Then click the **Add** button in the **Select Data Source** dialog box to add the next data series, which is "Tea."
- Add the "Tea, Decaf Coffee, and Herbal Tea" data series using the same method described for Coffee. For each data series, use "Sales in Cups" to define the Series X values and Price per Cup to define the Series Y values.
- Click the **OK** button at the bottom of the **Select Data Source** dialog box to complete the chart.

Figure 47 shows the completed **Edit Series** dialog box for the Coffee data series. Notice that it has input boxes for defining both the X- and Y-axes values. In addition, as you define a data series, you will see a sample of the values appear on the right side of the **Edit Series** dialog box as well as on the chart itself.

Figure 47 | **Edit Series Dialog Box for Scatter Plot Chart**

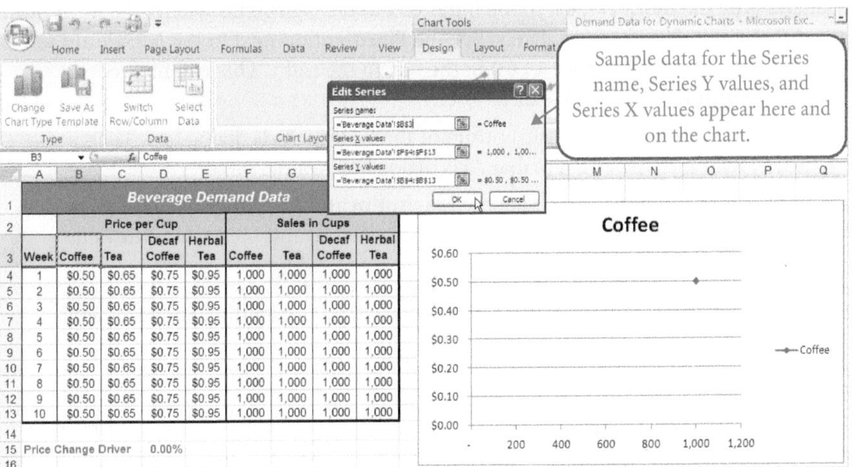


Figure 48 shows the completed **Select Data Source** dialog box after adding and defining each data series as shown in Figure 47. The name of each data series is listed on the left side of the **Select Data Source** dialog box. Notice that a unique marker is displayed for each data series, or beverage, in the plot area of the chart.

Figure 48 | **Final Settings in the Edit Data Source Dialog Box**

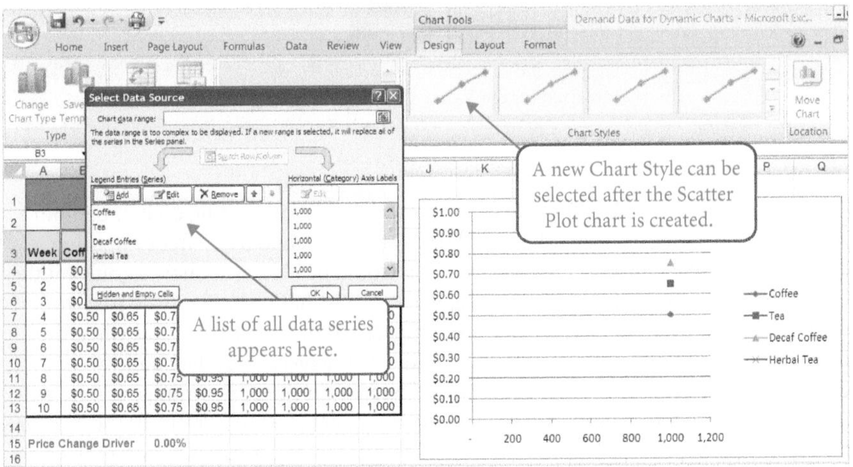


To complete the chart in Figure 48, several formatting techniques are applied such as adding titles, adjusting font sizes, and changing the color of the chart area. However, the most important formatting adjustment is fixing the scale of both the X- and Y-axes. The goal of this example is to show how the appearance of the chart changes when the formulas in the worksheet produce new outputs. Seeing how the data series changes, or moves, on the chart will provide insights as to how significant the Sales per Cup will change when the price is changed. However, the scale of the X- and Y-axes will constantly readjust when the data is changed, making it impossible to accurately read any data movements. Therefore, the scale of the X- and Y-axes must be fixed. You accomplish this as follows:

- Activate the Y-axis.
- Click the **Format** tab and then click the **Format Selection** icon. This will open the **Format Axis** dialog box, which was originally shown in Figure 29.

- In the **Axis Options** section, click the **Fixed** option next to the **Minimum** setting and type the number **.40** in the input box to the right. This will fix the **Minimum** value on the Y-axis at .40. Then click the **Fixed** option next to the **Maximum** setting and type the number **1.80** in the box to the right. This will fix the **Maximum** value of the Y-axis at 1.80.
- Click the **Close** button at the bottom of the **Format Axis** dialog box. Then activate the X-axis and open the **Format Axis** dialog box again.
- Use the same method for fixing the **Maximum** and **Minimum** values for the X-axis. The **Maximum** value should be set to 1,100 and the **Minimum** value should be set to 200.

Figure 49 shows the final scatter plot chart with all formatting enhancements added.

Figure 49 | **Final Scatter Plot Chart**

All beverages show sales of 1,000 cups before the price is changed.

| Beverage Demand Data | | | | | | | | |
|---|---|---|---|---|---|---|---|---|
| | Price per Cup | | | | Sales in Cups | | | |
| Week | Coffee | Tea | Decaf Coffee | Herbal Tea | Coffee | Tea | Decaf Coffee | Herbal Tea |
| 1 | $0.50 | $0.65 | $0.75 | $0.95 | 1,000 | 1,000 | 1,000 | 1,000 |
| 2 | $0.50 | $0.65 | $0.75 | $0.95 | 1,000 | 1,000 | 1,000 | 1,000 |
| 3 | $0.50 | $0.65 | $0.75 | $0.95 | 1,000 | 1,000 | 1,000 | 1,000 |
| 4 | $0.50 | $0.65 | $0.75 | $0.95 | 1,000 | 1,000 | 1,000 | 1,000 |
| 5 | $0.50 | $0.65 | $0.75 | $0.95 | 1,000 | 1,000 | 1,000 | 1,000 |
| 6 | $0.50 | $0.65 | $0.75 | $0.95 | 1,000 | 1,000 | 1,000 | 1,000 |
| 7 | $0.50 | $0.65 | $0.75 | $0.95 | 1,000 | 1,000 | 1,000 | 1,000 |
| 8 | $0.50 | $0.65 | $0.75 | $0.95 | 1,000 | 1,000 | 1,000 | 1,000 |
| 9 | $0.50 | $0.65 | $0.75 | $0.95 | 1,000 | 1,000 | 1,000 | 1,000 |
| 10 | $0.50 | $0.65 | $0.75 | $0.95 | 1,000 | 1,000 | 1,000 | 1,000 |

Price Change Driver 0.00%

The max and min values were fixed for the X-and Y-Axis scale.

Beverage Demand Analysis

Price per Cup: $1.80, $1.60, $1.40, $1.20, $1.00, $0.80, $0.60, $0.40

Sales in Cups: 200, 400, 600, 800, 1,000

Coffee, Tea, Decaf Coffee, Herbal Tea

Figures 50, 51, and 52 illustrate how the data series representing each of the four beverages moves on the chart when cell D15 is set to 1, 3, and 5%. After examining each of these three figures, a business manager would be able to see how significant the change in sales is as the price is increased. For example, notice in Figure 50 that the line for Herbal Tea extends farthest to the left compared to the other beverages when the price is increased by 1% per week for 10 weeks. This suggests that the quantity demanded for Herbal Tea is very sensitive to increases in price, assuming this data represents industrywide changes in price and quantity demanded. Conversely, the line for Coffee does not move nearly as far to the left because sales per cup are not significantly declining when the price is increased.

Figure 50 | **Sales in Cups When Price Is Increased 1%**

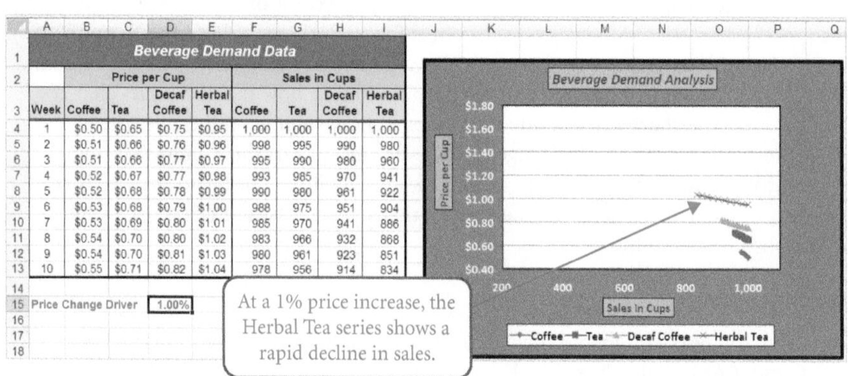

| Beverage Demand Data | | | | | | | | |
|---|---|---|---|---|---|---|---|---|
| | Price per Cup | | | | Sales in Cups | | | |
| Week | Coffee | Tea | Decaf Coffee | Herbal Tea | Coffee | Tea | Decaf Coffee | Herbal Tea |
| 1 | $0.50 | $0.65 | $0.75 | $0.95 | 1,000 | 1,000 | 1,000 | 1,000 |
| 2 | $0.51 | $0.66 | $0.76 | $0.96 | 998 | 995 | 990 | 980 |
| 3 | $0.51 | $0.66 | $0.77 | $0.97 | 995 | 990 | 980 | 960 |
| 4 | $0.52 | $0.67 | $0.77 | $0.98 | 993 | 985 | 970 | 941 |
| 5 | $0.52 | $0.68 | $0.78 | $0.99 | 990 | 980 | 961 | 922 |
| 6 | $0.53 | $0.68 | $0.79 | $1.00 | 988 | 975 | 951 | 904 |
| 7 | $0.53 | $0.69 | $0.80 | $1.01 | 985 | 970 | 941 | 886 |
| 8 | $0.54 | $0.70 | $0.80 | $1.02 | 983 | 966 | 932 | 868 |
| 9 | $0.54 | $0.70 | $0.81 | $1.03 | 980 | 961 | 923 | 851 |
| 10 | $0.55 | $0.71 | $0.82 | $1.04 | 978 | 956 | 914 | 834 |

Price Change Driver 1.00%

Figure 51 | **Sales in Cups When Price Is Increased 3%**

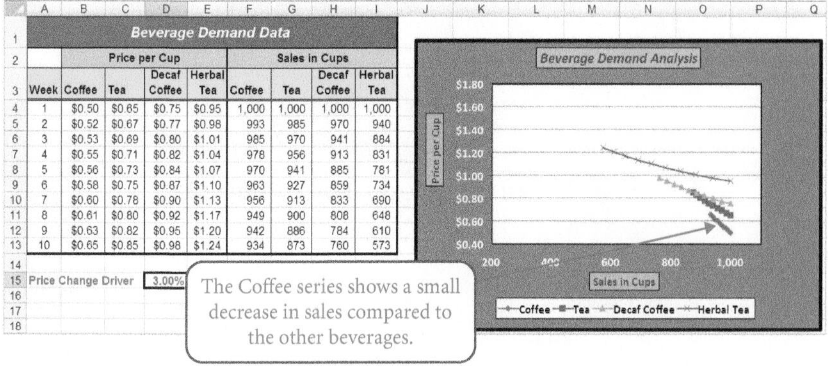

**Beverage Demand Data**

| | Price per Cup | | | | Sales in Cups | | | |
|---|---|---|---|---|---|---|---|---|
| Week | Coffee | Tea | Decaf Coffee | Herbal Tea | Coffee | Tea | Decaf Coffee | Herbal Tea |
| 1 | $0.50 | $0.65 | $0.75 | $0.95 | 1,000 | 1,000 | 1,000 | 1,000 |
| 2 | $0.52 | $0.67 | $0.77 | $0.98 | 993 | 985 | 970 | 940 |
| 3 | $0.53 | $0.69 | $0.80 | $1.01 | 985 | 970 | 941 | 884 |
| 4 | $0.55 | $0.71 | $0.82 | $1.04 | 978 | 956 | 913 | 831 |
| 5 | $0.56 | $0.73 | $0.84 | $1.07 | 970 | 941 | 885 | 781 |
| 6 | $0.58 | $0.75 | $0.87 | $1.10 | 963 | 927 | 859 | 734 |
| 7 | $0.60 | $0.78 | $0.90 | $1.13 | 956 | 913 | 833 | 690 |
| 8 | $0.61 | $0.80 | $0.92 | $1.17 | 949 | 900 | 808 | 648 |
| 9 | $0.63 | $0.82 | $0.95 | $1.20 | 942 | 886 | 784 | 610 |
| 10 | $0.65 | $0.85 | $0.98 | $1.24 | 934 | 873 | 760 | 573 |

Price Change Driver 3.00%



Figure 52 | **Sales in Cups When Price Is Increased 5%**

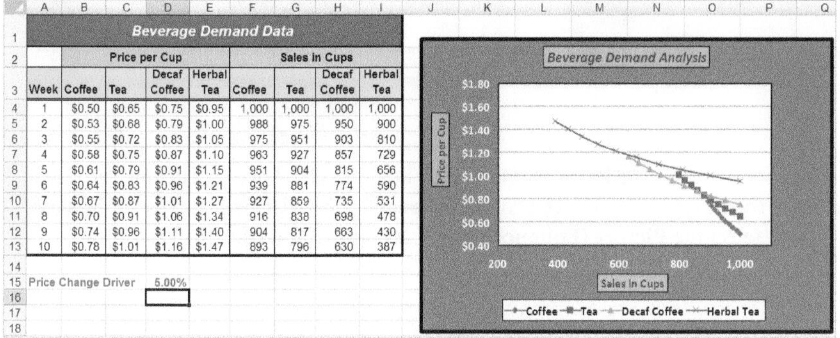

**Beverage Demand Data**

| | Price per Cup | | | | Sales in Cups | | | |
|---|---|---|---|---|---|---|---|---|
| Week | Coffee | Tea | Decaf Coffee | Herbal Tea | Coffee | Tea | Decaf Coffee | Herbal Tea |
| 1 | $0.50 | $0.65 | $0.75 | $0.95 | 1,000 | 1,000 | 1,000 | 1,000 |
| 2 | $0.53 | $0.68 | $0.79 | $1.00 | 988 | 975 | 950 | 900 |
| 3 | $0.55 | $0.72 | $0.83 | $1.05 | 975 | 951 | 903 | 810 |
| 4 | $0.58 | $0.75 | $0.87 | $1.10 | 963 | 927 | 857 | 729 |
| 5 | $0.61 | $0.79 | $0.91 | $1.15 | 951 | 904 | 815 | 656 |
| 6 | $0.64 | $0.83 | $0.96 | $1.21 | 939 | 881 | 774 | 590 |
| 7 | $0.67 | $0.87 | $1.01 | $1.27 | 927 | 859 | 735 | 531 |
| 8 | $0.70 | $0.91 | $1.06 | $1.34 | 916 | 838 | 698 | 478 |
| 9 | $0.74 | $0.96 | $1.11 | $1.40 | 904 | 817 | 663 | 430 |
| 10 | $0.78 | $1.01 | $1.16 | $1.47 | 893 | 796 | 630 | 387 |

Price Change Driver 5.00%



## Pasting Charts into PowerPoint and Word

Excel charts are frequently added to PowerPoint slides or Word documents for business presentations and reports. This section will demonstrate how you can copy and paste Excel charts into either a PowerPoint slide or Word document.

Figure 53 shows a PowerPoint slide that could be used by a business manager who is presenting the results of the column chart shown in Figure 30. The following steps explain how to copy and paste this chart into this slide:

- Open both the PowerPoint file and the Excel file containing the column chart.
- Activate the Excel file by clicking it in the taskbar at the bottom of the screen (see Figure 54).
- Activate the column chart and click the **Copy** icon.
- Activate the PowerPoint file by clicking it in the taskbar at the bottom of the screen.
- Select the **Paste Special** option in the **Paste** icon in **Home** tab on the Ribbon in the PowerPoint file. This will open the **Paste Special** dialog box.
- Select the **Picture** (**Enhanced Metafile**) option in the **Paste Special** dialog box and click the **OK** button. The chart will appear in the slide.
- Use the sizing handles on the chart to change the size of the chart and click and drag the chart to reposition on the slide if necessary.

>> ***Quick Reference***

### Scatter Plot Charts

1. Activate a blank cell on a worksheet. A blank column or a blank row must appear between the data on a worksheet and the blank cell that is activated.
2. Click the **Scatter** icon in the **Insert** tab on the Ribbon.
3. Select a chart format.
4. With the blank chart activated, click the **Select Data** icon in the **Design** tab on the Ribbon.
5. Click the **Add** button on the left side of the **Select Data Source** dialog box to add a data series.
6. Define the Series name in the **Edit Series** dialog box with one cell location or type a name in quotation marks.
7. Define the X Series values with a range of cells.
8. Define the Y Series values with a range of cells.
9. Click the **OK** button to close the **Edit Series** dialog box.
10. Repeat steps 5–9 to add additional data series if needed.
11. Click the **OK** button on the **Select Data Source** dialog box.

Figure 53 | **View of a PowerPoint Slide**

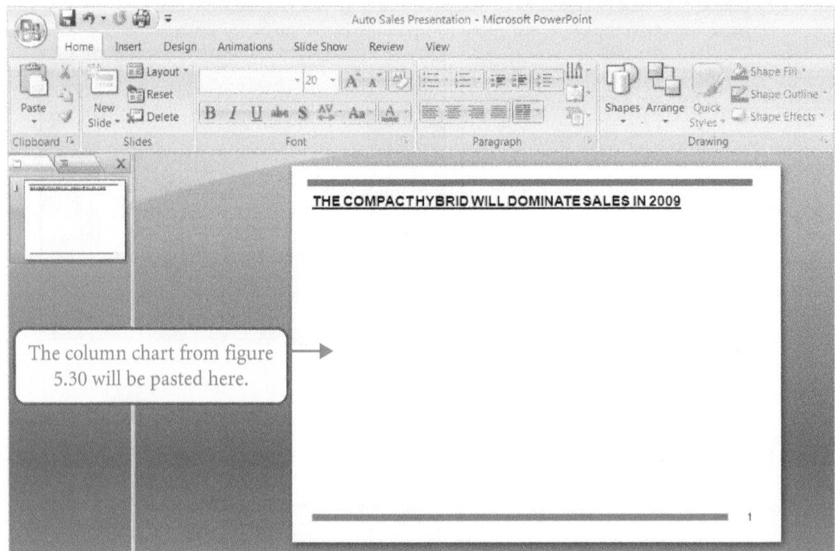


Figure 54 shows the **Paste Special** dialog box that is opened by clicking the down arrow of the **Paste** icon and selecting **Paste Special.** The chart will appear in the slide after you select the **Picture (Enhanced Metafile)** option and click the **OK** button.

Figure 54 | **Paste Special Dialog Box for Pasting a Chart**

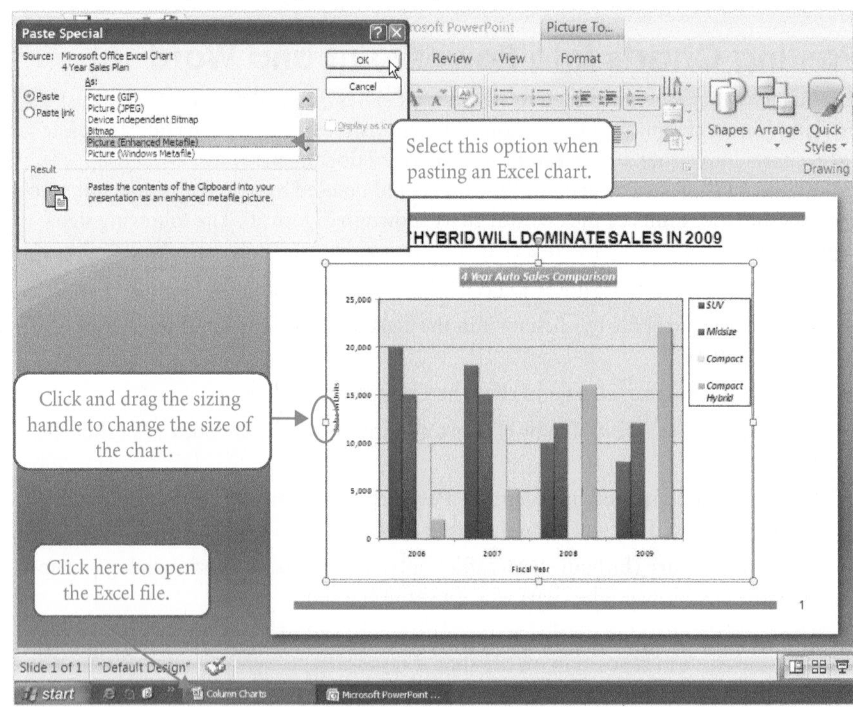


Figure 55 shows the final PowerPoint slide with the Excel chart. Notice that the chart was repositioned on the slide to make room for the triangle and text box.

Figure 55 | **Final PowerPoint Slide**

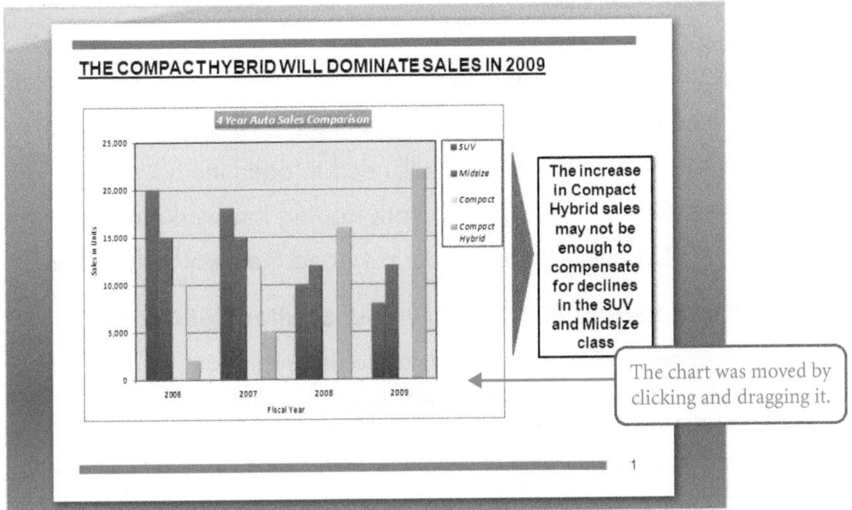


Figure 56 shows an example of pasting the 100% Stacked Column chart shown in Figure 37 into a Word document. This business research paper example demonstrates the trends in the Sporting Goods industry. The method for pasting this chart into the Word document is identical to the method illustrated for pasting a chart into a PowerPoint slide. After copying the chart in an Excel file, place the cursor in your Word document where you want the chart to appear. Then open the **Paste Special** dialog box and select the **Picture (Enhanced Metafile)** option.

Figure 56 | **Excel Chart Pasted into a Word Document**

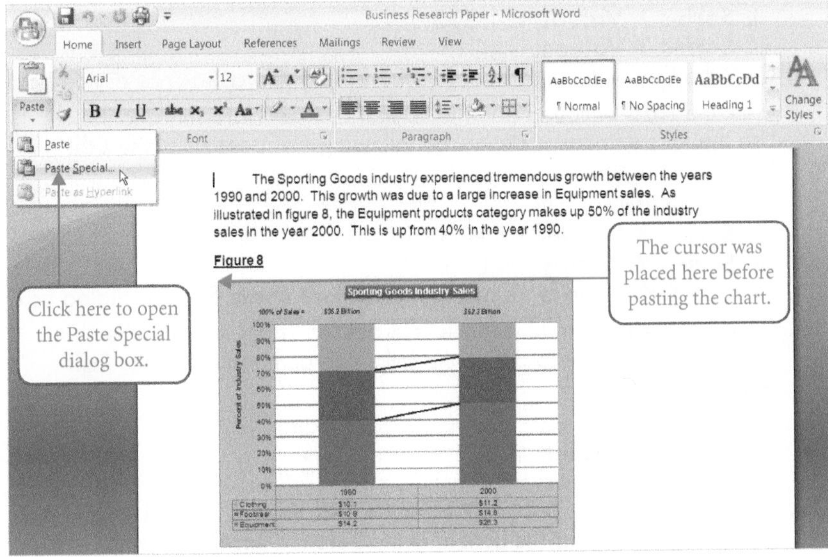


> **Quick Reference**
>
> **Pasting Charts into PowerPoint and Word**
>
> 1. Activate a chart in an Excel file and click the **Copy** icon.
> 2. Open a PowerPoint file to a slide where the chart should appear. For a Word document, place the cursor where the chart should appear.
> 3. Click the **Home** tab in the Ribbon.
> 4. Click the down arrow below the **Paste** icon.
> 5. Select the **Paste Special** option to open the **Paste Special** dialog box.
> 6. Select the **Picture (Enhanced Metafile)** option and click the **OK** button in the **Paste Special** dialog box.
> 7. Adjust the size of the chart by clicking and dragging the sizing handles as needed.

VIDEO WORKSHOP

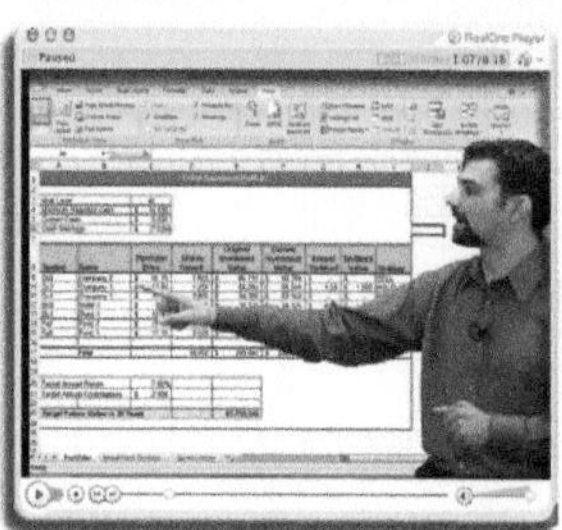

## >> Scatter Plot Charts

The purpose of this workshop is to review the construction of scatter plot charts. I will be demonstrating the tasks in this workshop on the video named **Scatter Plot Charts**. You will need to open the file named ib_e05_beveragedemandanalysis before starting this workshop. Try completing the following tasks on your own and then watch the video.

1. **Creating a Scatter Plot Chart (Video: Scatter Plot Charts)**
   a. Activate cell L1 on the worksheet named Beverage Data.
   b. Click the **Scatter** icon in the **Insert** tab on the Ribbon. Then select the **Scatter with Straight Lines and Markers** format option.
   c. Click and drag the frame of the blank chart so the upper-left corner is in cell J1.
   d. Click the **Select Data** icon in the **Design** tab on the Ribbon.
   e. Click the **Add** button to add the "Coffee" data series to the chart. Use the range finder to define the following components of the **Edit Series** dialog box:
      i. **Series name**: B3
      ii. **Series X Values**: F4:F13
      iii. **Series Y Values**: B4:B13
   f. Click the **OK** button to go back to the **Select Data Source** dialog box.
   g. Click the **Add** button to add the "Tea" data series to the chart. Use the range finder to define the following components of the **Edit Series** dialog box:
      i. **Series name**: C3
      ii. **Series X Values**: G4:G13
      iii. **Series Y Values**: C4:C13
   h. Click the **OK** button to go back to the **Select Data Source** dialog box.
   i. Click the **Add** button to add the "Decaf Coffee" data series to the chart. Use the range finder to define the following components of the **Edit Series** dialog box:
      i. **Series name**: D3
      ii. **Series X Values**: H4:H13
      iii. **Series Y Values**: D4:D13
   j. Click the **OK** button to go back to the **Select Data Source** dialog box.
   k. Click the **Add** button to add the "Herbal Tea" data series to the chart. Use the range finder to define the following components of the **Edit Series** dialog box:
      i. **Series name**: E3
      ii. **Series X Values**: I4:I13
      iii. **Series Y Values**: E4:E13
   l. Click the **OK** button at the bottom of the **Edit Series** dialog box and then click the **OK** button at the bottom of the **Select Data Source** dialog box.
   m. Select the **Style 18 Chart Styles** icon in the **Design** tab on the Ribbon.
   n. Click the **Legend** icon in the **Layout** tab and select the **Show Legend at Bottom** option.

o. Add the chart title `Beverage Demand Analysis`. Use the **Above chart** option.
p. Add the title `Price per Cup` to the Y-axis.
q. Add the title `Sales in Cups` to the X-axis.

2. **Formatting (Video: Scatter Plot Charts)**
   a. Center the title over the middle of the chart and then center the legend at the bottom of the chart.
   b. Format the chart title with a 12-point font, bold, italics, orange background, and black outline with a 1-point weight.
   c. Format the legend with a 10-point font, bold, white background, and black outline with a 1-point weight.
   d. Create space between the left side of the plot area and the Y-axis title. Decrease the plot area to the right and move the Y-axis title to the left.
   e. Make the same formatting enhancements to the X- and Y-axes titles as the chart title, except keep the font size at 10 points.
   f. Change the color of the chart area to green.
   g. Change the color of the Y-axis and X-axis values to white.

3. **Fixing the Scale for the X- and Y-Axes (Video: Scatter Plot Charts)**
   a. Click anywhere on the Y-axis and click the **Format Selection** icon in the **Format** tab on the Ribbon.
   b. Set the **Minimum** and **Maximum** options to **Fixed**. Then type the following values in the input box next to each option:
      i. **Minimum**: `.40`
      ii. **Maximum**: `1.80`
   c. Click the **Close** button at the bottom of the **Format Axis** dialog box.
   d. Click anywhere on the X-axis and click the **Format Selection** icon in the **Format** tab on the Ribbon.
   e. Set the **Minimum** and **Maximum** options to **Fixed**. Then type the following values in the input box next to each option:
      i. **Minimum**: `200`
      ii. **Maximum**: `1100`
   f. Click the **Close** button at the bottom of the **Format Axis** dialog box.
   g. Change the value in cell D15 to `1`. Then change it to `3`.
   h. Save and close your file.

## >> Pasting Charts into Word

**VIDEO WORKSHOP**

The purpose of this workshop is to demonstrate the method of pasting Excel charts into a Word document. I will be demonstrating the tasks in this workshop in the video named **Pasting Charts into Word**. You will need to open the Word file named ib_e05_businessplanpaper and the Excel file named ib_e05_costschart before starting this workshop. Try completing the following tasks on your own and then watch the video.

1. **Inserting Charts into Word Documents (Video: Pasting Charts into Word)**
   a. Activate the Excel file named ib_e05_costschart.
   b. Activate the pie chart named Startup Costs and copy it.
   c. Activate the Word document named ib_e05_businessplanpaper and place the cursor below the **Figure 2** heading along the left margin.
   d. Open the **Paste Special** dialog box by clicking the down arrow below the **Paste** icon.
   e. Select the **Picture (Enhanced Metafile)** option in the **Paste Special** dialog box and click the **OK** button.
   f. Select the chart and reduce the height of the pie chart to 2.5 inches using the **Height** icon in the **Format** tab on the Ribbon. This will automatically reduce the width to 4.06 inches.
   g. Save and close your file.

**EXERCISE**

**Why Do I Need This?**

## >> Analyzing Supply and Demand

Studying changes in supply and demand is a common area of research for professional economists and business analysts. Changes in supply and demand can impact decisions such as product pricing, entry into new markets, exiting existing markets, increasing product lines, or decreasing product lines. Having the ability to visually display these trends can not only serve as a powerful presentation tool, but can also serve as a powerful analytical tool.

### Exercise

The purpose of this exercise is to create a supply and demand chart using a scatter plot chart. In addition, this exercise will demonstrate how a change in price impacts the quantity supplied and the quantity demanded for a hypothetical industry. Your goal will be to change the price to identify where the demand and supply lines intersect, which is also known as *reaching equilibrium*. This data can be found in the file named ib_e05_supplyanddemand. Open this file before working on the following tasks:

1. Type the number `10` into cell C15. Note the price in cell B12 by typing it into a blank cell on the worksheet or jot it down on a piece of paper. You will need to know this number later in the exercise.

2. Type the number `-10` into cell C15. Note the quantity value in cell D12 by typing it into another blank cell on the worksheet or jot it down on a piece of paper. You will need to know this number later in the exercise.

3. Type the number `0` into cell C15. Then activate a blank cell for the purposes of creating a blank chart.

4. Create a blank **Scatter** chart using the **Scatter with Straight Lines and Markers** format option. After creating the blank chart, move it so the upper-left corner is in cell E1.

5. Open the **Select Data Source** dialog box and add the Supply data series to the chart. The settings in the **Edit Series** dialog box should be as follows:
   a. **Series name**: Cell C2, which contains the word *Supply*.
   b. **Series X values**: The range C3:C12, which contains the quantity supplied values.
   c. **Series Y values**: The range B3:B12, which contains the price.

6. Add the Demand data series to the chart using the following details in the **Edit Series** dialog box:
   a. **Series name**: Cell D2, which contains the word *Demand*.
   b. **Series X values**: The range D3:D12, which contains the quantity demand values.
   c. **Series Y values**: The range B3:B12, which contains the price.
7. Change the **Chart Style** of the chart to **Style 34**. This will change the color of the Demand data series to red and the Supply data series to blue.
8. Add the following titles to the chart:
   a. **Chart Title**: `Supply and Demand for Product A`
   b. **X-Axis Title**: `Quantity`
   c. **Y-Axis Title**: `Price`
9. Change the font size of the chart title to 14 points and change the font size of the X- and Y-axes titles to 12 points. Then move the Y-axis title to the left to create space between the title and Y-axis values.
10. Fix the scale of the Y-axis using the **Format Axis** dialog box. Use the number you identified in step 1 rounded *up* to the nearest dollar to set the **Maximum** value for the axis. Set the **Minimum** value of the axis to `0`.
11. Fix the scale of the X-axis using the **Format Axis** dialog box. Use the number you identified in step 2 to set the **Maximum** value for the axis. Set the **Minimum** value to `0`.
12. Type the number `3`, then `5`, and then `10` into cell C15. At what price (approximately) does the demand line intersect the supply line?
13. Enter the number `0`, then `-3`, then `-5`, and then `-10` into cell C15. Can the quantity supplied satisfy the quantity demanded at these prices?
14. Save and close your file.

## >> What's Wrong with This Spreadsheet?

**PROBLEM & EXERCISE**

### Problem

A coworker in your department is trying to create a chart for a strategy presentation being held tomorrow morning. She is having difficulty creating a column chart based on the sales results contained in an Excel file and has come to you for help. Her goal is to show the change in Net Sales from the year 2006 to 2007 for each company in her worksheet. Her conversation with you includes the following points:

1. I am trying to create a basic column chart that shows the Net Sales values along the Y-axis and the name of each company on the X-axis. Because I have two years' worth of data, I thought I would use the legend to show what bar pertains to what year.
2. A friend of mine showed me this trick in which you just highlight everything on the worksheet; click that chart icon in the Ribbon, and bingo, the chart appears. I did the same exact thing as my friend, but my chart is horrible!
3. The other thing I noticed is the Public Company indicator (Column B) keeps popping up in the chart. I just want the sales data in a simple column chart. However, I guess this is more complicated than I thought!

### Exercise

The chart your coworker tried to create is on the file named ib_e05_charttrouble. Open this file and take a look at the Chart1 chart sheet. Consider the following points:

1. What method is your coworker using to create the chart? Will this enable her to achieve her goals?
2. Why is the Public Company indicator (column B) appearing in the chart?
3. Your coworker is trying to create a column chart. Is that apparent in the chart that was attempted on the file?
4. Your coworker wants the year to be in the legend of the chart. How can this be accomplished?

What's wrong with this chart? Write a short answer to each of the points listed here. Then create a second chart in the ib_e05_charttrouble Excel file based on the requirements stated here. Apply any formatting features that you think will make the chart easier to read. The chart you create should appear in its own chart sheet.

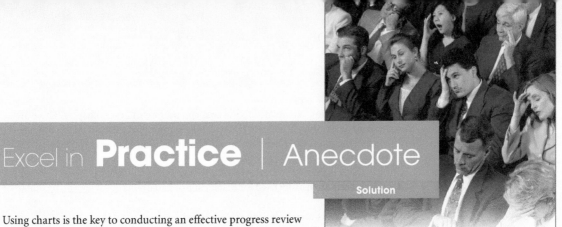

SuperStock, Inc

# Excel in Practice | Anecdote

Solution

Using charts is the key to conducting an effective progress review meeting. A well-constructed chart can explain trends, relationships, and results in a very short period time. Therefore, I converted the data calculated and evaluated in numerous Excel files to a few charts, pasted them into PowerPoint slides, and presented them at progress review meetings. Constructing charts this way not only increased the efficiency of the meetings, but also demonstrated a professional standard that my clients often appreciated.

## Assignment

1. The file named ib_e05_clientresearchdata contains data for a meeting with the executives of a major corporation.
2. Create a chart that will best display the sales trend by region in the Regional Sales worksheet. This chart should demonstrate how the overall sales of the company have shifted between the regions.
3. Use any annotations, objects, and formatting techniques to highlight changes in the company's sales by region. Note that the total sales for the company by year are in row 8 of the worksheet. Your chart must show these total sales results.
4. Create a PowerPoint slide with the title **`Region 4 Provides Future Growth`**. Display the chart you created in this slide. This PowerPoint slide as well as the chart should have a professional appearance.

## Questions for Discussion

1. Why are charts better to use in presentations as opposed to worksheets?
2. Is it possible to have too much formatting on a chart?
3. What do you need to know to create an effective chart?

# Review Questions

The following questions are related to the concepts addressed in this chapter. There are three types of questions: Short Answer, True or False, and Fill in the Blank. If your answer to a True or False question is False, write a short explanation as to why you think the statement is not true.

1. Excel charts are usually used for displaying and analyzing ____________ data.
2. How are charts used in business?
3. The ____________ tab on the Ribbon is used for creating charts.
4. True or False: You must *always* highlight data on a worksheet before creating a chart.
5. What three tabs are added to the Ribbon after you create a chart?
6. After you create a chart, if the data you wanted on the X-axis appears on the Y-axis, you can use the ____________ icon in the ____________ tab on the Ribbon.
7. Explain when you would use a 100% Stacked Column chart instead of a pie chart.
8. What is the purpose of adding lines to a 100% Stacked Column chart?
9. A ____________ chart is commonly used to display trends over time, such as stock prices or market indices.
10. A data table can be added to the bottom of a chart using the ____________ icon in the ____________ tab on the Ribbon.
11. Specific data values can be added to a chart by using the ____________ icon in the ____________ tab on the Ribbon.
12. True or False: The formatting icons in the **Home** tab cannot be used when formatting an area of a chart.
13. True or False: The data values or data table added to a chart cannot be formatted.
14. Explain when you would need to use the **Format Axis** dialog box when formatting either the X- or Y-axis.
15. How would you change the color of one individual bar on a column chart?
16. The ____________ icon in the ____________ tab is used for adding annotations to a chart.
17. Lines and arrows can be added to a chart by clicking the ____________ icon in the ____________tab on the Ribbon.
18. True or False: A **Format** dialog box can be opened for any area of the chart by activating that area, right clicking, and selecting the appropriate command.
19. Explain why you would want to manually define the data series, X-axis values, and Y-axis values for a chart.
20. True or False: For a column chart, both the X and Y series values can be defined for each data series added to the chart.

21. True or False: Once a chart is created, it will never change even if the data used to create it changes.

22. What chart would you need to use if you wanted to define X-axis and Y-axis values for each data series.

23. For you to see data moving on a chart, it is best to use the ____________ of the X- and Y-axes.

24. What option in the **Paste Special** dialog box should you use when pasting charts into a Word or PowerPoint file?

25. True or False: When you are pasting a chart into a Word file, the chart will always appear in the upper-left corner of the page that is currently visible on the screen.

# Skills Exam

The following exam is designed to test your ability to recognize and execute the Excel skills presented in this chapter. Read each question carefully and answer the questions in the order they are listed. You should be able to complete this exam in 60 minutes or less.

1. Open the ib_e05_skillsexam.
2. For the Global Sales worksheet, create a 100% Stacked Column chart that can be used to evaluate the sales growth of this company by country/region. The chart should include the following details:
   a. The X-axis should display the years in the range B3:E3.
   b. The Legend should display the name of the country or region from column A.
   c. The chart title above the chart should be **Global Net Sales**.
   d. The title for the Y-axis should be **Percent of Total Net Sales**.
   e. Data labels showing the sales value for each country should appear on the inside end of the bars.
   f. The chart should appear in its own chart sheet with the tab name **Global Sales Chart**.
3. Change the font size for the percentages along the Y-axis to 12 points.
4. Change the font size for the years along the X-axis to 14 points.
5. Make the following format adjustments to the Y-axis title:
   a. Add a black outline with a 1-point weight.
   b. Change the background color to blue.
   c. Change the font size to 12 and change the text color to white.
6. Make the following format adjustments to the chart title:
   a. Add a black outline with a 1-point weight.
   b. Change the background color to blue.
   c. Change the font size to 18 and change the text color to white.
7. Decrease the height of the plot area so there is approximately ½ inch of space between the top of the plot area and the chart title.
8. Make the following format adjustments to the chart legend:
   a. Add a black outline with a 1-point weight.
   b. Change the font size to 16 and bold the text.
   c. Move the legend next to the plot area.
   d. Increase the height of the legend so it is the same height as the plot area.
9. Change the color of the Europe data series to red, the Canada data series to orange, and the Asia Pacific data series to light green.
10. For all the data labels on the bars of the chart, increase the font size to 12 points.
11. Add the following annotation to the chart: **Dollars in U.S. Billions**. This annotation should appear in the upper-left corner of the chart area. Change the font size to 10 points and add italics.
12. Add the following annotation to the chart: **100% Net Sales =**. This annotation should appear next to the left border of the chart area above the Y-axis. The font size should be 10 points, bold, and italic.
13. Add an annotation to the top of each bar of the chart showing the total Net Sales for each year. The total sales for each year can be found in row 8 of the Global Sales worksheet. A dollar sign should appear in front of each number, and the font should be 12 points, bold, and italic. Make sure the number is completely visible.

14. Connect the top of each bar for the USA data series with a *black* line. Do the same for the Europe and Canada data series. Use a 1-point weight for all lines.
15. Create a line chart based on the data in the Income Summary worksheet. The chart should include the following details:
    a. The X-axis should display the years in the range B2:J2.
    b. The Legend should display the name of the income categories in column A.
    c. The chart title shouldbe **`Income Summary`**.
    d. The title for the Y-axis should be **`Percent Change at Year End`**.
    e. The legend should appear at the bottom of the chart.
    f. The chart should appear in its own chart sheet with the tab name **`Income Summary Chart`**.
    g. The Style of the chart should be set to the **Style 2** option.
16. Change the font size of the percentages and years on the Y- and X-axes to 12 points.
17. Make the following format adjustments to the chart legend:
    a. Add a black outline with a 1-point weight.
    b. Change the font size to 12 points and bold the text.
    c. Move the legend so that it is centered under the plot area.
18. Change the line weight for each data series to 2¼ points. Do not change the colors.
19. Fix the scale of the Y-axis as follows:
    a. **Minimum: `-.08`**
    b. **Maximum: `.16`**
    c. **Major Unit: `04`**
20. Open the Word document named ib_e05_internationalsalesreport.
21. Paste the **Global Sales Chart** from the Excel file into this Word document. The chart must appear below the words *Figure 1* in bold text. Leave one space between the chart and this heading.
22. Save and close both the Word file and the Excel file.

# Challenge Questions

The following questions are designed to test your ability to apply the Excel skills you have learned to complete a business objective. Use your knowledge of Excel as well as your creativity to answer these questions. For most questions, there are several possible ways to complete the objective.

1. If you are presenting data for an international company, what chart would you use to show the percent of sales generated by country for one year? Assume this company is operating in five countries. Create a spreadsheet showing one year of sales data for an international company by country. You can make up the countries and the sales numbers. Create a chart to present this data.

2. Pick two public companies and research the historical closing price of the stock for every month last year. In addition, research the historical adjusted closing price of the Dow Jones Industrial Average for every month last year. Record your data onto an Excel worksheet and create an appropriate chart to present this information. Your chart should have a professional appearance and should clearly highlight any significant trends displayed.

3. What chart would you use to show a two-year divisional sales trend of a corporation? The divisions of the corporation could be three different retail store chains such as clothing stores, jewelry stores, and sports equipment. Another example can be a corporation that sells different brands of candy such as a chocolate brand, a marshmallow brand, and a hard candy brand. Research the financial statement of a public company that operates several divisions such as these. Find and record two years' worth of sales data for each division on an Excel worksheet. Then create an appropriate chart to present this data and place it in a PowerPoint slide. Your chart, as well as the PowerPoint slide, should have a professional appearance.

4. The following formula is used to calculate the quantity supplied for a given market:

   $Q = P \times 27 - 5$, where Q = quantity supplied and P = price

   Create a spreadsheet with three columns of data. The first column should be labeled **Data Points** and should contain a list of numbers from 1 to 10. The second column should be labeled **Price**. The first value in the Price column should be **$3**. The third column should be **Quantity**. Use the supply formula shown here to calculate the data in this column. Create a formula for the remainder of the values in the Price column so that you can control how much the price increases for each of the remaining nine data points. You should be able to enter a percentage into another cell on the spreadsheet and have the Price column calculate a price each week based on the value you enter. A positive number will increase the price for every data point; a negative number will decrease the price for every data point. After constructing the spreadsheet, create an appropriate chart that can be used to study the data as the price is changed.

# Applying Core Competency Skills

## Financial Planning and Accounting

## Chapter Goals

The purpose of this chapter is to show how Excel can be applied to two common business practices. The first is financial planning. Business managers often use Excel to develop financial strategies for improving the performance and growth of existing businesses or for starting new ones. The second is constructing a full set of financial accounting statements. Excel is a great tool for building basic accounting spreadsheets, especially when you are working on assignments for accounting courses. You can accomplish both of these critical business exercises in Excel utilizing the core competency skills you have learned in previous chapters of this text. This chapter begins by demonstrating the technique of linking data between worksheets or workbooks. Worksheets are often linked when spreadsheets for financial planning or accounting are constructed, which is why they are covered in the first section of this chapter.

## >> Excel | Skill Sets

**Linking Data**
- Linking Worksheets and Workbooks
- Updating Workbook Links
- SUMIF Function

**Financial Planning**
- Financial Assumptions
- Freeze Panes
- Financial Data
- Cash Analysis (The NPV Function)

**Financial Accounting**
- T-Accounts
- Journals
- Ledgers
- Trial Balance and Work Sheets
- Statements

Corbis/Bettmann

## Excel in Practice | Anecdote

### My Role as a Strategic Planning Manager

When I worked as a strategic planning manager, I was responsible for developing business plans that demonstrated the financial potential of new businesses ideas and corporate initiatives. These plans were constructed from several assumptions related to almost every aspect of the business. Assumptions could include the cost of shipping goods, expected growth in sales, change in the cost of goods sold, the number of full-time employees, the wage per employee, and so on. The decision to invest in a new business or initiative depended on the result of a net present value analysis, which showed whether an investment could provide an adequate return. I would then present the completed business plans with net present value results to the directing officers of the company, which often included both the CEO and CFO. One of the biggest challenges in preparing for these meetings was to show different scenarios regarding the potential performance of a business idea. For example, the executives would often ask questions such as "What if the business requires more employees? What if the cost of construction goes over budget? What if sales come in lower than planned?" A negative change in any of these assumptions could reduce or eliminate any potential profits. Therefore, I had to construct and present several different plans showing a worst, best, and target case scenario. Constructing so many plans and being prepared to answer any question from the directing officers appeared to be in impossible task at first.

>> Continued later in this chapter

# Linking Data

**Skill Set**

***Linking*** data between multiple worksheets or workbooks is a common technique used in financial planning and financial accounting spreadsheets. This section will demonstrate how you can use the technique of linking data to construct a sales and gross profit plan for a division of a hypothetical manufacturing company. Linking data is also commonly used with the **SUMIF** function, which will also be introduced in this section.

## Linking Worksheets and Workbooks

Cell referencing is an important tool for working with formulas and functions on a specific worksheet. However, you can also use cell referencing to link data between two worksheets or workbooks. This is also referred to as a ***3-D reference.*** You may recall that to define the **table_array** argument of the **VLookup** function you highlighted a range of cells in a second worksheet. This is essentially how data is linked from one worksheet to another. Linking data is especially valuable when constructing financial plans because business managers are typically required to show various scenarios when planning the financial goals for their area of responsibility. Since linking data uses cell references, the business manager can change values in key cell locations to produce new outputs for the formulas and functions used to create the plan.

This example demonstrates the technique of linking data by creating a sales and gross profit plan for a division in a hypothetical manufacturing company (Division B). Large companies will typically require the managing director of each division to create a comprehensive financial plan which outlines all expenses, sales, and profits that will be generated by their product line or service. For example, a large electronics manufacturer might consist of four divisions: Personal Computers, Cameras, Corporate Services, and Copy Machines. The directors for each of these divisions would be required to develop and present a financial plan to the executive officers of the company. This demonstration will focus on the sales and gross profit portion of these financial plans. Figures 1 through 3 show the data that will be used for this example. The worksheet shown in Figure 3 is the blank financial plan that will be completed by creating links to the worksheets shown Figure 1 and 2.

Figure 1 | **Financial Results LY Workbook: Results for 2006 Worksheet**

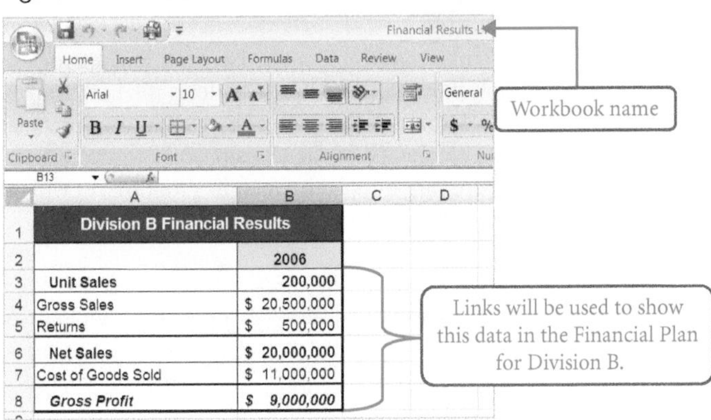

Figure 2 | **Division B Financial Plan Workbook: Plan Assumptions Worksheet**

| Division B Financial Plan Assumptions | | | |
|---|---|---|---|
| | 2007 | 2008 | 2009 |
| Returns (Percent of Gross Sales) | 2.00% | 2.00% | 2.00% |
| Gross Sales Change (Percent) | 10.00% | 5.00% | 5.00% |
| Average Price per Item | $100.00 | $102.50 | $102.50 |
| Cost of Goods Sold (Percent of Gross Sales) | 55.00% | 55.00% | 55.00% |

Division B Financial Plan

Workbook name

This data will be referenced in the formulas used to create the Financial Plan for Division B.

The Financial Plan for Division B is in this worksheet.

Plan Assumptions | Financial Plan

Figure 3 | **Division B Financial Plan Workbook: Financial Plan Worksheet**

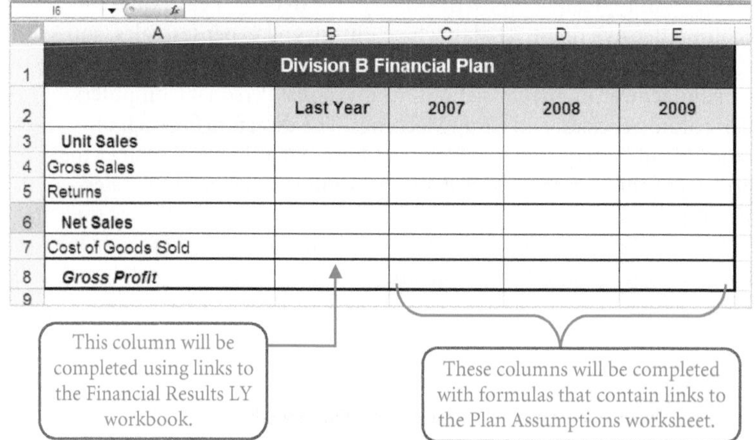

| Division B Financial Plan | | | | |
|---|---|---|---|---|
| | Last Year | 2007 | 2008 | 2009 |
| Unit Sales | | | | |
| Gross Sales | | | | |
| Returns | | | | |
| Net Sales | | | | |
| Cost of Goods Sold | | | | |
| *Gross Profit* | | | | |

This column will be completed using links to the Financial Results LY workbook.
These columns will be completed with formulas that contain links to the Plan Assumptions worksheet.

As mentioned, Figure 3 shows the blank Financial Plan for Division B. Creating a link to the Financial Results LY workbook shown in Figure 1 completes the Last Year column in this worksheet. Once the link is created, if the data is changed in the Financial Results LY workbook, those changes will be reflected in the Division B Financial Plan workbook. Adjustments to last year data are rare but can happen in situations in which a company moves a product line from one division to another. The following points explain how to create this link:

- Open the Division B Financial Plan workbook and then open the Financial Results LY workbook.
- Type an equal sign in cell B3 of the Financial Plan worksheet (see Figure 3). This cell represents the Unit Sales for Division B last year.
- Activate the Financial Results LY workbook by clicking the workbook name in the task bar (see Figure 4).

- Activate cell B3 in the Results for 2006 worksheet in the Financial Results LY workbook.
- Press the **Enter** key.

Figures 4 and 5 show the setup and results of creating a link between the Division B Financial Plan and Financial Results LY workbooks. Notice in Figure 5 that the workbook and worksheet name precede the cell location that was used to create the link in cell B3 to show the Unit Sales for Last Year.

Figure 4 | **Creating a Link in the Financial Plan Worksheet**

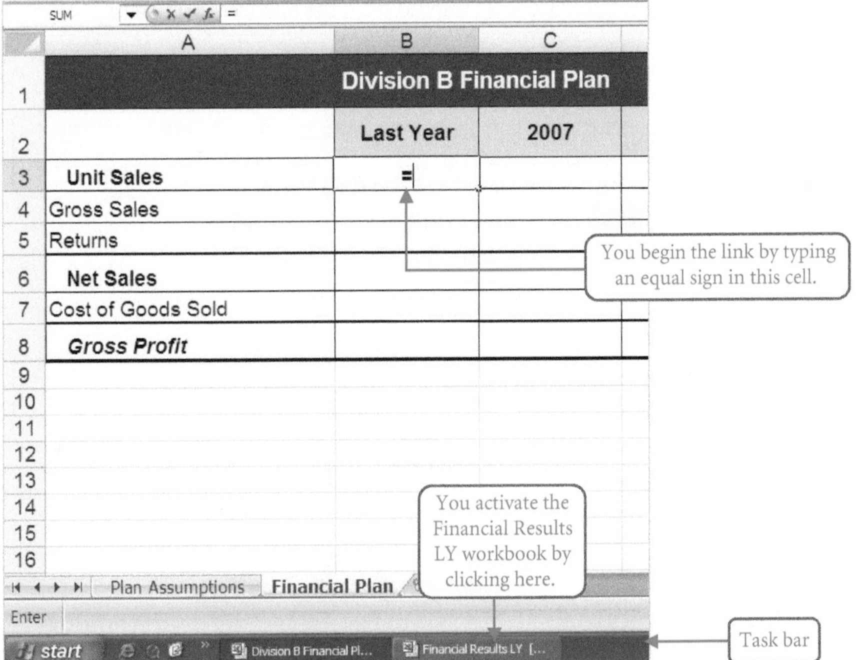


Figure 5 | **Results of Creating a Link in the Financial Plan Worksheet**

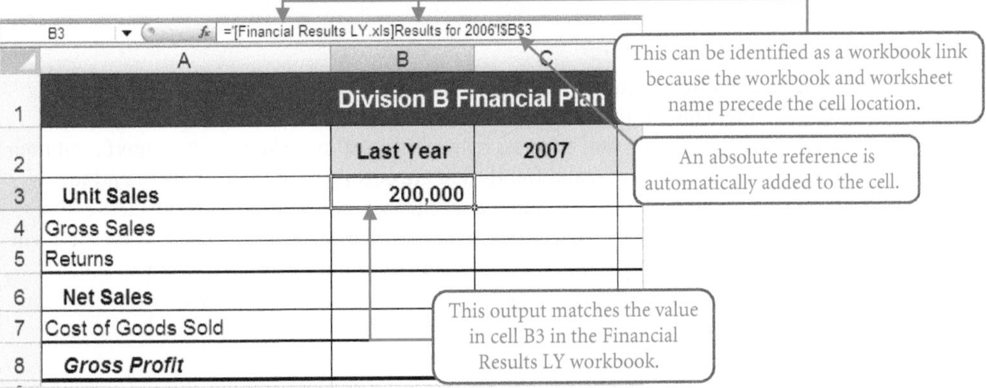


Copying the link that was created in cell B3 and pasting it to cells B4 through B8 completes the Last Year column in Figure 5. This example can use relative referencing to adjust the link because the financial items listed in the Financial Plan worksheet in Figure 5 are in the same sequence as the financial items listed in the Financial Results LY workbook in Figure 1. However, notice that the cell reference in the link shown in the formula bar of Figure 5 contains an absolute reference that must be removed before copying and pasting the link. You accomplish this by doing the following:

- Edit cell B3 in the Financial Plan worksheet to remove the absolute reference on cell B3 in the link.
- Copy cell B3 in the Financial Plan worksheet and then highlight the range B4:B8.
- Select the **Formulas** option from the **Paste** icon in the Ribbon. Using the **Formulas** option will paste the link without changing any of the formats in the worksheet.

Figure 6 shows the completed Last Year column in the Financial Plan worksheet. Notice that the absolute reference was removed from the link (see formula bar).

Figure 6 | **Completed Last Year Column in the Financial Plan Worksheet**

B3 ='[Financial Results LY.xls]Results for 2006'!B3

The absolute reference was removed from this cell before copying.

| | A | B | C |
|---|---|---|---|
| 1 | Division B Financial Plan | | |
| 2 | | Last Year | 2007 |
| 3 | Unit Sales | 200,000 | |
| 4 | Gross Sales | $ 20,500,000 | |
| 5 | Returns | $ 500,000 | |
| 6 | Net Sales | $ 20,000,000 | |
| 7 | Cost of Goods Sold | $ 11,000,000 | |
| 8 | *Gross Profit* | *$ 9,000,000* | |

Relative referencing automatically adjusts the link that was pasted into these cell locations.

## COMMON MISTAKES | Copying and Pasting Workbook Links

Excel will automatically place an absolute reference on cell references used to link data between two workbooks. Therefore, you must remove the absolute reference after creating the link if you intend to use relative referencing to automatically adjust the link when it is pasted to a new location on the worksheet.

The remaining columns in the Financial Plan worksheet will be completed using formulas that contain links to the Plan Assumptions worksheet in Figure 2. When developing a financial plan, business managers must make key assumptions about their business based on research and trends that are occurring in their industry and the overall economy. You will learn more about these techniques in your business courses. For example, a business manager might assume that the gross sales for his division will increase 10% next year based on current growth trends in the industry. The Plan Assumptions worksheet contains these types of assumptions and will be used to calculate data for the Financial Plan worksheet. The following points explain how data for the year 2007 (column C) is calculated in the Financial Plan worksheet:

- Activate cell C4 in the Financial Plan worksheet. Skip the Unit Sales formula for now because the Net Sales has not been calculated. That said, skipping this formula is not a requirement. You could still type the formula for Unit Sales, and a result will be produced once the Net Sales is calculated.
- Type an equal sign and the beginning of the formula B4 + B4*.
- Activate the Plan Assumptions worksheet and then activate cell B4, which contains the percent change for Gross Sales. This will place a link in the formula that will

reference the value in cell B4 in the Plan Assumptions worksheet. The formula will take the Gross Sales for Last Year (cell B4) in the Financial Plan worksheet and add to it the Gross Sales from Last Year multiplied by the percent change in Gross Sales on the Plan Assumptions worksheet.

- Press the **Enter** key.

Figure 7 shows the result of the formula calculating the Gross Sales for 2007. Notice in the formula bar that the worksheet name Plan Assumptions is enclosed in apostrophes and is followed by an exclamation point. This indicates that the formula will use the value in cell B4 in the Plan Assumptions worksheet. The first two cell references in the formula, which are also B4, are from the Financial Plan worksheet. Since these cell references are not preceded by a worksheet name, they relate to the current worksheet that contains this formula.

Figure 7 | **Calculating Gross Sales for 2007 in the Financial Plan Worksheet**

C4 =B4+B4*'Plan Assumptions'!B4

| | A | B | C |
|---|---|---|---|
| 1 | Division B Finar | | |
| 2 | | Last Year | |
| 3 | Unit Sales | 200,000 | |
| 4 | Gross Sales | $ 20,500,000 | $ 22,550,000 |
| 5 | Returns | $ 500,000 | |
| 6 | Net Sales | $ 20,000,000 | |
| 7 | Cost of Goods Sold | $ 11,000,000 | |
| 8 | *Gross Profit* | *$ 9,000,000* | |

This cell can be identified as a link because it is preceded by the worksheet name Plan Assumptions.

This output will change if the value in cell B4 in the Plan Assumptions worksheet is changed.

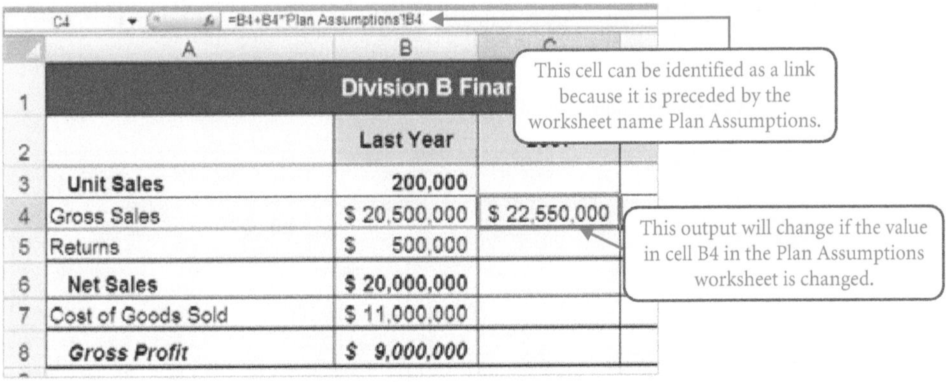

The following steps explain how to create formulas to complete the data for 2007 in the Financial Plan worksheet:

- Activate cell C5. This cell will contain the planned Returns for 2007.
- Type an equal sign and the beginning of the formula `C4 *`.
- Activate the Plan Assumptions worksheet and then activate cell B3. This formula will multiply the Gross Sales, which was calculated in cell C4 of the Financial Plan worksheet, by the percentage in cell B3 of the Plan Assumptions worksheet.
- Press the **Enter** key.
- Activate cell C6.
- Type an equal sign, type the formula `C4-C5`, and then press the **Enter** key. This formula will calculate the Net Sales by subtracting the Returns from the Gross Sales.
- Activate cell C3. Since the Net Sales are calculated, you can now calculate the Unit Sales.
- Type an equal sign and the beginning of the formula `C6/`(cell C6 divided by).
- Activate the Plan Assumptions worksheet and activate cell B5. This formula will take the Average Price per Item and divide it into the Net Sales to calculate the planned Unit Sales for the division.
- Press the **Enter** key.
- Activate cell C7.
- Type an equal sign and the beginning of the formula `C4 *`.
- Activate the Plan Assumptions worksheet and then activate cell B6. This formula will calculate the Cost of Goods Sold by multiplying the percentage in cell B6 of

> **Quick Reference**
>
> **Linking Data between Worksheets**
>
> 1. Activate a cell location where the data or output of a formula or functions should appear.
> 2. Type an equal sign, or type an equal sign and the beginning of a formula or function.
> 3. Click a **Worksheet** tab that contains the data you wish to display in the first worksheet or use in a formula or function.
> 4. Activate a cell location that contains the data you wish to display or use in a formula or function.
> 5. Press the **Enter** key, or complete the formula or function and then press the **Enter** key.

the Plan Assumptions worksheet by the Gross Sales in cell C4 of the Financial Plan worksheet.

- Press the **Enter** key.
- Activate cell C8.
- Type an equal sign, type the formula `C6-C7`, and then press the **Enter** key. This formula will calculate the Gross Profit by subtracting the Cost of Goods Sold from the Net Sales.
- Copy the range C3:C8. Then highlight cells D3 and E3 and select the **Formulas** option from the **Paste** icon. This will paste the formulas created for the year 2007 into the years 2008 and 2009 to complete the Financial Plan worksheet. Relative referencing will automatically adjust the cell references for the links and formulas to make the appropriate calculations for the years 2008 and 2009.

Figure 8 shows the completed Financial Plan worksheet. As previously mentioned, this represents part of a financial plan that the directing manager of a division in a large company would typically create. In addition, the formats and items included in a financial plan will vary depending on the business that is being managed.

Figure 8 | **Completed Financial Plan Worksheet**

This formula was originally created in cell C4 but was adjusted through relative referencing.

E4 =D4+D4*'Plan Assumptions'!D4

| | A | B | C | D | E |
|---|---|---|---|---|---|
| 1 | Division B Financial Plan | | | | |
| 2 | | Last Year | 2007 | 2008 | 2009 |
| 3 | **Unit Sales** | **200,000** | **220,990** | **226,380** | **237,699** |
| 4 | Gross Sales | $ 20,500,000 | $ 22,550,000 | $ 23,677,500 | $ 24,861,375 |
| 5 | Returns | $ 500,000 | $ 451,000 | $ 473,550 | $ 497,228 |
| 6 | **Net Sales** | **$ 20,000,000** | **$ 22,099,000** | **$ 23,203,950** | **$ 24,364,148** |
| 7 | Cost of Goods Sold | $ 11,000,000 | $ 12,402,500 | $ 13,022,625 | $ 13,673,756 |
| 8 | ***Gross Profit*** | ***$ 9,000,000*** | ***$ 9,696,500*** | ***$ 10,181,325*** | ***$ 10,690,391*** |
| 9 | | | | | |

Business managers will most likely be required to present their financial plans to the executive officers of the company. During this presentation, the business manager might be asked questions such as "What if our sales only increase 5% in 2007?" or "What if our cost of goods sold increases to 60%?" Simply typing new assumptions into the Plan Assumptions worksheet in Figure 2 easily answers these questions. Because of cell referencing, the outputs of the financial plan shown in Figure 8 will automatically change when the data in the Plan Assumptions worksheet is changed.

**Quick Reference**

**Linking Data between Workbooks**

1. Open two workbooks.
2. Activate a cell location in the workbook where the data or output of a formula or functions should appear.
3. Type an equal sign, or type an equal sign and the beginning of a formula or function.
4. Click the name of the second workbook in the task bar.
5. Click a **Worksheet** tab that contains the data you wish to display or use in a formula or function.
6. Activate a cell location that contains the data you wish to display or use in a formula or function.
7. Press the **Enter** key, or complete the formula or function and then press the **Enter** key.

## Updating Workbook Links

When an Excel file contains workbook links, a ***Security Alert*** prompt will appear just below the Ribbon of the Excel screen, as shown in Figure 9, when the file is opened. The purpose of this prompt is to inform you that data is being linked to an external workbook and to give you the option of updating these links. Workbook links must be updated to show any changes that might have occurred in the external workbook. You can use two methods for updating workbook links. The first is to click the **Options** button in the Security Alert prompt, as shown in Figure 9. After you click this button, a dialog box will open giving you the option to automatically update all workbook links. To update any workbook links, you click the *Enable this content* option and click the **OK** button in the dialog box. Once the workbook links are updated, or ***refreshed***, any changes that might have occurred in the external workbook will appear in the current workbook.

Figure 9 | **Updating Workbook Links Using the Security Alert Prompt**

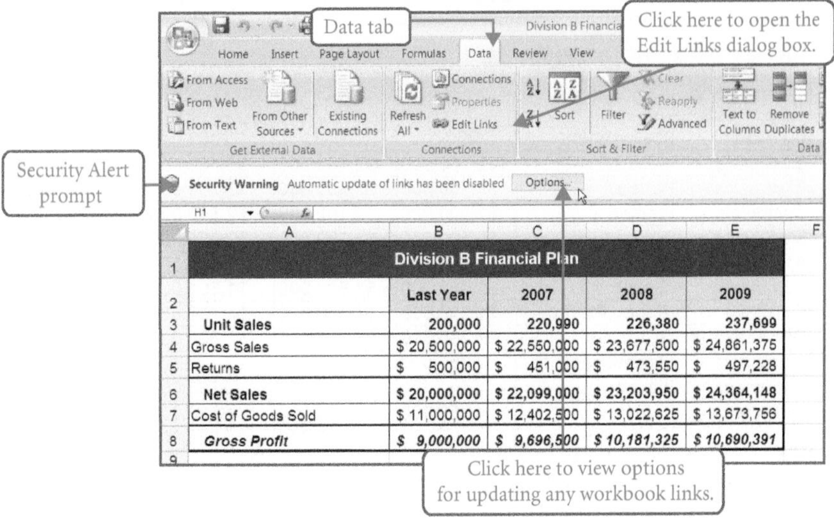


The second method for updating workbook links is through the **Edit Links** dialog box. You can open the **Edit Links** dialog box by clicking the **Edit Links** icon in the **Data** tab of the Ribbon (see Figure 9). As shown in Figure 10, this dialog box allows you to select and manually update any workbook links that are in your Excel file. In addition, it provides options for checking a selected workbook link to see if it needs to be updated, changing the source file for a selected workbook link, or breaking a workbook link.

Figure 10 | **Edit Links Dialog Box**

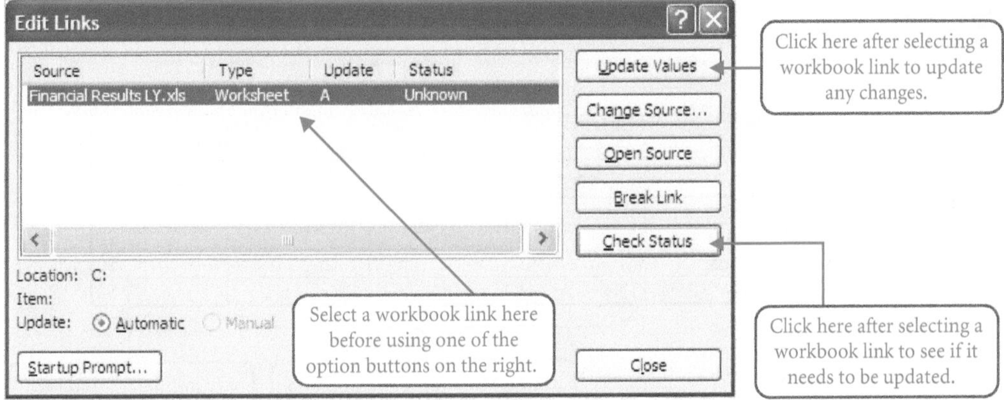


## SUMIF Function

The **SUMIF** function allows you to add specific values in a worksheet based on the results of a logical test. In business, this function is often used to summarize financial or statistical data. For example, Figure 11 shows a worksheet that contains gross sales projections for the departments of a hypothetical electronics retail company. Notice that several departments are assigned to each division. The **SUMIF** function will be used to total the gross sales projections for each division in the Sales Summary worksheet.

Figure 11 | **Gross Sales Projections by Division/Department**

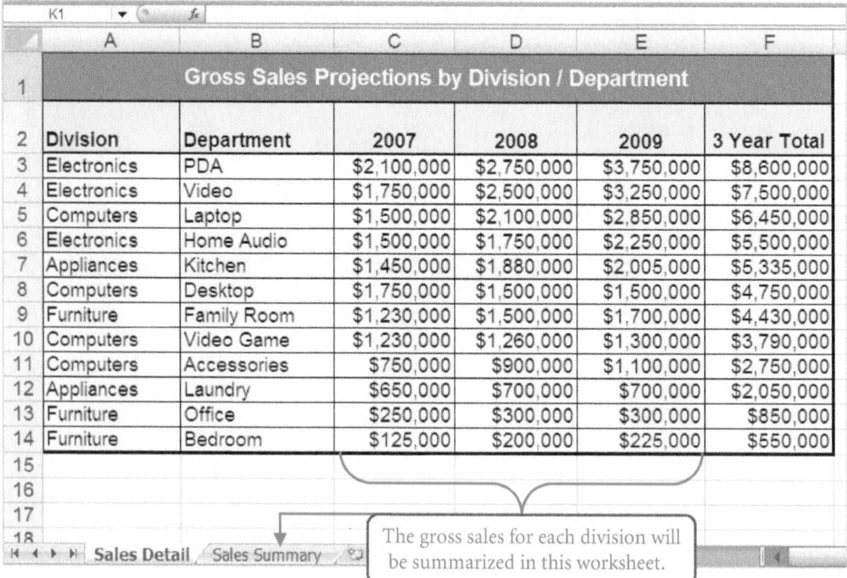

| Gross Sales Projections by Division / Department | | | | | |
|---|---|---|---|---|---|
| **Division** | **Department** | **2007** | **2008** | **2009** | **3 Year Total** |
| Electronics | PDA | $2,100,000 | $2,750,000 | $3,750,000 | $8,600,000 |
| Electronics | Video | $1,750,000 | $2,500,000 | $3,250,000 | $7,500,000 |
| Computers | Laptop | $1,500,000 | $2,100,000 | $2,850,000 | $6,450,000 |
| Electronics | Home Audio | $1,500,000 | $1,750,000 | $2,250,000 | $5,500,000 |
| Appliances | Kitchen | $1,450,000 | $1,880,000 | $2,005,000 | $5,335,000 |
| Computers | Desktop | $1,750,000 | $1,500,000 | $1,500,000 | $4,750,000 |
| Furniture | Family Room | $1,230,000 | $1,500,000 | $1,700,000 | $4,430,000 |
| Computers | Video Game | $1,230,000 | $1,260,000 | $1,300,000 | $3,790,000 |
| Computers | Accessories | $750,000 | $900,000 | $1,100,000 | $2,750,000 |
| Appliances | Laundry | $650,000 | $700,000 | $700,000 | $2,050,000 |
| Furniture | Office | $250,000 | $300,000 | $300,000 | $850,000 |
| Furniture | Bedroom | $125,000 | $200,000 | $225,000 | $550,000 |



Figure 12 shows the worksheet that will be used to summarize the gross sales projections for each division. Since this is a different worksheet, a link will be used in the **SUMIF** function to reference the data in the Sales Detail worksheet shown in Figure 11. Using links in the **SUMIF** function is a common technique, especially when you are creating summary reports such as the one shown in Figure 12. The **SUMIF** function will be used to search for the division listed in column A from the Sales Summary worksheet in the Sales Detail worksheet and calculate a total for each division for each year.

Figure 12 | **Sales Summary Worksheet**

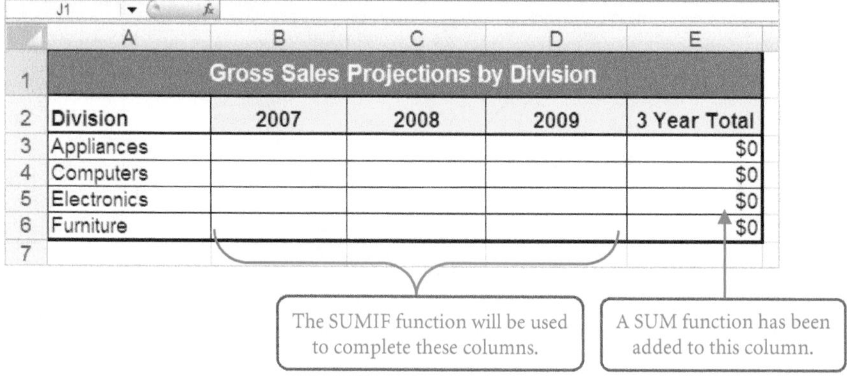

| Gross Sales Projections by Division | | | | |
|---|---|---|---|---|
| **Division** | **2007** | **2008** | **2009** | **3 Year Total** |
| Appliances | | | | $0 |
| Computers | | | | $0 |
| Electronics | | | | $0 |
| Furniture | | | | $0 |



As shown in Figure 13, the **SUMIF** function contains three arguments. Each of these arguments is defined as follows:

- **range**: The range of cells that will be evaluated by the logical test or data used to define the **criteria** argument. In some cases, this argument may be identical to the range of data that is being summed.
- **criteria**: The logical test or data that will be used to determine which values are summed. This is similar to the **logical_test** argument of the **IF** function. However, this argument can be defined by a particular value, cell location, text, and so on, without entering a complete logical test.

> **Quick Reference**
>
> **Updating Workbook Links**
>
> 1. Click the **Options** button in the Security Alert prompt.
> 2. Select the **Enable this content** option in the **Security Options** dialog box and click the **OK** button.
>
> Or
>
> 1. Click the **Data** tab of the Ribbon.
> 2. Click the **Edit Links** icon.
> 3. Select the workbook link you wish to update from the **Edit Links** dialog box.
> 4. Click the **Update Values** button on the right side of the **Edit Links** dialog box.
> 5. Click the **Close** button at the bottom of the **Edit Links** dialog box.

- **[sum_range]**: The range of cells that contain data that will be summed if the data in the **criteria** argument is found in the **range** argument. This argument is needed only if the range of cells used for the **range** argument does not contain the values that need to be summed. Otherwise, it can be omitted.

Figure 13 | **Arguments of the SUMIF Function**

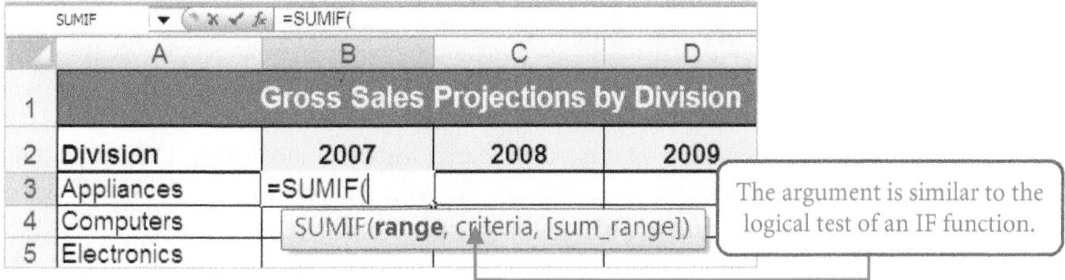


As mentioned, the Sales Summary worksheet in Figure 12 summarizes by division the gross sales projections by department (from Figure 11). The following steps explains how you accomplish this:

- Activate cell B3 in the Sales Summary worksheet. This cell will show the gross sales projections for the Appliances division for the year 2007.
- Type an equal sign, the function name SUMIF, and an open parenthesis.
- Define the **range** argument by clicking the Sales Detail worksheet and highlighting the range A3:A14. This will create a link to the Sales Detail worksheet. Type a comma after defining this argument.
- Type the cell location A3 to define the **criteria** argument. The function will search for the division name in cell A3 in the Sales Summary worksheet by looking in the range A3:A14 in the Sales Detail worksheet. Note that you will still be in the Sales Detail worksheet when you define this argument; therefore, you must type cell A3 instead of clicking it. Type a comma after defining this argument.
- Define the **[sum_range]** argument by highlighting the range C3:C14 in the Sales Detail worksheet, which contains the gross sales projections for the year 2007. You will still be in the Sales Detail worksheet, so you can simply click and drag over this range. This will create a second link in the function. When a match is found in the **criteria** argument, the function will add whatever value is in the same row in the range of cells used to define this argument.
- Type a closing parenthesis and press the **Enter** key. This will bring you back to the Sales Summary worksheet.

Figure 14 shows the results of the **SUMIF** function. The function found the word *Appliances* in column A of the Sales Detail worksheet and summed whatever value is in the same row in the range C3:C14, which contains the gross sales projections for 2007. Notice the links that are created in the **range** and **[sum_range]** arguments.

Figure 14 | **Results of the SUMIF Function**

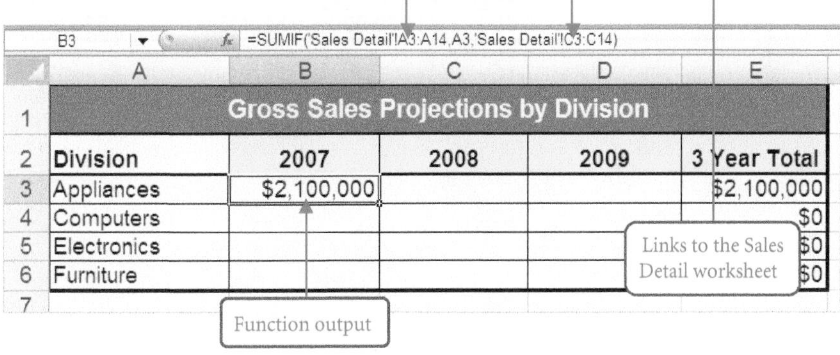

You can copy and paste the **SUMIF** function to calculate the gross sales projections for the rest of the divisions and years in Figure 14. However, you would need to add absolute references to the function to prevent relative referencing from making unwanted adjustments to the cell locations in each argument. You accomplish this as follows:

- Double click cell B3 in the Sales Summary worksheet to edit the function, or activate cell B3 and click in the formula bar.
- Place an absolute reference on the link used to define the **range** argument. Type a dollar sign in front of both the column letters and row numbers of the range A3:A14. The function will always need to search for the appropriate division name in column A of the Sales Detail worksheet. Therefore, this range cannot be adjusted by relative referencing when it is pasted to other cell locations on the worksheet.
- Type a dollar sign *only* in front of the column letter of cell A3 in the **criteria** argument. This argument requires a mixed reference because a different division is in each row in column A of the Sales Summary worksheet (see Figure 14). Therefore, it is important for relative referencing to adjust the row number when the function is pasted to a new location. However, the column letter must not change.
- Type a dollar sign *only* in front of the two row numbers in the link used to define the **[sum_range]** argument. This argument also requires a mixed reference because each year of sales projections is in a different column in the Sales Detail worksheet. Therefore, it is important for relative referencing to adjust the column letters when the function is pasted to columns C and D of the Sales Summary worksheet. However, the row numbers must not change. Press the **Enter** key after making this adjustment.
- Copy cell B3 and paste it down to cells B4 through B6. Then copy the range B3:B6 and paste it into the range C3:C6 and D3:D6.

Figure 15 shows the completed Sales Summary worksheet. Notice the mixed references that were placed on the **criteria** and **[sum_range]** arguments.

> **Quick Reference**
>
> **SUMIF Functions**
>
> 1. Activate the cell where output should appear.
> 2. Type an equal sign, the function name **SUMIF**, and an open parenthesis.
> 3. Define the following arguments:
>    a) **range**: A range of cells that will be evaluated by data used to define the **criteria** argument.
>    b) **criteria**: A logical test, cell location, value, and so on, that will be searched in the range used to define the **range** argument.
>    c) **[sum_range]**: A range of cells containing values that will be summed if the data in the **criteria** argument is found in the range used to define the **range** argument. Define this argument only if the **range** argument does not contain the values that need to be summed.
> 4. Type a closing parenthesis and press the **Enter** key.

Figure 15 | **Completed Sales Summary Worksheet**

Mixed references are used in these two arguments.

B3 =SUMIF('Sales Detail'!$A$3:$A$14,$A3,'Sales Detail'!C$3:C$14)

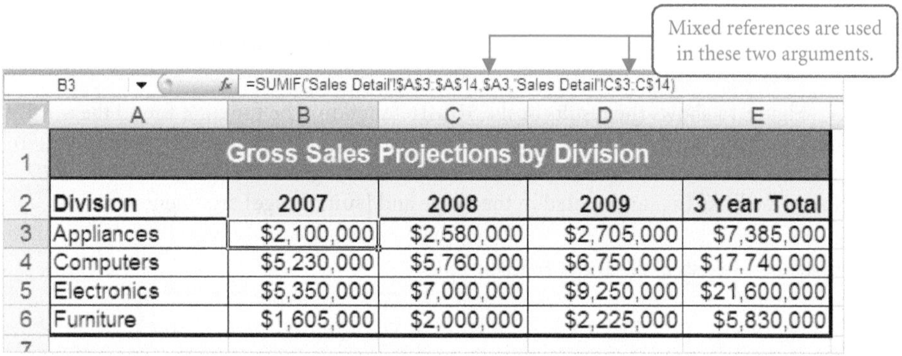

| | A | B | C | D | E |
|---|---|---|---|---|---|
| 1 | Gross Sales Projections by Division | | | | |
| 2 | Division | 2007 | 2008 | 2009 | 3 Year Total |
| 3 | Appliances | $2,100,000 | $2,580,000 | $2,705,000 | $7,385,000 |
| 4 | Computers | $5,230,000 | $5,760,000 | $6,750,000 | $17,740,000 |
| 5 | Electronics | $5,350,000 | $7,000,000 | $9,250,000 | $21,600,000 |
| 6 | Furniture | $1,605,000 | $2,000,000 | $2,225,000 | $5,830,000 |
| 7 | | | | | |

**COMMON MISTAKES | SUMIF Function**

When you are using both the **range** and the **[sum_range]** argument, make sure each range of cells used to define these arguments contains the same number of cells. Excel will automatically adjust the range in the **[sum_range]** argument to match the number of cells in the range used to define the `range` argument. If there are fewer cells in the range argument compared to the **[sum_range]** argument, Excel will add only the number of cells in the range used to define the **range** argument. For example, the following **SUMIF** function will add only values in the range C3:C7. The reason is that the range of cells used to define the **range** argument is smaller than the range of cells used to define the **[sum_range]** argument.

```
=SUMIF('Sales Detail'!A3:A7,A4,'Sales Detail'!C3:C14)
```

## >> Linking Data

**VIDEO WORKSHOP**

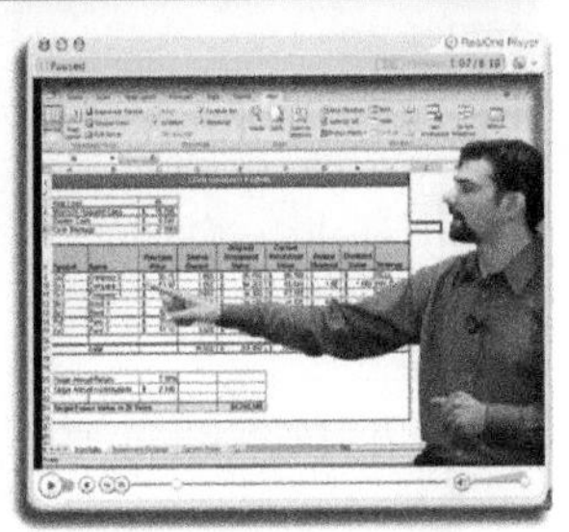

The purpose of this workshop is to review the techniques of linking data between workbooks and worksheets. I will be demonstrating the tasks in this workshop on the **Workbook Links** and **Worksheet Links** videos. After completing each section of tasks, watch the related video shown in parentheses. You will need to open the following two Excel files before starting this workshop: ib_e06_financialplan and ib_e06_lastyeardata. Both are identical to the example demonstrated earlier in this section. You must open both files before completing the tasks in this workshop.

1. **Linking Data between Two Workbooks (Video: Workbook Links)**
   a. Activate the Financial Plan workbook.
   b. Activate cell B3 in the Plan worksheet and type an equal sign.
   c. Activate the Last Year Data workbook, activate cell B3, and press the **Enter** key.
   d. Edit the workbook link that was created in cell B3 in the Plan worksheet to remove the absolute reference.
   e. Copy the workbook link in cell B3 of the Plan worksheet and paste it into cells B4 through B8 using the **Formulas** option in the **Paste** icon.
   f. Activate the Last Year Data workbook and close it.

2. **Linking Data between Two Worksheets (Video: Worksheet Links)**
   a. In cell C4 of the Plan worksheet, type the beginning of the formula `=B4 + B4 *`.
   b. Activate cell B4 in the Plan Assumptions worksheet and press the **Enter** key.
   c. In cell C5 of the Plan worksheet, type the beginning of the formula `=C4*`.
   d. Activate cell B3 in the Plan Assumptions worksheet and press the **Enter** key.
   e. Type the formula `=C4-C5` in cell C6 of the Plan worksheet.
   f. In cell C3 of the Plan worksheet, type the beginning of the formula `=C6/`.
   g. Activate cell B5 in the Plan Assumptions worksheet and press the **Enter** key.

h. In cell C7 of the Plan worksheet, type the beginning of the formula `=C4 *`.
i. Activate cell B6 in the Plan Assumptions worksheet and press the **Enter** key.
j. Type the formula `=C6 - C7` into cell C8 of the Plan worksheet.
k. Copy the range C3:C8 in the Plan worksheet. Using the **Paste Formulas** option, paste this range into cells D3 through D8 and cells E3 through E8.
l. Save and close your file.

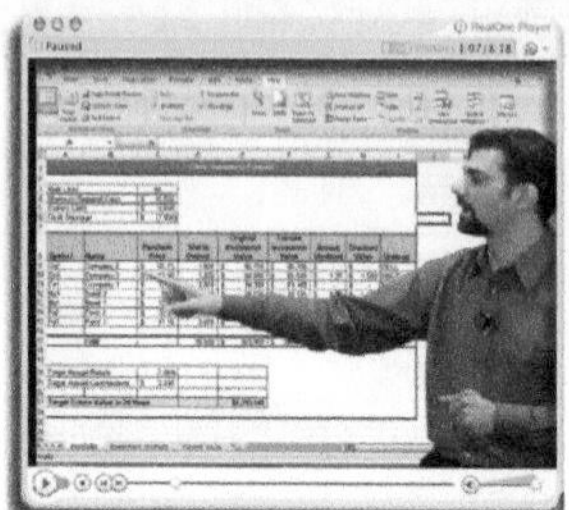

## >> SUMIF Function

The purpose of this workshop is to demonstrate the **SUMIF** function. I will be demonstrating the tasks in this workshop in the video named **SUMIF Function**. Open the file named ib_e06_divisionsalessummary and then complete the tasks in this workshop.

**SUMIF (Video: SUMIF Function)**

a. Activate cell B3 in the Sales Summary worksheet.
b. Type an equal sign, the function name **SUMIF**, and an open parenthesis.
c. Activate the Sales Detail worksheet and highlight the range A3:A14. Then type a comma.
d. Type the cell location A3 and then type a comma.
e. Highlight the range C3:C14 in the Sales Detail worksheet, type a closing parenthesis, and press the **Enter** key.
f. Add the following absolute and mixed references to the **SUMIF** function in cell B3 in the Sales Summary worksheet:
   i. Add an absolute reference to the worksheet link used to define the **range** argument. You will need to add four dollar signs to the range A3:A14 in this argument.
   ii. Add an absolute reference to the column letter only in the **criteria** argument (cell A3). The row number should remain a relative reference.
   iii. Add an absolute reference to the row numbers only in the worksheet link used to define the **[sum_range]** argument. You will need to add two dollar signs to the range C3:C14. The column letters for this range should remain a relative reference.
g. Copy cell B3 and paste it to cells B4:B6. Then copy the range B3:B6 and paste it into the range C3:D6.
h. Type a **SUM** function in cell E3 in the Sales Summary worksheet that totals the values in the range B3:D3. Then copy and paste this function into the range E4:E6.
i. Save and close your file.

# >> Store Construction Plans

This section demonstrated how linking data can be used to develop a financial plan for the division of a corporation. However, linking data can also be useful when planning other aspects of business such as the construction of stores, the distribution of merchandise, or the capacity of a distribution center. These exercises involve separate components or assumptions that have to be planned and then utilized to calculate a final output.

**EXERCISE**

**Why Do I Need This?**

## Exercise

The goal of this exercise is to develop a store construction plan for a hypothetical retail company. You will use the technique of linking data to calculate the construction cost of each store and also to produce a summary report. The summary report will use the **SUMIF** function to show how much total retail space is constructed or planned by state. To begin this exercise, open the file named ib_e06_storeconstruction.

1. Calculate the Construction Cost in cell G3 on the Construction Plan worksheet. You calculate this cost by multiplying the "Size (square feet)" column in the Construction Plan worksheet by the "Cost per Square Foot" column in the Cost by State worksheet. You will need to create this formula using the **VLookup** function to find the cost per square foot for each state listed in column C of the Construction Plan worksheet in column B of the Cost by State worksheet. The arguments of the **VLookup** function should be defined as followed:
   a. **lookup_value**: `C3`
   b. **table_array**: The range `A2:B12` in the Cost by State worksheet
   c. **col_index_num**: `2`
   d. **[range_lookup]**: `False`
2. Add an absolute reference to the range used to define the **table_array** argument of the VLookup portion of the formula you created in number 1. Then copy the formula and paste it into cells G4 through G25.
3. Type a formula into cell H3 in the Construction Plan worksheet that calculates the Total Cost to Open. Your formula should add the Construction Cost calculated in number 1 to the Inventory Value. Copy your formula and paste it into cells H4 through H25.
4. Create a link in cell A3 of the Store Summary worksheet to cell A2 in the Cost by State worksheet. Then copy this link and paste it into cells A4 through A12.
5. Type a **SUMIF** function in cell B3 of the Store Summary worksheet to calculate the total square feet of store space in the state of Massachusetts. The arguments of the function should be defined as follows:
   a. **range**: `C3:C30` in the Construction Plan worksheet
   b. **criteria**: `A3`
   c. **[sum_range]**: `E3:E30` in the Construction Plan worksheet
6. Add an absolute value to the link used to define the **range** and **[sum_range]** arguments of the **SUMIF** function created in step 5. Then copy the function and paste it into cells B4 through B12.
7. Type a **SUMIF** function in cell E33 of the Construction Plan worksheet. The purpose of this function is to add the total square footage of retail space that

exists for each size category of store. The definitions for each argument are listed here. Notice that only two of the three arguments are listed because the range that is used to define the **range** argument contains the values that are being summed.

a. **range** = `E3:E30`

b. **criteria** = `D33`

8. Place an absolute reference on the range E3:E30 in the **SUMIF** function that you created in step 7. Then copy the function and paste it into cells E34 through E36.

9. Which size category has the highest square footage of retail space for this company?

10. You may have noticed that the range used to define the **range** argument of the **SUMIF** function created in step 7 included blank cells. This is so the summary report will automatically include new stores when they are added. For example, type **VA** in cell A10 in the Cost by State worksheet and add a Cost per Square Foot of **32** in cell B10.

11. In row 26 of the Construction Plan spreadsheet, type open date: **3/23/2008**; store number: **2801**; state: **VA**; city: **Reston**; size: **15000**; and inventory value: **3700500**.

12. Copy cells G25 and H25 in the Construction Plan worksheet and paste them into cells G26 and H26.

13. Which size category has the highest total square footage?

14. Look at the Store Summary worksheet. Is Virginia (VA) added to the list? Sort this worksheet based on the values in the Total Space (sqr feet) column in descending order. Which state has the highest square footage of retail space?

15. Save and close your file.

PROBLEM & EXERCISE

## >> What's Wrong with This Spreadsheet?

### Problem

You are managing a department in a large public corporation. Each year the company holds a planning meeting to determine what sales targets will be announced to the stockholders. You receive an e-mail from a coworker who created an Excel spreadsheet to help you plan the sales of your department. He explains how the spreadsheet works as follows:

1. The spreadsheet shows two years of history (2005 and 2006) and three years of projections. The history is linked to another workbook named Sales History, which is attached to this e-mail. You do not have to enter any history data for your sales plan. The history workbooks for each department are maintained by the accounting department. As a result, if they make any adjustments to the results of your department (mostly returns), the changes will automatically show up on the Department Sales Plan workbook I attached to this e-mail.

2. The only things you have to enter in the Department Sales Plan workbook are the Growth of Gross Sales, percent of Returns, and the Average Price. These

items are in the Assumptions worksheet. When you change any of the numbers on this worksheet, it will automatically update the Sales Plan.

3. The Sales Plan worksheet contains all the plan data for the department. Just print this worksheet and bring it to the meeting. It's that easy!

### Exercise

Your coworker e-mailed you the Sales History and Department Sales Plan workbooks. Open the file named ib_e06_departmentsalesplan. Would you be comfortable printing the Sales Plan worksheet and presenting this data at the sales meeting? Consider the following points:

1. Do the numbers appear to make sense? For example, the formula to calculate Net Sales is `Gross Sales - Returns`. The Unit sales are calculated by dividing the Net Sales by the Average Price entered onto the Assumptions worksheet.

2. Give the spreadsheet a test drive. The coworker explained that changing the data in the Assumptions worksheet will produce new outputs on the Sales Plan worksheet. Change the data in the Assumptions worksheet one item at a time and check the Sales Plan worksheet. For example, change the Growth of Gross Sales percentages and check the Gross Sales results on the Sales Plan worksheet.

3. Does the historical data for 2005 and 2006 look suspicious?

4. Do the Net Sales results still make sense?

Write a short answer for each of the points listed here. Then fix any errors you find in the Department Sales Plan workbook.

## >> Financial Planning

Skill Set

The previous section demonstrated how the sales and gross profit portion of a financial plan is constructed in Excel using the technique of linking data. This section will provide an illustrative review of how you can use the core competency skills in this text to construct a comprehensive financial plan for starting a new business. A total of three worksheets will be used to construct this plan, as opposed to the two worksheets that were used in the previous section: Financial Assumptions, Financial Data, and Cash Analysis. In addition, this section introduces the **NPV** function, which you use to compute the net present value of an investment. It is important to note that this section will mention and work with several terms and rules that apply to the disciplines of finance, but they will not be explained in detail. You will receive more detailed instruction regarding these concepts in your financial accounting courses and reference material.

### Financial Assumptions

Figures 16 and 17 show the first component that will be demonstrated for the comprehensive financial plan: the Financial Assumptions worksheet. The purpose of this worksheet is identical to the Plan Assumptions worksheet that was shown in Figure 2.

All of the assumptions related to the financial plan will be entered into this worksheet. In addition, this will be the only worksheet in the plan that is used for any data entry needs. The other two worksheets, Financial Data and Cash Analysis, will be constructed using formulas and functions. A business manager would use the Financial Assumptions worksheet to enter all critical decisions required to develop the comprehensive financial plan such as startup investments, first-year sales estimates, sales growth rates, cost of goods sold, and so on.

The Financial Assumptions worksheet, shown in Figures 16 and 17, is designed to enter plan data for five financial categories. The number and types of categories that are used to create a financial plan will change depending on the business and purpose of the plan. As previously mentioned, this financial plan will be used for starting a new business. In addition, this example will assume that the business will be manufacturing a product that will be sold to retail stores. Therefore, items such as Cost of Goods Sold and Inventory are included on the Financial Assumptions spreadsheet. If you were planning a service business, these items would not be included in the design of the plan. The following five categories are used for the design of this plan:

- Startup Investments
- Sales Information
- Cost and Expense Information
- Asset Information
- Liability Information

Figure 16 | **Financial Assumptions Worksheet (Rows 1 – 25)**

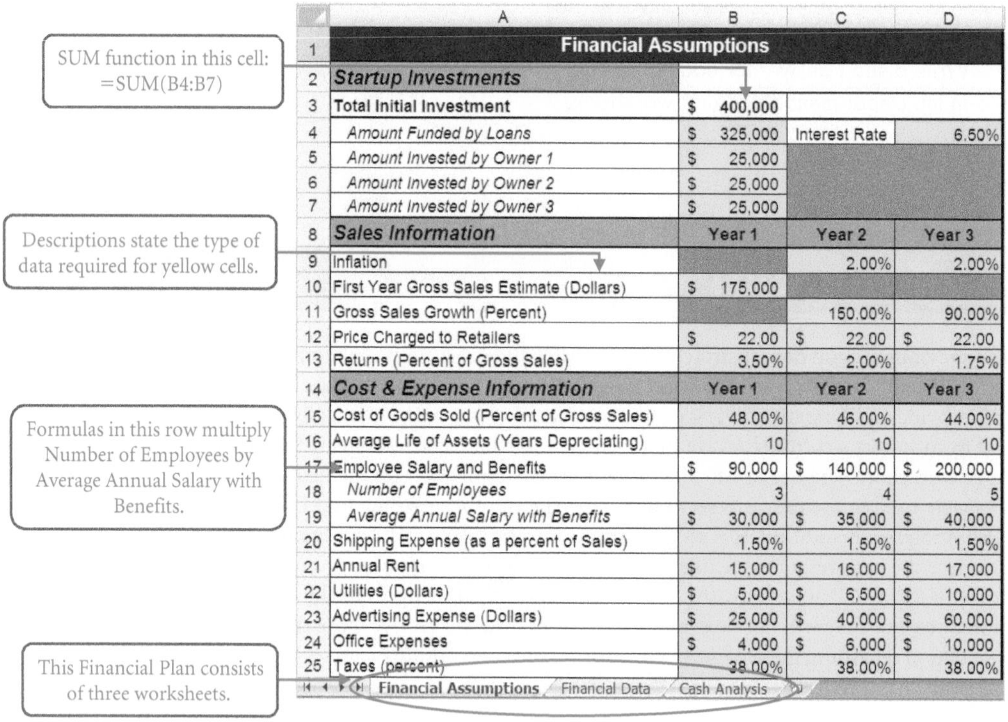

SUM function in this cell: =SUM(B4:B7)

Descriptions state the type of data required for yellow cells.

Formulas in this row multiply Number of Employees by Average Annual Salary with Benefits.

This Financial Plan consists of three worksheets.

| | A | B | C | D |
|---|---|---|---|---|
| 1 | **Financial Assumptions** | | | |
| 2 | ***Startup Investments*** | | | |
| 3 | **Total Initial Investment** | $ 400,000 | | |
| 4 | *Amount Funded by Loans* | $ 325,000 | Interest Rate | 6.50% |
| 5 | *Amount Invested by Owner 1* | $ 25,000 | | |
| 6 | *Amount Invested by Owner 2* | $ 25,000 | | |
| 7 | *Amount Invested by Owner 3* | $ 25,000 | | |
| 8 | ***Sales Information*** | **Year 1** | **Year 2** | **Year 3** |
| 9 | Inflation | | 2.00% | 2.00% |
| 10 | First Year Gross Sales Estimate (Dollars) | $ 175,000 | | |
| 11 | Gross Sales Growth (Percent) | | 150.00% | 90.00% |
| 12 | Price Charged to Retailers | $ 22.00 | $ 22.00 | $ 22.00 |
| 13 | Returns (Percent of Gross Sales) | 3.50% | 2.00% | 1.75% |
| 14 | ***Cost & Expense Information*** | **Year 1** | **Year 2** | **Year 3** |
| 15 | Cost of Goods Sold (Percent of Gross Sales) | 48.00% | 46.00% | 44.00% |
| 16 | Average Life of Assets (Years Depreciating) | 10 | 10 | 10 |
| 17 | Employee Salary and Benefits | $ 90,000 | $ 140,000 | $ 200,000 |
| 18 | *Number of Employees* | 3 | 4 | 5 |
| 19 | *Average Annual Salary with Benefits* | $ 30,000 | $ 35,000 | $ 40,000 |
| 20 | Shipping Expense (as a percent of Sales) | 1.50% | 1.50% | 1.50% |
| 21 | Annual Rent | $ 15,000 | $ 16,000 | $ 17,000 |
| 22 | Utilities (Dollars) | $ 5,000 | $ 6,500 | $ 10,000 |
| 23 | Advertising Expense (Dollars) | $ 25,000 | $ 40,000 | $ 60,000 |
| 24 | Office Expenses | $ 4,000 | $ 6,000 | $ 10,000 |
| 25 | Taxes (percent) | 38.00% | 38.00% | 38.00% |

Financial Assumptions / Financial Data / Cash Analysis

Figure 17 | **Financial Assumptions Worksheet (Rows 26 – 39)**

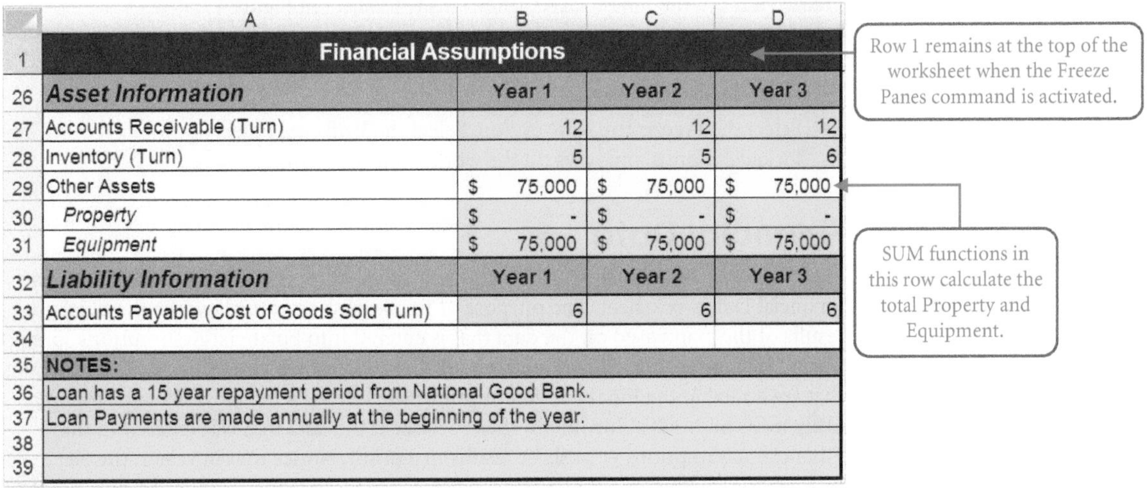

| | A | B | C | D |
|---|---|---|---|---|
| 1 | **Financial Assumptions** | | | |
| 26 | ***Asset Information*** | **Year 1** | **Year 2** | **Year 3** |
| 27 | Accounts Receivable (Turn) | 12 | 12 | 12 |
| 28 | Inventory (Turn) | 5 | 5 | 6 |
| 29 | Other Assets | $ 75,000 | $ 75,000 | $ 75,000 |
| 30 | *Property* | $ - | $ - | $ - |
| 31 | *Equipment* | $ 75,000 | $ 75,000 | $ 75,000 |
| 32 | ***Liability Information*** | **Year 1** | **Year 2** | **Year 3** |
| 33 | Accounts Payable (Cost of Goods Sold Turn) | 6 | 6 | 6 |
| 34 | | | | |
| 35 | **NOTES:** | | | |
| 36 | Loan has a 15 year repayment period from National Good Bank. | | | |
| 37 | Loan Payments are made annually at the beginning of the year. | | | |
| 38 | | | | |
| 39 | | | | |

Row 1 remains at the top of the worksheet when the Freeze Panes command is activated.

SUM functions in this row calculate the total Property and Equipment.

The following list highlights how a few of the core competency skills were used in the construction of the Financial Assumptions worksheet in Figures 16 and 17:

- **Formatting**: Besides the obvious use of formatting techniques such as borders, alignment, number formats, and so on, the use of cell color (also known as fill color) is used as a way of communicating how to use this worksheet. For example, the yellow cells indicate that a business manager must enter key financial data. The white cells indicate labels or calculations that should not be changed. The color grey identifies unused cells.
- **Formulas**: Basic formulas are used to calculate the cost of Employee Salary and Benefits in row 17. The formula multiplies the Number of Employees entered in row 18 by the Average Annual Salary with Benefits in row 19 for each year. If your project requires, you could add another worksheet to this workbook that is dedicated to calculating the employee costs for this business. The results of that worksheet would then be linked into the Financial Assumptions worksheet.
- **Functions**: Two **SUM** functions are used in this worksheet. The first is in cell B3, which calculates the total investments planned to start the business in the range B4:B7. Similar to the way you calculate employee costs, you could add another worksheet to this workbook that is dedicated for creating a more detailed plan of how investments are being obtained. This worksheet can include various types of loans and other investment arrangements. The results of this worksheet can then be linked into the Financial Assumptions worksheet. The second **SUM** function is used in row 29 to total the Other Assets in rows 30 and 31.

## Freeze Panes

You may have noticed in Figure 17 that the first row number showing on the left side of the figure is 1, but the second number is 26. Although it appears as if rows 2 through 25 are hidden, this is not the case. Since the Financial Assumptions spreadsheet is very long, a feature called **Freeze Panes** was used to prevent row 1 from moving off the screen when scrolling down the worksheet. Commonly used when working with long or wide worksheets, this feature allows you lock a specific row and column when

> ***Quick Reference***
>
> **Freeze Panes**
>
> 1. Activate a cell that is below the row and to the right of the column you wish to lock in place when scrolling (except cell A1).
> 2. Click the **View** tab in the Ribbon.
> 3. Click the **Freeze Panes** icon.
> 4. Select the **Freeze Panes** option (select the **Unfreeze Panes** option to remove any locked rows and columns).
> 5. Use the **Freeze Top Row** or **Freeze First Column** options to lock the first column or row.

scrolling up and down or left and right. The following steps explain how to apply **Freeze Panes** to the Financial Assumptions worksheet in Figure 17:

- Click the **View** tab of the Ribbon.
- Click the **Freeze Panes** icon.
- Select the **Freeze Top Row** option. Select the **Unfreeze Panes** option to remove any locked columns and rows on the worksheet.

## Financial Data

Figures 18 and 19 show the next component of the comprehensive financial plan: the Financial Data worksheet. The purpose of this worksheet is to show the financial results of the plan based on the data that is entered into Financial Assumptions spreadsheet. Most of the data shown in this worksheet is produced by formulas and functions that are linked to the Financial Assumptions worksheet. A business manager will most likely focus on the Net Income in row 14 to see if the data that was entered in the Financial Assumptions worksheet results in a profit. Notice that in year 1, the Net Income shows a loss of ($75,038), a small loss of ($1,432) in year 2, and a profit in year 3 of $87,365. This trend is typical for new businesses.

Figure 18 | **Financial Data Worksheet Rows 1 – 15**

Changes made to the data in the Financial Assumptions worksheet will produce new outputs in this worksheet.

The Net Income trend shown in this row is typical for new businesses.

| | A | B | C | D |
|---|---|---|---|---|
| 1 | Financial Data for Business Strategy | | | |
| 2 | *Sales and Income* | Year 1 | Year 2 | Year 3 |
| 3 | Unit Sales | 7,676 | 19,878 | 38,623 |
| 4 | Gross Sales | $ 175,000 | $ 446,250 | $ 864,833 |
| 5 | Returns | $ 6,125 | $ 8,925 | $ 15,135 |
| 6 | Net Sales | $ 168,875 | $ 437,325 | $ 849,698 |
| 7 | Cost of Goods Sold | $ 84,000 | $ 205,275 | $ 380,526 |
| 8 | Gross Profit | $ 84,875 | $ 232,050 | $ 469,172 |
| 9 | Depreciation | $ 7,500 | $ 7,500 | $ 7,500 |
| 10 | Selling, General & Admin. Expenses | $ 141,625 | $ 215,194 | $ 309,972 |
| 11 | Interest | $ 10,788 | $ 10,788 | $ 10,788 |
| 12 | Income Before Taxes | $ (75,038) | $ (1,432) | $ 140,911 |
| 13 | Taxes | $ - | $ - | $ 53,546 |
| 14 | Net Income | $ (75,038) | $ (1,432) | $ 87,365 |
| 15 | *Percent of Net Sales* | *-44.4%* | *-0.3%* | *10.3%* |

Figure 19 | **Financial Data Worksheet Rows 16 – 23**

The Freeze Panes command is locking this row at the top of the worksheet.

This row contains links to the Cash Analysis worksheet.

| | A | B | C | D |
|---|---|---|---|---|
| 1 | Financial Data for Business Strategy | | | |
| 16 | *Assets* | Year 1 | Year 2 | Year 3 |
| 17 | Cash | $ 189,423 | $ 106,394 | $ 108,242 |
| 18 | Accounts Receivable | $ 14,583 | $ 37,188 | $ 72,069 |
| 19 | Inventory | $ 35,000 | $ 89,250 | $ 144,139 |
| 20 | Other Assets | $ 75,000 | $ 75,000 | $ 75,000 |
| 21 | Total Assets | $ 314,007 | $ 307,832 | $ 399,450 |
| 22 | *Liabilities* | Year 1 | Year 2 | Year 3 |
| 23 | Accounts Payable | $ 14,000 | $ 34,213 | $ 63,421 |

As previously mentioned, the numbers shown on the Financial Data worksheet (Figures 18 and 19) are produced by formulas and functions, most of which contain links to the Financial Assumptions worksheet. The following lists each formula or function that was created for Year 1. These formulas and functions are copied and pasted to produce the results for Year 2 and Year 3 unless otherwise noted:

- **Unit Sales:** `B6/'Financial Assumptions'!B12` This formula takes the Net Sales value calculated in cell B6 of the Financial Data worksheet and divides it by the Price Charged to Retailers in cell B12 of the Financial Assumptions worksheet.
- **Gross Sales Year 1:** `'Financial Assumptions'!B10` Since this is a new business, the first year of sales is typed into cell B10 of the Financial Assumptions worksheet. Therefore, the Gross Sales for Year 1 on the Financial Data worksheet is simply a link to cell B10 on the Financial Assumptions worksheet.
- **Gross Sales Year 2 and 3:** `(B4 + B4*'Financial Assumptions'!C11)*(1 + 'Financial Assumptions'!C9)` The first part of this formula is identical to the one used in Figure 7 in the previous section, which calculates the Gross Sales based on a percentage change. However, in this example an adjustment is made for inflation. The percentage change in inflation, which is entered into cell C9 in the Financial Assumptions worksheet, is added to 1 and then multiplied by the result of calculating the Gross Sales. This formula is copied and pasted into to cell D4 to calculate the Gross Sales for Year 3.
- **Returns:** `B4*'Financial Assumptions'!B13` The returns are calculated by multiplying the percentage entered into cell B13 on the Financial Assumptions worksheet by the Gross Sales calculated in cell B4.
- **Net Sales:** `B4 - B5` This basic formula takes the Gross Sales calculated in cell B4 and subtracts the Returns calculated in cell B5.
- **Cost of Goods Sold:** `B4*'Financial Assumptions'!B15` The Cost of Goods Sold percentage in the Financial Assumptions worksheet is multiplied by the Gross Sales in cell B4.
- **Gross Profit:** `B6-B7` This basic formula subtracts the Cost of Goods Sold from the Net Sales.
- **Depreciation:** `'Financial Assumptions'!B29/'Financial Assumptions'!B16` This formula takes a straight-line depreciation method approach (depreciation methods will be covered in your accounting courses). The Other Assets calculated in cell B29 in the Financial Assumptions worksheet is simply divided by the number of years entered into cell B16 of the Financial Assumptions worksheet.
- **Selling, General & Admin. Expenses:** `'Financial Assumptions'!B17+('Financial Assumptions'!B20*B4)+SUM('Financial Assumptions'!B21:B24)` The first part of this formula is simply a link to the total Employee Salary and Benefits cost in cell B17 in the Financial Assumptions worksheet. This is added to the Shipping Expenses, which are calculated by multiplying the percentage in cell B20 of the Financial Assumptions worksheet by the Gross Sales in cell B4. This result is then added to the summation of all expenses in the range B21:B24 in the Financial Assumptions worksheet.
- **Interest:** `PMT('Financial Assumptions'!D4,15,-'Financial Assumptions'!B4)-('Financial Assumptions'!B4/15)` This formula estimates the interest expense paid on a loan entered into cell B4 in the Financial Assumptions worksheet. The annual payments calculated by the **PMT** function include the principal *and interest* of the loan. When the principal divided

by the number of periods is subtracted from this result, what is left is an estimate of the interest that is paid each year. Years 2 and 3 for the interest expense simply reference the output of this formula in cell B11.

- **Income Before Taxes:** `B8 – SUM(B9:B11)` The **SUM** function adds the expenses in the range B9:B11 and subtracts it from the Gross Profit calculated in cell B8.
- **Taxes:** `IF(B12 > 0,B12 * 'Financial Assumptions'!B25,0)` An **IF** function is used to calculate the projected tax expense. This function checks to see if the Income Before Taxes, which is calculated in cell B12, is greater than zero. If the Income Before Taxes is greater than 0, it is multiplied by the tax percentage entered into cell B25 in the Financial Assumptions worksheet. If the Income Before Taxes is not greater than 0, the tax expense is assumed to be 0. This is a rather simple approach to projecting tax expenses. Depending on your project, you may be required to apply other tax accounting methodologies.
- **Net Income:** `B12 – B13` The Net Income is calculated by taking the Income Before Taxes and subtracting any taxes calculated in cell B13.
- **Percent of Net Sales:** `B14 / B6` This formula calculates Net Income as a percentage of Net Sales.
- **Cash:** `'Cash Analysis'!B11` This is a link to cell B11 in the Cash Analysis worksheet. The methods of data calculation in the Cash Analysis worksheet will be covered in the next section.
- **Accounts Receivable:** `B4 / 'Financial Assumptions'!B27` This formula estimates the accounts receivable by dividing the Accounts Receivable Turn in cell B27 in the Financial Assumptions worksheet into the Gross Sales in cell B4.
- **Inventory:** `B4 / 'Financial Assumptions'!B28` This formula divides the Inventory Turn in cell B28 in the Financial Assumptions worksheet into the Gross Sales in cell B4.
- **Other Assets:** `'Financial Assumptions'!B29` This is simply a link to cell B29 in the Financial Assumptions worksheet.
- **Account Payable:** `B7 / 'Financial Assumptions'!B33` The accounts payable is calculated by dividing the Accounts Payable Turn in cell B33 in the Financial Assumptions worksheet into the Cost of Goods Sold calculated in cell B7.

## Cash Analysis (The NPV Function)

The third and final component of the comprehensive financial plan is the Cash Analysis worksheet, which is shown in Figure 20. The purpose of this worksheet is to show how much cash is used or accumulated as a result of the assumptions entered into the Financial Assumptions worksheet. Similar to the Financial Data worksheet, the Cash Analysis worksheet is created entirely of formulas and functions. In fact, most of the formulas and functions created in the Cash Analysis worksheet are linked to the Financial Data worksheet. Therefore, when the outputs of the formulas and functions change in the Financial Data worksheet, the outputs of the Cash Analysis worksheet will also change. The results of the Cash Analysis worksheet enable you to conduct a net present value analysis, which is a method used to determine the value of an investment or business. This will be calculated through the **NPV** function, which is covered in this section.

Figure 20 | **Cash Analysis Worksheet**

| | A | B | C | D |
|---|---|---|---|---|
| 1 | Cash Analysis | | | |
| 2 | | Year 1 | Year 2 | Year 3 |
| 3 | **Beginning Cash** | $ 400,000 | $ 189,423 | $ 106,394 |
| 4 | Net Income | $ (75,038) | $ (1,432) | $ 87,365 |
| 5 | Depreciation | $ 7,500 | $ 7,500 | $ 7,500 |
| 6 | Change in Inventory | $ (35,000) | $ (54,250) | $ (54,889) |
| 7 | Change in Accounts Receivable | $ (14,583) | $ (22,604) | $ (34,882) |
| 8 | Change in Accounts Payable | $ 14,000 | $ 20,213 | $ 29,209 |
| 9 | Capital Expenditures | $ (75,000) | $ - | $ - |
| 10 | Repayment of Debt | $ (32,455) | $ (32,455) | $ (32,455) |
| 11 | *Ending Cash* | *$ 189,423* | *$ 106,394* | *$ 108,242* |
| 12 | | | | |
| 13 | | | | |
| 14 | *Net Present Value of Plan for Three Years* | | $ (36,363) | |
| 15 | | | | |
| 16 | Net Present Value Assuming Ending Cash in Year 3 is Sustained 3 More Years | | $ 186,477 | |

The data in this area of the worksheet is produced by formulas and functions that contain links to the Financial Data worksheet.

The NPV function has been entered into these two cells.

The following is a list of the formulas and functions that were created for Year 2. In several cases, a different calculation method is required for Year 1 and is noted accordingly:

- **Beginning Cash:** `B11` The Beginning Cash for Year 2 references the Ending Cash from Year 1. The Beginning Cash for Year 1 is a link to cell B3 in the Financial Assumptions worksheet, which contains the Total Initial Investment to start the business.
- **Net Income:** `'Financial Data'!C14` The Net Income is a link to the Financial Data worksheet.
- **Depreciation:** `'Financial Data'!C9` This is also a link to the Financial Data worksheet.
- **Change in Inventory:** `'Financial Data'!B19 - 'Financial Data'!C19` This formula takes the inventory value in Year 2 from the Financial Data worksheet and subtracts it from the inventory value in Year 1. As inventory increases from one year to the next, the formula produces a negative number, which shows that more cash is absorbed from the business. For Year 1 the inventory value in cell B18 in the Financial Data worksheet is subtracted from 0. As a result, the entire inventory required to start the business in Year 1 absorbs cash from the business.
- **Change in Accounts Receivable:** `'Financial Data'!B18 - 'Financial Data'!C18` Similar to the Change in Inventory calculation, the Change in Accounts Receivable is calculated by subtracting the Accounts Receivable value in Year 2 in the Financial Data worksheet from Year 1. Year 1 is calculated by subtracting the Accounts Receivable value from 0.
- **Change in Accounts Payable:** `'Financial Data'!C23 - 'Financial Data'!B23` This formula subtracts the Accounts Payable value in Year 1 from Year 2 in the Financial Data worksheet. This calculation is the opposite of the calculations used for Change in Inventory and Change in Accounts Receivable because, as Accounts Payable increases, cash is added to the business. The value for

Year 1 is a link to the Accounts Payable value in Year 1 on the Financial Data worksheet.

- **Capital Expenditures:** `'Financial Data'!B20 - 'Financial Data'!C20` This formula subtracts the Other Assets value in Year 2 from Year 1 in the Financial Data worksheet. If the value of Other Assets increases in Year 2 over Year 1, a negative number will be produced, indicating cash was used. The value for Year 1 subtracts the Other Assets value in cell B20 in the Financial Data worksheet from 0.
- **Repayment of Debt:** `PMT('Financial Assumptions'!D4,15,-'Financial Assumptions'!B4,,1) * -1` The **Payment** function calculates the annual payments of the loan based on the details listed in the Financial Assumptions worksheet. The result of the function is multiplied by –1 because it reduces the cash available to the business.
- **Ending Cash:** `C3 + SUM(C4:C10)` The Ending Cash is calculated by adding all of the items that add or reduce the cash of the business and adding that number to the beginning cash value.

The final calculation shown on the Cash Analysis worksheet in Figure 20 is the net present value of the comprehensive financial plan. This value is calculated using the **NPV** function. Details regarding the concepts of a net present value analysis will be covered in your finance courses. However, the following definitions for the arguments of the **NPV** function will provide a few insights as to what a net present value analysis can tell a business manager:

- **rate:** This is the interest rate or cost of borrowing money for the business. The goal of the **NPV** function is to calculate the present value of cash that is generated by a business in the future. It might be best to think of this concept as the **Future Value** function in reverse. That is, the **Future Value** function calculates how much money will be worth in the future when interest is added to a principal value over a period of time. The **NPV** function takes cash that is expected to be generated in the future and calculates how much that money is worth today. A new business is often considered a worthy investment if the NPV is a positive number.
- **value1:** This is the initial investment required to start, rebuild, or enhance a business. A negative sign must be used when entering values or cell locations for this argument.
- [**value(n)**]: Each value entered into the function after the **value1** argument is the cash flow that is expected for the year. Therefore, if you are using the **NPV** function to calculate the net present value for a ten-year financial plan, you will have ten cash values after you input the initial investment for the **value1** argument.

The arguments for the **NPV** function entered into cell C14 in the Cash Analysis worksheet are defined as follows:

- **rate:** `'Financial Assumptions'!D4` This is the interest rate from the loan details on the Financial Assumptions spreadsheet. This rate is used as the cost of borrowing money for this business.
- **value1:** `'Financial Assumptions'!B3` This is the principal of the loan from the Financial Assumptions worksheet. Notice that a negative sign is placed in front of this link.
- [**value2**]: `B11` This is the Ending Cash value in Year 1 on the Cash Analysis worksheet.
- [**value3**]: `C11` This is the Ending Cash value in Year 2 on the Cash Analysis worksheet.
- [**value4**]: `D11` This is the Ending Cash value in Year 3 on the Cash Analysis worksheet.

**>> Quick Reference**

**NPV Function**

1. Activate cell where the output should appear.
2. Type an equal sign, the function name **NPV**, and an open parenthesis.
3. Define the following arguments:
   a. **rate**: The interest rate that is charged for a loan or a firm's cost to borrow money.
   b. **value1**: The initial investment for starting a new business or in an existing business. You must precede values or cell locations with a negative sign.
   c. **[value(n)]**: Cash generated by the end of the year for a new business or incremental cash generated by an existing business. Use a separate argument to add cash value for each year.
4. Type a closing parenthesis and press the **Enter** key.

The Cash Analysis worksheet also shows a second **NPV** function that was entered into cell C16. The purpose of this function is to show the net present value of the comprehensive financial plan if the Ending Cash in Year 3 were produced for another three years. As a result, the cell reference D11 is simply repeated for the **[value5]** through **[value7]** arguments. Notice that the output of the **NPV** function in cell C14 is negative. This suggests that the financial plan for this new business does not generate a substantial return if it were in operation only for three years. However, the second **NPV** function in cell C16 shows a substantial return if the business operates for six years and continues to generate the same Ending Cash in Year 3 for an additional three years.

One of the key benefits of setting up a comprehensive financial plan through the methods described in this section is that the outputs in the Financial Data worksheet and Cash Analysis worksheet will automatically change when you change the inputs in the Financial Assumptions worksheet. This feature allows you to evaluate multiple scenarios to determine what would happen to the profitability or net present value of the business when certain assumptions are changed. It is this process of evaluating several scenarios that helps business managers make key financial decisions, such as how much money can be spent on advertising, how many people should be hired, or how much equipment should be purchased. There is no way to say for certain what will happen in business. However, business managers will use Excel to construct plans similar to what was described in this section to determine what is possible with respect to various business initiatives and ultimately decide which initiatives to execute and which initiatives to drop.

## >> NPV Function

**VIDEO WORKSHOP**

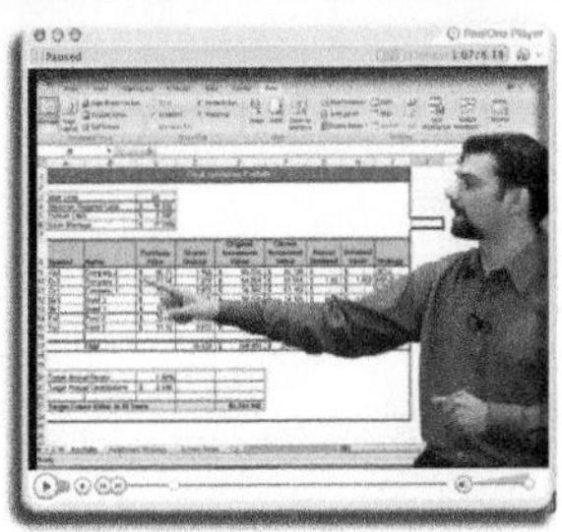

The purpose of this workshop is to demonstrate how the **NPV** function is used to evaluate an investment. I will be demonstrating the tasks in this workshop in the video named **NPV Function**. Open the file named ib_e06_investmentvalue and complete the tasks in this workshop.

1. **NPV Function (Video: NPV Function)**
   a. Activate cell E8 on the NPV Analysis worksheet.
   b. Type an equal sign, the function name **NPV**, and an open parenthesis.
   c. Click cell D3 to define the rate segment and type a comma.
   d. Type a negative sign and click cell D2. Then type a comma.
   e. Click cell A6 and type a comma.
   f. Click cell B6 and type a comma.
   g. Click cell C6 and type a comma.
   h. Click cell D6 and type a comma.
   i. Click cell E6 and type a closing parenthesis.
   j. Press the **Enter** key.
   k. Change the value in cell D2 to **975000**.
   l. Save and close your file.

**VIDEO WORKSHOP**

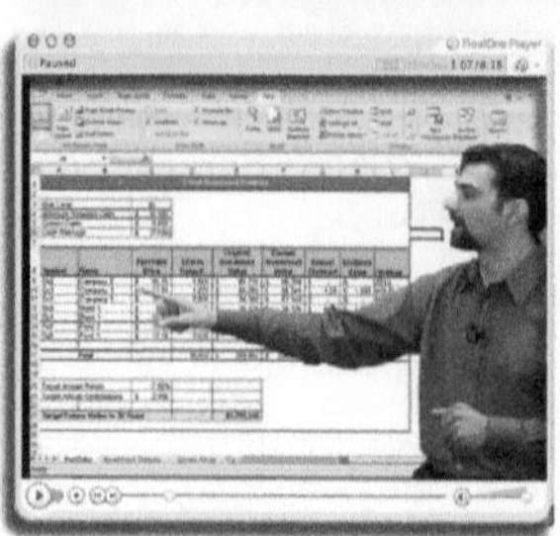

# >> Financial Plans

The purpose of this workshop is to construct the comprehensive financial plan that was presented in this section. I will be demonstrating the tasks in this workshop in the following three videos: **Financial Assumptions**, **Financial Data**, and **Cash Analysis**. These video names appear at the beginning of each section of tasks. Open the file named ib_e06_newbusinessfinancialplan. Complete each section of tasks and then watch the related video.

1. **Financial Assumptions (Video: Financial Assumptions)**
   - a. Activate the Financial Assumptions worksheet.
   - b. Type a **SUM** function in cell B3 that adds the values in the range B4:B7.
   - c. Type the formula `B18 * B19` in cell B17.
   - d. Copy the formula in cell B17 and paste it into cells C17 and D17 using the **Formulas** option.
   - e. Type a **SUM** function in cell B29 that adds the values in the range B30:B31.
   - f. Copy the **SUM** function in cell B29 and paste it into cells C29 and D29 using the **Formulas** option.
   - g. Type the following text in cell A38: **Target Scenario for New Business**.
   - h. Bold and italicize the text in cell A38 and change the text color to red.

2. **Financial Data (Video: Financial Data)**
   - a. Activate the Financial Data worksheet.
   - b. Type a link in cell B4 that displays the Gross Sales value in cell B10 in the Financial Assumptions worksheet.
   - c. Type a formula in cell C4 that calculates the Gross Sales for Year 2. Your formula should add to the Gross Sales value in cell B4 the result of multiplying the Gross Sales value in cell B4 by the Gross Sales Growth in cell C11 in the Financial Assumptions worksheet.
   - d. Edit the formula that was created in cell C4 to account for inflation. Place parentheses around the formula and then multiply it by the result of adding 1 to the inflation percentage in cell C9 of the Financial Assumptions worksheet.
   - e. Copy the formula in cell C4 and paste it into cell D4 using the **Formulas** option.
   - f. Type a formula in cell B5 that calculates the Returns for Year 1. Your formula should multiply the Gross Sales value in cell B4 by the Returns percent in cell B13 in the Financial Assumptions worksheet.
   - g. Copy the formula in cell B5 and paste it into cell C5 and D5 using the **Formulas** option.
   - h. Type a formula in cell B6 that calculates the Net Sales. Your formula should subtract the Returns from the Gross Sales. Then copy this formula and paste it into cells C6 and D6 using the **Formulas** option.
   - i. Type a formula in cell B3 that calculates the Unit Sales. Your formula should divide the Net Sales value in cell B6 by the Price Charged to Retailers in cell B12 in the Financial Assumptions worksheet.

j. Copy the formula in cell B3 and paste it into cells C3 and D3 using the **Formulas** option.

k. Type a formula in cell B7 that calculates the Cost of Goods Sold for Year 1. Your formula should multiply the Gross Sales value in cell B4 by the percentage in cell B15 in the Financial Assumptions worksheet.

l. Copy the formula in cell B7 and paste it into cells C7 and D7 using the **Formulas** option.

m. Type a formula in cell B8 that calculates the Gross Profit. Your formula should subtract the Cost of Goods Sold value in cell B7 from the Net Sales value in cell B6. Then copy this formula and paste it into cells C8 and D8 using the **Formulas** option.

n. Type a formula in cell B9 that calculates the Depreciation for Year 1. Your formula should divide the Other Assets value in cell B29 in the Financial Assumptions worksheet by the Average Life of Assets in cell B16, which is also in the Financial Assumptions worksheet.

o. Copy the formula in cell B9 and paste it into cells C9 and D9 using the **Formulas** option.

p. Type a formula in cell B10 that calculates the Selling, General & Admin. Expenses for Year 1. Your formula should add the Employee Salary and Benefits, the Shipping Expense, and all expenses in the range B21:B24 from the Financial Assumptions worksheet. Note that the Shipping Expense is calculated by multiplying the percentage in cell B20 in the Financial Assumptions worksheet by the Gross Sales value in cell B4 in the Financial Data worksheet.

q. Copy the formula in cell B10 and paste it into cells C10 and D10 using the **Formulas** option.

r. Type a formula in cell B11 that estimates the Interest Expense for Year 1. Your formula should first calculate the payments on the loan value in cell B4 in the Financial Assumptions worksheet using the **Payment** function. Use the Interest Rate in cell D4 of the Financial Assumptions worksheet to define the rate argument, use the number **15** to define the **nper** argument, and assume that payments are made at the beginning of the period. Then subtract from the output of this **Payment** function the result of dividing the loan value in cell B4 in the Financial Assumptions worksheet by 15.

s. Type the cell reference **B11** in cells C11 and D11 to display the output of the formula showing the Interest Expense in Year 1.

t. Type a formula in cell B12 to calculate the Income Before Taxes in Year 1. Your formula should subtract the sum of the expenses in the range B9:B11 from the Gross Profit value in cell B8. Then copy this formula and paste it into cells C12 and D12 using the **Formulas** option.

u. Type an **IF** function in cell B13 to calculate the Taxes for Year 1. If the Income Before Taxes is greater than 0, the function should multiply the Tax percent in cell B25 in the Financial Assumptions worksheet by the Income Before Taxes value in cell B12. Otherwise, the function should display a value of 0.

v. Copy the **IF** function in cell B13 and paste it into cells C13 and D13 using the **Formulas** option.

w. Type a formula in cell B14 to calculate the Net Income for Year 1. Your formula should subtract the Taxes value in cell B13 from the Income Before Taxes in cell B12. Then copy this formula and paste it into cells C14 and D14 using the **Formulas** option.

x. Type a formula in cell B15 to calculate the Percent of Net Sales for Year 1. Your formula should divide the Net Income value in cell B14 by the Net

Sales value in cell B6. Then copy this formula and paste it into cells C15 and D15 using the **Formulas** option.

y. Show the value of the Cash Assets in cell B17 by creating a link to cell B11 in the Cash Analysis worksheet. Then copy this link and paste it into cells C17 and D17 using the **Formulas** option.

z. Type a formula in cell B18 to calculate the Accounts Receivable for Year 1. Your formula should divide the Gross Sales value in cell B4 by the Accounts Receivable Turn in cell B27 in the Financial Assumptions worksheet.

aa. Copy the formula in cell B18 and paste it into cells C18 and D18 using the **Formulas** option.

bb. Type a formula in cell B19 to calculate the Inventory value for Year 1. Your formula should divide the Gross Sales in cell B4 by the Inventory Turn value in cell B28 in the Financial Assumptions worksheet.

cc. Copy the formula in cell B19 and paste it into cells C19 and D19 using the **Formulas** option.

dd. In cell B20, create a link to cell B29 in the Financial Assumptions worksheet. Then copy this link and paste it into cells C20 and D20 using the **Formulas** option.

ee. Type a **SUM** function in cell B21 that totals the values in the range B17:B20. Then copy the function and paste it into cells C21 and D21 using the **Formulas** option.

ff. Type a formula in cell B23 to calculate the Accounts Payable for Year 1. Your formula should divide the Cost of Goods Sold value in cell B7 by the Accounts Payable value in cell B33 in the Financial Assumptions worksheet.

gg. Copy the formula in cell B23 and paste it into cells C23 and D23 using the **Formulas** option.

3. **Cash Analysis (Video: Cash Analysis)**

a. Activate the Cash Analysis worksheet.

b. Create a link in cell B3 in the Cash Analysis worksheet that shows the value in cell B3 in the Financial Assumptions worksheet.

c. Type the cell reference `B11` in cell C3 to show the Ending Cash for Year 1. Then copy this cell reference and paste it into cell D3 using the **Formulas** option.

d. Create a link in cell B4 that shows the Net Income value in cell B14 in the Financial Data worksheet. Then copy this link and paste it into cells C4 and D4 using the **Formulas** option.

e. Create a link in cell B5 that shows the Depreciation value in cell B9 in the Financial Data worksheet. Then copy this link and paste it into cells C5 and D5 using the **Formulas** option.

f. Type a formula in cell B6 that calculates the Change in Inventory for Year 1. Your formula should subtract the value in cell B19 in the Financial Data worksheet from 0.

g. Type a formula in cell C6 that calculates the Change in Inventory for Year 2. Your formula should subtract the value in cell C19 in the Financial Data worksheet from the value in cell B19 in the Financial Data worksheet.

h. Copy the formula in cell C6 and paste it into cell D6 using the **Formulas** option.

i. Type a formula in cell B7 that calculates the Change in Accounts Receivable for Year 1. Your formula should subtract the value in cell B18 in the Financial Data worksheet from 0.

j. Type a formula in cell C7 that calculates the Change in Accounts Receivable for Year 2. Your formula should subtract the value in cell C18 in the Financial Data worksheet from the value in cell B18 in the Financial Data worksheet.
k. Copy the formula in cell C7 and paste it into cell D7 using the **Formulas** option.
l. Create a link in cell B8 that displays the value in cell B23 in the Financial Data worksheet.
m. Type a formula in cell C8 that calculates the Change in Accounts Payable for Year 2. Your formula should subtract the value in cell B23 in the Financial Data worksheet from the value in cell C23 in the Financial Data worksheet.
n. Copy the formula in cell C8 and paste it into cell D8 using the **Formulas** option.
o. Type a formula in cell B9 that calculates the Capital Expenditures for Year 1. Your formula should subtract the value in cell B20 in the Financial Data worksheet from 0.
p. Type a formula in cell C9 that calculates the Capital Expenditures for Year 2. Your formula should subtract the value in cell C20 in the Financial Data worksheet from the value in cell B20 in the Financial Data worksheet.
q. Copy the formula in cell C9 and paste it into cell D9 using the **Formulas** option.
r. Use the **Payment** function in cell B10 to calculate the Repayment of Debt in Year 1. Use the Interest Rate in cell D4 of the Financial Assumptions worksheet to define the **rate** argument, use the number `15` to define the **nper** argument, use the value in cell B4 in the Financial Assumptions worksheet to define the **pv** argument, and assume that payments are made at the beginning of the period. Multiply this function by −1 to show a negative number in cell B10.
s. Type the cell reference `B10` in cell C10 and D10.
t. Type a formula in cell B11 that adds the sum of the range B4:B10 to the value in cell B3. Then copy this formula and paste it into cells C11 and D11 using the **Formulas** option.
u. Type an **NPV** function into cell C14 to determine the net present value of the plan. Use the value in cell D4 in the Financial Assumptions worksheet to define the **rate** argument, the value in cell B3 in the Financial Assumptions worksheet to define the **[value1]** argument, and the Ending Cash values in the Cash Analysis worksheet to define the **[value2]**, **[value3]**, and **[value4]** arguments.
v. Save and close your file.

## >> Evaluating Business Initiatives Using Net Present Value

**EXERCISE**

**Why Do I Need This?**

Business managers frequently evaluate how various financial assumptions change the profitability and cash flow of a business. This information is vital before making critical investment or operational decisions. These decisions include areas such as acquiring new businesses, starting new businesses, or improving existing businesses. In addition, many businesses evaluate the quality of an investment through a net present value analysis.

## Exercise

The purpose of this exercise is to evaluate a decision to invest money in a new computer system that is expected to increase the productivity of a division within a major corporation. You will use a net present value analysis to evaluate the investment and its expected return. Open the file named ib_e06_systemimprovements.

1. Examine the formulas used to produce the data in the Revised Plan worksheet. What will happen if any value in the yellow cells of the Assumptions worksheet is changed?

2. Type a formula in cell B3 on the Change in Plan worksheet that subtracts cell B3 in the Current Plan worksheet from cell B3 in the Revised Plan worksheet. This will calculate the change in Gross Sales from the current to the revised plan. Copy this formula and paste it into the cells C3 through E3.

3. Type a formula in cell B4 in the Change in Plan worksheet to calculate the change in Returns by subtracting cell B4 in the Current Plan from cell B4 in the Revised Plan. Copy this formula and paste it into cells C4 through E4. What impact is the new system expected to have on returns?

4. Type a formula in cell B5 in the Change in Plan worksheet that shows the Change in Returns as a percent of Gross Sales. Your formula should subtract cell B5 in the Current Plan worksheet from cell B5 in the Revised Plan worksheet. Copy this formula and paste it into cells C5 through E5.

5. Copy the range B3:E3 and paste it into the range B6:E15. This will show the difference between the Current Plan and Revised Plan for each financial item listed in column A. You will want to use the Formulas option when pasting to maintain the formatting of the worksheet.

6. Type a **SUM** function in cell G3 on the Change in Plan worksheet that totals the values in the range B3:E3. What is the total increase in sales over four years the new system is expected to generate for the business?

7. Copy the **SUM** function in cell G3 and paste it in to cells G4, G6, G7, G9, and the range G11:G14. How much additional Net Income is the new system expected to generate for the business over a four-year period? Compare this number to the Total Initial Investment value in cell B2 in the Assumptions worksheet. Does this system seem be a good investment?

8. As previously mentioned, many business managers measure the quality of an investment based on the results of a net present value analysis. This will tell the business manager if the profits generated from an investment make sense given the time value of money. Therefore, type an **NPV** function in cell C18 on the Change in Plan worksheet. Define each argument of the function as follows:

   a. **Rate**: Cell B3 in the Assumptions worksheet. This is the division's cost to borrow money to pay for the initial cost of the new computer system.

   b. **value1**: Cell B2 in the Assumptions worksheet. This is the investment that is required to purchase and install the system.

   c. **[value2]**: The range B14:E14 in the Change in Plan worksheet. We will assume that the entire increase in Net Income will be incremental, or extra, cash added to the business as a result of the computer system.

9. Assume that this company has a policy that states all investments must prove that a minimum net present value of $5,000 is achievable over a four-year period. Should the manager of this division buy the computer system? Why?

10. In the Assumptions spreadsheet, change the values in the range B7:E7 to `15%`. This will assume that Gross Sales will increase 15% over the current

financial plan of the division. What is the total increase in Gross Sales (cell G3 in the Change in Plan worksheet) after making this change? Is the NPV of this investment positive or negative after making this change? Is it at least $5,000?

11. Change the Gross Sales percent values in the range B7:E7 on the Assumptions worksheet back to **10%**. Then change the values in the range B8:E8 to **2%**. This assumes that the new system will decrease the amount of Returns as a Percent of Gross Sales by 2% instead of 1%. Check the NPV on the Change in Plan worksheet. Is it positive or negative? Is it positive by at least $5,000?

12. Go back to the Assumptions worksheet and change the Gross Sales percent values in the range B7:E7 to **5%**. This assumes that the new system will increase Gross Sales over the current plan by only 5%. However, it will still assume that Returns as a Percent of Gross Sales will be reduced by 2%. Check the NPV of the investment. Is it positive or negative? Is it at least $5,000?

13. What does your assessment of step 12 tell you about the value of business initiatives that increase quality or reduce costs versus increasing sales?

14. Save and close your file.

## >> What's Wrong with This Spreadsheet?

**PROBLEM & EXERCISE**

### Problem

You are the CEO of a corporation. Your directors of Strategic Planning are presenting the results of a financial plan for starting a new business. This business will operate as a separate division and will add a new brand of merchandise to the current portfolio of the corporation. You have set the following NPV standard for evaluating investments made by the company:

1. For new businesses, the NPV must be positive by at least $10,000 considering three years of cash flow.

2. For existing businesses, the NPV must be positive by at least $5,000 considering four years of cash flow.

With these standards in mind, the directors of Strategic Planning are very excited to present this new business idea. They explain that a $2,500,000 investment will be required to start the business. In addition, the results of the plan show that the NPV is positive and well over $100,000. They explain that this business will generate Net Sales of over $3.3 million over a three-year period and will produce over $2 million in gross profit over the same time period. However, the directors point out that the business will lose a considerable amount of money in the first year and show that the Net Income is negative by over $600,000 in Year 1. That said, they also show that the Net Income makes a dramatic improvement in Year 2 and that the company is expected to show a profit in Year 3.

You look carefully at the spreadsheets the team has printed out for you, and they appear to be well constructed. As you glance at the numbers, they all appear to make sense. You congratulate the Strategic Planning team for a job well done and tell them that you would like to look at the plan one more time before approving the $2,500,000 investment. In addition, you ask the team to e-mail you the Excel file that was used to produce the spreadsheets in the meeting.

### Exercise

The Excel file that the Strategic Planning department e-mailed to you is named ib_e06_agreatbusinessidea. Would you let the team spend the $2,500,000? Consider the following points:

1. Look at the numbers in the Financial Data worksheet. This information was presented to you at the meeting. Do the numbers make sense?
2. The formulas in the Financial Data worksheet are based on the numbers entered on the Assumptions worksheet. Do the outputs on the Financial Data worksheet change when the assumptions are changed?
3. Is the NPV really positive and over $100,000?

What's wrong with this spreadsheet? Write a short answer for each of the points listed here and explain why you would or would not approve this investment? Then fix any errors you find in the workbook.

Skill Set

## Financial Accounting

The previous section illustrated how you can use the core competency skills in this text to construct a comprehensive financial plan. This section will provide an illustrative review of how you can use the core competency skills to construct spreadsheets used for financial accounting. Business professionals will typically use specialized software for managing the accounting needs of their business. However, for business students, Excel can be a very convenient and valuable tool for completing assignments typically required in accounting courses. As a result, several financial accounting concepts and rules will be mentioned but not explained in detail. You will receive more detailed instruction regarding these concepts in your financial accounting courses and reference material.

### T-Accounts

Many financial accounting courses include assignments related to T-accounts. T-accounts are often considered a teaching tool when you are learning how certain transactions are treated according to the rules of accounting. Figure 21 shows an example of a blank T-account that was created in Excel. You use the **Borders** command to create the "T," and cells at the top of the T-account are merged so the name of the account can be centered over the "T."

Figure 21 | **Blank T-Account**

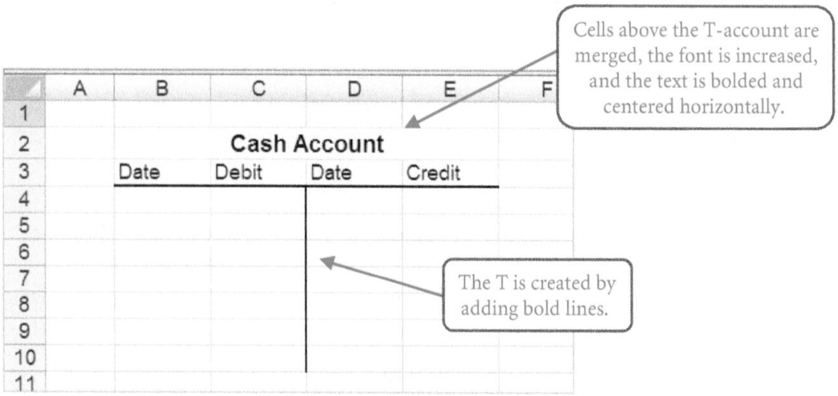

|  | A | B | C | D | E | F |
|---|---|---|---|---|---|---|
| 1 | | | | | | |
| 2 | | Cash Account | | | | |
| 3 | | Date | Debit | Date | Credit | |
| 4 | | | | | | |
| 5 | | | | | | |
| 6 | | | | | | |
| 7 | | | | | | |
| 8 | | | | | | |
| 9 | | | | | | |
| 10 | | | | | | |
| 11 | | | | | | |

Cells above the T-account are merged, the font is increased, and the text is bolded and centered horizontally.

The T is created by adding bold lines.

Figure 22 shows the T-account with dates and numbers entered into the debits and credits columns. A standard rule in accounting is that debits are always shown on the left and credits are always shown on the right. The **SUM** function is used at the bottom of the T-account to total the Debit and Credit columns.

Figure 22 | **T-Account with Dates and Dollar Entries**

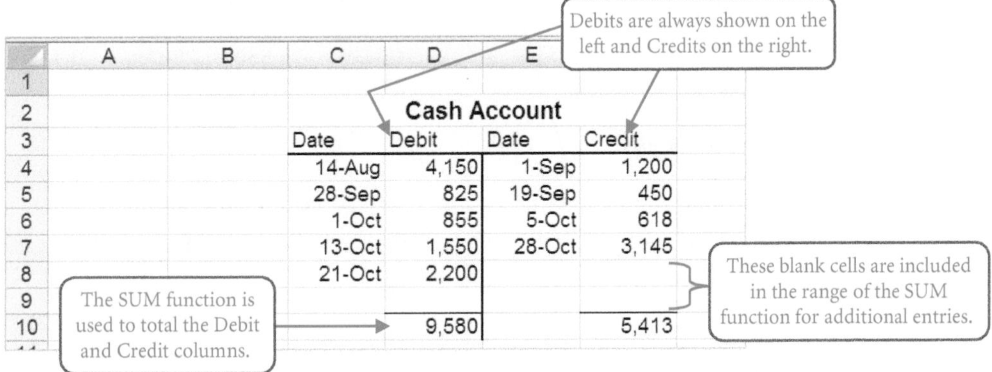

Debits are always shown on the left and Credits on the right.
Cash Account
Date
Debit
Date
Credit
14-Aug 4,150 1-Sep 1,200
28-Sep 825 19-Sep 450
1-Oct 855 5-Oct 618
13-Oct 1,550 28-Oct 3,145
21-Oct 2,200
9,580
5,413
These blank cells are included in the range of the SUM function for additional entries.
The SUM function is used to total the Debit and Credit columns.


Figure 23 shows a completed T-account which includes a formula that calculates the balance of the Cash Account (see cell B10). It is important to remember that the formula for calculating the balance of an account will change depending on the account. For example, Cash is an asset account, which means debits will increase the account and credits will decrease the account. For liability accounts, debits decrease the account and credits increase the account. These rules will be covered in your accounting courses.

Figure 23 | **Completed T-Account with Formula Calculating the Balance**

B10 =D10-F10

| | A | B | C | D | E | F |
|---|---|---|---|---|---|---|
| 2 | | | | Cash Account | | |
| 3 | | | Date | Debit | Date | Credit |
| 4 | | | 14-Aug | 4,150 | 1-Sep | 1,200 |
| 5 | | | 28-Sep | 825 | 19-Sep | 450 |
| 6 | | | 1-Oct | 855 | 5-Oct | 618 |
| 7 | | | 13-Oct | 1,550 | 28-Oct | 3,145 |
| 8 | | | 21-Oct | 2,200 | | |
| 9 | | | | | | |
| 10 | *Balance* | *4,167* | | 9,580 | | 5,413 |

For asset accounts, the balance is calculated by subtracting the total credits from the total debits.

A big benefit of doing T-accounts in Excel is that you can easily copy and paste them for other accounts. If you were assigned to do a T-account for another asset account, such as Accounts Receivables, you could copy the Cash Account, paste it to another location, delete the dates and numbers, and enter new dates and numbers. As shown in Figure 24, the **SUM** function totaling the debits and credits and the formula calculating the balance of the account produce new outputs when new data is entered. However, you must be careful when pasting a T-account from one account class to another. *The formula calculating the balance for an asset account will be different for a Liability account.* Therefore, if you are creating a Liability T-account from an asset account, you must delete the formula and re-create it to properly account for debits and credits.

Figure 24 | **Creating a New T-Account Using the Copy and Paste Commands**

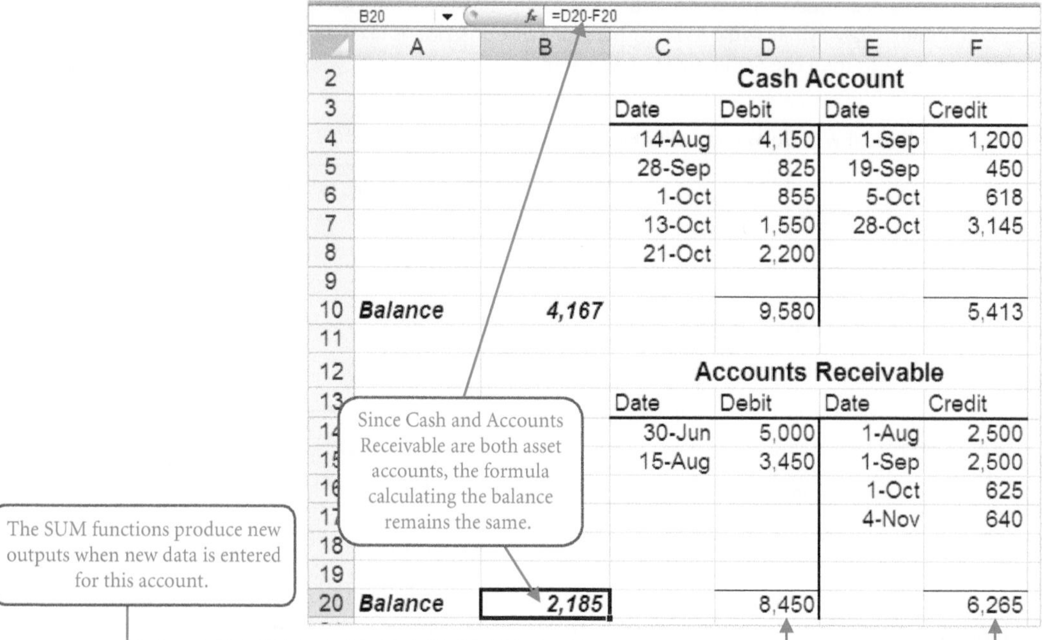

B20 =D20-F20

| | A | B | C | D | E | F |
|---|---|---|---|---|---|---|
| 2 | | | Cash Account | | | |
| 3 | | | Date | Debit | Date | Credit |
| 4 | | | 14-Aug | 4,150 | 1-Sep | 1,200 |
| 5 | | | 28-Sep | 825 | 19-Sep | 450 |
| 6 | | | 1-Oct | 855 | 5-Oct | 618 |
| 7 | | | 13-Oct | 1,550 | 28-Oct | 3,145 |
| 8 | | | 21-Oct | 2,200 | | |
| 9 | | | | | | |
| 10 | *Balance* | *4,167* | | 9,580 | | 5,413 |
| 11 | | | | | | |
| 12 | | | Accounts Receivable | | | |
| 13 | | | Date | Debit | Date | Credit |
| 14 | | | 30-Jun | 5,000 | 1-Aug | 2,500 |
| 15 | | | 15-Aug | 3,450 | 1-Sep | 2,500 |
| 16 | | | | | 1-Oct | 625 |
| 17 | | | | | 4-Nov | 640 |
| 18 | | | | | | |
| 19 | | | | | | |
| 20 | *Balance* | *2,185* | | 8,450 | | 6,265 |

Since Cash and Accounts Receivable are both asset accounts, the formula calculating the balance remains the same.
The SUM functions produce new outputs when new data is entered for this account.

## COMMON MISTAKES | T-Accounts

The most common mistake made when creating T-accounts in Excel is copying old T-accounts into different account classes. When you copy an old T-account to create a new one, *always check the formula that is calculating the balance of the account.* You may need to adjust the formula to properly account for debits and credits in order to calculate an accurate balance.

## Journals

Creating a journal is another common exercise that is required in accounting courses. A journal is used to keep track of all transactions that occur in a business and consists of the transaction date, the account description, and a monetary entry in either a Debit or Credit column. Figure 25 shows an example of a journal with several entries. Notice that each entry consists of at least two accounts (at least one debit and one credit), debit entries are listed before credit entries, and accounts with credit entries are indented.

Figure 26 shows the Accounting journal with the **SUM** function added to total the Debit and Credit columns. The amount of debits entered in a journal must equal the amount of credits. If the outputs of the two **SUM** functions are not identical, then there was most likely an error with one of the entries in the journal.

Figure 25 | **Accounting Journal**

| | A | B | C | D | E |
|---|---|---|---|---|---|
| 1 | JOURNAL | | | | |
| 2 | Date | Description | Post. Ref. | Debit | Credit |
| 3 | 10-Nov | Supplies | 14 | $ 1,350.00 | |
| 4 | 10-Nov | Accounts Payable | 21 | | $ 1,350.00 |
| 5 | | *Purchased supplies on account* | | | |
| 6 | | | | | |
| 7 | 18-Nov | Cash | 11 | $ 7,500.00 | |
| 8 | 18-Nov | Fees Earned | 41 | | $ 7,500.00 |
| 9 | | *Received fees from customers* | | | |
| 10 | | | | | |
| 11 | 30-Nov | Wages Expense | 51 | $ 2,125.00 | |
| 12 | 30-Nov | Rent Expense | 52 | $ 800.00 | |
| 13 | 30-Nov | Utilities Expense | 54 | $ 450.00 | |
| 14 | 30-Nov | Miscellaneous Expense | 59 | $ 275.00 | |
| 15 | 30-Nov | Cash | 11 | | $ 3,650.00 |
| 16 | | *Paid Expenses* | | | |
| 17 | | | | | |
| 18 | 30-Nov | Accounts Payable | 21 | $ 950.00 | |
| 19 | 30-Nov | Cash | 11 | | $ 950.00 |
| 20 | | *Paid creditors on account* | | | |

Accounts with a credit entry along with the transaction description are indented.

The Accounting number format is used for the dollar values in these columns.

Figure 26 | **The SUM Function Is Used to Total the Debit and Credit Entries**

D22 =SUM(D3:D18)

| | A | B | C | D | E |
|---|---|---|---|---|---|
| 1 | JOURNAL | | | | |
| 2 | Date | Description | Post. Ref. | Debit | Credit |
| 9 | | *Received fees from customers* | | | |
| 10 | | | | | |
| 11 | 30-Nov | Wages Expense | 51 | $ 2,125.00 | |
| 12 | 30-Nov | Rent Expense | 52 | $ 800.00 | |
| 13 | 30-Nov | Utilities Expense | 54 | $ 450.00 | |
| 14 | 30-Nov | Miscellaneous Expense | 59 | $ 275.00 | |
| 15 | 30-Nov | Cash | 11 | | $ 3,650.00 |
| 16 | | *Paid Expenses* | | | |
| 17 | | | | | |
| 18 | 30-Nov | Accounts Payable | 21 | $ 950.00 | |
| 19 | 30-Nov | Cash | 11 | | $ 950.00 |
| 20 | | *Paid creditors on account* | | | |
| 21 | | | | | |
| 22 | | | | $ 13,450.00 | $ 13,450.00 |

The Freeze Panes command was used to lock these two rows.

SUM functions are used to total all debit and credit entries.

## Ledgers

This section will illustrate how you use Excel to create an Accounting Ledger. A ledger is used to record all transactions for one specific account such as Cash, Accounts Payable, Inventory, and so on. Figure 27 shows an example of a blank ledger for the Cash account.

Figure 27 | **Blank Ledger for the Cash Account**

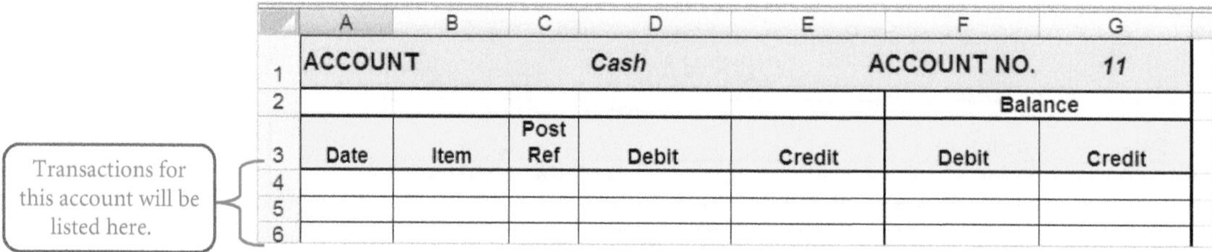

| | A | B | C | D | E | F | G |
|---|---|---|---|---|---|---|---|
| 1 | ACCOUNT | | | Cash | | ACCOUNT NO. | 11 |
| 2 | | | | | | Balance | |
| 3 | Date | Item | Post Ref | Debit | Credit | Debit | Credit |
| 4 | | | | | | | |
| 5 | | | | | | | |
| 6 | | | | | | | |

Transactions for this account will be listed here.

To complete the ledger shown in Figure 27, entries for the Cash Account are taken directly from the journal as shown in Figure 28. A copy of the journal is pasted into a new worksheet and then sorted by the Description and Date columns in ascending order. After the data is sorted, the Cash Account entries can be copied and pasted into the ledger. This eliminates the need to manually type the data into the ledger, which opens the possibility for data entry errors.

Figure 28 | **Journal Entries Sorted for Pasting Data into the Ledger**

These cash entries are grouped together after sorting the worksheet.

| | A | B | C | D | E |
|---|---|---|---|---|---|
| 1 | JOURNAL | | | | |
| 2 | Date | Description | Post. Ref. | Debit | Credit |
| 3 | 10-Nov | Accounts Payable | 21 | | $ 1,350.00 |
| 4 | 30-Nov | Accounts Payable | 21 | $ 950.00 | |
| 5 | 18-Nov | Cash | 11 | $ 7,500.00 | |
| 6 | 30-Nov | Cash | 11 | | $ 3,650.00 |
| 7 | 30-Nov | Cash | 11 | | $ 950.00 |
| 8 | 18-Nov | Fees Earned | 41 | | $ 7,500.00 |
| 9 | 30-Nov | Miscellaneous Expense | 59 | $ 275.00 | |
| 10 | | *Paid creditiors on account* | | | |

Figure 29 shows the entries that were pasted into the Cash account ledger from the journal in Figure 28. The next step will be to calculate the balance for the account. As previously mentioned, since Cash is an asset account, debits will increase the account and credits will decrease the account. Therefore, an **IF** function will be used to determine if the balance of the account should be increased or decreased based on the entry.

Figure 29 | **Cash Account Ledger with Entries Added**

| | A | B | C | D | E | F | G |
|---|---|---|---|---|---|---|---|
| 1 | ACCOUNT | | | Cash | | ACCOUNT NO. | 11 |
| 2 | | | | | | Balance | |
| 3 | Date | Item | Post Ref | Debit | Credit | Debit | Credit |
| 4 | 1-Nov | Balance | | | | $ - | |
| 5 | 18-Nov | | 1 | $ 7,500.00 | | | |
| 6 | 30-Nov | | 2 | | $ 3,650.00 | | |
| 7 | 30-Nov | | 2 | | $ 950.00 | | |
| 8 | | | | | | | |

The first entry reflects a beginning balance of 0.

An IF function will be created in this cell to calculate the balance.

The **IF** function is used to calculate the balance of the Cash ledger shown in Figure 29. The function will be created in cell F5 under the Debit column because asset accounts have a normal debit balance. Your accounting course will provide instruction on what the normal balance is for each type of account. The arguments of this **IF** function are defined as follows:

- **logical_test:** `D5 > 0` The logical test of the **IF** function will be used to determine if there is a value entered in the Debit column.
- **[value_if_true]:** `F4 + D5` If the logical test is true, it can be assumed that there is no entry in the Credit column. An entry *cannot* have a value in both the Debit and Credit columns. As a result, if the logical test is true, then this is a debit entry, which increases the balance of an asset account. Therefore, the value in cell D5 is added to the prior balance of the account, which is in cell F4.
- **[value_if_false]:** `F4 - E5` If the logical test is false, then it is assumed that there is a value in the Credit column. For asset accounts, credits decrease the balance. Therefore, the value in cell E5 is subtracted from cell F4, which is the prior balance of the account.

After the **IF** function is created in cell F5, it can be copied and pasted to the rest of the rows in the ledger. Figure 30 shows the completed ledger for the Cash account with the balance being calculated by the **IF** function.

Figure 30 | **Complete Ledger for the Cash Account**

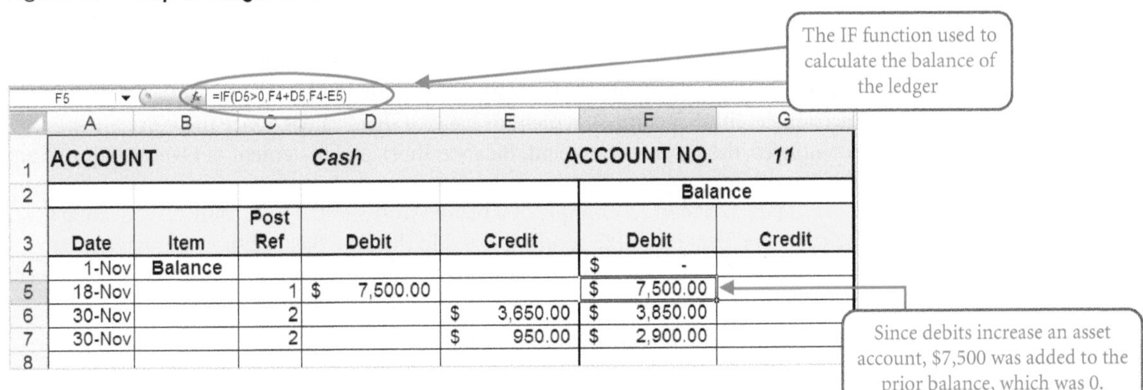

F5
=IF(D5>0,F4+D5,F4-E5)
The IF function used to calculate the balance of the ledger
Since debits increase an asset account, $7,500 was added to the prior balance, which was 0.

| | A | B | C | D | E | F | G |
|---|---|---|---|---|---|---|---|
| 1 | ACCOUNT | | | Cash | ACCOUNT NO. | | 11 |
| 2 | | | | | | Balance | |
| 3 | Date | Item | Post Ref | Debit | Credit | Debit | Credit |
| 4 | 1-Nov | Balance | | | | $ - | |
| 5 | 18-Nov | | 1 | $ 7,500.00 | | $ 7,500.00 | |
| 6 | 30-Nov | | 2 | | $ 3,650.00 | $ 3,850.00 | |
| 7 | 30-Nov | | 2 | | $ 950.00 | $ 2,900.00 | |
| 8 | | | | | | | |

## Trial Balance and Work Sheets

This section will illustrate two key components of the financial accounting system. The first is a Trial Balance. A Trial Balance is a list showing the current balance of all accounts for a particular business. The second is an accounting Work Sheet. Work Sheets are used to make any necessary adjustments and finalize the balance of all accounts for a business.

As previously mentioned, each account type has either a normal debit or credit balance. The purpose of the Trial Balance is to assess whether the total for all accounts that carry a debit balance are equal to the total for all accounts that carry a credit balance. Figure 31 shows an example of a completed Trial Balance. If a ledger was created in Excel for each account listed in column A, the balance can either be pasted, or preferably linked, into the Trial Balance. A **SUM** function is used to add both columns of the Trial Balance in row 20 to see whether they are equal. The double underline at the bottom of each result signifies that the accounts are balanced, meaning the sum of all debit balances is equal to the sum of all credit balances. You can access the double underline through the **Underline** icon.

Figure 31 | **Example of a Completed Trial Balance**

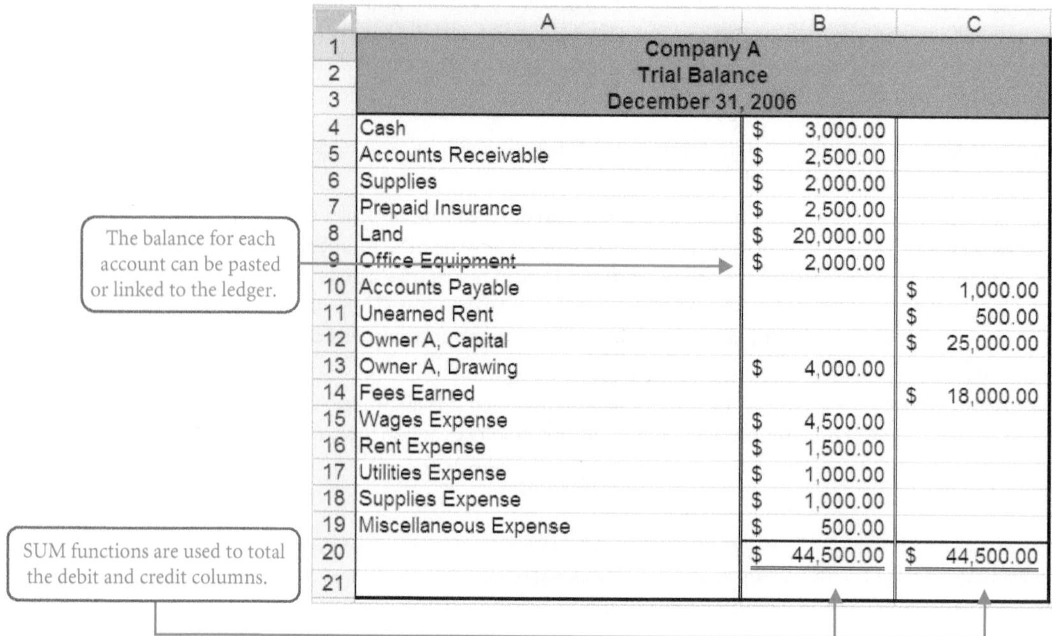

| | A | B | C |
|---|---|---|---|
| 1 | Company A | | |
| 2 | Trial Balance | | |
| 3 | December 31, 2006 | | |
| 4 | Cash | $ 3,000.00 | |
| 5 | Accounts Receivable | $ 2,500.00 | |
| 6 | Supplies | $ 2,000.00 | |
| 7 | Prepaid Insurance | $ 2,500.00 | |
| 8 | Land | $ 20,000.00 | |
| 9 | Office Equipment | $ 2,000.00 | |
| 10 | Accounts Payable | | $ 1,000.00 |
| 11 | Unearned Rent | | $ 500.00 |
| 12 | Owner A, Capital | | $ 25,000.00 |
| 13 | Owner A, Drawing | $ 4,000.00 | |
| 14 | Fees Earned | | $ 18,000.00 |
| 15 | Wages Expense | $ 4,500.00 | |
| 16 | Rent Expense | $ 1,500.00 | |
| 17 | Utilities Expense | $ 1,000.00 | |
| 18 | Supplies Expense | $ 1,000.00 | |
| 19 | Miscellaneous Expense | $ 500.00 | |
| 20 | | $ 44,500.00 | $ 44,500.00 |
| 21 | | | |

The balance for each account can be pasted or linked to the ledger.
SUM functions are used to total the debit and credit columns.

An accounting Work Sheet is used to make adjusting entries to the Trial Balance of each account and calculate a new balance if necessary. Not all accounts will have an adjusting entry; therefore, the calculated balance on the worksheet may be identical to the trial balance. In addition, the Work Sheet is used to identify the balance of each account as either income statement or balance sheet values. Once the Work Sheet is completed, the Income Statement, Balance Sheet, and Statement of Owners Equity can be created.

Figure 32 shows an example of a blank Work Sheet. The accounts listed along the left side are identical to the accounts listed in the Trial Balance shown in Figure 31; however, additional accounts can be added to the Work Sheet if necessary. The balance

Figure 32 | **Blank Accounting Work Sheet**

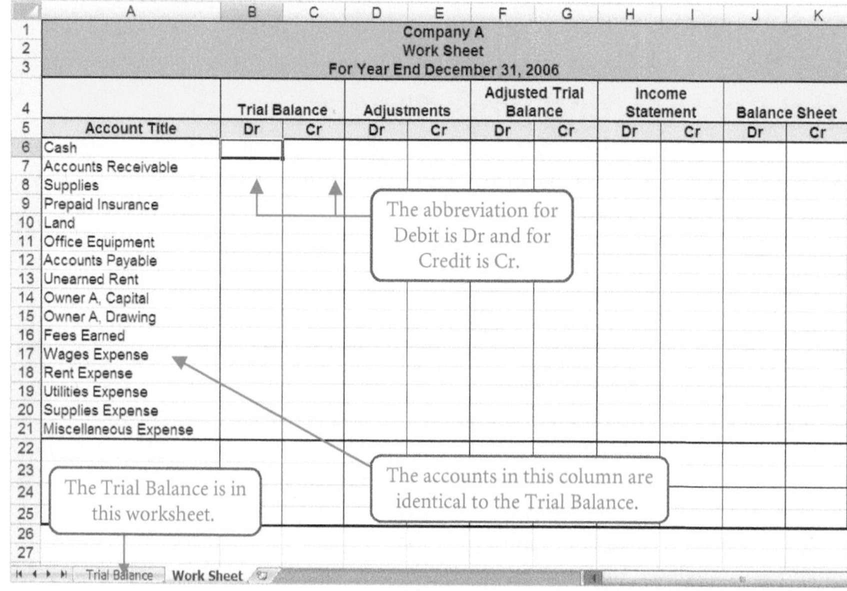

| | A | B | C | D | E | F | G | H | I | J | K |
|---|---|---|---|---|---|---|---|---|---|---|---|
| 1 | Company A | | | | | | | | | | |
| 2 | Work Sheet | | | | | | | | | | |
| 3 | For Year End December 31, 2006 | | | | | | | | | | |
| 4 | | Trial Balance | | Adjustments | | Adjusted Trial Balance | | Income Statement | | Balance Sheet | |
| 5 | Account Title | Dr | Cr | Dr | Cr | Dr | Cr | Dr | Cr | Dr | Cr |
| 6 | Cash | | | | | | | | | | |
| 7 | Accounts Receivable | | | | | | | | | | |
| 8 | Supplies | | | | | | | | | | |
| 9 | Prepaid Insurance | | | | | | | | | | |
| 10 | Land | | | | | | | | | | |
| 11 | Office Equipment | | | | | | | | | | |
| 12 | Accounts Payable | | | | | | | | | | |
| 13 | Unearned Rent | | | | | | | | | | |
| 14 | Owner A, Capital | | | | | | | | | | |
| 15 | Owner A, Drawing | | | | | | | | | | |
| 16 | Fees Earned | | | | | | | | | | |
| 17 | Wages Expense | | | | | | | | | | |
| 18 | Rent Expense | | | | | | | | | | |
| 19 | Utilities Expense | | | | | | | | | | |
| 20 | Supplies Expense | | | | | | | | | | |
| 21 | Miscellaneous Expense | | | | | | | | | | |
| 22 | | | | | | | | | | | |
| 23 | | | | | | | | | | | |
| 24 | | | | | | | | | | | |
| 25 | | | | | | | | | | | |
| 26 | | | | | | | | | | | |
| 27 | | | | | | | | | | | |

Trial Balance
Work Sheet
The abbreviation for Debit is Dr and for Credit is Cr.
The accounts in this column are identical to the Trial Balance.
The Trial Balance is in this worksheet.

for each account in the first two columns of the Work Sheet should be identical to the Trial Balance. The next set of columns is for adding any necessary adjustments. Columns F and G are used for calculating a new balance for each account to include any adjusting entries. The Income Statement and Balance Sheet columns are for categorizing the adjusted balance for each account in its respective financial statement. Therefore, the balance for each account used to construct an income statement will be shown in the Income Statement columns, and the balance for each account used to construct a balance sheet will be shown in the Balance Sheet columns.

As previously mentioned, the balance that appears in the first two columns of the Work Sheet must match the Trial Balance. Therefore, links are created in the Work Sheet to show the debit and credit values under the Trial Balance heading. If the order of the accounts in the Work Sheet is identical to the Trial Balance, the first link can be copied and pasted for the other accounts. Linking data in this situation ensures that the balance for each account in the Trial Balance matches the Work Sheet. If any changes are made to the Trial Balance, it will automatically be reflected in the Work Sheet. Figure 33 shows the links that were created in the Work Sheet.

Figure 33 | **Work Sheet with Links to the Trial Balance**

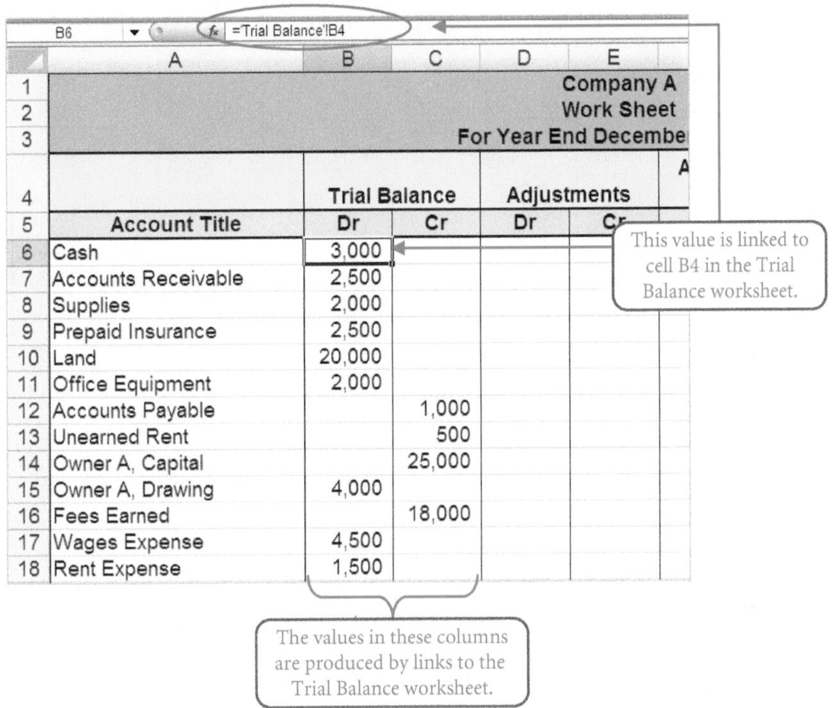

| | A | B | C | D | E |
|---|---|---|---|---|---|
| 1 | | | | | Company A |
| 2 | | | | | Work Sheet |
| 3 | | | | | For Year End Decembe |
| 4 | | Trial Balance | | Adjustments | |
| 5 | Account Title | Dr | Cr | Dr | Cr |
| 6 | Cash | 3,000 | | | |
| 7 | Accounts Receivable | 2,500 | | | |
| 8 | Supplies | 2,000 | | | |
| 9 | Prepaid Insurance | 2,500 | | | |
| 10 | Land | 20,000 | | | |
| 11 | Office Equipment | 2,000 | | | |
| 12 | Accounts Payable | | 1,000 | | |
| 13 | Unearned Rent | | 500 | | |
| 14 | Owner A, Capital | | 25,000 | | |
| 15 | Owner A, Drawing | 4,000 | | | |
| 16 | Fees Earned | | 18,000 | | |
| 17 | Wages Expense | 4,500 | | | |
| 18 | Rent Expense | 1,500 | | | |



The next set of columns in the Work Sheet is used for adding any adjusting entries for each account. Once the adjustments are added into the Work Sheet, an adjusted balance is calculated. Similar to calculating the balance on a ledger, the **IF** function will be used to calculate the adjusted balance on the Work Sheet by determining if the adjustments in columns D and E should be added or subtracted from the balance in the Trial Balance columns (columns B and C). To do this, you must first determine how debits and credits change the balance of an account. For the accounts on this Work Sheet, *debits will increase the balance of an account except for* Accounts Payable; Unearned Rent; Owner A, Capital; and Fees earned. For these accounts, the formula in the **IF** function must be adjusted so that any value in the Debit column is subtracted from the trial balance. Figure 34 shows an example of two **IF** functions that are used to calculate the Adjusted Trial Balance columns in the Work Sheet.

Figure 34 | **Using the IF Function to Calculate the Adjusted Trial Balance in the Work Sheet**

| Account | Trial Balance Cell Location | Adjusting Entry Cell Locations | Account Type | IF Function |
|---|---|---|---|---|
| Cash | **B6** | Debits = **D6**<br>Credits = **E6** | **Asset:** Debits increase the balance. | **=IF(D6 > 0,B6 + D6,B6 - E6)** |
| Accounts Payable | **C12** | Debits = **D12**<br>Credits = **E12** | **Liability:** Debits decrease the balance. | **=IF(D12 > 0,C12 - D12,C12 + E12)** |

Figure 35 shows the Work Sheet with adjusting entries added to columns D and E and the adjusted trial balance calculated by **IF** functions in columns F and G. In addition, **SUM** functions were added to row 22 to show the total debits and credits for each set of columns. Notice that the debits match the credits for each set of columns.

Figure 35 | **Work Sheet with Adjustments and Adjusted Trial Balance Added**

| | A | B | C | D | E | F | G | H | I | J | K |
|---|---|---|---|---|---|---|---|---|---|---|---|
| 1 | Company A | | | | | | | | | | |
| 2 | Work Sheet | | | | | | | | | | |
| 3 | For Year End December 31, 2006 | | | | | | | | | | |
| 4 | | Trial Balance | | Adjustments | | Adjusted Trial Balance | | Income Statement | | Balance Sheet | |
| 5 | Account Title | Dr | Cr | Dr | Cr | Dr | Cr | Dr | Cr | Dr | Cr |
| 6 | Cash | 3,000 | | | 500 | 2,500 | | | | | |
| 7 | Accounts Receivable | 2,500 | | 500 | | 3,000 | | | | | |
| 8 | Supplies | 2,000 | | | 500 | 1,500 | | | | | |
| 9 | Prepaid Insurance | 2,500 | | | | 2,500 | | | | | |
| 10 | Land | 20,000 | | | | 20,000 | | | | | |
| 11 | Office Equipment | 2,000 | | 500 | | 2,500 | | | | | |
| 12 | Accounts Payable | | 1,000 | 250 | | | 750 | | | | |
| 13 | Unearned Rent | | 500 | | | | 500 | | | | |
| 14 | Owner A, Capital | | 25,000 | | | | 25,000 | | | | |
| 15 | Owner A, Drawing | 4,000 | | | | 4,000 | | | | | |
| 16 | Fees Earned | | 18,000 | | 500 | | 18,500 | | | | |
| 17 | Wages Expense | 4,500 | | | | 4,500 | | | | | |
| 18 | Rent Expense | 1,500 | | | | 1,500 | | | | | |
| 19 | Utilities Expense | 1,000 | | | | 1,000 | | | | | |
| 20 | Supplies Expense | 1,000 | | 250 | | 1,250 | | | | | |
| 21 | Miscellaneous Expense | 500 | | | | 500 | | | | | |
| 22 | | 44,500 | 44,500 | 1,500 | 1,500 | 44,750 | 44,750 | | | | |

The IF function calculating the balance of this account is =IF(D12 > 0, C12 - D12,C12 + E 12).

The IF function calculating the balance of this account is =IF(D6 > 0,B6 + D6,B6 - E6).

SUM functions are used to add the total debits and credits for each set of columns.

The last columns to be completed on the Work Sheet are the Income Statement and Balance Sheet columns. These columns are used to classify the adjusted trial balances as either income statement or balance sheet accounts. This is accomplished by referencing the appropriate cell location in the Debit or Credit column of either the Income Statement or Balance Sheet headings. Your accounting course will provide details on which accounts are income statement or balance sheet accounts.

Figure 36 shows how each account in the Work Sheet is classified with respect to the Income Statement or Balance Sheet columns. For the first account, which is Cash, the cell reference =F6 is used to display the Adjusted Trial Balance in the Debit column under the Balance Sheet heading. As a result, any changes to the Adjusted Trial Balance for each account will be reflected in either the Income Statement or Balance Sheet columns.

## COMMON MISTAKES | Accounting Work Sheets

Make sure cell references are typed into the appropriate Debit or Credit column for the Income Statement or Balance Sheet columns of the Work Sheet. If an account shows a debit balance in the Adjusted Trial Balance column, then it must also have a debit balance in either the Income Statement or Balance Sheet columns. The same is true for accounts that have credit balances.

Figure 36 | **Work Sheet with Income Statement and Balance Sheet Columns Completed**

| | A | B | C | D | E | F | G | H | I | J | K |
|---|---|---|---|---|---|---|---|---|---|---|---|
| 1 | | | | | Company A | | | | | | |
| 2 | | | | | Work Sheet | | | | | | |
| 3 | | | | | For Year End December 31, 2006 | | | | | | |
| 4 | | Trial Balance | | Adjustments | | Adjusted Trial Balance | | Income Statement | | Balance Sheet | |
| 5 | Account Title | Dr | Cr | Dr | Cr | Dr | Cr | Dr | Cr | Dr | Cr |
| 6 | Cash | 3,000 | | | 500 | 2,500 | | | | 2,500 | |
| 7 | Accounts Receivable | 2,500 | | 500 | | 3,000 | | | | 3,000 | |
| 8 | Supplies | 2,000 | | | 500 | 1,500 | | | | 1,500 | |
| 9 | Prepaid Insurance | 2,500 | | | | 2,500 | | | | 2,500 | |
| 10 | Land | 20,000 | | | | 20,000 | | | | 20,000 | |
| 11 | Office Equipment | 2,000 | | 500 | | 2,500 | | | | 2,500 | |
| 12 | Accounts Payable | | 1,000 | 250 | | | 750 | | | | 750 |
| 13 | Unearned Rent | | 500 | | | | 500 | | | | 500 |
| 14 | Owner A, Capital | | 25,000 | | | | 25,000 | | | | 25,000 |
| 15 | Owner A, Drawing | 4,000 | | | | 4,000 | | | | 4,000 | |
| 16 | Fees Earned | | 18,000 | | 500 | | 18,500 | | 18,500 | | |
| 17 | Wages Expense | 4,500 | | | | 4,500 | | 4,500 | | | |
| 18 | Rent Expense | 1,500 | | | | 1,500 | | 1,500 | | | |
| 19 | Utilities Expense | 1,000 | | | | 1,000 | | 1,000 | | | |
| 20 | Supplies Expense | 1,000 | | 250 | | 1,250 | | 1,250 | | | |
| 21 | Miscellaneous Expense | 500 | | | | 500 | | 500 | | | |
| 22 | | 44,500 | 44,500 | 1,500 | 1,500 | 44,750 | 44,750 | 8,750 | 18,500 | 36,000 | 26,250 |

The cell reference =F6 is entered here.

SUM functions are used to total the debit and credit columns.

The final step in completing the Work Sheet is entering a formula to calculate the Net Income. You may have noticed in Figure 36 that the total debits and credits for the Income Statement and Balance Sheet columns do not match. This is why a double underline was not added to these results. For the Debit and Credit columns to match, the Net Income must be calculated and added to the Debit column of the Income Statement and to the Credit column of the Balance Sheet. This is done using basic formulas. For the Income Statement column, you calculate the Net Income by subtracting the total debits from the total credits. For the Balance Sheet column, you subtract the total credits from the total debits. You enter this formula in the Debit column for the Income Statement and in the Credit column for the Balance Sheet. When the net income is added to the total debits in the Income Statement column, the total debits will match the total credits. When the net income is added to the total credits of the Balance Sheet column, the total credits will match the total debits. The final Work Sheet is shown in Figure 37.

Figure 37 | **Final Work Sheet**

| | A | B | C | D | E | F | G | H | I | J | K |
|---|---|---|---|---|---|---|---|---|---|---|---|
| 1 | | | | | Company A | | | | | | |
| 2 | | | | | Work Sheet | | | | | | |
| 3 | | | | | For Year End December 31, 2006 | | | | | | |
| 4 | | Trial Balance | | Adjustments | | Adjusted Trial Balance | | Income Statement | | Balance Sheet | |
| 5 | Account Title | Dr | Cr | Dr | Cr | Dr | Cr | Dr | Cr | Dr | Cr |
| 6 | Cash | 3,000 | | | 500 | 2,500 | | | | 2,500 | |
| 7 | Accounts Receivable | 2,500 | | 500 | | 3,000 | | | | 3,000 | |
| 8 | Supplies | 2,000 | | | 500 | 1,500 | | | | 1,500 | |
| 9 | Prepaid Insurance | 2,500 | | | | 2,500 | | | | 2,500 | |
| 10 | Land | 20,000 | | | | 20,000 | | | | 20,000 | |
| 11 | Office Equipment | 2,000 | | 500 | | 2,500 | | | | 2,500 | |
| 12 | Accounts Payable | | 1,000 | 250 | | | 750 | | | | 750 |
| 13 | Unearned Rent | | 500 | | | | 500 | | | | 500 |
| 14 | Owner A, Capital | | 25,000 | | | | 25,000 | | | | 25,000 |
| 15 | Owner A, Drawing | 4,000 | | | | 4,000 | | | | 4,000 | |
| 16 | Fees Earned | | 18,000 | | 500 | | 18,500 | | 18,500 | | |
| 17 | Wages Expense | 4,500 | | | | 4,500 | | 4,500 | | | |
| 18 | Rent Expense | 1,500 | | | | 1,500 | | 1,500 | | | |
| 19 | Utilities Expense | 1,000 | | | | 1,000 | | 1,000 | | | |
| 20 | Supplies Expense | 1,000 | | 250 | | 1,250 | | 1,250 | | | |
| 21 | Miscellaneous Expense | 500 | | | | 500 | | 500 | | | |
| 22 | | 44,500 | 44,500 | 1,500 | 1,500 | 44,750 | 44,750 | 8,750 | 18,500 | 36,000 | 26,250 |
| 23 | | | | | | | | 9,750 | | | 9,750 |
| 24 | | | | | | | | 18,500 | 18,500 | 36,000 | 36,000 |
| 25 | | | | | | | | | | | |

The formula entered into this cell is =I22 - H22.

This is the output of a formula adding cells H22 and H23.

The formula entered into this cell is =J22 - K22.

## Statements

Once the Work Sheet is completed, you can create a set of financial statements. The data used to create these statements will be linked to the Work Sheet. As a result, when the data is changed in the Work Sheet, it will adjust the outputs of the financial statements. Three statements will be created from the Work Sheet shown in Figure 37: an Income Statement, a Balance Sheet, and a Statement of Owners Equity.

The purpose of an Income Statement is to report the profitability of a business by showing all sales and expenses incurred by a company. Figure 38 shows an example of a blank Income Statement. The first item listed in column A (cell A4) is Fees earned, which is typically used to represent the sales of a service business. The items listed in the range A7:A11 represent various expenses for this service business. The total expenses in row 12 will be subtracted from the Fees earned to calculate the Net Income.

Figure 38 | **Blank Income Statement**

| | A | B | C | D |
|---|---|---|---|---|
| 1 | Company A | | | |
| 2 | Income Statement | | | |
| 3 | For Year End December 31, 2006 | | | |
| 4 | Fees earned | | | |
| 5 | | | | |
| 6 | Expenses: | | | |
| 7 | Wages Expense | | | |
| 8 | Rent Expense | | | |
| 9 | Utilities Expense | | | |
| 10 | Supplies Expense | | | |
| 11 | Miscellaneous Expense | | | |
| 12 | Total Expenses | | | |
| 13 | Net Income | | | |
| 14 | | | | |

Balances for these accounts appear in the Income Statement columns on the worksheet.

Data will be displayed by creating links to the worksheet.

There are three accounting statements in this workbook.

Trial Balance | Work Sheet | Income Statement | Owners Equity | Balance Sheet

Figure 39 shows the completed Income Statement. The value for the Fees earned is the result of a link to cell I16 in the Work Sheet shown in Figure 37. Links are also created for each expense account listed in column A. A **SUM** function is used in cell C12 to calculate a total for all expenses. Then a formula is entered in cell C13 to calculate the Net Income; this formula subtracts the Total Expenses from the Fees earned.

Figure 39 | **Complete Income Statement**

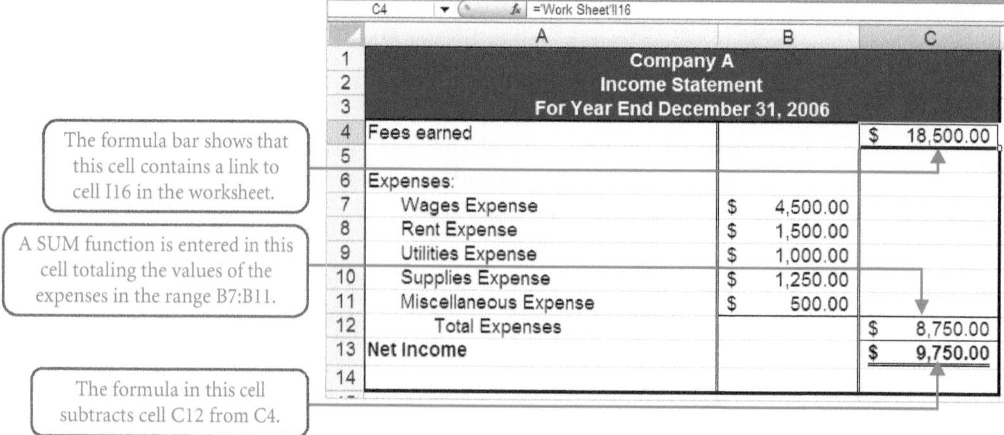

C4 =Work Sheet'!I16

| | A | B | C |
|---|---|---|---|
| 1 | Company A | | |
| 2 | Income Statement | | |
| 3 | For Year End December 31, 2006 | | |
| 4 | Fees earned | | $ 18,500.00 |
| 5 | | | |
| 6 | Expenses: | | |
| 7 | Wages Expense | $ 4,500.00 | |
| 8 | Rent Expense | $ 1,500.00 | |
| 9 | Utilities Expense | $ 1,000.00 | |
| 10 | Supplies Expense | $ 1,250.00 | |
| 11 | Miscellaneous Expense | $ 500.00 | |
| 12 | Total Expenses | | $ 8,750.00 |
| 13 | Net Income | | $ 9,750.00 |
| 14 | | | |

In your accounting classes, you will learn that the assets of a company are entitled to either owners or creditors. The Statement of Owners Equity presents the value of a company's assets that is entitled to the owners. Figure 40 shows a blank Statement of Owners Equity.

Figure 40 | **Blank Statement of Owners Equity**

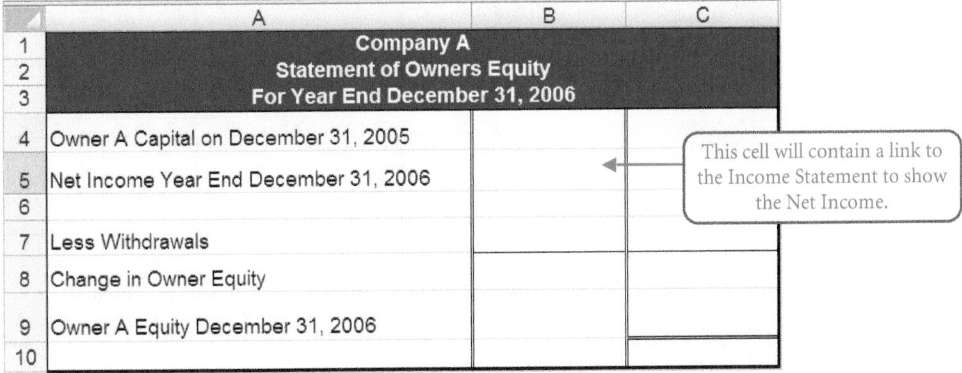

A
B
C
Company A
Statement of Owners Equity
For Year End December 31, 2006
Owner A Capital on December 31, 2005
Net Income Year End December 31, 2006
Less Withdrawals
Change in Owner Equity
Owner A Equity December 31, 2006
This cell will contain a link to the Income Statement to show the Net Income.


Figure 41 shows a completed Statement of Owners Equity. The value for the first item—Owner A Capital on December 31, 2005—is the result of link to cell K14 on the Work Sheet in Figure 37. This is the Owners Equity balance in the Balance Sheet column. The Withdrawals value in row 7 is linked to the Owner A Drawing account balance in cell J15 of the Work Sheet. The Net Income value in row 5 is linked to the Net Income that was calculated in cell C13 on the Income Statement in Figure 39. The Change in Owner Equity is calculated with a formula that subtracts the Withdrawals in row 7 from the Net Income in row 5. The Owners Equity for this period is calculated using a formula in cell C9 that adds the Change in Owner Equity in cell C8 from Owner's Capital in cell C4.

Figure 41 | **Completed Statement of Owners Equity**

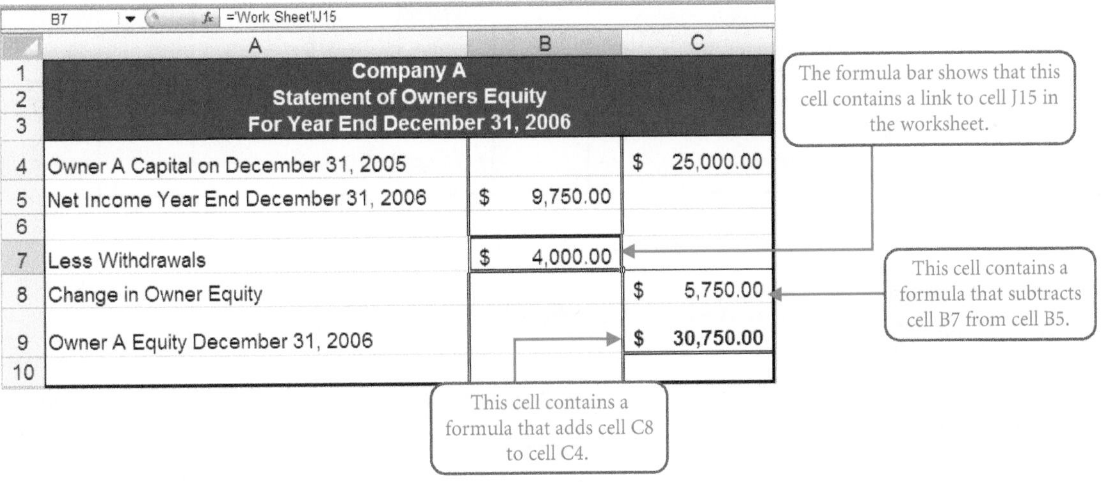

B7
='Work Sheet'!J15
A
B
C
Company A
Statement of Owners Equity
For Year End December 31, 2006
Owner A Capital on December 31, 2005
$ 25,000.00
Net Income Year End December 31, 2006
$ 9,750.00
Less Withdrawals
$ 4,000.00
Change in Owner Equity
$ 5,750.00
Owner A Equity December 31, 2006
$ 30,750.00
The formula bar shows that this cell contains a link to cell J15 in the worksheet.
This cell contains a formula that subtracts cell B7 from cell B5.
This cell contains a formula that adds cell C8 to cell C4.


Figure 42 shows an example of a blank Balance Sheet. The Balance Sheet contains current account balance information for all Asset accounts, Liability accounts, and Owners Equity. The Balance Sheet follows the accounting equation `Assets = Liabilities + Owners Equity`. Details regarding this equation will be covered in your accounting courses. However, a cursory knowledge of this equation is required when constructing a Balance Sheet. The data used for the Balance Sheet will come from links to the worksheet in Figure 37 and the Statement of Owners Equity in Figure 41.

Figure 42 | **Blank Balance Sheet**

| | A | B | C | D | E | F |
|---|---|---|---|---|---|---|
| 1 | | | Company A | | | |
| 2 | | | Balance Sheet | | | |
| 3 | | | December 31, 2006 | | | |
| 4 | Assets | | | Liabilities | | |
| 5 | Current assets: | | | Current liabilities: | | |
| 6 | Cash | | | Accounts payable | | |
| 7 | Accounts receivable | | | Unearned Rent | | |
| 8 | Supplies | | | Total liabilities | | |
| 9 | Prepaid insurance | | | | | |
| 10 | Total current assets | | | | | |
| 11 | Property, Plant, & Equipment (net of Accumulated Depreciation): | | | | | |
| 12 | Land | | | | | |
| 13 | Office equipment | | | Owners Equity | | |
| 14 | Total PP&E | | | Owner A, Capital | | |
| 15 | | | | | | |
| 16 | *Total assets* | | | *Total Liabilities and OE* | | |
| 17 | | | | | | |

Figure 43 shows a completed Balance Sheet. With the exception of the Owner A Capital, links for all accounts on the Balance Sheet can be found in the Balance Sheet column on the Work Sheet in Figure 37. The links for each account are created in columns B and E in Figure 43. The **SUM** function is used in column C to total each category of accounts such as Current assets and Property, Plant, & Equipment. At the bottom of the Balance Sheet, formulas are used to add the Total assets and the Total Liabilities and OE. The results of these formulas will match if the Balance Sheet, Work Sheet, Income Statement, and Statement of Owners Equity were properly constructed.

Figure 43 | **Completed Balance Sheet**

| | A | B | C | D | E | F |
|---|---|---|---|---|---|---|
| 1 | | | Company A | | | |
| 2 | | | Balance Sheet | | | |
| 3 | | | December 31, 2006 | | | |
| 4 | Assets | | | Liabilities | | |
| 5 | Current assets: | | | Current liabilities: | | |
| 6 | Cash | $ 2,500.00 | | Accounts payable | $ 750.00 | |
| 7 | Accounts receivable | $ 3,000.00 | | Unearned Rent | $ 500.00 | |
| 8 | Supplies | $ 1,500.00 | | Total liabilities | | $ 1,250.00 |
| 9 | Prepaid insurance | $ 2,500.00 | | | | |
| 10 | Total current assets | | $ 9,500.00 | | | |
| 11 | Property, Plant, & Equipment (net of Accumulated Depreciation): | | | | | |
| 12 | Land | $ 20,000.00 | | | | |
| 13 | Office equipment | $ 2,500.00 | | Owners Equity | | |
| 14 | Total PP&E | | $ 22,500.00 | Owner A, Capital | | $ 30,750.00 |
| 15 | | | | | | |
| 16 | *Total assets* | | $ 32,000.00 | *Total Liabilities and OE* | | $ 32,000.00 |
| 17 | | | | | | |

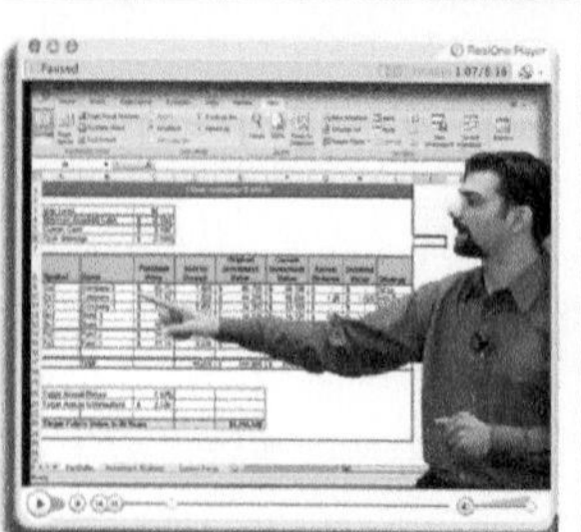

# >> Financial Accounting

The purpose of this workshop is to demonstrate how to use Excel to construct the financial accounting spreadsheets and statements illustrated in this section. I will be demonstrating the tasks in this workshop in the following seven videos: **T-Accounts**, **Journals**, **Ledgers**, **Trial Balance and Work Sheet**, **Income Statement**, **Owners Equity**, and **Balance Sheet**. The name of the video appears at the beginning of each section. At the beginning of each section, you will be instructed to open the Excel file that is required to complete the tasks. Complete each section and then watch the related video.

1. **T-Accounts (Video: T-Accounts)**
   a. Open the file named ib_e06_t-accounts.
   b. Type a **SUM** function in cell D12 that sums the values in the range D5:D11.
   c. Type a **SUM** function in cell F12 that sums the values in the range F5:F11.
   d. Type a formula in cell B12 that subtracts cell F12 from D12.
   e. Bold and italicize cell B12.
   f. Copy the range A3:F12 and paste it after activating cell A15.
   g. Type **`Accounts Receivable`** in cell C15.
   h. Delete the contents in the range C17:D21 and E17:F20.
   i. Type the data listed for the following cell locations:
      i. C17: **`June 30`**
      ii. C18: **`August 15`**
      iii. D17: **`5000`**
      iv. D18: **`3000`**
      v. E17: **`August 1`**
      vi. F17: **`2500`**
   j. Copy the range A15:F24 and paste it after activating cell H3.
   k. Delete the contents in J5:K6, L5:M5, and cell I12.
   l. Type **`Accounts Payable`** in cell J3.
   m. Type the data listed for the following cell locations:
      i. L5: **`June 1`**
      ii. L6: **`June 30`**
      iii. M5: **`3000`**
      iv. M6: **`3000`**
      v. J5: **`August 1`**
      vi. K5: **`1000`**
   n. Type a formula into cell I2 that subtracts cell K12 from M12.
   o. Save and close your file.

2. **Journals (Video: Journals)**
   a. Open the file named ib_e06_journals.
   b. Type the date **`November 30`** in cells A18 and A19.
   c. Type the data listed for the following cell locations:
      i. B18: **`Accounts Payable`**
      ii. C18: **`21`**
      iii. D18: **`950`**
      iv. B19: **`Cash`**
      v. C19: **`11`**
      vi. E19: **`950`**
      vii. B20: **`Paid creditors on account`**
   d. Indent cell B19 once and cell B20 twice. Then italicize the text in cell B20.
   e. Type a **SUM** function into cell D22 that totals the values in the range D3:D20.
   f. Copy the **SUM** function in cell D22 and paste it into cell E22 using the **Formulas** option.
   g. Save and close your file.

3. **Ledgers (Video: Ledgers)**
   a. Open the file named ib_e06_ledger.
   b. Type the word `Cash` in cell C1 in the Ledger worksheet.
   c. Add a new worksheet to the workbook.
   d. Copy the Journal worksheet and paste it into the new worksheet.
   e. Sort the Journal pasted in the new worksheet by the Description and Date column in ascending order.
   f. Copy cells A5:A7 in the copy of the Journal. Activate cell A5 on the Ledger worksheet and paste.
   g. Copy cells D5:E7 on the copy of the Journal. Activate cell D5 on the Ledger worksheet and paste.
   h. Type an **IF** function into cell F5 of the Ledger worksheet that tests whether the value in cell D5 is greater than 0. If the test is true, then have the function add the value in cell D5 to the value in cell F4. If the test is false, have the function subtract the value in cell E5 from the value in cell F4.
   i. Copy cell F5 in the Ledger worksheet and paste it to cells F6 through F8.
   j. Type the date `October 1` into cell A8 and the number 100 into cell E8. Then format cell E8 with the Accounting number format.
   k. Save and close your file.

4. **Trial Balance and Work Sheet (Video: Trial Balance and Work Sheet)**
   a. Open the file named ib_e06_trialbalanceandworksheet.
   b. Type a **SUM** function into cell B20 in the Trial Balance worksheet that totals the values in the range B4:B19. Then copy this function and paste it into cell C20 using the **Formulas** option.
   c. Add a double underline to cells B20 and C20.
   d. Activate the Work Sheet worksheet.
   e. Create a link in cell B6 that shows the value in cell B4 in the Trial Balance worksheet.
   f. Copy cell B6 and paste it into the range B7:C21 using the **Formulas** option. Then delete any links in the range B7:C21 that display a value of 0.
   g. Type a **SUM** function in cell B22 that totals the values in the range B6:B21. Then copy this function and paste it into the range C22:E22.
   h. Add a double underline to cells B22:E22.
   i. Type an **IF** function into cell F6. If the value in cell D6 is greater than 0, the function should add the value in cell B6 to the value in cell D6. Otherwise, the function should subtract the value in cell E6 from the value in cell B6.
   j. Copy the **IF** function in cell F6 and paste it into the range F7:F11, cell F15, and cells F17:F21.
   k. Type an **IF** function into cell G12. If the value in cell D12 is greater than 0, the function should subtract the value in cell D12 from the value in cell C12. Otherwise, the function should add the value in cell C12 to the value in cell E12.
   l. Copy cell G12 and paste it into G13, G14, and G16.
   m. Type the cell reference `=F6` into cell J6.
   n. Copy cell J6 and paste into the range J7:J11 and J15.
   o. Type the cell reference `=G12` into cell K12.

p. Copy cell K12 and paste it into cells K13 and K14.

q. Type the cell reference **=G16** into cell I16.

r. Type the cell reference **=F17** into cell H17. Then copy cell H17 and paste it into the range H18:H21.

s. Type a **SUM** function into cell F22 that totals the values in the range F6:F21.

t. Copy the **SUM** function in cell F22 and paste it into cells G22:K22.

u. Add a double accounting underline to cells F22 and G22.

v. Type a formula in cell H23 that subtracts H22 from I22.

w. Type a formula in cell K23 that subtracts K22 from J22.

x. Type a formula in cell H24 that adds cells H22 and H23. Then copy this formula and paste it into cell K24.

y. Type the cell reference **=I22** into cell I24. Then copy this cell reference and paste it into cell J24.

z. Add a double underline to the range H24:K24.

aa. Save and close your file.

## 5. Income Statement (Video: Income Statement)

a. Open the file named ib_e06_accountingstatements. Use this file for sections 5–7.

b. Activate the Income Statement worksheet.

c. Create a link in cell C4 that displays the value in cell I16 in the Work Sheet worksheet.

d. Create a link in cell B7 that displays the value in cell H17 in the Work Sheet worksheet. Then copy this link and paste it into the range B8:B11.

e. Type a **SUM** function in cell C12 that totals the values in the range B7:B11.

f. Type a formula in cell C13 that subtracts the value in cell C12 from the value in cell C4.

## 6. Owners Equity (Video: Owners Equity)

a. Activate the Owners Equity worksheet.

b. Create a link in cell C4 that displays the value in cell K14 in the Work Sheet worksheet.

c. Create a link in cell B5 that displays the value in cell C13 in the Income Statement worksheet.

d. Create a link in cell B7 that displays the value in cell J15 in the Work Sheet worksheet.

e. Type a formula in cell C8 that subtracts the value in cell B7 from the value in cell B5.

f. Type a formula in cell C9 that adds cells C4 and C8.

## 7. Balance Sheet (Video: Balance Sheet)

a. Activate the Balance Sheet worksheet.

b. Create a link in cell B6 that displays the value in cell J6 in the Work Sheet worksheet. Then copy this link and paste it into the range B7:B9.

c. Type a **SUM** function into cell C10 that totals the values in the range B6:B9.

d. Create a link in cell B12 that displays the value in cell J10 in the Work Sheet worksheet. Then copy this link and paste it into cell B13.
e. Type a **SUM** function into cell C14 that totals the values in the range B12:B13.
f. Type a formula into cell C16 that adds the value in cell C10 to the value in cell C14.
g. Create a link in cell E6 that displays the value in cell K12 in the Work Sheet worksheet. Then copy this link and paste it into cell E7.
h. Type a **SUM** function into cell F8 that totals the values in the range E6:E7.
i. Create a link in cell F14 that displays the value in cell C9 in the Owners Equity worksheet.
j. Type a formula in cell F16 that adds the value in cell F8 to the value in cell F14.
k. Add double underlines to cells C16 and F16.
l. Save and close your file.

**EXERCISE**
**Why Do I Need This?**

## >> Analyzing Adjusting Entries and Net Income

The benefits of Excel's cell referencing features are very apparent in the construction of financial accounting spreadsheets and statements. A change in the value of just one account can impact every accounting statement. As a result, this section demonstrated how to use linking techniques so that when the value of one account changes in the Trial Balance, or when adjustments are made on the Work Sheet, every statement will automatically calculate new outputs. Imagine doing these spreadsheets with paper and pencil! A change in one account would require you to erase, recalculate, and rewrite the outcome of every statement.

### Exercise

The purpose of this exercise is to show how to use cell referencing and linking techniques to analyze how adjustments to certain accounts impact the Net Income of a company. As a result, this exercise will focus on the construction of an accounting Work Sheet and the adjustment of various accounts. Open the file named ib_e06_accountinganalysis before starting this exercise.

1. Type an **IF** function in cell F6 of the Work Sheet to calculate the Adjusted Trial Balance of the Cash account. The arguments of the **IF** function should be defined as follows:
   a. **logical_test**: `D6 > 0`
   b. **[value_if_true]**: `B6 + D6`
   c. **[value_if_false]**: `B6 - E6`
2. The **IF** function you created in number 1 will add any debits in the Adjustment column to the Trial Balance for Cash (cell B6). If there are any credits in the Adjustment column, it will subtract them from the balance. This is because Cash is an Asset account and debits increase the value of the account and credits decrease the value of the account. Every account on the Work Sheet follows this rule except for Accounts Payable, Unearned Rent, Owner A Capital, and Fees earned. Therefore, copy cell F6 and paste it into the range F7:F11, cell F15, and the range F17:F21.

3. Type an **IF** function in cell G12 to calculate the Adjusted Trial Balance of the Accounts Payable account. The segments of the function should be defined as follows:
   a. **[logical_test]**: `D12 > 0`
   b. **[value_if_true]**: `C12 - D12`
   c. **[value_if_false]**: `C12 + E12`
4. Copy the **IF** function in cell G12 and paste it into cells G13, G14, and G16.
5. Create a **SUM** function in cell F22 that sums the values in the range F6:F21. Copy the function and paste it to cell G22. Add a double underline to cells F22 and G22.
6. Type a cell reference in cell J6 to show the Adjusted Trial balance for the Cash account in cell F6. Copy this cell reference and paste it into the range J7:J11 and into cell J15. These are all Balance Sheet accounts that carry a normal debit balance.
7. The Accounts Payable account is also a Balance Sheet account; however, it carries a normal credit balance. Therefore, type a cell reference into cell K12 that displays the value in cell G12. Copy this link to cells K13 and K14.
8. Fees earned is an Income Statement account, which carries a normal credit balance. Type a cell reference into cell I16 that shows the value in cell G16. The rest of the accounts on the Work Sheet from Wages Expense down to Selling Expense are also Income Statement accounts. Type a cell reference into cell H17 that shows the value in cell F17. Then copy this cell reference and paste it into the range H18:H21.
9. Create a **SUM** function in cell H22 that adds the values in the range H6:H21. Copy this function and paste it into the range I22:K22.
10. Calculate the Net Income in cell H23 using a formula that subtracts cell H22 from cell I22. Create another formula in cell K23 that subtracts cell K22 from J22.
11. Type a formula in cell H24 that adds cells H22 and H23. Copy this formula and paste it into cell K24.
12. Type a cell reference into cell I24 that displays the value in cell I22. Then type a cell reference into cell J24 that displays the value in cell J22. Add a double underline to the range H24:K24.
13. Assume that a customer was not satisfied with the service this company provided and demanded a refund. Type a **5000** debit adjustment for Fees earned in cell D16 and a **5000** credit to Accounts Receivable in cell E7. What was the change in Net Income?
14. Assume this company was issued a rent rebate from the landlord. Type a **3000** credit adjustment to Rent Expense in cell E18 and a **3000** debit adjustment to Cash in cell D6. What happened to the Net Income?
15. The CEO of this company promised its shareholders that it would achieve a target of $78,000 in Net Income. As you can see, this company is falling significantly short of this goal. An unethical accountant proposes an idea of reclassifying $50,000 in sales training expenses as Other Assets. Activate the Trial Balance worksheet and reduce the balance of selling expenses in cell B19 to **120000**. Then increase the balance of Other Assets in cell B7 to **52000**. Check to make sure the values in cell B20 and C20 match. What happened to the Net Income in cells H23 and K23 on the Work Sheet?
16. Save and close your file.

PROBLEM & EXERCISE

# >> What's Wrong with This Spreadsheet?

## Problem

You and two other classmates are working on a group project for a Financial Accounting class. The assignment includes a Trial Balance, T-accounts, and Ledgers. Your professor mentions the following list of key accounting rules for each of the three requirements of the project:

1. Trial Balance: The sum of the debits must equal the sum of the credits.

2. T-accounts and Ledgers: For Asset accounts (i.e., Cash and Accounts Receivable), the balance is calculated by subtracting total credits from total debits. For Liability accounts (i.e., Accounts Payable), the balance is calculated by subtracting the sum of all debits from the sum of all credits.

## Exercise

One of your teammates says that this project will be easy and offers to do the assignment for the team in Excel. She completes the project and e-mails a completed file to each team member to review before printing and handing in at class the next day. The file your teammate e-mailed is named ib_e06_accountingproject. Would you be comfortable printing each worksheet and handing them in for a grade? Consider the following points:

1. Compare the requirements listed in the Problems section to the data in each worksheet. Does the data in this file comply with these rules?
2. Your teammate thought this assignment would be easy to do in Excel. Why?

What's wrong with this spreadsheet? Write a short answer for each of the points listed here. Then correct any mistakes you find in the workbook.

Corbis/Bettmann

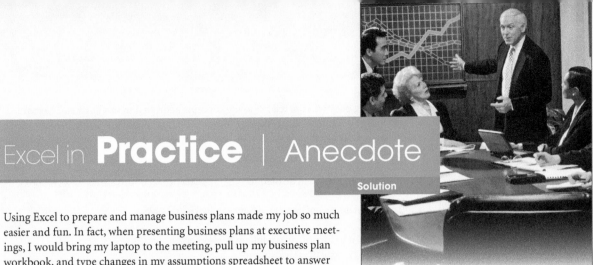

# Excel in **Practice** | Anecdote

**Solution**

Using Excel to prepare and manage business plans made my job so much easier and fun. In fact, when presenting business plans at executive meetings, I would bring my laptop to the meeting, pull up my business plan workbook, and type changes in my assumptions spreadsheet to answer any questions the directing officers asked. However, I had to make sure that all possible assumptions that were related to the business I was presenting were included in the spreadsheet. As a result, the details of every business plan I constructed were different, but the techniques I used to construct them in Excel were always the same.

## Assignment

1. Open the file named ib_e06_financialprojectionsfornewbusiness.
2. This file includes a worksheet showing five years' worth of financial assumptions for a new business. Construct a financial data and a cash analysis worksheet showing the five-year financial performance of this new business based on the assumptions included in this file.
3. The format of the financial data and cash analysis worksheets should be modeled after the example that was illustrated in the Financial Planning section of this chapter. This section also includes extensive details on how each financial statistic was calculated for each worksheet.
4. Adjust the assumptions in this file such that the NPV of this business achieves at least a positive $10,000 result.

## Questions for Discussion

1. This anecdote mentions that researching the assumptions for a business plan was one of the key factors for creating a successful business plan. What else is required to build a successful and accurate business plan?
2. How would you present a business plan to a group of executive officers? What Excel techniques can you use to build an effective and dynamic presentation?

# Review Questions

The following questions are related to the concepts addressed in this chapter. There are three types of questions: Short Answer, True or False, and Fill in the Blank. If your answer to a True or False question is False, write a short explanation as to why you think the statement is not true.

1. Cell referencing can be used to _______ data between worksheets or workbooks.
2. Explain how a link is created between two workbooks.
3. Data can be identified as a link to a workbook because the _______ and _______ names precede the cell location.
4. True or False: Data linked to another workbook will always be automatically updated.
5. True or False: Excel will automatically add an absolute value to any cell location that is linked to another workbook.
6. Explain how you can check the Status of data that is linked to other workbooks.
7. The three arguments of the **SUMIF** function are _______, _______, and _______.
8. What range of cells will be added in the following **SUMIF** function: `=SUMIF(A3:A6,D18,C3:C10)`
9. True or False: You must always complete all three arguments of the **SUMIF** function.
10. True or False: Creating ledgers in Excel is easy because after you create the first ledger, you can simply copy and paste it to another worksheet, delete all the entries and dates, enter new dates and entries, and the formulas and functions will automatically calculate a new output.
11. Why should you minimize the need to enter data manually into a worksheet when constructing financial plans?
12. What function can be used to calculate the balance on either a ledger or Work Sheet?
13. Explain the value in using links between the Trial Balance, Work Sheet, and Accounting Statements.
14. The _______ command in the _______ tab of the Ribbon is used to lock specific rows and columns when scrolling a worksheet.
15. What is the **value1** argument used for in the **NPV** function?
16. Why is it important to add a Notes section to the Assumptions worksheet of a financial plan?
17. True or False: The data-linking techniques used to construct financial plans do not work well with other business planning exercises.
18. True or False: An **NPV** function will always give you a positive number if you forget to add a negative sign in front of the **value1** argument.

# Skills Exam

The following exam is designed to test your ability to recognize and execute the Excel skills presented in this chapter. Read each question carefully and answer the questions in the order they are listed. You should be able to complete this exam in 60 minutes or less.

1. Open the ib_e06_skillsexam.
2. Calculate the construction cost for restaurant 11, which is cell D3 in the Restaurant Detail worksheet. Use a formula that multiplies the size of the restaurant in cell C3 by the cost listed for its appropriate state in the Cost by State worksheet. Use the **VLookup** function to find the cost for the appropriate state for restaurant 11 in the Cost by State worksheet and multiply it by the restaurant size in the Restaurant Detail Worksheet.
3. Copy the formula you created in cell D3 of the Restaurant Detail worksheet and paste it into the range D4:D12 using the **Formulas** option. Be sure to add absolute references where needed.
4. Use **SUMIF** functions to calculate the Total Profit per Square Foot for MD, which is cell F16 of the Restaurant Detail worksheet. This will require two **SUMIF** functions. The first **SUMIF** function will look for the state entered in cell E16 in the range B3:B12 and sum the corresponding values in the range F3:F12. This should be divided by a second **SUMIF** function that will look for the state entered in cell E16 in the range B3:B12 and sum the corresponding values in the range C3:C12.
5. Copy the formula created in cell F16 and paste it into cells F17 and F18 using the Formulas option. Add absolute references where needed.
6. Type a **SUM** function in cell B3 of the Assumptions worksheet that adds the values in the range D3:D12 in the Restaurant Detail worksheet.
7. Type a **SUM** function in cell B2 of the Sales and Profit Plan worksheet that adds the values in the range E3:E12 in the Restaurant Detail worksheet.
8. Type a formula in cell C2 of the Sales and Profit Plan worksheet that uses the percentage in cell B8 in the Assumptions worksheet to calculate the projected sales for Year 1. Copy this formula and paste it to cells D2 and E2.
9. Type a **SUM** function into cell B3 of the Sales and Profit Plan worksheet that adds the values in the range F3:F12 in the Restaurant Detail worksheet.
10. Type a formula into cell B4 of the Sales and Profit Plan worksheet that divides the value in cell B3 by the value in cell B2.
11. Create a formula into cell C3 that multiplies the sales value in cell C2 by the value in cell B4. Place an absolute reference on cell B4 in this formula. Then copy the formula and paste it into cells D3 and E3.
12. Copy cell B4 and paste it into the range C4:E4.
13. Type a formula into cell C5 of the Sales and Profit Plan worksheet that multiplies cell C2 by cell B9 in the Assumptions worksheet. Copy the formula and paste it into the range D5:E5.
14. Type a formula in cell B7 of the Sales and Profit Plan worksheet that subtracts the sum of the range B5:B6 from the value in cell B3.
15. Copy cell B7 and paste it into the range C7:E7.
16. Type an **IF** function into cell C8 of the Sales and Profit Plan worksheet that evaluates whether cell C7 is greater than 0. If it is, then multiply cell C7 by the value in cell B10 on the Assumptions worksheet. If the value in cell C7 is not greater than 0, then show 0. Copy this function and paste it into cells D8 and E8.
17. Type a formula into cell B9 of the Sales and Profit Plan worksheet that subtracts the value in cell B8 from the value in cell B7. Copy this formula and paste it into the range C9:E9.

18. Calculate the loan payments in cell B11 on the Sales and Profit Plan worksheet using the **PMT** function. You should use Cell B4 in the Assumptions worksheet for the rate, cell B5 in the Assumptions worksheet for the periods, and cell B3 for the principal of the loan. Assume that these loan payments are made annually at the beginning of each year.
19. For cells C11, D11, and E11 on the Sales and Profit plan worksheet, type a cell reference that shows the value in cell B11.
20. Type a formula into cell B13 that subtracts the value in cell B11 from the value in cell B9.
21. Type a formula into cell C13 that adds the value in cell B13 to the result of subtracting the value in cell C11 from cell C9.
22. Copy the formula in cell C13 and paste it into cells D13 and E13.
23. Type an **NPV** function in cell E16. The rate of the function should be cell B4 in the Assumptions worksheet, the initial investment value should be cell B3 in the Assumptions worksheet, the cash flow values should be the range B13:E13 in the Sales and Profit Plan worksheet.
24. Add any appropriate formats to the values in the Sales and Profit Plan worksheet. In addition, add formatting features that you think will enhance the appearance of the spreadsheet and make it easier to read.
25. Save and close your file.

# Challenge Questions

1. Open the file named ib_e06_companye. This is a completed Trial Balance. Use this Trial Balance to construct a worksheet and set of three financial statements (Income Statement, Statement of Owners Equity, and Balance Sheet). Model the worksheet and statements from the example that was illustrated in the Financial Accounting section of this chapter. After completing the Work Sheet, note the net income. Then add the following adjustments to the Work Sheet and note how the net income changes.

   a. **Fees earned:** Debit $500,000

   b. **Accounts Receivable:** Credit $500,000

   c. **Accounts Payable:** Debit $25,000

   d. **Office Equipment:** Credit $25,000

2. You are considering the purchase of a company that was offered to you at a price of $1,200,000. Your cost to borrow money to buy this firm, or the interest rate charged by a bank, will be 6.0%. Would you buy this company? Develop a spreadsheet to analyze this offer and explain why you would or would not buy this company from a purely five-year financial point of view. What other considerations might you make beyond this financial perspective when considering the purchase of a company? The company has been generating the following cash flows for the past five years:

   a. Year 1 = $150,000

   b. Year 2 = $175,000

   c. Year 3 = $250,000

   d. Year 4 = $350,000

   e. Year 5 = $550,000

3. This chapter illustrated that the balance of a ledger can be calculated using an **IF** function. In addition, you learned that there should never be a number entered for both a debit and credit for a single entry in a ledger. How would you calculate the balance of a ledger and show an error message if a person makes a mistake and enters both a debit and credit for a single entry on the ledger. Create a hypothetical ledger in Excel and type your solution in the balance column.

4. Get a financial statement from any public company. In an Excel spreadsheet, type the financial statistics for the current reporting year and the prior reporting year from the firm's Income Statement. Then create a second spreadsheet with assumptions estimating how you think this company will perform over the next three years. For example, do you think Gross Sales will increase 5% per year over the next three years, do you think the company will maintain its current cost of goods sold percentage of gross sales, and so on? Then create a third spreadsheet showing your projected financial statistics for each item on the firm's income statement.

# Date Text and IS Functions

## Chapter Goals

This chapter demonstrates how you can use advanced functions to develop sophisticated spreadsheets for making business decisions. The first section presents Date functions, which are used to calculate a person's age or determine the timing of certain events. The second section reviews various Text functions, which are used to isolate and extract specific parts of data that has been entered into a cell. The last section demonstrates IS functions, which are used to evaluate the type of data that is typed into a cell or the result produced by a function or formula.

A common theme for all of the functions in this chapter is that they are rarely used independently. That is to say, these functions are usually integrated with other functions such as the IF and VLOOKUP functions. Therefore, it will be important for you to review these functions before continuing.

## >> Advanced Excel | Skill Sets

**Date Functions**

- TODAY Function
- YEAR Function
- MONTH Function
- DATE and DAY Functions

**Text Functions**

- CONCATENATE Function
- SEARCH, LEFT, LEN, and MID Functions

**IS Functions**

- ISNUMBER and ISTEXT Functions
- ISERROR Function

Getty Images, Inc.—Photodisk

# Excel in Practice | Anecdote

**My Role as a Retirement Analyst**

Imagine using a calculator and a calendar to figure out when thousands of your customers would each turn 70.5 years old. That is the situation I encountered in one of my most challenging projects as a consultant.

I was hired by a firm that managed the distribution of IRA investments. IRA accounts are a popular way to save money for retirement because you do not have to pay taxes on the money you invest, and companies will usually invest money into an IRA account for their employees before taxes are deducted from employees' paychecks. Federal law mandates that after you reach the age of 70.5, you must withdraw money out of your IRA account the following year. And the amount of this withdrawal depends on your age. Over the years, the firm that hired me had calculated these withdrawal amounts manually (as described above). However, as the company grew larger and supported thousands of customers, this manual process became cumbersome. And even worse, customers would have to pay a tax penalty if they did not make their mandatory withdrawal on time. The company hired me to automate this manual process to improve accuracy and efficiency.

So there I was, trying to come up with a way to figure out which customers, out of several thousand, had reached 70.5 years of age the previous year. Then, out of these customers, I had to figure out how much money they needed to withdraw from their accounts. To do this, I had to calculate their exact age the previous year so I could determine how much money they needed to withdraw from their account this year. This was definitely a challenging problem to solve.

>> Continued later in this chapter

# Date Functions

Date functions are commonly used in business situations that are related to the management of human resources. This is because companies usually provide certain benefits to their employees based on years of service or age. For example, some companies offer employees additional vacation time the longer they remain employed by the firm. A human resource manager can use Date functions to calculate the number of years each employee has been working for the company to determine who is eligible for additional vacation time. This section will demonstrate how a human resource manager could use Date functions to administer the employee benefits of a company. The functions demonstrated in this section will be used to calculate the results for columns D through F in Figure 1.

Figure 1 | **HR Benefits Worksheet**

| | A | B | C | D | E | F | G |
|---|---|---|---|---|---|---|---|
| 1 | *Employee Benefits Analysis* | | | | | | |
| 2 | *Today's Date* | | | | | | |
| 3 | Employee Name | Birthdate | Date Employed | Years of Service | Early Retirement Year | Vacation Effective Year | 401K Vesting Date |
| 4 | Employee 1 | 6/29/1968 | 1/31/1986 | | | | |
| 5 | Employee 2 | 8/14/1977 | 11/17/2003 | | | | |
| 6 | Employee 3 | 12/5/1941 | 5/12/1993 | | | | |
| 7 | Employee 4 | 4/18/1964 | 9/21/2000 | | | | |
| 8 | Employee 5 | 7/22/1978 | 10/25/2002 | | | | |
| 9 | Employee 6 | 9/26/1983 | 12/29/2004 | | | | |
| 10 | Employee 7 | 3/16/1951 | 9/22/2000 | | | | |
| 11 | Employee 8 | 3/13/1961 | 7/17/1996 | | | | |
| 12 | Employee 9 | 6/21/1971 | 10/25/2002 | | | | |
| 13 | Employee 10 | 6/24/1957 | 12/30/2005 | | | | |
| 14 | Employee 11 | 1/3/1965 | 3/6/1989 | | | | |
| 15 | Employee 12 | 5/15/1952 | 11/21/2002 | | | | |
| 16 | Employee 13 | 3/10/1973 | 6/13/1994 | | | | |
| 17 | Employee 14 | 5/14/1977 | 7/16/1996 | | | | |
| 18 | Employee 15 | 8/5/1942 | 1/2/1986 | | | | |

Date functions will be used to complete these columns.

## TODAY Function

The purpose of the **TODAY** function is to display the current date on a worksheet. This is especially useful when you need to compare a historical date to the current date. For example, the first column we will complete in the HR Benefits Worksheet (Figure 1) is the Years of Service column. To do this, the employed dates in column C will be compared to today's date. The following explains how today's date is added to cell B2 using the **TODAY** function.

- Type an equal sign into cell B2 to begin the function.
- Type the function name TODAY.
- Type an open parenthesis and then a closing parenthesis. This function is unique because it does not require anything to be typed between the parentheses.
- Press the **Enter** key.

Figure 2 | **The TODAY Function**

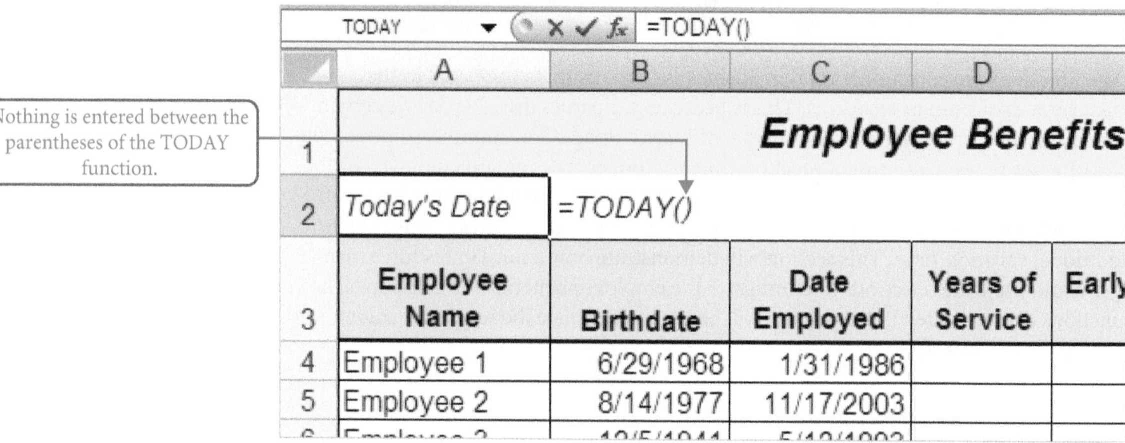


Figure 3 shows the results of the **TODAY** function after pressing the **Enter** key. The date displayed is the current date at the time this text was written. If you open this Excel file today, the function will show today's date.

Figure 3 | **Results of the TODAY Function**

This date will automatically change when the Excel file is opened at a future point in time.

J2 ▾ fx

| | A | B | C | D |
|---|---|---|---|---|
| 1 | | | | Employee Bene |
| 2 | Today's Date | 3/25/2007 | | |
| 3 | Employee Name | Birthdate | Date Employed | Years of Service |
| 4 | Employee 1 | 6/29/1968 | 1/31/1986 | |
| 5 | Employee 2 | 8/14/1977 | 11/17/2003 | |
| 6 | Employee 3 | 12/5/1941 | 5/12/1993 | |

The addition of the **TODAY** function to the HR Benefits Worksheet makes it possible to calculate the Years of Service for each employee in column D. These values are calculated by subtracting the dates in the Date Employed column (column C) from today's date in cell B2. A formula can be used to calculate these values because Excel stores every date as a unique ***Serial Number***. For example, Figure 4 shows the results of the **TODAY** function when the cell formatting is changed to a standard number with 0 decimal places. Notice that the Serial Number for 3/25/2007 is 39166. An increase in the Serial Number represents a date in the future, and a decrease in the Serial Number represents a date in the past. For example, Serial Number 39167 represents the date 3/26/2007, and Serial Number 39165 represents the date 3/24/2007. To change the Serial Number back to a date, select one of the **Date** options from the **Number Format** drop-down box in the **Home** tab of the Ribbon.

>> **Quick Reference**

**TODAY Function**

1. Activate a cell.
2. Type an equal sign.
3. Type the function name TODAY.
4. Type an open and then a closing parenthesis.
5. Press the **Enter** key.

Figure 4 | **Date Serial Number**

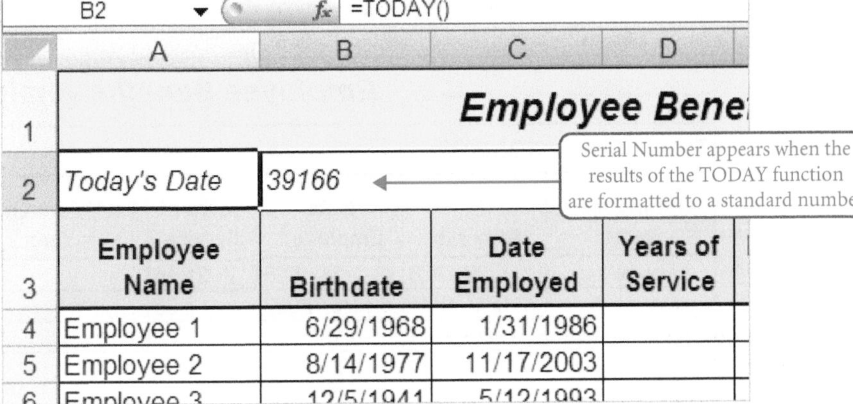


## COMMON MISTAKES | Dates and Formatting

People often mistake the date Serial Number as some type of error. However, this simply means that a cell containing a date has been formatted to a number. To convert the Serial Number to a date, choose one of the Date formats from the **Number Format** drop-down box in the **Home** tab of the Ribbon.

Figure 5 shows the results of subtracting the dates in the Date Employed column from today's date in cell B2 to calculate the Year of Service for each employee. Because the **TODAY** function always shows the current date, the formula will produce a new output each day the workbook is opened. The following explains how this formula was created.

- Type an equal sign in cell D4.
- Type the formula `($B$2 - C4)/365`. Because the date Serial Number represents a single day, subtracting C4 from B2 will provide the number of days each employee has worked for the company. To convert the days to years, this result is divided by 365. Also, notice that an absolute reference was placed on cell B2. This is because every date in the Date Employed column must be subtracted from B2. Therefore, an absolute reference is used to prevent cell B2 from changing because of relative referencing when the formula is pasted to the rest of the cells in the column.
- Format the results of the formula in cell B2 to a standard number with 2 decimal places.
- Copy cell D4 and paste it to the rest of the cells in the column.

Figure 5 | **Completed Years of Service Column**

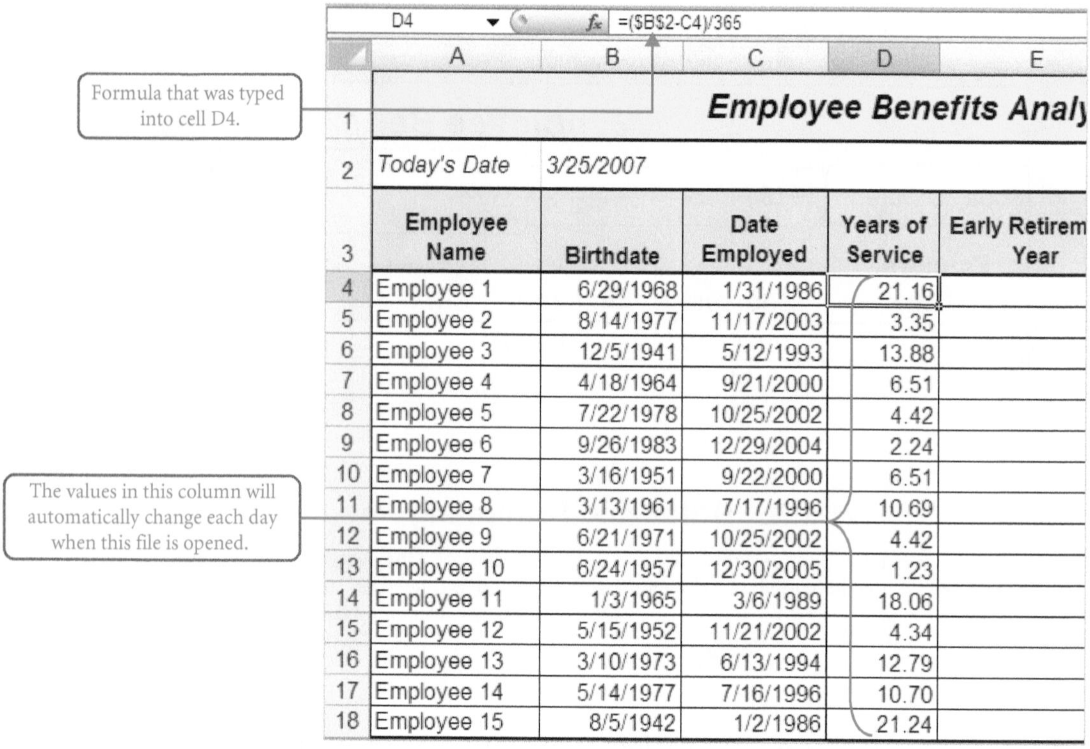

Formula that was typed into cell D4.

D4 | $f_x$ =($B$2-C4)/365

| | A | B | C | D | E |
|---|---|---|---|---|---|
| 1 | | | *Employee Benefits Analy* | | |
| 2 | *Today's Date* | *3/25/2007* | | | |
| 3 | Employee Name | Birthdate | Date Employed | Years of Service | Early Retirem Year |
| 4 | Employee 1 | 6/29/1968 | 1/31/1986 | 21.16 | |
| 5 | Employee 2 | 8/14/1977 | 11/17/2003 | 3.35 | |
| 6 | Employee 3 | 12/5/1941 | 5/12/1993 | 13.88 | |
| 7 | Employee 4 | 4/18/1964 | 9/21/2000 | 6.51 | |
| 8 | Employee 5 | 7/22/1978 | 10/25/2002 | 4.42 | |
| 9 | Employee 6 | 9/26/1983 | 12/29/2004 | 2.24 | |
| 10 | Employee 7 | 3/16/1951 | 9/22/2000 | 6.51 | |
| 11 | Employee 8 | 3/13/1961 | 7/17/1996 | 10.69 | |
| 12 | Employee 9 | 6/21/1971 | 10/25/2002 | 4.42 | |
| 13 | Employee 10 | 6/24/1957 | 12/30/2005 | 1.23 | |
| 14 | Employee 11 | 1/3/1965 | 3/6/1989 | 18.06 | |
| 15 | Employee 12 | 5/15/1952 | 11/21/2002 | 4.34 | |
| 16 | Employee 13 | 3/10/1973 | 6/13/1994 | 12.79 | |
| 17 | Employee 14 | 5/14/1977 | 7/16/1996 | 10.70 | |
| 18 | Employee 15 | 8/5/1942 | 1/2/1986 | 21.24 | |

The values in this column will automatically change each day when this file is opened.

**COMMON MISTAKES | Date Related Calculations**

If you are calculating data that relies on the current date, *do not* type the date into a cell and use that cell in a formula. The results that are produced by your formula will be valid for only one day. In addition, this forces you to type in a new date manually each time you open the file. For this type of calculation it is good practice to use the **TODAY** function. Using the **TODAY** function instead of typing the date will produce current results when the file is opened at a future point in time.

**>> Quick Reference**

**YEAR Function**

1. Activate a cell.
2. Type an equal sign.
3. Type the function name YEAR.
4. Type an open parenthesis.
5. Enter a cell location that contains a valid date Serial Number or type a valid date Serial Number.
6. Type a closing parenthesis. You can also type a date enclosed in quotations, i.e. "10/21/2006".
7. Press the **Enter** key.

## YEAR Function

The next column that will be completed in the HR Benefits Worksheet (see Figure 1) is the Early Retirement Year column. Some companies offer their employees the option to take an early retirement or to stop working and receive payments from their retirement pension before reaching the official retirement age of 65. The amount of income an employee receives from a pension usually depends on salary and years of service to the company. The purpose of column E in the HR Benefits Worksheet is to show what year each employee will qualify for early retirement. The age at which an employee qualifies for early retirement varies, depending on the plan offered by the company. For this example, we will assume an employee must be at least 55 years old.

The **YEAR** function isolates the year that is associated with a date Serial Number and displays it as a number. In this example, the **YEAR** function will be used in column E of the HR Benefits Worksheet to show the year each employee qualifies for early retirement. The following explains how the **YEAR** function is used to determine the year each employee becomes eligible for early retirement.

- Type an equal sign in cell E4.
- Type the function name YEAR and an open parenthesis.

- Type cell B4, and then type a closing parenthesis. Cell B4 contains the birth date of the first employee, which is required to determine the year of early retirement eligibility.
- Type a plus sign (+) after the **YEAR** function, and then type the number 55. As previously mentioned, we will assume that employees are eligible for early retirement when they reach the age of 55. To determine the year in which they become eligible, 55 is added to the year of their birth date (see Figure 6).
- Press the **Enter** key. The formula will calculate the year Employee 1 will turn 55. This formula can now be copied and pasted to show the early retirement year for the rest of the employees listed on the worksheet (see Figure 7).

Figure 6 | **YEAR Function Setup**

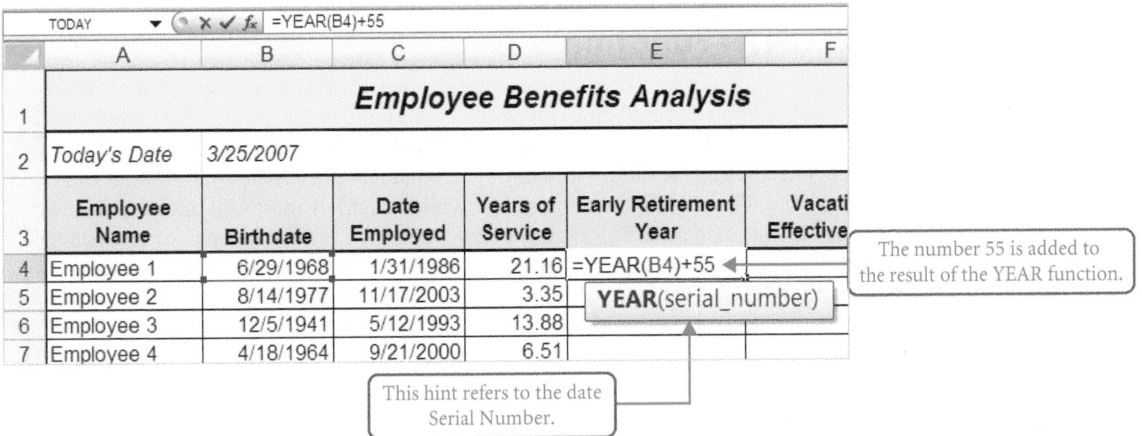

TODAY =YEAR(B4)+55

| | A | B | C | D | E | F |
|---|---|---|---|---|---|---|
| 1 | | | Employee Benefits Analysis | | | |
| 2 | Today's Date | 3/25/2007 | | | | |
| 3 | Employee Name | Birthdate | Date Employed | Years of Service | Early Retirement Year | Vacati Effective |
| 4 | Employee 1 | 6/29/1968 | 1/31/1986 | 21.16 | =YEAR(B4)+55 | |
| 5 | Employee 2 | 8/14/1977 | 11/17/2003 | 3.35 | YEAR(serial_number) | |
| 6 | Employee 3 | 12/5/1941 | 5/12/1993 | 13.88 | | |
| 7 | Employee 4 | 4/18/1964 | 9/21/2000 | 6.51 | | |



Figure 7 | **Results of the YEAR Function**

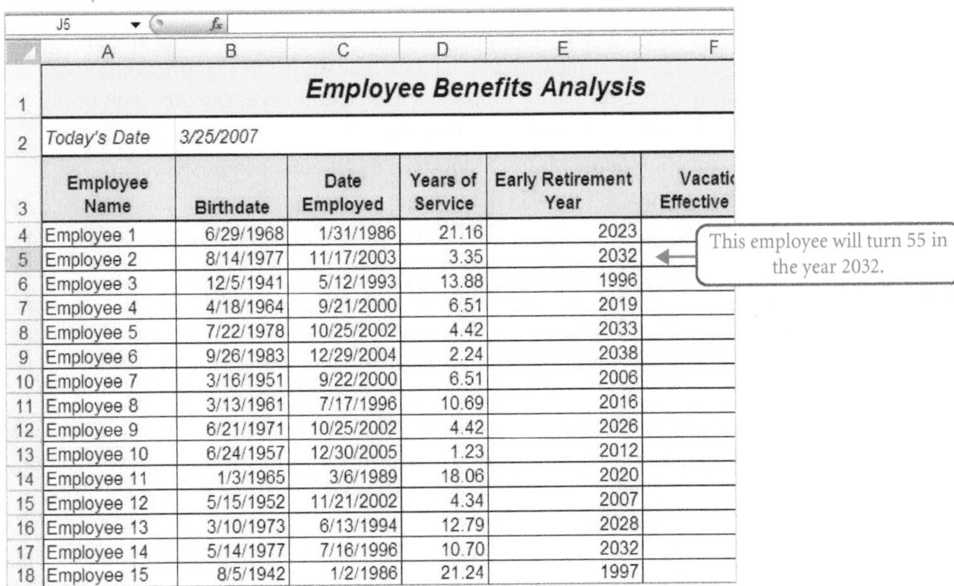

J5

| | A | B | C | D | E | F |
|---|---|---|---|---|---|---|
| 1 | | | Employee Benefits Analysis | | | |
| 2 | Today's Date | 3/25/2007 | | | | |
| 3 | Employee Name | Birthdate | Date Employed | Years of Service | Early Retirement Year | Vacatio Effective |
| 4 | Employee 1 | 6/29/1968 | 1/31/1986 | 21.16 | 2023 | |
| 5 | Employee 2 | 8/14/1977 | 11/17/2003 | 3.35 | 2032 | |
| 6 | Employee 3 | 12/5/1941 | 5/12/1993 | 13.88 | 1996 | |
| 7 | Employee 4 | 4/18/1964 | 9/21/2000 | 6.51 | 2019 | |
| 8 | Employee 5 | 7/22/1978 | 10/25/2002 | 4.42 | 2033 | |
| 9 | Employee 6 | 9/26/1983 | 12/29/2004 | 2.24 | 2038 | |
| 10 | Employee 7 | 3/16/1951 | 9/22/2000 | 6.51 | 2006 | |
| 11 | Employee 8 | 3/13/1961 | 7/17/1996 | 10.69 | 2016 | |
| 12 | Employee 9 | 6/21/1971 | 10/25/2002 | 4.42 | 2026 | |
| 13 | Employee 10 | 6/24/1957 | 12/30/2005 | 1.23 | 2012 | |
| 14 | Employee 11 | 1/3/1965 | 3/6/1989 | 18.06 | 2020 | |
| 15 | Employee 12 | 5/15/1952 | 11/21/2002 | 4.34 | 2007 | |
| 16 | Employee 13 | 3/10/1973 | 6/13/1994 | 12.79 | 2028 | |
| 17 | Employee 14 | 5/14/1977 | 7/16/1996 | 10.70 | 2032 | |
| 18 | Employee 15 | 8/5/1942 | 1/2/1986 | 21.24 | 1997 | |

**COMMON MISTAKES | The #Value! Error and Date Functions**

If the cell location or value you use in the parentheses of the **YEAR** function is not a valid date Serial Number, you will see the #Value! error. This error commonly occurs when the date on a spreadsheet is a text entry. For example, typing a space in front of a date will convert it to a text value. A date could also become a text value if it is produced from a text function. You can convert a text date to a valid Serial Number date by typing the appropriate cell location in the parentheses of the **DATEVALUE** function. This error will also occur when using date functions that are similar to the **YEAR** function, such as the **MONTH** and **DAY** functions.

## MONTH Function

The next column we will complete in the HR Benefits Worksheet (see Figure 1) is the Vacation Effective Year. Some companies have a policy to determine when employees can take vacations based on the date they were hired. This example will assume that employees hired during the months of January through July can use their vacation time in the year they were hired. However, employees hired after July must wait until the next year to use any vacation time. This type of policy is common in retail companies in which the Fall and Winter holiday seasons are critical to the overall success of the business.

The **MONTH** function will be used in the HR Benefits worksheet to identify the month each employee was hired. This function operates in the same manner as the **YEAR** function. When a valid date Serial Number is entered in the parentheses of the **MONTH** function, the month number of the date will be isolated and displayed in a cell. For example, if you entered the Serial Number representing the date 10/21/2006 (39011) in the parentheses of the **MONTH** function, the number 10 would be displayed in the cell.

The following explains how the **MONTH** function is used within an **IF** function to complete the Vacation Effective Year column on the HR Benefits Spreadsheet.

- Type an equal sign in cell F4, followed by the function name IF and an open parenthesis. This example will demonstrate how the **MONTH** function is used within an **IF** function. The **IF** function will be used to evaluate the result of the **MONTH** function and produce an output.
- Type the function name MONTH followed by an open parenthesis.
- Type cell location C4, followed by a closing parenthesis. This cell contains the date the employee was hired. The **MONTH** function will identify the month that is represented in this date.
- Type a greater-than sign followed by the number 7 and a comma. This completes the **logical_test** argument of the **IF** function, which assesses if the month number produced by the **MONTH** function is greater than 7 (because July is the 7th month).
- Type the words "Next Year" in quotations, and then type a comma. This completes the **value_if_true** argument of the **IF** function. As previously mentioned, if an employee is hired after the month of July, then vacation time will not become effective until next year.
- Type the words "This Year" in quotations, and then type a closing parenthesis. This completes the **value_if_false** argument of the **IF** function (see Figure 8). If the number produced by the **MONTH** function is not greater than 7, then the employee must have been hired in or before the month of July.
- Press the **Enter** key to complete the function. Then, copy cell F4 and paste it to the remaining cell locations in the column.

**>> Quick Reference**

**MONTH Function**

1. Activate a cell.
2. Type an equal sign and the function name MONTH.
3. Type an open parenthesis.
4. Enter a cell location that contains a valid date Serial Number or type a valid date Serial Number.
5. Type a closing parenthesis. You can also type a date enclosed in quotations, i.e. "10/21/2006".
6. Press the **Enter** key.

Figure 8 | **Setup of the MONTH Function within an IF Function**

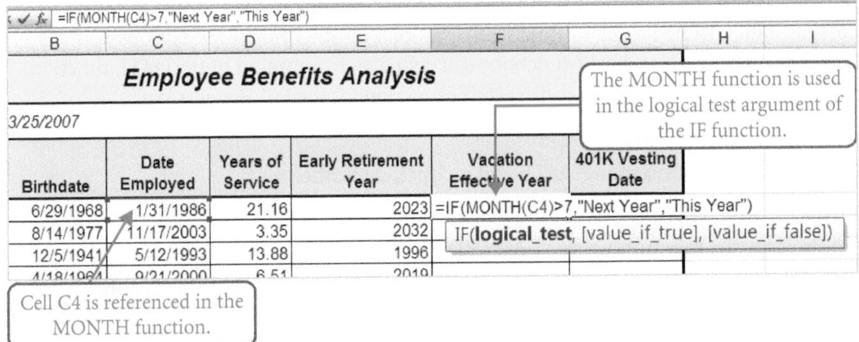


Figure 9 shows the results of the **MONTH / IF** function illustrated in Figure 8. Because Employee 1 was hired in the month of January (see cell C4), the **IF** function displays the words This Year. Therefore, this employee was entitled to use vacation time the same year he was hired. Conversely, Employee 2 was hired in the month of November and, therefore, unable to take any vacation time until the year after he was hired.

Figure 9 | **Results of the MONTH Function within an IF Function**

| | A | B | C | D | E | F | G |
|---|---|---|---|---|---|---|---|
| 1 | *Employee Benefits Analysis* | | | | | | |
| 2 | *Today's Date* | *3/25/2007* | | | | | |
| 3 | Employee Name | Birthdate | Date Employed | Years of Service | Early Retirement Year | Vacation Effective Year | 401K Vesting Date |
| 4 | Employee 1 | 6/29/1968 | 1/31/1986 | 21.16 | 2023 | This Year | |
| 5 | Employee 2 | 8/14/1977 | 11/17/2003 | 3.35 | 2032 | Next Year | |
| 6 | Employee 3 | 12/5/1941 | 5/12/1993 | 13.88 | 1996 | This Year | |
| 7 | Employee 4 | 4/18/1964 | 9/21/2000 | 6.51 | 2019 | Next Year | |
| 8 | Employee 5 | 7/22/1978 | 10/25/2002 | 4.42 | 2033 | Next Year | |
| 9 | Employee 6 | 9/26/1983 | 12/29/2004 | 2.24 | 2038 | Next Year | |
| 10 | Employee 7 | 3/16/1951 | 9/22/2000 | 6.51 | 2006 | Next Year | |
| 11 | Employee 8 | 3/13/1961 | 7/17/1996 | 10.69 | 2016 | This Year | |
| 12 | Employee 9 | 6/21/1971 | 10/25/2002 | 4.42 | 2026 | Next Year | |
| 13 | Employee 10 | 6/24/1957 | 12/30/2005 | 1.23 | 2012 | Next Year | |
| 14 | Employee 11 | 1/3/1965 | 3/6/1989 | 18.06 | 2020 | This Year | |
| 15 | Employee 12 | 5/15/1952 | 11/21/2002 | 4.34 | 2007 | Next Year | |
| 16 | Employee 13 | 3/10/1973 | 6/13/1994 | 12.79 | 2028 | This Year | |
| 17 | Employee 14 | 5/14/1977 | 7/16/1996 | 10.70 | 2032 | This Year | |
| 18 | Employee 15 | 8/5/1942 | 1/2/1986 | 21.24 | 1997 | This Year | |

Output of the IF function based on the month number in the Date Employed column

## DATE and DAY Functions

The last column to complete in the HR Benefits Worksheet (see Figure 1) is the 401K Vesting Date column. Employees invest a certain percentage of their salary into a 401K account to save money for their retirement. This is similar to the IRA accounts explained in the anecdote at the beginning of this chapter. In addition, many companies will add money to their employees' retirement accounts as an added form of compensation. For example, a company might contribute fifty cents for every dollar an employee invests in her 401K account. However, companies usually set a vesting period before an employee can actually own this money. For example, a 5-year vesting period means employees must stay with the company for at least 5 years in order to take ownership of any money that is contributed to their 401K account by the firm.

The **DATE** function will be used to calculate the dates for the 401K Vesting Date column in the HR Benefits worksheet. For this example, we will assume that employees will become vested if they work in the firm for 5 years. The **DATE** function converts numbers into a date Serial Number. The function has three arguments: **year**, **month**, and **day**. Like all other functions, these arguments can be defined by entering numeric values. However, they are most often defined using formulas, cell locations, or other functions. For this example, the **YEAR**, **MONTH**, and **DAY** functions will define each argument of the **DATE** function. The following explains how to construct this function for the HR Benefits Worksheet.

- Type an equal sign in cell G4.
- Type the function name DATE and an open parenthesis.
- Define the **year** argument as follows:
    - Type the function name YEAR followed by an open parenthesis.
    - Type the cell location C4 followed by a closing parenthesis. Cell C4 contains the date the employee was hired.
    - Type a plus sign (+) followed by the number 5. The goal for this column is to show the date exactly 5 years from the day the employee was hired. Therefore, the first argument of the **DATE** function is being defined by adding 5 years to the result of the **YEAR** function.
    - Type a comma.
- Define the **month** argument as follows:
    - Type the function name MONTH followed by an open parenthesis.
    - Type the cell location C4 followed by a closing parenthesis. This will add the exact month that is in the Date Employed column for each employee.
    - Type a comma.
- Define the **day** argument as follows:
    - Type the function name DAY followed by an open parenthesis. The **DAY** function operates exactly like the **MONTH** and **YEAR** functions. It will isolate the day that is contained in a date and display it as a number in a cell.
    - Type the cell location C4 followed by a closing parenthesis. This will add the exact day that is in the Date Employed column for each employee.
    - Type a comma.
- Type a closing parenthesis to complete the **DATE** function and press the **Enter** key.

Figure 10 shows the final setup of the **DATE** function. It is important to note that it is coincidental that the functions used to define the arguments of the **DATE** function have the same name as the arguments. You could define the arguments of the DATE using any function, formula, cell location, or numbers that satisfy the needs of your project.

Figure 10 | **Setup of the DATE Function**

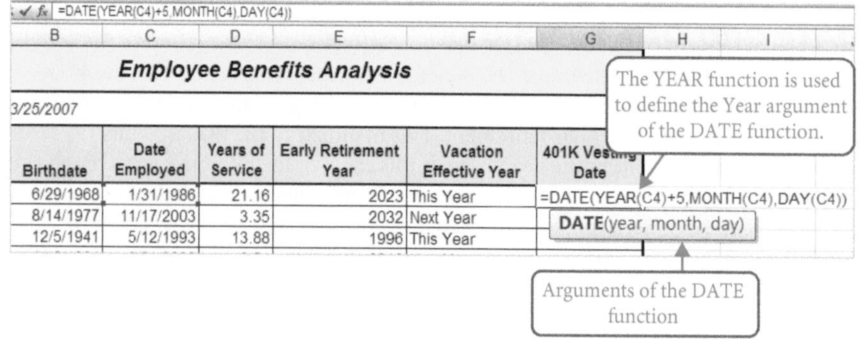

Figure 11 shows the results of the **DATE** function illustrated in Figure 10. Notice that the 401K Vesting Date for Employee 1 is exactly 5 years later than the Date Employed. This is because the number 5 was added to the result of the **YEAR** function in the **year** argument of the **DATE** function.

Figure 11 | **Results of the DATE Function for Calculating the 401K Vesting Dates**

G4 =DATE(YEAR(C4)+5,MONTH(C4),DAY(C4))

| | A | B | C | D | E | F | G |
|---|---|---|---|---|---|---|---|
| 1 | *Employee Benefits Analysis* | | | | | | |
| 2 | *Today's Date* | *3/25/2007* | | | | | |
| 3 | Employee Name | Birthdate | Date Employed | Years of Service | Early Retirement Year | Vacation Effective Year | 401K Vesting Date |
| 4 | Employee 1 | 6/29/1968 | 1/31/1986 | 21.16 | 2023 | This Year | 1/31/1991 |
| 5 | Employee 2 | 8/14/1977 | 11/17/2003 | 3.35 | 2032 | Next Year | 11/17/2008 |
| 6 | Employee 3 | 12/5/1941 | 5/12/1993 | 13.88 | 1996 | This Year | 5/12/1998 |
| 7 | Employee 4 | 4/18/1964 | 9/21/2000 | 6.51 | 2019 | Next Year | 9/21/2005 |
| 8 | Employee 5 | 7/22/1978 | 10/25/2002 | 4.42 | 2033 | Next Year | 10/25/2007 |
| 9 | Employee 6 | 9/26/1983 | 12/29/2004 | 2.24 | 2038 | Next Year | 12/29/2009 |
| 10 | Employee 7 | 3/16/1951 | 9/22/2000 | 6.51 | 2006 | Next Year | 9/22/2005 |
| 11 | Employee 8 | 3/13/1961 | 7/17/1996 | 10.69 | 2016 | This Year | 7/17/2001 |
| 12 | Employee 9 | 6/21/1971 | 10/25/2002 | 4.42 | 2026 | Next Year | 10/25/2007 |
| 13 | Employee 10 | 6/24/1957 | 12/30/2005 | 1.23 | 2012 | Next Year | 12/30/2010 |
| 14 | Employee 11 | 1/3/1965 | 3/6/1989 | 18.06 | 2020 | This Year | 3/6/1994 |
| 15 | Employee 12 | 5/15/1952 | 11/21/2002 | 4.34 | 2007 | Next Year | 11/21/2007 |
| 16 | Employee 13 | 3/10/1973 | 6/13/1994 | 12.79 | 2028 | This Year | 6/13/1999 |
| 17 | Employee 14 | 5/14/1977 | 7/16/1996 | 10.70 | 2032 | This Year | 7/16/2001 |
| 18 | Employee 15 | 8/5/1942 | 1/2/1986 | 21.24 | 1997 | This Year | 1/2/1991 |

The dates in the 401K Vesting column are exactly 5 years later than the dates in the Date Employed column.

## COMMON MISTAKES | Converting Years to Days and Adding to Date Serial Number

It might seem that a simple approach to calculating the dates for the 401K Vesting Date column in Figure 11 is to add 1825 days (365 × 5 years) to the date Serial Number in the Date Employed column. However, you will not get a date that is exactly 5 years from the Date Employed because of leap year. For example, notice that the 401K Vesting Date in Figure 12 is off by 1 day. You can increase a date Serial Number by converting and adding several years to days, but you will have to make adjustments to account for leap years. The **DATE** function method illustrated in Figure 10 does not require this type of adjustment.

Figure 12 | **Example of Adding Days to Date Serial Number**

| | | | | | |
|---|---|---|---|---|---|
| 3 | Employee Name | Birthdate | Date Employed | 401K Vesting Date | |
| 4 | Employee 1 | 6/29/1968 | 1/31/1986 | 1/30/1991 | 1/31/1991 |
| 5 | Employee 2 | 8/14/1977 | 11/17/2003 | | |
| 6 | Employee 3 | 12/5/1941 | 5/12/1993 | | |

Result of adding 1825 days to the Date Employed

Result using DATE function method from Figure 10

**>> Quick Reference**

**DAY Function**

1. Activate a cell.
2. Type an equal sign and the function name DAY.
3. Type an open parenthesis.
4. Enter a cell location that contains a valid date Serial Number or type a valid date Serial Number.
5. Type a closing parenthesis. You can also type a date enclosed in quotations, i.e. "10/21/2006".
6. Press the **Enter** key.

**>> Quick Reference**

**DATE Function**

1. Activate a cell.
2. Type an equal sign, the function name DATE, and an open parenthesis.
3. Define the **year**, **month**, and **day** arguments using numbers, cell locations, formulas, or functions.
4. Type a closing parenthesis.
5. Press the **Enter** key.

**VIDEO WORKSHOP**

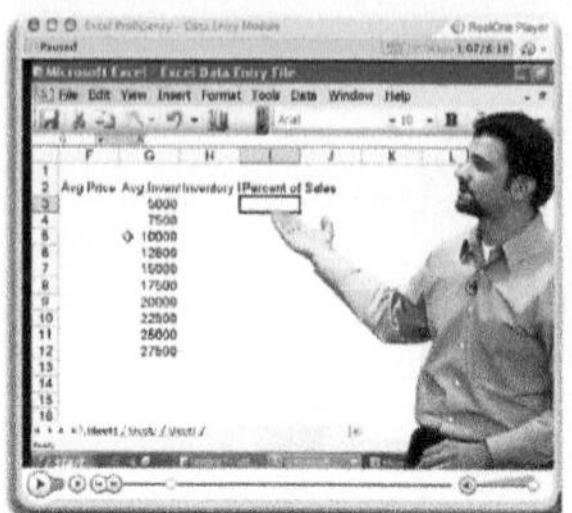

## >> DATE Functions

The purpose of this workshop is to demonstrate the use of **DATE** functions. The Excel workbook that will be used in this workshop is identical to the one shown in Figure 1. I will be demonstrating the tasks in this workshop in the following four videos named **TODAY Function**, **YEAR Function**, **MONTH Function**, and **DATE Function**. The name of the video appears in parentheses next to the relevant section heading. Open the Excel workbook named ib_e07_datefunctions. Complete each section of tasks first, and then watch the video pertaining to that section.

1. **TODAY Function (Video: TODAY Function)**
   a. Activate cell B2. Note that the cells in range B2:G2 are merged.
   b. Type an equal sign followed by the function name **TODAY**.
   c. Type an open then a closing parenthesis and press the **Enter** key.
   d. Format cell B2 to a number with 0 decimal places. Then, switch the format back to the Short Date format.
   e. Type an equal sign in cell D4 followed by the formula **($B$2 - C4) / 365**.
   f. Copy the formula in cell D4 and paste it into the range D5:D18 using the **Formulas** option in the **Paste** icon.

2. **YEAR Function (Video: YEAR Function)**
   a. Type an equal sign in cell E4 followed by the function name **YEAR**.
   b. Type an open parenthesis, cell location **B4**, and a closing parenthesis.
   c. Type a plus sign and the number **55**.
   d. Press the **Enter** key. Then, copy and paste the function in cell E4 to the range E5:E18 using the **Formulas** option in the **Paste** icon.

3. **MONTH Function (Video: MONTH Function)**
   a. Type an equal sign in cell F4 followed by the function name **IF** and an open parenthesis.
   b. For the **logical_test** argument, type the function name **MONTH** followed by an open parenthesis. Then, type **C4** followed by a closing parenthesis.
   c. Complete the **logical_test** argument by typing a greater-than sign **(>)** followed by the number **7** and a comma.
   d. Define the **value_if_true** argument with the words **"Next Year"**. Remember to use the quotations.
   e. Define the **value_if_false** argument with the words **"This Year"**.
   f. Complete the function by typing a closing parenthesis and press the **Enter** key.
   g. Copy cell F4 and paste it into the range F5:F18 using the **Formulas** option in the **Paste** icon.

4. **DATE Function (Video: DATE Function)**
   a. Type an equal sign in cell G4 followed by the function name **DATE** and an open parenthesis.

b. Define the **year** argument by typing the function name **YEAR** followed by an open parenthesis.
c. Type **C4** followed by a closing parenthesis. Then, type a plus sign followed by the number **5**. Complete the **year** argument by typing a comma.
d. Define the **month** argument by typing the function name **MONTH** followed by an open parenthesis. Then, type **C4** followed by a closing parenthesis and a comma.
e. Define the **day** argument by typing the function name **DAY** followed by an open parenthesis. Then, type **C4** followed by a closing parenthesis.
f. Complete the DATE function by typing a closing parenthesis and press the **Enter** key.
g. Copy cell G4 and paste it into the range G5:G18 using the **Formulas** option in the **Paste** icon.
h. Save and close the workbook.

## >> Project Management for a New Store

**EXERCISE**

**Why Do I Need This?**

Most executives agree that timing is one of the most critical success factors in business. Whether a company is launching a new product or opening a new store, the timing of when these events occur could mean the difference between making and losing money. As a result, business projects must be planned carefully. A project plan is a business manager's guide for making decisions, such as ordering supplies, hiring people, or buying inventory. This plan is critical to a business manager's decision process because a change in the completion date for just one component could change the execution of every task in the plan. Most business managers use project-planning software for large business projects. However, Excel is a great tool for planning small-to-medium projects.

### Exercise

The purpose of this exercise is to use Excel to plan the opening of a new retail store. In order for a store to open on a specific target date, several activities and events must take place. Planning these events is the focus of this exercise. To begin, open the Excel workbook named ib_e07_openinganewstore and continue with the tasks listed below.

1. The first event listed is Renovations in cell A3. Most retail stores require some type of construction renovations to suit the needs of the business. Cell B3 contains the target date of when these renovations will begin, which is March 1, 2007. Cell C3 shows how long it will take to complete the renovations, which is 90 days. Calculate the completion date of the renovations in cell D3 by adding cell C3 to cell B3.

2. The next event listed is Order Fixtures in cell A4. The fixtures include the shelves that will hold the products, the check-out counter, signs, etc. The goal is to have the fixtures delivered to the store the day the renovations are completed. Considering that it takes 45 days to receive the fixtures, calculate the order date in cell B4 by subtracting cell C4 from cell D3.

3. Calculate the delivery date for the fixtures in cell D4 by adding cell B4 to cell C4. The delivery date for the fixtures should match the completion date for renovations.

4. The next event listed is Assemble Fixtures in cell A5. The fixtures must first be received before they can be assembled. Therefore, the begin date in

cell B5 must be equal to the delivered date in cell D4. Use a link to show the completion date in D4 in cell B5.

5. Calculate the completion date for assembling the fixtures in cell D5 by adding cell B5 to cell C5.

6. The next event listed is Order Inventory in cell A6. The inventory must not be received before the fixtures are assembled. Therefore, calculate the order date by subtracting cell C6 from cell D5. Notice that inventory must be ordered before renovations begin.

7. Calculate the delivery date for the inventory in cell D6 by adding cell C6 to cell B6. The delivery date for the inventory should match the completion date for assembling the fixtures.

8. The next event listed is Order Cash Registers in cell A7. The cash registers should arrive at the same time as the inventory so they can be tested. Calculate the order date for the cash registers in cell B7 by subtracting cell C7 from cell D6.

9. Calculate the delivery date for the cash registers in cell D7 by adding cell B7 to cell C7. This date should match the delivery date of the inventory.

10. The final event listed is Assemble and Test Registers in cell A8. The registers must first be received before they can be assembled and tested. Therefore, link cell B8 to cell D7.

11. Calculate the completion date for assembling and testing the registers in cell D8 by adding cell C8 to cell B8.

12. Calculate the date the store will be open for business in cell C11. The store can open the day after the registers have been assembled and tested. Therefore, add 1 to cell D8.

13. You just received a call from the renovation contractor telling you that renovations cannot be started until March 14. Change the date in cell B3 to 3/14/2007. Given this date, when should you order inventory? When should you order fixtures? When will the store be open for business?

14. You find out that the inventory can be delivered in 110 days instead of 120. Will this allow you to open the store 10 days sooner? Why or why not?

15. For which events could you decrease the process time to compensate for the delay in renovations so the store could be opened sooner?

16. Save and close the workbook.

**PROBLEM & EXERCISE**

## >> What's Wrong with This Spreadsheet?

### Problem

You are managing a human resources department for a large company. Your department is currently in the process of constructing a benefits statement for each employee that includes information such as salary, vacation time, and health insurance plan. This statement also includes the date on which the employee will qualify for early retirement benefits. An employee is eligible for early retirement benefits on they day he reaches the age of 60. An intern working in your department constructs an Excel spreadsheet that calculates the early retirement date for each employee.

The information from this spreadsheet will be used to produce the final benefits statement, which will be mailed to each employee's home.

### Exercise

The Excel file created by the intern in your department is named ib_e07_earlyretirement. Open the file and examine the retirement dates that were calculated by the intern. Would you be comfortable using this information to produce each employee's benefit statement? Consider the following:

1. Look at the birth dates for the first few employees. Does the early retirement date fall on the employee's 60th birthday?
2. Explain how the early retirement dates in column C are being calculated for each employee.
3. Why would the method you identified in point 2 not produce an employee's exact 60th birthday?

What's wrong with this spreadsheet? Write a short answer for each of the points listed above. Create an alternate method in column D for calculating the date on which each employee will reach the age of 60.

## >> Text Functions

Skill Set

The previous section demonstrated how you can use Excel Date functions to manipulate dates and use them in calculations. Similarly, you can use Text functions to extract specific parts of data within a cell or combine data from multiple cells to match the data configuration you are currently using in a workbook. The commands and calculations executed in Excel are always applied to an entire cell or range of cells in a worksheet. However, there may be situations when you need to isolate a specific portion of data within a cell or combine data from multiple cells into one. These situations require the use of Text functions. This section will illustrate a variety of situations showing why and when text functions are useful when using Excel in business.

### CONCATENATE Function

You can use the **CONCATENATE** function to combine data from two or more cell locations into one. This function is often used when you require a unique value to reference data in a second worksheet using a **VLOOKUP** or **HLOOKUP** function. For example, let us assume you are a human resources manager and you receive a data file from your company's IT department listing all new employees hired in the past month. You open the file in Excel and realize that the name of every employee is separated into two columns (see Figure 13). The first column contains the employees' last names and the second column contains the employees' first names. You intend to add this data to an Excel file you created previously that contains a list of current employees (see Figure 14). However, this file has each employee's full name in one cell location. This is because there are several employees with the same last name and you frequently use the employee's name as the lookup value in a **VLOOKUP** function to reference data in other Excel files. Therefore, to make the data you received match the data in your current Excel file, you must combine each employee's first and last name together in one cell. This task is done using the **CONCATENATE** function.

Figure 13 | **New Employee List**

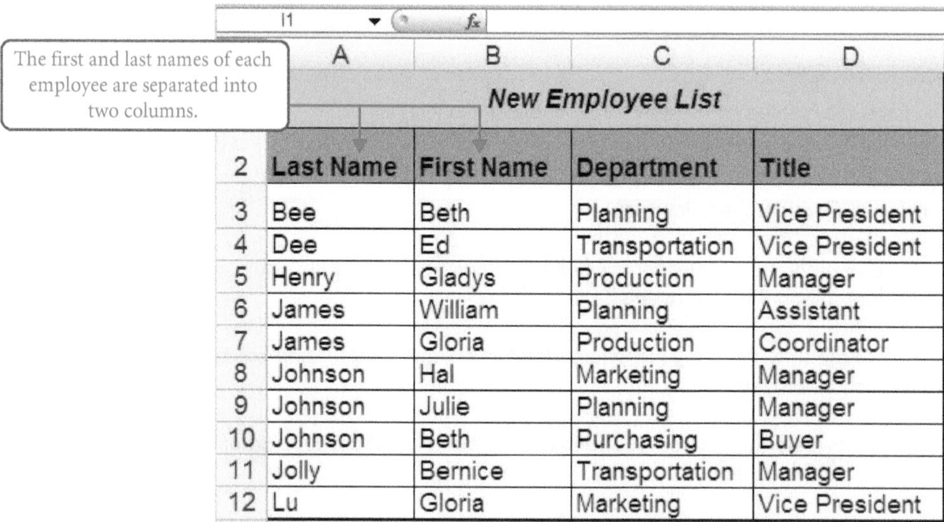


| | A | B | C | D |
|---|---|---|---|---|
| 1 | New Employee List | | | |
| 2 | Last Name | First Name | Department | Title |
| 3 | Bee | Beth | Planning | Vice President |
| 4 | Dee | Ed | Transportation | Vice President |
| 5 | Henry | Gladys | Production | Manager |
| 6 | James | William | Planning | Assistant |
| 7 | James | Gloria | Production | Coordinator |
| 8 | Johnson | Hal | Marketing | Manager |
| 9 | Johnson | Julie | Planning | Manager |
| 10 | Johnson | Beth | Purchasing | Buyer |
| 11 | Jolly | Bernice | Transportation | Manager |
| 12 | Lu | Gloria | Marketing | Vice President |

Figure 14 | **Previously Created List of Current Employees**

Each employee's name is combined into one column, last name followed by first name.

| | A | B | C |
|---|---|---|---|
| 1 | Current Employees | | |
| 2 | Full Name | Department | Title |
| 3 | Angello, Salvatore | Transportation | Manager |
| 4 | Ball, Gloria | Warehousing | Director |
| 5 | Bee, Bernice | Production | Vice President |
| 6 | Best, Jennifer | IT | Vice President |
| 7 | Blu, Natalie | Warehousing | Manager |
| 8 | Charles, Hale | Transportation | Assistant |
| 9 | Cowlins, John | Accounting | Director |
| 10 | Frank, Bill | Sales | Regional Director |
| 11 | Gil, Anthony | Production | President |
| 12 | Henry, Keith | IT | Programmer |
| 13 | Jay, Mary | Human Resources | Vice President |
| 14 | Keey, Mary | Accounting | Manager |

The new list of employees shown in Figure 13 cannot be added to the current list of employees in Figure 14 unless the first and last name of each employee is combined into one column. The following explains how the **CONCATENATE** function is used to accomplish this goal.

- Insert a new column between columns B and C in the New Employee List worksheet (Figure 13). This will create a new column C, which is blank.
- Type the column heading Full Name in cell C2.
- Type an equal sign in cell C3 followed by the function name CONCATENATE.
- Type an open parenthesis.
- Type cell location A3 followed by a comma.
- Type an open quotation mark followed by a comma, a space, and a closing quotation mark. This will add a comma and a space between the last and first names,

which is how the names are configured in column A of Figure 14. As with most other functions, in addition to using cell locations you can use numeric or text data to define each argument. However, if you are using text data or symbols, you must put them in quotations.

- Type a comma.
- Type cell location B3 followed by a closing parenthesis.
- Press the **Enter** key. Then, copy cell C3 and paste it to the rest of the cells in the list.

Figure 15 shows the setup of the **CONCATENATE** function that was added to the New Employee List worksheet in Figure 13. The comma and space enclosed in quotations in the middle of the function will separate the last and first names as shown in Figure 14.

Figure 15 | **Setup of the CONCATENATE Function**

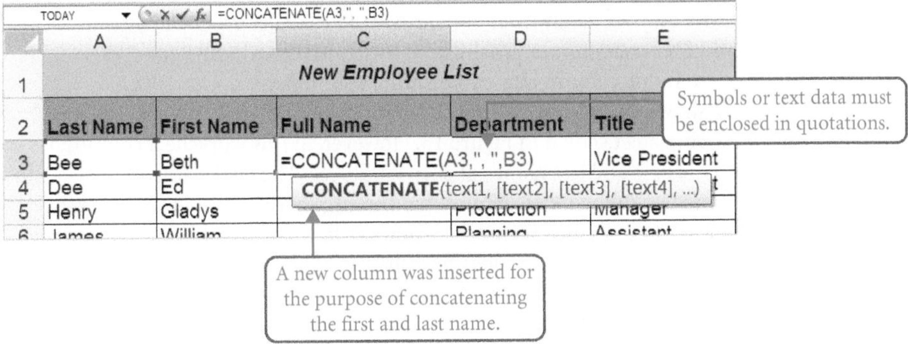


Figure 16 shows the results of the **CONCATENATE** function from Figure 15. Each employee's last and first names from columns A and B have been combined in column C. A comma and a space were added between the last and first names to match the configuration of the names in column A of Figure 14. The data in Figure 16 can now be copied and pasted into the Excel file shown in Figure 14. However, remember to use the **Paste Values** option in the **Paste** icon. If you use the regular paste command, you will be pasting the **CONCATENATE** function and not the names that were produced as a result of the function output.

Figure 16 | **Results of the CONCATENATE Function**

C3 | =CONCATENATE(A3,", ",B3) ← Concatenate function entered in cell C3.

| | A | B | C | D | E |
|---|---|---|---|---|---|
| 1 | New Employee List | | | | |
| 2 | Last Name | First Name | Full Name | Department | Title |
| 3 | Bee | Beth | Bee, Beth | Planning | Vice President |
| 4 | Dee | Ed | Dee, Ed | Transportation | Vice President |
| 5 | Henry | Gladys | Henry, Gladys | Production | Manager |
| 6 | James | William | James, William | Planning | Assistant |
| 7 | James | Gloria | James, Gloria | Production | Coordinator |
| 8 | Johnson | Hal | Johnson, Hal | Marketing | Manager |
| 9 | Johnson | Julie | Johnson, Julie | Planning | Manager |
| 10 | Johnson | Beth | Johnson, Beth | Purchasing | Buyer |
| 11 | Jolly | Bernice | Jolly, Bernice | Transportation | Manager |
| 12 | Lu | Gloria | Lu, Gloria | Marketing | Vice President |

Last and first names in columns A and B are now combined.

**COMMON MISTAKES | The #Name? Error and CONCATENATE Function**

If you see the #Name? error when using the **CONCATENATE** function, check to see that any text data is enclosed in quotations. Cell locations and numbers can be typed directly into the arguments of the function. However, you will see the #Name? error if you typed any symbols, words, or letters into one of the arguments without using quotations.

## SEARCH, LEFT, LEN, and MID Functions

In the previous segment, you saw how the **CONCATENATE** function enables you to combine a list of employee names from two columns into one. You will now learn how to use the **LEN**, **SEARCH**, **LEFT**, and **MID** functions to separate a list of employee names from one column into two. These four functions are being demonstrated together because they are rarely used individually. The results produced by the **SEARCH** and **LEN** functions are usually used by the **MID** and **LEFT** functions to separate data from one column into two or more columns.

Figure 17 shows an Excel worksheet containing a list of new employees that is similar to the worksheet shown in Figure 13. However, in this worksheet column A contains both the first and last names of each employee. The goal is to add this data to the worksheet shown in Figure 18. Notice that the employee names in this worksheet are separated into two columns (columns B and C). In this example, the HR manager uses an ID number (column A) to identify each employee. This eliminates the need to combine the first and last names of each employee into one column. As a result, the employee names in Figure 17 need to be separated into two columns before they can be pasted into the worksheet shown in Figure 18.

Figure 17 | **Worksheet with Employee Names in One Column**

F1 fx

| | A | B | C |
|---|---|---|---|
| 1 | *New Employee List* | | |
| 2 | **Name** | **Department** | **Title** |
| 3 | Bee, Beth | Planning | Vice President |
| 4 | Dee, Ed | Transportation | Vice President |
| 5 | Henry, Gladys | Production | Manager |
| 6 | James, William | Planning | Assistant |
| 7 | James, Gloria | Production | Coordinator |
| 8 | Johnson, Hal | Marketing | Manager |
| 9 | Johnson, Julie | Planning | Manager |
| 10 | Johnson, Beth | Purchasing | Buyer |
| 11 | Jolly, Bernice | Transportation | Manager |
| 12 | Lu, Gloria | Marketing | Vice President |

Employee names are combined into one column.

>> **Quick Reference**

**CONCATENATE Function**

1. Activate a cell.
2. Type an equal sign followed by the function name CONCATENATE and an open parenthesis.
3. Identify data that you wish to combine and enter it into each argument of the function, followed by commas. Remember to use quotation marks if you are typing words or text into an argument.
4. Type a closing parenthesis.
5. Press the **Enter** key.

Figure 18 | **Worksheet with Employee Names in Two Columns**

| | A | B | C | D | E |
|---|---|---|---|---|---|
| 1 | *Current Employees* | | | | |
| 2 | ID Number | Last Name | First Name | Department | Title |
| 3 | 101401 | Angello | Salvatore | Transportation | Manager |
| 4 | 592889 | Ball | Gloria | Warehousing | Director |
| 5 | 845966 | Bee | Bernice | Production | Vice President |
| 6 | 110602 | Best | Jennifer | IT | Vice President |
| 7 | 576409 | Blu | Natalie | Warehousing | Manager |
| 8 | 855442 | Charles | Hale | Transportation | Assistant |
| 9 | 671718 | Cowlins | John | Accounting | Director |
| 10 | 665153 | Frank | Bill | Sales | Regional Director |
| 11 | 401034 | Gil | Anthony | Production | President |
| 12 | 265349 | Henry | Keith | IT | Programmer |
| 13 | 244502 | Jay | Mary | Human Resources | Vice President |
| 14 | 876674 | Keey | Mary | Accounting | Manager |
| 15 | 763649 | Lite | Bruce | Human Resources | Recruiting Manager |
| 16 | 125544 | Love | Bill | Planning | Manager |

Employee names are separated into two columns.

As mentioned previously, the **SEARCH**, **LEN**, **LEFT**, and **MID** functions will be used to separate the employee names in column A of Figure 17 into two columns. The following provides a brief definition of these four functions and explains how they are used together to separate data contained in one column into two or more columns.

- **LEN:** The **LEN** function is used to count the total number of characters of data that is entered into a cell location. The function has one argument, which is usually defined by a cell location that contains text data. The number of characters produced by this function can be used in the **LEFT** or **MID** function to select specific characters from data that is entered into a target cell location.
- **SEARCH:** The **SEARCH** function is used to count the number of characters up to and including a target symbol for data contained in a cell. The function counts the number of characters up to the target symbol from left to right. For example, column A in Figure 17 contains each employee's last and first names separated by a comma. The letters preceding the comma make up the employee's last name. The **SEARCH** function can be used to count the number of characters that precede and include the comma. This number can then be used in one of the arguments of the **LEFT** function to separate the employee's last name and place it into another cell location. The following are the three arguments of the **SEARCH** function.
  - **find_text:** Type the symbol or character you are searching for and enclose it in quotation marks. For example, if you wanted to count the number of characters up to and including a comma, you would type a comma enclosed in quotation marks. You can also type a cell location that contains a character or symbol into this argument. However, quotation marks are not required if you are using cell locations.
  - **within_text:** Type the cell location that contains the text entry you are searching. You can also type a word into this segment, but it must be enclosed in quotation marks.
  - **[start_num]:** The **SEARCH** function will automatically look for the character used to define the **find_text** argument beginning with the first character. Use this argument if you want to begin searching after the first character of a text string, or when the character used to define the **find_text** argument appears multiple times in a text string.

- **LEFT:** The **LEFT** function is used to select a specific number of characters from a text entry beginning from left to right. The number of characters this function selects is usually determined by using a function such as the **SEARCH** function. For example, to select only the last name from column A in Figure 17, you can use the **SEARCH** function to determine how many letters appear before the comma. The number produced by the **SEARCH** function can then be used in the **LEFT** function to select only the last name from each name listed in column A. This function contains the following two arguments.
    - **text:** Type the cell location containing text data from which the function will select characters. You can also type a text entry directly into this argument, but it must be enclosed in quotation marks.
    - **[num_chars]:** Type the cell location, formula, or number that contains the number of characters the **LEFT** function will select from a text entry. The function will select the first character of a text entry and continue selecting, from left to right, the number of characters defined by this argument.
- **MID:** The **MID** function serves the same purpose as the **LEFT** function. However, the **LEFT** function will always select the *first character of a text entry* and continue selecting characters from left to right. The **MID** function allows you to start selecting characters at a specific point in a text entry. For example, after the last name is selected from column A in Figure 17, characters after the comma must be selected to separate the first name. The **MID** function can be used to start selecting characters after the comma so that only the first name is selected and placed into a separate cell location. The following are the three arguments of this function.
    - **text:** Identical to the **text** argument in the **LEFT** function.
    - **start_num:** Type the cell location, formula, or number that defines where the function should begin selecting characters from the data used to define the **text** argument. The function will use the number in this argument to select the starting character by counting from left to right. For example, if the number 3 is typed into this argument, the function will begin selecting characters from left to right beginning with the third character.
    - **[num_chars]:** Identical to the **num_chars** argument in the **LEFT** function.

As mentioned previously, the **SEARCH, LEN, LEFT**, and **MID** functions will be used to separate the names listed in column A in Figure 17 into two columns. This is necessary in order to paste the data shown in Figure 17 into the worksheet shown in Figure 18. The following explains how these four functions are used to accomplish this task.

- Insert 4 columns between columns A and B in the New Employee List worksheet (see Figure 17).
- Type the column heading Last Name in cell D2 and the column heading First Name in cell E2.
- Type an equal sign followed by the function name **LEN** and an open parenthesis in cell B3.
- Type the cell location A3 followed by a closing parenthesis. This will count the number of characters in the first employee's name (see Figure 19).
- Copy the function in cell B3 and paste it to the rest of the cells in the list.

**>> Quick Reference**

**LEN Function**

1. Activate a cell.
2. Type an equal sign followed by the function name LEN.
3. Type an open parenthesis followed by a cell location containing text data, or type a text entry enclosed in quotation marks.
4. Type a closing parenthesis and press the **Enter** key.

Figure 19 | **Setup of the LEN Function**

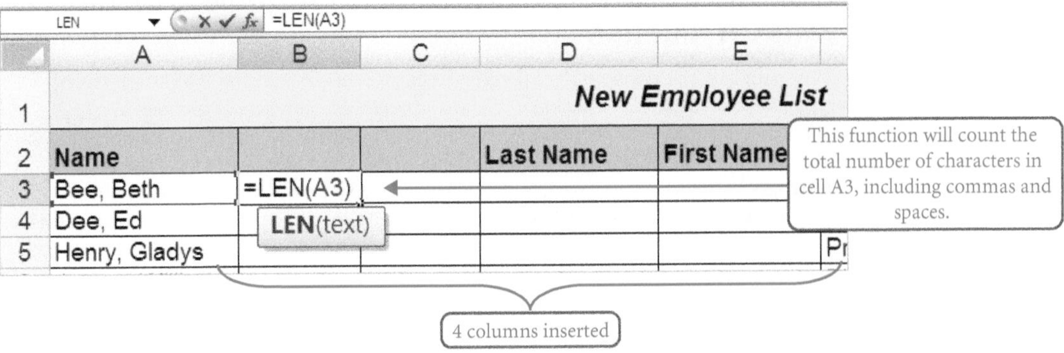


The following explains how the **SEARCH** function is added to the New Employee List worksheet:

- Type an equal sign in cell C3, followed by the function name SEARCH and an open parenthesis. This function will be used to count the number of characters preceding and including the comma in the first employee's name in cell A3. Define the three arguments of this function as follows.
  - **find_text:** Type an open quotation mark followed by a comma and then a closing quotation mark. The function will stop counting characters from left to right when it encounters a comma. Type a comma to complete this argument.
  - **within_text:** Type cell location A3 followed by a closing parenthesis.
  - **[start_num]:** Because a comma appears only one time in the names listed in column A, there is no need to define this argument. The function will begin searching for a comma after the first letter of the employee's name. This is why a closing parenthesis was typed after the **within_text** argument (see Figure 20).
- Copy the **SEARCH** function in cell C3 and paste it to the rest of the cells in the list.

Figure 20 | **SEARCH Function Setup and LEN Function Results**

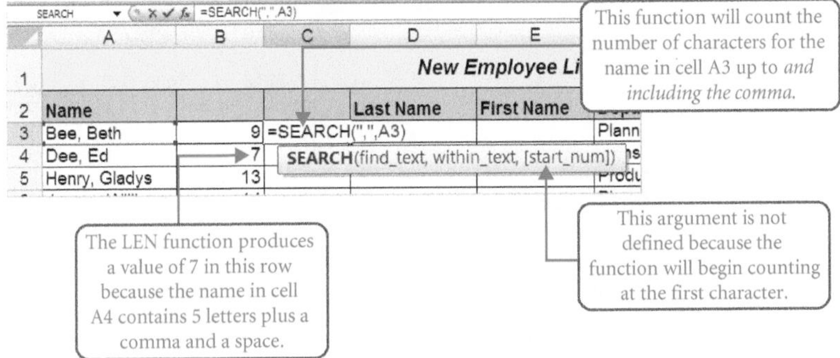


>> **Quick Reference**

**SEARCH Function**

1. Activate a cell.
2. Type an equal sign followed by the function name SEARCH.
3. Type an open parenthesis and define the following three arguments:
   a. **find_text:** The character the function will search for in a text entry. Characters typed into this argument must be enclosed in quotation marks.
   b. **within_text:** The characters of the text data used to define this argument will be counted.
   c. **[start_num]:** Position in a text entry at which the function will begin searching for the character in the **find_text** argument. The function assumes 1 if not defined.
4. Type a closing parenthesis and press the **Enter** key.

## COMMON MISTAKES | (start_num) Argument in the SEARCH function

Most people confuse the result of the **SEARCH** function when using the **[start_num]** argument. The **SEARCH** function will *always* count the number of characters in a text string beginning with the first character. The **[start_num]** argument changes only the point at which the function will begin looking for the character used to define the **find_text** argument. For example, the function listed below will return the number 9. This is because there are 9 characters preceding the *second comma* in the **within_text** argument. Because the number 6 is entered in the **[start_num]** argument, the function will begin looking for a comma starting with the letter T in the word Two.

```
=SEARCH(",","One, Two, Three",6)
```

The following explains how the **LEFT** function is added and used in the New Employee List worksheet:

- Type an equal sign in cell D3 followed by the function name LEFT and an open parenthesis. Define the two arguments of this function as follows (see Figure 21).
  - **text:** Type cell location A3 followed by a comma. This function will be used to select only the last name of the employee entered in cell A3.
  - **[num_chars]:** Type cell location C3 followed by a subtraction sign and the number 1. The **SEARCH** function in C3 is providing the number of characters that precedes the comma for the first employee, which is the employee's last name. However, this number also includes the comma. Therefore, the number 1 is subtracted from cell C3 so that the **LEFT** function does not include the comma when selecting the employee's last name.
- Type a closing parenthesis to complete the **LEFT** function and press the **Enter** key.
- Copy the **LEFT** function in cell D3 to the rest of the cells in the list.

> **Quick Reference**
>
> **LEFT Function**
>
> 1. Activate a cell.
> 2. Type an equal sign followed by the function name LEFT.
> 3. Type an open parenthesis and define the following two arguments:
>    a. **text:** Cell location containing text data or typed text in quotation marks.
>    b. **[num_chars]:** Number of characters the function will select from the text data in the **text** argument beginning from left to right.
> 4. Type a closing parenthesis and press the **Enter** key.

Figure 21 | **LEFT Function Setup and SEARCH Function Results**

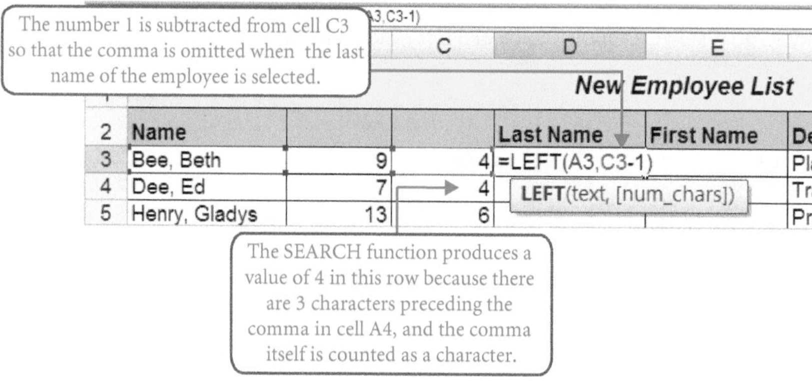


The following explains how the **MID** function is added and used in the New Employee List worksheet:

- Type an equal sign in cell E3 followed by the function name MID and an open parenthesis. Define the three arguments of this function as follows (see Figure 22).
  - **text:** Type cell location A3 followed by a comma. This function will be used to select the first name of the employee entered in cell A3.
  - **[start_num]:** Type cell location C3, a plus sign, and the number 2. The goal for this function is to begin selecting the letters of the employee's first name. Cell

C3 contains the results of the **SEARCH** function, which is counting the letters of the employee's last name plus the comma. After the comma there is a space, and the next letter begins the employee's first name. Therefore, the number 2 is added to the result of the **SEARCH** function so that this function can select characters beginning with the first letter of the employee's first name. Complete this argument by typing a comma.

- **[num_chars]:** Type cell location B3-C3 enclosed in parentheses. Then, type a subtraction sign and the number 1. Cell B3 contains the result of the LEN function, which is counting all of the characters for the employee's name in cell A3. The result of the **SEARCH** function in cell C3 is counting all of the characters in the employee's last name including the comma. Therefore, the number of characters calculated by subtracting the **SEARCH** function in cell C3 from the **LEN** function in cell B3 is the employee's first name. However, to account for the space after the comma, the number 1 is subtracted from this result.

- Type a closing parenthesis to complete the **MID** function and press the **Enter** key.
- Copy the **MID** function in cell E3 and paste it to the rest of the cell locations in the list.

Figure 22 | **MID Function Setup and LEFT Function Results**

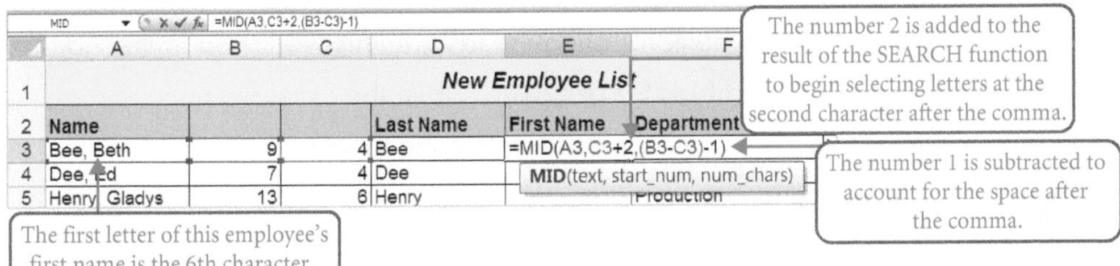


## COMMON MISTAKES | Each Space Is Counted as a Character

It is important to remember that when working with text functions, each space counts as one character. Many people make the mistake of using a number in the **[num_chars]** argument of the **MID** or **LEFT** function that is too high. In order to select the exact number of characters in a text entry, you must account for any spaces in the data that is used to define the **text** argument.

Figure 23 shows the final results of using the **LEN**, **SEARCH**, **LEFT**, and **MID** functions to separate each of the employee names in column A into columns D and E. Columns D, E, F, and G can now be pasted into the worksheet shown in Figure 18. However, these columns must be pasted using the **Paste Values** option in the **Paste** icon because the names in columns D and E are being produced by functions.

>> **Quick Reference**

**MID Function**

1. Type an equal sign followed by the function name MID.
2. Type an open parenthesis and define the following three arguments:
   a. **text:** Cell location containing text data or typed text in quotation marks.
   b. **[start_num]:** Number of the first character that will be selected counting from left to right.
   c. **[num_chars]:** Number of characters that will be selected from the text data in the **text** argument beginning from the character number in the **[start_num]** argument from left to right.
3. Type a closing parenthesis and press the **Enter** key.

Figure 23 | **Final Results of Separating Names with the LEN, SEARCH, LEFT, and MID Functions**

Each name in column A is separated into two columns.

| | A | B | C | D | E | F | G |
|---|---|---|---|---|---|---|---|
| 1 | | | | New Employee List | | | |
| 2 | Name | | | Last Name | First Name | Department | Title |
| 3 | Bee, Beth | 9 | 4 | Bee | Beth | Planning | Vice President |
| 4 | Dee, Ed | 7 | 4 | Dee | Ed | Transportation | Vice President |
| 5 | Henry, Gladys | 13 | 6 | Henry | Gladys | Production | Manager |
| 6 | James, William | 14 | 6 | James | William | Planning | Assistant |
| 7 | James, Gloria | 13 | 6 | James | Gloria | Production | Coordinator |
| 8 | Johnson, Hal | 12 | 8 | Johnson | Hal | Marketing | Manager |
| 9 | Johnson, Julie | 14 | 8 | Johnson | Julie | Planning | Manager |
| 10 | Johnson, Beth | 13 | 8 | Johnson | Beth | Purchasing | Buyer |
| 11 | Jolly, Bernice | 14 | 6 | Jolly | Bernice | Transportation | Manager |
| 12 | Lu, Gloria | 10 | 3 | Lu | Gloria | Marketing | Vice President |

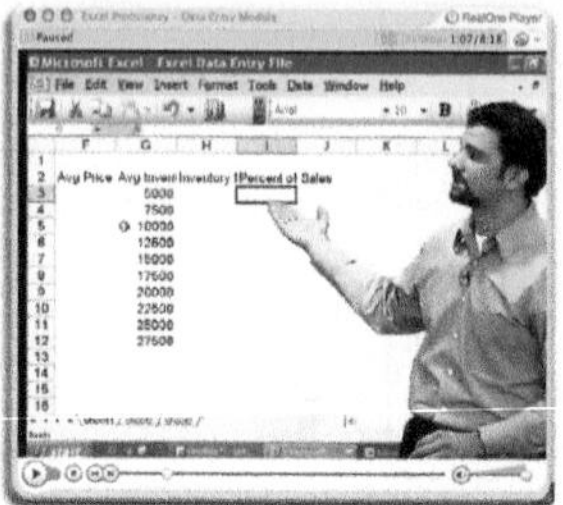

## >> CONCATENATE Function

The purpose of this workshop is to demonstrate the **CONCATENATE** function. I will be demonstrating the tasks in this workshop in the video named **CONCATENATE Function.** Open the Excel file named ib_e07_concatenatefunction. Complete the tasks below first, and then watch the video.

1. **Concatenating Data (Video: CONCATENATE Function)**
   a. Activate the New Employees List worksheet.
   b. Activate cell C2 and Insert a column.
   c. Type the column heading `Full Name` in cell C2.
   d. Type an equal sign in cell C3 followed by the function name `CONCATENATE` and an open parenthesis.
   e. Type cell `A3` followed by a comma.
   f. Type an opening quotation mark, a comma, a space, and a closing quotation mark.
   g. Type a comma.
   h. Type cell `B3` followed by a closing parenthesis. Then press the **Enter** key.
   i. Copy cell C3 and paste it into the range C4:C12.
   j. Copy the range C3:E12.
   k. Activate the Current Employees worksheet and activate cell A22.
   l. Paste the data using the **Paste Values** option in the **Paste** icon on the **Home** tab of the Ribbon.
   m. Highlight the range A22:C31. Then, add a dark line to the right side, left side, and bottom of the range and a regular line on the inside of the range.
   n. Sort the data in the Current Employees worksheet based on the Full Name column in ascending order.
   o. Save and close your file.

## »LEN, SEARCH, LEFT and MID Functions

**VIDEO WORKSHOP**

The purpose of this workshop is to demonstrate the use of the **LEN**, **SEARCH**, **LEFT**, and **MID** functions. I will be demonstrating the tasks in this workshop in the four videos named **LEN Function**, **SEARCH Function**, **LEFT Function**, and **MID Function**. The name of the video will appear in parentheses next to the relevant section heading. Open the Excel workbook named ib_e07_separatingdata. Complete each section of tasks first, and then watch the video pertaining to that section.

1. **Counting All Characters in a Cell (Video: LEN Function)**
   a. Activate the New Employees worksheet and activate cell B3.
   b. Insert 4 columns.
   c. Type the column heading **`Last Name`** in cell D2 and type the column heading **`First Name`** in cell E2.
   d. Type an equal sign in cell B3 followed by the function name **`LEN`** and an open parenthesis.
   e. Type cell **`A3`** followed by a closing parenthesis and press the **Enter** key.
   f. Copy cell B3 and paste it into the range B4:B12.

2. **Counting Target Characters in a Cell (Video: SEARCH Function)**
   a. Type an equal sign in cell C3 followed by the function name **`SEARCH`** and an open parenthesis.
   b. Define the **find_text** argument by typing an opening quotation mark, a comma, and a closing quotation mark. Complete the argument by typing a comma.
   c. Define the **within_text** argument by typing cell **`A3`**.
   d. Complete the function by typing a closing parenthesis and press the **Enter** key.
   e. Copy cell C3 and paste it into the range C4:C12.

3. **Selecting Characters from the Beginning of Text (Video: LEFT Function)**
   a. Type an equal sign in cell D3 followed by the function name **`LEFT`** and an open parenthesis.
   b. Define the text argument by typing cell **`A3`** followed by a comma.
   c. Define the **[num_chars]** argument by typing the formula **`C3-1`**.
   d. Complete the function by typing a closing parenthesis and press the **Enter** key.
   e. Copy cell D3 and paste it into the range D4:D12.

4. **Selecting Characters from the Middle of Text (Video: MID Function)**
   a. Type an equal sign in cell E3 followed by the function name **`MID`** and an open parenthesis.
   b. Define the text argument by typing cell **`A3`** followed by a comma.
   c. Define the **[start_num]** argument by typing the formula **`C3 + 2`** followed by a comma.

d. Define the **[num_chars]** argument by typing the formula `(B3 - C3) -1`.
e. Complete the function by typing a closing parenthesis and press the **Enter** key.
f. Copy cell E3 and paste it into the range E4:E12.
g. Save and close the workbook.

**EXERCISE**

**Why Do I Need This?**

## >> Calculating Cubic Capacity

The data that business managers use in Excel spreadsheets can come from a variety of sources. In some cases data might be manually typed into a spreadsheet. However, manually typing large amounts of data into an Excel spreadsheet increases the risk of data entry errors. Therefore, many business managers receive data from other sources such as the Internet or from their company's database system. This eliminates the risk of data entry errors. However, a potential challenge with this data is that it may not be in a format that is usable in mathematical formulas and functions. For example, the term 9′ is usually used to indicate a dimension of 9 feet. Excel will read 9′ as a text value that would not be usable in any mathematical formulas or functions. In these situations, text functions can transform a term such as 9′ into just the number 9.

### Exercise

The purpose of this exercise is to calculate the cubic capacity for a fleet of trucks. Open the Excel workbook named ib_e07_trailercapacity. The data in this worksheet is similar to what a transportation manager might receive from a database system. The following tasks will feature the use of text functions to convert data in this worksheet into numeric values to calculate the cubic capacities in column E.

1. Column A contains the ID number for each trailer. Each ID number ends in a 3-digit number. The first two digits of this number is the length of the trailer. Use the MID function in cell B3 to select the trailer length from the ID number in cell A3. Define each argument of the MID function as follows:
   a. **text**: `A3`
   b. **start_num:** `SEARCH(" ",A3) + 1` Notice that the **find_text** argument of the **SEARCH** function is a space enclosed in parentheses. This is because the trailer length begins after the space in the trailer ID number. The **MID** function will begin selecting numbers one character after the space of the trailer ID number in cell A3.
   c. **num_chars:** `2` The first two digits of the ending 3-digit number in cell A3 is the length of the trailer.
2. Copy cell B3 and paste it into the range B4:B26.
3. Calculate the cubic capacity in cell E3 by multiplying the trailer length in cell B3 by the trailer height in cell C3 by the trailer width in cell D3. However, use the **LEFT** function to select only the first character in cells C3 and D3 because the apostrophe sign cannot be used in formulas (i.e., B3 * LEFT(C3,1) * LEFT(D3,1)).
4. Copy your formula in cell E3 and paste it into the range E4:E26.
5. What is the total cubic capacity of the entire fleet?
6. Save and close your file.

## >> What's Wrong with This Spreadsheet?

PROBLEM & EXERCISE

### Problem

You are directing the strategic planning department for a large textile manufacturing corporation that produces a variety of fabrics used in the production of clothes. Your department was asked to evaluate the capacity of a textile dying and finishing factory that might be acquired as part of a growth strategy. You receive a file listing the dyeing machines in the factory and the number of batches each machine is capable of producing per day. Given the cost to maintain and operate the factory, the machines must be able to process at least 50,000 pounds of fabric per day. You ask one of the analysts in your department to calculate the total capacity of the factory to see if the machines can produce this minimum target. He completes his analysis and mentions the following points in an e-mail message.

1. Unfortunately, the results of my analysis show that this factory is falling significantly short of our minimum capacity target. Looks like we should probably pass on buying this factory.
2. I calculated the daily production per machine by multiplying the machine capacity by the batches per day as per your instructions. I had a slight problem with the machine capacity because the data you gave me had only a listing of the machine ID numbers. However, I spoke to a manager at the factory and he told me that the machine capacity is the number after the space in the Machine ID number.
3. I attached the Excel file containing my analysis to this e-mail. Let me know if you have any questions.

### Exercise

The Excel file your analyst attached to his e-mail in named ib_e07_textileincapacity. Do you agree with your analyst's assessment that this factory is incapable of producing the minimum 50,000 pounds of fabric per day? Consider the following points:

1. The analyst stated that the capacity for each machine is the number that follows the space in the Machine ID number (column A). Calculate the daily capacity of the first machine by multiplying this number by the batch number in column B. Does your calculation match the number the analyst calculated?
2. Look at the formula in cell C3. Explain how this formula is producing the number that is being multiplied by cell B3.
3. Is the calculation you analyzed in point 2 producing an accurate result of each machine's daily capacity?

What's wrong with this spreadsheet? Write a short answer for each of the points listed above. Then, fix the calculation in cell C3 and paste it into the range C4:C38. What is the total capacity of the factory?

## >> IS Functions

Skill Set

The previous section demonstrated how you can use text functions to manipulate data within a cell. **IS** functions (pronounced like the word "is") are used to determine the type of data within a cell or establish whether the result of a formula or function is an error. These functions are often used with the **IF**, **AND**, and **OR** functions to develop advanced spreadsheets in which different outputs are produced based on the type of data that is entered into a cell. Combining these functions allows you to build flexible spreadsheets in which users are required to type data into one or more cell locations to produce calculated results. This section illustrates how **IS** functions are used in various business situations and demonstrates how they are used to handle errors that might be produced by formulas and functions based on what the user types into a cell location.

## ISNUMBER and ISTEXT Functions

You can use the **ISNUMBER** and **ISTEXT** functions to determine if the data typed into a cell is either numeric data or text data. The output of both functions is either TRUE or FALSE depending on the data contained in a cell. These functions are frequently used together and will be demonstrated in a spreadsheet that might be used by a human resources manager to discuss a company's retirement plan with an employee. As mentioned earlier in this chapter, many companies offer some type of retirement plan for their employees. This example assumes that a company will contribute fifty cents for every dollar the employee contributes to his retirement plan. The worksheet shown in Figure 24 could be used by a human resources manger to show an employee the total annual investment that would be made into his retirement account. The **ISNUMBER** and **ISTEXT** functions will be used to display a message in cell B6 depending on the data that is entered into the spreadsheet.

Figure 24 | **Retirement Investment Worksheet**

| | A | B | C | D | E | F |
|---|---|---|---|---|---|---|
| 1 | Retirement Plan | | | | | |
| 2 | Salary | Percent of Salary | Your Annual Investment | Company Annual Contribution | Total Annual Investment | Monthly Investment |
| 3 | | | $0 | $0 | $0 | $0 |
| 4 | | | | | | |
| 5 | | | | | | |
| 6 | Message: | | | | | |
| 7 | | | | | | |

The ISNUMBER and ISTEXT functions will be used in an IF function to produce instructions for using this worksheet here.

Formulas have been created in these cells to calculate an employee's retirement investment based on the salary and percent that is entered in cells A3 and B3.

Again, the output of the **ISNUMBER** or **ISTEXT** function is the word TRUE or the word FALSE. Figures 25 and 26 show the setup and results of these functions using a basic example. Notice that Figure 25 demonstrates only one argument for each function, which is usually defined by typing a cell location.

Figure 25 | **Setup of Basic ISNUMBER and ISTEXT Example**

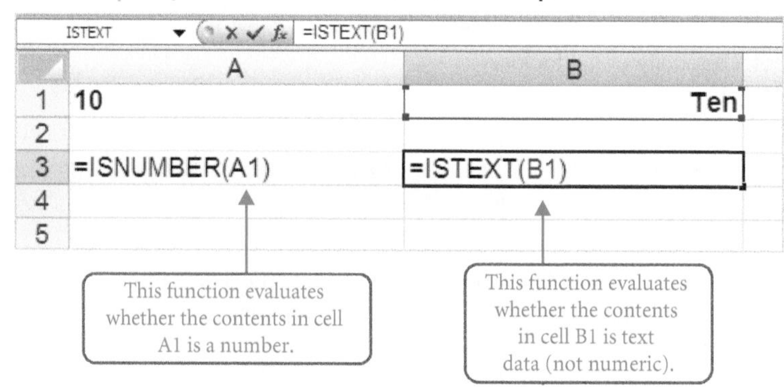
ISTEXT
=ISTEXT(B1)
A
B
10
Ten
=ISNUMBER(A1)
=ISTEXT(B1)
This function evaluates whether the contents in cell A1 is a number.
This function evaluates whether the contents in cell B1 is text data (not numeric).

Figure 26 | **Results of Basic ISNUMBER and ISTEXT Example**

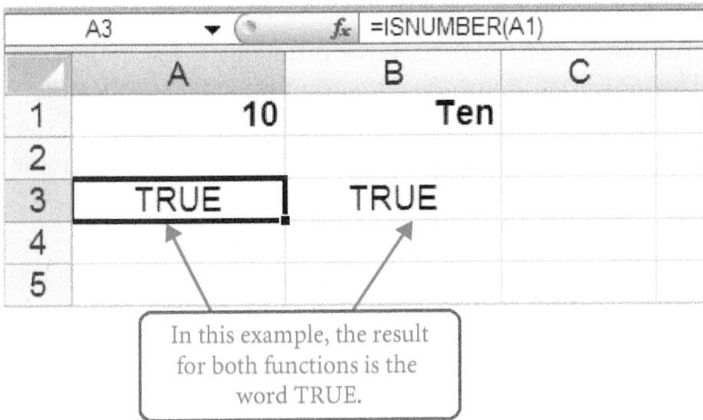


Figures 25 and 26 demonstrate the results of the **ISNUMBER** and **ISTEXT** functions when they are used independently. However, these functions are often used with an **IF** function to produce various outputs based on what is typed into a cell. The following explains how the **ISNUMBER** and **ISTEXT** functions are used with the **IF**, **AND**, and **OR** functions to produce instructions in cell B6 of the worksheet shown in Figure 24. The purpose of these instructions is to inform the employee what to type into cells A3 and B3 to calculate the amount of money that will be invested into a retirement account. A secondary goal is to inform the employee if the wrong information has been typed into a cell.

- Type an equal sign in cell B6 followed by the function name IF and an open parenthesis. The instructions displayed on this worksheet will be the output of a three-part nested **IF** function. The following is the **logical_test** and **value_if_true** arguments for the first **IF** function.
  - **logical_test:** `OR(ISTEXT(A3),ISTEXT(B3))=TRUE` This logical test is using a combination of the **OR** function and the **ISTEXT** function. The **OR** function is evaluating if *either* of the **ISTEXT** functions produces an output of TRUE. If either **ISTEXT** function is true, then the result of the **OR** function will be TRUE. If the result of the **OR** function is TRUE, the output of the function will be the instruction in the **value_if_true** argument. Type a comma at the end of this argument.
  - **value_if_true:** "You can only enter numeric values in cells A3 and B3." If the first logical test is true, then the function will tell the employee that only numbers can be entered into cells A3 and B3. As illustrated later in this segment, typing words into either cell A3 or cell B3 will produce errors in the formulas that were created in the worksheet. The **ISTEXT** function is being used to determine whether the employee inadvertently typed words or symbols into these cells. Type a comma to complete this argument.
- Define the **value_if_false** argument for the first **IF** function by starting a second **IF** function. The following is how the **logical_test** and **value_if_true** arguments should be defined for this second **IF** function.
  - **logical_test:** `AND (ISNUMBER(A3),ISNUMBER(B3))=TRUE` This is the second logical test in the nested IF function. The **AND** function is evaluating whether a number has been typed into both cells A3 and B3. If both **ISNUMBER** functions are true, then the **AND** function and this logical test are true. Type a comma to complete this argument.
  - **value_if_true:** `" "` If the second logical test is true, then the output of the function will be a blank cell. This is why this argument is defined using two quotation marks. Once numbers are typed into both cells A3 and B3, there are no required instructions or messages. Type a comma to complete this argument.

- Define the **value_if_false** argument for the second **IF** function by starting a third **IF** function. The three arguments for the third IF function are defined as follows.
    - **logical_test:** `ISNUMBER(A3)=FALSE` This is the third logical test in the nested **IF** function. The ISNUMBER function is determining if a number has been entered into cell A3. If a number has not been typed into cell A3, then the **ISNUMBER** function will be false. If the **ISNUMBER** function is false, then the logical test is *true*. Type a comma at the end of this argument.
    - **value_if_true:** `"Enter your annual salary in cell A3."` If the third logical test is true, then the employee has not entered a number in cell A3. Therefore, the instructions will tell the employee to enter an annual salary into cell A3.
    - **value_if_false:** `"Enter the percentage of your salary you wish to invest in cell B3."` If all three logical tests are false, then we can assume that a number has not been entered into cell B3, which is the percentage of the employee's salary that will be invested.
- Type three closing parentheses to complete the nested **IF** function and press the **Enter** key.

## COMMON MISTAKES | Evaluating the Result of ISNUMBER/ISTEXT

When evaluating the result of an **ISNUMBER** or **ISTEXT** function in the logical test argument of an **IF** function, *do not use quotation marks.* Quotation marks are used to evaluate text data that is entered in a cell except when it is a TRUE or FALSE output from a function or formula.

Figure 27 shows the setup of the nested **IF** function in the Retirement Plan worksheet. Figures 28 through 30 show the results of the nested **IF** function as data is typed into cells A3 and B3.

Figure 27 | **Setup of Nested IF Function with ISNUMBER and ISTEXT Functions**

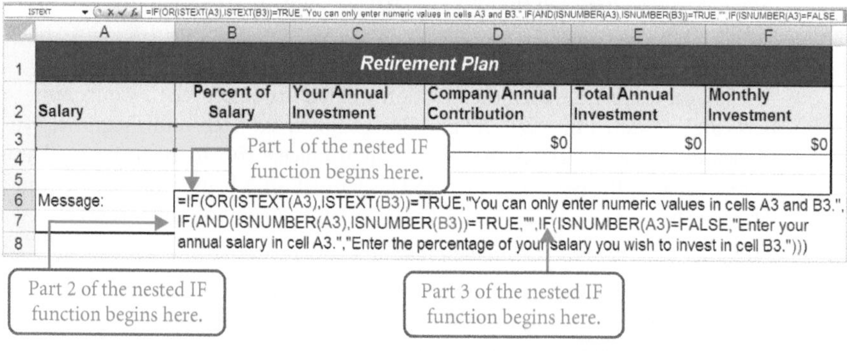


Figure 28 | **Results of Nested IF Function with ISNUMBER and ISTEXT Functions, Part 1**

| | A | B | C | D | E | F |
|---|---|---|---|---|---|---|
| 1 | Retirement Plan | | | | | |
| 2 | Salary | Percent of Salary | Your Annual Investment | Company Annual Contribution | Total Annual Investment | Monthly Investment |
| 3 | | | $0 | $0 | $0 | $0 |
| 4 | | | | | | |
| 5 | | | | | | |
| 6 | Message: | Enter your annual salary in cell A3. | | | | |
| 7 | | | | | | |

The function shows the third value_if_true argument because cell A3 is empty.

Figure 29 | **Results of Nested IF Function with ISNUMBER and ISTEXT Functions, Part 2**

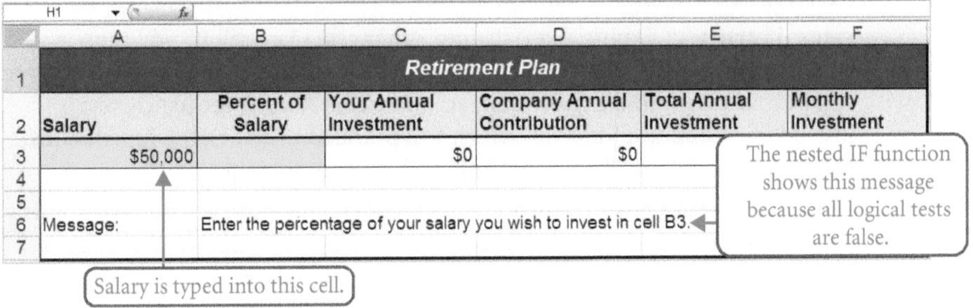

| | A | B | C | D | E | F |
|---|---|---|---|---|---|---|
| 1 | Retirement Plan | | | | | |
| 2 | Salary | Percent of Salary | Your Annual Investment | Company Annual Contribution | Total Annual Investment | Monthly Investment |
| 3 | $50,000 | | $0 | $0 | | |
| 4 | | | | | | |
| 5 | | | | | | |
| 6 | Message: | Enter the percentage of your salary you wish to invest in cell B3. | | | | |
| 7 | | | | | | |



Figure 30 | **Results of Nested IF Function with ISNUMBER and ISTEXT Functions, Part 3**

| | A | B | C | D | E | F |
|---|---|---|---|---|---|---|
| 1 | Retirement Plan | | | | | |
| 2 | Salary | Percent of Salary | Your Annual Investment | Company Annual Contribution | Total Annual Investment | Monthly Investment |
| 3 | $50,000 | 10.00% | $5,000 | $2,500 | $7,500 | $625 |
| 4 | | | | | | |
| 5 | | | | | | |
| 6 | Message: | | | | | |
| 7 | | | | | | |

The output of the function is a blank cell since both cells A3 and B3 contain a number.

Figures 28 through 30 show the output of the nested **IF** function as numbers are being typed into cells A3 and B3. Figure 31 shows what will happen if the employee makes a mistake and types text data into cell B3. Notice that instead of typing a number, the employee typed 10 Percent. Notice that this causes an error in the formulas in the range C3:F3.

Figure 31 | **Results When Text Is Typed into Cell B3**

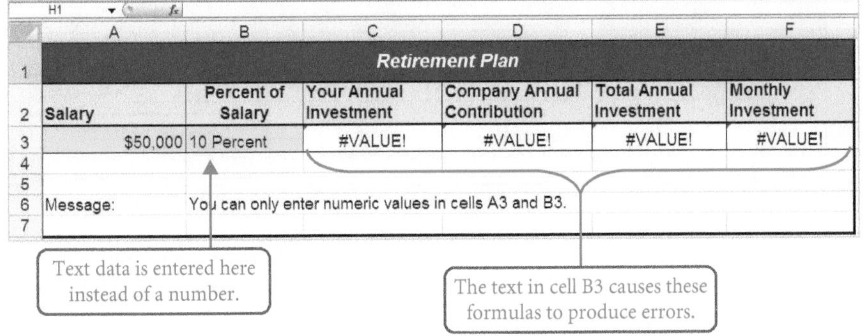

| | A | B | C | D | E | F |
|---|---|---|---|---|---|---|
| 1 | Retirement Plan | | | | | |
| 2 | Salary | Percent of Salary | Your Annual Investment | Company Annual Contribution | Total Annual Investment | Monthly Investment |
| 3 | $50,000 | 10 Percent | #VALUE! | #VALUE! | #VALUE! | #VALUE! |
| 4 | | | | | | |
| 5 | | | | | | |
| 6 | Message: | You can only enter numeric values in cells A3 and B3. | | | | |
| 7 | | | | | | |



You can use the **ISTEXT** function to prevent the #VALUE! error codes from being displayed in the range C3:F3 in Figure 31. These errors appear in the figure because text data was typed into cell B3 instead of a number. The following explains how the **ISTEXT** function is used along with the **OR** and **IF** functions to recreate the formulas in the range C3:F3 in Figure 31.

- Type an equal sign in cell C3 followed by the function name IF and an open parenthesis. The following text explains how each of the arguments in the **IF** function is defined.
  - **logical_test:** `OR(ISTEXT(A3),ISTEXT(B3))=TRUE` The **OR** function in this logical test is evaluating if either ISTEXT function is true. If text has been

typed into either cell A3 or cell B3, the **OR** function and the logical test will be true. Type a comma after this argument.

- **value_if_true:** `""` Typing text data into either cell A3 or cell B3 will cause an error to occur in the formula that calculates the amount of money the employee will be investing into the retirement account. Therefore, if the logical test is true, instead of executing a formula (which will produce an error), the function displays nothing in the cell. Type a comma after this argument.
- **value_if_false:** `B3 * A3` If the logical test for this function is false, either numbers or nothing has been typed into cell B3 or cell A3. Therefore, the formula for calculating how much money the employee is investing into a retirement account can be executed. This formula is taking the percent typed into cell B3 and multiplying it by the salary typed into cell A3.

- Type a closing parenthesis and press the **Enter** key to complete this **IF** function.

Figure 32 and 33 show the setup and results of the **IF** function used to calculate the amount of money the employee is investing into the retirement account. Notice that cell C3 in Figure 33 is blank. This is because text data is typed into cell B3.

Figure 32 | **Setup of the IF and ISTEXT Functions**

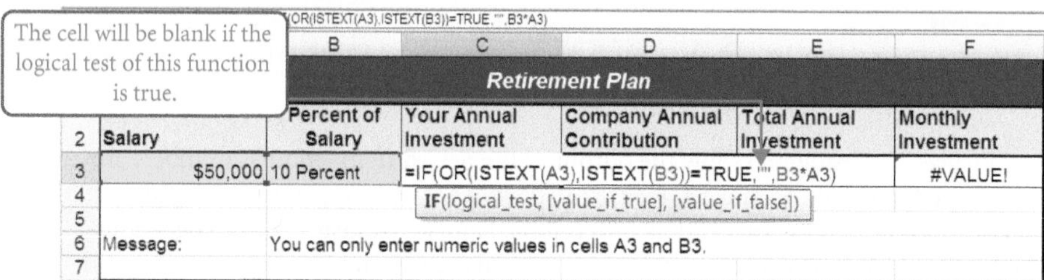


Figure 33 | **Results of the IF and ISTEXT Functions**

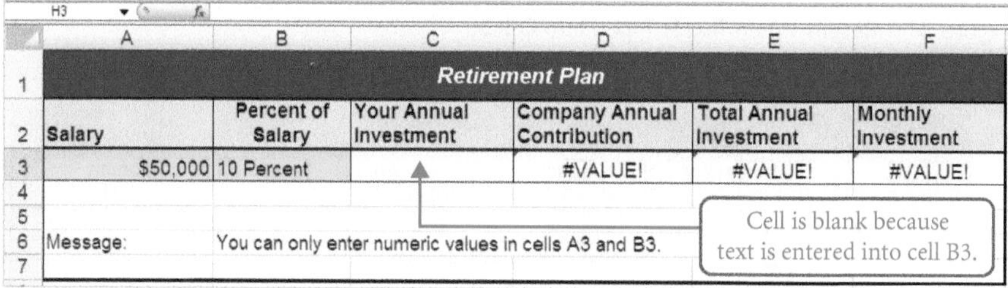


Figure 34 shows the final adjustments that were made to all of the formulas in the range C3:F3 in the Retirement Plan worksheet. Because text is entered into cell B3, these cells are now blank instead of displaying the #Value! error code. The following lists the IF functions that are used for cells D3, E3, and F3.

- **Cell D3:** `IF(OR(ISTEXT(A3),ISTEXT(B3))=TRUE,"",(A3 * B3) / 2)` This function will calculate the amount of money the company will contribute to the employee's retirement account if the logical test is not true. It was mentioned at the beginning of this section that the company will contribute fifty cents for every dollar invested by the employee. The formula takes the result of the employee's investment, which is the salary in cell A3 multiplied by the percent in cell B3, and divides it by 2.
- **Cell E3:** `IF(OR(ISTEXT(A3),ISTEXT(B3))=TRUE,"",C3+D3)` This function will calculate the total investment that will be made into the employee's retirement account if the logical test is false. The formula is adding the employee's investment in cell C3 to the Company's contribution in cell D3.

- **Cell F3:** `IF(OR(ISTEXT(A3),ISTEXT(B3))=TRUE,"",E3/12)` This function will calculate the monthly investment that will be made into the employees retirement account if the logical test is false. The formula is taking the total annual investment in cell E3 and dividing it by 12.

Figure 34 | **Final Results of the Retirement Plan Spreadsheet**

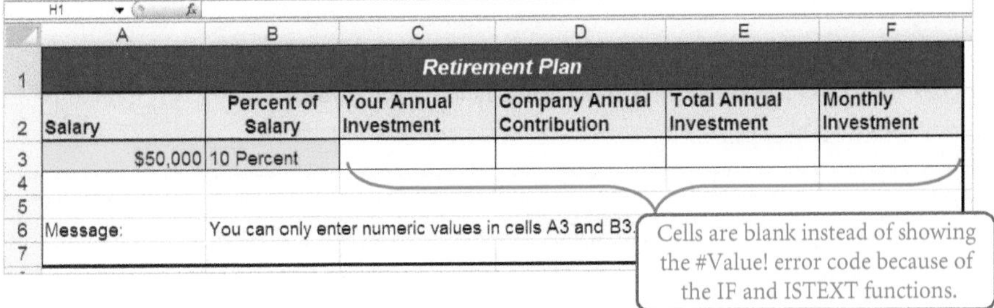


## ISERROR Function

The **ISERROR** function is used to identify if the result of a formula or function produces an error. In Figure 32 the **ISTEXT** function was used in an **IF** function to prevent the formula from calculating the result of the employee's retirement investment if cells A3 and B3 contained text. The **ISERROR** function could have been used in this situation to serve the same purpose. However, in the case of Figure 32, the error occurs only if text data is typed into either cell A3 or B3. The **ISERROR** function is used in situations in which you may not know when or what will cause a formula or function to produce an error. As with the **ISTEXT** and **ISNUMBER** functions, the output of the **ISERROR** function is either TRUE or FALSE. Like most IS functions, the **ISERROR** function is rarely used independently and is usually used with an **IF** function.

Figure 35 shows a worksheet that will be used to demonstrate the **ISERROR** function. A human resources manager might use this worksheet to show an employee the current value of a retirement account. The worksheet also shows an employee how funds in her retirement account are invested. Companies often work with financial firms to offer their employees a variety of investment options for their retirement accounts. For example, one option could be a mutual fund that is a medium-risk investment with slow and steady growth. Another option could be a high-risk fund with the potential for either large gains or large losses.

>> **Quick Reference**

**ISNUMBER Function**

1. Activate a cell.
2. Type an equal sign.
3. Type the function name ISNUMBER and open parenthesis.
4. Type a cell location.
5. Type a closing parenthesis.
6. Press the **Enter** key.

Figure 35 | **Retirement Investment Details Worksheet**

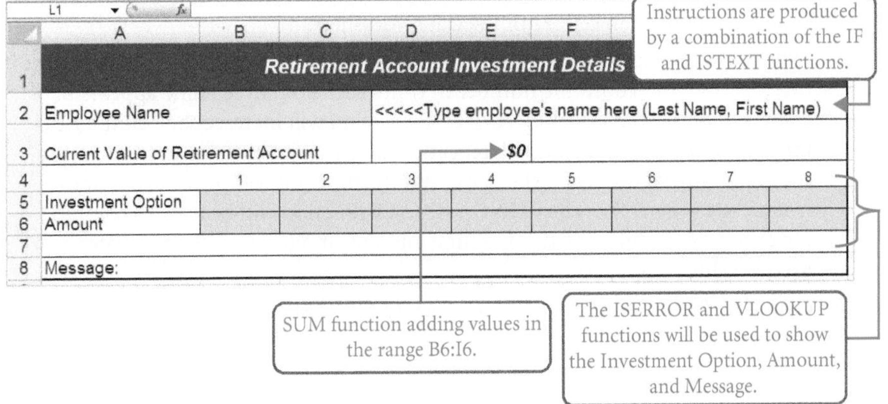


>> **Quick Reference**

**ISTEXT Function**

1. Activate a cell.
2. Type an equal sign.
3. Type the function name ISTEXT and an open parenthesis.
4. Type a cell location.
5. Type a closing parenthesis.
6. Press the **Enter** key.

Figure 36 shows the data that will be used to populate the worksheet in Figure 35. Notice that the investment options for each employee are listed vertically in column B. However, these options are listed horizontally in row 5 in Figure 35. This example will demonstrate how to display data that is listed in vertical columns in rows. This is a common problem in business because mangers typically receive data from a database system arranged in columns. However, they frequently work with spreadsheets that require the same data to be arranged in rows.

Figure 36 | **Data Worksheet with Investment Details by Employee**

| | A | B | C |
|---|---|---|---|
| 1 | **Name** | **Investment Option** | **Amount Invested** |
| 2 | Charles, Louis | Blue Chip Fund | $3,300 |
| 3 | Jay, Jackie | Blue Chip Fund | $1,500 |
| 4 | Ray, David | Blue Chip Fund | $4,400 |
| 5 | Bee, Bernice | Company Stock | $4,500 |
| 6 | Dee, Ed | Company Stock | $10,000 |
| 7 | Charles, Louis | High Risk Fund | $1,800 |
| 8 | Jay, Jackie | High Risk Fund | $2,500 |
| 9 | Dee, Ed | Low Risk Fund | $5,000 |
| 10 | Dee, Ed | Med Risk Fund | $5,000 |
| 11 | Jay, Jackie | Money Market | $5,000 |
| 12 | Bee, Bernice | Over Seas Fund | $3,200 |
| 13 | Jay, Jackie | Over Seas Fund | $2,200 |
| 14 | | | |

The data in these two columns is displayed horizontally in rows 5 and 6 in Figure 35.

The following explains how the **ISERROR, VLOOKUP, CONCATENATE,** and **IF** functions are used to display data from the worksheet shown in Figure 36 to the worksheet shown in Figure 35. The data displayed in the Retirement Investment Details worksheet (Figure 35) will be based on the name that is typed into cell B2. The purpose of the first several points for this example is to prepare the Data worksheet in Figure 36. Then, the use of the **ISERROR** function combined with the **IF** and **VLOOKUP** functions are explained in the next part of this example.

- Sort the Data worksheet (Figure 36) based on the Name column in ascending order and the Amount Invested column in descending order. After sorting the worksheet, you will see the name of each employee appear several times. This is because an employee can invest their retirement money into eight different investment options.
- Type the number 1 in cell D2 in the Data worksheet.
- Type the following IF function in cell D3: `IF(A3=A2,1+D2,1)` The purpose of this function is to count the number of times each employee name appears in column A of the Data worksheet. The IF function will increase the count by 1 if the employee name in column A repeats. When a different name appears in column A, the logical test will be false and the function will start the count over from 1 (see Figure 37). The **CONCATENATE** function will be used to combine the numbers produced by this function and the employee's name to create a unique value in every row.
- Copy the **IF** function in cell D3 and paste it to the rest of the cells in the worksheet (see Figure 38).

Figure 37 | **Setup of IF Function to Count Duplicate Employee Names**

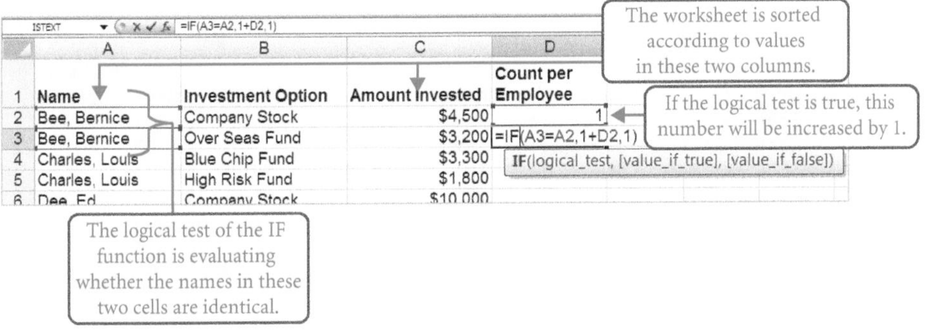


Figure 38 | **Results of IF Function to Count Duplicate Employee Names**

| | A | B | C | D |
|---|---|---|---|---|
| 1 | Name | Investment Option | Amount Invested | Count per Employee |
| 2 | Bee, Bernice | Company Stock | $4,500 | 1 |
| 3 | Bee, Bernice | Over Seas Fund | $3,200 | 2 |
| 4 | Charles, Louis | Blue Chip Fund | $3,300 | 1 |
| 5 | Charles, Louis | High Risk Fund | $1,800 | 2 |
| 6 | Dee, Ed | Company Stock | $10,000 | 1 |
| 7 | Dee, Ed | Low Risk Fund | $5,000 | 2 |
| 8 | Dee, Ed | Med Risk Fund | $5,000 | 3 |
| 9 | Jay, Jackie | Blue Chip Fund | $1,500 | 1 |
| 10 | Jay, Jackie | High Risk Fund | $2,500 | 2 |
| 11 | Jay, Jackie | Money Market | $5,000 | 3 |
| 12 | Jay, Jackie | Over Seas Fund | $2,200 | 4 |
| 13 | Ray, David | Blue Chip Fund | $4,400 | 1 |

This number is the result of the formula 1+D2, which is the value_if_true argument of the IF function.

Because the name in cell A9 does not equal the name in A8, the number 1 appears here, which is the value_if_false argument.

The following explains how the **CONCATENATE** function is used for this example:

- Insert a column to the left of column A in the Data worksheet (Figure 38).
- Type the following **CONCATENATE** function in cell A2: `CONCATENATE(E2,B2)` The purpose of this function is to combine the number produced by the IF function in cell E2 with the employee's name in cell B2. This creates a unique value in each row of the Data worksheet (see Figure 39). The reason for creating this unique value will become evident when the **VLOOKUP** function is used later in this example.
- Copy the **CONCATENATE** function in cell A2 and paste it to the rest of the cells in the worksheet (see Figure 40).

Figure 39 | **Setup of CONCATENATE Function Combining Count and Employee Name**

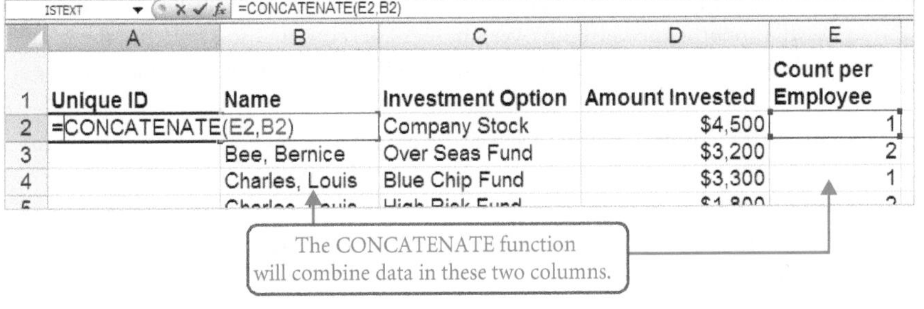

Figure 40 | **Results of CONCATENATE Function Combining Count and Employee Name**

The data in this column makes every row in the worksheet unique.

| | A | B | C | D | E |
|---|---|---|---|---|---|
| 1 | Unique ID | Name | Investment Option | Amount Invested | Count per Employee |
| 2 | 1Bee, Bernice | Bee, Bernice | Company Stock | $4,500 | 1 |
| 3 | 2Bee, Bernice | Bee, Bernice | Over Seas Fund | $3,200 | 2 |
| 4 | 1Charles, Louis | Charles, Louis | Blue Chip Fund | $3,300 | 1 |
| 5 | 2Charles, Louis | Charles, Louis | High Risk Fund | $1,800 | 2 |
| 6 | 1Dee, Ed | Dee, Ed | Company Stock | $10,000 | 1 |
| 7 | 2Dee, Ed | Dee, Ed | Low Risk Fund | $5,000 | 2 |
| 8 | 3Dee, Ed | Dee, Ed | Med Risk Fund | $5,000 | 3 |
| 9 | 1Jay, Jackie | Jay, Jackie | Money Market | $5,000 | 1 |
| 10 | 2Jay, Jackie | Jay, Jackie | High Risk Fund | $2,500 | 2 |
| 11 | 3Jay, Jackie | Jay, Jackie | Over Seas Fund | $2,200 | 3 |
| 12 | 4Jay, Jackie | Jay, Jackie | Blue Chip Fund | $1,500 | 4 |
| 13 | 1Ray, David | Ray, David | Blue Chip Fund | $4,400 | 1 |

## COMMON MISTAKES | Sorting Duplicate Data in a Worksheet

Figure 40 shows the results of counting duplicate data entries in a column for the purposes of creating a unique ID value for each row. The most critical step in this process is sorting the data. You must remember to sort the worksheet using the column that contains duplicate values. Forgetting this step makes it impossible to accurately count the number of times an entry is duplicated in a column.

The following points explain why and how the **ISERROR** function is used for this example. The first set of points is designed to show you what happens if the ISERROR function is not used. The second set of points will then integrate the **ISERROR** function to complete this example.

- Type an equal sign in cell B5 of the Retirement Investment Details worksheet (see Figure 35) followed by the function name VLOOKUP and an open parenthesis. The following shows how each argument of the **VLOOKUP** function is defined.
  - **lookup_value:** `CONCATENATE(B4,$B$2)` The **CONCATENATE** function is defining the lookup value by combining the number in cell B4 with the employee's name in cell B2. Because this example assumes that employees can choose up to eight different options for investing their retirement money, row 4 contains cell locations numbered 1 through 8. The absolute reference used in cell B2 allows the function to be copied and pasted to the rest of the cells in row 5. Type a comma after this argument.
  - **table_array:** `Data!$A$2:$D$13` The table array is the range A2:D13 in the Data worksheet (Figure 40). Both the Data worksheet and the Retirement Investment Details worksheet are in the same workbook. The first column in the table array argument is the combination of the count number produced by the IF function and the employee's name. This combination matches the result of the CONCATENATE function, which is used in the **lookup_value** argument. Type a comma after this argument.
  - **col_index_num:** `3` This will select the employee's investment option, which is column C in the Data worksheet (Figure 40). Type a comma after this argument.
  - **[range_lookup]:** `False` This forces the function to search for exact matches to the lookup value.

- Complete the **VLOOKUP** function by typing a closing parenthesis (see Figure 41) and then press the **Enter** key.
- Copy the **VLOOKUP** function in cell B5 and paste it into the range C5:I5 (see Figure 42).

Figure 41 | **Setup of VLOOKUP Function in Retirement Investment Details Worksheet**

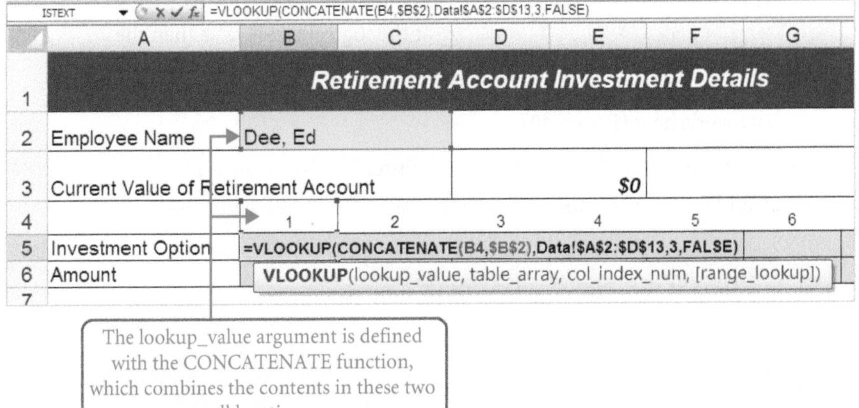


Figure 42 shows the results of the **VLOOKUP** function when it is pasted into the range C5:I5. A different investment option appears in each cell in row 5 because the **CONCATENATE** function is combining a different number with the employee name as the **VLOOKUP** function is pasted to the rest of the cells in the row. However, notice that in the range E5:I5, the error #N/A is displayed. This is because the employee entered into cell B5 is investing his retirement money in only three of the eight available options. In cell 5, the **VLOOKUP** function is looking for 4Dee, Ed in column A of the Data worksheet (see Figure 40), but it does not exist. This produces the #N/A error.

Figure 42 | **Results of VLOOKUP Function in Retirement Investment Details Worksheet**

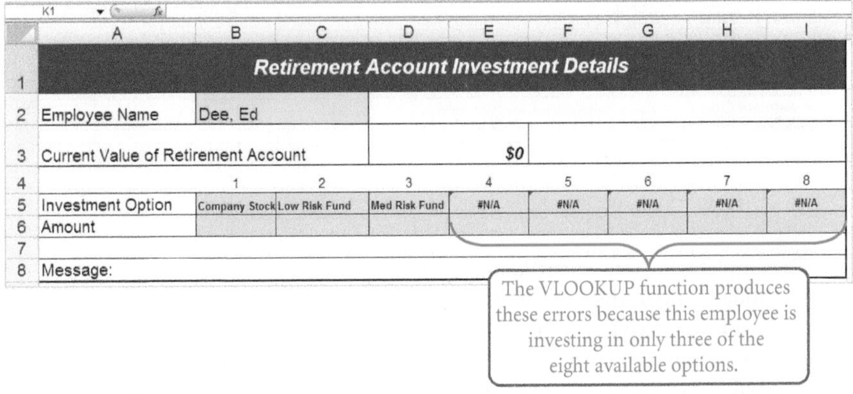


The errors displayed in Figure 42 can be removed by using the **VLOOKUP** function with the **ISERROR** and **IF** functions. The following explains how to recreate the function in cell B5 to display either the employee's investment option or a blank cell.

- Type an equal sign in cell B5 followed by the function name IF and an open parenthesis. The following explains how each argument of the function is defined.
  - **logical_test:** `ISERROR(VLOOKUP(CONCATENATE(B4,$B$2), Data!$A$2:$D$13,3,FALSE))=TRUE` The logical test is evaluating

whether the result of the **ISERROR** function is true. The **ISERROR** function is evaluating the **VLOOKUP** function that was illustrated in Figure 41. If the **VLOOKUP** function produces a #N/A error, the result of the **ISERROR** function will be true, which makes the logical test true. Type a comma after this argument.

- **value_if_true:** " " If the logical test is true, then the IF function will leave the cell blank. Type a comma after this argument.
- **value_if_false:** `VLOOKUP(CONCATENATE(B4,$B$2), Data!$A$2:$D$13,3,FALSE)` If the logical test is false then the **VLOOKUP** function is not producing an error. Therefore, the **VLOOKUP** function will be executed to pull the employee's investment option from the Data worksheet (Figure 40).

- Type a closing parenthesis and press the **Enter** key (see Figure 43).
- Copy and paste the **IF** function into the range C5:I5 (see Figure 44).

Figure 43 | **Setup of IF, ISERROR, and VLOOKUP Functions**

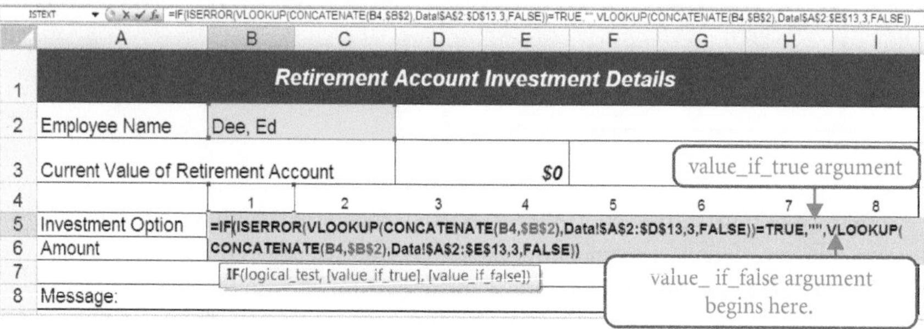


Figure 44 | **Results of the IF, ISERROR, and VLOOKUP Functions**

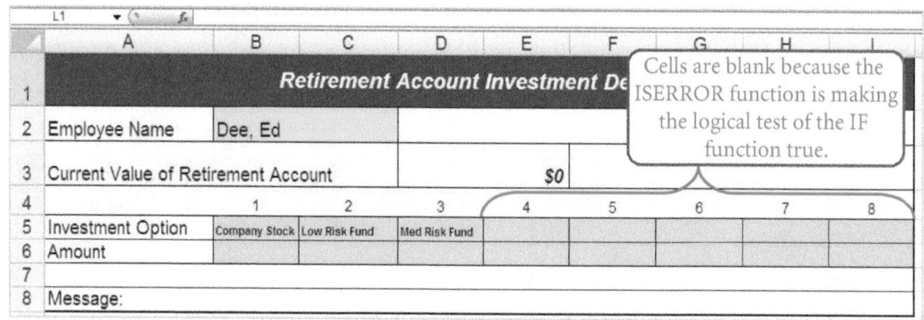


To complete the Retirement Account Investment Details worksheet, functions must be added for the Amount row and the Message. The function used to complete the Amount row, which begins in cell B6, is identical to the function used for the Investment Option row. However, the column index argument for the **VLOOKUP** function will be 4 instead of 3. The purpose of the Message row is to tell the user if a name that was typed into cell B2 does not exist in the Data worksheet (see Figure 40). The following explains these functions and the functions that were created in cells D2 and D3.

- **Amount Row** (begins with cell B6): `IF(ISERROR(VLOOKUP(CONCATENATE(B4,$B$2),Data!$A$2:$D$13,4,FALSE))=TRUE,"",VLOOKUP(CONCATENATE(B4,$B$2),Data!$A$2:$E$13,4,FALSE))`

As previously mentioned, this function is identical to the one illustrated in Figure 43. However, the column index number is changed from 3 to 4. This will pull the dollar amount for each employee's investment.

- **Message** (cell B8): IF(ISTEXT(B2)=FALSE,"",IF(ISERROR (VLOOKUP(CONCATENATE(B4,B2),Data!A2:A13,1,FALSE))=TRUE, "There is no match for the name you entered. Check the spelling or type a new name.","")) The purpose of this function is to check if the name typed into cell B2 is listed at least one time in the Data worksheet. However, the function must first check if anything has been typed into cell B2. If the **ISTEXT** function in the first logical test is false, the cell will be left blank. If the **ISERROR** function in the second logical test is true, the message will tell the user that the name typed into the worksheet could not be found. If the result of the **ISERROR** function is false, the cell will be left blank.
- **Current Value of Retirement Account** (cell D3): Sum(B6:I6) The **SUM** function is totaling all of the values in the Amount row.
- **Initial Instructions** (cell D2): IF(ISTEXT(B2)=TRUE,"","<<<<<Type employee's name here (Last Name, First Name)") This function is evaluating if text data has been typed into cell B2. If cell B2 contains text data, cell D2 will be blank. If there is no text typed into cell B2, instructions will be provided in cell D2 telling the user to type an employee's name. Notice that the greater-than sign is used at the beginning of the message to create an arrow (see Figure 35).

Figure 45 shows the completed Retirement Account Investment Details worksheet. Figure 46 shows how the worksheet appears if a name typed into cell B2 does not match the name from the Data worksheet.

Figure 45 | **Completed Retirement Investment Details Worksheet**

| | A | B | C | D | E | F | G | H | I |
|---|---|---|---|---|---|---|---|---|---|
| 1 | Retirement Account Investment Details | | | | | | | | |
| 2 | Employee Name | Dee, Ed | | | | | | | |
| 3 | Current Value of Retirement Account | | | | $20,000 | | | | |
| 4 | | 1 | 2 | 3 | 4 | 5 | 6 | 7 | 8 |
| 5 | Investment Option | Company Stock | Low Risk Fund | Med Risk Fund | | | | | |
| 6 | Amount | $10,000 | $5,000 | $5,000 | | | | | |
| 7 | | | | | | | | | |
| 8 | Message: | | | | | | | | |

Sum function is adding the values in the range B6:I6.

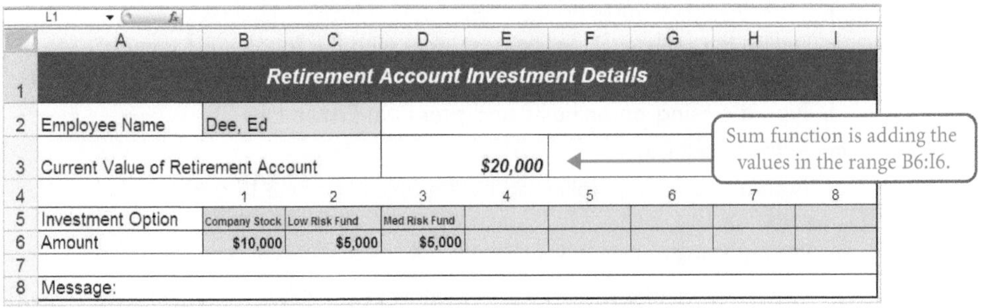

Figure 46 | **Retirement Investment Details Worksheet with Unknown Name**

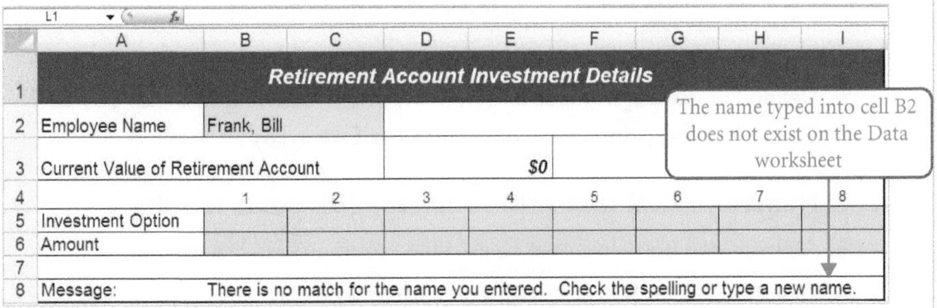

| | A | B | C | D | E | F | G | H | I |
|---|---|---|---|---|---|---|---|---|---|
| 1 | Retirement Account Investment Details | | | | | | | | |
| 2 | Employee Name | Frank, Bill | | | | | | | |
| 3 | Current Value of Retirement Account | | | | $0 | | | | |
| 4 | | 1 | 2 | 3 | 4 | 5 | 6 | 7 | 8 |
| 5 | Investment Option | | | | | | | | |
| 6 | Amount | | | | | | | | |
| 7 | | | | | | | | | |
| 8 | Message: | There is no match for the name you entered. Check the spelling or type a new name. | | | | | | | |

The name typed into cell B2 does not exist on the Data worksheet

>> **Quick Reference**

**ISERROR Function**

1. Activate a cell.
2. Type an equal sign.
3. Type the function name ISERROR and open parenthesis.
4. Type a cell location that contains a formula or function or type a formula or function.
5. Type a closing parenthesis.
6. Press the **Enter** key.

VIDEO WORKSHOP

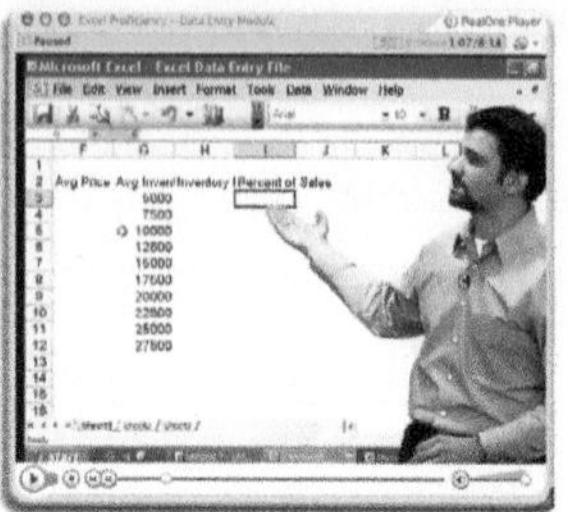

# >> IS Text/IS Number Functions

The purpose of this workshop is to demonstrate the **IS TEXT** and **ISNUMBER** functions. I will be demonstrating the tasks in this workshop on the **IS Text** and **IS Number** videos. The name of the video will appear in parentheses next to the relevant section heading. Open the Excel workbook named ib_e07_istextisnumber. Complete each section of tasks first, and then watch the video pertaining to that section.

1. **IS Text with IF and OR Functions (Video: IS Text)**
   a. Activate cell C3.
   b. Type an equal sign followed by the function name **IF** and an open parenthesis.
   c. Define the logical test of the IF function by typing the following **OR** function: **OR(ISTEXT(A3),ISTEXT(B3))**.
   d. Complete the logical test by typing an equal sign and the word **TRUE**. Then, type a comma.
   e. Define the **value_if_true** argument by typing two quotation marks followed by a comma.
   f. Define the **value_if_false** argument with the following formula: **B3 * A3**.
   g. Type a closing parenthesis and press the **Enter** key.
   h. Activate cell D3.
   i. Type an equal sign followed by the function name **IF** and an open parenthesis.
   j. Repeat steps c. through e.
   k. Define the **value_if_false** argument with the following formula: **(A3 * B3) / 2**.
   l. Type a closing parenthesis and press the **Enter** key.
   m. Activate cell E3.
   n. Type an equal sign followed by the function name **IF** and an open parenthesis.
   o. Repeat steps c. through e.
   p. Define the **value_if_false** argument with the following formula: **C3 + D3**.
   q. Type a closing parenthesis and press the **Enter** key.
   r. Activate cell F3
   s. Type an equal sign followed by the function name **IF** and an open parenthesis.
   t. Repeat steps c. through e.
   u. Define the **value_if_false** argument with the following formula: **E3/12**.
   v. Type a closing parenthesis and press the **Enter** key.

2. **IS Number with IF and AND Functions (Video: IS Number)**
   a. Activate cell B6. Note that cells in the range B6:F6 are merged.
   b. Begin a nested **IF** function by typing an equal sign followed by the function name **IF** and an open parenthesis.
   c. Define the first **logical_test** argument as follows: **OR(ISTEXT(A3),ISTEXT(B3))=TRUE,**

d. Type the following phrase in the first **value_if_true** argument: **"You can only enter numeric values in cells A3 and B3."** Complete the argument by typing a comma.
e. For the **value_if_false** argument, begin a second **IF** function by typing the function name IF followed by an open parenthesis.
f. Define the **logical_test** of the second **IF** function as follows: **AND(ISNUMBER(A3),ISNUMBER(B3))=TRUE,**
g. Define the **value_if_true** argument of the second **IF** function by typing two quotation marks followed by a comma.
h. For the **value_if_false** argument of the second **IF** function, begin a third **IF** function by typing the function name **IF** followed by an open parenthesis.
i. Define the **logical_test** argument of the third **IF** function by typing the following: **ISNUMBER(A3)=FALSE,**
j. Type the following phrase in the **value_if_true** argument for the third **IF** function: **"Enter your annual salary in cell A3."** Complete the argument by typing a comma.
k. Type the following phrase in the **value_if_false** argument: **"Enter the percentage of your salary you wish to invest in cell B3."**.
l. Complete the nested **IF** function by typing three closing parentheses.
m. Type the number **50000** in cell A3.
n. Type the number **10** in cell B3.
o. Type **10 Percent** in cell B3.
p. Save and close the workbook.

## >> IS Error Function

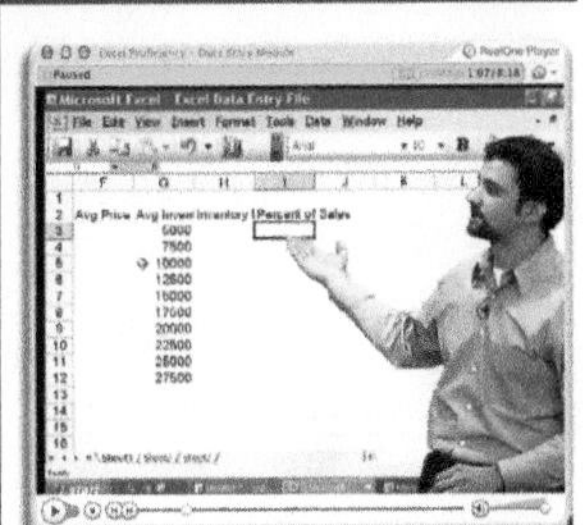

The purpose of this workshop is to demonstrate the IS Error function. I will be demonstrating the tasks in this workshop in the three videos named: **Unique Sequencing**, **IS Error**, and **IS Error and IS Text**. The name of the video will appear in parentheses next to the relevant section heading. Open the Excel file named ib_e07_iserror. Complete each section of tasks first, and then watch the video pertaining to that section.

### 1. Creating a Unique Sequence (Video: Unique Sequencing)

a. Activate the Data worksheet and highlight the range A1:C13.
b. Sort the data based on the Name column in ascending order and the Amount Invested column in descending order.
c. Type the column heading **Count per Employee** in cell D1.
d. Type the number **1** in cell D2.
e. Type an equal sign in cell D3 followed by the function name **IF** and an open parenthesis.
f. Define the logical test of the function with the formula **A3=A2** and type a comma.
g. Define the **value_if_true** argument with the formula **1 + D2** and type a comma.

h. Define the **value_if_false** by typing the number **1**. Complete the function by typing a closing parenthesis and press the **Enter** key.
i. Copy cell D3 and paste it into the range D4:D13.
j. Activate cell A2 and insert a column.
k. Type the column heading **Unique ID** in cell A1.
l. Type an equal sign in cell A2 followed by the function name **CONCATENATE** and an open parenthesis.
m. Type cell **E2** followed by a comma and then cell **B2**.
n. Complete the function by typing a closing parenthesis and press the **Enter** key.
o. Copy cell A2 and paste it into cell A3:A13.

**2. Displaying Vertical Data Horizontally (Video: IS Error)**

a. Activate the Investment Detail worksheet.
b. Activate cell B5 and type an equal sign followed by the function name **IF** and an open parenthesis.
c. Define the logical test of the **IF** function by typing the function name **ISERROR** followed by an open parenthesis.
d. Type the following **VLOOKUP** function after the open parenthesis of the **ISERROR** function: **VLOOKUP(CONCATENATE(B4,$B$2),Data!$A$2:$D$13,3,FALSE)**
e. Complete the **ISERROR** function by typing a closing parenthesis.
f. Complete the logical test of the **IF** function by typing an equal sign followed by the word **TRUE** and a comma.
g. Define the **value_if_true** argument by typing two quotation marks followed by a comma.
h. Define the **value_if_false** argument by typing the same **VLOOKUP** function listed in step d.
i. Complete the **IF** function by typing a closing parenthesis and press the **Enter** key.
j. Copy cell B5 and paste it into the range C5:I5 using the **Formulas** option from the **Paste** icon.
k. Activate cell B6 and type an equal sign followed by the function name **IF** and an open parenthesis.
l. Define the logical test of the **IF** function by typing the function name **ISERROR** followed by an open parenthesis.
m. Type the following **VLOOKUP** function after the open parenthesis of the ISERROR function: **VLOOKUP(CONCATENATE(B4,$B$2),Data!$A$2:$D$13,4,FALSE)**
n. Complete the **ISERROR** function by typing a closing parenthesis.
o. Complete the logical test of the **IF** function by typing an equal sign followed by the word **TRUE** and a comma.
p. Define the **value_if_true** argument by typing two quotation marks followed by a comma.
q. Define the **value_if_false** argument by typing the same **VLOOKUP** function listed in step m.
r. Complete the **IF** function by typing a closing parenthesis and press the **Enter** key.
s. Copy cell B6 and paste it into the range C6:I6 using the **Formulas** option from the **Paste** icon.

**3. Instructions and Messages (Video: IS Error and IS Text)**

a. Activate the Investment Detail worksheet.

b. Activate cell D3 and use the **SUM** function to total the values in the range B6:I6.

c. Activate cell D2 and type an equal sign followed by the function name `IF` and an open parenthesis.

d. Define the **logical_test** argument by typing the following function: `ISTEXT(B2)`.

e. Complete the logical test by typing an equal sign followed by the word `TRUE` and a comma.

f. Define the **value_if_true** argument by typing two quotation marks and a comma.

g. Define the **value_if_false** argument by typing the following phrase: `"<<<<<Type employee's name here (Last Name, First Name)"`

h. Complete the **IF** function by typing a closing parenthesis and press the **Enter** key.

i. Activate cell B8 and begin a nested **IF** function by typing an equal sign, the word `IF`, and an open parenthesis.

j. Define the first **logical_test** argument by typing the following function: `ISTEXT(B2)`

k. Complete the first **logical_test** argument by typing an equal sign followed by the word `FALSE` and a comma.

l. Define the first **value_if_true** argument by typing two quotation marks and a comma.

m. Start the second **IF** function by typing the function name `IF` followed by an open parenthesis.

n. Define the second **logical_test** argument by typing the function name `ISERROR` followed by an open parenthesis.

o. Type the following **VLOOKUP** function after the open parenthesis of the ISERROR function: `VLOOKUP(CONCATENATE(B4,B2),Data!A2:A13,1,FALSE)`

p. Complete the **ISERROR** function by typing a closing parenthesis.

q. Complete the second **logical_test** argument by typing an equal sign followed by the word `TRUE` and a comma.

r. Define the second **value_if_true** argument by typing the following phrase: `"There is no match for the name you entered. Check the spelling or type a new name."`

s. Type a comma and define the **value_if_false** argument by typing two quotation marks.

t. Complete the nested **IF** function by typing two closing parentheses and press the **Enter** key.

u. Type the name `Dee, Ed` in cell B2.

v. Type the name `Charles, Louis` in cell B2.

w. Type your name in cell B2 (Last Name, First Name).

x. Save and close the workbook.

**EXERCISE**

**Why Do I Need This?**

# >> Sales and Profit Plans

One of the key benefits of using Excel to make business decisions is that one spreadsheet design can be used by all managers in a department. This makes it possible for a department or company to execute consistent standards for calculating certain business metrics. For example, a business might have a specific profit requirement for every product it sells. You can design an Excel spreadsheet that includes the calculations for this profit requirement that can be used by every manager making product decisions in the company. However, the challenge of designing a spreadsheet that will be used by other people is that it must provide some direction as to the type of data that needs to be typed into certain cells, and it must notify the user if any data has been typed incorrectly. Without these instructions, you may be looking into many false claims that your spreadsheet does not work. Many instructions and messages can be added to a spreadsheet using the **ISNUMBER**, **ISTEXT**, and **ISERROR** functions.

## Exercise

The purpose of this exercise is to develop a spreadsheet that might be used by the buyers of a small retail company. This spreadsheet will help the buyers plan the price and unit sales for items that will be sold in their company's retail stores. Open the Excel workbook named ib_e07_salesandprofittargets before completing the tasks listed below.

1. Enter the first set of instructions in cell C3 (cells C3:E3 are merged). Use an **IF** function to instruct the user to enter the Item Cost into cell B3. Define each of the arguments for this function as follows:
   a. **logical_test:** `ISNUMBER(B3)=TRUE` Use the **ISNUMBER** function to determine if a number has been typed into cell B3.
   b. **value_if_true:** `""` If a number has been typed into cell B3, then the function should leave the cell blank.
   c. **value_if_false: "<<<Enter the item cost here."** If a number has not been typed into cell B3, then the function should display the instructions. The less-than signs are used to point to cell B3.
2. Use the same **IF** function you created in step 1 to display instructions for the Retail Price in cell C4 (cells C4:E4 are merged). **The logical_test** argument should determine if a number has been typed into cell B4. The **value_if_false** argument should read `"<<<Enter the planned retail price here."`
3. Calculate the Gross Profit in cell B5 using the **ISERROR** and **IF** functions. The formula for calculating the Gross Profit is `B4-B3`. However, if the user types text data in cells B3 or B4, the formula will produce an error. Therefore, use the **ISERROR** function in the **logical_test** argument to determine if the formula B4-B3 produces an error. If the formula produces an error, then leave the cell blank. Otherwise, calculate the Gross Profit.
4. Calculate the Net Profit in cell B6 using the same method described in step 3. The formula for calculating the Net Profit is `B5 - (B4 * 0.1)`. This formula is taking 10% of the retail price and subtracting it from the Gross Profit. The 10% is accounting for any freight, warehousing, and stocking costs. As stated in step 3, use the **ISERROR** function in the **logical_test** argument to check if the formula produces an error. If so, then leave the cell blank.
5. Use an **IF** function to provide instructions in cell D7 (cells D7:E7 are merged). This **IF** function is identical to the one described in step 1. However, the

**ISNUMBER** function in the **logical_test** argument will be evaluating cell C7. The **value_if_false** argument should read **`"<<Override unit sales here."`** The purpose of cell C7 is to allow the buyer to overwrite the calculated Planned Unit Sales number in cell B7 (see next step).

6. Create a three-part nested IF function in cell B7 to calculate the Planned Unit Sales. The purpose of cell B7 is to show the buyer the minimum number of units that must be sold to reach the company's minimum profit target of $10,000 per item. However, as stated in step 5, the buyer can override this number by typing a new sales plan number in cell C7. The following shows how each argument of this nested **IF** function should be defined.
   a. **logical_test:** **`B6<=0`** This test is evaluating if the value in cell B6, which is the Net Profit, is less than or equal to 0. If the net profit is not greater than 0, then the item should not be sold.
   b. **value_if_true:** **`""`** If the first logical test is true, then the function will leave the cell blank. This will prevent the buyer from planning any unit sales because the item is losing money for the company.
   c. **logical_test 2:** **`ISNUMBER(C7)=TRUE`** This is the second **logical_test** of the nested IF function. This logical test is evaluating whether the buyer typed a number into C7. If the buyer wants to overwrite the calculated Planned Unit Sales, a number can be typed into cell C7, which will be displayed in this cell.
   d. **value_if_true 2:** **`C7`** This is the second **value_if_true** argument for the nested IF function. If the buyer typed a number in cell C7, then it will be displayed in this cell.
   e. **logical_test 3:** **`ISERROR(10000/B6)`** This is the third **logical_test** of the **nested IF** function. This logical test will evaluate whether the formula for calculating the Planned Unit Sales produces an error.
   f. **value_if_true 3:** **`""`** This is the third **value_if_true** argument of the nested IF function. If the third logical test is true, then the function will leave the cell blank.
   g. **value_if_false:** **`10000/B6`** This is the **value_if_false** argument for the third IF function. This is the formula for calculating the number of units that must be sold to reach the company's minimum profit target of $10,000. Therefore, the number 10000 is divided by the value in cell B6, which is the Net Profit for the item.

7. Create an **IF** function in cell B8 to calculate the Planned Profit. This **IF** function serves the same purpose as the one created in step 3. Use the **ISERROR** function in the **logical_test** argument to determine if the formula produces an error. If the logical test is true, leave the cell blank. The Planned Profit is calculated by multiplying the Net Profit in cell B6 by the Planned Unit Sales in cell B7 (B6 * B7).

8. Create a four-part nested **IF** function to display a message in cell B10 based on what the buyer types into cells B3, B4, and C7 (cells B10:E10 are merged). Define each argument of the function as follows.
   a. **logical_test:** **`OR(ISTEXT(B3),ISTEXT(B4))=TRUE`** This test is determining whether the buyer typed text data into either cell B3 or cell B4.
   b. **value_if_true:** **`"This spreadsheet will accept only numeric values."`** If the first logical test is true, then the function will display this message telling the buyer that only numeric values can be typed into the spreadsheet.
   c. **logical_test 2:** **`AND(ISNUMBER(B3),ISNUMBER(B4))=FALSE`** This is the second logical test of the **nested IF** function. This is determining if a number has been typed into *both* cells B3 and B4.

d. **value_if_true 2:** `""` This is the second **value_if_true** argument for the **nested IF** function. If the second logical test is true, it is assumed that the buyer has not finished typing the cost and retail price information into cells B3 and B4. Therefore, the cell will be left blank.

e. **logical_test 3:** `B6 <= 0` This is the third logical test for the **nested IF** function. This test is determining if the Net Profit is less than or equal to 0. This is the same logical test that was used in step 6a.

f. **value_if_true 3:** `"Net Profit is negative—Do not purchase this item at the current plan."` This is the third **value_if_true** argument for the **nested IF** function. If the third logical test is true, then the function will notify the buyer that the company will lose money if this item is sold.

g. **logical_test 4:** `B8 < 10000` This is the fourth logical test of the **nested IF** function. This test will determine if the Planned Profit in cell B8 is less than the company's minimum profit target of $10,000. The reason for this test is to ensure that any sales number the buyer types into cell C7 achieves the company's minimum profit target of $10,000.

h. **value_if_true 4:** `"Item is currently planned below the company's minimum profit standard of $10,000."` This is the fourth value_if_true argument of the **nested IF** function. If the fourth logical test is true, then the function will notify the buyer that the current plan is not sufficient to achieve the company's minimum profit target.

i. **value_if_false:** `""` This is the **value_if_false** argument for the fourth **IF** function. If all logical tests in the function are false, then there is no need to display a message. Therefore, the cell will be left blank.

9. Type an Item Cost of **12.35** in cell B3 and a Retail Price of **15.99** in cell B4. What is the minimum number of units that must be sold to reach the company's minimum profit target of $10,000?
10. Type the number **2500** in cell C7. Notice the message in cell B10 stating that the current plan is below the company's minimum profit target.
11. Determine how much the buyer can pay a supplier for this item by decreasing the item cost in cell B3. At what cost will the item achieve the minimum profit target of $10,000?
12. Type a retail price of **9.99** in cell B4. Notice the message informing the buyer that the Net Profit is negative. In addition, notice that the Planned Unit Sales in cell B7 is blank.
13. Type the word **"Ten"** in cell B3. Notice the message in cell B10.
14. Type an item cost of **11.39** in cell B3. What retail price should the buyer charge if he is trying to generate $25,000 of profit on planned unit sales of 2,500?
15. Delete the values in cells B3, B4, and C7.
16. Save and close the workbook.

# >> What's Wrong with This Spreadsheet?

PROBLEM & EXERCISE

## Problem

You are working as a director for a small finance company that manages investments for approximately 100 customers. These customers trust your firm to invest money they will need for future events such as retirement, children's college tuition, or a new home purchase. One of the analysts in the firm creates an Excel spreadsheet to help the company manage these investments more efficiently. He explains that a customer's investments will automatically be grouped and displayed into six investment categories. He attaches the Excel file to an e-mail and includes the following points in his message.

1. I developed this Excel spreadsheet using data for only a few customers so you can see how it works. I added the investment information for the following customers to the Data worksheet: Bill Frank, Louis Charles, Olivia Angelo, Bernice Blu, and Albert Henry.
2. Type a customer's name in cell B2 and you will see his investments displayed in rows 5 and 6. Row 7 shows the percentage each investment category contributes to the customer's total account value. You must type the customer's last name first followed by a comma and then the first name.
3. Thanks for looking at this file! I really think this Excel spreadsheet will help us stay on top of the market by evaluating more investments over a shorter period of time.

## Exercise

The Excel file the analyst attached to the e-mail is named ib_e07_customerinvestments. Would you be comfortable using this file to make investment decisions for your customers? Consider the following points:

1. Test the spreadsheet by typing a few names listed at the end of point 1 above into cell B2 in the Investment Detail worksheet. Follow the directions the analyst provides in point 2. Does the spreadsheet work? Do you see the customer's investments in rows 5 and 6?
2. Does the spreadsheet accurately display and total a customer's investments?
3. Does the spreadsheet show any error codes? Why?
4. Try typing your own name in cell B2. What happens?
5. Did the spreadsheet provide any instructions or messages as you typed names into B2? What messages or instructions would you add?

What's wrong with this spreadsheet? Write a short answer for each of the questions listed above. Then, fix any errors you find. In addition, add any instructions or messages to the Investment Detail worksheet that you identified in question 5.

Getty Images, Inc.—Photodisk

## Excel in Practice | Anecdote

**Solution**

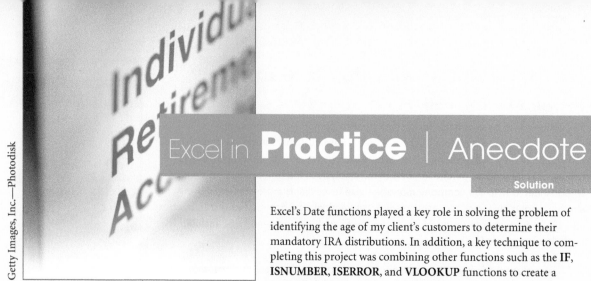

Excel's Date functions played a key role in solving the problem of identifying the age of my client's customers to determine their mandatory IRA distributions. In addition, a key technique to completing this project was combining other functions such as the **IF**, **ISNUMBER**, **ISERROR**, and **VLOOKUP** functions to create a spreadsheet that would be easy to use by other analysts working in the firm. After completing the project, we ran several tests to ensure that the spreadsheet was accurately calculating each customer's age and the required withdrawal amounts from the IRA accounts.

## Assignment

1. Open the file named ib_e07_iraproject. This file contains data similar to that used in the project that was explained in the anecdote.
2. The purpose of this assignment is to complete the IRA Analysis worksheet. This worksheet contains four items in column A that need to be displayed when a customer's name is typed into cell B2. The following is a list of formulas and features that must be designed into this worksheet:
   a. Cell B3 should display the date the customer will reach the age of 70.5.
   b. Cell B4 should indicate (Yes or No) if the customer is required to withdraw money from her IRA. Customers must make a withdrawal if they reached the age of 70.5 on or before December 31 last year.
   c. Cell B5 should calculate the required withdrawal amount if cell B4 indicates Yes. This is calculated by dividing the current value of the IRA account (column C in the Customer Data worksheet) by one of the distribution factors in column B of the Distribution Factor worksheet. The formula is `Current Value of IRA Account / Distribution Factor`. You will need to determine the customer's age *on his birthday last year* to identify the distribution factor that should be used in this calculation.
   d. Cell C5 in the IRA Analysis worksheet should allow the user to type an alternate IRA Distribution Amount. If a number is typed into cell C5, it should appear in cell B5.
   e. Cell B7 should be used to notify the user if the customer name typed into cell B2 does not exist, or if the alternate distribution amount typed into cell C5 is less than the required distribution that is calculated in item 2**c**.
3. Add any instructions you think are appropriate to the worksheet.
4. Format the spreadsheet so that it has a professional appearance and is easy to read.

## Questions for Discussion

1. The anecdote discussed freeing up the analysts' time through the use of Excel. What other benefits can electronic spreadsheets bring to a company like an investment firm?

2. The author mentions in the anecdote that the spreadsheet was tested. Explain why it is important to test a spreadsheet such as the one described in this anecdote. What are some key points you would hope to learn or validate from testing a spreadsheet?

3. The anecdote mentioned that several functions were used together to produce a spreadsheet that could be used by any analyst in the firm. What are the benefits of creating a spreadsheet that can be used by several people? What techniques can you apply that will make a spreadsheet flexible and easy to use?

# > Review Questions

The following questions are related to the concepts addressed in this chapter. There are three types of questions: Short Answer, True or False, and Fill in the Blank. If your answer to a True or False question is False, write a short explanation as to why you think the statement is not true.

1. The ____________ function will always display the current date in a cell.

2. Explain why it is best not type the current date into a cell when calculating data such as a person's age or the amount of time a machine has been in use at a factory.

3. The date Serial Number for September 15, 2007, is 39340. What is the date Serial Number for October 15, 2007?

4. True or False: If a number appears in a cell after typing a date, the date was typed incorrectly. For example, 4/12/2007 will appear as a number instead of a date.

5. True or False: The **YEAR, MONTH,** and **DAY** functions are used only to define the three arguments of the **DATE** function.

6. If you wanted to add 10 years to the date 10/21/2007, explain why adding 3650 days would not give you a result of 10/21/2017.

7. What would be the result of the following **CONCATENATE** function if it were typed into a cell: =CONCATENATE("A3"," ","B3")

8. True or False: If the **#Name?** error appears in a cell when using the **CONCATENATE** function, there is an error in one of the cells that is used in the arguments of the function.

9. The number ____________ will appear in a cell as a result of the following **LEN** function: `=LEN("Vice President")`

10. The number ____________ will appear in a cell as a result of the following **SEARCH** function: `=SEARCH(",","Birds, And, Trees",9)`

11. True or False: Spaces cannot be used in the **find_text** argument of a **SEARCH** function because spaces are not recognized as characters in Text functions.

12. The letter ____________ will appear in a cell as a result of the following **MID** function: `=MID("Outstanding",5,1)`

13. True or False: The following **IF** function can be used to evaluate if a number was typed into cell A3: `=IF(ISNUMBER(A3)="True","Yes","No")`

14. Explain how the **ISERROR** function can be used to prevent an error code from appearing in a cell.

15. To create a column of unique values in a worksheet that contains data that is duplicated several times, the worksheet must be ____________ based on the column that contains ____________ data.

# Skills Exam

The following exam is designed to test your ability to recognize and execute the Excel skills presented in this chapter. Read each question carefully and answer the questions in the order they are listed. You should be able to complete this exam in 60 minutes or less.

1. Open the file named ib_e07_chapter7skillsexam.
2. Activate the Color Detail worksheet and use the **CONCATENATE** function in cell A2 to combine the data in cells B2 and D2. The data in cell B2 must appear first.
3. Copy cell A2 and paste it into the range A3:A23.
4. Activate the Order Worksheet and enter the **TODAY** function in cell B6.
5. Calculate the Delivery Date in cell B8 by adding cell B7 to today's date in cell B6. Format the date in cell B8 to the Short Date format.
6. Use the **DATE** function to calculate the In Store Date in cell B9. The In Store Date will be exactly 3 months after the Received Date in cell B8. Use the **YEAR**, **MONTH**, and **DAY** functions to define the **year**, **month**, and **day** arguments of the **DATE** function.
7. In cell D11, enter the **LEN** function to count the characters in cell B5.
8. In cell C11, use the **SEARCH** function to count the number of characters in cell B5 up to and including the space. The function should begin counting from the first character in the cell. Note that there is only one space in the Manufacturer Model Number entered in cell B5.
9. In cell B11, use the **MID** function to select only the last two digits of the Manufacturer Model Number entered in cell B5. You must use cells C11 and D11 when defining the arguments of this function.
10. Use an **IF** function in cell B13 to calculate the Order Quantity in Cartons. Use the **ISNUMBER** function in the **logical_test** argument to determine if a number has been typed into cell C13. If the logical test is true, then display whatever number had been typed into cell C13. If the logical test is false, calculate the Order Quantity in Cartons by dividing B11 into B10.
11. Create a two-part nested **IF** function in cell B17 to display one of three different outputs. Use the **ISTEXT** function in the first logical test to determine if text data has been typed into cell C13. If the first logical test is true, display the message **"You can type only numeric data into cell C13."** The second logical test should evaluate whether cell B14 is equal to cell B10. If cell B14 does not equal B10, display the message **"Order quantity does not match unit sales plan."** If both logical tests are false, leave cell B17 blank.
12. Use an **IF** function to display instructions in cell A2. Use the **OR** function in the **logical_test** argument to determine if a number or text data has been typed into cell B4. If the logical test is true, leave cell A2 blank. If the logical test is false, display the instruction **"Enter an item description or number in cell B4."**
13. Use the **VLOOKUP**, **ISERROR**, and **IF** functions in cell C4 to display the colors of the item typed into cell B4. Use an **ISERROR** function in the **logical_test** argument of an **IF** function to determine whether the **VLOOKUP** function produces an error. If the logical test is true, then leave cell C4 blank. If the logical test is false, then execute the **VLOOKUP** function. The following explains how each argument of the **VLOOKUP** function should be defined.
    a. **lookup_value:** Use the **CONCATENATE** function to combine the data in cells B4 and C3. Cell B4 must be added to the function first followed by cell C3. Add an absolute reference to cell B4.
    b. **table_array:** The range A2:D23 in the Color Detail worksheet. You must use an absolute reference on this range.
    c. **col_index**_num: **3**
    d. [**range_lookup**]: **FALSE**
14. Copy cell C4 and paste it into the range D4:I4 using the **Formulas** option.
15. Save and close your workbook.

# Challenge Questions

The following questions are designed to test your ability to apply the Excel skills you have learned to complete a business objective. Use your knowledge of Excel and your creativity to answer these questions. For most questions, there are several possible ways to complete the objective.

1. Open the Excel workbook named ib_e07_challengea. This file contains a list of machine serial numbers in column A. The serial number is divided into four parts separated by one space. The first part is the model number of the machine. The second part is the capacity of the machine in pounds. The third part is the year the machine was manufactured. The fourth part is the processing time of the machine in hours. Use the information contained in these serial numbers to create a spreadsheet with the following information and features:

   a. Show the model number for each machine in a separate column.

   b. Show the age of the machine based on today's date in a separate column.

   c. Calculate the number of batches *each* machine can produce depending on the operating hours of the factory. A batch is calculated by dividing the processing time of the machine in hours into the factory operating hours. Create the spreadsheet so that a user can enter the factory operating hours in one cell that will be used to calculate the batches for all machines.

   d. Calculate the total capacity for each machine by multiplying the capacity of each machine in pounds by the number of batches you calculated in step 1c.

   e. Show the total capacity of the factory by summing the total capacity for all machines.

   f. Include any formatting and instructions that would make your spreadsheet easy to read and use.

2. Open the Excel workbook named ib_e07_challengeb. The DJIA Trend worksheet shows the adjusted average close of the Dow Jones Industrial Average every month for the past 4 years. Create a spreadsheet using this data that contains the following information and features:

   a. Allow the user to type a year into a cell that will be used to display the data in step b.

   b. Display the adjusted closing price of the DJIA *horizontally in a row* for 12 months based on the year that was typed into a cell by a user in step a.

   c. Calculate the percent change of the DJIA for all 12 months in a row below the adjusted closing price that was constructed in step b.

   d. Construct your spreadsheet so that no error codes appear in any cell displaying data.

   e. Include any formatting and instructions that would make your spreadsheet easy to read and use.

3. Research the *monthly* adjusted closing stock price for any three public companies for the years 2004 and 2005. Place your data into an Excel worksheet (you can download this data from the Internet for free from a site such as Yahoo Finance). Construct a spreadsheet that allows the user to type a stock symbol in one cell and the year in another. Display the adjusted closing price for the stock and the year typed by the user. Your spreadsheet should include the same information and features listed in steps b through e in question 2.

# Managing Large Volumes of Data

## Chapter Goals

The purpose of this chapter is to review tools that you can use to manage large volumes of data in Excel. Excel can store over 1 million rows of data in a single worksheet; however, summarizing and analyzing this volume of data can be challenging. Although Microsoft Access is usually the tool of choice to manage and analyze large volumes of data, Excel includes several tools you can use to perform this task. In the first section of this chapter, you will learn how PivotTables summarize large amounts of data into a two dimensional grid using various mathematical computations such as Sum, Average, Count, and so on. The second section of this chapter will then review three additional tools that are used to apply specific functions to analyze large volumes of data: Filters, Subtotals, and List Boxes.

## >> Excel | Skill Sets

**PivotTables**

- Creating a New PivotTable
- Adding Fields and Changing Field Settings
- Applying Filters to Fields
- Adding and Removing Report Totals
- Adding Formulas (Calculated Fields)
- Sorting Data
- PivotCharts

**Tools for Selecting and Summarizing Data**

- Filters
- Subtotals
- Adding the Developer Tab
- List Boxes

Getty Images, Inc.—Digital Vision

## Excel in Practice | Anecdote

### Managing Data for a Strategy Team

When I worked in the Strategic Planning department for a large retail corporation, we frequently worked with large volumes of data. The company managed almost 2,000 stores and collected customer transaction data from every cash register in every store. This amounted to almost 10,000 cash registers transmitting sales transactions to the company's database everyday. As a result, most analytical projects that I managed usually involved thousands of rows of data. To analyze this volume of data, I usually used tools such as Microsoft Access. For one project in particular, however, the team asked me to use Excel to analyze over 7,500 rows of data. This was a large project that was managed by a team of 20 people, and involved the financial and physical evaluation of over 1,500 stores across the U.S. The data assembled for this project included five years of key statistics for every store in the company, such as population growth, sales, number of competitor stores, and the average distance customers traveled to get to the store. Most members on the team were not familiar with Access, but they all used Excel. In addition, the type of analysis that a team member needed to conduct would vary depending on the district of stores that was being evaluated. For example, some team members needed to focus on statistics such as population growth; others needed to focus on the growth in the number of competitors. I knew how to do this type of analysis in Access, but was not sure if I could accomplish the same results using Excel.

>> Continued later in this chapter

# PivotTables

Skill Set

PivotTables are a valuable Excel feature used for summarizing and analyzing large volumes of data. This section demonstrates how a PivotTable is used to evaluate customer shopping patterns for a large retail corporation. Most business executives would agree that the level of success you achieve in any industry depends on how well you listen to and stay in touch with your customers. This usually requires the collection and evaluation of large amounts of data. For example, Figure 1 shows a worksheet containing customer shopping patterns for stores in three regions of a hypothetical retail corporation (East, West, and South). The worksheet contains five years of data for each region, and 750 rows of data. It can be a challenge to evaluate this data and identify any significant trends in customer buying patterns; however, a PivotTable can quickly turn this large volume of data into valuable trend information.

Figure 1 | **Retail Customer Data**

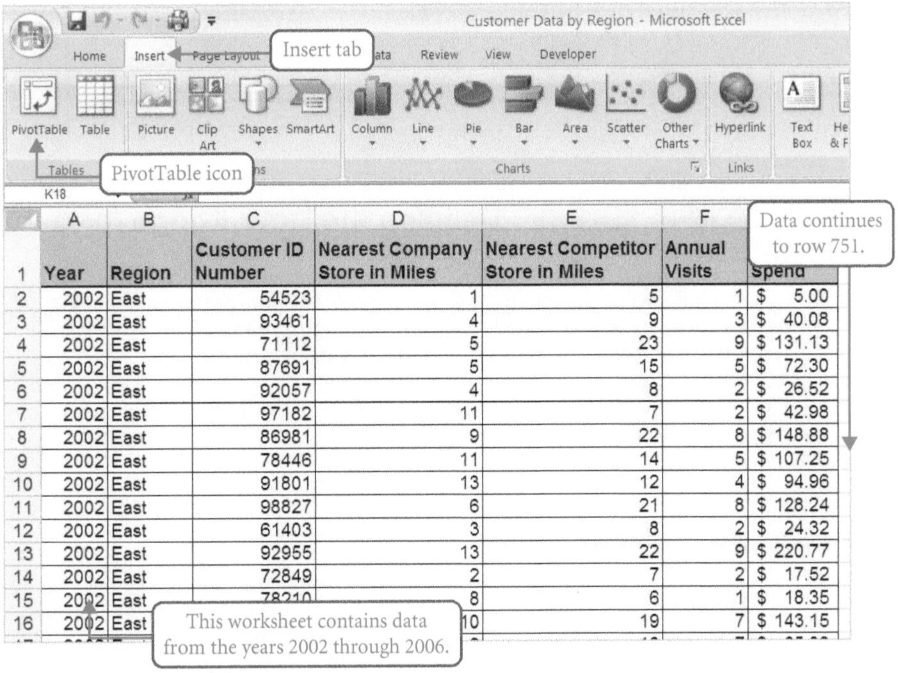

Customer Data by Region - Microsoft Excel

Home | Insert | Page Layout | Data | Review | View | Developer

Insert tab

PivotTable | Table | Picture | Clip Art | Shapes | SmartArt | Column | Line | Pie | Bar | Area | Scatter | Other Charts | Hyperlink | Text Box | He & F

Tables | Charts | Links

PivotTable icon

K18

Data continues to row 751.

| | A | B | C | D | E | F | G |
|---|---|---|---|---|---|---|---|
| 1 | Year | Region | Customer ID Number | Nearest Company Store in Miles | Nearest Competitor Store in Miles | Annual Visits | Spend |
| 2 | 2002 | East | 54523 | 1 | 5 | 1 | $ 5.00 |
| 3 | 2002 | East | 93461 | 4 | 9 | 3 | $ 40.08 |
| 4 | 2002 | East | 71112 | 5 | 23 | 9 | $ 131.13 |
| 5 | 2002 | East | 87691 | 5 | 15 | 5 | $ 72.30 |
| 6 | 2002 | East | 92057 | 4 | 8 | 2 | $ 26.52 |
| 7 | 2002 | East | 97182 | 11 | 7 | 2 | $ 42.98 |
| 8 | 2002 | East | 86981 | 9 | 22 | 8 | $ 148.88 |
| 9 | 2002 | East | 78446 | 11 | 14 | 5 | $ 107.25 |
| 10 | 2002 | East | 91801 | 13 | 12 | 4 | $ 94.96 |
| 11 | 2002 | East | 98827 | 6 | 21 | 8 | $ 128.24 |
| 12 | 2002 | East | 61403 | 3 | 8 | 2 | $ 24.32 |
| 13 | 2002 | East | 92955 | 13 | 22 | 9 | $ 220.77 |
| 14 | 2002 | East | 72849 | 2 | 7 | 2 | $ 17.52 |
| 15 | 2002 | East | 78210 | 8 | 6 | 1 | $ 18.35 |
| 16 | 2002 | East | [illegible] | 10 | 19 | 7 | $ 143.15 |

This worksheet contains data from the years 2002 through 2006.

## Creating a New PivotTable

This example shows the construction of a PivotTable using the data in Figure 1 to summarize the five-year trend in Annual Visits (column F) and Annual Spend (column G) for each region. In addition, the distance the customers live from the company's stores is compared to the distance they live to a competitor's store (column D vs. E). The results of this analysis could be used by a marketing manager to develop specialized advertising and promotional strategies for each region to maintain and grow a company's business. The following explains how the PivotTable is initially created.

- Click the down arrow of the **PivotTable** icon in the **Insert** tab of the Ribbon and then select the **PivotTable** option. This will open the **Create PivotTable** dialog box.
- Click the range finder next to the **Table/Range** box. Highlight all of the data on the worksheet including the column headings and then press the **Enter** key. If you activated any cell location in your data range prior to opening the **PivotTable** dialog box, Excel will come up with a suggested cell range. Check this range to ensure it covers all the data you need to create your PivotTable.

- Select the New Worksheet option near the bottom of the **Create PivotTable** dialog box (see Figure 2). This will place the PivotTable in a new worksheet in the workbook.
- Click the **OK** button at the bottom of the **Create PivotTable** dialog box. This will add a new worksheet that contains the tools you need to build the PivotTable (see Figure 3).

Figure 2 | **Settings in the Create PivotTable Dialog Box**

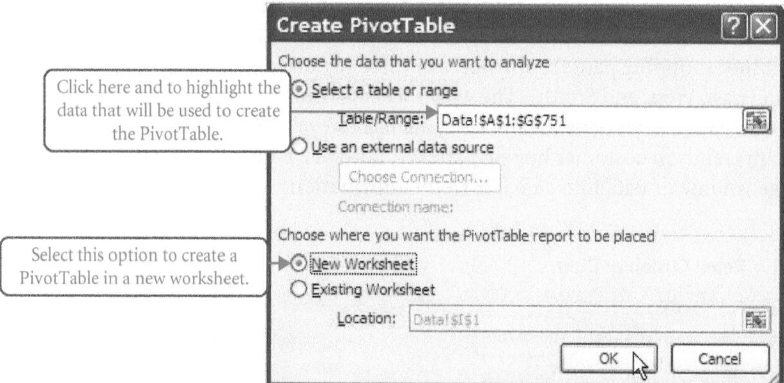


## COMMON MISTAKES | Defining the Data Range for a PivotTable

When defining the Table/Range in the **Create PivotTable** dialog box, be sure to include the column headings in the first row of the range. These column headings will become the field names in the PivotTable Field List. If there are no column headings included in your data range, the PivotTable Field List will show the value that is typed into the first cell of each column. This will make it difficult to identify what data you are placing into the PivotTable Report.

Figure 3 | **Tools for Creating a PivotTable**

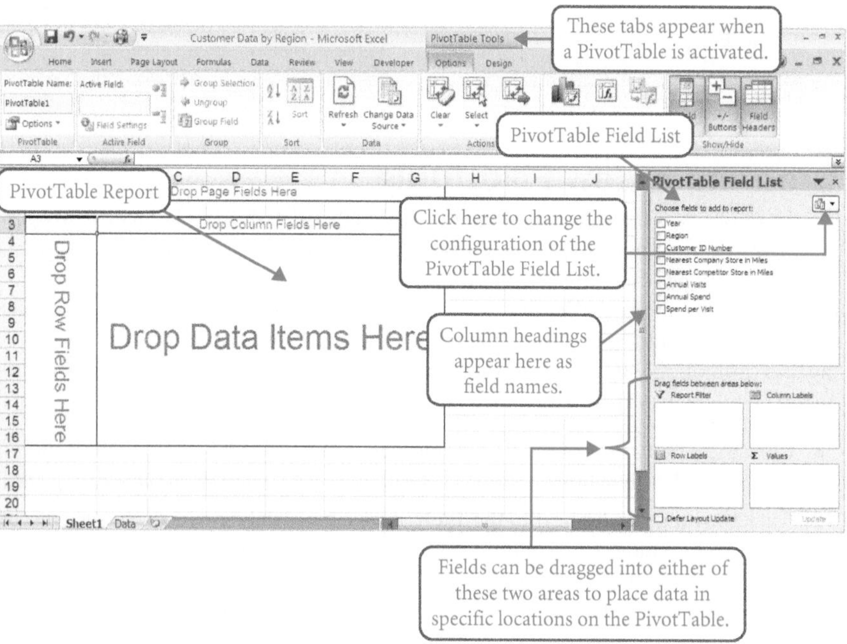

## COMMON MISTAKES | You Can't Drag Fields onto This PivotTable

If your PivotTable looks similar the following figure, you will not be able to click and drag fields onto it from the PivotTable Field List. You must first change the settings in the **PivotTable Options** dialog box. To do this, click anywhere in the blank PivotTable and then click the **Options** icon in the **Options** tab of the Ribbon. This will open the **PivotTable Options** dialog box. Click the **Display** tab at the top of the **PivotTable Options** dialog box, and select the **Classic PivotTable layout (enables dragging of fields in the grid)** option; then, click the **OK** button at the bottom of the dialog box to apply this setting to your PivotTable.

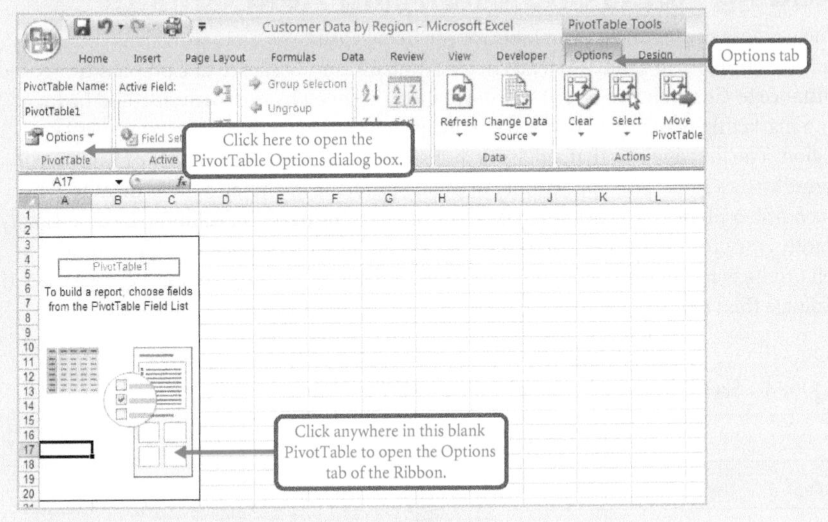


Figure 3 shows the tools that are used to construct a PivotTable. The following is a brief definition of each one:

- **PivotTable Field List:** This is a list of the column headings that are contained in the first row of the Table/Range in the **Create PivotTable** dialog box (see Figure 2). When building PivotTables, each column of data is referred to as a *field*. For example, the column heading Annual Visits in cell F1 in Figure 1 is considered the Annual Visits field when constructing a PivotTable. Fields from the upper area of the PivotTable Field List can be dragged down to one of the four locations in the lower section to place data onto the PivotTable Report.
- **PivotTable Report:** This area is used to construct and analyze the final results of the PivotTable. Fields can be dragged from the PivotTable Field List over to the PivotTable Report to place data in specific locations.
- **PivotTable Tools:** When a PivotTable is created or activated, the **Options** and **Design** tabs get added to the Ribbon (see Figure 3). These tabs contain commands that are used to adjust the settings and appearance of the PivotTable.

>> **Quick Reference**

**Creating a New PivotTable**

1. Click the drop-down arrow of the **PivotTable** icon in the **Insert** tab of the Ribbon and then select the **PivotTable** option.
2. Define the Table/Range in the **Create PivotTable** dialog box. If a range is provided, check it to ensure it contains all the data that is required for your PivotTable. To create a new range, click the range finder, highlight the range of cells that contain data for the PivotTable, and press the **Enter** key.
3. Select either New Worksheet or Existing Worksheet near the bottom of the **Create PivotTable** dialog box.
4. Click the **OK** button at the bottom of the **Create PivotTable** dialog box.

> **COMMON MISTAKES | Data Consistency Within a Column**
>
> Each column of data that is used for a PivotTable must contain only numeric or text data and not a combination of both. If a column contains a mix of both types of data, the PivotTable will not be able to conduct mathematical calculations and summaries. This problem occurs mostly in situations where the letters NA are used for a numeric value that is not available for specific row of data. Instead of using the letters NA, it is better to leave the cell blank or use the number zero.

## Adding Fields and Changing Field Settings

The purpose of creating a PivotTable for the Retail Customer Data worksheet (Figure 1) in this example is to evaluate trends in the Annual Visits, Distance to Company Store, and Distance to Competitor Store. The information provided by this analysis could be used by a marketing manager to develop specific promotion and advertising strategies by region. The first analysis that will be demonstrated is the average number of times a customer visits a store. The opportunity of selling products in a retail store is measured by the number of visits a customer makes to a store. If this trend is declining, it could significantly compromise the growth of the business because there are fewer opportunities to sell products to a customer. Figure 4 provides a sketch of how a PivotTable can be used to evaluate this trend.

Figure 4 | **Sketch Showing Design of Annual Visit Trend Table**

| | 2002 | 2003 | 2004 | 2005 | 2006 |
|---|---|---|---|---|---|
| East | | | | | |
| West | | Average store visits per customer will be displayed here | | | |
| South | | | | | |
| Total Company | | | | | |

Each row will show the five-year store visit trend for each region and for the entire company.

The following explains how the sketch in Figure 4 is produced by using the PivotTable tools shown in Figure 3.

- Click anywhere in the PivotTable Report section. This will show the PivotTable Field List, and activate the **Options** and **Design** tabs on the Ribbon.
- Click the Year field in the PivotTable Field List and then drag it over to the Column Fields section of the PivotTable report. This will show the years 2002 through 2006 across the top of the PivotTable report (see Figure 8). You can also click and drag the Year field into the Column Labels section in the lower area of the PivotTable Field List. This will place the years 2002 through 2006 across the top of the PivotTable report.
- Click the Region field in the PivotTable Field List, and drag it over to the Row Fields section of the PivotTable Report. This will list the three regions down the left side of the report. You can also click and drag this field into the Row Labels section in the lower area of the PivotTable Field list.
- Click the Annual Visits field in the PivotTable Field List, and drag it to the Data section of the PivotTable Report. As soon as this field is dragged into the PivotTable Report, all 750 rows of data are immediately summed for each region for every year. This data will be changed to *average* visits per customer by adjusting the field properties, which is covered next. You can also click and drag this field into the Values section in the lower area of the PivotTable Field list.

Figure 5 shows the process of dragging fields from the PivotTable Field List to the PivotTable Report. Notice that an icon appears when a field is dragged over to the PivotTable Report indicating where a field is being placed.

Figure 5 | **Dragging Fields into the PivotTable Report**

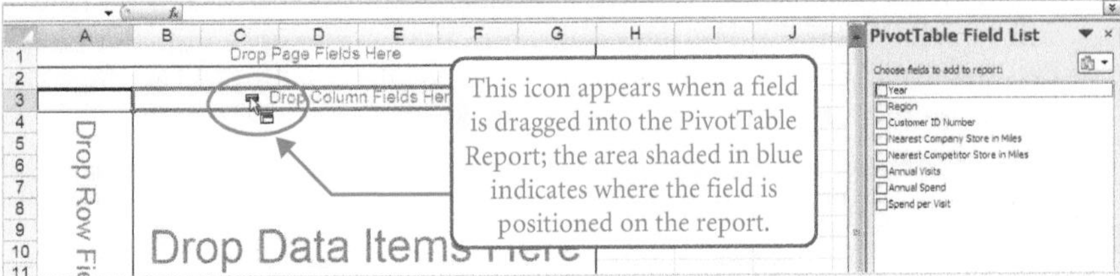


Figure 6 shows the results of adding the Year field to the Column Fields section of the PivotTable report. Notice that this field also appears in the Column Labels section in the lower area of the PivotTable Field List.

Figure 6 | **Column Fields Section of the PivotTable Report**

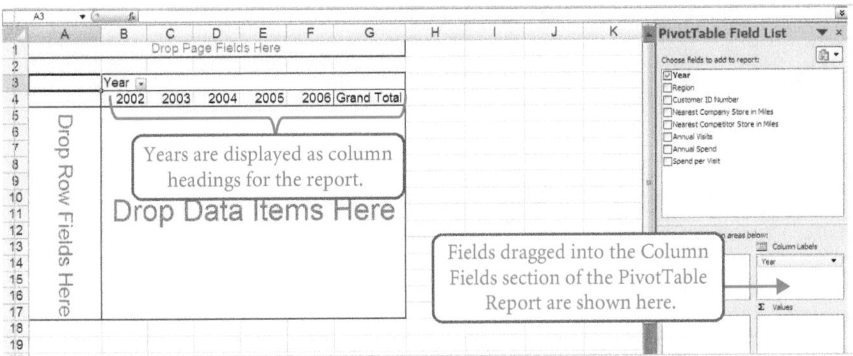


Figure 7 shows the completed PivotTable designed to match the sketch shown in Figure 4. Notice that the Annual Visits field, which was dragged into the Data section of the PivotTable Report, is shown in the Values section in the lower area of the PivotTable Field List. The words *Sum of* precede the field name because the PivotTable is showing the sum of all the Annual visits.

Figure 7 | **Region and Annual Visits Fields Added to the PivotTable Report**

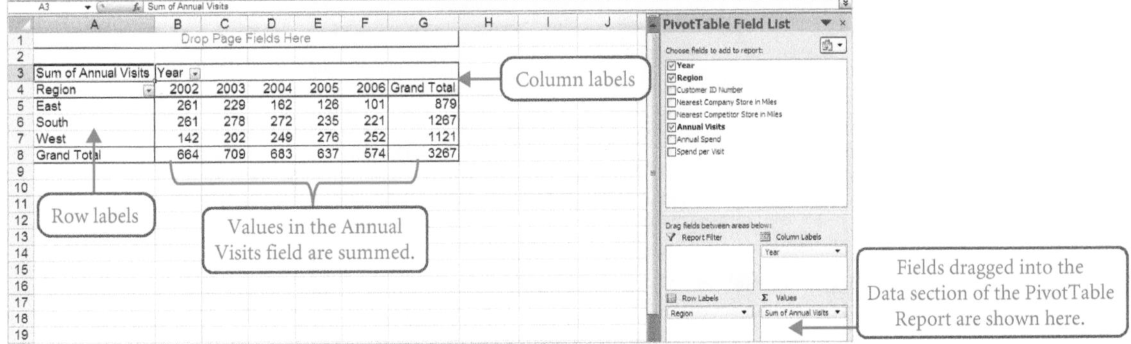

| Sum of Annual Visits | Year | | | | | |
|---|---|---|---|---|---|---|
| Region | 2002 | 2003 | 2004 | 2005 | 2006 | Grand Total |
| East | 261 | 229 | 162 | 126 | 101 | 879 |
| South | 261 | 278 | 272 | 235 | 221 | 1267 |
| West | 142 | 202 | 249 | 276 | 252 | 1121 |
| Grand Total | 664 | 709 | 683 | 637 | 574 | 3267 |

The goal for the PivotTable sketch shown in Figure 4 is to show the average customer visits per store. The sum of the Annual Visits field in Figure 7 will be changed to an average by adjusting the field settings. The following explains how this is accomplished.

- Double-click the Annual Visits field in the PivotTable Report (see cell A3 in Figure 7). Because the annual visits are being summed for all customers by region by year, Excel renames the field Sum of Annual Visits. Double-clicking the field will open the **Value Field Settings** dialog box. You can also open the **Value Field Settings** dialog box by clicking the field and then selecting the **Field Settings** icon in the **Options** tab of the Ribbon (see Figure 8).
- Click the **Average** option from the list of mathematical functions in **Summarize by** tab in the dialog box (see Figure 9).
- Click the **Number Format** button at the bottom of the dialog box. This will open the **Number** tab of the **Format Cells** dialog box. Select the **Number** option and set the decimal places to 1.
- Click the **OK** button at the bottom of the **Value Field Settings** dialog box. This will change the results in the PivotTable to show an average of the values in the Annual Visits field.

Figure 8 | **Opening the Value Field Settings Dialog Box**

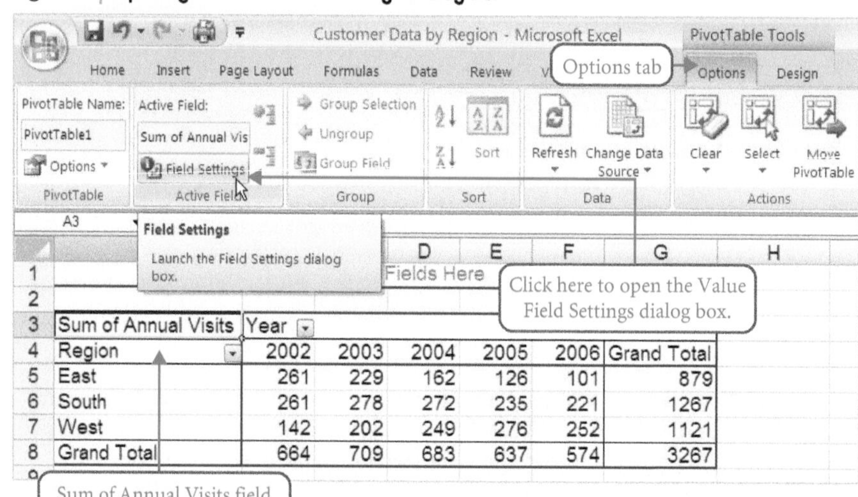


| | A | B | C | D | E | F | G |
|---|---|---|---|---|---|---|---|
| 3 | Sum of Annual Visits | Year | | | | | |
| 4 | Region | 2002 | 2003 | 2004 | 2005 | 2006 | Grand Total |
| 5 | East | 261 | 229 | 162 | 126 | 101 | 879 |
| 6 | South | 261 | 278 | 272 | 235 | 221 | 1267 |
| 7 | West | 142 | 202 | 249 | 276 | 252 | 1121 |
| 8 | Grand Total | 664 | 709 | 683 | 637 | 574 | 3267 |

Figure 9 | **Value Field Settings Dialog Box**

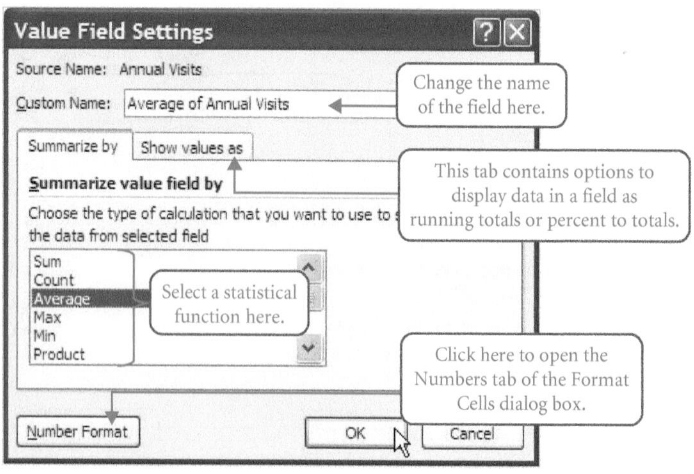

Figure 10 shows the results of computing the average number of times a customer visits a company store per region. A marketing manager can immediately see that the East region is experiencing a significant decline in customer visits. In the year 2002, a customer visited a company store in the East region an average of 5.2 times per year. By the year 2006, however, this number drops to 2.0. A marketing manager for this company will need to analyze additional data for this region to understand why customers are not visiting the company's stores as often as they did in 2002.

Figure 10 | **Results of Changing the Annual Visits Field Properties**

A3 fx Average of Annual Visits

| | A | B | C | D | E | F | G |
|---|---|---|---|---|---|---|---|
| 1 | | Drop Page Fields Here | | | | | |
| 2 | | | | | | | |
| 3 | Average of Annual Visits | Year | | | | | |
| 4 | Region | 2002 | 2003 | 2004 | 2005 | 2006 | Grand Total |
| 5 | East | 5.2 | 4.6 | 3.2 | 2.5 | 2.0 | 3.5 |
| 6 | South | 5.2 | 5.6 | 5.4 | 4.7 | 4.4 | 5.1 |
| 7 | West | 2.8 | 4.0 | 5.0 | 5.5 | 5.0 | 4.5 |
| 8 | Grand Total | 4.4 | 4.7 | 4.6 | 4.2 | 3.8 | 4.4 |
| 9 | | | | | | | |
| 10 | | | | | | | |

The trend for the East region shows a significant decline in customer visits.

The arrangement of the PivotTable in Figure 10 assumed that a marketing manager could easily evaluate the annual visit trends by placing the years across the top and listing the region names down the left side. However, after the PivotTable is constructed, the data can be manipulated into a few different configurations depending on your preference. For example, the PivotTable shown in Figure 11 was created by clicking the Year field in the Column Fields section and then dragging it over to the Row Fields section. This adjustment is also known as *pivoting*, which is why this is called a PivotTable. This can also be accomplished from the lower area of the PivotTable Field List. You can click and drag the Year field from the Column Labels section to the Row Labels section.

Figure 11 | **Results of Pivoting the Year Field**

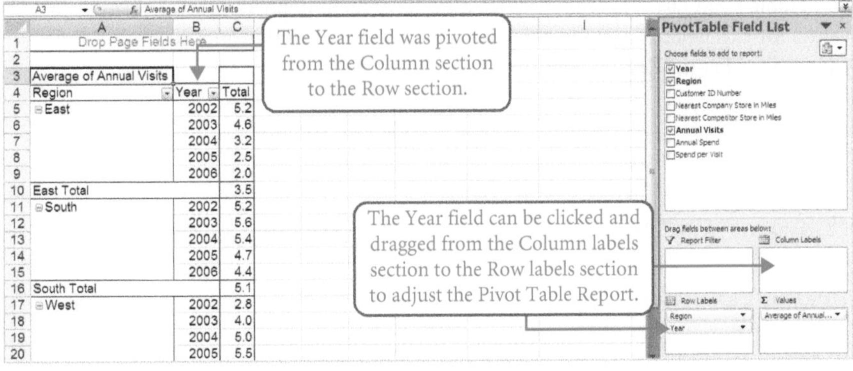

| | A | B | C |
|---|---|---|---|
| 1 | Drop Page Fields Here | | |
| 2 | | | |
| 3 | Average of Annual Visits | | |
| 4 | Region | Year | Total |
| 5 | East | 2002 | 5.2 |
| 6 | | 2003 | 4.6 |
| 7 | | 2004 | 3.2 |
| 8 | | 2005 | 2.5 |
| 9 | | 2006 | 2.0 |
| 10 | East Total | | 3.5 |
| 11 | South | 2002 | 5.2 |
| 12 | | 2003 | 5.6 |
| 13 | | 2004 | 5.4 |
| 14 | | 2005 | 4.7 |
| 15 | | 2006 | 4.4 |
| 16 | South Total | | 5.1 |
| 17 | West | 2002 | 2.8 |
| 18 | | 2003 | 4.0 |
| 19 | | 2004 | 5.0 |
| 20 | | 2005 | 5.5 |

The Year field was pivoted from the Column section to the Row section.
The Year field can be clicked and dragged from the Column labels section to the Row labels section to adjust the Pivot Table Report.
PivotTable Field List
Year
Region
Annual Visits
Row Labels
Column Labels
Values

## Applying Filters to Fields

As previously mentioned, the PivotTable in Figure 10 reveals a significant decline in the number of visits a customer makes to stores in the East region. A marketing manager can apply a filter to the Region field in the PivotTable to isolate the East region and add more fields to determine why this decline is taking place. The following explains how this filter is applied.

- Click the drop-down arrow next to the Region field in the PivotTable Report area. This will open a list of filter options for this field (see Figure 12).

>> **Quick Reference**

### Adding Data to a PivotTable

1. Click anywhere in the PivotTable Report to open the PivotTable Field. List and activate the **PivotTable Tools** tabs of the Ribbon.
2. Click a field in the PivotTable Field List, and drag it over to one of the sections of the PivotTable Report. You can also click and drag a field to one of the sections in the lower area of the PivotTable Field List.

>> **Quick Reference**

### Changing Field Settings

1. Click a field name in one of the sections of the PivotTable Report.
2. Click the **Field Settings** icon in the **Options** tab of the Ribbon.
3. Select a statistical function in the **Summarize by** tab in the **Value Field Settings** dialog box.
4. Click the **Number Format** button to open the **Number** tab of the **Format Cells** dialog box to format the values in a field.
5. Click the **OK** button in the **Format Cell** dialog box (if opened).
6. Click the **OK** button in the **Value Field Settings** dialog box.

- Click the box next to the (**Select All**) option. This will remove the check marks next to each region.
- Click the box next to the East region. A black check mark will appear.
- Click the **OK** button. The PivotTable will be reduced to only the East region (see Figure 13).

Figure 12 | **Applying a Filter to the Region Field**

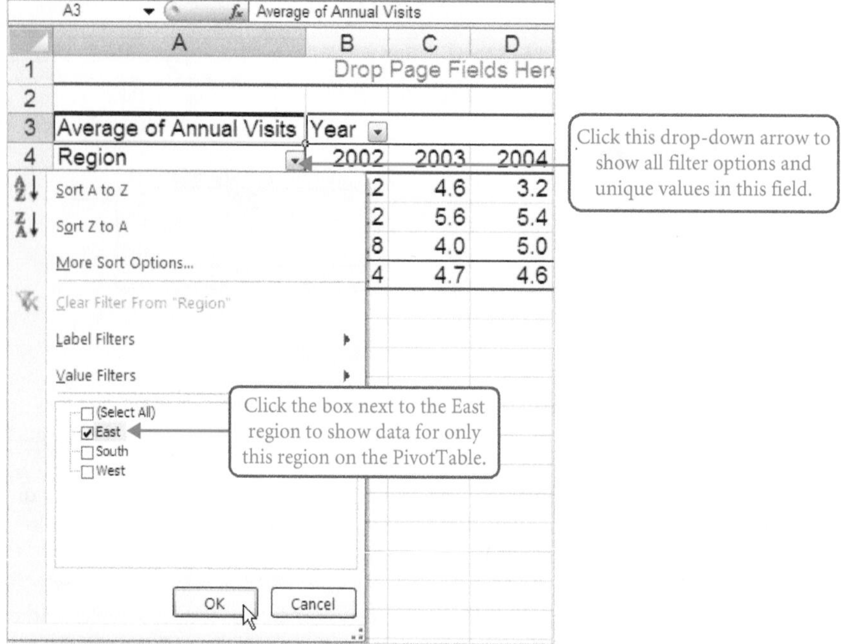


Figure 13 shows the results of applying a filter to the Region field. Notice the symbol that appears next to the Region field on the PivotTable Report and in the PivotTable Field List. This indicates that the PivotTable Report is showing only selected values for this field. To remove this filter, click the filter symbol and then select the **Clear Filter From "Region"** option.

Figure 13 | **Results of Isolating the East Region**

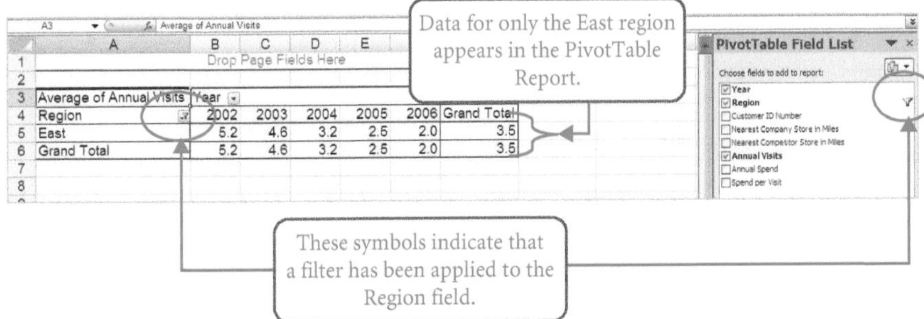
Data for only the East region appears in the PivotTable Report.
These symbols indicate that a filter has been applied to the Region field.
PivotTable Field List

After you have isolated the East region on the PivotTable Report, you can add more fields to determine why the annual visits are declining. For example, fields that a marketing manager might want to add are the Nearest Company Store in Miles and Nearest Competitor Store in Miles. Store location is especially critical in the retail industry. The purpose of this analysis is to compare data for two years: 2002 and 2006. This trend will indicate if competitors have built stores in more valuable locations compared to the company stores. The following explains how this analysis is constructed.

- Click and drag the Nearest Company Store in Miles field from the PivotTable Field List to the Data section of the PivotTable Report.
- Change the field settings for the Nearest Company Store in Miles by double-clicking the field name on the PivotTable Report. This will open the **Value Field Settings** dialog box.
- Select the Average option from the **Value Field Settings** dialog box; then, click the **Number Format** button and select the Number format with 1 decimal place.
- Click the **OK** button on the **Format Cells** dialog box and then click the **OK** button on the **Value Field Settings** dialog box. This will calculate the average distance each customer needs to travel to get to the nearest company store.
- Add the Nearest Competitor Store in Miles field to the Data section of the PivotTable Report; then, open the **Value Field Settings** dialog box, select the average mathematical function, and format the values using the Number format with 1 decimal place. This will show the average distance a customer must travel to get to a competitor's store.
- Click the drop-down arrow next to the Year field, and click the box next to the (**Select All**) option. Click the box next to the years 2002 and 2006 and then click the **OK** button. This will apply a filter to the Year field so the PivotTable Report shows values only for the years 2002 and 2006.

Figure 14 shows the results of adding two more fields to the PivotTable Report shown in Figure 13. Data is shown only for the years 2002 and 2006 for the East region. The trend shows that when customers were visiting stores in the East region 5.2 times per year in 2002, the average distance they traveled to get to the store was 8.1 miles. If they wanted to visit the competitor's store, they had to drive 14.4 miles. However, this distance to a competitor's store declines to 8.3 miles by the year 2006. In addition, the average distance a customer must travel to get to a company store increases to 10.6 miles in the year 2006. This suggests that the competition might be building stores in better locations, and could partially explain why the average number of visits a customer makes to the company store declines to 2.0 in the year 2006.

>> **Quick Reference**

**Filters**

1. Click the down arrow next to a field added to the PivotTable Report.
2. Select a filter option or specific value by clicking a check box.
3. Click the **OK** button.
4. Click the filter symbol next to a field and select the **Clear Filter** option to remove a filter.

Figure 14 | **Results of Adding Additional Fields to Evaluate the East Region**

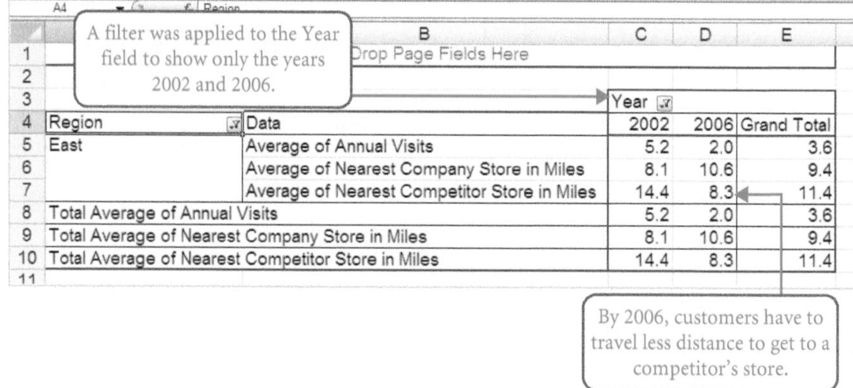

| | A | B | C | D | E |
|---|---|---|---|---|---|
| 1 | | Drop Page Fields Here | | | |
| 2 | | | | | |
| 3 | | | Year | | |
| 4 | Region | Data | 2002 | 2006 | Grand Total |
| 5 | East | Average of Annual Visits | 5.2 | 2.0 | 3.6 |
| 6 | | Average of Nearest Company Store in Miles | 8.1 | 10.6 | 9.4 |
| 7 | | Average of Nearest Competitor Store in Miles | 14.4 | 8.3 | 11.4 |
| 8 | Total Average of Annual Visits | | 5.2 | 2.0 | 3.6 |
| 9 | Total Average of Nearest Company Store in Miles | | 8.1 | 10.6 | 9.4 |
| 10 | Total Average of Nearest Competitor Store in Miles | | 14.4 | 8.3 | 11.4 |
| 11 | | | | | |

A filter was applied to the Year field to show only the years 2002 and 2006.
By 2006, customers have to travel less distance to get to a competitor's store.

## Adding and Removing Report Totals

Looking at Figure 14, you may have noticed that the three totals beginning in row 8 are merely duplicating the data in rows 5, 6, and 7. When multiple items are listed in the Row Fields section, these totals are very helpful. However, in this example they are not necessary because we are isolating only one item in the row fields section, which is the East region. You can adjust the totals in the PivotTable Report by using the **PivotTable Options** dialog box. The following explains how this is used to remove the totals listed in rows 8, 9, and 10 in Figure 14.

- Click anywhere in the PivotTable Report to activate the **PivotTable Tools** tabs of the Ribbon.
- Click the **Options** icon in the **Options** tab of the Ribbon. This will open the **PivotTable Options** dialog box.
- Click the **Totals & Filters** tab near the top of the dialog box.
- Click in the box next to the **Show grand totals for columns** option (see Figure 15). This will remove the green check that appears when the dialog box is opened.
- Click the **OK** button at the bottom of the dialog box. This will remove the totals at the bottom of the PivotTable Report which is shown in Figure 16.

Figure 15 | **PivotTable Options Dialog Box**

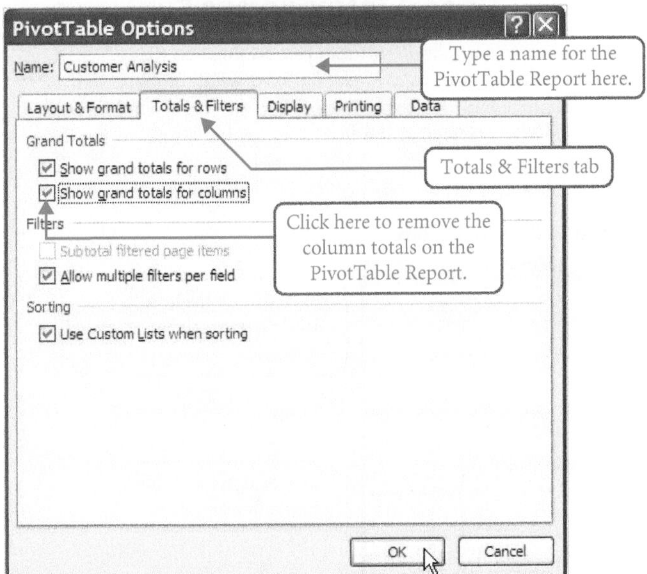


Figure 16 | **PivotTable Report Without Column Totals**

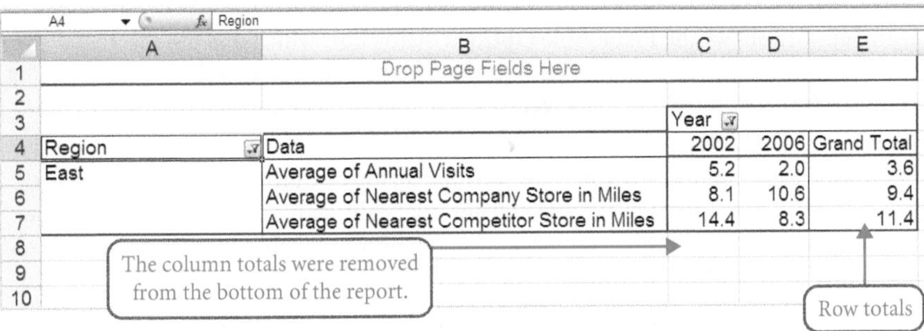


| | A | B | C | D | E |
|---|---|---|---|---|---|
| 1 | Drop Page Fields Here | | | | |
| 2 | | | | | |
| 3 | | | Year | | |
| 4 | Region | Data | 2002 | 2006 | Grand Total |
| 5 | East | Average of Annual Visits | 5.2 | 2.0 | 3.6 |
| 6 | | Average of Nearest Company Store in Miles | 8.1 | 10.6 | 9.4 |
| 7 | | Average of Nearest Competitor Store in Miles | 14.4 | 8.3 | 11.4 |
| 8 | | | | | |
| 9 | | | | | |
| 10 | | | | | |

## COMMON MISTAKES | Report Totals versus Subtotals

You can not add or remove subtotals on the PivotTable Report through the **PivotTable Options** dialog box. Subtotals are usually used when multiple fields are added to the Row Labels section of the PivotTable Report and are controlled through the Field Settings dialog box. When adjusting the field settings for a field in the Row Label section of the PivotTable, the dialog box is named Field Settings instead of Value Field Settings. Figure 17 shows an example of this dialog box.

Figure 17 | **Field Settings Dialog Box**

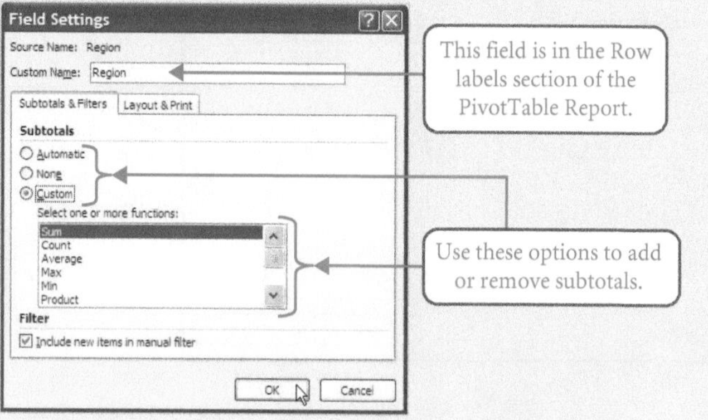


> **Quick Reference**
>
> **Adding and Removing Report Totals**
>
> 1. Click anywhere in the PivotTable Report to activate the **PivotTable Tools** tabs on the Ribbon.
> 2. Click the **Options** icon in the **Options** tab of the Ribbon.
> 3. Click the **Totals & Filters** tab near the top of the dialog box.
> 4. Click the box next to the **Show grand totals for columns** or **Show grand totals for rows** to add or remove the check mark. When the check mark appears in the box, totals will be added to the PivotTable Report.
> 5. Click the **OK** button at the bottom of the **PivotTable Options** dialog box.

Figure 15 shows the **PivotTable Options** dialog box, which was used to remove the column totals in Figure 16. However, this dialog box contains several tabs for accessing commands that control other key features. The following defines a few of these commonly used features.

- **Name:** The top of the **PivotTable Options** dialog box provides a space to type a name for your PivotTable. Excel will automatically assign a name to a PivotTable such as PivotTable1, PivotTable2, and so on; however, you can type a unique name, which is helpful when working with multiple tables in a workbook.
- **Show grand totals for rows:** This command is in the **Totals & Filters** tab of the dialog box and is used to add or remove totals for all rows in the PivotTable Report.
- **Refresh data when opening the file:** This command is in the **Data** tab of the dialog box, and will automatically update a PivotTable when the Excel workbook is opened. If you change data in the range of cells that is used to create a PivotTable, the changes *will not* appear in the PivotTable unless you click the **Refresh** icon in the **Data** group in the **Options** tab of the Ribbon.
- **Sort A to Z (Field List):** This option is in the **Display** tab of the **PivotTable Options** dialog box in the Field List section. This is used to show the fields in the PivotTable Field List window in alphabetical order. Excel will automatically show fields in the PivotTable Field List in the order in which they appear in the source range of cells. If your project uses many fields, however, it may be easier to find what you need if the fields are shown in alphabetical order.
- **Classic PivotTable layout (enables dragging of fields in the grid):** This option is also in the **Display** tab of the PivotTable options dialog box. This option must be selected if you want to click and drag fields from the PivotTable Field List into the PivotTable Report.

## COMMON MISTAKES | Refresh the PivotTable Report

You must click the **Refresh** icon in the **Options** tab of the Ribbon to show any data revisions in the PivotTable Report. People often make revisions in the range of cells that is used to supply data for a PivotTable and expect to see changes in the PivotTable Report; however, the PivotTable Report will not change unless the data is refreshed. In addition, if you select the **Refresh data when opening the file** option in the **Data** tab of the **PivotTable Options** dialog box, the data will refresh only when you open the workbook, but not immediately when the data is changed.

# Adding Formulas (Calculated Fields)

The PivotTable shown in Figure 16 reveals that a customer needed to travel less distance to get to a competitor's store compared to the company's store in the year 2006. This might explain why the customer visits to a company store in the East region declined significantly from the year 2002 to 2006. Another key statistic that might also explain this decline is the amount of money customers spend per visit. This is calculated by taking the Annual Spend field and dividing it by the Annual Visits field; however, creating a formula in the PivotTable Report is *not* the same as typing a formula into the cell of a worksheet. To produce mathematical results on the PivotTable Report, a calculated field must be created. The following explains how a calculated field is added to the PivotTable Report shown in Figure 16 to calculate the average spend per visit.

- Click anywhere in the PivotTable Report to activate the **PivotTable Tools** tabs on the Ribbon.
- Click the **Formulas** icon in the **Options** tab of the Ribbon and then select the **Calculated Field** option to open the **Insert Calculated Field** dialog box.
- Type the name Spend per Visit in the **Name** input box at the top of the **Insert Calculated Field** dialog box.
- Double-click the Annual Spend field from the list of fields in the lower area of the **Insert Calculated Field** dialog box.
- Type the slash symbol for division in the formula input box. Double-click the Annual visits field from the list in the lower area of the **Insert Calculated Field** dialog box.
- Click the **OK** button at the bottom of the dialog box. This will add the new field to the PivotTable Field List.
- Click and drag the Spend per Visit calculated field from the PivotTable Field List into the Data section of the PivotTable Report.

Figure 18 | **Opening the Insert Calculated Field Dialog Box**

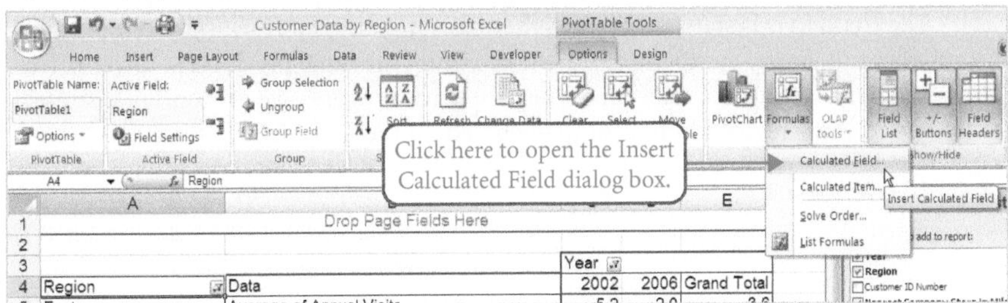

Figure 19 | **The Insert Calculated Field Dialog Box**

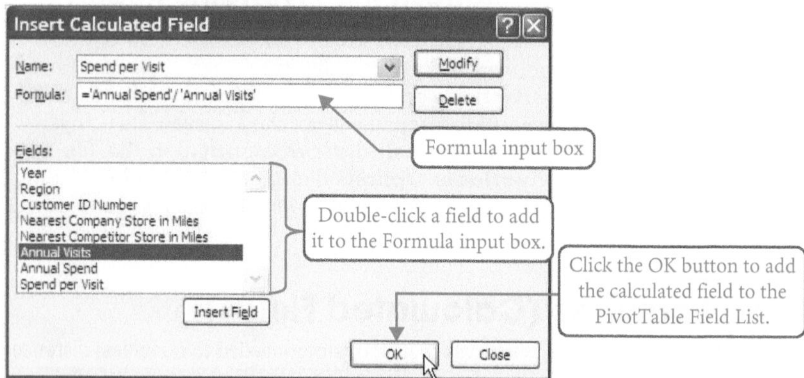


Figure 20 shows the appearance of the PivotTable Report after adding the Spend per Visit calculated field to the Data section. Notice the PivotTable renames the field **Sum of Spend per Visit.** This is because all fields, including calculated fields, are automatically summed when they are added to the PivotTable Report; however, this calculated field is actually producing an *average* for the amount of money a customer spends when they visit the store, even though Excel is summing the results. In other words, the sum of the Annual Spend divided by the sum of the Annual Visits is still an average. Therefore, the name of this field is changed in the **Value Field Settings** dialog box after double-clicking the field.

> **Quick Reference**
>
> **Adding Formulas (Calculated Fields)**
>
> 1. Click anywhere in the PivotTable Report to activate the **PivotTable Tools** tabs on the Ribbon.
> 2. Click the **Formulas** icon in the **Options** tab of the Ribbon.
> 3. Select the **Calculated Field** option.
> 4. Type a name for the calculated field at the top of the **Insert Calculated Field** dialog box.
> 5. Build a formula by double-clicking the fields in the field list and typing mathematical operators in the formula input box.
> 6. Click the **OK** button to add the calculated field to the PivotTable Field List.
> 7. Click and drag the calculated field from the PivotTable Field List into the Data section of the PivotTable Report.

Figure 20 | **Adding the Spend per Visit Calculated Field to the PivotTable Report**

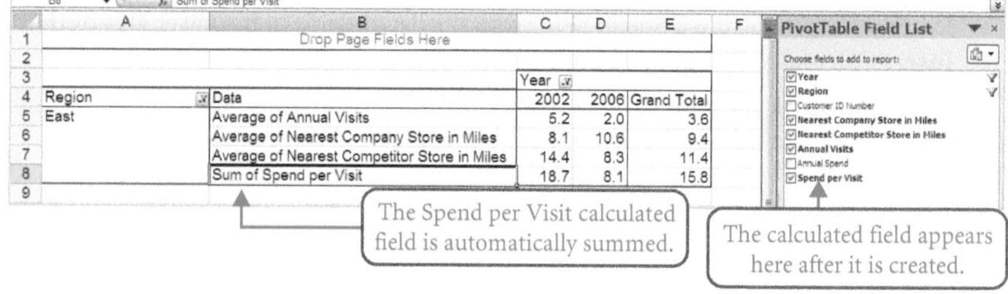


The final result of adding the Spend per Visit calculated field to the PivotTable Report is shown in Figure 21. Notice that in the year 2002, customers were spending on average $18.70 per visit; however, this is reduced by over 50 percent in the year 2006 to $8.10. The trend in this statistic suggests that the company is not selling products that customers want, or the competition might be selling the same products at lower prices. Therefore, a marketing manager might develop a more aggressive promotional strategy compared to other regions in the company based on these results.

Figure 21 | **Final Results of the Spend per Visit Calculated Field**

| | A | B | C | D | E |
|---|---|---|---|---|---|
| 1 | | Drop Page Fields Here | | | |
| 2 | | | | | |
| 3 | | | Year | | |
| 4 | Region | Data | 2002 | 2006 | Grand Total |
| 5 | East | Average of Annual Visits | 5.2 | 2.0 | 3.6 |
| 6 | | Average of Nearest Company Store in Miles | 8.1 | 10.6 | 9.4 |
| 7 | | Average of Nearest Competitor Store in Miles | 14.4 | 8.3 | 11.4 |
| 8 | | Average Spend per Visit | 18.7 | 8.1 | 15.8 |
| 9 | | | | | |

Customers are spending less money per visit in 2006 compared to 2002.

## Sorting Data

PivotTables provide the option of sorting fields in either the Row Fields section or the Column Fields section based on values in the Data section. The sorting commands will be demonstrated using the configuration of the PivotTable shown in Figure 11. The following explains how the Year field is sorted based on the data in the Annual Visits field.

- Click the Year field in cell B4.
- Click the **Sort** icon in the **Options** tab of the Ribbon. This will open the **Sort (Year)** dialog box. The field you are sorting will appear in the parentheses of the dialog box title.
- Click the circle next to the **Descending (Z to A) by** option, which is near the center of the dialog box.
- Click the drop-down arrow next to the box below the **Descending (Z to A) by** option and then select the **Average of Annual Visits** option. This will sort the years for each region based on the average values in the Annual Visits field.
- Click the **OK** button at the bottom of the **Sort (Year)** dialog box.

Figures 22 and 23 show the setup and results of sorting the PivotTable shown in Figure 11. Notice in Figure 22, the Summary section near the bottom of the **Sort (Year)** dialog box describes how your data will be sorted based on the options selected. In Figure 23 you will see that the years for each region are sorted based on the values for the Average of Annual Visits field in descending order.

Figure 22 | **Sort (Year) Dialog Box**

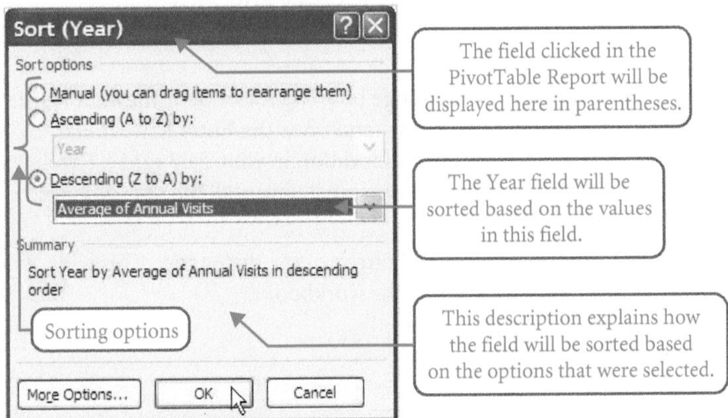


>> **Quick Reference**

**Sorting Data**

1. Click a field in either the Row Fields or Column Fields section on the PivotTable Report.
2. Click the **Sort** icon in the **Options** tab of the Ribbon.
3. Select one of the sort options in the **Sort** dialog box.
4. If you selected the **Ascending or Descending** option in Step 3, click the down arrow next to the box below these options and then select a field that will be used to set the sort sequence.
5. Click the **OK** button.

Figure 23 | **Results of Sorting the Year Field Based on Values in the Average Annual Visits Field**

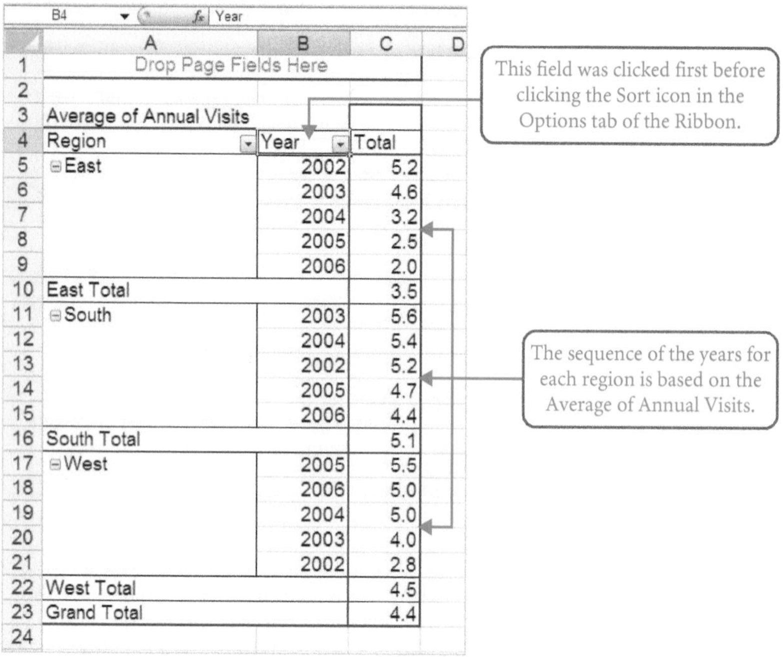

| | A | B | C |
|---|---|---|---|
| 1 | Drop Page Fields Here | | |
| 2 | | | |
| 3 | Average of Annual Visits | | |
| 4 | Region | Year | Total |
| 5 | ⊟East | 2002 | 5.2 |
| 6 | | 2003 | 4.6 |
| 7 | | 2004 | 3.2 |
| 8 | | 2005 | 2.5 |
| 9 | | 2006 | 2.0 |
| 10 | East Total | | 3.5 |
| 11 | ⊟South | 2003 | 5.6 |
| 12 | | 2004 | 5.4 |
| 13 | | 2002 | 5.2 |
| 14 | | 2005 | 4.7 |
| 15 | | 2006 | 4.4 |
| 16 | South Total | | 5.1 |
| 17 | ⊟West | 2005 | 5.5 |
| 18 | | 2006 | 5.0 |
| 19 | | 2004 | 5.0 |
| 20 | | 2003 | 4.0 |
| 21 | | 2002 | 2.8 |
| 22 | West Total | | 4.5 |
| 23 | Grand Total | | 4.4 |
| 24 | | | |

This field was clicked first before clicking the Sort icon in the Options tab of the Ribbon.

The sequence of the years for each region is based on the Average of Annual Visits.

## PivotCharts

The **PivotTable** icon in the **Insert** tab of the Ribbon contains an option for creating a PivotChart as well as a PivotTable. The mechanics and features of a PivotChart are similar to a PivotTable; however, instead of summarizing data in the form of a grid, the PivotChart displays data graphically in the form of a chart. You can use these charts for comparing data across multiple categories and for business presentations. This segment will demonstrate how to construct a PivotChart using the Retail Customer Data shown in Figure 1. The following explains how the PivotChart is initially created.

- Click the down arrow of the **PivotTable** icon in the **Insert** tab of the Ribbon, and select the **PivotChart** option. This will open the Create PivotTable with **PivotChart** dialog box, which is identical to the **Create PivotTable** dialog box (see Figure 2).
- Click the range finder next to the **Table/Range** box. Highlight all of the data on the worksheet—including the column headings—and press the **Enter** key. Similar to creating a PivotTable, if you activated any cell location in your data range, Excel will suggest a cell range. Check this range to ensure it covers all the data you need to create your PivotChart.
- Select the **New Worksheet** option near the bottom of the dialog box. This will place the PivotChart in a new worksheet in the workbook.

- Click the **OK** button at the bottom of the dialog box. This will add a new worksheet to the workbook that contains the tools you need to build the PivotChart (see Figure 24).
- Figure 24 shows the tools that are displayed for constructing a PivotChart after clicking the **OK** button in the Create PivotTable with **PivotChart** dialog box. These tools appear on a separate worksheet that is added to the workbook. In addition, a blank PivotTable will appear on the left side of the worksheet because a PivotChart is always associated with a PivotTable. In fact, the PivotTable will be used during the process of constructing the PivotChart for this example.

## COMMON MISTAKES | PivotCharts are Linked to a PivotTable

Any change you make to a PivotTable that is associated to a PivotChart will change the PivotChart. If you intend to use a PivotChart and a PivotTable to show different statistics for the same project, you will need to add a separate and independent PivotTable. This means your workbook will have two PivotTables: one which is independent and a second which is associated to the PivotChart.

Figure 24 | **Tools for Building a PivotChart**

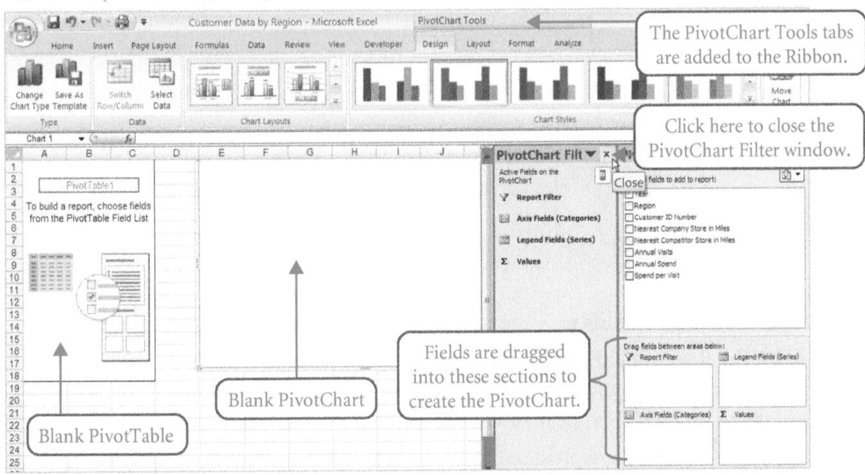


As shown in Figure 24, the **PivotChart Filter** window will be opened when the PivotChart is initially created. To see the PivotChart as it is being constructed, close this window by clicking the X in the upper-right corner.

Looking at Figure 24, you may have noticed the instructions in the blank PivotTable that state you can simply select fields in the PivotTable Field List to build a chart. Although this is true, there is no guarantee Excel will build the chart that you need for your project. The following method will provide you with the most control for placing data exactly where you want to see it on a chart. The goal for this example is to construct a PivotChart that compares the average number of visits per store by region for a selected year.

- Click the Year field in the PivotTable Field List, and drag it into the Report Filter section in the lower area of the PivotTable Field List. Placing fields in this section will allow you to focus the data displayed on the chart for one specific item or category, or for this example, a specific year. When creating a PivotTable, you can click and drag fields from the PivotTable Field List directly onto the PivotTable Report; however, you cannot drag fields directly onto a PivotChart. When building a PivotChart you will click and drag fields into the sections in the lower area of the PivotTable Field List.
- Click the down arrow next to the Year field on the *PivotTable* and then select the year 2002 (see Figure 25). This will show data only for the year 2002 on the PivotChart. Other years of data can be viewed on the chart by changing the filter to a different year.

Figure 25 shows the appearance of the PivotTable and PivotChart when the Year field is dragged into the Report Filter section of the PivotTable Field List. Notice that the PivotChart is still blank. Objects on the chart will not be visible until fields are added to the Values section of the PivotTable Field List.

Figure 25 | **Adding Fields to the Report Filter Section**

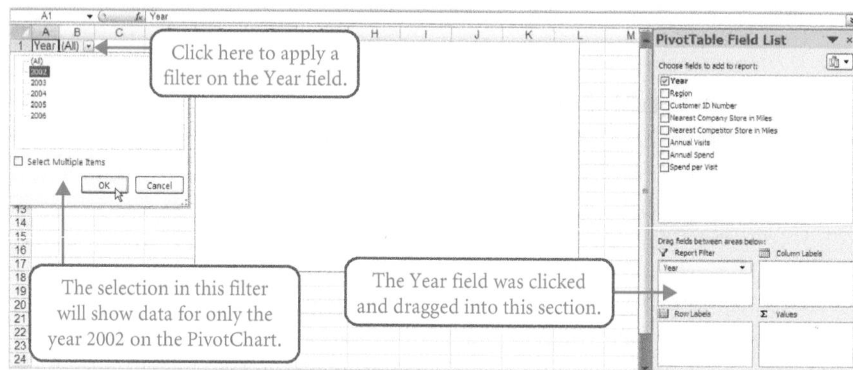


The following explains how the rest of the PivotChart is created for this example.

- Click the Region field in the PivotTable Field List and then drag it into the Axis Fields (Categories) section in the lower area of the PivotTable Field List. You will see the three regions appear in the PivotTable to the left of the PivotChart.
- Click the Annual Visits field in the PivotTable Field List and then drag it into the Values section in the lower area of the PivotTable Field List. The PivotChart will automatically sum the total number of customer visits for each region, and bars for each region will appear on the chart.
- Double-click the Sum of Annual Visits field in the PivotTable to open the **Value Field Settings** dialog box. Select the Average option in the **Summarize by** tab, and click the **OK** button at the bottom of the dialog box. Because the objective for this chart is to compare the *average* number of times a customer visits the company's stores, the field settings are changed to Average.
- Click and drag the chart down and to the left until it is full view. To view the entire chart after it is created, you will have to move it or close the PivotTable Field List so it is fully visible.

## COMMON MISTAKES | Opening the PivotTable Field List

If you close the PivotTable Field List, you must activate either the PivotTable or PivotChart and then click the **Field List** icon in either the **Options** or **Analyze** tabs of the Ribbon to open it again. People often find it difficult to open the PivotTable Field List after closing it. If you close the PivotTable Field List by clicking the X in the upper-right corner, it will not appear when you activate the PivotTable Report or PivotChart unless you click the **Field List** icon.

Figure 26 shows the results of PivotChart comparing the average annual visits by region for the year 2002. The chart can be changed to a different year by clicking the filter icon next to the Year field in the PivotTable and selecting a different year. In addition, a filter can be placed on the Region field by clicking the down arrow next to the Row Labels heading in the PivotTable. Notice that the **PivotChart Tools** tabs are added to the Ribbon when the PivotChart is activated. The **Design**, **Layout**, and **Format** tabs contain commands that can be used to adjust the design or select a different chart type. The PivotChart will automatically use the Clustered Column chart type when it is created.

Figure 26 | **Results of the PivotChart**

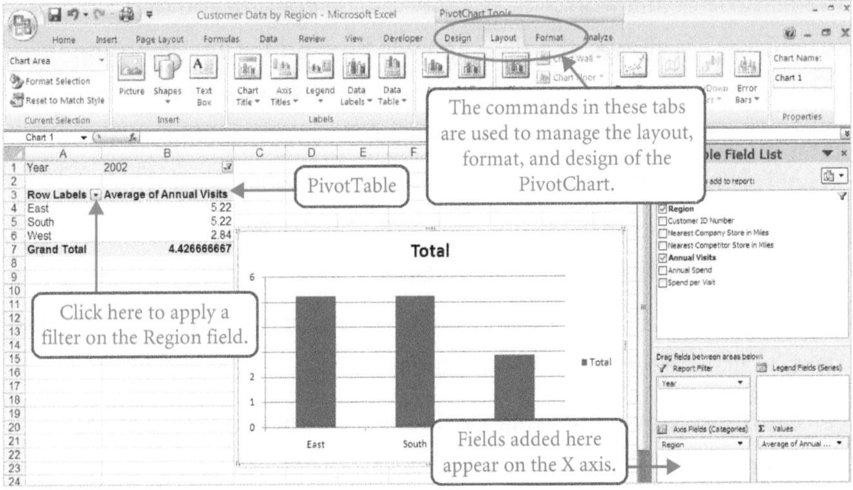


Figure 27 shows a variation of the PivotChart shown in Figure 26, and includes formatting adjustments. In this chart the Year field was clicked and dragged from the Report Filter section into the Legend Fields (Series) section in the lower area of the PivotTable Field List. This creates a bar on the PivotChart for each year by region, and the legend shows the color associated with each year.

>> Quick Reference

### Creating a New PivotChart

1. Click the drop-down arrow of the **PivotTable** icon in the Insert tab of the Ribbon, and select the **PivotChart** option.
2. Define the Table/Range in the **Create PivotTable with PivotChart** dialog box. If a range is provided, check it to ensure it contains all the data that is required for your PivotChart. To create a new range, click the range finder, highlight the range of cells that contain data for the PivotChart, and press the **Enter** key.
3. Select either New Worksheet or Existing Worksheet near the bottom of the **Create PivotTable with PivotChart** dialog box and then click the **OK** button.
4. Click and drag fields from the upper area of the PivotTable Field List into one of the sections in the lower area.
5. Make any formatting adjustments to the PivotChart using the same commands and techniques that would be used for any Excel chart.

Figure 27 | **PivotChart Variation with Formatting**

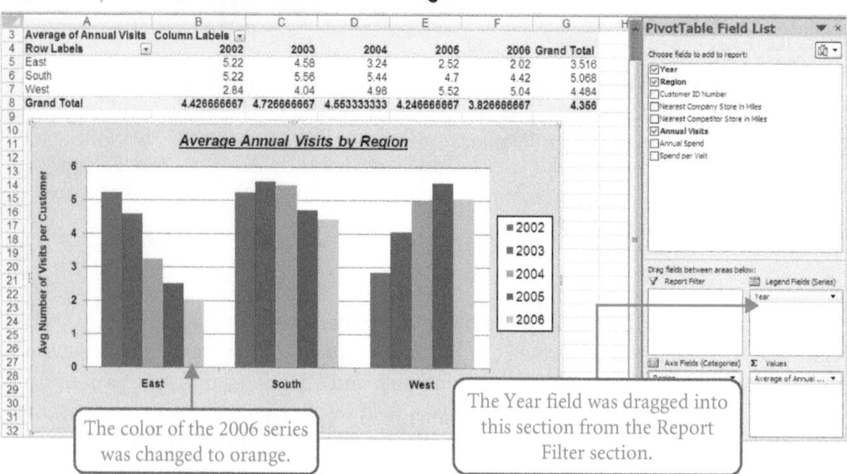


**VIDEO WORKSHOP**

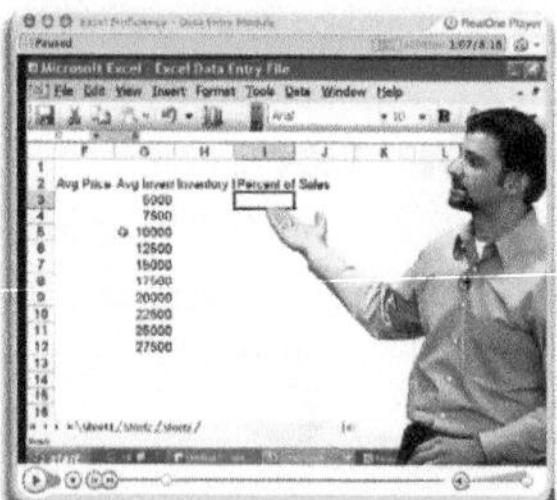

## >> PivotTables

The purpose of this workshop is to review the construction and features of an Excel PivotTable. The data that will be used for this workshop is identical to the data used in this section of the chapter. I will be demonstrating the tasks in this workshop in the following five videos: **PivotTables: Initial Setup; PivotTables: Fields and Settings; PivotTables: Report Totals and Subtotals; PivotTables: Calculated Fields; and PivotTables: Sorting Data.** Open the Excel file named ib_e08_customerdata. After completing each section of tasks, watch the related video in parentheses.

1. **Create a New PivotTable (Video: PivotTables: Initial Setup)**
   a. Activate cell A1 in the Data worksheet.
   b. Click the down arrow on the **PivotTable** icon in the **Insert** tab of the Ribbon, and select the **PivotTable** option.
   c. In the Create **PivotTable** dialog box, check that the range in the **Table/Range** box is Data!$A$1:$G$751. Select the New Worksheet option near the bottom of the dialog box and then click the **OK** button.
   d. Click the **Options** icon in the **Options** tab of the Ribbon.
   e. Click the **Display** tab near the top of the **PivotTable Options** dialog box. A check mark should appear next to the Classic PivotTable layout (enables dragging of fields in the grid) option. If you do not see a check mark, click the box next to this option.
   f. Click the **OK** button at the bottom of the **PivotTable Options** dialog box.

2. **Adding Fields (Video: PivotTables: Fields and Settings)**
   a. Click anywhere in the PivotTable Report area in the Sheet1 worksheet.
   b. Click the Year field in the PivotTable Field List and drag it into the Column Fields section of the PivotTable Report.

c. Click the Region field in the PivotTable Field List and drag it into the Row Fields section of the PivotTable Report.

d. Click the Annual Visits field in the PivotTable Field List and drag it into the Data section of the PivotTable Report.

e. Double-click the Sum of Annual Visits field name in cell A3 on the PivotTable Report.

f. Select the Average option in the **Summarize by** tab in the **Value Field Settings** dialog box.

g. Click the **Number Format** button at the bottom of the **Value Field Settings** dialog box; then, select the **Number** option and set the decimal places to 1 in the **Format Cells** dialog box.

h. Click the **OK** button in the **Format Cells** dialog box and then on the **Value Field Settings** dialog box.

i. Click the drop down arrow next to the Region field name on the PivotTable Report, and set the filter for the East region.

j. Click and drag the Nearest Company Store in Miles field from the PivotTable Field List into the Data section of the PivotTable Report.

k. Look in the Column Labels section in the lower area of the PivotTable Field List. If the Values field appears in this section below the Year field, click and drag it into the Row Labels section below the Region field.

l. Change the field settings for the Nearest Company Store in Miles from Sum to Average, and format the values in this field using the Number format with 1 decimal place.

m. Click and drag the Nearest Competitor Store in Miles field from the PivotTable Field List into the Data section of the PivotTable Report.

n. Change the field settings for the Nearest Competitor Store in Miles from Sum to Average, and format the values in this field using the Number format with 1 decimal place.

**3. Report Totals (Video: PivotTables: Report Totals and Subtotals)**

a. Click anywhere on the PivotTable Report in the Sheet1 worksheet.

b. Click the **Options** icon in the **Options** tab of the Ribbon.

c. At the top of the **PivotTable Options** dialog box, change the name of the PivotTable in the Name: input box to `Customer Analysis`.

d. Click the **Totals & Filters** tab in the **PivotTable Options** dialog box, and then click the box next to the Show grand totals for columns option to remove the check mark. Click the **OK** button at the bottom of the **PivotTable Options** dialog box.

e. Click the filter symbol next to the Region field on the PivotTable Report, and remove the filter by selecting the **Clear Filter From "Region"** option.

f. In the lower area of the PivotTable Field List, click the Year field in the Column Labels section. Drag it between the Region and Values fields in the Row Labels section.

g. In the lower area of the PivotTable Field List, click the Values field in the Row Labels section and then drag it into the Column Labels section

h. Double-click the Region field name in the PivotTable Report (cell A4).

i. In the Subtotals & Filters tab of the **Field Settings** dialog box, click the Custom option and then select the Average function. Click the **OK** button at the bottom of the dialog box.

**4. Adding Formulas (Video: PivotTables: Calculated Fields)**

a. Click anywhere on the PivotTable Report in the Sheet1 worksheet.

b. In the lower area of the PivotTable Field List, click and drag the Year field into the Column Labels section, and then click and drag the Values field into the Row Labels section below the Region field.
c. Click the **Formulas** icon in the **Options** tab of the Ribbon, and select the **Calculated Field** option.
d. Type the name `Spend per Visit` in the Name: input box at the top of the **Insert Calculated Field** dialog box. Delete the name Field1 before typing the field name.
e. Double-click the Annual Spend field from the field list, type a slash symbol, and double-click the Annual Visits field.
f. Click the **OK** button at the bottom of the **Insert Calculated Field** dialog box.
g. Double-click the Sum of Spend per Visit field name in the PivotTable Report (cell B8). Change the name of the field to **`Average Spend per Visit`**; then, click the **Number Format** button, select the **Currency** option, and set the decimal places to 2.
h. Click the **OK** button on the **Format Cells** dialog box and again on the **Value Field Settings** dialog box.

5. **Sorting (Video: PivotTables: Sorting Data)**
   a. Click anywhere on the PivotTable Report in the Sheet1 worksheet.
   b. In the PivotTable Field List, click the box next to the Nearest Company Store in Miles, Nearest Competitor Store in Miles, and Spend per Visit fields to remove the check mark.
   c. Click the Year field name in the PivotTable Report (cell B3), and drag it over to the Row Fields section next to the regions.
   d. Click the Year field name in the PivotTable report (cell B4) and then click the Sort icon in the **Options** tab of the Ribbon.
   e. Click the Descending (Z to A) option in the center of the Sort (Year) dialog box. Click the drop-down arrow next to the box below this option, and select the Average of Annual Visits field.
   f. Click the **OK** button on the **Sort (Year)** dialog box.
   g. Save and close your file.

**VIDEO WORKSHOP**

## >> PivotCharts

The purpose of this workshop is to review the construction and features of a PivotChart. This workshop will use the same Excel file that was used for the PivotTable workshop. I will be demonstrating the tasks in this workshop in the video named **PivotCharts**. Open the ib_e08_customerdata file, and begin the workshop.

1. **PivotCharts (Video: PivotCharts)**
   a. Activate cell A1 in the Data worksheet.
   b. Click the down arrow on the **PivotTable** icon in the **Insert** tab of the Ribbon, and select the **PivotChart** option.
   c. In the **Create PivotTable** dialog box, check that the range in the **Table/Range** box is Data!$A$1:$G$751. Select the New Worksheet option near the bottom of the dialog box and then click the **OK** button.

d. Close the **PivotChart Filter** window by clicking the X in the upper-right corner of the window.
e. Click the Year field in the PivotTable Field List and drag it into the Report Filter section in the lower area of the PivotTable Field List.
f. Click the drop-down arrow next to the Year field on the PivotTable, and set the filter for the year 2002.
g. Click anywhere in the blank PivotChart and then click the Region field in the PivotTable Field List. Drag it into the Axis Fields (Categories) section in the lower area of the PivotTable Field List.
h. Click the Annual Visits field in the PivotTable Field List, and drag it into the Values section in the lower area of the PivotTable Field List.
i. Double-click the Sum of Annual Visits field in cell B3. Change the field settings to Average, and format the values using the Number format with 1 decimal place.
j. Change the filter on the Year field in the PivotTable to the year 2006.
k. Save and close your file.

## >> Analyzing Customer Survey Data

**EXERCISE**

**Why Do I Need This?**

Data plays a critical role in the decision making process of most businesses; however, most business managers struggle to turn large volumes of data into information they can use for making decisions. The amount and type of data business managers evaluate depends on the function they serve within a company. For example, marketing mangers might work with large volumes of data, especially if they are conducting and evaluating consumer surveys. These surveys are sometimes administered over the Internet, mailed to consumers' homes, or conducted in person as customers leave a retail store. Companies can use these survey methods to collect data from thousands of customers. Business managers can then use tools such as Excel PivotTables to convert this data into valuable information.

### Exercise

The purpose of this exercise is to use a PivotTable to evaluate the results of a survey that was conducted as customers were leaving the stores of a home furnishings retail company. The data collected from this survey is contained in the Excel file named ib_e08_customersurveyresults. Open the file and complete the following tasks.

1. Create a new PivotTable using the range A1:G751 on the Data worksheet. This PivotTable should appear in a new worksheet in the workbook. Note: If you do not see the layout of the PivotTable Report that allows you to click and drag fields into it, check the **Classic PivotTable layout (enables dragging of fields in the grid)** option in the **Display** tab of the **PivotTable Options** dialog box.

2. The fields in the PivotTable Field List contain data pertaining to the sales growth of each store in the company as well as the scores from the customer survey. The goal of this analysis is to determine if the results of the survey can explain the sales growth trends of the stores. Therefore, the first step of this exercise will be to analyze the sales growth trends of the stores. To accomplish this, arrange the PivotTable Report as follows.
   a. Use the Store field to establish the Row Labels.
   b. Use the Year field to establish the Column Labels.
   c. Use the Sales Growth field for the values of the report.

3. Change the field settings of the Sales Growth field to Average, and format the numbers in this field to Currency with 0 decimal places.

4. Sort the stores in the Row Labels section of the PivotTable in Descending order based on the values in the Sales Growth field. Remember to click the Store field name first in the PivotTable Report. This will enable a business manager to quickly identify stores with the highest and lowest sales growth results.

5. Store 2 should be the last store listed in the PivotTable Report because it had the largest sales decrease over the years 2004 through 2006. Set a filter on the Store field so only this store appears in the PivotTable report.

6. Add the In Stock, Price, and Associates fields to the Values section of the PivotTable Report. Move the Values field from the Column Labels section in the lower area of the PivotTable Field List to the Row Labels section. Change the field settings for these fields to Average, and format the numbers to a regular Number format with 1 decimal place. The data in these three fields will now show the average score that was surveyed for this store by its customers. Customers rated the store on a 10 point scale (1=Poor, 10=Superior). The In Stock score is the customers' response to the question: "Did you find the product you wanted?" The Price score is in response to the question: "Do you think products in the store are fairly priced?" The Associates score is in response to the question "Do think the associates are friendly and helpful?" Given the results of these scores, does it make sense that this store experienced the most significant sales decline compared to the other stores?

7. Remove the report totals at the bottom of the PivotTable Report. Because there is only one store in the PivotTable report, these totals are not necessary.

8. Adjust the filter on the Store field to show Stores 2 and 7 on the PivotTable Report. Store 7 has also experienced a significant decline in sales. Compare the data for the In Stock, Price, and Associates fields for both stores. Based on this comparison, explain why you think sales in Store 7 are declining.

9. Adjust the Store field filter to add Store 5 to the PivotTable Report. The PivotTable Report should now show three stores (5, 7, and 2). Based on the Price field scores, which store did customers rate as having the best prices? Why do you think the sales growth for Store 5 is much higher than store 7?

10. Adjust the Store field filter to add Store 6 to the PivotTable Report. If you are the president of this company and can invest money to improve either the Price score or the Associates score for this store, which would you choose? Why?

11. If you could only invest money to improve two scores to improve the sales of Store 2, which would you choose? Why?

12. Save and close your file.

**PROBLEM & EXERCISE**

## >> What's Wrong with This Spreadsheet?

### Problem

You are working in the marketing and sales division of a large retail corporation and receive an e-mail from your boss who needs help putting together a presentation for the firm's executive officers. The purpose of the presentation is to show the three-year trend in customer survey scores and change in sales for the company's stores. Your boss explains the following in an e-mail.

1. Please take a look at the Excel file attached to this e-mail. I am trying to use a PivotTable and a PivotChart to show the results of the customer survey results in the Data worksheet.

2. The first problem is that there are few fields in the PivotTable Field List that do not match the column headings in the Data worksheet. I can't figure out why some fields match the column headings, and some don't.

3. The second problem is that the PivotChart keeps changing on me! I want to show the executives an overview of the *Average* sales results by store for all three years on a basic column chart. Then I want to use the PivotTable to show the Average sales and the *Average* survey scores for the *three stores that had the biggest decrease* in sales for each year. However, every time I change the PivotTable, the PivotChart changes.

4. You will see the PivotChart that I attempted to create in Sheet2 of the workbook. Is there any way to make this look better and move it to separate worksheet so I can use it for a presentation?

### Exercise

The Excel file that was attached to the e-mail sent by your boss in named ib_e08_pivotcharttroubles. Open this file and look at the PivotChart in the Sheet2 worksheet. What's wrong with this PivotChart? Consider the following points.

1. Your boss mentioned that some of the field names in the PivotTable Field List do not match the column headings in the Data worksheet. Why is this happening?

2. Why is the PivotChart changing when your boss tries to show the average sales and survey score results on the PivotTable in Sheet2?

3. Is it possible to move a PivotChart to a separate worksheet or chart sheet and apply formatting enhancements as you would any other Excel chart?

Write a short answer for each of these points; then, help your boss complete this presentation by fixing any errors you find. The PivotChart should show the average sales results for each year for all stores *sorted in descending order*. Also, make any formatting enhancements to this chart so it has a professional appearance (for example, add a title, adjust font sizes, color, and so on) and place it in a separate chart sheet. Finally, the workbook should include a PivotTable that shows the average sales and survey scores *by year* for the three stores with the lowest sales results.

## >> Tools for Selecting and Summarizing Data

Skill Set

The previous section demonstrated how you can use PivotTables to execute a variety of mathematical functions and data processes when analyzing large volumes of data. The purpose of this section is to demonstrate three other tools that can also be used for this purpose. Each tool covered in this section is used to apply one specific function or process to a large data set. The section begins with the **Filter** tool, which is designed to select a specific number of rows from a large data set based on criteria that you define. The next tool is Subtotals, which is designed to provide a mathematical summary for specified columns within a large dataset. The last tool that will be demonstrated is the List Box, which allows you to select specific values from a large column of data.

## Filters

Excel's **Filter** tool is a way to identify and select key data points from large volumes of data contained in a worksheet. Similar to the example demonstrated in the PivotTable section, this tool is also helpful when analyzing data that might be used by a marketing manager. One of the most important goals of a marketing manager is to determine where a company's products should be promoted and sold; however, finding the best markets to sell products is sometimes like finding a needle in a haystack. Marketing managers might collect and analyze thousands of rows of data to decide which markets best represent a firm's target customer. For example, Figure 28 shows age of population and household income statistics for 500 hypothetical markets or locations. A marketing manager would analyze this data to determine which markets might provide a company with the best potential for promoting and selling its products. This example assumes that the marketing manager's goal is to promote products to consumers between the ages of 25 to 35 with a household income of at least $70,000.

Figure 28 | **Hypothetical Market Data**

Market Data - Microsoft Excel

| | A | B | C | D | E |
|---|---|---|---|---|---|
| 1 | Market | Total Population | Percent of Population Age 25-35 | Growth in Population Age 25-35 | Household Income |
| 2 | Market 441 | 215,036 | 16.10% | 4.00% | 44,327 |
| 3 | Market 156 | 66,587 | 27.32% | 22.00% | 96,089 |
| 4 | Market 378 | 101,452 | 10.57% | 13.00% | 70,156 |
| 5 | Market 464 | 94,184 | 20.41% | 6.00% | 50,932 |
| 6 | Market 450 | 100,144 | 8.47% | 14.00% | 72,494 |
| 7 | Market 197 | 70,463 | 11.79% | -2.00% | 29,066 |
| 8 | Market 483 | 100,615 | 27.80% | 23.00% | 98,375 |
| 9 | Market 291 | 101,875 | 21.77% | 10.00% | 63,770 |
| 10 | Market 91 | 81,710 | 12.45% | -3.00% | 26,706 |
| 11 | Market 239 | 141,594 | 26.90% | 1.00% | 35,819 |
| 12 | Market 374 | 100,820 | 23.47% | 20.00% | 92,027 |

Filter icon

Data continues to row 501.

The following explains how a marketing manger could use the **Filter** tool to decide which of the 500 markets shown in Figure 28 best represent the firm's target customer.

- Click any cell that contains data. If you are using a worksheet that contains several adjacent columns of data as shown in Figure 28, you can click any cell that contains data and Excel will automatically configure the **Filter** tool.
- Click the **Filter** icon in the **Data** tab of the Ribbon (see Figure 28).

Figure 29 shows the Market Data worksheet after applying the **Filter** tool. Notice that drop-down arrows appear next to each column heading in row 1 of the worksheet. This figure also shows the list of options that appear when an arrow is clicked.

Figure 29 | **Filter Options**

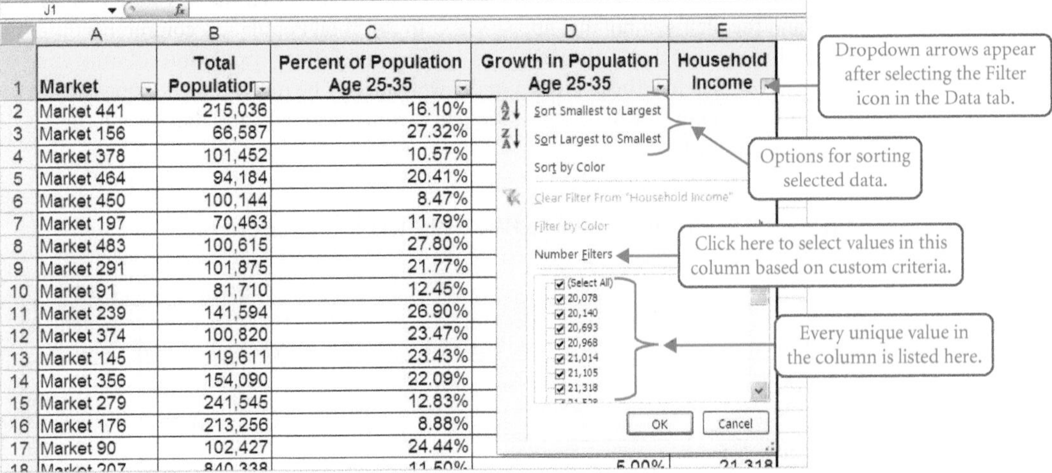


As shown in Figure 29, the **Filter** tool provides several options for selecting values in a column of data. Notice that when the drop-down arrow is clicked, every unique value in the column is displayed. The **Number Filters** option is used to select multiple values that meet the conditions of a logical test that you define. The following explains how this option is used to select markets that represent the best opportunities to sell products based on a target customer that is between the age of 25 to 35 with a household income of at least $70,000.

- Click the down arrow next to the Total Population column heading in cell B1 and then place the cursor over the **Number Filters** option.
- Select the **Custom Filter** from the list of options. This will open the **Custom AutoFilter** dialog box (see Figure 30).
- Click the drop-down arrow to the left of the box in the upper-left area of the **Custom AutoFilter** dialog box. Select the **greater than or equal to** comparison criterion.
- Click the drop-down arrow next to the box to the right of the comparison criterion, and select the value 100,002. This will reduce the data shown in Figure 28 to those rows where the total population is greater than or equal to the 100,002 people. A marketing manager might use this type of criterion to set an overall minimum market size standard.
- Click the **OK** button at the bottom of the **Custom AutoFilter** dialog box.

Figure 30 | **Custom AutoFilter Window for the Total Population Column**

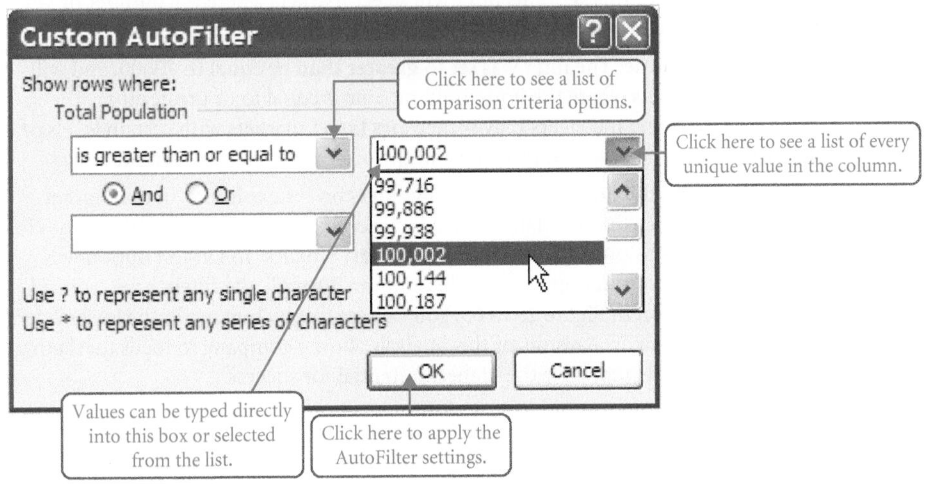

Figure 31 shows the results of the Hypothetical Market data after applying the AutoFilter settings to the Total Population column. Notice that the row numbers are blue and the filter symbol that appears next to the Total Population column heading is blue. This signifies that a filter has been applied to the Total Population column, and that rows of data have been hidden in the worksheet. The row numbers along the left side of the worksheet will be out of sequence, which also indicates that several rows have been hidden.

Figure 31 | **Results After Applying a Filter on the Total Population Column**

| | A | B | C | D | E |
|---|---|---|---|---|---|
| 1 | Market | Total Population | Percent of Population Age 25-35 | Growth in Population Age 25-35 | Household Income |
| 2 | Market 441 | 215,036 | 16.10% | 4.00% | 44,327 |
| 4 | Market 378 | 101,452 | 10.57% | 13.00% | 70,156 |
| 6 | Market 450 | 100,144 | 8.47% | 14.00% | 72,494 |
| 8 | Market 483 | 100,615 | 27.80% | 23.00% | 98,375 |
| 9 | Market 291 | 101,875 | 21.77% | 10.00% | 63,770 |
| 11 | Market 239 | 141,594 | 26.90% | 1.00% | 35,819 |
| 12 | Market 374 | 100,820 | 23.47% | 20.00% | 92,027 |
| 13 | Market 145 | 119,611 | 23.43% | -4.00% | 21,528 |
| 14 | Market 356 | 154,090 | 22.09% | 2.00% | 40,444 |

Row numbers are out of sequence.

Data is reduced to only rows where the total population is greater than or equal to 100,002.

This symbol indicates a filter is applied to this column.

The following explains how filters are applied to three more columns to further reduce the data shown in Figure 31 to markets that best represent the company's target customer.

- **Percent of Population Age 25–35:** The filter was set to **greater than or equal to** .20. This will select rows of data where at least 20 percent of the population is between the ages of 25 and 35. Notice that 20 percent in decimal form is used to set this filter. Based on the filter that was applied to the Total Population field, this ensures the company is selecting markets where there are at least 20,000 potential customers. Marketing managers will usually calculate what the minimum number of potential customers must be to enter a market based on factors such as number of competitors, industry growth trends, and their company's past performance in new markets.
- **Growth in Population Age 25–35:** The filter was set to **greater than** .05. The purpose of this filter is to ensure that the number of people age 25 to 35 is growing within a particular market. This filter will select markets where the number of people age 25 to 35 has grown by more than 5 percent in the past year.
- **Household Income:** The filter was set to **greater than or equal to** 70000, and will select only markets where the household income is equal to or greater than $70,000. Marketing managers may sometimes target markets with certain levels of household income based on research and the price of their firm's product.

Figure 32 shows the final results of setting filters on four columns in the Market Data worksheet. Notice that the data is sorted in ascending order based on the values in the Total Population column. This is because the Sort Smallest to Largest option was selected from the list of filter options for this column. Overall, the filters have reduced the 500 markets shown in Figure 28 to 63. You can see this by looking in the lower-left corner of the status bar. The results of this analysis allow a company to focus marketing investments in markets that have the highest potential for success.

**>> Quick Reference**

**Applying Filters**

1. Click any cell containing data in a worksheet with several adjacent columns.
2. Click the **Filter** icon in the **Data** tab of the Ribbon.
3. Click the drop-down arrow next to any of the column headings and select a filter option.

Figure 32 | **Final Results After Applying Filters on Four Columns of Data**

| | A | B | C | D | E |
|---|---|---|---|---|---|
| 1 | Market | Total Population | Percent of Population Age 25-35 | Growth in Population Age 25-35 | Household Income |
| 8 | Market 483 | 100,615 | 27.80% | 23.00% | 98,375 |
| 12 | Market 374 | 100,820 | 23.47% | 20.00% | 92,027 |
| 17 | Market 90 | 102,427 | 24.44% | 18.00% | 83,978 |
| 24 | Market 131 | 104,713 | 24.80% | 17.00% | 83,677 |
| 41 | Market 440 | 109,007 | 24.67% | 14.00% | 73,780 |
| 54 | Market 163 | 113,004 | 25.11% | 18.00% | 85,124 |
| 65 | Market 421 | 113,516 | 24.97% | 15.00% | 75,350 |
| 66 | Market 234 | 113,742 | 20.64% | 13.00% | 72,400 |
| 94 | Market 407 | 116,768 | 28.61% | 19.00% | 87,477 |
| 95 | Market 165 | 116,801 | 24.71% | 23.00% | 98,152 |
| 96 | Market 146 | 122,404 | 28.63% | 14.00% | 72,559 |
| 100 | Market 476 | 132,641 | 28.67% | 24.00% | 102,562 |
| 101 | Market 424 | 135,367 | 23.22% | 13.00% | 72,302 |
| 107 | Market 231 | 141,057 | 22.04% | 22.00% | 97,511 |
| 113 | Market 437 | 142,136 | 20.00% | 18.00% | 84,976 |

Sheet1 Sheet2 Sheet3

Ready 63 of 500 records found

A total of 63 markets are listed in the worksheet.

Data is sorted by values in this column.

## COMMON MISTAKES | Identifying Number of Rows Using the Filter Tool

It is sometimes difficult to determine how many rows of data you have after applying the Filter to data in a worksheet. Because the **Filter** tool hides rows of data, you cannot use the row number next to your last row of data to determine the size of a filtered set of data. Instead, you need to look in the lower-left corner of the status bar, or you can copy and paste the data into a new worksheet. When you copy and paste filtered data to a new worksheet, Excel will only paste the data from rows that are not hidden. This allows you to use either the row numbers or use a count function to determine how many rows of data you have.

## Subtotals

One of the key challenges when working with large volumes of data in Excel is summarizing totals and subtotals for multiple categories. This is one of the key benefits of using a PivotTable to analyze large sets of data; however, subtotals can be added directly to a large data set contained in a worksheet. This might be a better option compared to a PivotTable if you need to analyze the details that make up the total result for a particular category in your data set. For example, Figure 33 contains category sales data for the stores of a hypothetical electronics retail company. The company sells three categories of merchandise in every store, and there are 80 stores in the company. Every store is assigned to a district and each district is assigned to a region. Overall, there are 241 rows of data in this example. The **Subtotal** tool will be used to analyze the sales performance of this company by summing the sales results in columns E, F, and G by region, district, and store.

Figure 33 | **Merchandise Sales for a Hypothetical Electronics Retail Store**

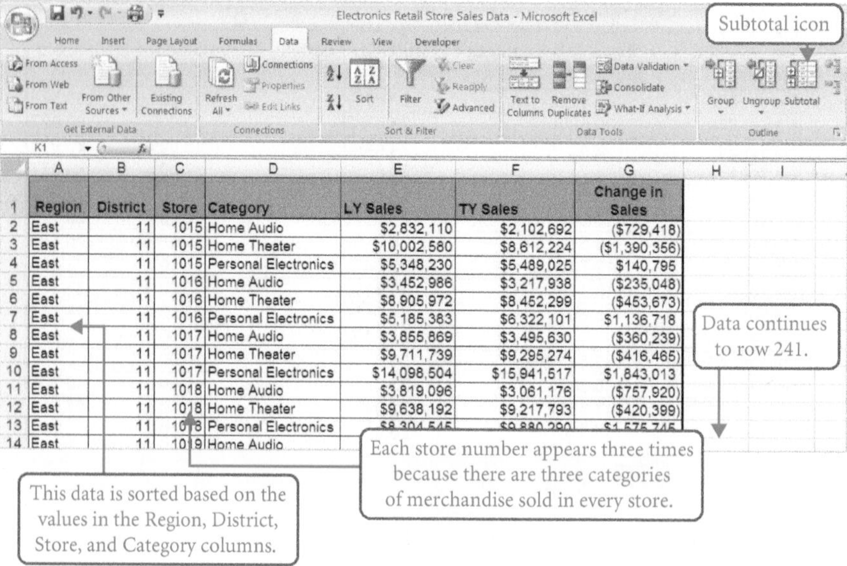


| Region | District | Store | Category | LY Sales | TY Sales | Change in Sales |
|---|---|---|---|---|---|---|
| East | 11 | 1015 | Home Audio | $2,832,110 | $2,102,692 | ($729,418) |
| East | 11 | 1015 | Home Theater | $10,002,580 | $8,612,224 | ($1,390,356) |
| East | 11 | 1015 | Personal Electronics | $5,348,230 | $5,489,025 | $140,795 |
| East | 11 | 1016 | Home Audio | $3,452,986 | $3,217,938 | ($235,048) |
| East | 11 | 1016 | Home Theater | $8,905,972 | $8,452,299 | ($453,673) |
| East | 11 | 1016 | Personal Electronics | $5,185,383 | $6,322,101 | $1,136,718 |
| East | 11 | 1017 | Home Audio | $3,855,869 | $3,495,630 | ($360,239) |
| East | 11 | 1017 | Home Theater | $9,711,739 | $9,295,274 | ($416,465) |
| East | 11 | 1017 | Personal Electronics | $14,098,504 | $15,941,517 | $1,843,013 |
| East | 11 | 1018 | Home Audio | $3,819,096 | $3,061,176 | ($757,920) |
| East | 11 | 1018 | Home Theater | $9,638,192 | $9,217,793 | ($420,399) |
| East | 11 | 1018 | Personal Electronics | $8,304,545 | $9,880,290 | $1,575,745 |
| East | 11 | 1019 | Home Audio | | | |

The first step in analyzing the sales data from Figure 33 is to add subtotals to the Region column. This will provide an overall view of the sales performance of the company by summarizing 241 rows of data into 5. The following explains how this is accomplished.

- Sort the data in the worksheet in ascending order based on values in the following columns: Region, District, Store, and Category. The data in a worksheet must be sorted for the **Subtotal** tool to work properly. The sort order should be based on the subtotals you need to analyze for your project.
- Click any cell that contains data. If you are using a worksheet that contains several adjacent columns of data as shown in Figure 33, you can click any cell that contains data and Excel will automatically configure the **Subtotal** tool.
- Click the **Subtotal** icon in the **Data** tab of the Ribbon. This will open the **Subtotal** dialog box (see Figure 34).
- Click the drop-down arrow next to the first box labeled **At each change in:** and select Region. This will add a subtotal after the last row of each region.
- Click the drop-down arrow next to the second box labeled **Use function:** and select Sum. The drop-down arrow for this box will list several different mathematical functions that can be processed through the Subtotal tool.
- The third box in this window lists all the column headings from the worksheet in Figure 33. The check mark next to a column heading shows what data Excel will be subtotaling. The checks can be added or removed by clicking in the box next to the column heading. For this example, the LY Sales, TY Sales, and Change in Sales columns are selected.
- Click the **OK** button at the bottom of the **Subtotal** dialog box.

Figure 34 | **Subtotal Dialog Box**

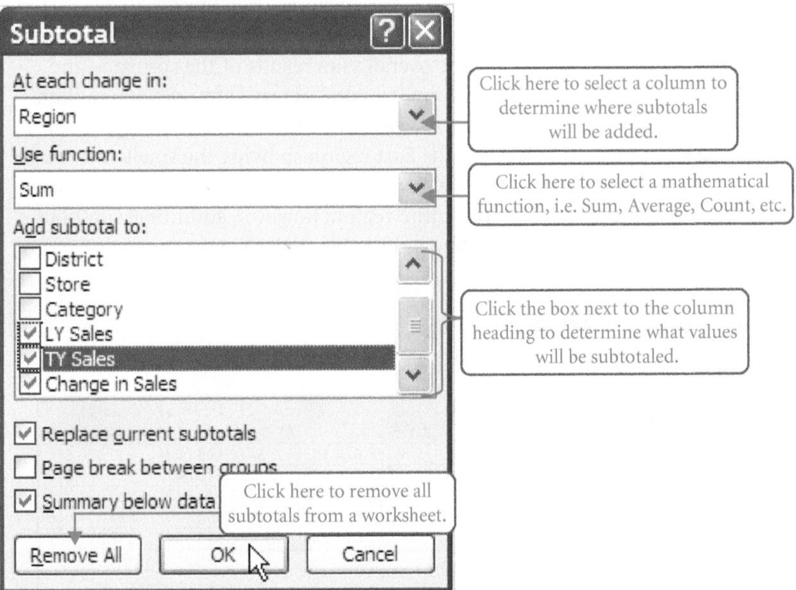


## COMMON MISTAKES | Sorting Data Before Using Subtotals

The data in a worksheet must be sorted in a logical sequence before using the **Subtotal** tool. The **Subtotal** tool will subtotal data based on the way data is sorted. Therefore, before adding subtotals make sure the data in your worksheet is sorted based on the columns that will be used for adding subtotals.

Figure 35 shows the results of adding subtotals to the data shown in Figure 33. Notice that a button with a minus sign appears to the left of the subtotal. This is one of two types of buttons that are used to control the rows of detail that are displayed on the worksheet. These buttons are as follows:

- **Hide/Show Detail Buttons:** These buttons appear next to each subtotal that is added to the worksheet. They are used to hide or show all the values that make up the subtotal for a particular category.
- **Level Buttons:** These buttons appear at the top-left side of the worksheet. They are used to hide or show details for an entire level of subtotals. For example, these buttons can be used to hide or show details for the subtotals of every region in Figure 35.

Figure 35 | **Results of Adding Subtotals to the Region Column**

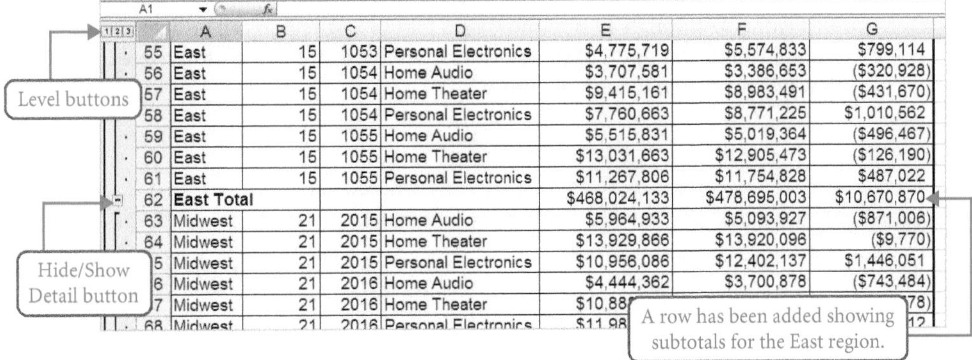

| | A | B | C | D | E | F | G |
|---|---|---|---|---|---|---|---|
| 55 | East | 15 | 1053 | Personal Electronics | $4,775,719 | $5,574,833 | $799,114 |
| 56 | East | 15 | 1054 | Home Audio | $3,707,581 | $3,386,653 | ($320,928) |
| 57 | East | 15 | 1054 | Home Theater | $9,415,161 | $8,983,491 | ($431,670) |
| 58 | East | 15 | 1054 | Personal Electronics | $7,760,663 | $8,771,225 | $1,010,562 |
| 59 | East | 15 | 1055 | Home Audio | $5,515,831 | $5,019,364 | ($496,467) |
| 60 | East | 15 | 1055 | Home Theater | $13,031,663 | $12,905,473 | ($126,190) |
| 61 | East | 15 | 1055 | Personal Electronics | $11,267,806 | $11,754,828 | $487,022 |
| 62 | East Total | | | | $468,024,133 | $478,695,003 | $10,670,870 |
| 63 | Midwest | 21 | 2015 | Home Audio | $5,964,933 | $5,093,927 | ($871,006) |
| 64 | Midwest | 21 | 2015 | Home Theater | $13,929,866 | $13,920,096 | ($9,770) |
| 5 | Midwest | 21 | 2015 | Personal Electronics | $10,956,086 | $12,402,137 | $1,446,051 |
| 6 | Midwest | 21 | 2016 | Home Audio | $4,444,362 | $3,700,878 | ($743,484) |
| 7 | Midwest | 21 | 2016 | Home Theater | $10,88 | | 78) |
| 68 | Midwest | 21 | 2016 | Personal Electronics | $11,98 | | 12 |

Figure 36 shows a variation of the results shown in Figure 35. The Level 2 button was clicked to hide all of the details in the worksheet so the only rows showing are the subtotals for each region and the grand total results for the entire company. Removing the detail allows a manager to evaluate the overall sales results of the company and identify any key trends. Notice that the company sales increased by over $65 million dollars and that almost 50 percent of this increase came from the South region. All regions showed an increase in sales with the East region showing the smallest increase. A manager might want to look at more details for the East region to see if there is any one district that is lowering sales for the entire region; however, additional subtotals will need to be added to the worksheet to conduct this analysis.

Figure 36 | **Hiding Details for All Subtotals**

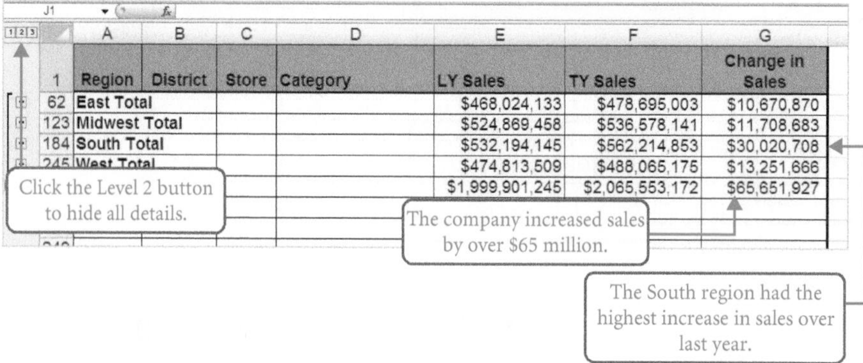


As previously mentioned, to evaluate the sales results by region, additional subtotals need to be added to the worksheet in Figure 36. The following explains how subtotals are added for the District and Store columns.

- Click any cell that contains data in the worksheet.
- Click the **Subtotal** icon in the **Data** tab of the Ribbon.
- Select the District column in the first drop-down box of the **Subtotal** dialog box.
- Set the function to Sum in the second drop-down box.
- Check to see that a check mark appears next to the LY Sales, TY Sales, and Change in Sales fields in the **Add subtotal to** box. You can add a check mark by clicking the box next to the field.
- Click the box next to the **Replace Current Subtotals** option to *remove* the check mark. This option must *not* be selected or the subtotals for the Region column will be removed.
- Click the **OK** button at the bottom of the **Subtotal** dialog box.
- Add a subtotal for the Store column by opening the **Subtotal** dialog box again, and repeat the same process that was explained for the District column.

Figures 37 through 40 show how sales for the East region can be analyzed by examining different levels of subtotals. The Level 5, 4, 3, and 2 buttons were clicked to show just the region totals in Figure 37.

Figure 37 | **Subtotals Added for Three Additional Columns**

| | Region | District | Store | Category | LY Sales | TY Sales | Change in Sales |
|---|---|---|---|---|---|---|---|
| 87 | East Total | | | | $468,024,133 | $478,695,003 | $10,670,870 |
| 173 | Midwest Total | | | | $524,869,458 | $536,578,141 | $11,708,683 |
| 259 | South Total | | | | $532,194,145 | $562,214,853 | $30,020,708 |
| 345 | West Total | | | | $474,813,509 | $488,065,175 | $13,251,666 |
| 346 | Grand Total | | | | $1,999,901,245 | $2,065,553,172 | $65,651,927 |

Additional Level Buttons are added to the worksheet.

Click here to view details for the East region.

Notice in Figure 38 that District 14 is showing a significant decline in sales. Sales declined over 1.7 million dollars from last year.

Figure 38 | **Details for the East Region**

| | Region | District | Store | Category | LY Sales | TY Sales | Change in Sales |
|---|---|---|---|---|---|---|---|
| 22 | | 11 Total | | | $101,915,039 | $102,033,116 | $118,077 |
| 35 | | 12 Total | | | $81,628,605 | $84,361,667 | $2,733,062 |
| 52 | | 13 Total | | | $108,623,073 | $117,419,182 | $8,796,109 |
| 73 | | 14 Total | | | $103,547,560 | $101,823,067 | ($1,724,493) |
| 86 | | 15 Total | | | $72,309,856 | $73,057,971 | $748,115 |
| 87 | East Total | | | | $468,024,133 | $478,695,003 | $10,670,870 |
| 173 | Midwest Total | | | | $524,869,458 | $536,578,141 | $11,708,683 |
| | | | | | $532,194,145 | $562,214,853 | $30,020,708 |
| | | | | | $474,813,509 | $488,065,175 | $13,251,666 |
| | | | | | $1,999,901,245 | $2,065,553,172 | $65,651,927 |

Click here to hide details for the East region.

Subtotals for all districts in the East region.

District 14 shows the largest decrease in sales compared to other districts in the East region.

Figure 39 shows that Store 1044 had the largest decrease in sales for District 14. Sales declined in this store over $900,000.

Figure 39 | **Details for District 14**

| | Region | District | Store | Category | LY Sales | TY Sales | Change in Sales |
|---|---|---|---|---|---|---|---|
| 22 | | 11 Total | | | $101,915,039 | $102,033,116 | $118,077 |
| 35 | | 12 Total | | | $81,628,605 | $84,361,667 | $2,733,062 |
| 52 | | 13 Total | | | $108,623,073 | $117,419,182 | $8,796,109 |
| 56 | | | 1040 Total | | $10,860,900 | $10,862,649 | $1,749 |
| 60 | | | 1041 Total | | $18,769,919 | $18,447,657 | ($322,262) |
| 64 | | | 1042 Total | | $29,937,133 | $29,298,804 | ($638,329) |
| 68 | | | 1043 Total | | $18,442,508 | $18,578,249 | $135,741 |
| 72 | | | 1044 Total | | $25,537,100 | $24,635,708 | ($901,392) |
| 73 | | 14 Total | | | 3,547,560 | $101,823,067 | ($1,724,493) |
| 86 | | 15 Total | | | 2,309,856 | $73,057,971 | $748,115 |
| | | | | | 8,024,133 | $478,695,003 | $10,670,870 |

Click here to hide details for district 14.

Subtotals for all stores in district 14

Store 1044 shows the largest sales decrease in the district.

Figure 40 shows that all of the sales decrease for Store 1044 is coming from the Home Audio merchandise category. This decrease might be the result of a strong competitor opening one or several stores in this market. A marketing manager might use this information to create an aggressive promotional campaign for Home Audio merchandise to regain this business.

>> ***Quick Reference***

**Applying Subtotals**

1. Sort your data based on columns where subtotals will be applied.
2. Click any cell containing data in a worksheet with several adjacent columns.
3. Click the **Subtotal** icon in the **Data** tab of the Ribbon.
4. Select a column where a subtotal will be added in the first drop-down box of the **Subtotal** dialog box.
5. Select a mathematical function in the second drop-down box.
6. Select columns that contain data to be subtotaled in the third box.
7. If you are adding multiple subtotals to a worksheet, make sure the Replace Current Subtotals is not selected.
8. Click the **OK** button in the **Subtotal** dialog box.
9. Use the +/− buttons to show or hide details for a specific subtotal.

Figure 40 | **Details for Store 1044**

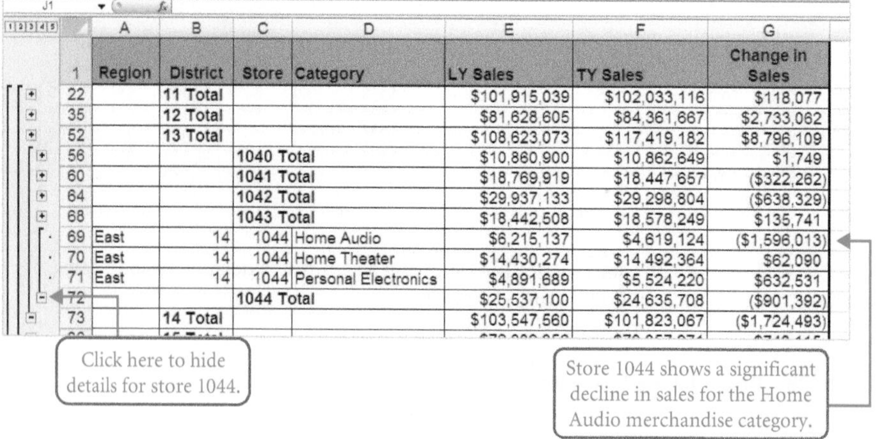

| | Region | District | Store | Category | LY Sales | TY Sales | Change in Sales |
|---|---|---|---|---|---|---|---|
| 22 | | 11 Total | | | $101,915,039 | $102,033,116 | $118,077 |
| 35 | | 12 Total | | | $81,628,605 | $84,361,667 | $2,733,062 |
| 52 | | 13 Total | | | $108,623,073 | $117,419,182 | $8,796,109 |
| 56 | | | 1040 Total | | $10,860,900 | $10,862,649 | $1,749 |
| 60 | | | 1041 Total | | $18,769,919 | $18,447,657 | ($322,262) |
| 64 | | | 1042 Total | | $29,937,133 | $29,298,804 | ($638,329) |
| 68 | | | 1043 Total | | $18,442,508 | $18,578,249 | $135,741 |
| 69 | East | 14 | 1044 | Home Audio | $6,215,137 | $4,619,124 | ($1,596,013) |
| 70 | East | 14 | 1044 | Home Theater | $14,430,274 | $14,492,364 | $62,090 |
| 71 | East | 14 | 1044 | Personal Electronics | $4,891,689 | $5,524,220 | $632,531 |
| 72 | | | 1044 Total | | $25,537,100 | $24,635,708 | ($901,392) |
| 73 | | 14 Total | | | $103,547,560 | $101,823,067 | ($1,724,493) |



## Adding the Developer Tab

You will need to add the **Developer** tab to the Ribbon before reviewing the next tool in this section. The Developer tab contains advanced features for creating macros and adding controls to a worksheet. The following explains how this tab is added to the Ribbon.

- Click the **Office Button.**
- Click the **Excel Options** button to open the **Excel Options** dialog box.
- Click the Popular option on the left side of the **Excel Options** dialog box.
- Click the box next to the **Show Developer tab in the Ribbon** option to add a check mark (see Figure 41).
- Click the **OK** button at the bottom of the **Excel Options** dialog box.

Figure 41 shows the Developer tab option in the **Excel Options** dialog box. After the **OK** button is clicked, the **Developer** tab will be added to the Ribbon.

Figure 41 | **The Excel Options Dialog Box**

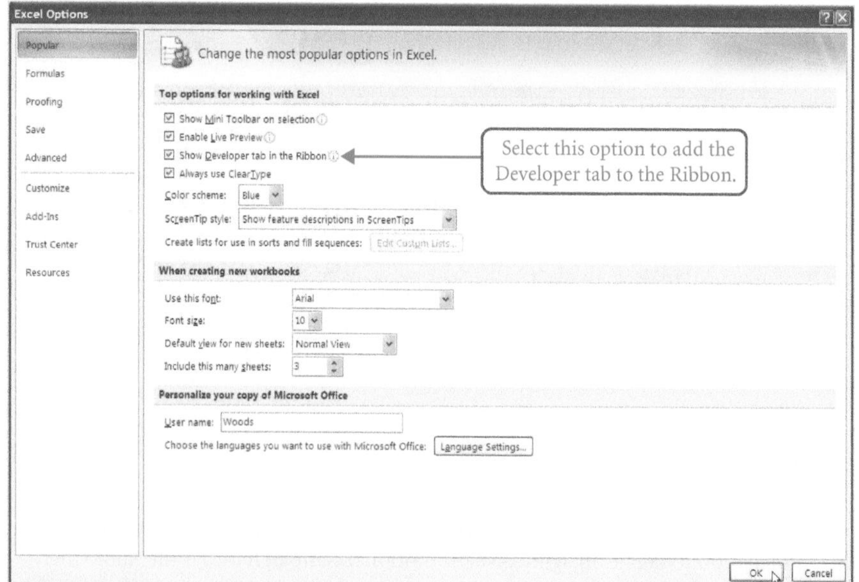

## List Boxes

The last tool that will be demonstrated in this section is the List Box. The List Box is used to select specific values from a column of data. Similar to the other tools covered in this chapter, this demonstration shows how a business manager can evaluate specific trend information from a large dataset. The List Box is often used with the **Vlookup** function because values can be selected by pointing and clicking from a list of options instead of typing them into a cell. This eliminates spelling error problems or typing wrong data into the lookup cell of a **Vlookup** function. This feature will be demonstrated using a variation of the Electronics Retail Store Sales data shown in Figure 33. Figure 42 shows the same data; however, sales for each store is shown for each month of the year and there is no merchandise category detail. The purpose of this demonstration is to evaluate the monthly and overall sales trend for specific stores.

Figure 42 | **Electronics Retail Store Data by Month**

| | A | B | C | D | E | F | G |
|---|---|---|---|---|---|---|---|
| 1 | Store/Month | Region | District | Store | Month | LY Sales | TY Sales |
| 2 | 1015January | 1 | 11 | 1015 | January | $1,876,167 | $824,674 |
| 3 | 1015February | 1 | 11 | 1015 | February | $632,782 | $625,750 |
| 4 | 1015March | 1 | 11 | 1015 | March | $900,681 | $1,001,241 |
| 5 | 1015April | 1 | 11 | 1015 | April | $1,026,778 | $1,020,506 |
| 6 | 1015May | 1 | 11 | 1015 | May | $1,171,174 | $1,059,090 |
| 7 | 1015June | 1 | 11 | 1015 | June | $1,165,468 | $1,043,707 |
| 8 | 1015July | 1 | 11 | 1015 | July | $1,214,917 | $1,296,513 |
| 9 | 1015August | 1 | 11 | 1015 | August | $1,992,039 | $2,095,867 |
| 10 | 1015September | 1 | 11 | 1015 | September | $2,503,066 | $2,152,621 |
| 11 | 1015October | 1 | 11 | 1015 | October | $1,866,679 | $1,635,170 |
| 12 | 1015November | 1 | 11 | 1015 | November | $1,772,117 | $1,663,390 |
| 13 | 1015December | 1 | 11 | 1015 | December | $2,061,052 | $1,785,413 |
| 14 | 1016January | 1 | 11 | 1016 | January | $1,810,277 | $915,691 |
| 15 | 1016February | 1 | 11 | 1016 | February | $610,559 | $694,813 |
| 16 | 1016March | 1 | 11 | 1016 | March | $869,049 | $1,111,746 |
| 17 | 1016April | 1 | 11 | 1016 | April | $990,718 | $1,133,137 |

Store List | Store Sales | Store Analysis

Data continues to row 961.

Concatenate function was used to combine the store and month.

Each unique store number is listed in this worksheet.

This worksheet will be used to display store sales data by month.

Figure 42 shows the *Store Sales* worksheet from the workbook that will be used to demonstrate the List Box. Notice that the Store Number and Month columns are concatenated together in column A. This will enable a Vlookup function to select sales for a specific month for each store. This example will utilize two other worksheets in this workbook. The Store List worksheet contains a list of every unique store in the company, which will be used to populate the window of the List Box. The stores in this column will be used to populate the window of the List Box. The *Store Analysis* worksheet is shown in Figure 43. This worksheet will be the focus of this demonstration and will be used to display the monthly sales results for a selected store by using a combination of the List Box and the **Vookup** function.

Figure 43 | **Store Analysis Worksheet**

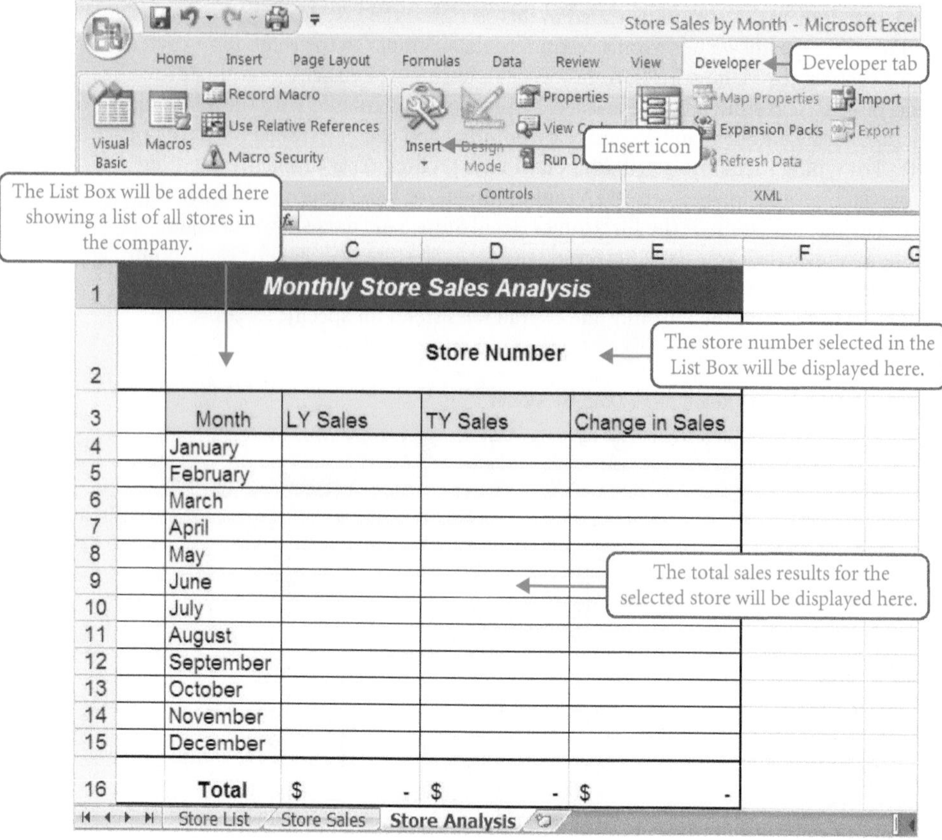


Figure 43 shows the worksheet that will be used to show the monthly sales results for a store that is selected using the List Box. The following explains how the List Box is added to this worksheet in the area of cells B2 and C2.

- Click the **Insert** icon in the **Developer** tab of the Ribbon.
- Click the **List Box** icon from the **Form Controls** options.
- Click and drag a square over cells B2 and C2 in the Store Analysis worksheet. The List Box will appear after releasing the mouse button. White circles will appear around the perimeter of the List Box indicating it is ready to be configured (see Figure 44).

Figure 44 | **Adding a List Box to the Store Analysis Worksheet**

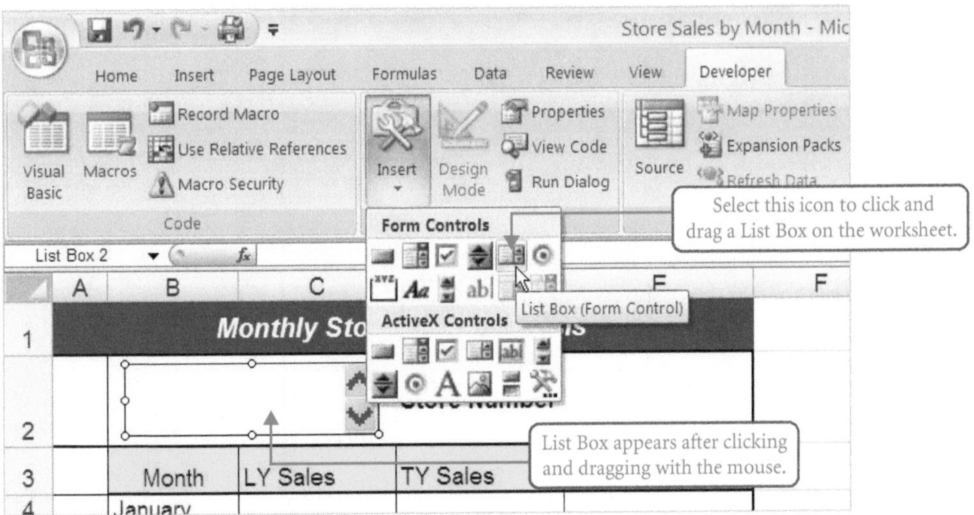


Figure 44 shows the results of adding an empty List Box to the Store Analysis worksheet. The List Box must be configured for store numbers to appear in the List Box window. The following explains how this is accomplished.

- Make sure the List Box is not active. If white circles appear around the perimeter of the List Box, the box is not active and can be configured. If the List Box *is* active (no white circles around the perimeter) hold down the **Ctrl** key and click the box.
- Click the **Properties** icon in the **Developer** tab of the Ribbon. This will open the **Format Control** dialog box (see Figure 45).
- Click the **Control** tab at the top of the **Format Control** dialog box.
- Click the range finder next to the **Input Range** box, highlight the range B2:B81 on the Store List worksheet, and press the **Enter** key. The stores contained in this range will appear in the window of the List Box when it is activated.
- Click the range finder next to the **Cell Link** box, activate cell A2 on the Store Analysis worksheet, and press the **Enter** key. When a store is selected in the List Box, the sequence number of where that store appears in the list in the Store List worksheet will be displayed in cell A2 of the Store Analysis worksheet. This number will be used in a **Vlookup** function to display the store number that was selected in the List Box in cell E2 of the Store Analysis worksheet.
- Select the Single option in the Selection Type options area of the **Format Control** dialog box. This will allow only one store to be selected at a time.
- Click the **OK** button at the bottom of the **Format Control** dialog box and then click anywhere on the Store Analysis worksheet to activate the List Box.

Figure 45 shows the settings that were made in the **Format Control** dialog box for this example.

Figure 45 | **Format Control Dialog Box for a List Box**

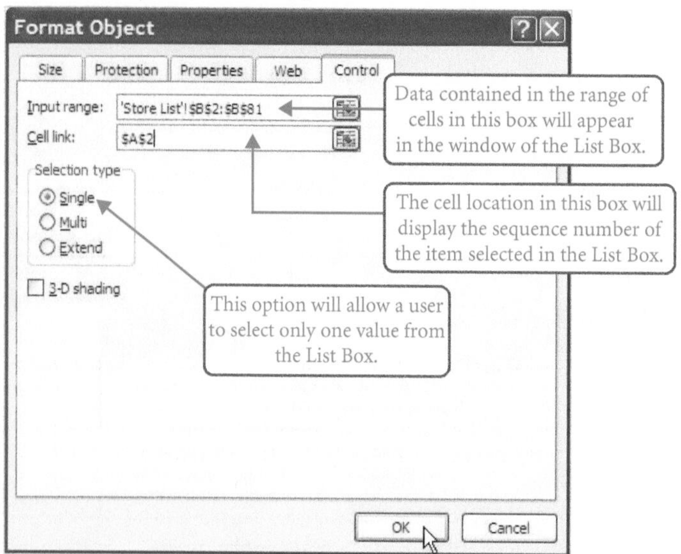


Figure 46 shows the List Box activated in the Store Analysis worksheet. Store 1015 has been selected from the List Box. Notice that the number 1 appears in cell A2. This is because store 1015 is listed first in the list of stores contained in the range B2:B81 in the Store List worksheet (see Figure 47).

Figure 46 | **Active List Box in the Store Analysis Worksheet**

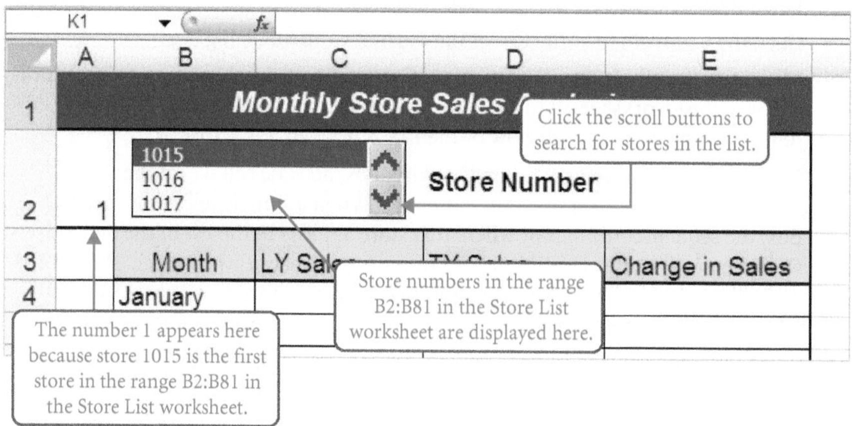

Figure 47 | **Data from the Store List Worksheet**

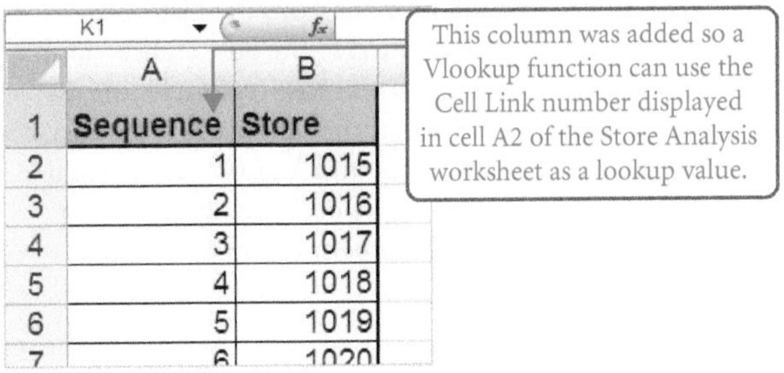

| | A | B |
|---|---|---|
| 1 | Sequence | Store |
| 2 | 1 | 1015 |
| 3 | 2 | 1016 |
| 4 | 3 | 1017 |
| 5 | 4 | 1018 |
| 6 | 5 | 1019 |
| 7 | 6 | 1020 |

This column was added so a Vlookup function can use the Cell Link number displayed in cell A2 of the Store Analysis worksheet as a lookup value.

After the List Box is configured and activated, the Store Analysis worksheet can be completed by using **Vlookup** functions to find and display sales data for the store that is selected. The **Vlookup** functions that will be added to the Store Analysis worksheet will serve two purposes. The first purpose is to display the store number that was selected in the List Box in cell location E2. This is done to display the store prominently on the spreadsheet so it can be easily identified when the worksheet is printed. The following is how each argument of this **Vlookup** function is defined.

- **lookup_value:** `A2` Cell A2 contains the sequence number that is displayed in the Store Analysis worksheet (see Figure 46). The function will look for the number that is displayed in this cell in Column A of the Store List worksheet (see Figure 47).
- **table_array:** `'Store List'!A2:B81` This is the range of data that contains the sequence number and the store numbers in the Store List worksheet.
- **col_index_num:** `2` The store numbers are in the second column to the right of the first column in the table array range.
- **[range_lookup]:** `False` The function will only look for exact values.

The second purpose the **Vlookup** functions will serve is to display the sales data that pertains to each month for the store selected in the List Box. The lookup value for these **Vlookup** functions will be created by concatenating the store number displayed in cell E2 with the month displayed in Column B of the Sales Analysis worksheet (see Figure 48). The following is how each of the arguments of this function is constructed for the LY Sales column. The **Vlookup** function that is used for the TY Sales column is identical to the LY Sales column except the column index number is 7 instead of 6.

- **lookup_value:** `CONCATENATE($E$2,B4)` The function will look for the combination of the store number displayed in cell E2 and the month displayed in cell B4, which is January. Notice that an absolute reference is placed on cell E2 but not B4. This is because when the function is pasted to the rest of the cells in the LY Sales column, a different month will be concatenated with the store number.
- **table_array:** `'Store Sales'!$A$2:$G$961` The function will search for the lookup value in Column A of the Store Sales worksheet (see Figure 42). As previously mentioned, this column was added to the worksheet by concatenating the values in the Store Number column with the Month column. This makes it possible for sales data to be matched up with the store number selected in the Store Analysis worksheet for each month of the year.
- **col_index_num:** `6` The sales data for Last Year in the Store Sales worksheet is six columns to the right of Column A which is the first column in the table array range.
- **[range_lookup]:** `False` The function will only look for exact values.

**>> Quick Reference**

**List Box**

1. Click the **Insert** icon in the **Developer** tab of the Ribbon.
2. Click the **List Box** icon from the **Form Controls** options.
3. Click and drag the desired size of the List Box on your worksheet.
4. Click the **Properties** icon in the **Developer** tab of the Ribbon.
5. Click the **Control** tab at the top of the **Format Control** dialog box.
6. Click the range finder next to the **Input Range** box and then highlight a range of cells in one column that contains data displayed in the **List Box** window.
7. Click the range finder next to the **Cell Link** box and then activate a cell location that will be used to display the sequence number of the item selected in the List Box.
8. Choose a Selection Type.
9. Click the **OK** button in the **Format Control** dialog box.
10. Click any cell location on your worksheet to activate the List Box.

Figure 48 shows the completed Sales Analysis worksheet. Noticed that Column A is hidden. The only value in this column is the Cell Link number from the List Box, which is not necessary for the reader to see. It was mentioned in the Subtotal section that Store 1044 showed a considerable decrease in sales for the East region. Figure 48 shows this store selected in the List Box. Notice that most of the sales decline for this store occurred in the month of January. In fact, March, July, and August were particularly strong months for this store; however, sales for this store declined again during September through December. This might suggest that competing stores had an aggressive Fall/Holiday promotional marketing strategy.

Figure 48 | **Completed Store Analysis Worksheet**

K1

| | B | C | D | E |
|---|---|---|---|---|
| 1 | **Monthly Store Sales Analysis** | | | |
| 2 | 1042<br>1043<br>1044 | | **Store Number** | **1044** |
| 3 | Month | LY Sales | TY Sales | Change in Sales |
| 4 | January | $ 2,634,993 | $ 1,253,795 | $ (1,381,198) |
| 5 | February | $ 888,714 | $ 951,361 | $ 62,647 |
| 6 | March | $ 1,264,966 | $ 1,522,240 | $ 257,274 |
| 7 | April | $ 1,442,063 | $ 1,551,529 | $ 109,466 |
| 8 | May | $ 1,644,862 | $ 1,610,190 | $ (34,672) |
| 9 | June | $ 1,636,848 | $ 1,586,803 | $ (50,045) |
| 10 | July | $ 1,706,297 | $ 1,971,157 | $ 264,860 |
| 11 | August | $ 2,797,730 | $ 3,186,457 | $ 388,727 |
| 12 | September | $ 3,515,445 | $ 3,272,743 | $ (242,702) |
| 13 | October | $ 2,621,667 | $ 2,486,036 | $ (135,631) |
| 14 | November | $ 2,488,860 | $ 2,528,940 | $ 40,080 |
| 15 | December | $ 2,894,655 | $ 2,714,458 | $ (180,197) |
| 16 | **Total** | $25,537,100 | $ 24,635,709 | $ (901,391) |

Store List | Store Sales | **Store Analysis**

Formulas subtracting LY Sales from TY Sales are used in this column.

Sum functions are used in these cells.

Most of the sales decline for this store occurred in January.

**VIDEO WORKSHOP**

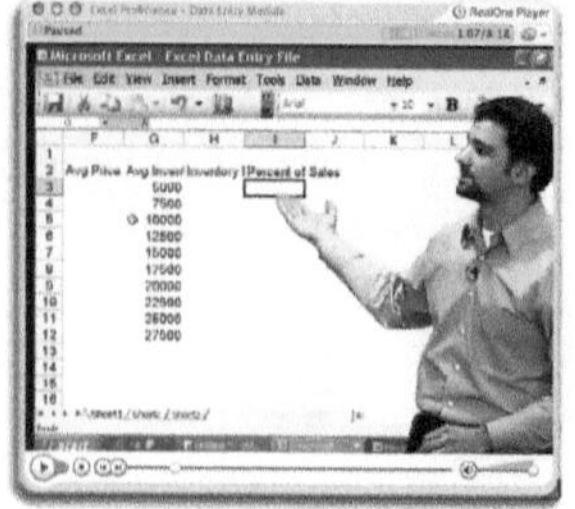

## >> Filters

The purpose of this workshop is to review the setup and use of the **Filter** tool. This workshop will use the same data that was shown in the Filters segment. I will be demonstrating the tasks in this workshop in the video named **Filters**. Open the Excel file named ib_e08_marketanalysis and then complete the tasks in the workshop.

1. **Applying Filters (Video: Filters)**
   a. Activate cell location A1 on the Data worksheet.
   b. Click the **Filter** icon in the **Data** tab of the Ribbon.
   c. Click the drop-down arrow next to the Total Population column heading, place the cursor over the **Number Filters** option, and select the **Custom Filter** option.
   d. Click the drop-down arrow next to the first box in the **Custom AutoFilter** dialog box, and select the is greater than or equal to option.
   e. Click the drop-down arrow next to the second box in the **Custom AutoFilter** dialog box, and select the value 100,002; then click the **OK** button.
   f. Open the **Custom AutoFilter** dialog box for the Percent of Population Age 25–35 column. Set the filter for any values greater than or equal to .20.
   g. Open the **Custom AutoFilter** dialog box for the Growth in Population Age 25–35 column. Set the filter for any values greater than .05
   h. Open the **Custom AutoFilter** dialog box for the Household Income column. Set the filter for any values greater than or equal to 70000.
   i. Insert a new worksheet in the workbook. Copy the range A1:A501 in the Data worksheet and paste it into cell A1 of the new worksheet.
   j. Save and close your workbook.

## Subtotals

**VIDEO WORKSHOP**

The purpose of this workshop is to review the setup and use of Subtotals. This workshop will use the same data that was shown in the Subtotals segment. I will be demonstrating the tasks in this workshop in the video named **Subtotals.** Open the Excel file named ib_e08_electronicsstoreanalysis and then complete the tasks in the workshop.

1. **Applying Subtotals to Data (Video: Subtotals)**
   a. Sort the range A1:G241 based on values in the Region, District, and Stores columns. Set the sort option for each column to ascending or smallest to largest.
   b. Activate cell A1 in the Data worksheet.
   c. Click the **Subtotals** icon in the **Data** tab of the Ribbon.
   d. Select the Region column for the first drop-down box in the **Subtotal** dialog box.
   e. Select the **Sum** function in the second drop-down box in the **Subtotal** dialog box.
   f. In the **Add subtotal to** box, check marks should appear next to the LY Sales, TY Sales, and Change in Sales columns. Click the box next to the column name to add a check mark, if necessary.
   g. Click the **OK** button at the bottom of the **Subtotal** dialog box.
   h. Click the **Level 2** button in the upper-left margin of the worksheet.
   i. Activate cell A1 and then open the **Subtotal** dialog box.
   j. Select the District column for the first drop-down box in the **Subtotal** dialog box and repeat Steps e and f.

k. Click the box next to the Replace current subtotals option to remove the check mark and then click the **OK** button.
l. Click the **Level 2** button and then activate cell A1.
m. Open the **Subtotal** dialog box, select the Store column, and repeat Steps e and f; then click the **OK** button.
n. In this order, click the **Level 4, 3**, and **2** buttons.
o. Click the **Show Details** button next to the East region.
p. Click the **Show Details** button next to District 14.
q. Click the **Show Details** button next to Store 1044.
r. Save and close your workbook.

## » List Boxes

The purpose of this workshop is to review the setup and use of List Boxes. This workshop will use the same data that was shown in the List Boxes segment. I will be demonstrating the tasks in this workshop in the video named **List Boxes**. Open the Excel file named ib_e08_storesalesbymonth and complete the tasks in the workshop.

1. **List Boxes (Video: List Boxes)**

a. Activate the Store Analysis worksheet.
b. Click the **Insert** icon in the **Developer** tab of the Ribbon.
c. Click the **List Box** icon from the **Form Controls** set of options.
d. Click and drag a rectangle in the space between cells B2 and C2.
e. Click the **Properties** icon in the **Developer** tab of the Ribbon.
f. In the **Control** tab of the **Format Control** dialog box, click the range finder next to the Input range box, highlight the range B2:B81 in the Store List worksheet, and press the **Enter** key.
g. Click the range finder next to the **Cell link** box, activate cell A2 in the Store Analysis worksheet, and press the **Enter** key.
h. Click the **OK** button in the **Format Objects** dialog box, and then activate cell F1 in the Store Analysis worksheet.
i. Select Store 1015 in the List Box.
j. Type a **VLOOKUP** function in cell E2 on the Store Analysis worksheet, defining each argument as follows:
   i. lookup_value: Cell A2 in the Store Analysis worksheet
   ii. table_array: A2:B81 in the Store List worksheet
   iii. col_index_num: 2
   iv. [range_lookup]: False
k. Type a **VLOOKUP** function in cell C4 on the Store Analysis worksheet defining each argument as follows (use absolute references as shown):
   i. lookup_value: Concatenate($E$2,B4)
   ii. table_array: $A$2:$G$961 in the Store Sales worksheet
   iii. col_index_num: 6
   iv. [range_lookup]: False
l. Copy the **VLOOKUP** function in cell C4 and paste it into the range C5:C15 in the Store Analysis worksheet.

m. Type a **VLOOKUP** function in cell D4 on the Store Analysis worksheet defining each argument as follows:
   i. lookup_value: Concatenate($E$2,B4)
   ii. table_array: $A$2:$G$961 in the Store Sales worksheet
   iii. col_index_num: 7
   iv. [range_lookup]: False
n. Copy the **VLOOKUP** function in cell D4 and paste it into the range D5:D15 in the Store Analysis worksheet.
o. Type the formula `D4-C4` in cell E4 of the Store Analysis worksheet; then copy and paste this formula into the range E5:E15.
p. Type a sum function in cells C16, D16, and E16 to add the values in rows 4 through 15 for each column.
q. Hide column A in the Store Analysis worksheet.
r. Select Store 1044 in the List Box.
s. Save and close your workbook.

## >> Summarizing the Sales Performance of a Business

**EXERCISE**

**Why Do I Need This?**

Attention to detail is often the difference between success and failure in any business. Business mangers working in today's corporations have access to enormous amounts of data. However, it is impossible for a person to evaluate every row of data that is collected for their business or industry every day. As a result, business managers must determine what details they need to evaluate to improve their firm's business. This usually begins with some type of general performance report for the business they are managing, which then directs them to areas where more detailed information is needed. For example, if a business manager is running a division of company that sells five categories of products, a general performance report might show the overall sales results of the division by category. If one of the categories is showing a significant decline in sales, the manager will research more details for that category. This type of analysis can be conducted using Excel's AutoFilter and Subtotal tools.

### Exercise

The purpose of this exercise is to use Excel's **Subtotal** and **Filter** tools to evaluate the sales performance of a clothing business. Open the Excel file named ib_e08_salesbyitem before completing the following tasks.

1. Activate cell A1 in the Data for Subtotals worksheet. This worksheet contains almost 500 rows of data showing the sales results for this year and last year for every item sold by this clothing business for each month of the year. The data is sorted in month order and then by the Category and Item columns in ascending order. The first goal of this analysis is to use the Subtotal tool to evaluate the overall sales performance of the business by month.
2. Open the **Subtotal** dialog box. Create a subtotal for each month of sales data. Sum the values in the LY Sales, TY Sales, and Change in Sales columns.
3. Click the **Level 2** button to hide all the details in the worksheet except for the subtotals by month. Are the overall sales for this business increasing or decreasing? Which month is showing a decrease in sales?
4. Add a second subtotal to this worksheet for the Category column. Make sure the **Replace Current Subtotals** is *not* checked. Click the box next to this option to remove the check.

5. Add a third subtotal for the Item column. There should be a total of three subtotals on this worksheet.
6. In this order, click the **Level 5, 4, 3**, and **2** buttons. The worksheet should be back to showing just the overall sales result of the business by month.
7. Click the **Show Details** button for the month you identified in number 3. Are all categories showing a decrease in sales? Which category is showing the biggest decrease in sales?
8. Click the **Show Details** button for the category you identified in number 7. Are all items in this category showing a decrease in sales? Which item is showing the largest decrease in sales?
9. Click the **Show Details** button for the item you identified in number 8. Which colors for this item are showing a decrease in sales?
10. Activate cell A1 in the Data for AutoFilter worksheet.
11. Click the **Filter** icon in the **Data** tab of the Ribbon.
12. Click the drop-down arrow next to the Change in Sales column heading. Place the cursor over the **Number Filters** option and select the **Top 10** option. The goal of this task is to identify items in the business with largest decline in sales compared to last year. Select the **Bottom** option in the first drop-down box in the **Top 10 AutoFilter** dialog box and then click the **OK** button.
13. Sort the items selected by the filter based on the values in the Change in Sales column in ascending order—smallest to largest. Which item/color appears most frequently in this list? Based on these sales results, do you think this item should be discontinued?
14. Remove the filter on the Change in Sales column.
15. Set a filter on the Sales TY column to show the top ten highest sales results. Sort the values in this column in descending order—largest to smallest. Are all the items showing an increase in sales over last year? Would you still consider discontinuing the item you identified in number 13?
16. Set a filter on the Change in Sales column to show any item where the sales increased by more than $100,000 (you will need to remove the filter from the Sales TY column). Which category appears to have the best potential for increasing sales for the company?
17. Save and close your file.

PROBLEM & EXERCISE

## >> What's Wrong with This Spreadsheet?

### Problem

You are working as a business analyst in the buying division of a large retail company. Your coworker sends you an e-mail asking for help on a report he is trying to put together for a purchasing meeting. He is trying to use the **Subtotal** tool to summarize the sales results of the division by month. The following points are included in his e-mail.

- Can you do me a huge favor and take a look at the Excel file I attached to this e-mail? Someone told me that I would be able to summarize the total sales results by month for each category by using this **Subtotal** tool, but I can't figure out why this is not working.

- I am trying to show the total sales results for the company by month. I would also like to click on a month and see a summary of the sales results by category just for that month. Then, I want to see a summary of the sales results by item within the category.

- I set up the **Subtotal** tool on the attached file. I thought this was working fine because the total results for the divisions are correct. However, when I clicked on the box with the plus sign, the spreadsheet grew to almost 1900 rows. I thought this was odd because I started with less than 500 rows of data. Please help!

### Exercise

The Excel file your coworker attached to the e-mail is named ib_e08_suspicioussubtotals. Open this file and examine the subtotals that were added in the Data worksheet. What's wrong with this spreadsheet? Consider the following points.

1. Test the worksheet by clicking the **Show Details** button. What happens? Does the worksheet show a summary of the total sales results by month?
2. Continue to test the worksheet by clicking the show details button for the first month, then the category, and then the item. What do you notice about the sales results as you show more details?
3. Why would the number of rows increase by such a large amount after applying the subtotals?

Write a short answer for each of these points; then fix the spreadsheet so the subtotals provide the proper sales summaries as described in the second point of your coworker's e-mail.

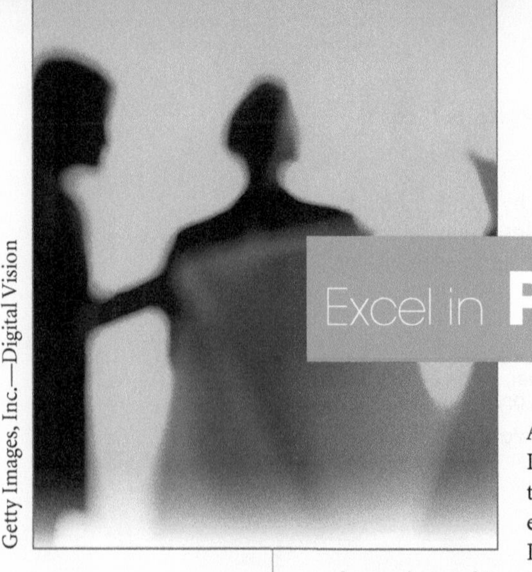

Getty Images, Inc.—Digital Vision

# Excel in **Practice** | Anecdote

**Solution**

After investigating Excel's features for managing large datasets, I found a few tools that were perfect for this project. Everyone on the team found these tools easy to use, and they were flexible enough to solve each team member's unique analytical needs.

I took the original worksheet which contained the 7,500 rows of data and copied it to two other worksheets. I then set up a different tool in each worksheet so each team member had a choice of using any of these tools to analyze the data based on their needs and preferences.

## Assignment

1. Open the Excel file named ib_e08_storeevaluations. The data contained in this file is similar to the data that was explained in the anecdote.
2. Use any of the tools covered in this chapter to analyze the data in the Sheet1 worksheet to answer the follow questions and tasks.
   a. Analyze the overall sales performance of the business. Are sales increasing every year? Which year is showing the greatest increase in sales?
   b. Analyze the population statistics for the overall business. The products sold in the stores of this business are targeted for children between the ages of 4 and 11. Overall, are these stores located in areas where the Total Population and the Population Age 4–11 is increasing every year?
   c. Analyze the sales performance of this business by Region. Which region is showing the strongest sales growth from 2004 to 2006? Which region is showing the largest sales decline?
   d. Compare the population and competition trends between the region with the largest sales increase and the region with the largest sales decrease. Explain the difference in the trends between these two regions and explain why you think sales are increasing or decreasing for these regions.
   e. Add a new worksheet to the Store Evaluations workbook. Create a list of stores in this worksheet where the Population Age 4–11 is equal to or less than 15 percent of the Total Population in the year 2006. In addition, these stores should be in areas were the competition has less than or equal to two stores. Sort this list based on values in the Population Age 4–11 column. How many stores are on your list?
   f. Save and close your file.

## Questions for Discussion

1. The anecdote suggests that both Access and Excel can be used to analyze large volumes of data. What are the benefits of being able to analyze data and get the same results using different tools and methods?

2. The main theme of this chapter is managing and analyzing large volumes of data. Why do companies collect so much data? What purpose does this data serve in a business?

3. Can companies achieve a competitive advantage if they collect and store more data than their competitors?

# Review Questions

The following questions are related to the concepts addressed in this chapter. There are three types of questions: Short Answer, True or False, and Fill in the Blank. If your answer to a True or False question is False, write a short explanation as to why you think the statement is not true.

1. The ________ icon in the ________ tab of the Ribbon is used to create a PivotChart.
2. You must click anywhere in the ________ ________ to see the PivotTable Field List as well as the ________ and ________ tabs of the Ribbon.
3. True or False: The PivotTable Field names must be typed into the **Field Settings** dialog box before they appear in the PivotTable Field List.
4. How can you count the values in a field that is added to the Data section of the PivotTable Report instead of summing them?
5. The ________ button in the ________ dialog box can be used to format numbers to currency in the Data section of the PivotTable Report.
6. How can you reduce the data on a PivotTable to a specific item from a field that is dragged into the Row Fields section?
7. True or False: To adjust the subtotals shown on a PivotTable Report, double-click the field name that was added to the Data or Values section to open the **Value Field Settings** dialog box.
8. True or False: Similar to most other Excel operations, a key benefit of PivotTables is that if the source data is changed, the change will immediately be seen in the values and calculations on the PivotTable Report.
9. Explain how you would use two fields in the Data section of a PivotTable Report to create a formula.
10. The grand totals on a PivotTable can be added or removed by selecting the appropriate options in the ________ tab in the ________ dialog box.
11. True or False: A PivotTable is always added to your workbook when you create a PivotChart, and the PivotChart can be created by adding and manipulating fields in this PivotTable.
12. True or False: When using the **Filter** tool, you must highlight the first row containing column headings in your worksheet for the drop-down arrows to appear in the proper place.
13. How can you sort the results that are displayed using the **Filter** tool?
14. True or False: When using Filters, after you apply a filter rule to a specific column, you can *not* sort the data based on values in that column.
15. Before using the **Subtotals** tool, you must ________ all the data in your worksheet.
16. True or False: You can only set subtotals for one column at a time in **Subtotals** dialog box; therefore, you will need to open the **Subtotals** dialog box multiple times to create subtotals for multiple columns.

17. The ________ ________ are used to either hide or show all details from a column that has been subtotaled using the **Subtotals** tool.

18. If store number 6215 is the 12th store in a list of 100 stores, what number will appear in the Cell Link cell when this store is selected from a List Box?

19. How do you know if a List Box is inactive, which means the controls for the List Box can be set or modified?

20. You must hold down the ________ ________ before clicking a List Box to deactivate it.

# Skills Exam

The following exam is designed to test your ability to recognize and execute the Excel skills presented in this chapter. Read each question carefully and answer the questions in the order they are listed. You should be able to complete this exam in 60 minutes or less.

1. Open the ib_e08_chapter8skillsexam Excel file.
2. Apply the **Filter** tool to the data in the Filter worksheet.
3. Apply the following filters to these columns:
   a. Year: equal to 2002
   b. Gross Sales: less than 1000000000
4. Sort results from number 3 in ascending order based on the values in the Gross Sales column.
5. Sort the data in the Subtotal worksheet so subtotals can be calculated for the Industry and Company columns.
6. Use the **Subtotals** tool to subtotal the values in the Gross Sales column for each industry.
7. Add a *second* subtotal to the data in the Subtotal worksheet for the Company column. Subtotal the values in the Gross Sales column for each company.
8. Use the **Level** buttons to hide all details for the Industry column in the Subtotals worksheet. The worksheet should show the subtotals for only the four industries and the Grand Totals.
9. Show the details for the Specialty Retail Industry.
10. Show the details for Sp Retail Company 1.
11. Use the data in the PivotTable worksheet to create a blank PivotTable Report in a new worksheet that is added to the workbook.
12. Add the following fields to the PivotTable Report in the locations specified:
    a. Year field: Column Labels section
    b. Industry field: Row Labels section
    c. Gross Sales field: Values section
13. Change the field settings for the Gross Sales field so the values are averaged instead of summed. Format the values in this field to a Currency format with 0 decimal places.
14. Add the Company field to the Values section of the PivotTable Report.
15. Change the name of the Company field to Number of Companies and make sure the field settings are set to Count.
16. Add a calculated field to the Values section of the PivotTable Report that divides the Gross Sales field by 52. Name this calculated field `Industry Weekly Sales`.
17. Show only the Computer Hardware industry on the PivotTable Report.
18. Remove the report totals for the columns on the PivotTable Report.
19. Adjust the PivotTable Report so the years are shown as row labels instead of column labels.
20. Sort the Year field based on the values in the Gross Sales field in Ascending order.
21. Add a Format Control List Box to the Company Analysis worksheet over cell locations B2 and C2.
22. Set the controls of the List Box you added in number 21 to show the list of companies in the range B3:B35 in the Company List worksheet. Use cell location A2 in the Company Analysis worksheet to define the Cell Link of the control. Set the Selection Type to Single.

23. Use a **VLOOKUP** function to display the company that is selected in the List Box in cell D2 of the Company Analysis worksheet.

24. Use a **VLOOKUP** function to display the industry sales for the appropriate year in cells C4 through C7 based on the company that is selected in the List Box. Industry sales data for each company can be found in the List Box Data worksheet.

25. Use the **VLOOKUP** function to show the Gross Sales for the company selected in the List Box for the appropriate year in cells D4 through D7. Gross sales data for each company can be found in the List Box data worksheet.

26. Use a formula to calculate the market share in cells E4 through E7 in the Company Analysis worksheet. Your formula should divide the industry sales into the gross sales for each year. Format the results to a percentage with 1 decimal place.

27. Hide Column A on the Company Analysis worksheet; then select the Restaurant 6 company from the List Box.

28. Save and close your file.

# Challenge Questions

The following questions are designed to test your ability to apply the Excel skills you have learned to complete a business objective. Use your knowledge of Excel as well as your creativity to answer these questions. For most questions, there are several possible ways to complete the objective.

**1.** Open the Excel file named ib_e08_challengea. This is the same data that was used in the subtotals workshop. Analyze the sales performance of this business by category through the following points:

a. Identify the total change in sales *by category* for the entire company.

b. Identify the category that experienced the largest decrease in sales and show the change in sales for each region just for this category.

c. Identify the region from letter b that experienced the largest decrease in sales and show the change in sales for every district in this region. Are the sales decreasing for all districts in this region?

**2.** Open the Excel file named ib_e08_challengeb. The data in this file is identical to the ib_e08_challengea file. Design a worksheet where a business manager can select a store number from a List Box to analyze sales data by category. Each unique store number in Column C should appear in the List Box only one time. After the store is selected, the following information should be displayed on the worksheet:

a. The region number and district number for the store.

b. The store's TY Sales and Change in Sales by category.

c. The TY Sales for the store's region by category.

d. The percentage of TY Sales the store contributes to the region (store TY Sales/region TY Sales) by category.

e. Total Change in Sales and TY Sales for the store and region as well as the total percentage of TY Sales the store contributes to the region.

# Scenario Tools and Advanced Statistics

## Chapter Goals

This chapter will demonstrate tools designed for conducting "What if" scenarios and advanced statistical computations. Excel's cell-referencing abilities have been used throughout this text to conduct a variety of business scenarios. The first section of this chapter also presents business scenarios, but through the use of tools that can provide greater flexibility and speed. The second section will introduce data analysis tools that can provide an entire range of descriptive statistics outputs at one time or execute other statistical methods such as regression and histograms. Finally, the third section will demonstrate the Solver tool, which is used to calculate minimum or maximum outputs given certain constraints or conditions that exist for a specific business situation.

This chapter will touch on fundamental concepts used in Cost Accounting and Economics. Although mastering these disciplines is *not* a prerequisite for learning the content in this chapter, you should have a working knowledge of each from your Accounting, Economics, and/or Statistics courses. This text will not provide in-depth explanations or instructions regarding the practice and theory of these disciplines.

## >> Excel | Skill Sets

**Scenario Tools**
- Scroll Bar
- Conditional Formatting
- Data Tables
- Goal Seek
- Scenario Manager

**Data Analysis Tools**
- Add-Ins
- Descriptive Statistics
- Histogram
- Regression

**Solver**
- Defining Constraints
- Defining Solver Parameters

Getty Images, Inc.—StockByte

# Excel in **Practice** | Anecdote

### My Role as a Profit Analyst

One of the most intense jobs I have had in my career was working as a profit analyst in the women's fashion industry. The company I worked for manufactured and sold women's fashion clothes in specialty stores across the United States. I was responsible for planning the sales and profits for all merchandise purchased in my department. I worked closely with the designers and production coordinators to develop a financial plan for merchandise that was purchased at the beginning of each season. This plan, along with the merchandise line, was presented to the executive officers of the company. It was at these meetings that I was constantly asked several "What if" questions. For example, "What if you have to sell 50% of this item at a 40% markdown." In other words, if an item we purchased, such as a printed skirt, did not meet our sales expectations, we would reduce the price to sell as much of the remaining inventory as possible. Depending on how much inventory we sold at full price, the amount of remaining inventory sold at the reduced price could decrease or eliminate any planned profits. As a result, the executive officers frequently wanted to know "the worst-case scenario." Therefore, I had to prepare almost every possible profit scenario for each item in the line and for the overall department. The kicker was that for some meetings, I would prepare what seemed to be hundreds of scenarios, and the executive officers would not ask one question. However, I was sure that if I came to a meeting without my "What if" scenarios, I would get questions on every item in the line.

>> Continued later in this chapter

# Scenario Tools

Skill Set

Excel provides several tools that can use cell referencing to enhance your ability to evaluate multiple "What if" scenarios when making business decisions. This section will demonstrate four of these tools and explain how business managers use them to set prices, manage profits, and evaluate the return on investments. You will need to add the **Developer** tab to the Ribbon to access the tools covered in this section. To do this, click the **Office Button**, click the **Excel Options** button, and select the **Show Developer** tab in the Ribbon option in the Popular section of the **Excel Options** dialog box.

## Scroll Bar

You may have learned about adding the **Developer** tab to the Ribbon to access the Form Controls. The Form Controls also contains an option called Scroll Bar, which can be used as a scenario tool. You can use the Scroll Bar to change a number in a target cell location in single-unit increments. This allows you to produce various outputs in other cells that are referencing the target cell in formulas and functions. This tool can be especially helpful when conducting a break-even analysis for a new business or product line. The goal of a break-even analysis is to determine the product price and unit sales required to meet or exceed the costs of production. For example, Figure 1 shows the sales and costs of a new hypothetical shirt company. Based on the cost of producing a shirt, a business manager will need to know how many shirts need to be sold and at what price for the company to produce a profit. However, determining the price of the shirt can be tricky, because as the price increases, the total number of shirts that can be sold will decrease. Therefore, this example uses the Scroll Bar to change the price in cell B2 of Figure 1 gradually to determine when the business will meet and exceed its costs.

Figure 1 | **Sales and Costs for a Shirt-Manufacturing Company**

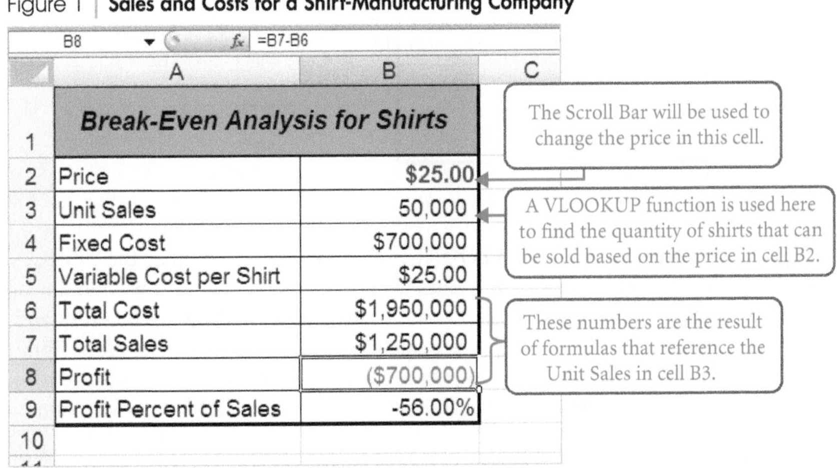

The Scroll Bar will be used to change the price in cell B2 in the worksheet shown in Figure 1. A second worksheet in this workbook shows how many shirts can be sold based on the price that is entered in cell B2 (see Figure 2). Following basic economic principles, as the price of the shirt increases, the quantity demanded for the shirt decreases. As a result, a VLOOKUP function is used in cell B3 to show the unit sales based on the price that is entered in cell B2 (see Figure 3).

Figure 2 | **Price and Sales Units Worksheet**

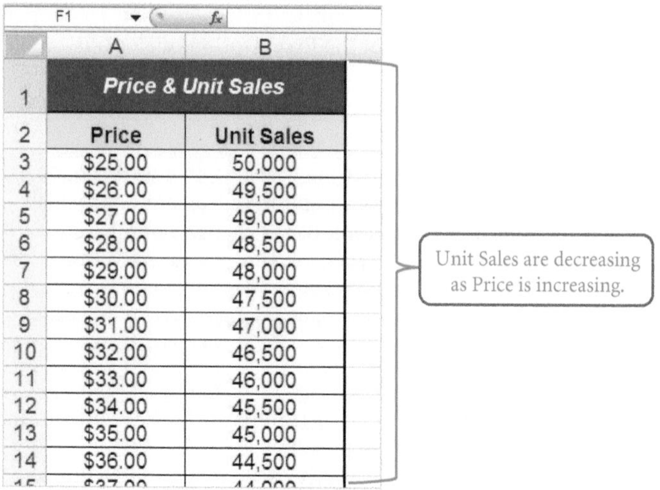

| | A | B |
|---|---|---|
| 1 | Price & Unit Sales | |
| 2 | Price | Unit Sales |
| 3 | $25.00 | 50,000 |
| 4 | $26.00 | 49,500 |
| 5 | $27.00 | 49,000 |
| 6 | $28.00 | 48,500 |
| 7 | $29.00 | 48,000 |
| 8 | $30.00 | 47,500 |
| 9 | $31.00 | 47,000 |
| 10 | $32.00 | 46,500 |
| 11 | $33.00 | 46,000 |
| 12 | $34.00 | 45,500 |
| 13 | $35.00 | 45,000 |
| 14 | $36.00 | 44,500 |



Figure 3 | **VLOOKUP Referencing Unit Sales from the Price and Sales Units Worksheet**

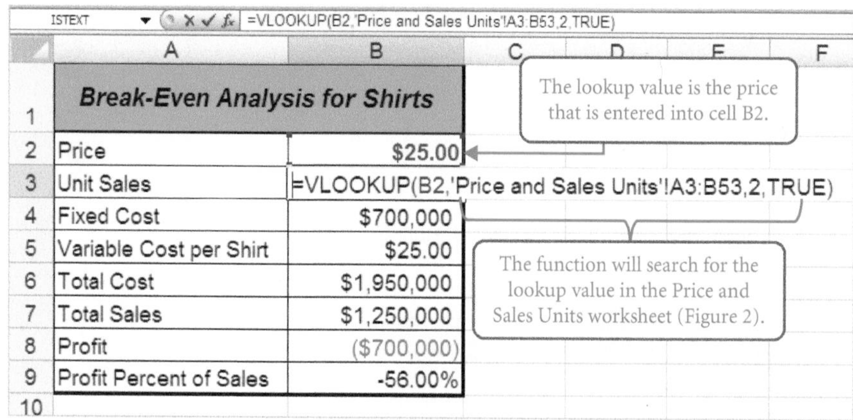

| | A | B |
|---|---|---|
| 1 | Break-Even Analysis for Shirts | |
| 2 | Price | $25.00 |
| 3 | Unit Sales | =VLOOKUP(B2,'Price and Sales Units'!A3:B53,2,TRUE) |
| 4 | Fixed Cost | $700,000 |
| 5 | Variable Cost per Shirt | $25.00 |
| 6 | Total Cost | $1,950,000 |
| 7 | Total Sales | $1,250,000 |
| 8 | Profit | ($700,000) |
| 9 | Profit Percent of Sales | -56.00% |
| 10 | | |



Figure 3 shows the setup of the **VLOOKUP** function that will display the Unit Sales value in cell B3 from the Price and Sales Units worksheet. Cell B3 is used in formulas to calculate the Total Cost in cell B6 and the Total Sales in cell B7. The Profit and Profit Percent of Sales in cells B8 and B9 are calculated based on the results of the Total Cost and Total Sales formulas. As a result, when the price is changed in cell B2, the **VLOOKUP** function will display a new value for Unit Sales in cell B3. When the value in cell B3 is changed, the results of the formulas calculating Total Cost, Total Sales, Profit, and Profit Percent of Sales will also change. Therefore, a business manager can keep typing different prices into cell B2 to see when the company produces a profit. However, instead of typing different prices, the Scroll Bar will be used to change the price gradually to see when profits become positive. The following explains how this is accomplished.

- Click the **Insert** icon in the **Controls** group on the **Developer** tab of the Ribbon.
- Click the **Scroll Bar** icon in the Form Controls set of options. Then, click and drag the shape of a vertical rectangle in the area of cells C2 through C9 (see Figure 4).

Figure 4 | **Adding a Scroll Bar to the Sales and Costs Worksheet**

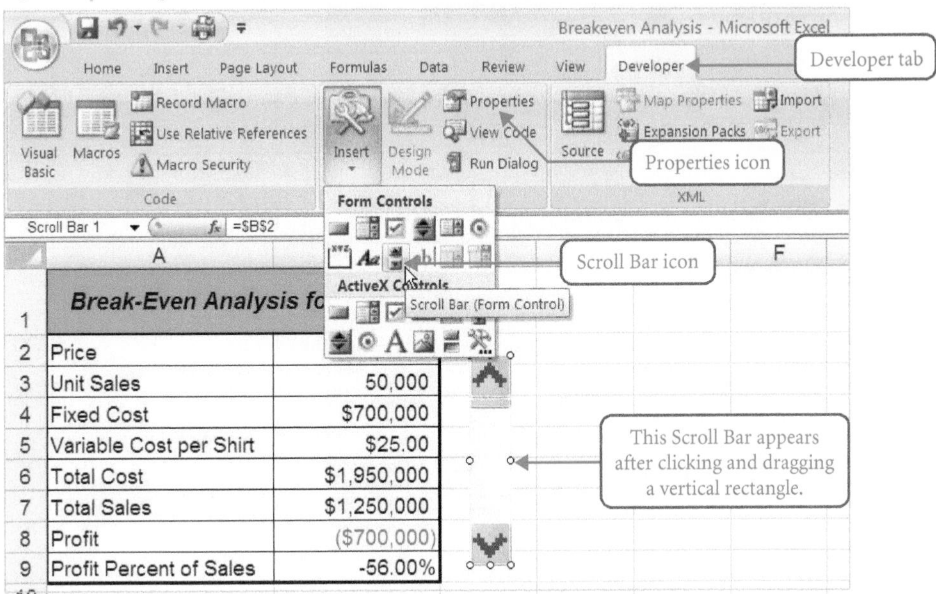


Figure 4 shows the results of adding a Scroll Bar to the worksheet that is calculating the profitability of a shirt manufacturing company. The white dots around the perimeter of the Scroll Bar signify that it is deactivated. Before the Scroll Bar is activated, it must be configured to change the price in cell B2 when either the Up or the Down arrow is clicked or the slide is dragged. The following explains how the Scroll Bar is configured for this example.

- Make sure the Scroll Bar is deactivated. White dots will appear around the perimeter of the Scroll Bar if it is deactivated. If the Scroll Bar is active, click it while holding the **Ctrl** key.
- Click the **Properties** icon in the **Developer** tab of the Ribbon (see Figure 4). This will open the **Format Control** dialog box.
- Click the **Control** tab at the top of the **Format Control** dialog box. Then, type the number 25 in the box labeled Current Value. The number 25 is typed into this box because it is the value that is currently entered into cell B2 (see Figure 3).
- Type the number 25 in the box labeled Minimum Value. As shown in Figure 3, at a price of $25 the company is losing a substantial amount of money. Therefore, there is no need to go below $25.
- Type the number 75 in the box labeled Maximum Value. For this example we will assume that there is very little demand for shirts priced more than $75.
- Type the number 1 in the box labeled Incremental Change. This will increase or decrease the price by $1 when either the Up arrow or the Down arrow is clicked.
- Type the number 5 in the box labeled Page Change. This will increase or decrease the price by $5 when the space above or below the slide in the Scroll Bar is clicked.
- Click the range finder next to the box labeled Cell Link, click cell B2, and press the **Enter** key. This connects the Scroll Bar to cell B2, which contains the price of the shirt.

- Click the **OK** button on the **Format Control** dialog box and then click anywhere on the worksheet to activate the Scroll Bar. Figure 5 shows the final setup of the **Format Control** dialog box for the Scroll Bar.

Figure 5 | **Format Control Settings for the Scroll Bar**

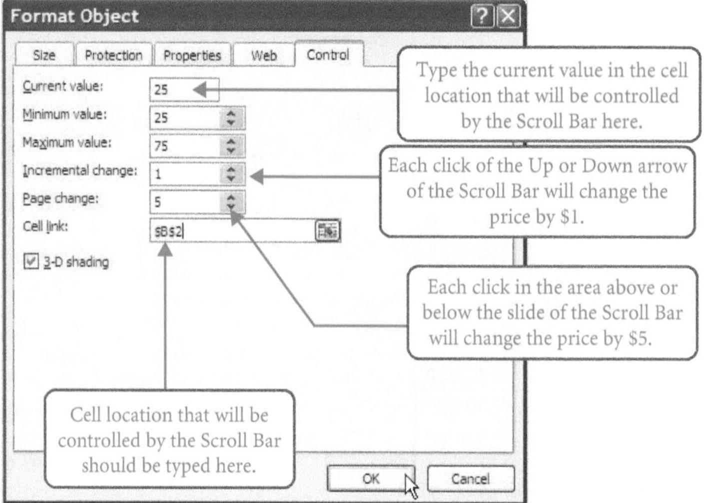


## COMMON MISTAKES | Setting Increment Values for the Scroll Bar

The Scroll Bar can increase or decrease the value in a target cell location only by whole-number increments. Therefore, you cannot type a number with a decimal point in either the **Incremental Change** box or the **Page Change** box in the Format Control dialog box for a Scroll Bar. Excel will automatically round numbers with decimal places to the nearest whole unit. In addition, if you enter a number such as .25 in either the Incremental **Change** box or the **Page Change** box, Excel will round this number to 0 and the Scroll Bar will not work. Finally, only positive numbers can be used in the Scroll bar control settings, and the settings must be in the range of 0 to 30,000.

Figure 6 shows the results of using the Scroll Bar to change the price in cell B2 to determine at what price the shirt company produces a profit. The slide in the middle of the Scroll Bar was clicked and dragged to gradually change the price to determine when the profit value in cell B8 becomes positive. As shown in the figure, the company begins to produce a profit when a price of $43 is charged for the shirt.

Figure 6 | **Using the Scroll Bar to Set the Prices**

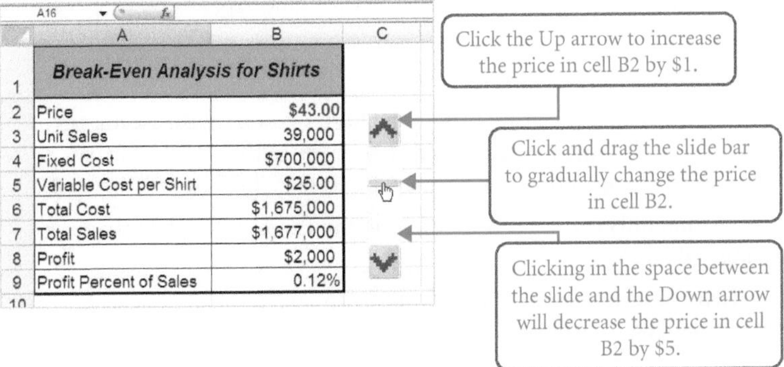

| Break-Even Analysis for Shirts | |
|---|---|
| Price | $43.00 |
| Unit Sales | 39,000 |
| Fixed Cost | $700,000 |
| Variable Cost per Shirt | $25.00 |
| Total Cost | $1,675,000 |
| Total Sales | $1,677,000 |
| Profit | $2,000 |
| Profit Percent of Sales | 0.12% |

Click the Up arrow to increase the price in cell B2 by $1.
Click and drag the slide bar to gradually change the price in cell B2.
Clicking in the space between the slide and the Down arrow will decrease the price in cell B2 by $5.

## Conditional Formatting

Looking at Figure 4 in the previous segment, you might have noticed that the profit value in cell B8 is in parentheses with a red font color. However, when the profit becomes positive in Figure 6, the value in cell B8 is no longer in parentheses and the font color changes to black. This is because the Currency category in the **Format Cells** dialog box provides an option to show negative values in parentheses with a red font color (see Figure 7). Managers frequently use this format option in business reporting because it helps draw the reader's attention to negative numbers that probably need to be addressed. However, this option is not available for all types of numbers. For example, in Figure 4 the profit value in cell B8 is red, but the percentage is still black. To change the percentage to a red font color to match the profit value, the **Conditional Formatting** features will need to be used.

Figure 7 | **Negative Currency Option in the Format Cells Dialog Box**

This option will show negative currency values in parentheses and will change the font color to red.

The Conditional Formatting feature will be used to set any negative percentage values in cell B9 in Figure 4 to a red font color. The following explains how this is accomplished.

- Activate cell B9 (see Figure 4).
- Click the **Conditional Formatting** icon in the **Styles** group on the **Home** tab of the Ribbon. Then, click the **New Rule** option near the bottom of the format options list. This will open the **New Formatting Rule** dialog box (see Figure 8).
- Select the **Format only cells that contain** option in the top section of the **New Formatting Rule** dialog box.
- Select the **Cell Value** option in the first drop-down box in the bottom section of the **New Formatting Rule** dialog box.
- Select the **Less Than** option in the second drop-down box at the bottom of the dialog box.
- Type the number 0 in the third box. This will complete the criteria that will be used to apply a format to the value in cell B9. Excel will apply a designated format when the value in cell B9 is less than 0.
- Click the **Format** button near the bottom of the **New Formatting Rule** dialog box. This will open the **Format Cells** dialog box. Change the color to red in the **Font** tab of the dialog box.
- Click the **OK** button in the **Format Cells** dialog box and then the **OK** button at the bottom of the **New Formatting Rule** dialog box. The text color will be changed to red for any value in cell B9 that is less than 0.

Figure 8 shows the options that appear after the **Conditional Formatting** icon is selected. Click the **New Rule** option to set criteria that will be used to apply a designated format to a cell or range of cells.

> **Quick Reference**
>
> **Scroll Bar**
>
> 1. Click the **Insert** icon in the **Developer** tab of the Ribbon.
> 2. Click the **Scroll Bar** icon from the **Form Controls** options.
> 3. Click and drag a vertical rectangle on your worksheet to define the size and placement of the Scroll Bar.
> 4. With the Scroll Bar deactivated, click the **Properties** icon in the **Developer** tab of the Ribbon to open the **Format Control** dialog box.
> 5. Set the Current Value, Minimum Value, and Maximum Value based on the needs of your project (must be between 0 and 30,000).
> 6. Type a whole number in the **Incremental Change** box.
> 7. Type a whole number in the **Page Change** box.
> 8. Type the target cell location in the **Cell Link** box or use the range finder.
> 9. Click the **OK** button on the **Format Control** dialog box.
> 10. Click anywhere on your worksheet to activate the Scroll Bar.

Figure 8 | **Creating a New Conditional Formatting Rule**

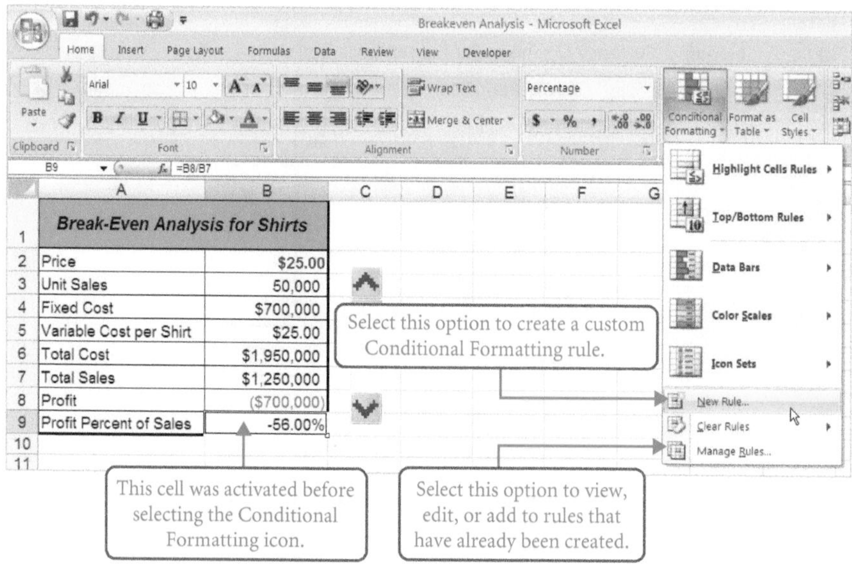


Figure 9 shows the final settings in the **New Formatting Rule** dialog box. If the criteria at the bottom of this dialog box are true, the formats selected in the **Format Cells** dialog box will be applied to cell B9.

Figure 9 | **New Formatting Rule Dialog Box**

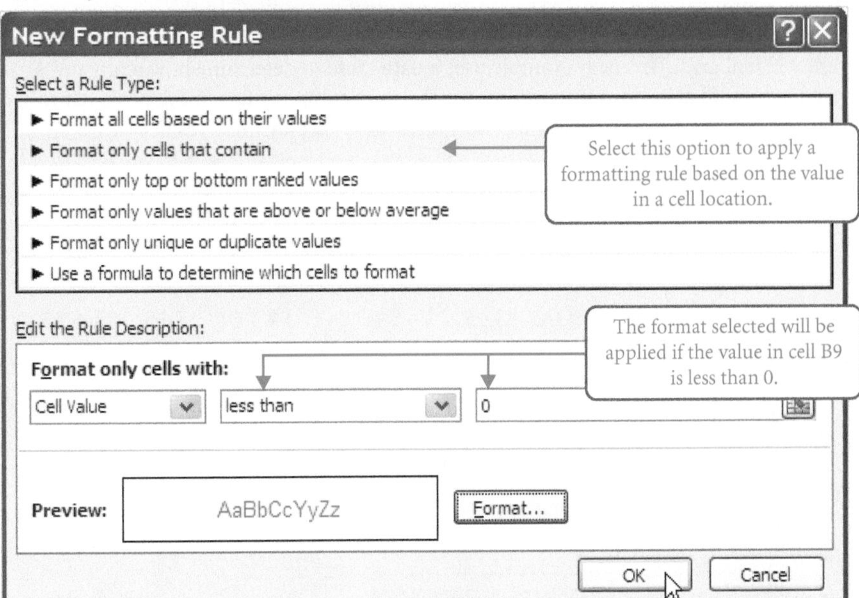


Figure 10 shows the final results of the break-even analysis worksheet with the conditional formatting rule applied. Because the value in cell B9 is less than 0, the font color was changed to red. To view or edit any conditional formatting rules that have been applied to a worksheet, click the **Manage Rules** option after clicking the **Conditional Formatting** icon in the **Home** tab of the Ribbon (see Figure 8).

Figure 10 | **Break-Even Worksheet with Conditional Formats**

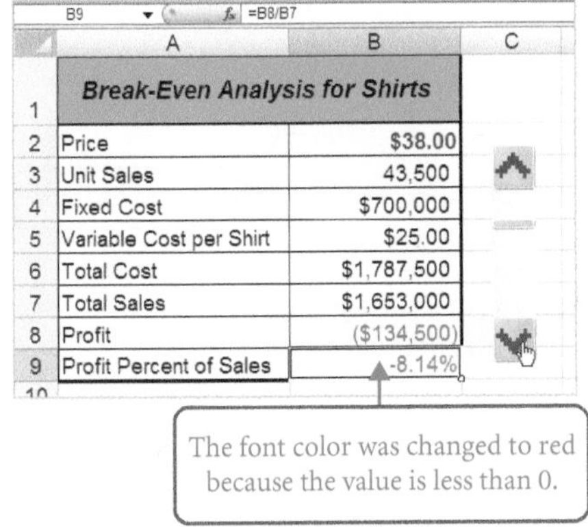


## Data Tables

The previous segment demonstrated how the Scroll Bar can be used to assess the profitability of a shirt company by changing the selling price of the product. This example assumed that a specific number of units could be sold based on the price that was charged. As a result, the **VLOOKUP** function was used in a second worksheet to find the exact number of units that could be sold based on the price that was entered in the first worksheet. However, what if you were not sure how many shirts you could sell at

>> ***Quick Reference***

### Conditional Formatting

1. Activate the cell location where the conditional format will be applied.
2. Click the **Conditional Formatting** icon in the **Styles** group on **Home** tab of the Ribbon.
3. Select the **New Rule** option near the bottom of the **Conditional Format** list.
4. Select the **Format only cells that contain** option in the top section of the **New Formatting Rule** dialog box if your criteria are based on the value in a cell location.
5. Set the first drop-down box to **Cell Value**.
6. Select a comparison operator in the second drop-down box.
7. Type a value in the third box or use the range finder to select a cell location on your worksheet.
8. Click the **Format** button to open the **Format Cells** dialog box.
9. Set the formatting options that will be applied to the cell activated in step 1 if the conditions defined in steps 6 and 7 are true.
10. Click the **OK** button on the **Format Cells** dialog box.
11. Click the **OK** button on the **New Formatting Rule** dialog box.
12. Click the **Conditional Formatting** icon and select the **Manage Rules** option to edit or add additional rules to the same cell location.

different prices? In this case, you might need to ask the question, "If I charge a price of X, how many units do I need to sell to achieve positive profits?" In this situation you would need to use a data table. Data tables show multiple results of a formula in a two-dimensional grid. This next example uses a data table to determine how many units need to be sold at various price points for the shirt company to achieve positive profits. Figure 11 shows a sketch of how a Data Table would display these results.

Figure 11 | **Data-Table Sketch**

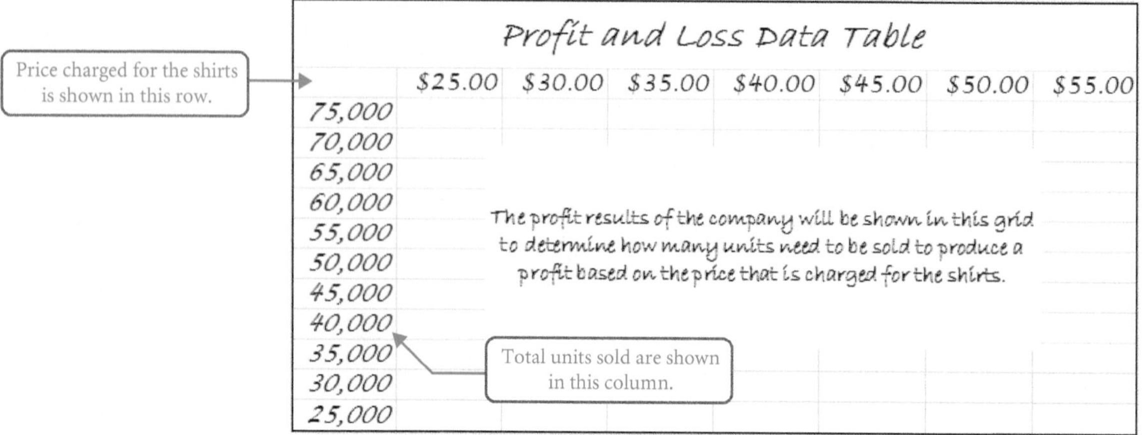


Figure 12 shows the setup of the worksheet that will be used to construct the data table that is sketched in Figure 11. As mentioned, the data table will be used to show the profit results of the company when a certain price is charged and a certain number of units are sold. For this example we will assume that the company cannot produce more than 75,000 shirts a year and will need to produce a minimum of 25,000 shirts to operate the factory for at least one shift throughout the year. This is why the numbers along the left side of the sketch in Figure 11 are between 75,000 and 25,000.

Figure 12 | **Worksheet for Profit and Loss Table**

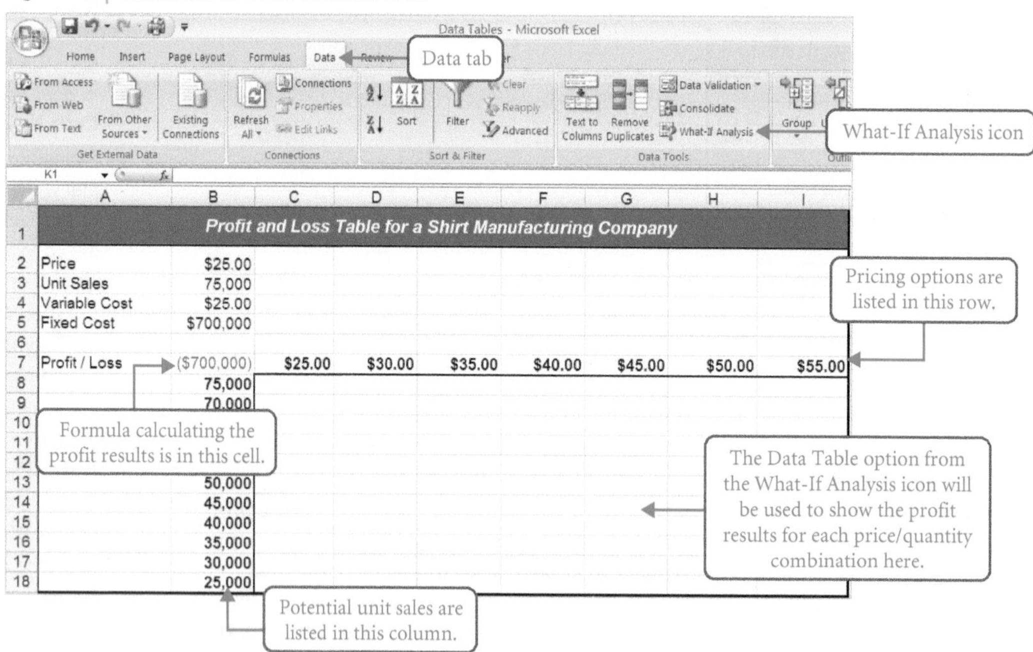

The **Data Table** option from the **What-If Analysis** icon will be used to calculate the profit of the shirt company for each combination of price and quantity in the range C8:I18 in Figure 12. These calculations will be made using the formula = `(B2 * B3) - ((B4 * B3) + B5)` in cell B7. To calculate the total sales of the business, the shirt price is multiplied by the unit sales, which are in cells B2 and B3: `(B2 * B3)`. The total cost of manufacturing the shirts is subtracted from the total sales to calculate the profit or loss for the business. The costs are calculated by multiplying the unit sales by the variable cost of producing each shirt (cell B4) and then adding the fixed costs in cell B5: `(B4 * B3) + B5`. The variable cost for manufacturing each shirt includes items such as fabric, thread, and buttons. The fixed cost includes items such as cutting and sewing machines. Your Managerial Accounting or Cost Accounting courses will provide more details on the nature of these costs. For now it is important to understand that the profit or loss for the business is calculated by subtracting these costs from the total sales. The following explains how you can use the **Data Table** feature to complete the profit calculations in the range C8:I18 in Figure 12.

- Define the table range by highlighting cells B7 through I18. Notice that this range includes the formula in cell B7 and the price and quantity options in the ranges B8:B18 and C7:I7.
- Click the **What-If Analysis** icon in the **Data** tab of the Ribbon and select the **Data Table** option. This will open the **Data Table** dialog box.
- Click the range finder next to the **Row Input Cell** box, click cell B2 on the worksheet, and press the **Enter** key. Excel will substitute any values in the first row of the table range (C7:I7) into cell B2 when using the formula in cell B7 to calculate the profit or loss.
- Click the range finder next to the **Column Input Cell** box, click cell B3, and press the **Enter** key. Excel will substitute any values in the left column of the table range (B8:B18) into cell B3 when using the formula in cell B7 to calculate the profit or loss. As a result, Excel will be substituting price values in cell B2 and unit sales values in cell B3 simultaneously when calculating the profit or loss of the business (see Figure 13).
- Click the **OK** button on the **Data Table** dialog box.

Figure 13 | **The Data Table Window**

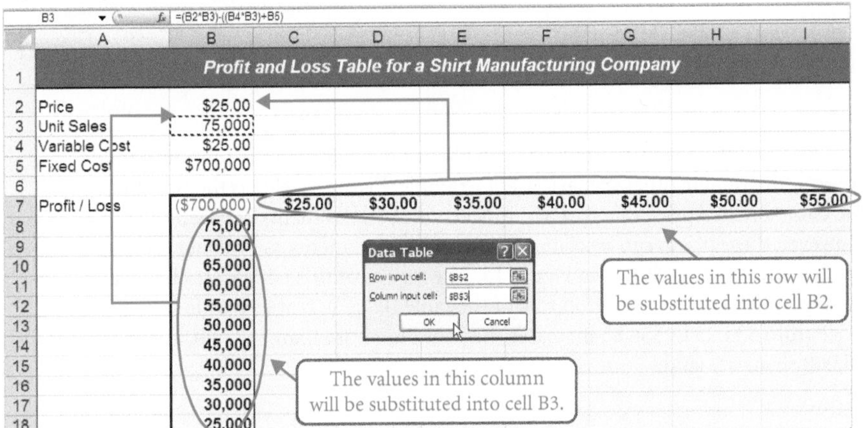

## COMMON MISTAKES | Defining the Cell Range for a Data Table

The cell range highlighted before selecting the **Data Table** option from the **What-If Analysis** icon must include the formula that will produce the results of the table. People often make the mistake of highlighting only the range of cells in which the results of the table should appear. However, the Data Table feature will not produce any results if the cell range does not begin with a formula.

>> **Quick Reference**

### Data Tables

1. Create a formula that will be used to produce the results of the table. Your formula *must* use cell references.
2. Type one set of alternate values, which will be substituted into one of the cell locations referenced by the formula in step 1. These values must be typed in *a row* to the right and *adjacent to* the formula created in step 1.
3. Type a second set of alternate values, which will be substituted into a second cell location that is referenced by the formula created in step 1. These values must be typed in the *column* directly below and *adjacent to* the formula created in step 1.
4. Highlight a range of cells that begins with the formula created in step 1 and covers all of the values typed for steps 2 and 3.
5. Click the **What-If Analysis** icon in the **Data** tab of the Ribbon and select the **Data Table** option.
6. In the **Data Table** dialog box, define the Row Input Cell with a cell location that will be used to substitute the values you typed for step 2.
7. Define the Column Input Cell with a cell location that will be used to substitute the values typed for step 3.
8. Click the **OK** button on the **Data Table** dialog box.

Figure 14 shows the results of the Data Table. Negative values are shown in red because the parentheses/red font option was selected for negative values in the numbers tab of the **Format Cells** dialog box. Notice that when the company charges $25, the profit is negative for all quantities sold. This makes sense considering that the variable cost to produce each shirt is $25. Therefore, the company is not able to recover any of the $700,000 in fixed costs. According to this table, the company does not cover both the variable and fixed costs until a price of $35 is charged. At this price, the company must sell at least 70,000 shirts to meet all costs, and 75,000 shirts to produce a profit of $50,000. As the company increases the price, it needs to sell fewer shirts to produce a profit.

Figure 14 | **Data Table Results**

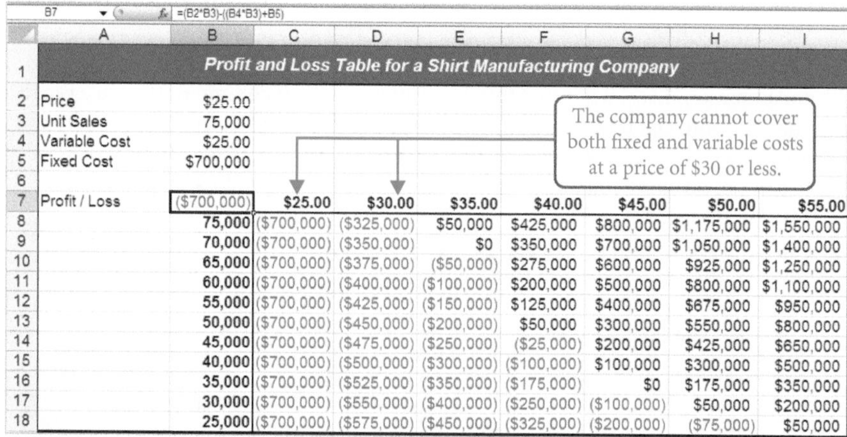


| | A | B | C | D | E | F | G | H | I |
|---|---|---|---|---|---|---|---|---|---|
| 1 | Profit and Loss Table for a Shirt Manufacturing Company | | | | | | | | |
| 2 | Price | $25.00 | | | | | | | |
| 3 | Unit Sales | 75,000 | | | | | | | |
| 4 | Variable Cost | $25.00 | | | | | | | |
| 5 | Fixed Cost | $700,000 | | | | | | | |
| 6 | | | | | | | | | |
| 7 | Profit / Loss | ($700,000) | $25.00 | $30.00 | $35.00 | $40.00 | $45.00 | $50.00 | $55.00 |
| 8 | | 75,000 | ($700,000) | ($325,000) | $50,000 | $425,000 | $800,000 | $1,175,000 | $1,550,000 |
| 9 | | 70,000 | ($700,000) | ($350,000) | $0 | $350,000 | $700,000 | $1,050,000 | $1,400,000 |
| 10 | | 65,000 | ($700,000) | ($375,000) | ($50,000) | $275,000 | $600,000 | $925,000 | $1,250,000 |
| 11 | | 60,000 | ($700,000) | ($400,000) | ($100,000) | $200,000 | $500,000 | $800,000 | $1,100,000 |
| 12 | | 55,000 | ($700,000) | ($425,000) | ($150,000) | $125,000 | $400,000 | $675,000 | $950,000 |
| 13 | | 50,000 | ($700,000) | ($450,000) | ($200,000) | $50,000 | $300,000 | $550,000 | $800,000 |
| 14 | | 45,000 | ($700,000) | ($475,000) | ($250,000) | ($25,000) | $200,000 | $425,000 | $650,000 |
| 15 | | 40,000 | ($700,000) | ($500,000) | ($300,000) | ($100,000) | $100,000 | $300,000 | $500,000 |
| 16 | | 35,000 | ($700,000) | ($525,000) | ($350,000) | ($175,000) | $0 | $175,000 | $350,000 |
| 17 | | 30,000 | ($700,000) | ($550,000) | ($400,000) | ($250,000) | ($100,000) | $50,000 | $200,000 |
| 18 | | 25,000 | ($700,000) | ($575,000) | ($450,000) | ($325,000) | ($200,000) | ($75,000) | $50,000 |

After a data table is created, you can change the values in the top row and left column to evaluate other scenarios. For example, Figure 14 shows the profit results of the company in a price range of $25 to $55 with $5 increments between each price. However, these prices can be changed to smaller increments to evaluate more specific pricing strategies, as shown in Figure 15. The results of this table were changed by simply typing new prices in the top row of the table (C7:I7). Notice that increasing the price from $34.25 to $34.85 increases the profit by more than $40,000, assuming that 75,000 shirts are sold.

Figure 15 | **Data Table Results with New Prices**

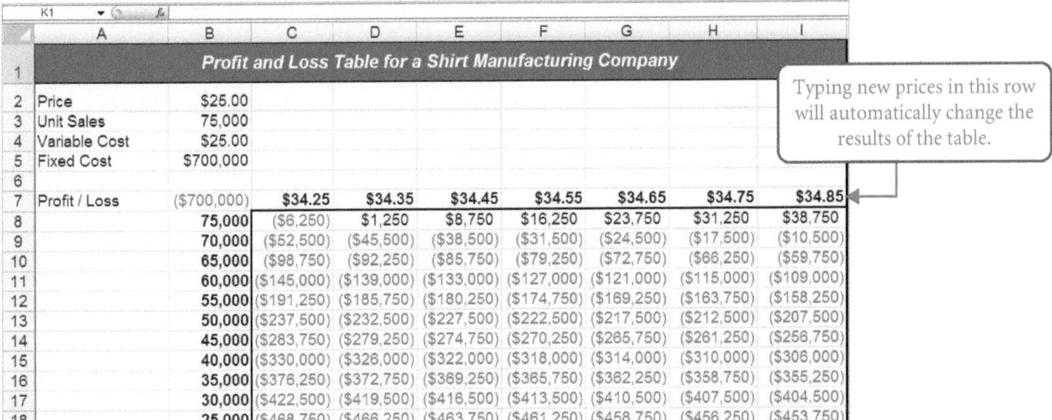

| | A | B | C | D | E | F | G | H | I |
|---|---|---|---|---|---|---|---|---|---|
| 1 | Profit and Loss Table for a Shirt Manufacturing Company | | | | | | | | |
| 2 | Price | $25.00 | | | | | | | |
| 3 | Unit Sales | 75,000 | | | | | | | |
| 4 | Variable Cost | $25.00 | | | | | | | |
| 5 | Fixed Cost | $700,000 | | | | | | | |
| 6 | | | | | | | | | |
| 7 | Profit / Loss | ($700,000) | $34.25 | $34.35 | $34.45 | $34.55 | $34.65 | $34.75 | $34.85 |
| 8 | | 75,000 | ($6,250) | $1,250 | $8,750 | $16,250 | $23,750 | $31,250 | $38,750 |
| 9 | | 70,000 | ($52,500) | ($45,500) | ($38,500) | ($31,500) | ($24,500) | ($17,500) | ($10,500) |
| 10 | | 65,000 | ($98,750) | ($92,250) | ($85,750) | ($79,250) | ($72,750) | ($66,250) | ($59,750) |
| 11 | | 60,000 | ($145,000) | ($139,000) | ($133,000) | ($127,000) | ($121,000) | ($115,000) | ($109,000) |
| 12 | | 55,000 | ($191,250) | ($185,750) | ($180,250) | ($174,750) | ($169,250) | ($163,750) | ($158,250) |
| 13 | | 50,000 | ($237,500) | ($232,500) | ($227,500) | ($222,500) | ($217,500) | ($212,500) | ($207,500) |
| 14 | | 45,000 | ($283,750) | ($279,250) | ($274,750) | ($270,250) | ($265,750) | ($261,250) | ($256,750) |
| 15 | | 40,000 | ($330,000) | ($326,000) | ($322,000) | ($318,000) | ($314,000) | ($310,000) | ($306,000) |
| 16 | | 35,000 | ($376,250) | ($372,750) | ($369,250) | ($365,750) | ($362,250) | ($358,750) | ($355,250) |
| 17 | | 30,000 | ($422,500) | ($419,500) | ($416,500) | ($413,500) | ($410,500) | ($407,500) | ($404,500) |
| 18 | | 25,000 | ($468,750) | ($466,250) | ($463,750) | ($461,250) | ($458,750) | ($456,250) | ($453,750) |

Typing new prices in this row will automatically change the results of the table.



## Goal Seek

Similar to the Scroll Bar and the Data Table tools, Goal Seek is another valuable scenario tool that maximizes Excel's cell-referencing capabilities. Goal Seek allows a business manager to target a specific outcome by changing the value in a cell location that is used in a formula or function. For example, Figure 16 shows a worksheet that uses the Future Value function to calculate the value of a person's monthly retirement investments. The example assumes that the person is 25 years old and will retire at the age of 65. Therefore, the monthly investment in cell B3 will be made over a 40-year period. This is calculated using a formula that subtracts the person's age in cell B2 from 65.

Figure 16 | **Investing for Retirement Worksheet**

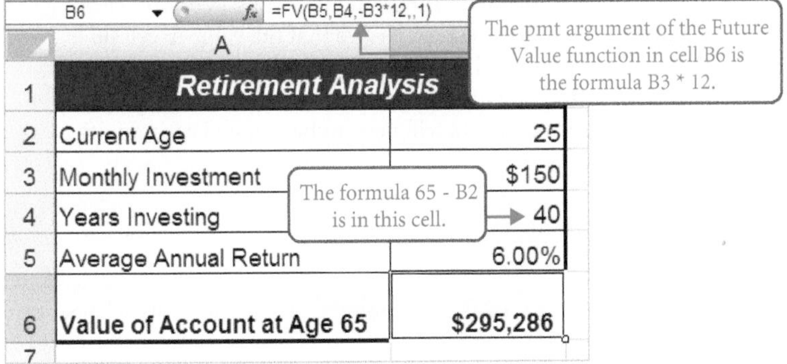

B6 =FV(B5,B4,-B3*12,,1)

| | A | B |
|---|---|---|
| 1 | Retirement Analysis | |
| 2 | Current Age | 25 |
| 3 | Monthly Investment | $150 |
| 4 | Years Investing | 40 |
| 5 | Average Annual Return | 6.00% |
| 6 | Value of Account at Age 65 | $295,286 |
| 7 | | |



The formula 65 - B2 is in this cell.

The result of the **Future Value** function displayed in cell B6 of Figure 16 shows that the value of this person's investments will be more than $295,000 at the age of 65. However, what if this person has a goal of reaching $1 million by the age of 65? How much money will need to be invested each month? What if this person could invest money in a mutual fund that provides a higher rate of return? What would the rate of return have to be to reach $1 million? All of these questions can be answered using the **Goal Seek** tool.

Using the data in Figure 16, the following explains how you can use the **Goal Seek** tool to determine how much money a person should invest per month assuming that the annual rate of return and the number of years investing cannot change.

- Select the **Goal Seek** option after clicking the **What-If Analysis** icon in the **Data** tab of the Ribbon. This will open the **Goal Seek** dialog box.

**>> Quick Reference**

**Goal Seek**

1. Create a formula or function that uses cell references to produce a mathematical result.
2. Select the **Goal Seek** option from the **What-If Analysis** icon in the **Data** tab of the Ribbon.
3. Type a cell location into the **Set Cell** box or use the range finder to click a cell on your worksheet. This cell location should contain the formula or function you created in step 1.
4. Type a number in the **To Value** box that you want the formula or function you created in step 1 to produce.
5. Type a cell location into the **By Changing Cell** box or use the range finder to click a cell on your worksheet. The cell location in this box must be a cell that is referenced in the formula or function created in step 1.
6. Click the **OK** button on the **Goal Seek** dialog box.
7. Click the **OK** button on the **Goal Seek Status** dialog box.

- Click the range finder next to the **Set Cell** box, click cell B6 on the worksheet, and press the **Enter** key. This will set cell B6 to the value that will be typed into the To Value box.
- Type 1000000 in the **To Value** box. This will set cell B6 to $1,000,000 by changing the value in the cell location that is entered into the **By Changing Cell** box.
- Click the range finder next to the **By Changing Cell** box, click cell B3 on the worksheet, and press the **Enter** key. The Goal Seek tool will change cell B6 to $1,000,000 by changing the value in cell B3, which is the monthly investment.
- Click the **OK** button on the **Goal Seek** dialog box.
- Click the **OK** button on the **Goal Seek Status** dialog box. This notifies you if a solution was found for the value that was typed into the **To Value** box of the **Goal Seek** dialog box.

Figure 17 shows the setup of the **Goal Seek** dialog box. Goal Seek will determine the value that should appear in cell B3 so that the output of the **Future Value** function in cell B6 is equal to 1,000,000.

Figure 17 | **Setup of the Goal Seek Window**

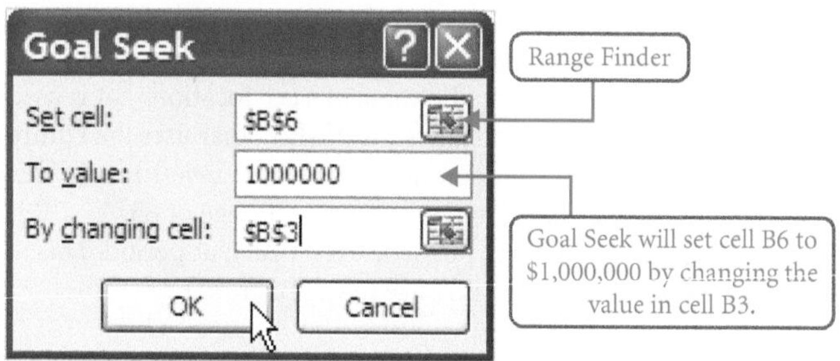


Figure 18 shows the results of the Retirement Analysis worksheet after clicking the **OK** button on the **Goal Seek Status** dialog box. Notice that the value in cell B6 is $1,000,000. This is because the monthly investment in cell B3 was changed to $508. Therefore, if this person wants to grow his retirement investments to $1 million over 40 years at a 6% rate of return, $508 dollars will need to be invested each month.

Figure 18 | **Monthly Investments Calculated by Goal Seek**

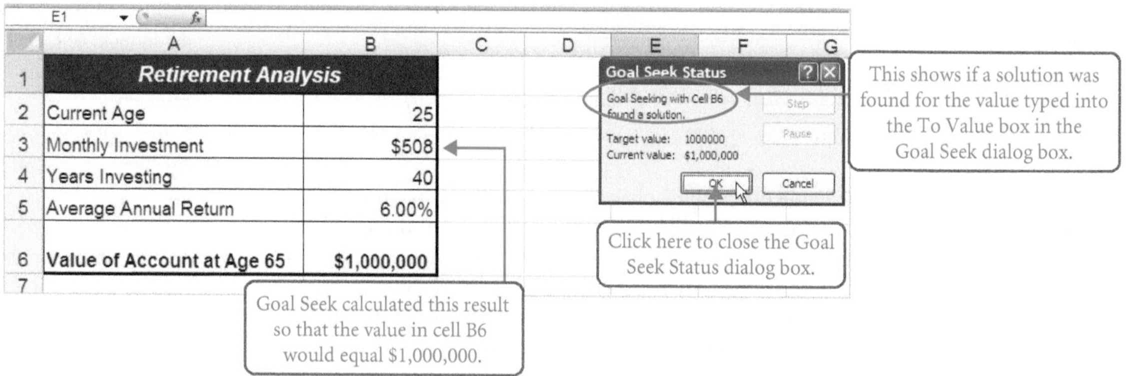


As previously mentioned, you can also use the **Goal Seek** tool to determine what rate would grow the retirement investments in Figure 16 to $1 million if the monthly investment is $150 and the years investing remains at 40. Figure 19 shows the settings in the Goal Seek dialog box and the results in the Retirement Analysis worksheet. Notice that the settings in the Goal Seek dialog box are identical to those in Figure 17 except the **By Changing Cell** box, which is set to cell B5. Goal Seek will change the rate of return in cell B5 so that the output of the Future Value function in cell B6 is $1,000,000. The results in the worksheet show that a 10.47% growth rate is required to achieve an investment value of $1 million by investing $150 a month over 40 years.

Figure 19 | **Annual Rate of Return Calculated by Goal Seek**

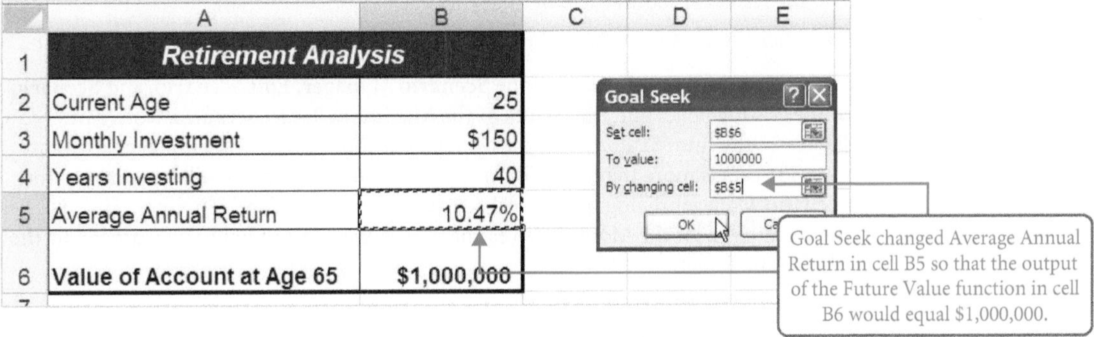


## Scenario Manager

The **Goal Seek** tool allows you to change one of the cell locations or variables in a formula to produce the results of a "What if" scenario. However, you may need to change more than one variable when conducting these scenarios. With the Scenario Manager, you can assign numbers to several variables or cell locations that are referenced in a formula or function. You can also assign several different numbers to a single variable or cell location. For example, suppose you wanted to use the investment data in Figure 16 to create three different scenarios for your retirement. The first scenario could calculate the future value of investing $200 per month at a 12% return over 40 years. The second scenario could show the results of investing $175 per month at a 9% return over 40 years, and the third scenario could show the results of investing $150 per month at a 6% return over 40 years. Each of these scenarios requires you to assign several different numbers to two variables or cell locations that are referenced by the Future Value function in cell B7 of Figure 16. In addition, the results of these scenarios can show you how much money you could make by looking at three different monthly investment and rate-of-return options.

The following explains how you can use the Scenario Manager to build three distinct retirement scenarios for the data in Figure 16. The first scenario will assume a monthly investment of $200 per month at a 12% average annual return.

- Select the **Scenario Manager** option from the **What-If Analysis** icon in the **Data** tab of the Ribbon. This will open the **Scenario Manager** dialog box (see Figure 20).
- Click the Add button on the right side of the **Scenario Manager** dialog box. This will open the **Add Scenario** dialog box.
- Type Maximum Target in the box labeled Scenario Name at the top of the **Add Scenario** dialog box. As mentioned, you can assign several different numbers to a single variable or cell reference used in a formula or function. However, a separately named scenario must be added in the **Add Scenario** dialog box for each number that is assigned to the same cell location. In this first scenario, we will assume that $200 per month is the maximum investment this person can afford and 12% is the highest estimated growth rate based on this person's investment decisions. Therefore, this scenario is named "Maximum Target."
- Click the range finder next to the box labeled Changing Cells. Click cell B3, hold the **Ctrl** key down, click cell B5, and press the **Enter** key. This will allow values to be defined for each of these cell locations in the Scenario Values dialog box. Once cell locations are added to the **Changing Cells** box, the name of the dialog box will change to Edit Scenario (see Figure 21).

- Click the **OK** button at the bottom of the **Edit Scenario** dialog box. This will open the **Scenario Values** dialog box.
- Type the number 200 in the box labeled $B$3 and .12 in the box labeled $B$5.
- Click the **OK** button in the **Scenario Values** dialog box. This will bring you back to the **Scenario Manager** dialog box.
- Click the **Show** button at the bottom of the **Scenario Manager** dialog box to show the results of the scenario on the worksheet.
- Click the **Close** button to close the **Scenario Manager** dialog box.

Figures 20 through 23 show the **Scenario Manager**, **Edit Scenario**, and **Scenario Values** dialog boxes and the results of the Maximum Target scenario. Notice in Figure 23 the future value of investing $200 per month at a 12% annual growth rate over 40 years is more than $2 million. Two additional scenarios will be added to the Scenario Manager dialog box to evaluate what the value of the retirement investments might be if the Monthly Investment and Average Annual Return are below the Maximum Target.

Figure 20 | **The Scenario Manager Dialog Box**

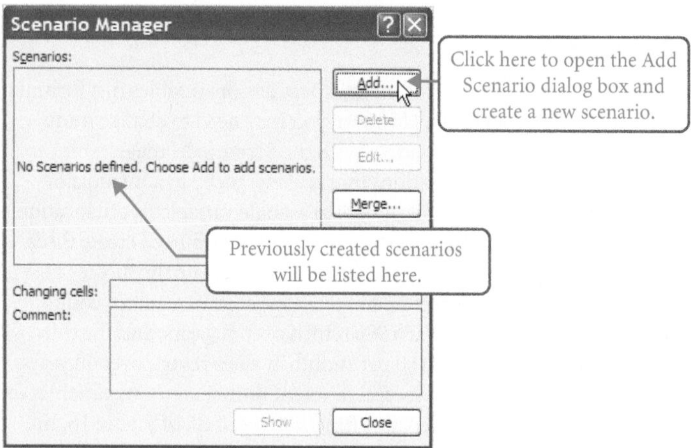


Figure 21 | **The Add/Edit Scenario Dialog Box**

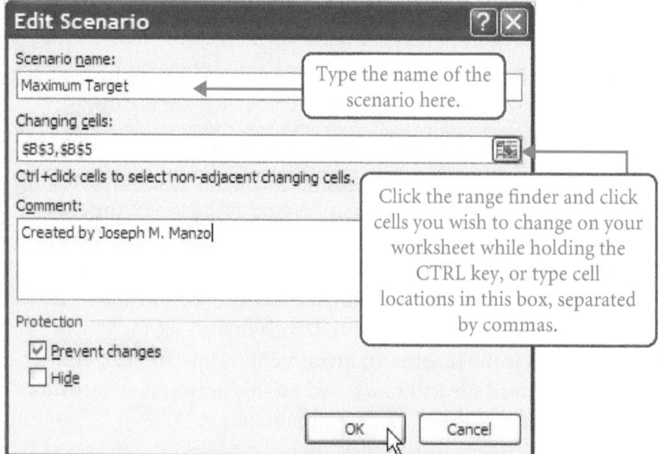

Figure 22 | **The Scenario Values Dialog Box**

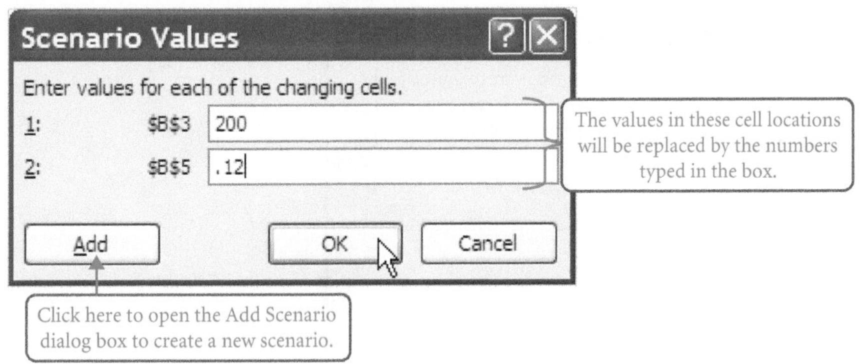

Scenario Values
Enter values for each of the changing cells.
1: $B$3 200
2: $B$5 .12
Add
OK
Cancel
The values in these cell locations will be replaced by the numbers typed in the box.
Click here to open the Add Scenario dialog box to create a new scenario.

Figure 23 | **Results of the Maximum Target Scenario**

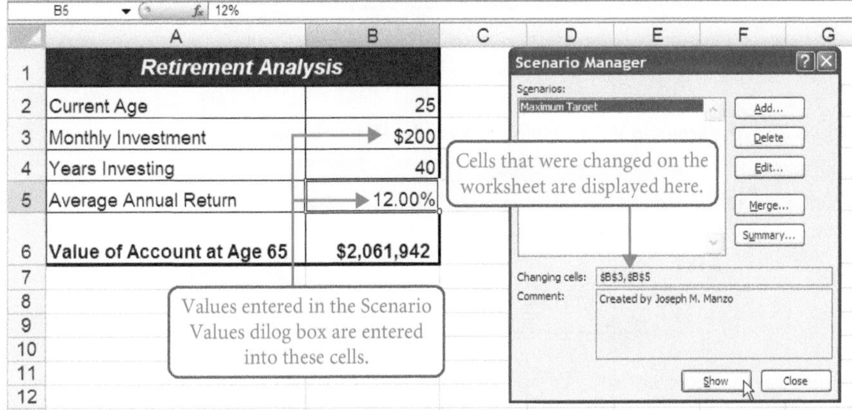

Retirement Analysis
Current Age 25
Monthly Investment $200
Years Investing 40
Average Annual Return 12.00%
Value of Account at Age 65 $2,061,942
Scenario Manager
Maximum Target
Cells that were changed on the worksheet are displayed here.
Values entered in the Scenario Values dilog box are entered into these cells.
Changing cells: $B$3,$B$5
Comment: Created by Joseph M. Manzo
Show
Close

Figures 24 through 26 show the setup and results of a second scenario that was added to the **Scenario Manager** dialog box. This scenario calculates the future value of an investment if a person can invest only $175 per month and is expecting a lower annual growth rate of 9%. Notice in Figure 26 that the **Scenario Manager** dialog box shows both scenarios that have been created for this example. To show the results of a scenario on a worksheet, click the scenario name and then click the **Show** button on the right side of the **Scenario Manager** dialog box.

>> ***Quick Reference***

**Scenario Manager**

1. Create a formula or function that uses cell references to produce a mathematical result.
2. Select the **Scenario Manager** option from the **What-If Analysis** icon in the **Data** tab of the Ribbon.
3. Click the **Add** button in the **Scenario Manager** dialog box.
4. Type a name for the scenario in the **Scenario Name** box.

*(Continued)*

**Scenario Manager**
*(Continued)*

5. Select cells that are referenced by the formula or function in step 1 by using the range finder, or type cells into the **Changing Cells** box, separating each cell location with a comma.
6. Click the **OK** button at the bottom of the **Edit Scenarios** dialog box.
7. Type values in the box next to each cell location that appears in the **Scenario Values** dialog box, then click the **OK** button.
8. Click the name of the Scenario you wish to apply to your worksheet in the **Scenario Manager** dialog box.
9. Click the **Show** button to apply the scenario selected in step 8 to your worksheet.
10. Click the **Close** button to close the Scenario Manager.

Figure 24 | **Add/Edit Scenario Dialog Box for the Middle Target**

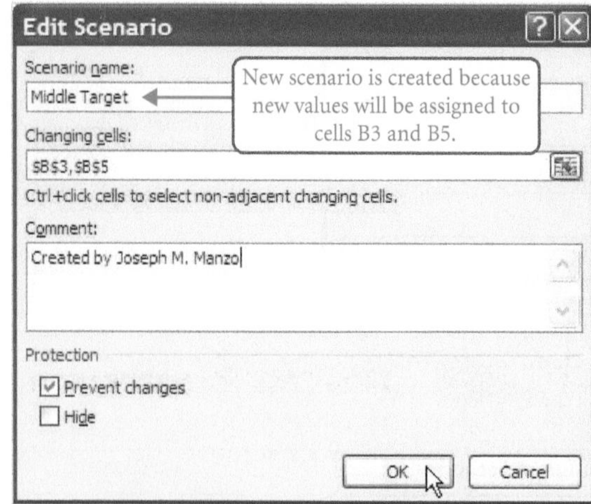


Figure 25 | **The Scenario Values Dialog Box for the Middle Target**

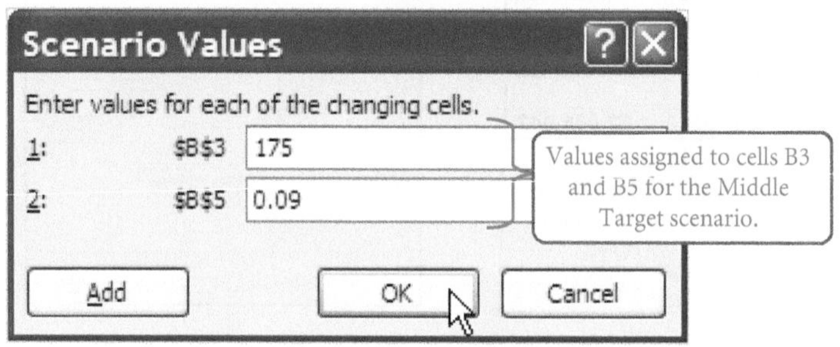


Figure 26 | **Results of the Middle Target Scenario**

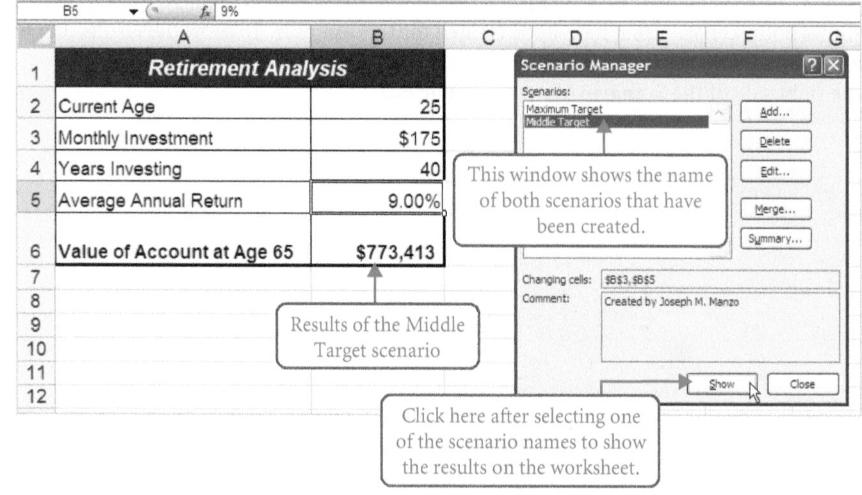

Next, we will add a third scenario to the **Scenario Manager** dialog box that will calculate the value of the retirement investments assuming that $150 is invested every month at an annual growth rate of 6% over 40 years. These are the original Monthly Investment and Average Annual Return values that were used in Figure 16, and they represent the minimum expectations for this person's retirement investments. Therefore, Figure 27 shows a third scenario in the **Scenario Manager** dialog box labeled Minimum Target. A report showing the results of all three scenarios can be created by clicking the **Summary** button on the right side of the **Scenario Manager** dialog box.

Figure 27 | **Results of the Minimum Target Scenario**

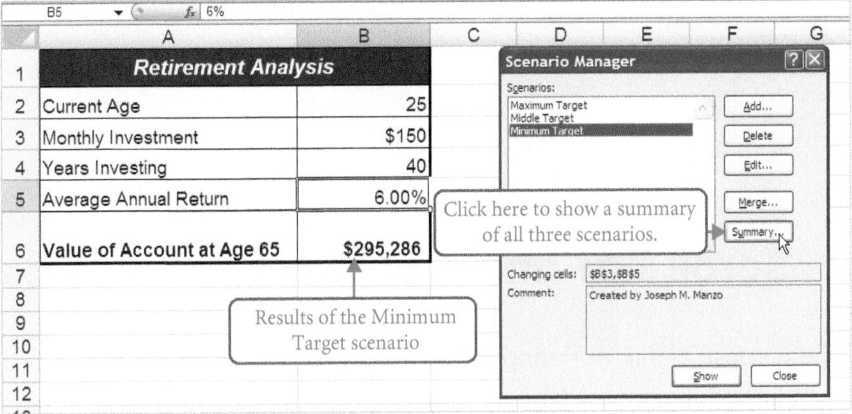


The Scenario Manager will automatically create a report showing the results of all scenarios that have been created when you click the **Summary** button. The **Summary** button will open the **Scenario Summary** dialog box, which gives you the option of creating a PivotTable or a worksheet with subtotals showing the results of the scenarios. Figures 28 and 29 show the **Scenario Summary** dialog box and the Summary Report for the three scenarios shown in Figure 27.

Figure 28 | **Scenario Summary Dialog Box**

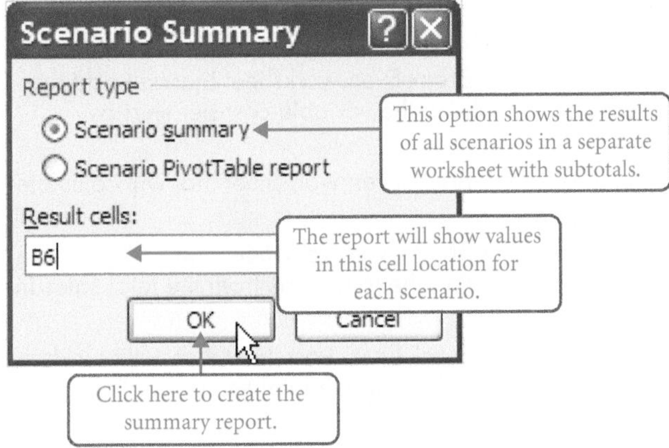

Figure 29 | **Scenario Summary Report**

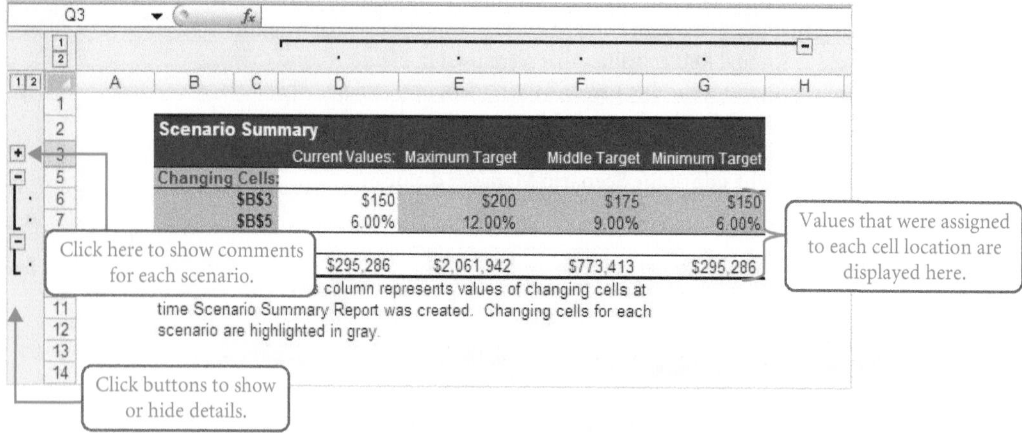


**VIDEO WORKSHOP**

## Scroll Bar and Conditional Formats

The purpose of this workshop is to demonstrate the Scroll Bar and Conditional Formatting features. I will be demonstrating the tasks in this workshop in the **Scroll Bar** and **Conditional Formatting** videos. After completing each section of tasks, watch the related video shown in parentheses. Open the Excel file named ib_e09_profitanalysis before starting this workshop.

1. **Scroll Bar (Video: Scroll Bar)**
   a. Enter a **VLOOKUP** function in cell B3 of the Break-Even worksheet that will find the value in cell B2 in the Price and Sales Units worksheet. The function should return the exact value in the Unit Sales column from the Price and Sales Units worksheet.
   b. Enter a formula in cell B6 of the Break-Even worksheet that will add the fixed costs to the result of multiplying the variable cost per shirt by the unit sales.
   c. Enter a formula in cell B7 of the Break-Even worksheet that will calculate the total sales in dollars.
   d. Enter a formula in cell B8 of the Break-Even worksheet that will calculate the total profit dollars by subtracting the total costs from the total sales in dollars.
   e. Enter a formula in cell B9 of the Break-Even worksheet that will calculate the profit as a percent of sales by dividing the total sales in dollars into the total profit dollars.
   f. Select the Scroll Bar form control from the **Insert** icon in the **Developer** tab of the Ribbon.
   g. Click and drag a vertical rectangle between cells C2 and C8.
   h. Click the **Properties** icon in the **Developer** tab of the Ribbon.
   i. Click the **Control** tab at the top of the **Format Control** dialog box.
   j. Type the number 25 in the **Current Value** box.
   k. Use the arrows or type the number 25 in the **Minimum Value** box.

l. Use the arrows or type the number `75` in the **Maximum Value** box.
m. Use the arrows or type the number `5` in the **Page Change** box.
n. Use the range finder or type cell location `B2` in the **Cell Link** box.
o. Click the **OK** button, and then click on any cell on the worksheet.
p. Click the Down arrow of the Scroll Bar until the profit in cell B8 reads $2,000.
q. Use the Scroll Bar slide to increase the price in cell B2 to any value greater than $65. Notice the profit value in cell B8.

2. **Conditional Formatting (Video: Conditional Formatting)**
   a. Activate cell B9 in the Break-Even worksheet.
   b. Select the **New Rule** option from the **Conditional Formatting** icon in the **Home** tab of the Ribbon.
   c. Select the **Format only cells that contain** option in the top section of the **New Formatting Rule** dialog box.
   d. Set the first drop-down box in the bottom section of the **New Formatting Rule** dialog box to Cell Value.
   e. Set the second drop-down box to Less Than, and then type `0` in the third box.
   f. Click the **Format** button, set the font color to red, and then click the **OK** button in the **Format Cells** dialog box.
   g. Click the **OK** button in the **New Formatting Rule** dialog box.
   h. Save and close your file.

# >> Data Tables

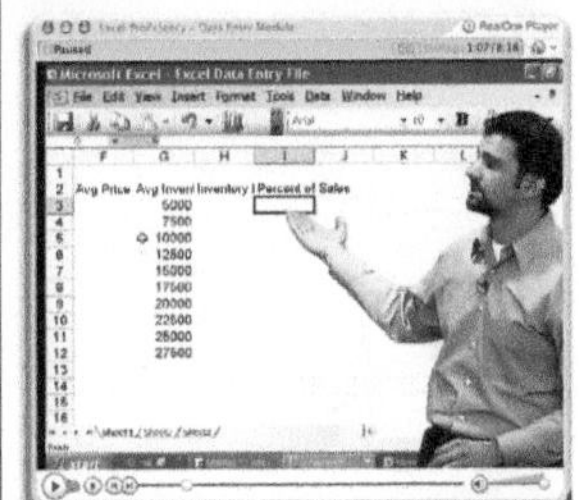

The purpose of this workshop is to demonstrate how data tables are used to assess the profitability of a business. I will be demonstrating the tasks in this workshop in the video named **Data Table**. Open the Excel file named ib_e09_profitandloss before starting this workshop. Complete the tasks below first, and then watch the video.

1. **Data Tables (Video: Data Table)**
   a. Enter the following formula in cell B7 in the Profit Table worksheet: `(B2 * B3) - (B5 + (B4 * B3)).`
   b. Type the following values in cells C7 through I7: `25, 30, 35, 40, 45, 50, 55.`
   c. Type the following values in cells B8 through B18: `75000, 70000, 65000, 60000, 55000, 50000, 45000, 40000, 35000, 30000, 25000.`
   d. Highlight the range C8:I18 and place a bold line on the top and left side of the range.
   e. Highlight the range B7:I18.
   f. Select the **Data Table** option from the **What-If Analysis** icon in the **Data** tab of the Ribbon.
   g. Use the range finder or type cell location `B2` in the **Row Input Cell** box of the **Data Table** dialog box.

h. Use the range finder or type cell location `B3` in the **Column Input Cell** box of the **Data Table** dialog box.
i. Click the **OK** button on the **Data Table** dialog box.
j. Change the value in cell F7 to `35.50`, G7 to `36.00`, H7 to `36.50`, and I7 to `37.00`.
k. Save and close your file.

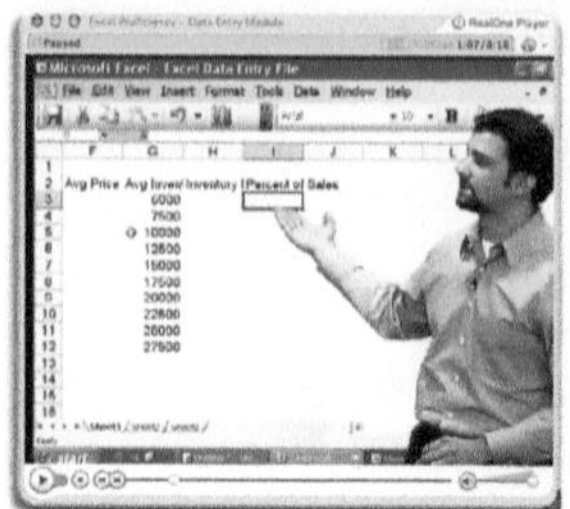

## >> Goal Seek

The purpose of this workshop is to demonstrate how the Goal Seek tool is used to assess the future value of investments. I will be demonstrating the tasks in this workshop in the video named **Goal Seek**. Open the Excel file named ib_e09_retirementanalysis. Complete the tasks below first, and then watch the video.

1. **Goal Seek (Video: Goal Seek)**
   a. Use the **FV** function in cell B6 of the Retirement Value worksheet to calculate the future value of the investment given the values in cells B3, B4, and B5. Note that the value in cell B3 represents monthly investments. Assume that investments are made at the beginning of each month.
   b. Select the **Goal Seek** option from the **What-If Analysis** icon in the **Data** tab of the Ribbon.
   c. Use the range finder or type cell location `B6` in the **Set Cell** box of the **Goal Seek** dialog box.
   d. Type the number `1000000` in the **To Value** box in the **Goal Seek** dialog box.
   e. Use the range finder or type cell location `B3` in the **By Changing Cell** box of the **Goal Seek** window.
   f. Click the **OK** button in the **Goal Seek** dialog box.
   g. Click the **OK** button in the **Goal Seek Status** dialog box.
   h. Type the number `150` in cell B3.
   i. Use Goal Seek to determine what annual growth rate would be required to achieve a future value of $1 million given a $150-a-month investment for 40 years.
   j. Save and close your file.

VIDEO
WORKSHOP

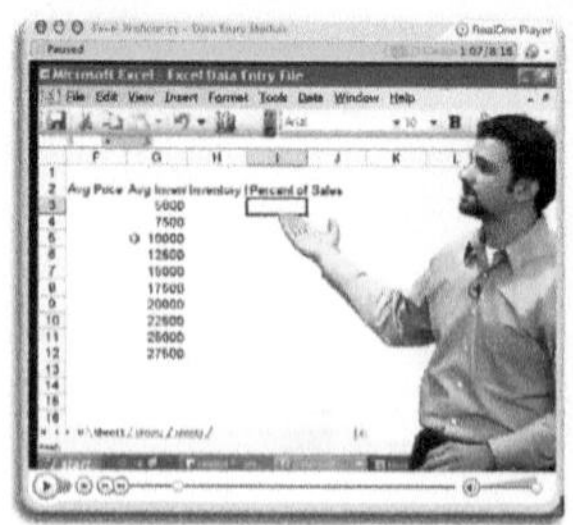

## >> Scenario Manager

The purpose of this workshop is to demonstrate how the Scenario Manager is used to establish a variety of investment scenarios. I will be demonstrating the tasks in this workshop in the video named **Scenario Manager**. Open the Excel file named ib_e09_investmentscenarios. Complete the tasks below first, and then watch the video.

1. **Scenario Manager (Video: Scenario Manager)**
   a. Select the **Scenario Manager** option from the **What-If Analysis** icon in the **Data** tab of the Ribbon.
   b. Click the **Add** button on the **Scenario Manager** dialog box.
   c. Type `Maximum Target` in the **Scenario Name** box of the **Add Scenario** dialog box.
   d. Use the range finder or type cell locations `B3` and `B5` in the **Changing Cells** box of the **Add Scenario** dialog box. Use a comma to separate each cell location if you are typing them into the box.
   e. Click the **OK** button on the **Edit Scenario** dialog box.
   f. Type `200` in the box next to cell $B$3 and `.12` in the box next to cell $B$5 in the **Scenario Values** dialog box. Delete any numbers that appear in the boxes before typing these values.
   g. Click the **OK** button in the **Scenario Values** dialog box.
   h. Click the **Show** button in the **Scenario Manager** dialog box.
   i. Click the **Add** button in the **Scenario Manager** dialog box.
   j. Type `Middle Target` in the **Scenario Name** box of the **Add Scenario** dialog box.
   k. Click the **OK** button on the **Add Scenario** dialog box.
   l. Type `175` in the box next tko cell $B$3 and `.09` in the box next to cell $B$5 in the **Scenario Values** dialog box. Delete any numbers that appear in the boxes before typing these values.
   m. Click the **OK** button in the **Scenario Values** dialog box.
   n. Click the **Show** button in the **Scenario Manager** window.
   o. Create a third scenario called `Minimum Target`. This scenario should assign the value `150` to cell B3 and `.06` to cell B5. Show the results of this scenario on the worksheet.
   p. Click the **Summary** button in the **Scenario Manager** dialog box.
   q. Select the **Scenario Summary** option in the **Scenario Summary** dialog box and click the **OK** button.
   r. Save and close your file.

## >> Sales Scenarios for Grocery Merchandise

**EXERCISE**

**Why Do I Need This?**

Uncertainty is one of the biggest challenges business managers face when launching new products or developing new businesses. A great business idea does not automatically produce great profits when it is executed by a company. As a result, most prudent business executives will test new ideas before launching them on a grand scale. A well-designed test can provide valuable information about a new business and can also help produce substantial growth in sales and profit for a company. The results of a test might tell a business manager whether the company should launch or abandon a new idea. However, in most instances managers use these results to determine *how* to execute a new business to maximize its profit potential. For example, the sales from a test might show a business manager which products in a new line of merchandise should be dropped. Or, the test results could indicate whether the amount of space allotted for a product line in a retail store should be increased or decreased. Consequently, business managers will analyze several "What if" scenarios before a test ever takes place, then compare these results with the results of the test, before making decisions about either implementing the business idea or determining how it should be implemented to produce a profit. Excel's scenario tools are valuable when developing the criteria that support a variety of decisions that are made on the basis of the results of a business test.

## Exercise

The purpose of this exercise is to develop scenarios for a new line of merchandise that will be launched in a grocery store. The results of these scenarios can be compared with the results of a test to determine if this new line of merchandise can be sold successfully and how the company should purchase and display the line to maximize its profit potential. Open the file named ib_e09_grocerymerchandisetest before starting this exercise.

1. Activate the Sales Mix worksheet. The line of merchandise to be tested involves two main categories: Cookware and Utensils. The results of this business will change dramatically depending on how much Cookware sells versus Utensils because the profit margins for these two categories are different. Therefore, the next several tasks of this exercise will focus on setting up the formulas for the Sales Mix worksheet so you can better understand how the sales combination of the two categories impact the overall results of the business.
2. Type a formula in cell C5 of the Sales Mix worksheet that calculates the Unit Sales of the Utensils category. This formula should subtract the sales of the Cookware category in cell C4 from the overall unit sales of both categories in cell B2. As a result, when the Unit Sales of the Cookware category is changed, the sales for the Utensils category will also change.
3. Type a formula in cell B5 that calculates the total percent of sales for the Utensils category. This formula should divide the sales results in cell C5 by the total sales in cell B2.
4. Type a formula in cell F4 that calculates the Sales Dollars for the Cookware category. This formula should multiply the Average Price in cell D4 by the Unit Sales in cell C4. Then, copy this formula and paste it into cell F5.
5. Type a formula in cell G4 that calculates the Profit Dollars for the Cookware category. This formula should first subtract the Average Cost in cell E4 from the Average Price in cell D4, and then this result should be multiplied by the Unit Sales in cell C4. Copy this formula and paste it into cell G5.
6. Type a formula in cell H4 that calculates the Profit Percent of Sales for the Cookware category. This formula should divide the Profit Dollars in cell G4 by the Sales Dollars in cell F4. Copy this formula and paste it into cell H5. Notice that the profit percent for the Cookware category is lower than for the Utensils category.
7. Type a **SUM** function in cells F6 and G6 to calculate the total Sales Dollars and Profit Dollars.
8. Type a formula in cell H6 that calculates the total Profit Percent of Sales by dividing the value in cell G6 by the value in cell F6.
9. Type a formula in cell D6 that calculates the total Average Price. This formula should divide the total Sales Dollars in cell F6 by the total Unit Sales in cell C6.
10. Type a formula in cell E6 that calculates the total Average Cost. This formula should first subtract the total Profit Dollars in cell G6 from the total Sales Dollars in cell F6, and then divide this result by the total Unit Sales in cell C6.

11. The total profit as a percent of sales in cell H6 should be 49.3%. However, this profit rate will decrease as sales in the Cookware category increases. The next several tasks will focus on adding a Scroll Bar to determine the maximum percent of Cookware sales needed to achieve at least a 40% profit rate for both categories. Begin by selecting the Scroll Bar format control from the **Insert** icon in the **Developer** tab of the Ribbon.
12. Add the Scroll Bar in the area of B8:B15.
13. Open the **Format Control** dialog box for the Scroll Bar and enter the following settings in the **Control** tab.
    a. Current Value: `100`
    b. Minimum Value: `100`
    c. Maximum Value: `14900`
    d. Incremental Change: `100`
    e. Page Change: `500`
    f. Cell Link: `C4`
14. Click the **OK** button of the **Format Control** dialog box and then click a cell location to activate the Scroll Bar.
15. Use the Scroll Bar to get the percentage in cell H6 as close as possible to 40%. What sales mix must the grocery store achieve (percent of total sales for Cookware and Utensils) if the company is targeting an overall profit rate of 40% or higher?
16. What is the profit rate in cell H6 if the grocery store achieves a sales mix of approximately 50% Cookware and 50% Utensils?
17. If this company has a profit rate target of 41.5% for all general-merchandise sales, what sales mix must be achieved to reach this goal? You may notice that getting the profit rate in cell H6 to read exactly 41.5% is difficult using the Scroll Bar. In these situations, Goal Seek is a better tool. Therefore, use the **Goal Seek** tool to answer this question by entering the following criteria in the **Goal Seek** dialog box.
    a. Set Cell: `H6`
    b. To Value: `.415`
    c. By Changing Cell: `C4`
18. The Average Price values showing in cells D4 and D5 are an important assumption made in this analysis. However, these prices could change depending on the mix of items that are sold within each category. If customers buy more of the lower-priced merchandise, the average price could decline. If customers buy more of the higher priced merchandise in the assortment, the average price could increase. As a result, the following tasks will focus on using the Scenario Manager to analyze the impact a change in the average price might have on the overall sales and profit of the business.
19. Create three different scenarios that will change the values in cell locations D4 and D5. Use the following scenario names and values for these cell locations.
    a. `Maximum Price`: `D4:45, D5:15`
    b. `Base Scenario`: `D4:35, D5:10`
    c. `Worst Case`: `D4:30, D5:8`

20. Select the Maximum Price scenario in the **Scenario Manager** dialog box and click the **Show** button. Then, close the **Scenario Manager** dialog box and use the Scroll Bar to set the sales mix to 40% Cookware and 60% Utensils. What is the overall profit rate of the business?

21. Activate the Sales per Square Foot worksheet. A key metric that many grocers use to measure the productivity of a product line is the sales per square foot. Maintaining space in any retail store is a significant cost. As a result, retailers usually set sales-per-square-foot targets to ensure that the appropriate amount of space is given to a line of products. A data table will be constructed in this worksheet to evaluate how much space should be allocated for the Cookware and Utensils product line.

22. Use a link to show the total average price in cell D6 of the Sales Mix worksheet in cell B3 of the Sales per Square Foot worksheet.

23. Type a formula in cell B4 of the Sales per Square Foot worksheet that calculates the Total Sales. This formula should multiply the Average Price in cell B3 by the Total Unit Sales in cell B2.

24. Type a formula in cell B7 of the Sales per Square Foot worksheet that calculates the Sales per Square Foot. This formula should divide the Space in Square Feet in cell B5 into the total sales in cell B4.

25. Highlight the range B7:H16 and use a Data Table to produce a sales-per-square-foot grid. Use cell B2 for the Row Input Cell and cell B5 for the Column Input Cell.

26. This company has a goal of maintaining at least $500 per square foot for the Cookware and Utensils merchandise. Use Conditional Formatting to color any value less than $500 in red within the data table results (C8:H16).

27. Based on the scenario that was selected in the Price Mix worksheet (should be the Maximum Price scenario, Cookware 40% of sales, and Utensils 60% of sales), will the company achieve at least $500 per square foot if it uses 1200 square feet of space to display this merchandise, assuming unit sales are 15,000? If sales are 15,000 units, what is the maximum amount of space the company should use to achieve at least $500 per square foot? What if sales drop to 10,000 units?

28. Go back to the Sales Mix worksheet and open the **Scenario Manager** dialog box. Select the Worst Case scenario and click the **Show** button. Then, close the **Scenario Manager** dialog box.

29. Use the Scroll Bar to change the sales mix to 25% Cookware and 75% Utensils. Then, activate the Sales per Square Foot worksheet. What is the maximum amount of space the company could dedicate to this product line if total unit sales are 15,000? What would the minimum percent of Cookware sales have to be to achieve at least $500 per square foot should sales drop to 10,000 units?

30. Save and close your file.

## >> What's Wrong with This Spreadsheet?

PROBLEM & EXERCISE

### Problem

You are the director of a product development division for a large retail corporation. You are about to give the president of the company an overview of a test your division will be conducting to determine if a new line of products has the potential of increasing the company's overall sales and profit. You have worked with this president for a few years and know that he is notorious for asking "What if" questions and wanting the "worst-case scenario." You give one of the analysts in your division instructions to assemble financial scenarios regarding this test. You inform the analyst that the president will be interested in seeing how the new product lines will reach the company standard of $600 per square foot and an overall profit margin of 47.5%. The analyst e-mails an Excel workbook to you and mentions the following points in his message.

1. The workbook attached to this e-mail contains two worksheets. The Sales Mix worksheet shows the sales and profit estimates for the two product lines. You need to change only the sales in cell C4 (shaded yellow) to change the overall Sales Mix.
2. The average price can be changed by typing new values in cells D4 and D5 (also shaded yellow) in the Sales Mix worksheet. I spoke to marketing and they expect the average price to be $42 for Line A and said that should be accurate within plus or minus $5. They expect the average price for Line B to be $18 and that should be accurate within plus or minus $3.
3. All of the data that is calculated in the Sales Mix worksheet is linked to the second worksheet (cells B2:B4). Therefore, any changes you make in the Sales Mix worksheet will automatically carry over into the Sales per Square Foot worksheet. I created a data table showing the sales per square foot at different unit sales and space allocations.
4. I think the profit target is a slam dunk. My estimates show us at 50%. However, I am concerned about the space. The good news is that it looks like the sales per square foot data is consistent no matter how many units we sell. However, I think the space will have to be reduced to 1,000 square feet.

### Exercise

The Excel file the analyst attached to your e-mail is named ib_e09_producttest. Would you be comfortable presenting this information to the president of the company? Review the file and consider the following points:

1. Look at the Sales Mix worksheet. Do the calculations and data in this worksheet make sense?
2. Look at the data table in the Sales per Square Foot worksheet. The analyst mentioned that the sales per square foot results do not change when the unit sales change. Does this make sense? Why or why not?
3. Can the current results in this workbook be used to explain a "worst-case scenario" to the president? Why or why not?

Write a short answer for each of the points above. Fix any errors you find in the workbook and prepare what you think would be a worst-case scenario. Write a short justification explaining why you think your adjustments better address a worst-case scenario. Make any other enhancements or adjustments you think would improve your meeting with the president.

Skill Set

# Data Analysis Tools

As you may have learned, Excel provides several functions for conducting statistical calculations. However, Excel also provides an entire suite of tools for conducting statistical analyses called **Data Analysis Tools**. The **Data Analysis Tools** provide 19 options for conducting statistical calculations using data that is contained in a worksheet. This section will focus on three of these options: Descriptive Statistics, Histogram, and Regression.

## Add-Ins

You may need to activate the **Data Analysis Tools** and **Solver** features on your computer before continuing with this section. Figure 30 shows how the **Data** tab of the Ribbon will appear if these tools are currently activated on your computer. You should see both the **Data Analysis** and **Solver** options in the **Analysis** group of icons.

Figure 30 | **Data Tab after the Data Analysis Tools and Solver Are Activated**

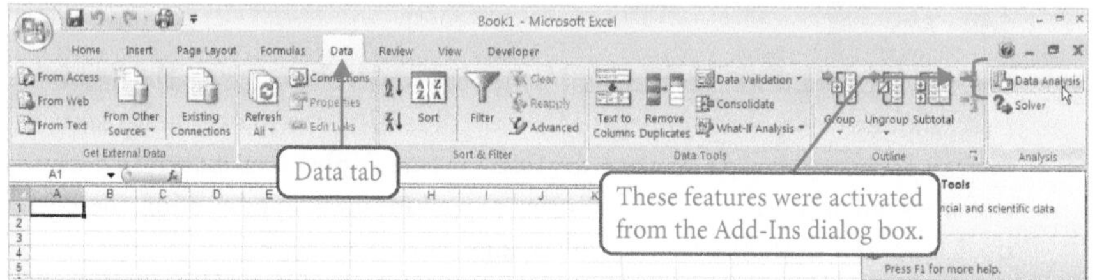


If you do not see the **Analysis** group of icons on your computer, you must activate the **Data Analysis Tools** and **Solver**. The following points explain how this is done:

- Click the **Office** icon and then the **Excel Options** button.
- Click the Add-Ins category on the left side of the **Excel Options** dialog box (see Figure 31).
- Make sure the **Manage** drop-down box at the bottom of the **Excel Options** dialog box is set to **Excel Add-Ins,** and then click the **Go** button. This will open the **Add-Ins** dialog box (see Figure 32).
- Click the **Analysis Toolpak** and **Solver Add-in** options in the **Add-Ins** dialog box.
- Click the **OK** button in the **Add-Ins** dialog box. This will add both features to your computer as shown in Figure 30.

**Quick Reference**

**Add-Ins**

1. Click the **Office** icon.
2. Click the **Excel Options** button.
3. Click the **Add-Ins** category on the left side of the **Excel Options** dialog box.
4. Set the **Manage** drop-down box to **Excel Add-Ins**.
5. Click the **Go** button.
6. Select the desired feature(s) in the **Add-Ins** dialog box and click the **OK** button.

Figure 31 | **Excel Options Dialog Box**

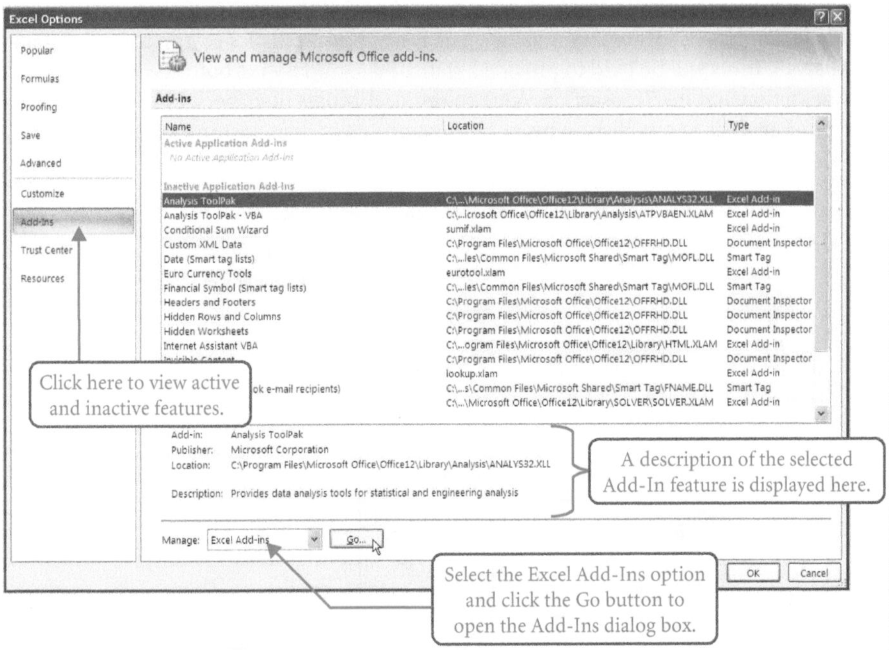

Click here to view active and inactive features.

A description of the selected Add-In feature is displayed here.

Select the Excel Add-Ins option and click the Go button to open the Add-Ins dialog box.

Figure 32 | **Add-Ins Dialog Box**

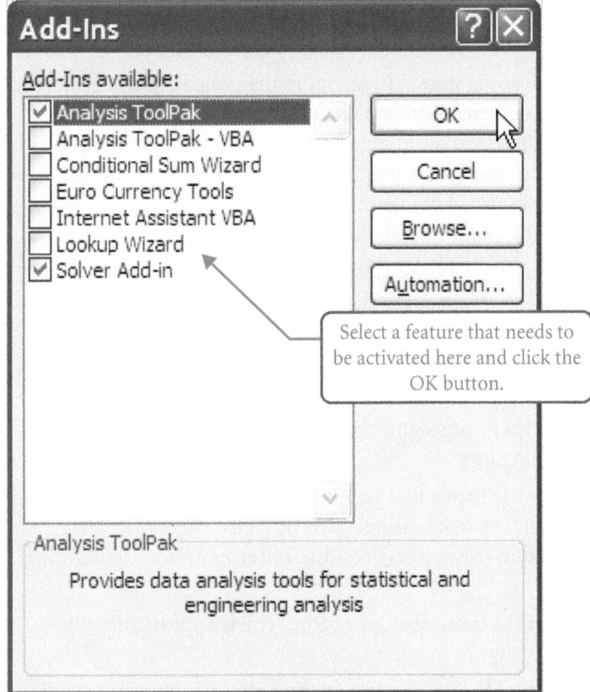


## Descriptive Statistics

Statistical calculations can be conducted using functions such as SUM, AVERAGE, MAX, MIN, etc. However, these functions must be added to a worksheet one at a time. You can use the **Descriptive Statistics** option from the **Data Analysis Tools** to conduct more than 13 different statistical calculations at the same time. In addition, this option also makes it easier to apply statistical calculations to a large data set. For example, Figure 33 shows 200 transactions from a general-merchandise retail company. Each transaction represents a customer's cash-register receipt. For each transaction number, the worksheet shows the number of items purchased (Items per Transaction) and the total dollars spent (Transaction Value). The Descriptive statistics option from the **Data Analysis Tools** will be used to provide a statistical summary for both the Items per Transaction and the Transaction Value columns. Business managers often conduct this type of analysis to establish an overall buying profile of their customers.

Figure 33 | **Transaction Data for a General-Merchandise Retailer**

K18

| | A | B | C |
|---|---|---|---|
| 1 | *Transaction Data* | | |
| 2 | Transaction Number | Items per Transaction | Transaction Value |
| 3 | 1001648 | 3 | 8.07 |
| 4 | 1875667 | 1 | 17.77 |
| 5 | 1374004 | 2 | 20.78 |
| 6 | 1746146 | 1 | 15.31 |
| 7 | 1844141 | 1 | 17.06 |
| 8 | 1959196 | 3 | 62.13 |
| 9 | 1730216 | 2 | 30.14 |
| 10 | 1538621 | 2 | 24.96 |
| 11 | 1838404 | 3 | 50.82 |
| 12 | 1996123 | 3 | 75.93 |
| 13 | 1156072 | 5 | [illegible] |
| 14 | 1864314 | 5 | [illegible] |
| 15 | 1413007 | 2 | [illegible] |
| 16 | 1533341 | 5 | 62.1 |

Each Transaction Number represents a customer's purchase.

Total dollars spent for each transaction is shown in this column.

Number of items purchased for each transaction is shown here.

A common goal for most retail companies is to sell more than one item to a customer each time she visits the store. For a large retailer servicing millions of customers per year, an increase of just one item per transaction could significantly boost sales and profits. As a result, business managers in these companies frequently conduct statistical assessments of transaction data similar to what is displayed in Figure 33. The following explains how the Descriptive Statistics option from the Data Analysis Tools is used to analyze this data.

- Click the **Data Analysis** icon in the **Analysis** group on the **Data** tab of the Ribbon (see Figure 30). This will open the **Data Analysis** dialog box, which lists a number of options for applying statistical methods to the data in a worksheet (see Figure 34). Most concepts that are covered in a fundamental Statistics course are listed in this dialog box.
- Select the **Descriptive Statistics** options and click the **OK** button. This will open the **Descriptive Statistics** dialog box.
- Click the range finder next to the **Input Range** box at the top of the dialog box and highlight the range B2:C202 in the worksheet shown in Figure 33. Notice that the column headings are included in this range. Press the **Enter** key after highlighting this range.
- Select the **Columns** option in the Grouped By section, which appears directly below the **Input Range** box.
- Make sure a green check appears in the box next to the **Labels in First Row** option. Click the box to add or remove a check. Because the column headings were highlighted when the Input Range was defined, this option must be checked.
- Select the **New Worksheet Ply** option in the Output Options section. This will add a new worksheet to the workbook showing the results of the statistical analysis. You can also enter a worksheet tab name in the box next to this option.
- Click the box next to the **Summary Statistics** option. A green check should appear in this box. You must select this box to produce a statistical summary of the data you are analyzing.

- Below the Summary Statistics check box are options for adjusting the confidence level for the Mean and for displaying the largest and smallest values in your data set. The confidence level for the mean will automatically be set to 95%. In addition, the summary will automatically show the largest and smallest values from the data set you are analyzing. However, by checking the box next to these options, you can type a value in the input box to show any number from the top and bottom of the dataset (i.e., 3rd largest value, 4th largest value, 5th smallest value, etc.).
- Click the **OK** button. This will add a new worksheet to the workbook and display several statistical outputs for the data in the range entered in the **Input Range** box.

Figure 34 | **Data Analysis Dialog Box**

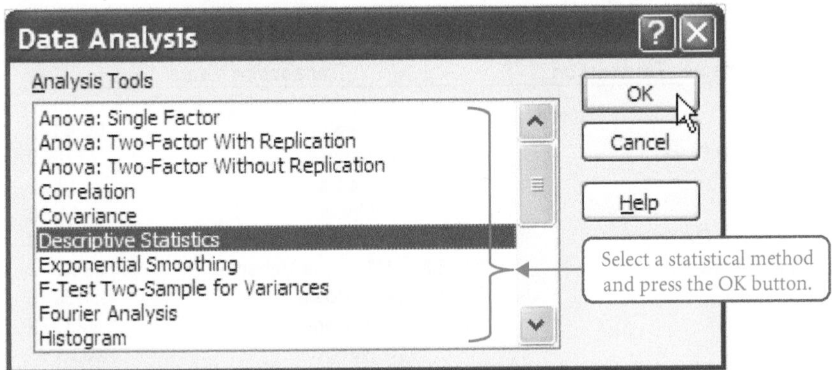


Figure 35 | **Descriptive Statistics Dialog Box**

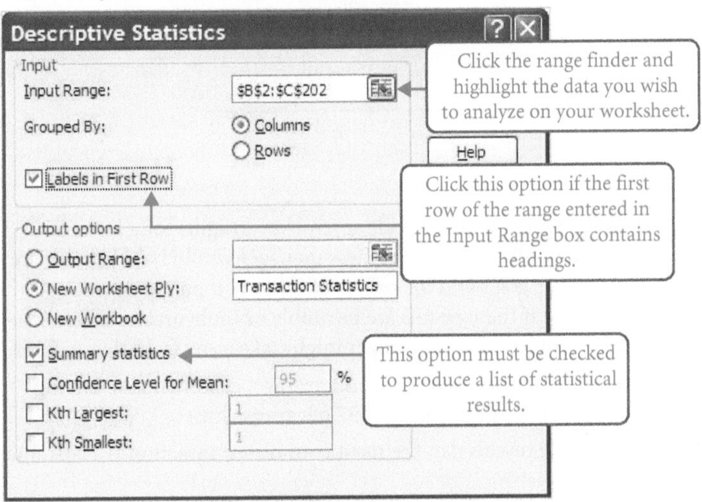


Figure 36 shows the Descriptive Statistics output for the transaction data in Figure 33. These results are automatically placed into a new worksheet if the New Worksheet Ply is selected in the **Descriptive Statistics** dialog box. In addition, adjustments can be made to the number formats and to the visual appearance (i.e., borders, font color, cell shading, etc.) as needed. Notice that there are two sets of statistics showing in this worksheet. This is because two columns of data were highlighted when the **Input Range** box was defined in the **Descriptive Statistics** dialog box.

## COMMON MISTAKES | Descriptive Statistics Window Settings

A green check must appear next to the **Summary Statistics** option in the **Descriptive Statistics** dialog box to produce the comprehensive output of statistical results. If you wish to see only the Confidence Level for Mean, the Kth Largest value, or the Kth Smallest value, then select these options without selecting the Summary Statistics. You can also select all four options if needed.

Figure 36 | **Descriptive Statistics Output**

Column heading pertaining to each set of statistics is shown in this row.

| | A | B | C | D |
|---|---|---|---|---|
| 1 | *Items per Transaction* | | *Transaction Value* | |
| 2 | | | | |
| 3 | Mean | 4.61 | Mean | 56.6133 |
| 4 | Standard Error | 0.268795 | Standard Error | 3.777009 |
| 5 | Median | 3 | Median | 42.29 |
| 6 | Mode | 1 | Mode | 11.66 |
| 7 | Standard Deviation | 3.8013354 | Standard Deviation | 53.41498 |
| 8 | Sample Variance | 14.450151 | Sample Variance | 2853.16 |
| 9 | Kurtosis | 2.8387259 | Kurtosis | 4.505986 |
| 10 | Skewness | 1.6071632 | Skewness | 1.923072 |
| 11 | Range | 19 | Range | 313.96 |
| 12 | Minimum | 1 | Minimum | 0.87 |
| 13 | Maximum | 20 | Maximum | 314.83 |
| 14 | Sum | 922 | Sum | 11322.66 |
| 15 | Count | 200 | Count | 200 |
| 16 | | | | |

Separate results are calculated for each column of data highlighted in the dialog box.

The statistics shown in Figure 36 can provide several key insights for a business manager in this retail company. Ultimately, a business manager would have to compare these results with the company's goals and the results of other companies operating in the same industry to determine if these results are favorable or unfavorable. The following are some key highlights that a business manager might take away from this analysis.

- **Mean (Row 3):** The Mean statistics show that on average, customers are buying between 4 and 5 items and spending almost $57 per transaction.
- **Mode (Cell B6):** The Mode reveals that the most common transaction is a customer buying only one item.
- **Standard Deviation (Cell D7) and Range (Cell D11):** The Standard Deviation and Range for the Transaction Value data is fairly high. This indicates a wide disparity in the amount of money customers spend when they visit the store.
- **Sum (Row 14):** The transactions analyzed in this example represent total sales of 922 items at $11,322.66. Depending on the size of this company, these transactions may or may not provide sufficient representation of this business.

## COMMON MISTAKES | Using the Currency Format

You will most likely need to expand the column width of the Descriptive Statistics output to see all the data. If the results appear distorted after clicking the **OK** button on the **Descriptive Statistics** window, expand the column widths on the output worksheet. You can also apply any of Excel's formatting features to enhance the appearance of a Descriptive Statistics output.

## Histogram

Business managers use histograms to calculate the frequency or number of occurrences within certain categories of data. For example, a retail business manager will often measure how many items are purchased by price point. As with the example illustrated in the previous segment, this type of analysis will give a business manager an understanding of how customers are buying products in the company's stores. In addition, this analysis can also provide valuable insights into a company's strength in selling certain products or categories of merchandise.

Figure 37 shows transaction data that is similar to the data shown in Figure 33. However, in this worksheet the transaction number is duplicated for each item the customer purchased. For example, if a customer purchased three items, the transaction number will be listed three times. As a result, there are 650 rows of data in this worksheet. Next to each transaction number is the price the customer paid for the item purchased. You will also see seven price categories listed in column D. With the exception of the first two price categories, each category is in $10 increments. The **Histogram** option from the **Data Analysis Tools** will be used to calculate how many items were purchased in each of these price categories.

Figure 37 | **Transactions and Price Points**

| | A | B | C | D |
|---|---|---|---|---|
| 1 | Transaction Details | | | |
| 2 | Transaction Number | Price | | Price Categories |
| 3 | 101483 | $2.00 | | $4.99 |
| 4 | 107334 | $9.29 | | $9.99 |
| 5 | 110245 | $7.82 | | $19.99 |
| 6 | 110245 | $8.28 | | $29.99 |
| 7 | 110245 | $8.95 | | $39.99 |
| 8 | 110245 | $12.76 | | $49.99 |
| 9 | 110245 | $19.68 | | $59.99 |
| 10 | 110245 | $3.30 | | |
| 11 | 110245 | $25.30 | | |
| 12 | 110245 | $31.08 | | |
| 13 | 110245 | $38.29 | | |
| 14 | 110739 | $9.14 | | |
| 15 | 111701 | $3.17 | | |
| 16 | 111701 | $7.62 | | |
| 17 | | | | |
| 18 | | | | |

The Histogram will count the number of transactions with a price between $0 and $4.99 and assign the number to this group.

This transaction is listed 9 times because the customer purchased 9 different items.

> **Quick Reference**
>
> **Data Analysis Tools: Descriptive Statistics**
>
> 1. Click the **Data Analysis** icon from the **Analysis** group on the **Data** tab of the Ribbon.
> 2. Select **Descriptive Statistics** from the **Data Analysis** dialog box and click the **OK** button.
> 3. Click the range finder next to the **Input Range** box and highlight the range of data you wish to analyze on your worksheet or type the range in the box.
> 4. Select either Columns or Rows based on the orientation of your data.
> 5. If you highlighted labels in step 3, click the box next to the **Labels in First Row** option.
> 6. Select an option designating where the output calculations will appear.
> 7. Select **Summary Statistics** to produce a comprehensive output of statistical calculations.
> 8. Select any or all of the three remaining output options if necessary.
> 9. Click the **OK** button.
> 10. Apply formatting adjustments to the output as needed.

The Histogram feature will be used to count the price frequency for each of the categories listed in column D using the prices in column B of Figure 37. The following explains how this is accomplished.

- Click the **Data Analysis** icon in the **Data** tab of the Ribbon.
- Select the **Histogram** option from the **Data Analysis** dialog box. This will open the **Histogram** dialog box shown in Figure 38.
- Click the range finder next to the **Input Range** box and highlight the range B2:B652. Notice that this range includes data in only the Price column (see Figure 37).
- Click the range finder next to the **Bin Range** box and highlight the range D2:D9. This is the range of price categories listed in column D. The Histogram will count the frequency of prices in the range of cells used to define the Input Range box based on the values that are contained in the range of cells entered for the Bin Range box.
- Select the **Labels** option, which is directly below the **Bin Range** box. Because the column headings were included in the range of cells used to define both the **Input Range** and **Bin Range** boxes, this option is selected.
- Select the **New Worksheet Ply** option in the center of the **Histogram** options window. The box next to this option is used for naming the worksheet that will be added to the workbook.
- Select the **Cumulative Percentage** and **Chart Output** options at the bottom of the **Histogram** dialog box. The Cumulative Percentage will display the price frequency for each of the groups in the Bin Range and show the cumulative percentage for each group.
- Click the **OK** button in the **Histogram** dialog box. This will add a new worksheet to the workbook showing the frequency results along with a histogram chart.

Figure 38 | **Settings in the Histogram Dialog Box**

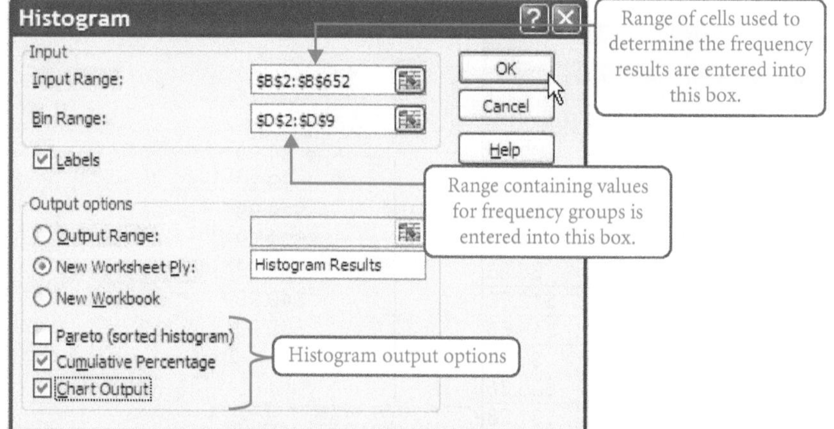


Figure 39 shows the Histogram output. Because of the options selected at the bottom of the **Histogram** dialog box shown in Figure 38, the price frequency is shown in category order (i.e., 4.99, 9.99, 19.99, etc.). In addition, a chart displaying the frequency data is also included. Note that both the data output and the histogram chart in Figure 39 have been formatted. You will most likely need to expand the column widths of the histogram data output to see the results. You will also need to resize and format the chart.

Figure 39 | **Histogram Output**

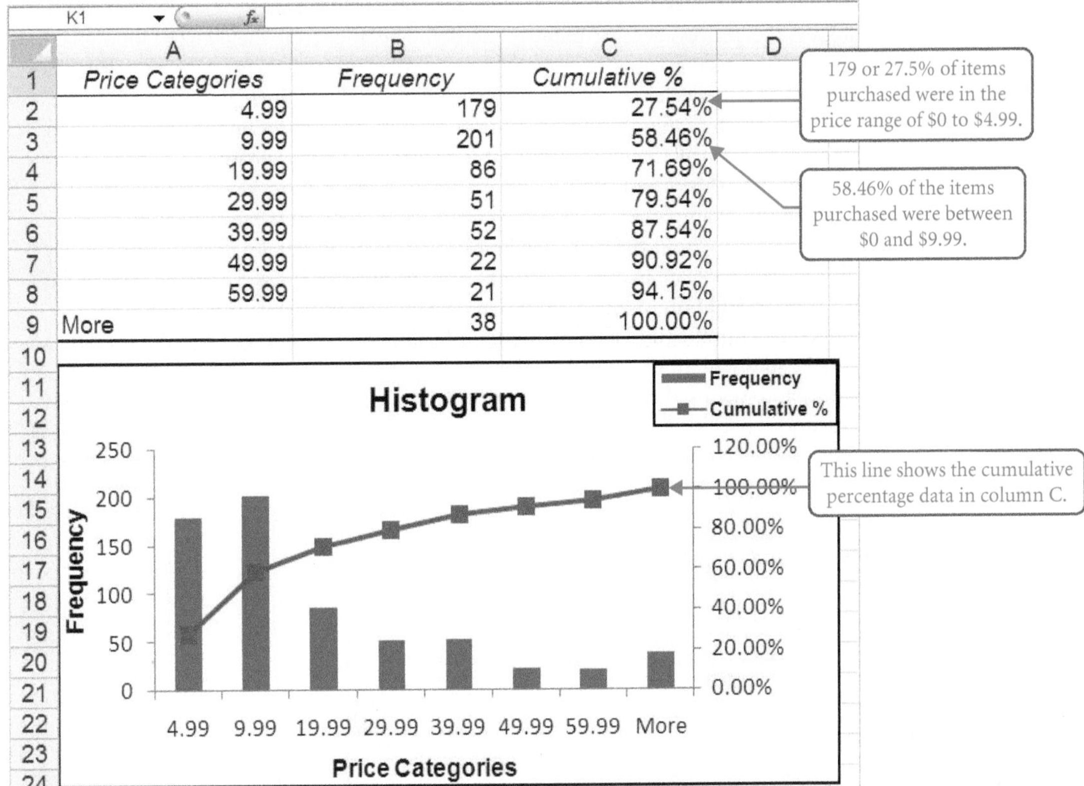

| | A | B | C |
|---|---|---|---|
| 1 | *Price Categories* | *Frequency* | *Cumulative %* |
| 2 | 4.99 | 179 | 27.54% |
| 3 | 9.99 | 201 | 58.46% |
| 4 | 19.99 | 86 | 71.69% |
| 5 | 29.99 | 51 | 79.54% |
| 6 | 39.99 | 52 | 87.54% |
| 7 | 49.99 | 22 | 90.92% |
| 8 | 59.99 | 21 | 94.15% |
| 9 | More | 38 | 100.00% |



## COMMON MISTAKES | Setting the Histogram Bin Range Values

Most mistakes with histograms occur when setting the category values that will be used for defining the **Bin Range** box in the **Histogram** dialog box. The category values should be the highest value in a group range. For example, if you wish to count the frequency of prices in a range of $0 to $4.99, the Bin Range value would be 4.99. If you wish to add a second category that counts the number of prices in the range $5.00 to $9.99, the Bin Range value would be 9.99. You can create any number of categories that suit the needs of your project. Any values that exceed the category values that are used to define the Bin Range will automatically be placed into a group called "More."

>> **Quick Reference**

### Data Analysis Tools: Histograms

1. Click the **Data Analysis** icon from the **Analysis** group on the **Data** tab of the Ribbon.
2. Select **Histogram** from the **Data Analysis** dialog box and click the **OK** button.
3. Click the range finder next to the **Input Range** box and highlight the range of data for which you wish to calculate the frequency on your worksheet.
4. Click the range finder next to the **Bin Range** box and highlight the range of data that contains values that will be used for grouping the frequency results.
5. If you highlighted labels in step 3 and 4, click the box next to the **Labels** option.

*(Continued)*

The results in Figure 39 show that 58.46% of all the items purchased are within the price range of $0 to $9.99. This result is also displayed visually in the histogram chart. Notice that the chart bars for price categories $19.99 and greater are considerably lower than in the $4.99 and $9.99 categories. A business manager might be concerned that customers are reluctant to purchase more-expensive products from the store. However, this depends on how much inventory the company owns at prices greater than $9.99. If more than 50% of this company's inventory is priced higher than $9.99, then a business manager will need to investigate why almost 60% of the company's sales are coming from products priced below $9.99. This analysis may ultimately change the way this company buys its inventory.

## Regression

Business managers use regression analysis in situations that require the measurement of how much the change in one performance metric, such as Unit Sales, can be explained by other events related to the business. For example, a marketing manager might want

**Histograms** *(Continued)*

6. Select a placement option for the Histogram results.
7. Select any combination of output options. You must select at least one option.
8. Click the **OK** button.
9. Apply formatting adjustments to the data output and/or chart as needed.

to know if certain advertising strategies have a statistically significant impact on the change of Unit Sales. In addition, a business manager will usually include several variables in this process because many events could be impacting the demand for a specific product at the same time. These variables could include price, competitor's prices, display enhancements, or changes in inventory. The results of the regression can tell the manager which of these events has the most significant impact on the change of sales when changes in all the other events, or variables, are held constant.

The data shown in Figure 40 represents the sales of chocolate bars in a grocery store. In this example we will assume a marketing manager is executing two marketing strategies throughout the year. The first strategy is setting up an in-store sign display promoting chocolate bars to customers. The second strategy is running a radio advertisement in addition to the in-store sign display. This data is shown in columns F and G. The number 0 in either column indicates that the marketing activity is not executed and the number 1 indicates that the marketing activity is being executed. In addition to the marketing data, the worksheet also contains prices from two similar grocery store competitors selling the same or similar chocolate bars. Column C shows the price the grocery store is charging for the chocolate bars each week and column B shows the unit sales each week.

Figure 40 | **Chocolate-Bar-Demand Data from a Grocery Store**

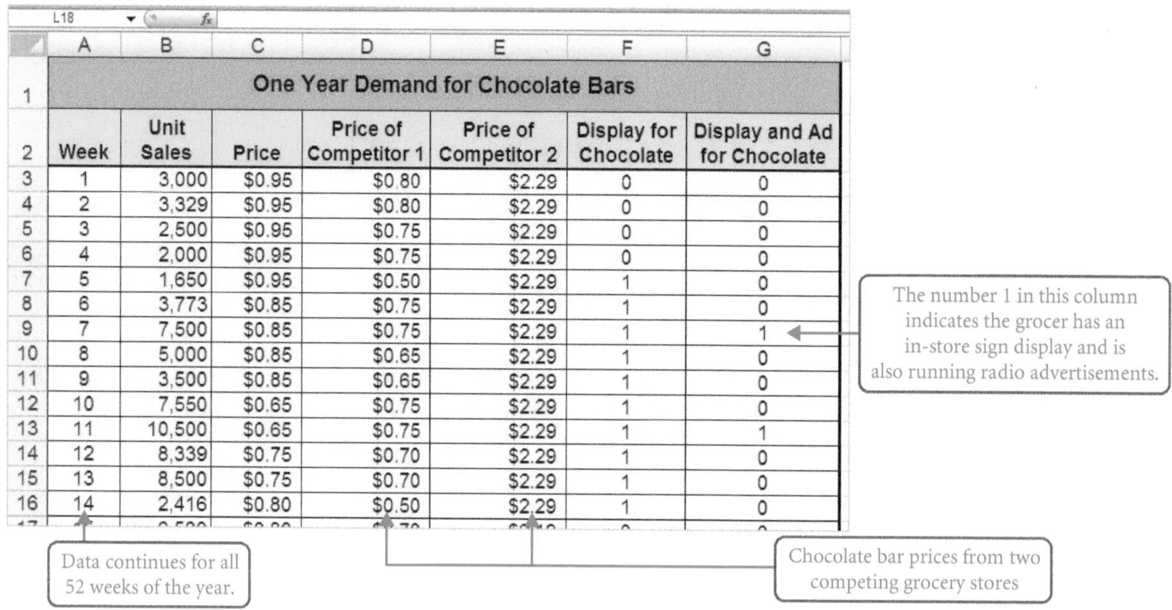

| | A | B | C | D | E | F | G |
|---|---|---|---|---|---|---|---|
| 1 | One Year Demand for Chocolate Bars | | | | | | |
| 2 | Week | Unit Sales | Price | Price of Competitor 1 | Price of Competitor 2 | Display for Chocolate | Display and Ad for Chocolate |
| 3 | 1 | 3,000 | $0.95 | $0.80 | $2.29 | 0 | 0 |
| 4 | 2 | 3,329 | $0.95 | $0.80 | $2.29 | 0 | 0 |
| 5 | 3 | 2,500 | $0.95 | $0.75 | $2.29 | 0 | 0 |
| 6 | 4 | 2,000 | $0.95 | $0.75 | $2.29 | 0 | 0 |
| 7 | 5 | 1,650 | $0.95 | $0.50 | $2.29 | 1 | 0 |
| 8 | 6 | 3,773 | $0.85 | $0.75 | $2.29 | 1 | 0 |
| 9 | 7 | 7,500 | $0.85 | $0.75 | $2.29 | 1 | 1 |
| 10 | 8 | 5,000 | $0.85 | $0.65 | $2.29 | 1 | 0 |
| 11 | 9 | 3,500 | $0.85 | $0.65 | $2.29 | 1 | 0 |
| 12 | 10 | 7,550 | $0.65 | $0.75 | $2.29 | 1 | 0 |
| 13 | 11 | 10,500 | $0.65 | $0.75 | $2.29 | 1 | 1 |
| 14 | 12 | 8,339 | $0.75 | $0.70 | $2.29 | 1 | 0 |
| 15 | 13 | 8,500 | $0.75 | $0.70 | $2.29 | 1 | 0 |
| 16 | 14 | 2,416 | $0.80 | $0.50 | $2.29 | 1 | 0 |

L18
The number 1 in this column indicates the grocer has an in-store sign display and is also running radio advertisements.
Data continues for all 52 weeks of the year.
Chocolate bar prices from two competing grocery stores

The following explains how the Regression option from the **Data Analysis Tools** is used to determine which of the five variables, or columns, in Figure 40 are statistically significant in explaining the change in Unit Sales shown in column B. As a result, the dependent variable in this example is Units Sales, and the five independent variables are Price, Price of Competitor 1, Price of Competitor 2, Display for Chocolate, and Display and Ad for Chocolate. It is important to note that this example will briefly discuss the regression results but will not provide in-depth interpretations. It is assumed that you have some knowledge of the terms and principles of regression.

- Click the **Data Analysis** icon in the **Data** tab of the Ribbon. Then, select the **Regression** option from the **Data Analysis** dialog box. This will open the **Regression** dialog box.
- Click the range finder next to the **Input Y Range** box and highlight the range B2:B54. This range contains the data for the dependent variable of the regression. Press the **Enter** key after highlighting this range.

- Click the range finder next to the **Input X Range** box, highlight the range C2:G54, and press the **Enter** key. This range contains the data for all five independent variables of the regression.
- Click the box next to the **Labels** option so that a green check appears. Because column headings were included in the range defining the dependent and independent variables, this option must be selected.
- Click the New Worksheet Ply in the Output Options area.
- Click the **OK** button in the **Regression** dialog box.

Figure 41 shows the settings that we made in the **Regression** dialog box for this example. Although they are not used for this example, there are options at the bottom of the dialog box for producing plot charts as part of the regression output. **Chart** options include line fit plots, residual plots, and normal probability plots.

## COMMON MISTAKES | Configuring Data Columns for Regression

When regressions are conducted in Excel, columns of data used for the independent variables must be adjacent. People often make the mistake of highlighting non-adjacent columns of data while holding the **CTRL** key when defining the independent variables, or Input X Range. However, this will produce the error shown below. Therefore, make sure the columns of data used to define the Input X Range are all adjacent.

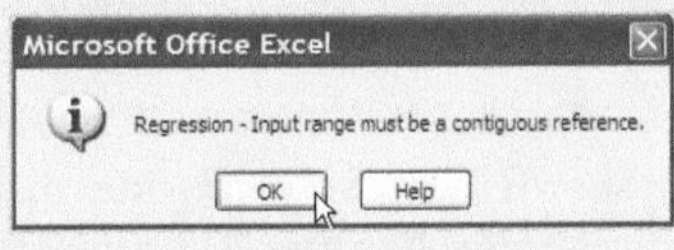


Figure 41 | **Settings in the Regression Options Window**

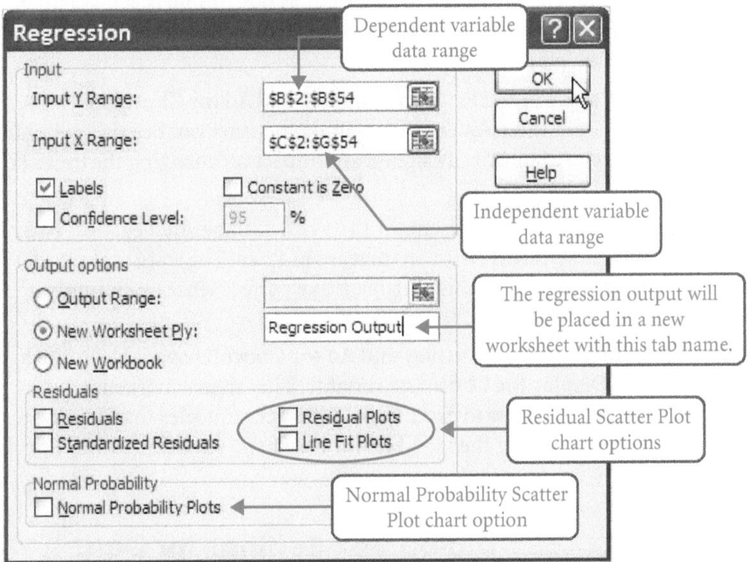


Figure 42 shows the regression output. As with the output for Descriptive Statistics and Histograms, the Regression output will most likely need to be formatted, especially with regard to column widths. Figure 42 shows the regression output after several formatting adjustments are made.

Figure 42 | **Regression Output**

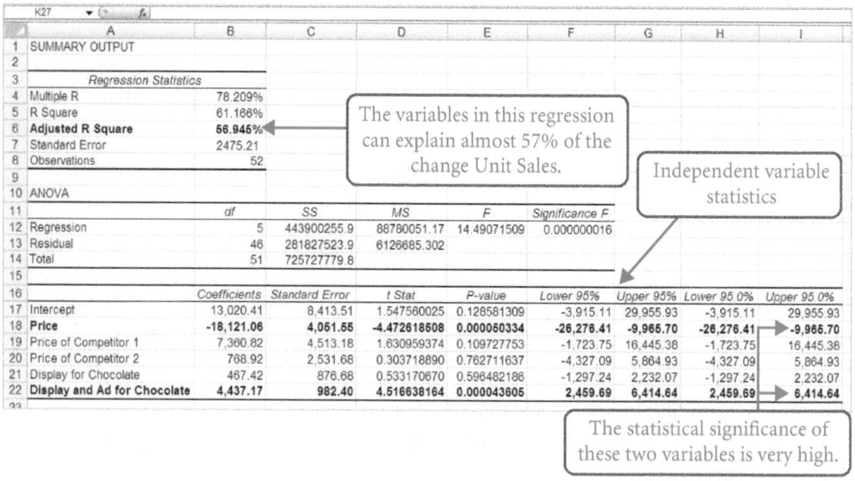

| | A | B | C | D | E | F | G | H | I |
|---|---|---|---|---|---|---|---|---|---|
| 1 | SUMMARY OUTPUT | | | | | | | | |
| 2 | | | | | | | | | |
| 3 | *Regression Statistics* | | | | | | | | |
| 4 | Multiple R | 78.209% | | | | | | | |
| 5 | R Square | 61.166% | | | | | | | |
| 6 | **Adjusted R Square** | **56.945%** | | | | | | | |
| 7 | Standard Error | 2475.21 | | | | | | | |
| 8 | Observations | 52 | | | | | | | |
| 9 | | | | | | | | | |
| 10 | ANOVA | | | | | | | | |
| 11 | | *df* | *SS* | *MS* | *F* | *Significance F* | | | |
| 12 | Regression | 5 | 443900255.9 | 88780051.17 | 14.49071509 | 0.000000016 | | | |
| 13 | Residual | 46 | 281827523.9 | 6126685.302 | | | | | |
| 14 | Total | 51 | 725727779.8 | | | | | | |
| 15 | | | | | | | | | |
| 16 | | *Coefficients* | *Standard Error* | *t Stat* | *P-value* | *Lower 95%* | *Upper 95%* | *Lower 95.0%* | *Upper 95.0%* |
| 17 | Intercept | 13,020.41 | 8,413.51 | 1.547560025 | 0.128581309 | -3,915.11 | 29,955.93 | -3,915.11 | 29,955.93 |
| 18 | **Price** | **-18,121.06** | **4,051.55** | **-4.472618508** | **0.000050334** | **-26,276.41** | **-9,965.70** | **-26,276.41** | **-9,965.70** |
| 19 | Price of Competitor 1 | 7,360.82 | 4,513.18 | 1.630959374 | 0.109727753 | -1,723.75 | 16,445.38 | -1,723.75 | 16,445.38 |
| 20 | Price of Competitor 2 | 768.92 | 2,531.68 | 0.303718890 | 0.762711637 | -4,327.09 | 5,864.93 | -4,327.09 | 5,864.93 |
| 21 | Display for Chocolate | 467.42 | 876.68 | 0.533170670 | 0.596482186 | -1,297.24 | 2,232.07 | -1,297.24 | 2,232.07 |
| 22 | **Display and Ad for Chocolate** | **4,437.17** | **982.40** | **4.516638164** | **0.000043605** | **2,459.69** | **6,414.64** | **2,459.69** | **6,414.64** |



### COMMON MISTAKES | Independent Variable Limit

You can define only 16 independent variables when using the **Regression** option from the Data Analysis Tool Pack. Excel will give you an error message and will not provide an output if you try to add more than 16 columns in the range of cells defining the Input X Range.

The regression output shown in Figure 42 provides many valuable insights with regard to marketing initiatives of this business. The following are a few key findings a marketing manager might take away from this analysis.

- The **Adjusted R Square** shows that the variables in this regression can explain almost 57% percent of the variation, or change in Unit Sales. Considering all of the factors that can influence a customer's decision to buy products, a marketing manager might be fairly satisfied that more than half of the variation in Unit Sales can be explained by these five variables.
- The statistical significance of the **Price** and **Display and Ad for Chocolate** variables are very high. Given these results, a marketing manager can be fairly certain that these variables have a statistically significant impact on changing the unit sales for chocolate.
- Notice that the t Stat and the Coefficient for the **Price** variable are negative. This indicates that Unit Sales decrease with an increase in Price. The statistical significance and negative correlation of this variable make perfect sense given fundamental economic principles.
- The statistical significance of the **Display and Ad for Chocolate** variable is much greater than for the **Display for Chocolate** variable. This gives a marketing manager a valuable insight as to how to execute promotional strategies that provide the greatest potential for increasing the sales of chocolate bars.

### COMMON MISTAKES | Dialog Box Settings for Data Analysis Tools

The settings you enter into the **Regression**, **Histogram**, **Descriptive Statistics**, or any **Data Analysis** tools dialog boxes will remain in the dialog box until you close Excel. Therefore, you must check these dialog boxes carefully before starting a new project.

>> **Quick Reference**

**Data Analysis: Regression**

1. Click the **Data Analysis** icon in the **Analysis** group on the **Data** tab of the Ribbon.
2. Select **Regression** from the **Data Analysis** dialog box and click the **OK** button.
3. Click the range finder next to the **Input Y Range** box and highlight the range of cells that contain data for the dependent variable on your worksheet.
4. Click the range finder next to the **Input X Range** box and highlight the range of cells that contain data for up to 16 independent variables on your worksheet.
5. If you highlighted column headings in steps 3 and 4, click the box next to the **Labels** option.
6. Select a placement option for the Regression output.
7. Select any of the **Residual** and/or **Normal Probability** chart options at the bottom of the **Regression** dialog box.
8. Click the **OK** button.
9. Apply formatting adjustments to the data output and/or charts as needed.

# >> Descriptive Statistics

VIDEO WORKSHOP

The purpose of this workshop is to demonstrate how the Descriptive Statistics option from the Data Analysis Tools is used to analyze transactions from a retail company. I will be demonstrating the tasks in this workshop in the video named **Descriptive Statistics**. Open the Excel file named ib_e09_transactionanalysis. Complete the tasks below first, and then watch the video.

1. **Descriptive Statistics (Video: Descriptive Statistics)**
   a. Click the **Data Analysis** icon from the **Data** tab of the Ribbon.
   b. Select the **Descriptive Statistics** option from the **Data Analysis** dialog box and click the **OK** button.
   c. Click the range finder next to the **Input Range** box in the **Descriptive Statistics** dialog box. Highlight the range B2:C202 in the Data worksheet and press the **Enter** key.
   d. Check that the **Columns** option is selected in the Grouped By section.
   e. Click the box next to the Labels in **First Row** option to place a checkmark in the box.
   f. Select the **New Worksheet Ply** option in the Output Options section. Type the name `Transaction Stats` in the box next to the **New Worksheet Ply** option.
   g. Select the **Summary Statistics** option at the bottom of the **Descriptive Statistics** dialog box.
   h. Select the **Kth Largest** option and type the number 2 in the box next to this option.
   i. Select the **Kth Smallest** option and type the number 2 in the box next to this option.
   j. Click the **OK** button on the **Descriptive Statistics** dialog box.
   k. Increase the width of the columns in the Transaction Stats worksheet so that all the data is visible.
   l. Save and close your worksheet.

# >> Histograms

VIDEO WORKSHOP

The purpose of this workshop is to demonstrate how the **Histograms** option from the Data Analysis Tools is used to determine the purchase frequency of retail items by price point. I will be demonstrating the tasks in this workshop in the video named **Histograms**. Open the Excel file named ib_e09_pricefrequency before starting this workshop. Complete the tasks below first, and then watch the video.

1. **Histograms (Video: Histograms)**
    a. Click the **Data Analysis** icon from the **Data** tab of the Ribbon.
    b. Select the **Histogram** option from the **Data Analysis** dialog box and click the **OK** button.
    c. Click the range finder next to the **Input Range** box in the **Histogram** dialog box. Then, highlight the range B2:B652 on the Data worksheet and press the **Enter** key.
    d. Click the range finder next to the **Bin Range** box in the **Histogram** dialog box. Then, highlight the range E2:E9 on the Data worksheet and press the **Enter** key.
    e. Click the box next the **Labels** options so that a green check appears.
    f. Select the **New Worksheet Ply** option in the Output Options section and type the name `Price Frequency` in the box next to the right.
    g. Select the **Cumulative Percentage** and **Chart Output** options at the bottom of the dialog box and click the **OK** button.
    h. In the Price Frequency worksheet, move the chart under the data to row 12. Then, increase the width of columns A, B, and C so that all the data is visible.
    i. Increase the overall height and width of the chart and change the position of the legend to the bottom. Then, increase the height and width of the plot area so that all the bars are clearly visible. Make any additional formatting adjustments to the chart so that it is easy to see and read.
    j. Save and close your file.

## >> Regression

The purpose of this workshop is to demonstrate how the **Regression** option from the Data Analysis Tools is used to measure the statistical significance of various marketing tactics. I will be demonstrating the tasks in this workshop in the video named **Regression**. Open the Excel file named ib_e09_marketinganalysis. Complete the tasks below first, and then watch the video.

1. **Regression (Video: Regression)**
    a. Click the **Data Analysis** icon from the **Data** tab of the Ribbon.
    b. Select the **Regression** option from the **Data Analysis** dialog box and click the **OK** button.
    c. Click the range finder next to the **Input Y Range** box in the **Regression** dialog box. Then, highlight the range B2:B54 on the Data worksheet and press the **Enter** key.
    d. Click the range finder next to the **Input X Range** box in the **Regression** dialog box. Then, highlight the range C2:G54 on the Data worksheet and press the **Enter** key.
    e. Click the box next the **Labels** options so that a green check appears.
    f. Select the **New Worksheet Ply** option in the Output Options section of the **Regression** dialog box. Then, type the name `Regression Results` in the box next to the **New Worksheet Ply** option.
    g. Click the **OK** button in the **Regression** dialog box.

h. Increase the width of columns of A through I in the Regression Results worksheet so that all the data is visible.

i. Change the font to bold for the rows containing the two variables in the regression output that have the highest t Stat score.

j. Save and close your file.

## >> Evaluating Historical Performance and Strategic Decisions

**EXERCISE**

**Why Do I Need This?**

Rebuilding or turning around a failing business can be a formidable challenge for any business executive. First, it might not always be clear why a business is failing. Many businesses suddenly fail after enjoying years of profitable success. Factors that might contribute to this decline include a drastic change in consumer demand, increased competition, or technological innovations that make a firm's product obsolete. In some cases, the reason for a company's decline is more tactical. For example, strategies that are executed to boost a firm's profits in the short term might cripple its long-term sales growth. As a result, executives might decide to hire a consulting firm to evaluate their company and determine why their business is declining. A common approach most consulting firms take when evaluating a company's business is to collect and analyze historical data to identify key trends and relationships. An analyst working on a consulting team could use many of Excel's statistical tools to conduct this type of analysis.

### Exercise

The purpose of this exercise is to evaluate 3 years of sales and cost data for a hypothetical home-audio manufacturing company. This company experienced rapid sales growth up to the year 2004. In 2004, the company's profit fell short of Wall Street's expectations, and the executive officers took action to increase the firm's profit for 2005. However, although the profit rate increased in 2005, sales declined. As a result, you will be taking on the role of an analyst in a consulting firm to determine why this company's sales are declining. To begin this exercise, open the file named ib_e09_businessevaluation.

1. Activate the Cost Demand Data worksheet. This worksheet contains 3 years of Unit Sales by month along with data for three key cost categories: Advertising, Human Resources, and Warehousing. The first tasks of this exercise will focus on using the **Descriptive Statistics** option from the **Data Analysis Tools** to summarize the data in this worksheet for each year. The data produced by this tool can be used to identify key trends that have occurred over the past 3 years.

2. Use the **Descriptive Statistics** option from the **Data Analysis Tools** to produce a statistical summary output for the cell range C2:C14 in the Cost Demand Data worksheet. This represents the Unit Sales history for the year 2004. Note that this range includes the column heading. The output should appear in the Sales Summary worksheet beginning in cell A2. This can be accomplished using the **Output Range** option (click the range finder and selected cell A2 in the Sales Summary worksheet).

3. Format the statistics in the range B4:B16 in the Sales Summary worksheet to a standard number with commas, and 0 decimal places.

4. Type a formula in cell B18 that multiples the sum of the sales units in cell B15 by 150, which is the average selling price this company charges per unit.

5. Type a formula in cell B19 that divides the result in cell B18 by 12. This will show on average how much revenue the company generates per month.

6. Activate the Cost Demand Data worksheet. Repeat steps 2, 3, and 4 to produce and format a statistical summary for the unit sales in the years 2005 (C15:C26) and 2006 (C27:C38). Note that these ranges *do not* include column headings. The output for the year 2005 should begin in cell C2 in the Sales Summary worksheet, and the output for the year 2006 should begin in cell E2.

7. Delete the descriptions in cells C2 and E2 in the Sales Summary worksheet. These descriptions are automatically created by the Descriptive Statistics output and are not needed.

8. Copy the formulas in cells B18 and B19 in the Sales Summary worksheet and paste them into cells D18 and D19, and F18 and F19.

9. Type formulas in cells D20 and F20 to calculate the percent change in sales revenue from the year 2004 to the year 2006. How much have sales declined from the year 2004 to 2006 in dollars? Compare the average (Mean) Unit Sales per month in the year 2004 and 2006. How much has the average monthly Unit Sales declined between these years?

10. Activate the Cost Summary worksheet. The **Descriptive Statistics** tool was used to create a 3-year summary for each of the cost categories in the Cost Demand Data worksheet. Type a formula in cell D18 to compare the percent change in Advertising Costs from the year 2004 to 2005. Copy this formula and paste it to cell F18. When did Advertising Costs increase, and by how much?

11. Copy the formula you created in step 10 and paste it to cells D36, F36, D54, and F54 to analyze the change in Human Resource and Warehousing costs. Explain the trend that has occurred in these two cost categories from 2004 to 2006. State the specific percent change and dollar change for both categories.

12. Activate the Receiving Data worksheet. From your analysis in step 11, you should have found that Warehousing costs of have increased from 2004 to 2006. The managers of this company were surprised at this statistic because the warehouse has an abundance of surplus space and the company pays for this space whether they use it or not. However, one of the key cost drivers in warehousing operations is the number of unique items the warehouse receives per inbound shipment. As a result, the **Histogram** tool will be used to analyze the inbound shipment data in this worksheet. Begin by opening the **Histogram** dialog box.

13. Define the Input Range in the **Histogram** dialog box using cells B2:B102 on the Receiving Data worksheet. This range contains the number of unique items received for a sample of 100 manifests taken from the years 2005 and 2006.

14. Define the Bin Range in the **Histogram** dialog box using cells E2:E7 on the Receiving Data worksheet. The frequency of the data in the Input Range will be categorized into the groups in this range. Other analysts on your consulting team have concluded that labor costs increase significantly when a shipment contains more than 15 unique items.

15. Select the Labels option in the **Histogram** dialog box and place the output in a new worksheet with a tab named `Item Frequency`. The Histogram output should include a cumulative percentage for each category as well as a chart. Produce this output by clicking the **OK** button on the dialog box.

16. Move the chart in the Item Frequency worksheet to row 10 beginning in column A. Then, increase the widths of columns A, B, and C so that all the frequency data in rows 1 through 7 are visible.

17. Increase the height of the Histogram chart and reposition the legend to the bottom of the chart. Apply any necessary formatting features so that the bars and trend lines are clear and easy to read. On the basis of the Histogram output and the information explained in step 14, what might be contributing to the increase in warehousing costs?

18. Activate the Cost Demand Data worksheet. The last goal of this analysis is to determine which of the three cost categories in this worksheet are statistically significant in explaining changes in unit sales. This will require the use of the Regression tool from the Data Analysis Tools. The results of this analysis will tell management the impact a change in one of the three costs categories has on the sales performance of the company. Begin by opening the **Regression** dialog box.

19. Define the Input Y Range (dependent variable) in the **Regression** dialog box using the range C2:C38 on the Cost Demand Data worksheet.

20. Define the Input X Range (independent variables) using the range D2:F38 on the Cost Demand Data worksheet.

21. Finish the Regression by selecting the **Labels** option and place the output in a new worksheet with the tab name `Regression Output`. Produce the output by clicking the **OK** button in the dialog box.

22. Expand the columns in the Regression Output worksheet so that all the data is visible. What are the t Stat results for each of the three cost variables (Advertising, Human Resources, and Warehousing)? Notice that Advertising has the lowest t Stat or statistical significance to Unit Sales. What does this suggest about the impact the company's advertising investments have on sales?

23. The t-Stat results for the Warehouse variable should be a negative number, suggesting that as warehousing costs increase, unit sales decrease. Why do you think this is so?

24. Which of the three independent variables has the highest t Stat?

25. The executive officers of this company are optimistic about sales and profit in the year 2007. They believe the primary reason for the company's sales decline is that advertising investments were too low. They plan to increase the amount of money invested in advertising and intend to fund this investment by reducing costs in Human Resource benefits and Warehousing. Considering the data you analyzed in this exercise, do you agree with management that this strategy will increase sales? Why or why not?

26. Save and close your file.

## >> What's Wrong with This Spreadsheet?

PROBLEM & EXERCISE

### Problem

You are working as a business analyst in the marketing department of retail company that sells kitchen and bathroom f urnishings. One of your coworkers is analyzing data regarding the annual spending of customers enrolled in the company's frequent shopper program. She is having trouble using Excel to put together a project for the vice president of your division and asks for your help. She sends you an e-mail with an Excel file attached and mentions the following points.

- Thank you so much for helping me with this project! The vice president of our division asked for a report showing the number of customers that fit into seven different annual spend categories. He gave me a list of these categories, which I typed into the Excel file attached to this e-mail.
- The data I am analyzing is a sample of 100 customers from our Frequent Shopper database. I found this Histogram feature in Excel and thought this would be a great way to put the annual-spend data into groups. However, I cannot get this thing to work. I keep getting this error message that says something like "bin range cannot have non-numeric data." What does that mean? If this is too much trouble I'll do this manually, but I figured I would ask anyway.
- By the way, he also asked for a statistical summary of the annual-spend data for the customers in my sample. Do you know what he is talking about? He was in a rush when he asked me to do this so I didn't have time to ask. He wants this done before noon and the only thing I can think of is adding an AVERAGE function.

### Exercise

The Excel file that was attached to your coworker's e-mail is named ib_e09_annualcustomerspendfrequency. What's wrong with this spreadsheet? Consider the following points:

1. Take a look at the annual-spend categories that were typed into the Excel worksheet. Why is a bin error occurring?
2. Your coworker mentioned that she would count the annual-spend frequency manually if she could not get the Histogram feature to work. What are the downsides of doing this type of project manually?
3. With regard to your coworker's last point, what could you recommend as an alternative to merely calculating the average of the annual customer spend?

Write a short answer for each of the points listed above. Then, fix any errors in the worksheet that are causing the bin range error. In addition, include the alternative you identified in point 3 above in the workbook.

Skill Set

## Solver

The **Solver** tool is very similar to the scenario tools demonstrated in the first section of this chapter. Business managers use Solver in situations that require an output to be maximized or minimized given various constraints. For example, a finance manager might use Solver to determine an investment strategy that maximizes the potential return given certain investment requirements and risks. Solver could also be used by a production manager to determine which combination of raw materials minimizes the cost of producing a product. This section will show how a financial planning manager might use Solver to create a basic investment strategy that maximizes the potential return given a specific level of risk.

## Defining Constraints

This example of the Solver tool involves a basic investment strategy that maximizes potential returns given a target level of risk. Financial planning managers usually plan investments on the basis of their clients' risk preference. In other words, some people might be averse to risk and concerned about losing money during market downturns. Therefore, these people might prefer slow-growing investments that will not be severely impacted by market fluctuations. Other people might prefer high-risk investments in hopes of achieving higher-than-average returns during market upswings. As a result, an investment manager will develop a strategy that suits the preferences of their clients. How does a financial planner know if an investment strategy is maximizing the potential return for a person's portfolio? Solver is one of several tools that a financial planner might use to answer this question.

Figure 43 shows hypothetical data of a basic personal-investment strategy. This example assumes that a financial planner will invest a person's money in four main categories: Bonds, Balanced Funds, Growth Funds, and Common Stocks. The column next to each investment category is a risk level based on a 10-point scale. Each investment category is assigned a value based on a person's potential risk of losing money. For example, Bonds are given a low-risk rating of 2 because they provide a fixed rate of return. Common Stocks are given a high-risk rating of 10 because these investments are focused on specific companies. If for some reason a company experiences any operational hardships, a person could lose a significant percentage of his investment. The remaining columns of data show the amount of money invested in each category, the percent each investment represents to the entire portfolio, the Estimated Annual Return, the Estimated Future Value in 3 Years, and the overall Portfolio Risk. The Estimated Future Value in 3 Years is calculated using the **future value (FV)** function. The overall Portfolio Risk (column G) is calculated by multiplying the Percent of Portfolio (column D) by the Risk Level (column B). Each of the values in column G is then summed to determine an overall risk level for the portfolio.

Figure 43 | **Personal Investment Strategy**

F6 =FV(E6,3,,-C6,1)

| | A | B | C | D | E | F | G |
|---|---|---|---|---|---|---|---|
| 1 | *Investment Strategy* | | | | | | |
| 2 | Investment Type | Risk Level | Investment | Percent of Portfolio | Estimated Annual Return | Estimated Future Value in 3 Years | Portfolio Risk |
| 3 | Bonds | 2 | 5,000 | 6.3% | 3.25% | $5,504 | 0.13 |
| 4 | Balanced Funds | 5 | 5,000 | 6.3% | 6.50% | $6,040 | 0.31 |
| 5 | Growth Funds | 7 | 5,000 | 6.3% | 10.50% | $6,746 | 0.44 |
| 6 | Common Stocks | 10 | 65,000 | 81.3% | 16.50% | $102,776 | 8.13 |
| 7 | *Total* | | *80,000* | | | *$121,065* | *9.00* |
| 8 | | | | | | | |

These values are calculated by multiplying the Percent of Portfolio by the Risk Level.

The FV function in this column uses the values from column C to define the pv argument.

These values are calculated by dividing each value in column C by the total value in cell C7.

The investment strategy in Figure 43 shows that a person's investment of $80,000 (cell C7) could potentially grow to $121,065 (cell F7) in 3 years. However, notice that the overall Portfolio Risk of this strategy is 9 (cell G7). As a result, whereas this strategy seems like it could provide significant growth, it could also result in a significant loss given the high level of risk. What if a person wanted to cut the overall risk of the portfolio in half to 4.5? What combination of investments would maximize the potential return at this target risk level? Solver can be used to answer this question; however, the constraints of this problem should be defined first.

The constraints of a Solver problem are any rules that *cannot* be broken in order to produce a result. For example, the following rules or constraints must be followed when determining an investment strategy that satisfies an overall portfolio risk level of 4.5 while maximizing the potential future value.

- The total dollars invested in the four categories listed in column A of Figure 43 must equal $80,000. This example will assume that the person has only $80,000 that can be invested. Therefore, the **SUM** function in cell C7 that is totaling the values in cells C3 through C6 must equal 80000.
- A minimum investment of $5,000 must be made in each category. This example assumes that a diversified investment strategy is desired. Therefore, the goal is to make a minimum investment of $5,000 in each of the four categories listed in column A.
- Investments must not exceed $40,000, or 50% of the portfolio in any category. For the purposes of moderating risk, this example will assume that 50% of the portfolio cannot be invested in any one category.
- The risk value in cell G7 must equal 4.5.

### COMMON MISTAKES | Cell References for Solver Problems

You must use formulas and/or functions with cell references in order to use the **Solver** tool. The **Solver** tool works by changing the values in cells referenced by a formula or function until the result is minimized, is maximized, or reaches a target value.

## Defining Solver Parameters

Once you have defined the constraints or the rules that must be followed when determining the optimal solution for a problem, you are ready to open the Solver tool. Each of the constraints defined in the previous segment of this example will be entered into the Solver Parameters dialog box. Therefore, it is good practice to define the constraints of the problem *before* opening the tool. The following explains how to open and set up the **Solver** tool.

- Click the **Solver** icon in the Analysis group on the **Data** tab of the Ribbon (see Figure 30). This will open the **Solver Parameters** dialog box.
- Click the range finder next to the **Set Target Cell** box at the top of the **Solver Parameters** dialog box and highlight cell F7 on the Personal Investment Strategy worksheet (Figure 43). This cell contains a SUM function, which is adding all of the values in the range F3:F6. Therefore, this cell contains the estimated 3-year future value of the entire portfolio. Press the **Enter** key after highlighting this cell.
- Click the **Max** option, which is one of the **Equal To** options listed below the **Set Target Cell** box. The goal is to maximize the value of the portfolio given a specific risk value. Therefore, the **Max** option is selected for this example. There are also options for minimizing the value of a target cell or setting a specific value for a target cell.
- Click the range finder next to the **By Changing Cells** box, highlight the range C3:C6, and press the **Enter** key. Solver will change the values in these cells, which contain the amount of money invested in each category, to maximize the future value of the portfolio given at a specific target risk value.

Figure 44 shows the initial setup of the **Solver Parameters** dialog box before adding any constraints. The settings in this window show that Solver will maximize the output in cell F7 by changing the values in cells C3 through C6 in Figure 43. Changing the values in these cells will directly impact the outputs in the Estimated Future Value in 3 Years column, and indirectly impact the values in the Portfolio Risk column. As previously mentioned, the values in the Portfolio Risk column are calculated by multiplying the values in the Percent of Portfolio column by the values in the Risk Level column.

Figure 44 | **Solver Parameters before Adding Constraints**

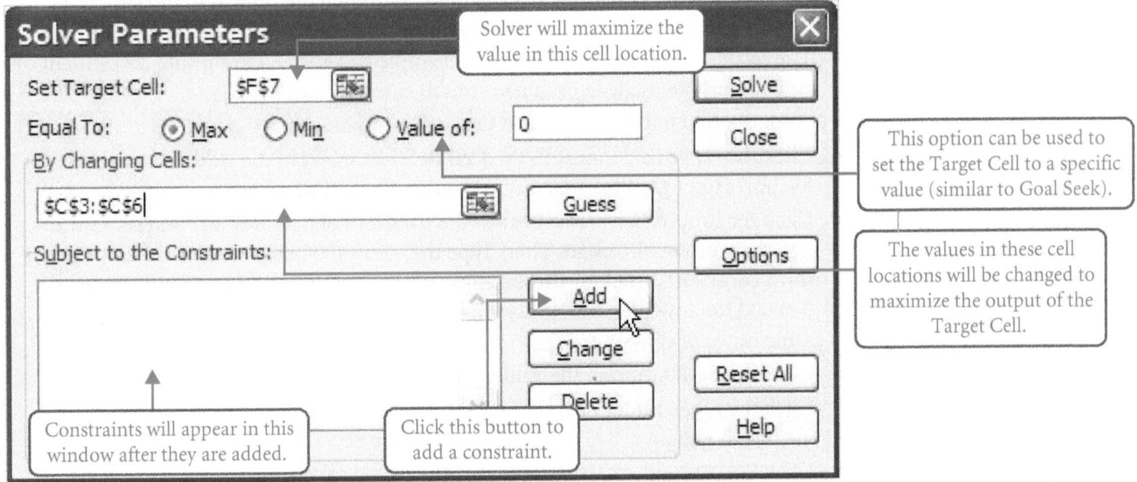


After making the initial settings in the **Solver Parameters** dialog box as shown in Figure 44, you are ready to begin adding constraints. The constraints for this example were defined in the previous segment. The following explains how the first constraint is added to the **Solver Parameters** dialog box.

- Click the **Add** button next to the **Subject to Constraints** box. This will open the **Add Constraint** dialog box.
- Click the range finder next to the **Cell Reference** box, highlight cell C7, and press the **Enter** key. Cell C7 is the output of the **SUM** function totaling the amount of money invested in all four investment categories.
- Click the drop-down arrow next to the conditional operator box and select the equal sign. Then, type the value 80000 in the **Constraint** box. As previously mentioned, the amount of money invested in all four categories must equal $80,000. Therefore, this constraint will ensure Solver provides a solution in which the total money invested is equal to $80,000.
- Click the Add button in the **Add Constraint** dialog box. This will add the first constraint to the **Solver Parameters** dialog box and clear the **Add Constraint** dialog box so that a second constraint can be added (see Figure 45).

Figure 45 shows the settings in the **Add Constraint** dialog box for the first constraint. Additional constraints can be added by clicking the **Add** button in this dialog box.

Figure 45 | **Add Constraint Dialog Box**

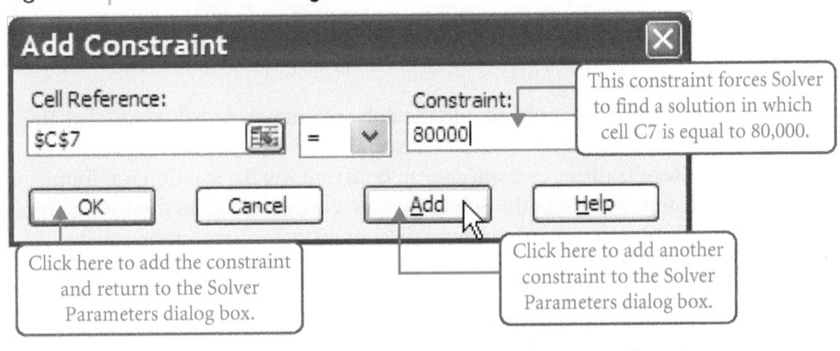

The following points explain how the remaining three constraints for this example are added to the **Solver Parameters** dialog box.

- Click the range finder next to the **Cell Reference** box in the **Add Constraints** dialog box. Highlight the range C3:C6, and press the **Enter** key. The range C3:C6 contains the investment values for the portfolio.
- Click the drop-down arrow next to the conditional operator box and select the greater-than-or-equal-to sign. Then, type the value 5000 in the **Constraint** box. The second constraint listed for this example states that a minimum investment of $5,000 must be made in each investment category.
- Click the Add button in the **Add Constraints** dialog box.
- Click the range finder next to the **Cell Reference** box in the **Add Constraints** dialog box. Highlight the range C3:C6, and press the **Enter** key.
- Click the drop-down arrow next to the conditional operator box and select the less-than-or-equal-to sign. Then, type the value 40000 in the **Constraint** box. The third constraint listed for this example states that an investment cannot exceed $40,000 for any category. Notice that we added two separate constraints to the same range of cells.
- Click the Add button in the **Add Constraints** dialog box.
- Click the range finder next to the **Cell Reference** box in the **Add Constraints** dialog box, highlight cell G7, and press the **Enter** key.
- Click the drop-down arrow next to the conditional operator box and select the equal sign. Then, type the value 4.5 in the **Constraint** box. The fourth constraint listed for this example states that the overall risk target for the portfolio is 4.5.
- Click the **OK** button in the **Add Constraint** dialog box. This will bring you back to the **Solver Parameters** dialog box.

Figure 46 shows the final settings in the **Solver Parameters** dialog box. Notice that all four constraints are listed in the **Subject to the Constraints** box. These constraints can be changed or deleted by highlighting a constraint and clicking either the **Change** or **Delete** button.

Figure 46 | **Final Solver Parameters Settings**

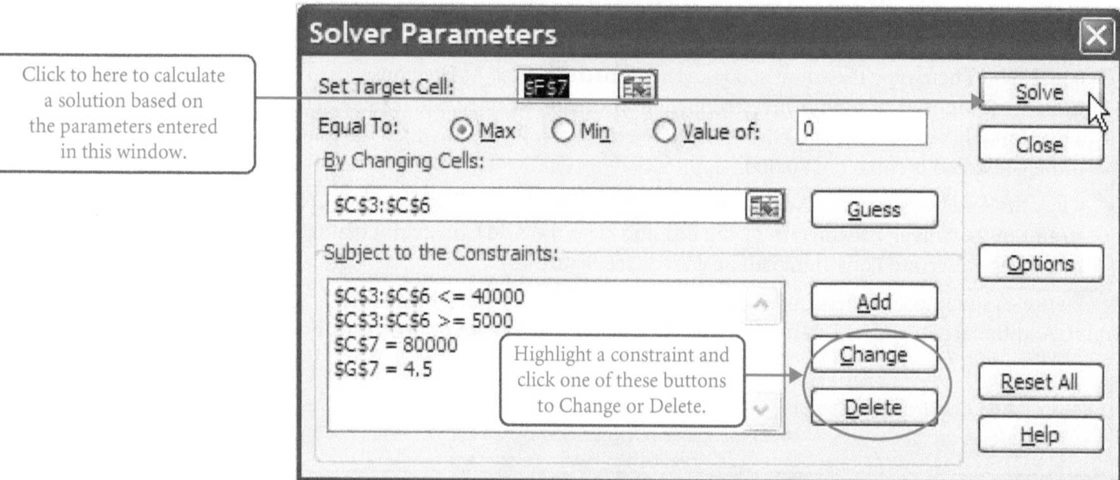


Once all the parameters are entered into the **Solver Parameters** dialog box, click the Solve button to show the new investment strategy for Figure 43. After clicking the **Solve** button, the **Solver Results** dialog box will appear, notifying you if a solution was found based on the constraints entered in the **Solver Parameters** dialog box. In this dialog box, you can apply the Solver solution to your worksheet or restore your worksheet to its original values. In addition, you can also create reports showing the mathematical details of how Solver arrived at the solution. As shown in Figure 47, Solver found a solution for the problem, and the **Keep Solver Solution** option has been selected.

Figure 47 | **Solver Results Dialog Box**

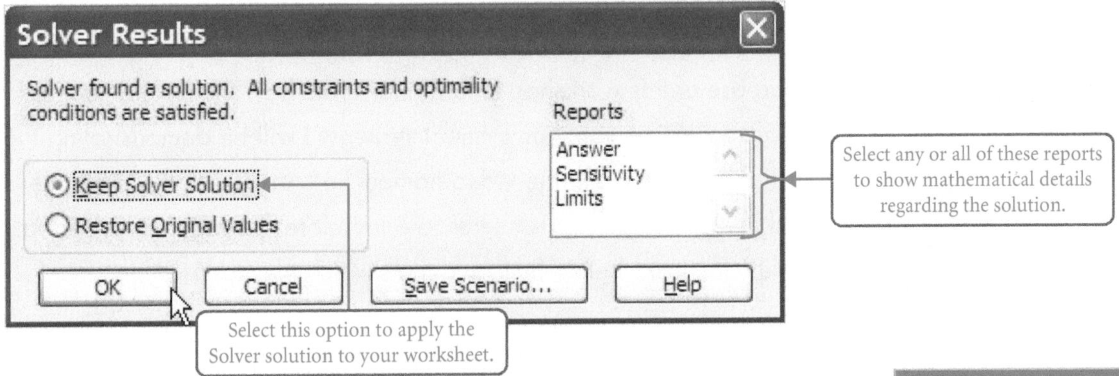


Figure 48 shows the values Solver applied to the range C3:C6 in Figure 43. Notice that more than 75% of the portfolio is invested in the Bonds and Balanced Funds categories. This strategy maximizes this person's portfolio return while achieving a risk level of 4.5. As a result, the future value of the portfolio in cell F7 is lower than what was originally shown in Figure 43. However, the risk level of this investment strategy is lowered to the target of 4.5, which is 50% less than the original risk level. A financial planning analyst could use Solver to run other scenarios showing a client how the future value of the portfolio changes at different risk levels.

## COMMON MISTAKES | Solver Iterations and Time Limits

After clicking the **Solve** button in the **Solver Parameters** dialog box, the dialog box shown below may appear. This is because Solver will automatically run through 100 solution iterations and/or calculate solutions for 100 seconds. However, your problem might require more than 100 iterations or 100 seconds to calculate an optimal solution. Solver will continue to calculate the optimal solution for your problem if you click the Continue button in this dialog box. However, Solver will not stop calculating iterations until an optimal solution is found, which might take a long period of time. To increase the number of iterations or seconds to calculate a solution, click the Options button in the Solver Parameters dialog box.

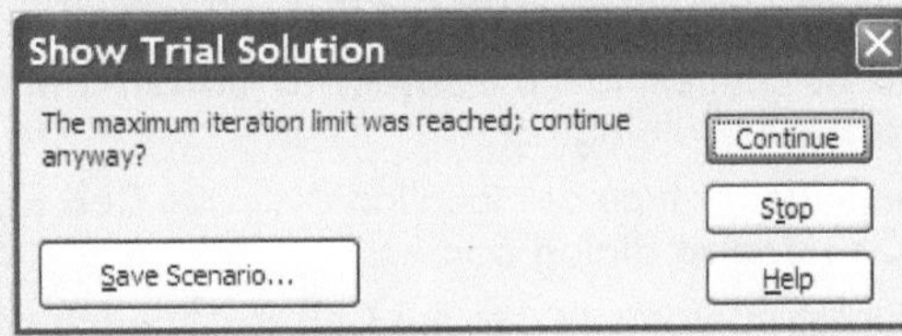


Figure 48 | **Solver Results**

| | A | B | C | D | E | F | G |
|---|---|---|---|---|---|---|---|
| 1 | *Investment Strategy* | | | | | | |
| 2 | Investment Type | Risk Level | Investment | Percent of Portfolio | Estimated Annual Return | Estimated Future Value in 3 Years | Portfolio Risk |
| 3 | Bonds | 2 | 40,000 | 50.0% | 3.25% | $44,028 | 1.00 |
| 4 | Balanced Funds | 5 | 21,000 | 26.2% | 6.50% | $25,367 | 1.31 |
| 5 | Growth Funds | 7 | 5,000 | 6.3% | 10.50% | $6,746 | 0.44 |
| 6 | Common Stocks | 10 | 14,000 | 17.5% | 16.50% | $22,136 | 1.75 |
| 7 | *Total* | | *80,000* | | | *$98,278* | *4.50* |
| 8 | | | | | | | |

Target risk level which was one of the constraints

Maximum and minimum constraints were used for these cell locations.

Maximum return value given the constraints entered for this problem

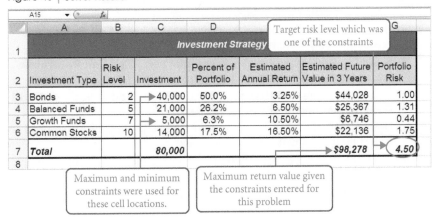

**>> Quick Reference**

**Solver**

1. Create a formula or function that uses cell references to produce a mathematical result.
2. Click the **Solver** icon in the **Analysis** group on the **Data** tab of the Ribbon to open the **Solver Parameters** dialog box.
3. Click the range finder next to the **Set Target Cell** box and highlight a cell location on your worksheet. This cell location should contain the formula or function you created in step 1.
4. Select one of the **Equal To** options based on the goals of your project. If you select the **Value Of** option, type a value in the box.
5. Click the range finder next to the **By Changing Cells** box and highlight cell locations that are directly or indirectly referenced by the formula you created in step 1.
6. Click the **Add** button in the **Solver Parameters** dialog box to enter any required constraints for your project.
7. Click the **Solve** button to calculate a solution.
8. Select either the **Keep Solver Solution** or **Restore Original Values** options in the **Solver Results** dialog box.
9. Click the **OK** button in the **Solver Results** dialog box.

VIDEO WORKSHOP

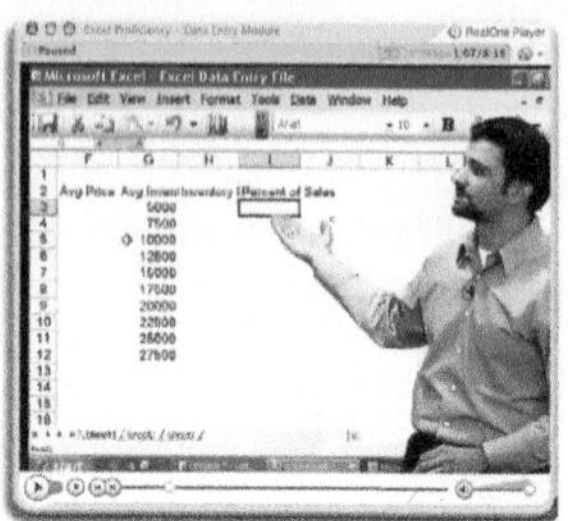

# >> Solver

The purpose of this workshop is to demonstrate how the **Solver** tool is used to create a personal investment strategy. I will be demonstrating the tasks in this workshop in the video named **Solver**. Open the Excel file named ib_e09_optimalinvestmentstrategy before starting this workshop. Complete the tasks below first, and then watch the video.

1. **Solver (Video: Solver)**
   a. Type a **SUM** function in cell C7 of the Investments worksheet that adds the values in the range C3:C6.
   b. Type a formula in cell D3 that divides the value in cell C3 by the output of the **SUM** function in cell C7. Place an absolute reference on cell C7 in this formula. Then, copy the formula and paste it into the range D4:D6 using the **Formulas paste** option.
   c. Enter a Future Value function in cell F3 that will determine the value of the investment in column C in 3 years. There are no periodic investments. Assume that the investment will be made at one time at the beginning of the period. Copy and paste this function into cells F4:F6.
   d. Type a **SUM** function in cell F7 that adds the values in cell F3:F6.
   e. Type a formula in cell G3 that multiplies the value in cell D3 by the value in cell B3. Copy this formula and paste it into the range G4:G6.
   f. Type a **SUM** function in cell G7 that adds the values in the range G3:G6.
   g. Click the **Solver** icon in the **Data** tab of the Ribbon.
   h. Use the range finder or type cell location `F7` in the **Set Target Cell** box of the **Solver Parameters** dialog box.
   i. Check to see that the **Max** option is selected in the **Equal To** options of the **Solver Parameters** dialog box.
   j. Use the range finder or type the range `C3:C6` in the **By Changing Cells** box of the **Solver Parameters** dialog box.
   k. Click the **Add** button next to the **Subject to Constraints** box in the **Solver Parameters** dialog box.
   l. Use the range finder or type cell location `C7` in the **Cell Reference** box of the **Add Constraint** dialog box.
   m. Select the equal-to operator next to the **Cell Reference** box of the **Add Constraint** dialog box.
   n. Type `80000` in the **Constraint** box and click the **Add** button in the **Add Constraint** dialog box.
   o. Use the range finder or type the range `C3:C6` in the **Cell Reference** box of the **Add Constraint** dialog box.
   p. Select the greater-than-or-equal-to operator next to the **Cell Reference** Box in the **Add Constraint** dialog box.
   q. Type `5000` in the **Constraint** box and click the **Add** button in the **Add Constraint** dialog box.
   r. Use the range finder or type the range `C3:C6` in the **Cell Reference** box of the **Add Constraint** dialog box.
   s. Select the less-than-or-equal-to operator next to the **Cell Reference** box in the **Add Constraint** dialog box.
   t. Type `40000` in the **Constraint** box and click the **Add** button in the **Add Constraint** dialog box.

u. Use the range finder or type cell location `G7` in the **Cell Reference** box of the **Add Constraint** dialog box.
v. Select the equal-to operator next to the **Cell Reference** box of the **Add Constraint** dialog box.
w. Type `4.5` in the **Constraint** box and click the **OK** button in the **Add Constraint** dialog box.
x. Click the **Solve** button on the **Solver Parameters** dialog box.
y. Click the **OK** button on the **Solver Results** dialog box.
z. Save and close your file.

## >> Optimizing Pick Costs in a Distribution Center

**EXERCISE**

**Why Do I Need This?**

Managing the efficiency and costs of a merchandise warehouse can be a challenging task. In some cases, a warehouse, commonly referred to as a distribution center (DC), can encompass more than 1 million square feet and extend several stories in height. The size of a distribution center usually depends on the amount of merchandise shipped as well as the type of merchandise sold by a company. Initially, many people think that the operations of a DC are very simple. Cartons come off a truck, are put on a shelf, and then are taken off a shelf when whatever is inside the carton is sold or shipped to a store. In theory, this is correct. However, decisions such as where cartons are stored in a DC can drastically change the costs and efficiency of the entire operation. For example, there is a significant cost difference between storing an item on the floor of the DC and on a shelf four stories high. When a carton is stored on the floor of the DC, a person can literally walk to that location, place the carton on a hand truck, and wheel it over to an outbound truck. However, the same carton stored on a shelf four stories high requires a special machine that must be operated by a skilled and licensed operator. Therefore, the cost of the machine, skilled operator, and added time increases the cost of picking a carton in the DC. As a result, the decision of where cartons are stored in a DC can have huge cost implications. A tool such as Solver can give DC managers valuable insights in developing a storage plan that minimizes the cost of picking cartons.

### Exercise

The purpose of this exercise is to use Solver to create a storage plan that minimizes carton picking costs for a DC. This DC is operated by a relatively small manufacturing company that sells 20 products. To begin this exercise, open the file named ib_e09_storageoptions.

1. Activate the Storage and Pick Data worksheet. This worksheet is divided into two parts. The top part (rows 1–24) shows the location and the number of cartons stored for each of the 20 products sold by this company, which are listed in column A. Row 2 shows the cost of picking cartons from each location listed in row 3. **SUM** functions are used in column F (F4:F23) to add the total number of cartons stored in all locations for each product. This number must match the Inventory in Cartons values in column G. Column H shows the weekly sales for each product in cartons. This is how many cartons of each product the DC will need to pick and ship out each week.

2. Scroll down the worksheet so that rows 26 through 48 are visible. This is the second part of the worksheet, which shows the number of cartons picked by location based on the product sales listed in the range H4:H23. The cells in range B28:E47 contain IF functions that compare the number of cartons stored in each location with the sales for each product in column H. The range F28:F47

contains formulas that calculate the Total Pick Cost for each product. Cell F48 shows the total cost of picking all required cartons to satisfy 1 week of sales. Notice that it costs this company more than $37,000 to pick and ship cartons for 1 week of sales. Multiplied by 52, this amounts to almost $2 million per year.

3. Notice that the Total Pick Cost for product 1 in cell F28 is $150. This is because all cartons for this product are stored on the Ground Level, which has a pick cost of $1.50 per carton. Change the value in cell B4 to `0` and type `300` in cell E4. Notice that the Total Pick Cost for product 1 is now $1,200. This is because the cost of picking a carton out of level 3 is $12.00 per carton. The next tasks of this exercise will use Solver to determine how cartons should be stored in cells B4:E23 to minimize the total cost calculated in cell F48.
4. Insert a new worksheet in this workbook. Rename the worksheet tab `Original Cost`. Copy all of the data in the Storage and Pick Data worksheet and paste it into the Original Cost worksheet.
5. Activate the Storage and Pick Data worksheet. Then, open the **Solver Parameters** dialog box.
6. Use the range finder or type cell location `F48` in the **Set Target Cell** box in the **Solver Parameters** dialog box.
7. Select Min in the set of **Equal To** options in the **Solver Parameters** dialog box.
8. Click the range finder next to the **By Changing Cells** box in the **Solver Parameters** dialog box and highlight the range B4:E23 in the Storage and Pick Data worksheet. Based on the settings you entered in the **Solver Parameters** dialog box to this point, Solver will minimize the output of the formula in cell F48 by changing the values in the range B4:E23, which contain the number of cartons stored for each location. However, there are several rules or constraints Solver will have to consider when calculating this solution. These constraints will be entered into the **Solver Parameters** dialog box next.
9. Click the **Add** button in the **Solver Parameters** dialog box. Then, click the range finder next to the **Cell Reference** box in the **Add Constraint** dialog box. Highlight the range B4:E23 on the Storage and Pick Data worksheet. Click the Down arrow next the comparison operator box and select **int**. Notice that the word "integer" automatically appears in the constraint box. This constraint will ensure that Solver does not place any partial cartons in a location (e.g., 1.4). Click the **Add** button in the **Add Constraint** dialog box.
10. Add a second constraint that requires Solver to use only positive numbers when assigning values to the range B4:E23. Therefore, any values Solver assigns to this range must be greater than or equal to 0.
11. As mentioned in step 1, the values in the range F4:F23 must match the values in the range G4:G23. Add a constraint to Solver that ensures that the values in these two cell ranges are equal to each other.
12. Each location in this DC can hold a maximum of 5000 cartons. As a result, each of the SUM functions in the range B24:E24 must be less than or equal to 5000. Add these constraints to Solver and then return to the **Solver Parameters** dialog box.
13. Click the **Options** button on the **Solver Parameters** dialog box. Type the number `300` in the **Max Time** box of the **Solver Options** dialog box and click the **OK** button. Given the complexity of this problem, it may take Solver several minutes to calculate a final solution.
14. Click the **Solve** button in the **Solver Parameters** dialog box. When the **Show Trial Solution** dialog box appears notifying you that the maximum *iterations* was reached, click the **Continue** button.

15. If the **Show Trial Solution** window appears again notifying you that the time limit has expired, click the **Continue** button. Solver should come up with a solution after a few more minutes. Processing times will vary depending on the type of computer you are using. The Branch number in the lower left corner of the Excel screen will reach 156 before Solver completes the solution.

16. Click the **Keep Solver Solution** option when the **Solver Results** dialog box appears and click the **OK** button.

17. Compare the Total Pick Cost in cell F48 between the Storage and Pick Data worksheet and the Original Cost worksheet. How much did the cost decrease? Compare the difference in cost between these two worksheets on an annual basis assuming cell F48 represents the weekly cost of the DC's picking operation. How much was the cost reduced on an annualized basis.

18. Save and close your file.

## >> What's Wrong with This Spreadsheet

PROBLEM & EXERCISE

### Problem

You are the director of a small hardware store. You asked one of your assistant managers to develop a purchasing plan for several items that will maximize the potential profits of the business. You give the assistant a list showing the cost and retail price of 16 different items in 4 different merchandise categories. In addition, you tell the assistant not to buy more than 1500 units of any one item and that the total units purchased for all items combined should not be greater than 10,000. Finally, you mention that most suppliers require a minimum purchase of 250 units per item. Your assistant works on developing a purchasing plan for the 16 items in Excel and attaches the file in an e-mail. He mentions the following points in his message.

- Thank you for giving me this assignment. I just learned how to use this cool tool in Excel called Solver and it can tell me exactly how many units we should be buying for each item.
- I typed all the items along with the cost and retail price information into an Excel spreadsheet. I calculated the profit dollars and profit rate for each item. Then, I calculated the profit rate for each category and for the entire purchase. You will notice that the last row of the spreadsheet labeled Grand Total shows the total sales and profit potential of this purchasing strategy.
- It's interesting how this math works. The Solver calculations are basically saying we can maximize our profits if we buy 1500 units of everything. Overall, it makes sense because if we sell everything we buy, we will maximize the profits of the store.

### Exercise

The Excel file your assistant attached to the e-mail is named ib_e09_purchaseplan. What's wrong with this spreadsheet? Consider the following points.

1. Take a look at the assistant's plan. Does the data make sense?
2. The settings the assistant used for the **Solver Parameters** window should still be visible. Open the **Solver** tool and look at these settings. Do they make sense?
3. Are there any flaws in the overall logic of this plan? Why or why not?

Write a short answer for each of the points listed above. Then, make any necessary adjustments to the Solver settings and come up with a new solution for this plan.

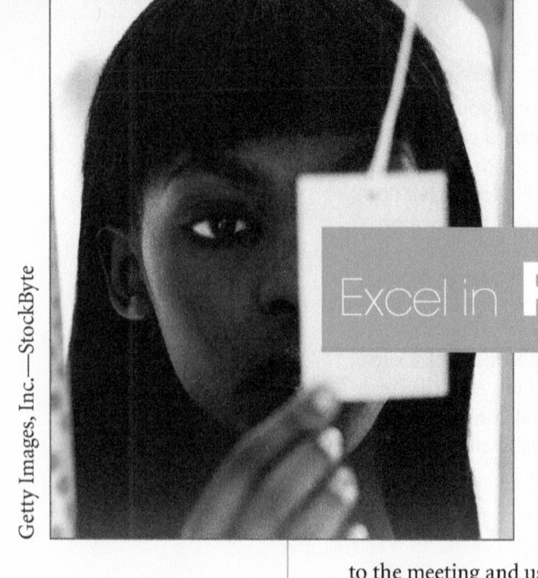
Getty Images, Inc.—StockByte

# Excel in **Practice** | Anecdotes

**Solution**

Excel's scenario tools were amazing in helping me put together all the information I needed for my merchandise plans. These tools were great for putting together reports that were reviewed by the executive officers at the merchandise planning meetings. However, what I liked most about these tools is that I could bring my laptop to the meeting and use the Excel tools to answer any questions that were raised by the executives. I would create spreadsheets with tools such as the Scroll Bar or Scenario Manager setup and be ready to go if someone asked the infamous question "What if. . . ?"

## Assignment

1. Open the file named ib_e09_merchandiseplanningmeeting. The data in this workbook is very similar to what appeared in the merchandise financial plans that were mentioned in the anecdote. The purpose of this assignment is to prepare various financial scenarios as if you were presenting this plan to the executive officers of an apparel retail company.
2. Add the necessary formulas and functions to complete the Item List worksheet including the Department Grand Totals (row 23). The following are a few formulas used for this type of analysis:
   a. `Units Sold at Full Price = Percent Sold at Full Price × Units Purchased`
   b. `Units Sold at Markdown Price = Units Purchased - Units Sold at Full Price`
   c. `Markdown Price = Retail Price × (1-Percent Markdown)`
3. Every year the executives are concerned about all velvet products in the line. Prepare the following three scenarios for all velvet items. Assume all other products in the department are sold at 65% of the full price with the remainder being sold at 30% off the original retail price. What is the *department profit rate* for each scenario?
   a. Best Case: 75% Full Price Sales selling remaining inventory at 25% off.
   b. Average Case: 60% Full Price Sales selling remainder at 40% off.
   c. Worst Case: 40% Full Price Sales selling remainder at 55% off.
4. The profit rate for the Printed Rayon Skirts is fairly strong; however, 15,000 units were purchased. Assuming the average markdown rate for this item is 50% off, what will the full price sales units need to be to achieve at least a 43.5% overall profit rate for this item?
5. The executives usually ask questions regarding the overall profit rate for the department when the average Percent Sold at Full Price and the average Percent Markdown *for the department* changes. For example, a typical question might be, "What if the department sells 60% of all merchandise at full price and sells the remaining inventory at an average of 40% off the original retail price?" They are most concerned about what combination of Percent Sold at Full Price and Percent of Markdown for the department will drive the profit rate of the entire department below 45%. Prepare a scenario that can answer these types of questions.

## Questions for Discussion

1. The anecdote mentions that several scenarios were created before money was spent to purchase a line of merchandise. Why would business managers need to evaluate so many scenarios before making inventory investments? What questions are they trying to answer?

2. Most business executives would agree that the process of evaluating scenarios can potentially improve the decisions a company makes. However, what key issues could undermine the integrity and value of scenario analysis?

# Review Questions

The following questions are related to the concepts addressed in this chapter. There are three types of questions: Short Answer, True or False, and Fill in the Blank. If your answer to a True or False question is False, write a short explanation as to why you think the statement is not true.

1. You must use ________ ________ in formulas or functions in order to use any of Excel's scenario tools.

2. The Scroll Bar is accessed from the ________ tab of the Ribbon.

3. List three limitations of which you must be aware when setting up the controls of a Scroll Bar.

4. True or False: Once a Scroll Bar is activated, you cannot go back and change any of the controls. If the controls need to be changed, you must delete the Scroll Bar and create a new one.

5. Explain how you can delete a Scroll Bar without deleting any columns or rows.

6. True or False: The use of the Conditional Formatting feature is somewhat limited because you can set only one condition for any given cell.

7. When creating a two-dimensional data table, if the formula used to create the output or results of the table is located in cell D5, the values that make up the top row and left column of the table must begin in cells ________ and ________.

8. When highlighting a range of cells before creating a two-dimensional data table, the first cell in the range must contain either a ________ or a ________.

9. True or False: After creating a Data Table, you cannot change any of the values along the top row or left column. Changing these values could create an error in the table results.

10. True or False: You can use both Solver and Goal Seek to set a specific value for a target cell location. Therefore, both of these tools can be used to accomplish the same tasks.

11. What is the difference between Scenario Manager and Goal Seek?

12. Tools for analyzing data using various statistical methods can be accessed by selecting the ________ ________ icon from the ________ tab of the Ribbon.

13. True or False: When using any option from the Data Analysis Tools, the output will automatically be formatted based on the results that are produced.

14. If you are using the **Histogram** tool, what bin range value should be entered into a cell location if the following is one of the groups you are using to count the frequency of purchases by price point: 15.99 and 19.99?

15. True or False: When defining the input X range of a regression, you can highlight a range of cells extending over continuous columns or hold down the Control key and highlight specific columns.

16. What is the maximum independent variable limit when running a regression in Excel?

# Skills Exam

The following exam is designed to test your ability to recognize and execute the Excel skills presented in this chapter. Read each question carefully and answer the questions in the order they are listed. You should be able to complete this exam in 60 minutes or less.

1. Open the file named ib_e09_chapter9skillsexam.
2. Activate the Fleet Details worksheet. Use Solver to maximize the Total Cartons in cell E27 by changing the Trips per Year in the range D3:D26. The solution must include the following constraints:
   a. Each trailer must make at least 24 trips per year.
   b. The maximum number of trips a trailer can make per year is 100.
   c. The total number of trips per year for all trailers must equal 1500.
   d. There cannot be any partial trips (e.g., 1.5).
3. Activate the Capacity worksheet. Type a formula in cell B6 that calculates the total cubic feet of freight capacity. This formula should first multiply the Average Capacity in cell B2 by the Number of Trucks in cell B3, and then multiply this result by the Number of Trips per Year in cell B4.
4. Create a Data Table that shows the total cubic feet of freight capacity when the values in the range D6:I6 are substituted for the number of trucks in cell B3 and the values in the range B7:B18 are substituted for the Total Trips per Year in cell B4.
5. Activate the Break-Even worksheet. Use Conditional Formatting to change the color of the value in cell B8 to red for any output that is less than 0.
6. Add a Scroll Bar to the Break-Even worksheet.
7. Set the controls of the Scroll Bar added in question 6 to change the value in cell B5. The value in cell B5 should not be less than 10,000 and should not be greater than 30,000. For each click of the arrow on the Scroll Bar, the value in cell B5 should increase 100 miles. For each page click of the Scroll Bar (space between the arrows), the value in cell B5 should change by 500 miles.
8. Use the Scroll Bar or type the value **20000** in cell B5.
9. Open the Scenario Manager and enter the following three scenarios, which assign different values to the Cost per Mile and Cost per Truck variables in the Break-Even worksheet. Use the scenario names listed below in the Scenario Manager.
   a. Target Scenario: Cost per Mile = **.40**; Cost per Truck = **40000**
   b. Best Scenario: Cost per Mile = **.25**; Cost per Truck = **30000**
   c. Worst Scenario: Cost per Mile = **.55**; Cost per Truck = **50000**
10. Create a Scenario Summary report showing the results of cell B7 for the three scenarios created in question 9.
11. Activate the Break-Even worksheet and show the results of the Worst Scenario that you created in question 9.
12. Use the Goal Seek tool to set the value in cell B8 of the Break-Even worksheet to 14.34% by changing the value in cell B4.
13. Activate the Store Sales Data worksheet. Use the Descriptive Statistics option from the Data Analysis Tools to provide a statistical summary for the Total Population and Population Age 4–11 data. The statistics output should appear in a new worksheet with the tab name **Population Stats**. Format the output so that all data is visible and numbers are formatted.
14. Activate the Store Sales Data worksheet. Create a Histogram for the Sales data in column B. Your histogram should count the number of stores in the sales groups listed below. The Histogram output should include the Cumulative Percentage as well as a Histogram chart. The output should appear in a new worksheet with the tab name **Sales Frequency**.

a. $0 – $3,000,000

b. $3,000,001 – $6,000,000

c. $6,000,001 – $9,000,000

d. Greater than $9,000,000

15. Format the Histogram data output that was created in question 14 so that all data is visible and easy to read. Then, format the Histogram chart. Expand the chart and add any formatting enhancements so that all the data is visible and easy to read.

16. Use the **Regression** option from the Data Analysis Tools to evaluate if Total Population, Population Age 4–11, and Competitor within 5 Miles can explain variations in the Sales data found in the Store Sales Data worksheet. The Sales data should be the dependent variable (Y Range) and the Total Population, Population Age 4–11, and Competitor within 5 Miles should be the independent variables (X Range). The regression output should appear in a new worksheet with the tab name `Regression Output`.

17. Format the data produced by the regression output in question 16. All data should be visible and numbers formatted with no more than 4 decimal places.

18. Save and close your file.

# Challenge Questions

The following questions are designed to test your ability to apply the Excel skills you have learned to complete a business objective. Use your knowledge of Excel and your creativity to answer these questions. For most questions, there are several possible ways to complete the objective.

1. The example shown in the Data Table segment suggested that, based on the price that was charged for a shirt, a business manager could determine how many units need to be sold to achieve a positive profit. The example also shows that the price of the shirt must exceed the variable cost to generate a profit. What other factors do you think need to be taken into consideration when setting the price of a product? Explain why a company might sell a product at a price that only meets its variable cost. Create an Excel spreadsheet with examples that support your answer.

2. As mentioned in the Scenario Tools segment of this chapter, the controls for the Scroll Bar can be set to change a value only in whole-number increments. However, with some creative thinking, you can use the Scroll Bar to increment the value in a target cell in fractional units. Open the file named ib_e09_challengea. The data in this file shows a simple investment analysis for a common stock. As the future price of the stock increases in cell B3, a formula in cell B7 calculates the Investment Gain/Loss. Add a Scroll Bar to increase the Future Price in cell B3 in $.10 increments. Set up the controls of the Scroll Bar so that the price can decrease as low as $5.00 and increase as high as $75.00.

3. It was mentioned in the Descriptive Statistics segment that the results shown in Figure 36 would have to be compared with company goals and statistics of other firms operating in the same industry. Research the annual reports of any two general-merchandise retail firms or a report on the General Merchandise industry published by a financial institution. Compare the results of your research with the results in Figure 36. If you were the president of a general-merchandise retail company, would you consider these results desirable? Why or why not? Assume that the transactions analyzed in Figure 36 provide sufficient representation of this company's business.

4. Open the Excel file named ib_e09_challengeb. This is the same data that was used in the Histogram workshop. Show the following statistics for this data in the Transaction Summary worksheet:

   - Total number of unique transactions.
   - The average dollars spent for each transaction.
   - The average number of items purchased per transaction. Assume that the transaction number is repeated for each item purchased.

# Working with External Data

## Chapter Goals

As demonstrated throughout this text, Excel is the primary analytical tool for most business managers. However, the data that business managers need to analyze typically exists in formats other than Excel. For example, most companies store data for their business on database systems. The data in these systems typically changes on a daily basis. In some cases, a business manager might need to place a sample set of data from a database system into an Excel worksheet for a one-time analysis. However, in many cases he needs to connect to an external data source, such as a database system, to conduct routine analytical projects that are required to make daily business decisions. This chapter will review tools a business manager can use to access and establish connections in Excel to data that exists in external sources such as text files, database systems, and the Internet.

## >> Excel | Skill Sets

**Opening Text Files**
- Delimited Text Files
- Fixed-Width Text Files

**Connecting to External Data Sources**
- Importing Data from an Access Database
- Importing Data from the Internet (Web Queries)
- Importing Text Files

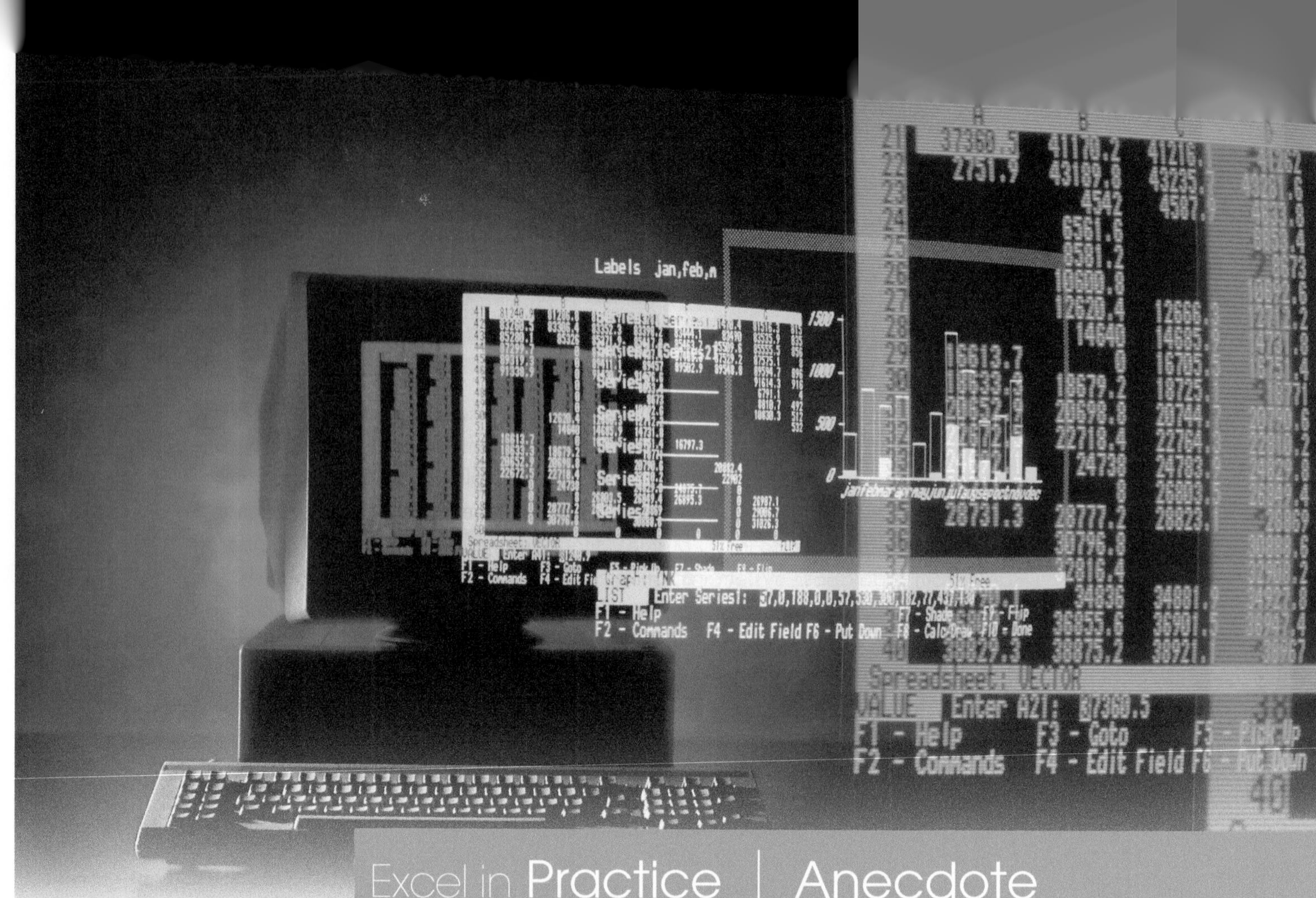

Getty Images, Inc.—Stone Allstock

## Excel in Practice | Anecdote

### My Role as an Information Systems Advisor

The cliché that information is power became very evident to me when I worked as an Information Systems Advisor in the retail industry. An Information Systems Advisor might not sound like a position directly involved in the day-to-day action of a business; however, this job provided me with opportunities to interact with executives who were making decisions at the highest level of a multi-billion-dollar corporation. My role was to help business managers access and analyze the data they needed to make critical business decisions every day. I studied and mastered the data the company stored in its massive database system and perfected my skills with tools such as Excel and Access, which helped me to quickly develop a reputation of being able to provide accurate data for almost every facet of the company's business. As a result, I received daily calls from employees across the company, ranging from assistant buyers to executive officers. One of my biggest challenges was not just supplying the data, but supplying it in a format the business manager could use easily. For example, one day I received a call from the Vice President of Merchandising. He wanted a way to compare the year-to-date sales, this year versus last year, for the company each week by division and category. This data was fairly easy to obtain with a simple database query. However, this person had never used database tools such as Access and rarely used Excel. I had my work cut out for me.

>> Continued later in this chapter

# Opening Text Files

Skill Set

Business managers often receive data in the form of a text file but need to use that data in an Excel worksheet. Text files are considered a universal format for data and can be opened in Excel as well as in many other software programs. File names that end in a .txt or .csv are examples of text files. For some text files, spaces, tabs, or symbols are used to separate data into columns. These are known as ***delimited text files.*** Text files containing data that is not separated into columns are known as ***fixed-width text files.*** This section will review how to open both delimited and fixed-width text files using Excel.

## Delimited Text Files

The ***comma-delimited*** file is one of the most common types of text files used by business managers and can be identified by the .csv extension that follows the file name. The term *comma delimited* means that the columns of data in a text file are delimited, or separated, by commas. Each comma in a .csv file signals the beginning of a new column of data. Excel will use the commas in a .csv text file to place data into columns on a worksheet. Figure 1 shows an example of a comma-delimited text file that will be opened using Excel. This will enable a business manager to add mathematical calculations and manipulate the data as necessary in an Excel worksheet. This file contains financial data for 15 public companies including stock symbols, current stock prices, and net income. A financial analyst would use this data to assess the financial performance of these firms or to construct an investment portfolio in Excel.

Figure 1 | **Comma-Delimited Text File**

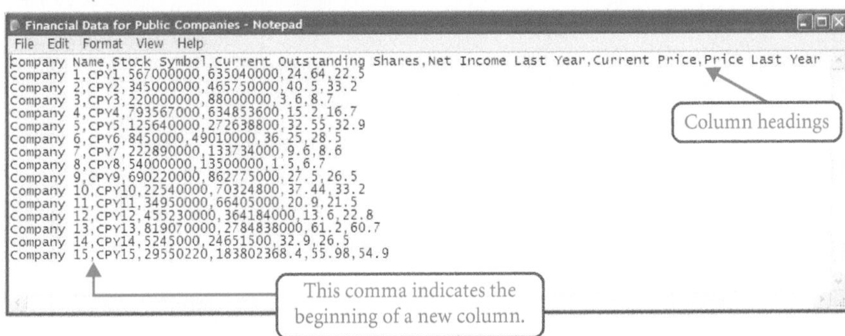


The following points explain how a business manager uses Excel to open the text file shown in Figure 1:

- Launch Excel and click the **Office Button.** Select the **Open** command.
- Set the file type at the bottom of the **Open** dialog box to Text Files (see Figure 2). You will not see any text files on your computer or network unless the file type in the **Open** dialog box is adjusted to either Text Files or All Files.
- Select a text file on your computer or network and click the **Open** button at the bottom of the **Open** dialog box. This will open the Text Import Wizard (see Figure 3).

Figure 2 | **Setting the File Type for Text Files**

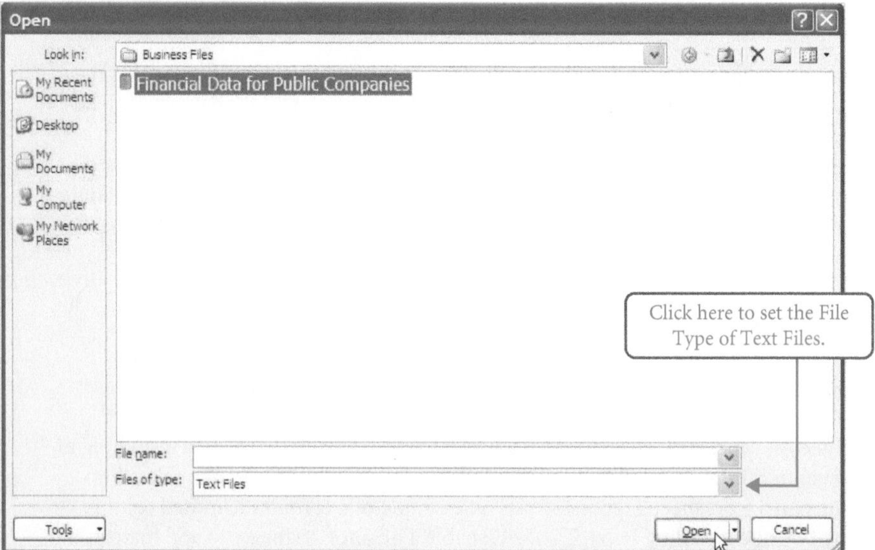


Figure 3 | **Step 1 of the Text Import Wizard**

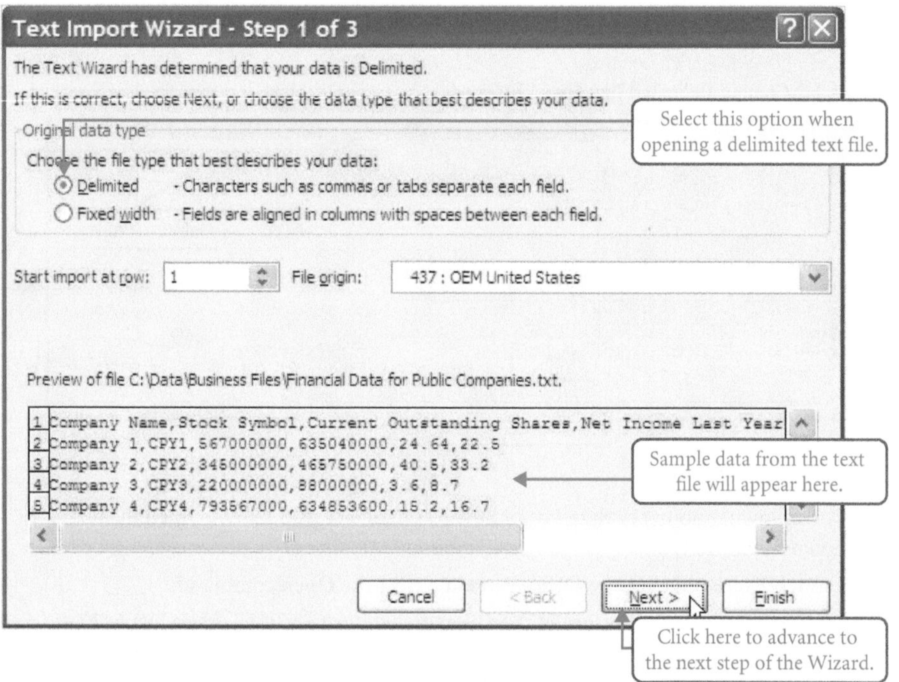


The following points explain the three steps of the Text Import Wizard, which appears when you open text files in Excel:

- Select the **Delimited** option in the first step of the Text Import Wizard when opening any type of delimited text file (see Figure 3). Excel will usually recognize a delimited text file and automatically select this option for you. You will see a sample of what is contained in the text file at the bottom of this step of the Text Import Wizard.
- Click the **Next** button to advance to step 2 of the Text Import Wizard.

- Click the box next to the **Tab delimiter** option to deselect it, and then click the box next to the **Comma delimited** option. This will tell Excel that commas are separating the data in the text file into columns. You should see the sample data from the text file separated into columns at the bottom of the Wizard screen. If you are opening a delimited text file, you will need to check the appropriate option so that Excel will know how the data is separated into columns. For example, if you were opening a Tab-delimited file, you would select the **Tab** option.
- Click the **Next** button to advance to step 3 of the Text Import Wizard. This step allows you to format each column of data before the file is opened in an Excel workbook. However, it might be easier to format this data once it is in Excel.
- Click the **Finish** button at the bottom of step 3 of the Wizard. This will open the text file in an Excel workbook.

Figures 4 and 5 show steps 2 and 3 of the Text Import Wizard. Once the **Finish** button is clicked in step 3 of the Wizard, the text file will appear in an Excel worksheet.

Figure 4 | **Step 2 of the Text Import Wizard**

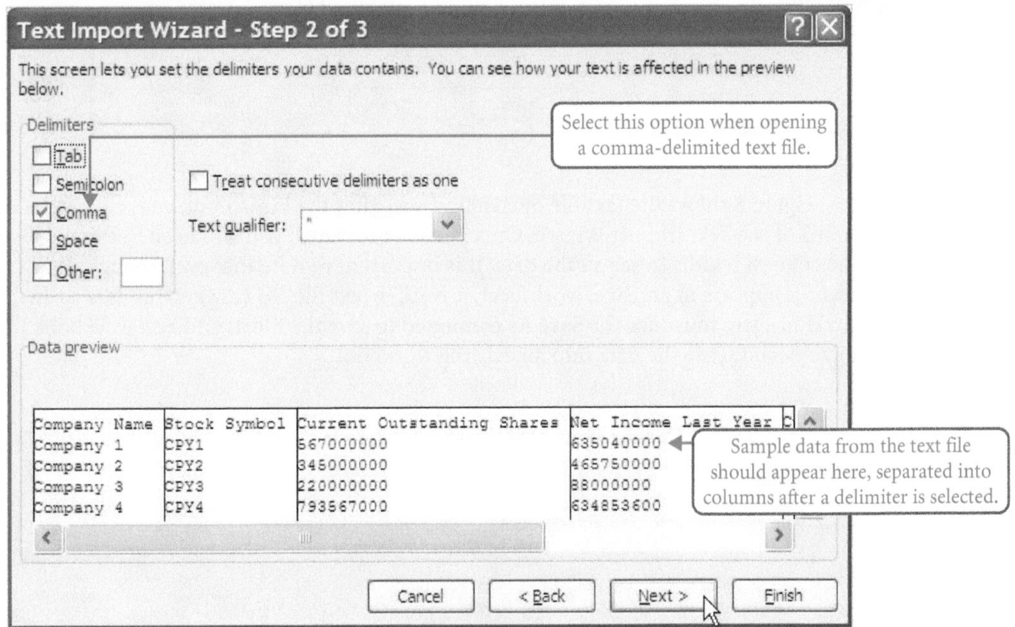

Figure 5 | **Step 3 of the Text Import Wizard**

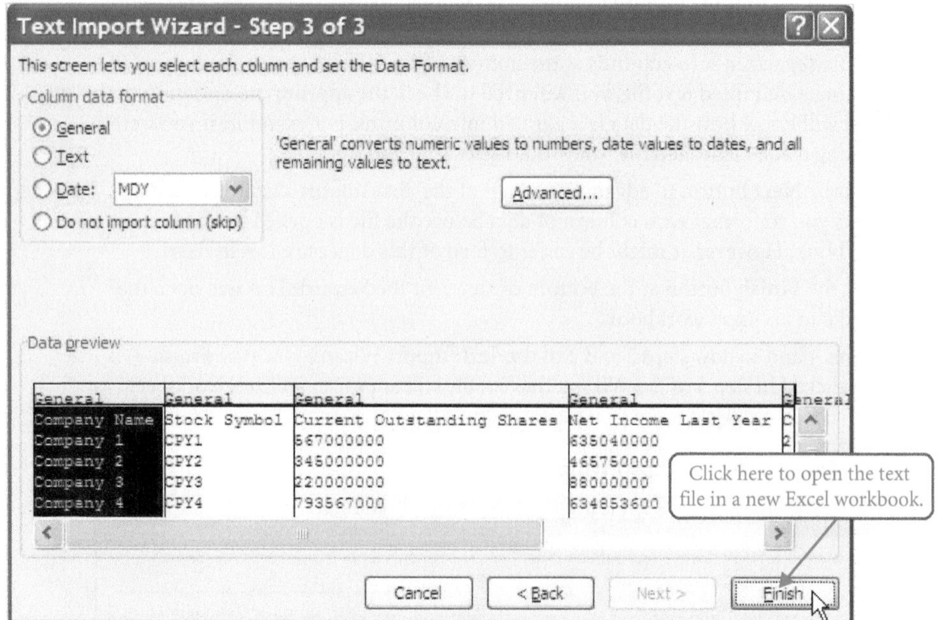


Figure 6 shows the text file opened in Excel after the **Finish** button is clicked in step 3 of the Text Import Wizard. Once the file is opened, you will need to expand the column widths to see all the data. It is important to note that even though the text file appears in an Excel worksheet, it is still a text file. To convert this data to an Excel file, you must use the **Save As** command to save the file as an Excel workbook or copy and paste the data into an existing workbook.

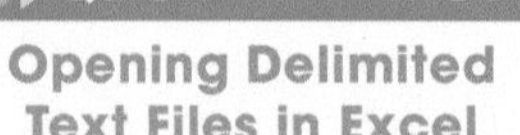

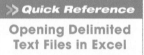

**>> Quick Reference**

**Opening Delimited Text Files in Excel**

1. Click the **Office Button** and select the **Open** option.
2. Set the file type on the **Open** dialog box to Text Files.
3. Select a text file on your computer or network and click the **Open** button.
4. Select the **Delimited** option in step 1 of the Text Import Wizard.
5. Select a delimiter option in step 2 of the Text Import Wizard (i.e., select Comma for comma-delimited files, Tab for tab-delimited files, etc.).
6. If needed, make any format adjustments in step 3 of the Text Import Wizard.
7. Click the **Finish** button in step 3 of the Text Import Wizard.

Figure 6 | **Text File Opened in an Excel Workbook**

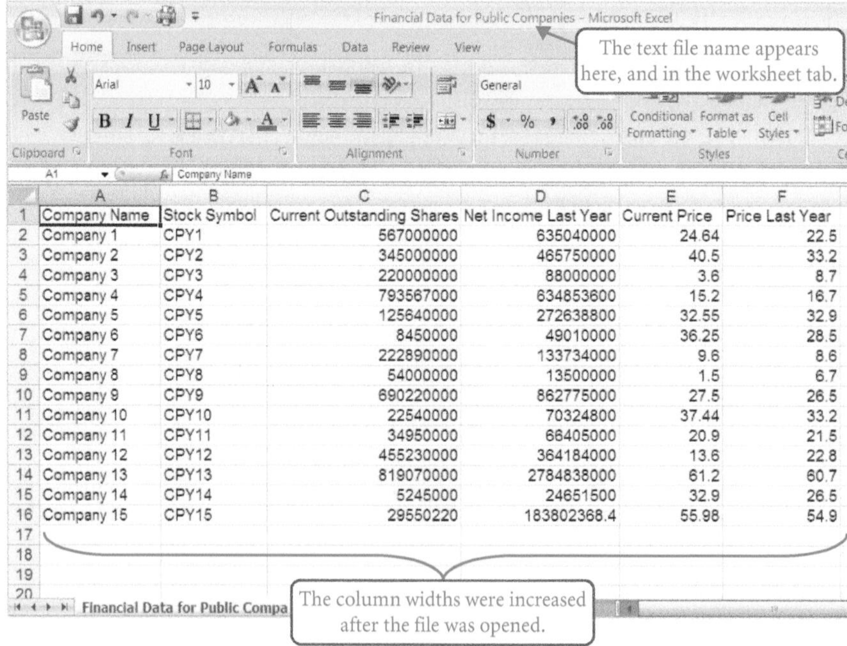

| Company Name | Stock Symbol | Current Outstanding Shares | Net Income Last Year | Current Price | Price Last Year |
|---|---|---|---|---|---|
| Company 1 | CPY1 | 567000000 | 635040000 | 24.64 | 22.5 |
| Company 2 | CPY2 | 345000000 | 465750000 | 40.5 | 33.2 |
| Company 3 | CPY3 | 220000000 | 88000000 | 3.6 | 8.7 |
| Company 4 | CPY4 | 793567000 | 634853600 | 15.2 | 16.7 |
| Company 5 | CPY5 | 125640000 | 272638800 | 32.55 | 32.9 |
| Company 6 | CPY6 | 8450000 | 49010000 | 36.25 | 28.5 |
| Company 7 | CPY7 | 222890000 | 133734000 | 9.6 | 8.6 |
| Company 8 | CPY8 | 54000000 | 13500000 | 1.5 | 6.7 |
| Company 9 | CPY9 | 690220000 | 862775000 | 27.5 | 26.5 |
| Company 10 | CPY10 | 22540000 | 70324800 | 37.44 | 33.2 |
| Company 11 | CPY11 | 34950000 | 66405000 | 20.9 | 21.5 |
| Company 12 | CPY12 | 455230000 | 364184000 | 13.6 | 22.8 |
| Company 13 | CPY13 | 819070000 | 2784838000 | 61.2 | 60.7 |
| Company 14 | CPY14 | 5245000 | 24651500 | 32.9 | 26.5 |
| Company 15 | CPY15 | 29550220 | 183802368.4 | 55.98 | 54.9 |

## COMMON MISTAKES | Saving Text Files as Excel Workbooks

People often make the mistake of thinking that after a text file is opened in Excel, it is now an Excel workbook. This is not true. Once a text file is opened in Excel, the data will be visible in a worksheet, but it is still a text file. In order to convert the text file to a workbook, you must use the **Save As** command and set the file type to Excel Workbook. You can also copy the data and paste it into an existing workbook.

# Fixed-Width Text Files

Another common format for text files is fixed width. Data that is contained in a fixed-width file is not separated into columns. Instead, the data appears as one long string of characters and a key is required to indicate where each column begins and ends. The key for a fixed-width text file will contain a column or field name, the starting and ending position for each column in characters, and the number of characters contained in each column. Figures 7 and 8 show the fixed-width text file and the key that will be used in this segment. The data shown in Figure 7 is identical to the data shown in Figure 1; however, there are no symbols indicating the beginning and end of each column. In addition, notice that there are no column heading descriptions in this file.

Figure 7 | **Fixed-Width Text File**

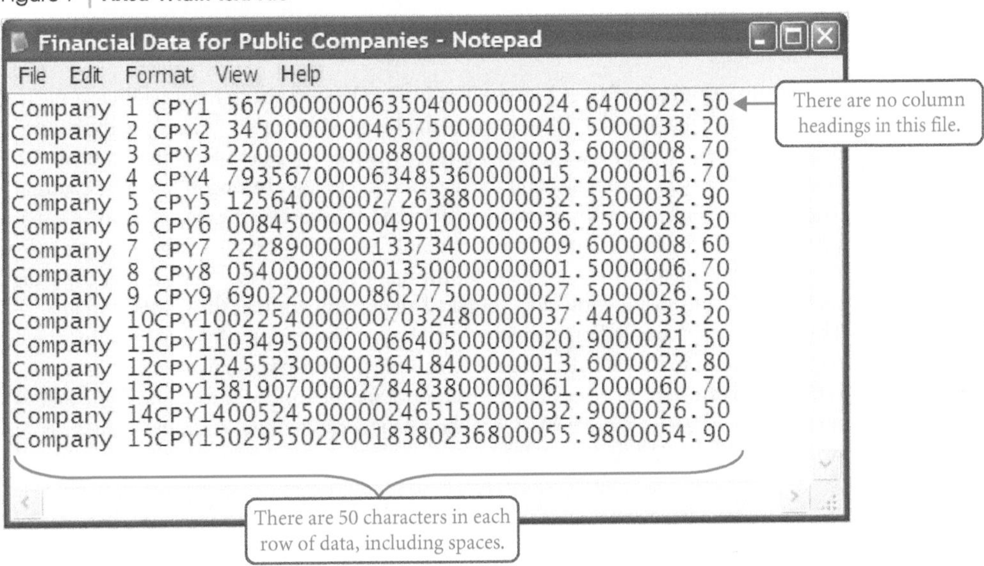


Figure 8 shows the key for the fixed-width text file shown in Figure 7. Each column in a fixed-width file is known as a field, and each character in the file is assigned a field position number. There are a total of 50 characters per row in this fixed-width file. The first column in this file is the Company Name field. Notice that the Field Positions for this column are characters 1 through10. This means that the Company Name column begins with the 1st character of each row and continues through the 10th character. Therefore, this column or field will always contain 10 characters. It is important to note that spaces are also counted as a character for each field.

Figure 8 | **Fixed Width Key**

| Financial Data for Public Companies Fixed Width Key | | |
|---|---|---|
| Field Name | Field Positions | Field Width |
| Company Name | 1 - 10 | 10 |
| Stock Symbol | 11 - 15 | 5 |
| Current Outstanding Shares | 16 - 24 | 9 |
| Net Income Last Year | 25 - 34 | 10 |
| Current Price | 35 - 42 | 8 |
| Price Last Year | 43 - 50 | 8 |

Values in both columns are expressed in number of characters.

The following explains how to open the fixed-width file shown in Figure 7 using Excel.

- Launch Excel and click the **Office Button**. Then, select the **Open** command.
- Set the file type at the bottom of the **Open** dialog box to Text Files (see Figure 2).
- Select a text file on your computer or network and click the **Open** button at the bottom of the **Open** dialog box. This will open the Text Import Wizard.
- Select the **Fixed width** option near the top of step 1 of the Text Import Wizard.
- Click the **Next** button at the bottom of the Text Import Wizard to advance to the next step.

Figure 9 shows the first step of the Text Import Wizard after a fixed-width text file is opened. Notice that the description next to the **Fixed width** option states that the columns or fields are separated by spaces. This is not always true. For example, in the Company Name field, the word Company and the number that follows belong in the same column. The space is added purely for formatting purposes. In addition, there appears to be a space between the Company Name and Stock Symbol field. This is because there is only a 1-digit number following the word Company for the first 9 rows. A space is added after the 1-digit numbers because ensuing rows will contain 2-digit numbers after the word Company. Therefore, the space will disappear after the 9th row. There are no spaces separating the remaining fields in this file. Because the remaining fields contain only numeric data, leading zeros are used as place holders to account for the variety of numeric digits that might be contained in these fields. Once the data is separated into columns in an Excel worksheet, the leading zeros will disappear.

Figure 9 | **Step 1 of the Text Import Wizard for a Fixed-Width Text File**

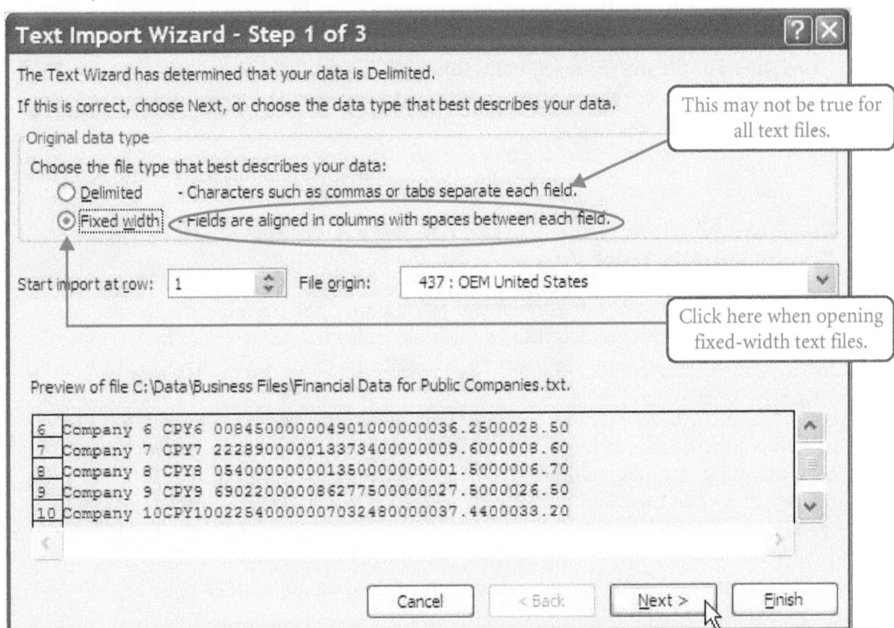


Step 2 of the Text Import Wizard is used to separate the data in fixed-width text files into columns. This is where you will need the key shown in Figure 8. The following explains how data is separated into columns using the information provided in the key.

- Remove the arrow pointing up toward the ruler in the lower left area of step 2 in the Text Import Wizard by double clicking it. The arrows, or **break lines**, are used in fixed-width files to mark the end of one column and the beginning of another (see Figure 10). Excel will automatically place ***break lines*** where there are spaces in the file. However, as previously mentioned, spaces that appear in a fixed-width file do not always indicate where columns should begin and end. In this case, the space is there simply for formatting purposes, so the arrow is removed.
- Click the number 10 on the ruler to add a break line. The numbers on the ruler show the number of characters in the file. Because the key shown in Figure 8 specifies that the Company Name field begins with the 1st character and ends after the 10th, and arrow should be placed after the 10th character by clicking the number 10 on the ruler.
- Click the number 15 on the ruler to mark the end of the Stock Symbol field and the beginning of the Current Outstanding Shares field. According to the key, the Stock Symbol field begins at the 11th character and continues through the 15th character.
- Click the number 24 on the ruler to mark the end of the Current Outstanding Shares field and the beginning of the Net Income Last Year field.
- Click the number 34 on the ruler to mark the end of the Net Income Last Year field and the beginning of the Current Price field.
- Click the number 42 on the ruler to mark the end of the Current Price field and the beginning of the Price Last Year.
- Click the **Next** button at the bottom of the Text Import Wizard. Because the Price Last Year field ends with character 50, which is the last character position on the file, there is no need to add a break line after this field (see Figure 11).
- Preview the data separated into columns near the bottom of step 3 of the Text Import Wizard (see Figure 12). If there is a need to change any of the break lines that were set in step 2 of the Wizard, you can click the Back button. There are

no data format settings that need to be set in this step, so the **Finish** button is clicked to complete the process. After you click the **Finish** button, the data from the fixed-width text file will appear in an Excel worksheet, separated into columns. As stated in the previous segment, this is still a text file. You will need to save this file as an Excel workbook if you wish to add any calculations or use any of Excel's formatting features.

## COMMON MISTAKES | Get a Key before Opening a Fixed-Width Text File

It is very important to obtain a character key before opening a fixed-width text file in Excel. Without a key, not only will you have to guess the point where break lines need to be added to separate the data into columns, but you will have to guess at the type of data the file contains. Because most fixed-width text files do not have column headings, there is no way to accurately define the data that is contained in each column. The fixed-width file key will provide a heading or description for each column of data as well as the beginning and ending characters for each column. A fixed-width file key should be obtained from the person or department that is responsible for creating the fixed-width file.

Figure 10 shows the initial appearance of step 2 of the Text Import Wizard. Notice that Excel places a break line after the first space in the file. This break line is removed by double clicking it.

Figure 10 | **Initial Appearance of Step 2 of the Text Import Wizard**

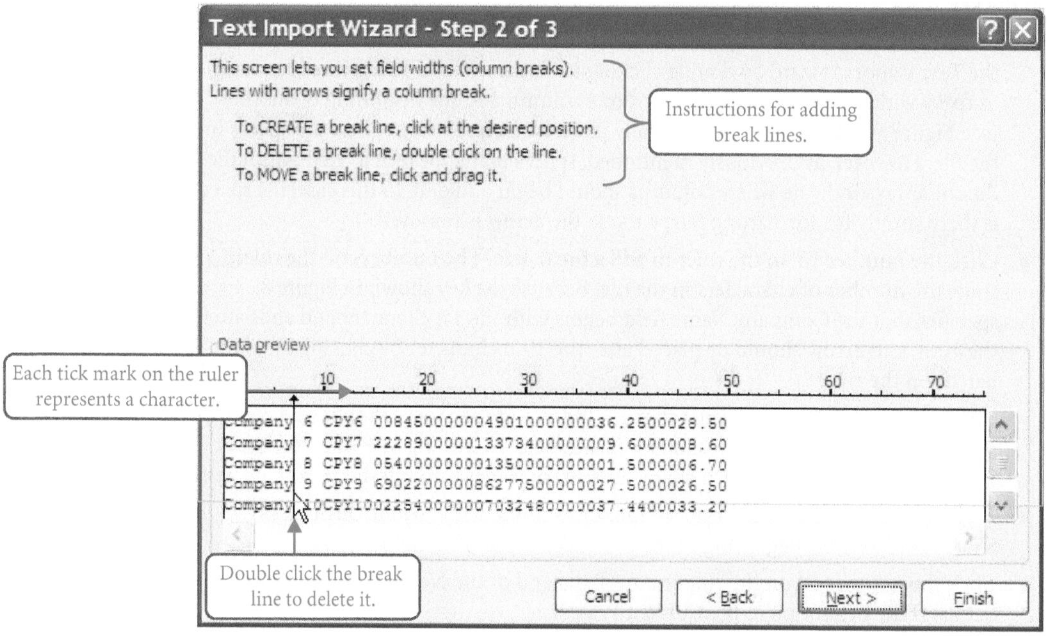

Figure 11 shows the final break lines that were added in step 2 of the Text Import Wizard. Each tick mark on the ruler represents one character in the file. Clicking on a tick mark or number will place the break line after the character. With the exception of the Price Last Year field, notice that the break lines fall on the second number of the character range listed in the Field Positions column in the key shown in Figure 8.

Figure 11 | **Break Line Positions in Step 2 of the Text Import Wizard**

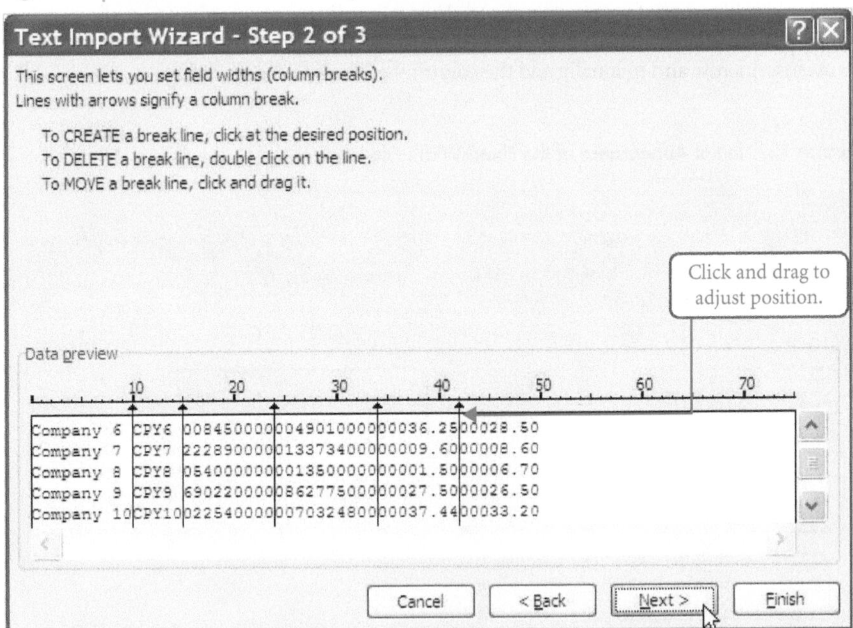


Figure 12 shows step 3 of the Text Import Wizard for the fixed-width text file. The columns that are created from the break lines in step 2 of the Text Import Wizard can be previewed in this step. Excel will convert all numeric values in a text file to numbers when the data is placed into a worksheet. This will remove any leading zeros that precede a value. However, if you do not want the values in a field converted to numeric values, select the field in this step of the Text Import Wizard and click the Text Column data format near the top left of the Wizard. This would be used when working with values such as zip codes.

Figure 12 | **Column Preview in Step 3 of the Text Import Wizard**

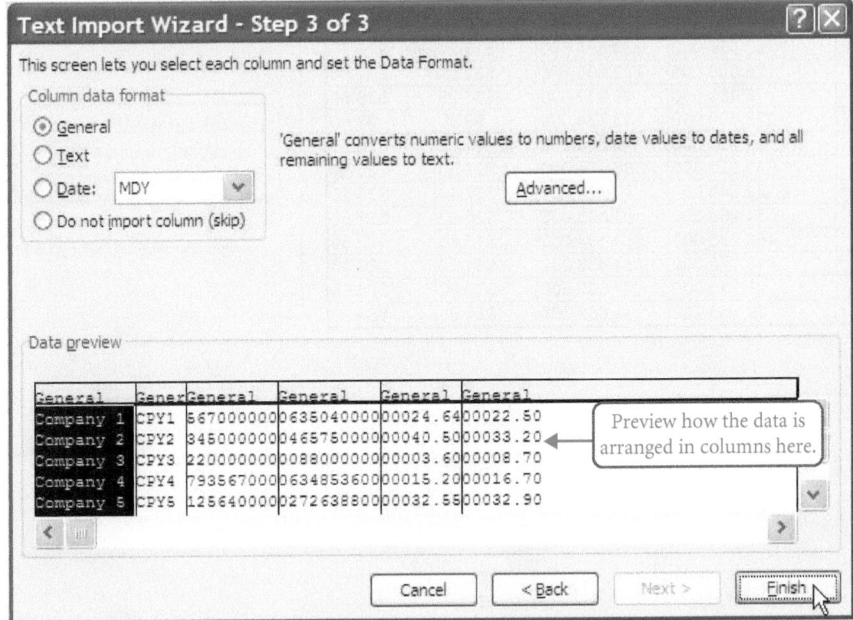


>> **Quick Reference**

**Opening Fixed-Width Files in Excel**

1. Obtain a key that identifies the character position for each column in a fixed-width file.
2. Click the **Office Button** and select the **Open** command.
3. Set the file type on the **Open** dialog box to Text Files.
4. Select a fixed-width text file on your computer or network and click the **Open** button.
5. Select the **Fixed width** option in step 1 of the Text Import Wizard.
6. Set break lines in step 2 of the Text Import Wizard by clicking on the character numbers on the ruler.
7. Preview the arrangement of data in columns and make any necessary format adjustments in step 3 of the Text Import Wizard.
8. Click the **Finish** button in step 3 of the Text Import Wizard.

Figure 13 shows the initial appearance of the Financial Data for Public Companies fixed-width file when it is opened in Excel. Notice that there are no column headings in the worksheet. Fixed-width files typically do not contain column headings. Therefore, you must insert a row and manually add the column headings to the worksheet.

Figure 13 | **Initial Appearance of the Fixed-Width File in Excel**

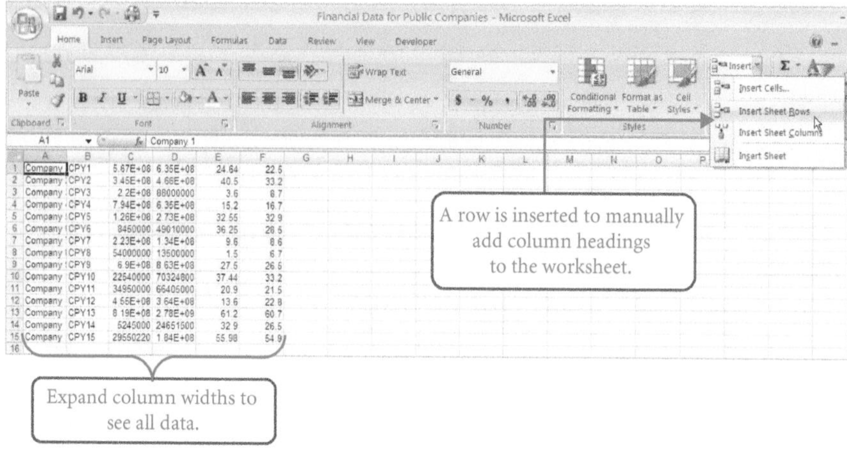
Financial Data for Public Companies - Microsoft Excel
A row is inserted to manually add column headings to the worksheet.
Expand column widths to see all data.

Figure 14 shows the final appearance of the Financial Data for Public Companies fixed-width file in Excel. This file was saved as an Excel Workbook and then formatting enhancements were added. Notice the column headings that were typed into the first row.

Figure 14 | **Final Appearance after the Fixed-Width File is Saved as an Excel Workbook**

K19

| | A | B | C | D | E | F |
|---|---|---|---|---|---|---|
| 1 | Company Name | Stock Symbol | Current Shares Outstanding | Net Income Last Year | Current Price | Price Last Year |
| 2 | Company 1 | CPY1 | 567,000,000 | 635,040,000 | $24.64 | $22.50 |
| 3 | Company 2 | CPY2 | 345,000,000 | 465,750,000 | $40.50 | $33.20 |
| 4 | Company 3 | CPY3 | 220,000,000 | 88,000,000 | $3.60 | $8.70 |
| 5 | Company 4 | CPY4 | 793,567,000 | 634,853,600 | $15.20 | $16.70 |
| 6 | Company 5 | CPY5 | 125,640,000 | 272,638,800 | $32.55 | $32.90 |
| 7 | Company 6 | CPY6 | 8,450,000 | 49,010,000 | $36.25 | $28.50 |
| 8 | Company 7 | CPY7 | 222,890,000 | 133,734,000 | $9.60 | $8.60 |
| 9 | Company 8 | CPY8 | 54,000,000 | 13,500,000 | $1.50 | $6.70 |
| 10 | Company 9 | CPY9 | 690,220,000 | 862,775,000 | $27.50 | $26.50 |
| 11 | Company 10 | CPY10 | 22,540,000 | 70,324,800 | $37.44 | $33.20 |
| 12 | Company 11 | CPY11 | 34,950,000 | 66,405,000 | $20.90 | $21.50 |
| 13 | Company 12 | CPY12 | 455,230,000 | 364,184,000 | $13.60 | $22.80 |
| 14 | Company 13 | CPY13 | 819,070,000 | 2,784,838,000 | $61.20 | $60.70 |
| 15 | Company 14 | CPY14 | 5,245,000 | 24,651,500 | $32.90 | $26.50 |
| 16 | Company 15 | CPY15 | 29,550,220 | 183,802,368 | $55.98 | $54.90 |
| 17 | | | | | | |

These column headings were typed into the worksheet after a row was inserted.

This file was saved as an Excel workbook to retain these formatting enhancements.

# >> Opening Text Files

**VIDEO WORKSHOP**

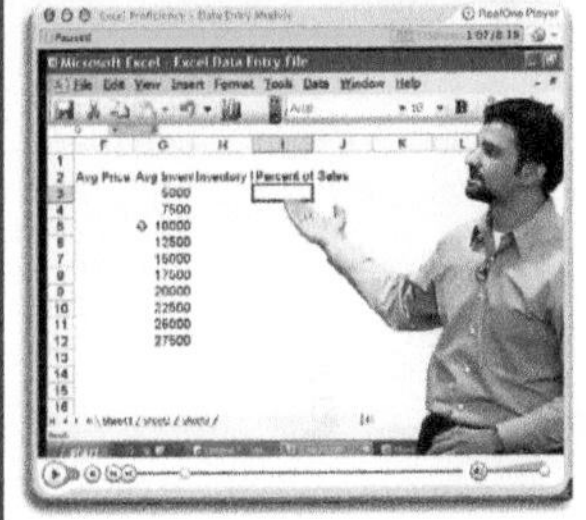

The purpose of this workshop is to demonstrate how text files are opened using Excel. I will be demonstrating the tasks in this workshop in the following two videos: **Opening Delimited Text Files** and **Opening Fixed-Width Files**. Complete the tasks in this workshop and then watch the related video.

1. **Delimited Text Files (Video: Opening Delimited Text Files)**
   a. Launch Excel and open the ib_e10_financialdatadelimited text file.
   b. Check that the **Delimited** option is selected in step 1 of the Text Import Wizard and click the **Next** button.
   c. Click the box next to the **Tab** option in step 2 of the Text Import Wizard to remove the check mark. Select the **Comma** option and click the **Next** button.
   d. Click the **Finish** button at the bottom of step 3 of the Text Import Wizard.
   e. Save the file as an Excel workbook on your computer or network.
   f. Bold the column headings and increase the row height of row 1 to 24 points.
   g. Increase the column widths so that all column headings and data are visible.
   h. Format the values in the Current Outstanding Shares and Net Income Last Year columns to a standard number with commas and 0 decimal places.
   i. Format the values in the Current Price and Price Last Year columns to Currency with 2 decimal places.
   j. Save and close your file.

2. **Fixed-Width Text Files (Video: Opening Fixed-Width Text Files)**
   a. Open the Excel file named ib_e10_fixedwidthkey.
   b. Open the ib_e10_financialdatafixedwidth text file.
   c. Select the **Fixed width** option in step 1 of the Text Import Wizard and click the **Next** button.
   d. Remove the break line that appears in step 2 of the Text Import Wizard by double-clicking it.
   e. Use the ib_e10_fixedwidthkey Excel file to determine the placement of break lines for each field in step 2 of the Text Import Wizard. Click the **Next** button after setting the break lines.
   f. Click the **Finish** button in step 3 of the Text Import Wizard.
   g. Save the file as an Excel workbook on your computer or network.
   h. Insert a row above row 1.
   i. Type the column headings listed in the Field Name column of the ib_e10_fixedwidthkey file in row 1 of the appropriate columns.
   j. Bold the column headings and increase the row height of row 1 to 24 points.
   k. Increase the column widths so that all column headings and data are visible.
   l. Format the values in the Current Outstanding Shares and Net Income Last Year columns to a standard number with commas and 0 decimal places.
   m. Format the values in the Current Price and Price Last Year columns to Currency with 2 decimal places.
   n. Save and close your file.

**EXERCISE**

**Why Do I Need This?**

# >> Evaluating Vendor-Managed Inventory

As demonstrated throughout this text, business managers frequently use Excel to analyze data in order to make informed decisions for their business. However, data is not always available in an Excel file. In fact, if a business manager needs to use data that is produced from an external company, the data will likely be in the form of a text file. This is because text files are created in a universal format that can be produced and used by the information systems maintained in most firms. Sharing data between companies is a common practice in industries in which firms are trying to increase the speed, accuracy, and efficiency of their supply chain. For example, a supplier might take responsibility for controlling the flow of inventory into a retailer's warehouse. However, in order to do this the supplier will need to analyze the retailer's sales by item and the current inventory status by item on a weekly or daily basis. One of the tools that the retailer can use to produce and distribute this information to the supplier is text files.

## Exercise

The purpose of this exercise is to use a delimited text file to evaluate the sales and inventory status of a hypothetical retailer. The goal of this project is to determine how many units per item must be shipped to the retailer in order to maintain a minimum of 4 weeks of supply for every item.

1. Open the comma-delimited text file named ib_e10_retailerdata in Excel. Then, save this file as an Excel workbook.
2. Bold the column headings in row 1 and set the alignment to wrap text. Then, increase the column widths so that partial words for the column headings are not wrapped to two lines.
3. Add a column heading to cell E1 named **`Weeks of Supply`**. This column will contain the current weeks of supply based on the sales units last week.
4. Calculate the weeks of supply values in column E using a formula that divides the Unit Sales Last Week into the Current Warehouse Inventory Units. Format these results to a standard number with one decimal place.
5. Add a column heading to cell F1 named **`Ship Unit Quantity`**. This column will contain the number of units that need to be shipped to the retailer.
6. Use an **IF** function to determine how many units need to be shipped to the retailer for each item. You must maintain a target of 4 weeks of supply for each item. If the inventory for any item is less than 4 weeks of supply, calculate the total units that must be shipped to the retailer. For example, if an item has 58 units in the warehouse and the unit sales last week were 29, the current weeks of supply is 2. Therefore, you need to ship 58 units to bring the total inventory in the warehouse up to 4 weeks of supply.
7. On a separate worksheet, show the items that need to be shipped to the retailer. Show only those items for which the ship quantity is greater than 10. How many items need to be shipped to the retailer? What is the total unit quantity that needs to be shipped to the retailer?
8. Save and close your file.

## >> What's Wrong with This Spreadsheet?

PROBLEM & EXERCISE

### Problem

You are working as a Senior Team Leader for a large consulting firm. Your team has just been assigned to a corporation that owns and operates a large chain of retail stores that sells children's products. The team's first objective is to assemble a 3-year sales-and-profit trend report for each of the merchandise categories sold by the company. Your team will have 1 week to complete the project and present the findings to the CEO of the company. You assign one of the analysts on your team to find the data that will be needed to complete this phase of the project. By the end of the day, the analyst sends you an e-mail explaining that she was able to find all of the data that the team will need. She explains the following in her e-mail:

- I worked with one the managers in the merchandise department who gave me a fixed-width text file that contains 3 years of data by month. He said that someone in the IT department sent him this file several months ago, but he was never able to use it.

- I opened the file in Excel and was able to figure out how to break down the data into columns on a worksheet. It was pretty easy to see where columns such as the year, month, and category began and ended. With regard to the numbers, the file contained leading zeros that made it easy to see where each column began.

- There were no column headings in the file, but I did a few math calculations and was able to back into the Cost, Retail, and Units Sold columns on the worksheet. This should give us everything we need to get a head start on the project so we can meet our deadline for the presentation to the CEO.

### Exercise

The analyst on your team attached an Excel workbook and a fixed-width text file to the e-mail she sent to you. The Excel workbook attached to the e-mail is named ib_e10_dataforhistoryanalysis. The text file attached to the e-mail is named ib_e10_fpsalesyearmonth. Would you be comfortable using the data contained in the Excel workbook for your presentation to the CEO? Consider the following points:

1. The analyst explained that the first three columns in the text file contained the year, month, and merchandise categories. Does this appear to be the case after you have reviewed the data in the Excel workbook?
2. Look at the values in the Total Cost, Total Sales, and Profit columns. Do these values make sense given the values in the Cost, Retail, and Units Sold columns?
3. Open the fixed-width text file in Excel and examine the data in step 2 of the Text Import Wizard. Does it appear that the analyst accurately separated the data into columns?

What's wrong with this spreadsheet? Write a short answer for each of the points listed above and explain why you would or would not be comfortable using the data in the Excel workbook for your presentation to the CEO.

Skill Set

# Connecting to External Data Sources

The previous segment explained how text files can be opened in Excel. However, once the text file is opened and saved as an Excel workbook, the data is static and will not change. If a business manager needs to update the data contained in a text file on a frequent basis, a new text file must be opened in Excel and converted to a workbook. As a result, a business manager might want to create a connection to an external data source, such as text files, so that any updates that are made in the external source can be automatically updated in an Excel workbook. This section will review how these connections are established for three common external data sources: Access databases, the Internet, and text files.

## Importing Data from an Access Database

This segment will demonstrate how you can connect to, and import data from, a query or table contained in a Microsoft Access database. Once you establish a connection to a table or query in an Access database, you can ***refresh*** your Excel workbook to show any changes that occur in that table or query. This allows you to use Excel features with data that can automatically be accessed and updated. For example, in the chapter "Managing Large Volumes of Data," the List Box was used to select a specific store to show a sales comparison by month between the current and previous years. The limitation of this design is that the data will always be static and can be used only to produce a historical analysis. However, a business manager in this industry would most likely monitor sales on at least a weekly or daily basis. This segment will demonstrate how data can be supplied in a similar analysis by creating a connection to an Access database. It is important to note that this segment will mention features and objects related to Microsoft Access. It would be beneficial if you have a basic understanding of Access tables and queries before proceeding.

Figure 15 shows a worksheet that could be used by a retail business executive to evaluate the sales performance for every store by district on a weekly basis. The List Box is displaying the district names for this business that were added to the District List worksheet. Cells F2 and G2 contain **VLOOKUP** functions that use the Cell Link value in cell A2 to look up and display the district name and district number from the District List worksheet. The data for columns C through F will be imported from an Access database and placed into the Sales Data worksheet. The goal for this example is to show sales results last week and last week last year for all of the stores in the district selected in the List Box.

Figure 15 | **Blank-Sales-Results Worksheet**

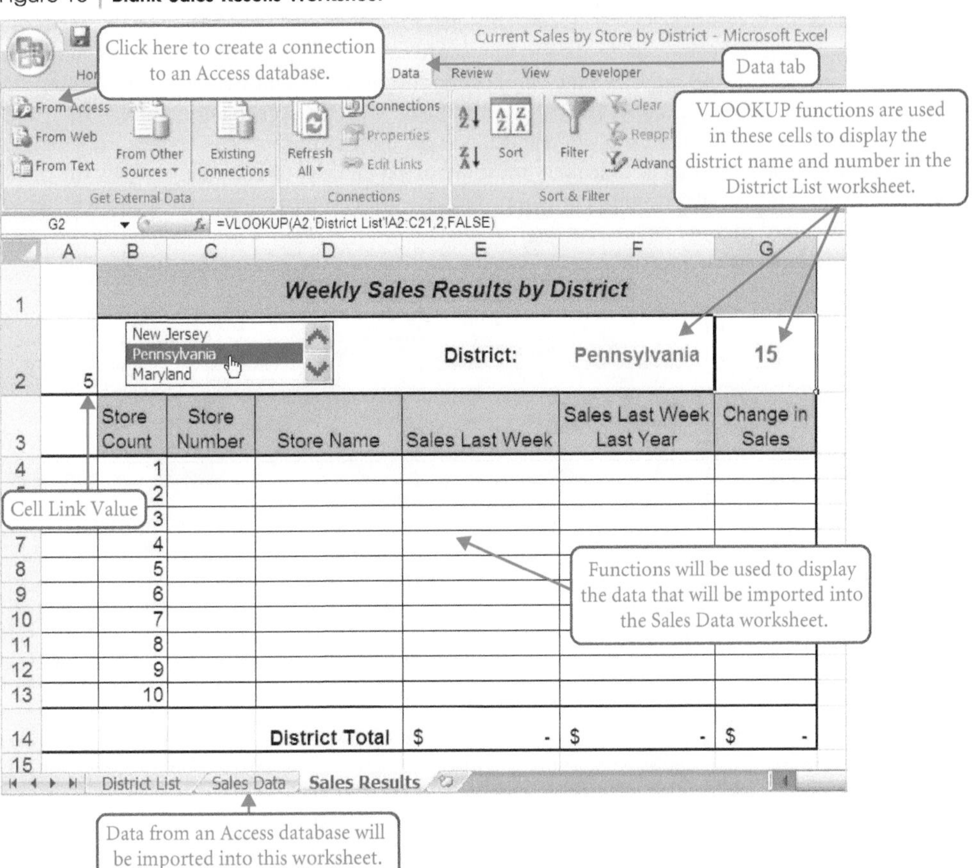


Figure 16 shows the first several rows of the District List worksheet. The input range for the List Box shown in Figure 15 is the range C2:C21 on this worksheet. This example assumes that the districts established for this retail company will not change. However, this list could also be created by importing data from an Access database. This would be the preferred method if the company was expanding its store base and adding more districts.

Figure 16 | **District List Worksheet**

The List Box in the Sales Results worksheet is displaying the districts in this column.

| | A | B | C |
|---|---|---|---|
| 1 | Sequence | District Number | District Name |
| 2 | 1 | 11 | Massachusetts |
| 3 | 2 | 12 | Connecticut |
| 4 | 3 | 13 | New York |
| 5 | 4 | 14 | New Jersey |
| 6 | 5 | 15 | Pennsylvania |
| 7 | 6 | 21 | Maryland |
| 8 | 7 | 22 | Virginia |
| 9 | 8 | 23 | Georgia |
| 10 | 9 | 24 | Florida |
| 11 | 10 | 25 | Tennessee |
| 12 | 11 | 31 | Illinois |

Figure 17 shows the query in the Access database that will be used to provide the data for the Sales Data worksheet. This query was designed specifically for the needs of this project. Each week the data in the record set of this query will change to reflect the most recent week of sales data. Once the connection is established between this query and the Excel workbook, any change in the query record set can automatically be updated in the Sales Data worksheet. Look carefully at the Sort row in the query design grid. The record set of this query must be sorted in order to accurately display the values in the Sales Results worksheet. This is a critical step in this project and will be discussed in more detail later.

Figure 17 | **Weekly Sales Results Query in the Access Database**

Database file name

The record set of this query must be sorted in order to produce accurate results for this project.

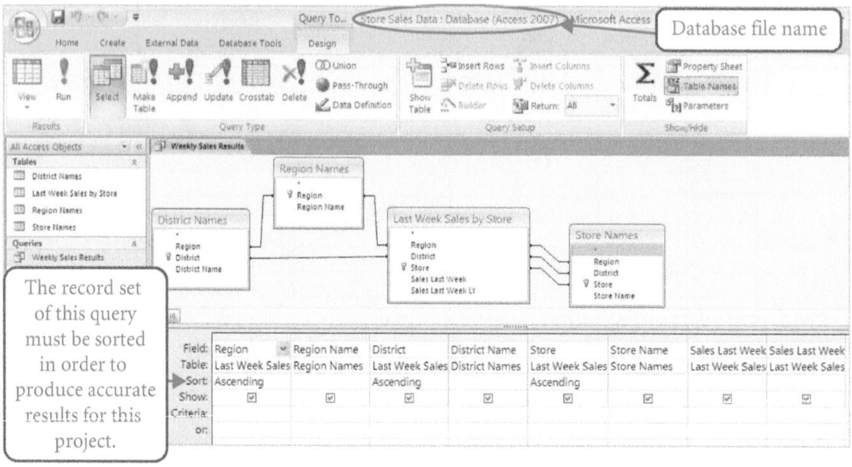

The following points explain how a connection is established between the Excel workbook shown in 15 and the Access query shown in Figure 17.

- Activate cell B1 in the Sales Data worksheet. The data will be imported into the Sales Data worksheet beginning with column B. Column A will contain a **CONCATENATE** function that will provide a way to look up the stores that exist for any district selected in the List Box shown in Figure 15.
- Click the **From Access** icon in the **Data** tab of the Ribbon (see Figure 15). This will open the **Select Data Source** dialog box.
- Select an Access database on your computer or network using the **Select Data Source** dialog box. For this example, the Store Sales Data database shown in Figure 17 will be selected. Click the **Open** button at the bottom of the **Select Data Source** dialog box after selecting an Access database. This will open the **Select Table** dialog box.
- Select the Weekly Sales Results query in the **Select Table** dialog box and click the **OK** button. The symbol to the left of the Access object indicates whether the object is a table or query (see Figure 18). After clicking the **OK** button, the **Import Data** dialog box will open.
- The selection at the top of the **Import Data** dialog box should be set to **Table.** The cell location in the **Existing worksheet** input box should be cell B1, which was activated before clicking the **From Access** icon (see Figure 19). Click the **OK** button at the bottom of the dialog box. This will import that record set of the Weekly Sales Results query into the Sales Data worksheet in the form of a table.

- Click the **Properties** icon in the **Design** tab of the Ribbon (the **Design** tab will be visible only if one of the cells in the table is activated). This will open the **External Data Properties** dialog box. Select the **Overwrite existing cells with new data, clear unused cells** option near the bottom of the dialog box and click the **OK** button (see Figure 20). This is a critical adjustment if you need to add formulas to the adjacent columns of the imported data. If this setting is not made, Excel will insert and delete cells in the worksheet when the data is refreshed, which can corrupt any formulas that are created in adjacent columns.

Figure 18 shows the **Select Table** dialog box. This will show a list of any tables and queries that are contained in the Access database that is selected in the **Select Data Source** dialog box. The symbol to the left of the object indicates the object type.

Figure 18 | **Select Table Dialog Box**

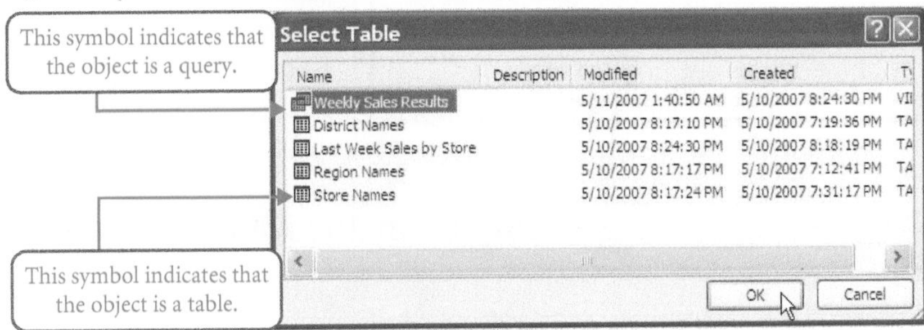


Figure 19 shows the **Import Data** dialog box. Notice that there are options for importing data into a PivotTable or PivotChart. If you want the data to appear in a worksheet, use the **Table** option.

Figure 19 | **Import Data Dialog Box**

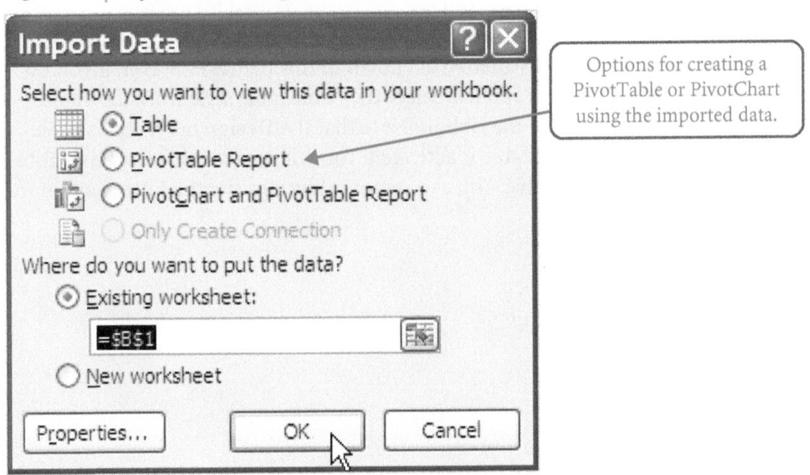


Figure 20 shows the **External Data Properties** dialog box. The **Overwrite existing cells with new data, clear unused cells** option is selected for this example because formulas will be added in two columns that are adjacent to the imported data. If this option is not selected, the formulas can be corrupted when the data is refreshed.

Figure 20 | **External Data Properties Dialog Box**

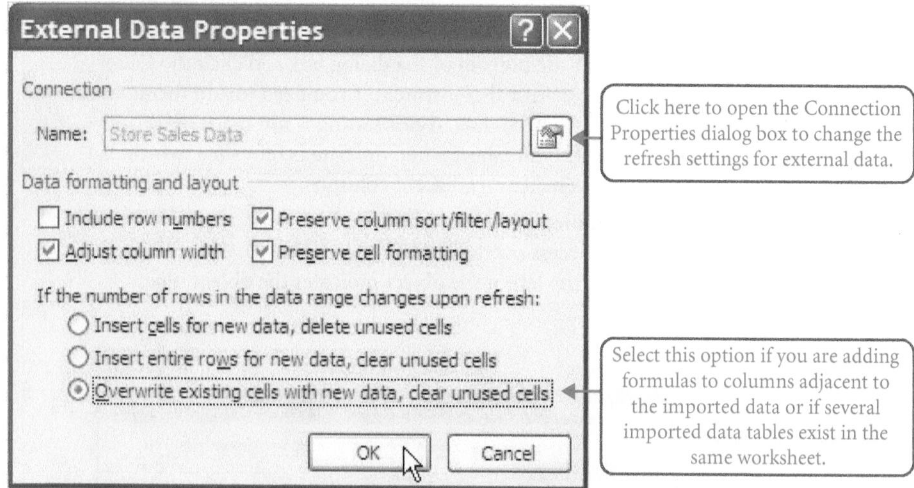


## COMMON MISTAKES | Using Formulas with Imported Data

If you intend to use formulas in columns adjacent to a table containing imported data, you must select the **Overwrite existing cells with new data, clear unused cells** option in the **External Data Properties** dialog box. To open this dialog box, click any cell on the table that contains imported data and then click the **Properties** icon in the **Design** tab of the Ribbon.

Figure 21 shows the table that is created in the Sales Data worksheet after the data is imported from the Access database. You can make any desired formatting adjustments to this table and delete any columns that are not required for your project. The table may automatically be formatted as shown in this figure. However, if you do not want any formatting features applied, select the **None** table style from the Table Styles group in the **Design** tab of the ribbon. Note that the **Design** tab will be visible only when one of the cells in the table is activated. You will also see that the **Filter** tool is automatically applied to the table. You can remove it by clicking the **Filter** icon in the **Data** tab of the Ribbon.

Figure 21 | **Imported Data Table**

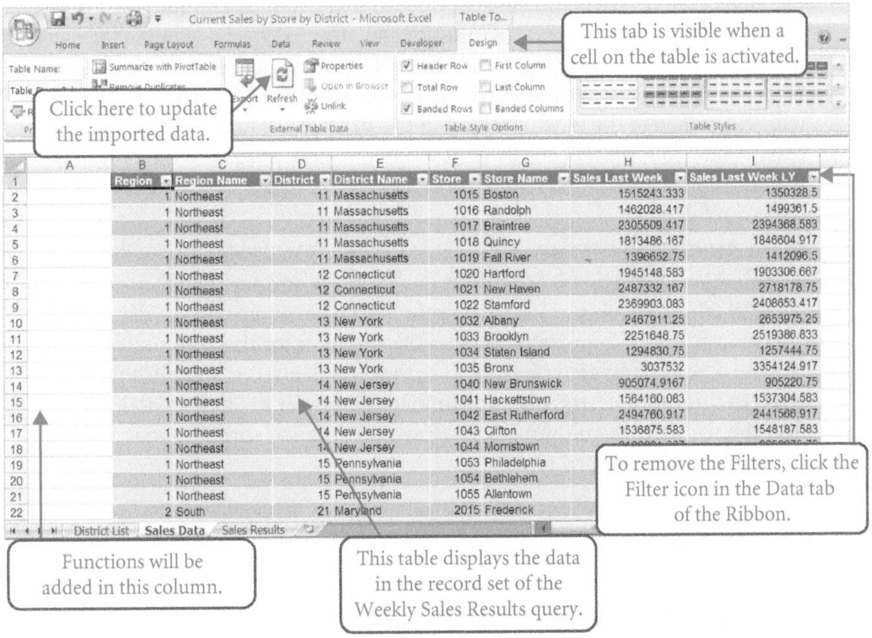

This tab is visible when a cell on the table is activated.

Click here to update the imported data.

| | A | B | C | D | E | F | G | H | I |
|---|---|---|---|---|---|---|---|---|---|
| 1 | | Region | Region Name | District | District Name | Store | Store Name | Sales Last Week | Sales Last Week LY |
| 2 | | 1 | Northeast | 11 | Massachusetts | 1015 | Boston | 1515243.333 | 1350328.5 |
| 3 | | 1 | Northeast | 11 | Massachusetts | 1016 | Randolph | 1462028.417 | 1499361.5 |
| 4 | | 1 | Northeast | 11 | Massachusetts | 1017 | Braintree | 2305509.417 | 2394368.583 |
| 5 | | 1 | Northeast | 11 | Massachusetts | 1018 | Quincy | 1813486.167 | 1846604.917 |
| 6 | | 1 | Northeast | 11 | Massachusetts | 1019 | Fall River | 1396652.75 | 1412096.5 |
| 7 | | 1 | Northeast | 12 | Connecticut | 1020 | Hartford | 1945148.583 | 1903306.667 |
| 8 | | 1 | Northeast | 12 | Connecticut | 1021 | New Haven | 2487332.167 | 2718178.75 |
| 9 | | 1 | Northeast | 12 | Connecticut | 1022 | Stamford | 2369903.083 | 2408653.417 |
| 10 | | 1 | Northeast | 13 | New York | 1032 | Albany | 2467911.25 | 2653975.25 |
| 11 | | 1 | Northeast | 13 | New York | 1033 | Brooklyn | 2251648.75 | 2519386.833 |
| 12 | | 1 | Northeast | 13 | New York | 1034 | Staten Island | 1294830.75 | 1257444.75 |
| 13 | | 1 | Northeast | 13 | New York | 1035 | Bronx | 3037532 | 3354124.917 |
| 14 | | 1 | Northeast | 14 | New Jersey | 1040 | New Brunswick | 905074.9167 | 905220.75 |
| 15 | | 1 | Northeast | 14 | New Jersey | 1041 | Hackettstown | 1564160.083 | 1537304.583 |
| 16 | | 1 | Northeast | 14 | New Jersey | 1042 | East Rutherford | 2494760.917 | 2441566.917 |
| 17 | | 1 | Northeast | 14 | New Jersey | 1043 | Clifton | 1536875.583 | 1548187.583 |
| 18 | | 1 | Northeast | 14 | New Jersey | 1044 | Morristown | | |
| 19 | | 1 | Northeast | 15 | Pennsylvania | 1053 | Philadelphia | | |
| 20 | | 1 | Northeast | 15 | Pennsylvania | 1054 | Bethlehem | | |
| 21 | | 1 | Northeast | 15 | Pennsylvania | 1055 | Allentown | | |
| 22 | | 2 | South | 21 | Maryland | 2015 | Frederick | | |

District List | Sales Data | Sales Results

To remove the Filters, click the Filter icon in the Data tab of the Ribbon.

Functions will be added in this column.

This table displays the data in the record set of the Weekly Sales Results query.

There are two columns of functions that must be added to the Sales Data worksheet in order to complete the objective for this segment. The purpose of these functions is to create a unique value for every row of data in the Sales Data worksheet so that the data for each store is accurately displayed in the Sales Results worksheet. The following points explain how this is accomplished.

- Type the column heading Unique District/Store in cell J1 of the Sales Data worksheet. Then, click the **Auto Correct Options** icon that appears to the right of the column heading and select the **Undo Table AutoExpansion** option. When a column heading is added to an adjacent column to the right of the table, it will automatically become part of the table. However, this column must not be added to the table for this type of project design. After adding the column heading, type the number 1 in cell J2.
- Type the following **IF** function into cell J3: =IF(D3=D2,J2+1,1). Then, copy the function and paste it into the range J4: J500. It was mentioned earlier in this segment that it is critical for the data imported from the Weekly Sales Results query to be sorted based on the Region, District, and Store column. The reason is that you need a way of identifying which stores belong to each district. The **IF** function that is created in cell J3 is evaluating whether the district number in cell D3 is equal to the district number in cell D2. If so, then the **IF** function will create a sequence by incrementing the value in cell J2, which is the number 1, by 1. Once the **IF** function is copied and pasted, each district will have a numbered sequence that can be matched to the Store Count column (column B) in the Sales Results worksheet (see Figure 15). Also, notice that the function is pasted well beyond the last row of the table, which ends at row 81. This is to account for the possibility that the company adds more stores, which would add additional rows to the table. This technique is known as adding capacity to the project design.
- Type the column heading Unique District Sequence in cell A1 of the Sales Data worksheet. This column will not become part of the table because it is to the left of the table.

- Type the following function into cell A2: =IF(ISBLANK(B2)=TRUE,"", CONCATENATE(D2,J2)). Then, copy the function and paste it into the range A2:A500. This function creates a unique value next to every row in the table if there is a value in the first column. If the cell in the first column of the table is blank, the function will leave the cell in column A blank. The values in column A will be matched to the look up values in the **VLOOKUP** functions that will be entered into column C of the Sales Results worksheet. Similar to the **IF** function, this function is also pasted well beyond the last row of the table to add capacity to the project design.

Figure 22 shows the first several rows of the completed Sales Data worksheet. The combination of the district numbers in column D and the sequence produced by the **IF** functions in column J create a unique value for every row of data in the table in column A. It is important to stress that in order for this technique to work, the data must be sorted based on the values that will be used to establish the sequence. In this example, the district numbers were used in the **IF** function to establish the sequence in column J. Therefore, the data was sorted so that all the district numbers are grouped together.

Figure 22 | **Final Setup of the Sales Data Worksheet**

A2 =CONCATENATE(D2,J2)

| | A | B | C | D | E | F | G | H | I | J |
|---|---|---|---|---|---|---|---|---|---|---|
| 1 | Unique District Sequence | Region | Region Name | District | District Name | Store | Store Name | Sales Last Week | Sales Last Week LY | Unique District/Store |
| 2 | 111 | 1 | Northeast | 11 | Massachusetts | 1015 | Boston | 1515243.333 | 1350328.5 | 1 |
| 3 | 112 | 1 | Northeast | 11 | Massachusetts | 1016 | Randolph | 1462028.417 | 1499361.5 | 2 |
| 4 | 113 | 1 | Northeast | 11 | Massachusetts | 1017 | Braintree | 2305509.417 | 2394368.583 | 3 |
| 5 | 114 | 1 | Northeast | 11 | Massachusetts | 1018 | Quincy | 1813486.167 | 1846604.917 | 4 |
| 6 | 115 | 1 | Northeast | 11 | Massachusetts | 1019 | Fall River | 1396652.75 | 1412096.5 | 5 |
| 7 | 121 | 1 | Northeast | 12 | Connecticut | 1020 | Hartford | 1945148.583 | 1903306.667 | 1 |
| 8 | 122 | 1 | Northeast | 12 | Connecticut | 1021 | New Haven | 2487332.167 | 2718178.75 | 2 |
| | | | | 12 | Connecticut | 1022 | Stamford | 2369903.083 | 2408653.417 | 3 |
| | | | | 13 | New York | 1032 | Albany | 2467911.25 | 2653975.25 | 1 |

The CONCATENATE function produces a unique value for every row.

The districts are sorted in ascending order.

The IF function resets the sequence to 1 here because the district number changed from 11 to 12.

## COMMON MISTAKES | Refreshing Data Imported from an Access Database

You will not see any changes to data that is imported from an Access database unless you click the **Refresh** icon in the **Design** tab of the Ribbon. People often make the mistake of assuming that data imported from an external data source will automatically be updated when an Excel workbook is opened. However, this will not happen unless you make the appropriate settings in the **Connection Properties** dialog box. This is opened by clicking the Properties icon in the **Design** tab of the Ribbon, and then clicking the **Connection Properties** button in the upper right area of the **External Data Properties** dialog box (see Figure 20). Remember that a cell in the imported external data table must be activated in order to see the Design tab of the Ribbon. Figure 23 shows the **Connection Properties** dialog box. To refresh the data from an external data source when opening a workbook, select the **Refresh data when opening the file** option. Notice that you can also select the **Refresh every** option and adjust the minutes to continuously refresh external data while the workbook is open.

Figure 23 | **Connection Properties Dialog Box**

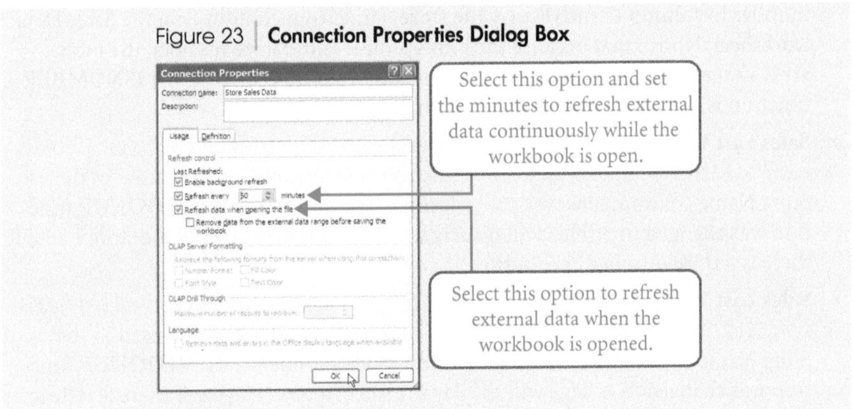
Connection Properties
Select this option and set the minutes to refresh external data continuously while the workbook is open.
Select this option to refresh external data when the workbook is opened.

To complete the business objective for this segment, functions are added to columns C, D, E, F, and G in the Sales Results worksheet (see Figure 15). These functions include the **IF** and **VLOOKUP**, and the **ISERRROR**, **ISNUMBER**, and **CONCATENATE**. The following specifies the details of each function by column.

**Store Number (Column C):** =IF(ISERROR((VLOOKUP(CONCATENATE ($G$2,B4),'SALES DATA'!$A$2:$J$500,6,FALSE))=TRUE,"",VLOOKUP(CONCATENATE ($G$2,B4),'SALES DATA'!$A$2:$J$500,6,FALSE)) This **IF** function uses the **ISERROR** function to determine if the **VLOOKUP** function produces an error. If the **VLOOKUP** function produces an error, the cell will be left blank. This is necessary because not all districts have the same number of stores. This example assumes that the maximum number of stores a district can have is 10. This is why the Store Count column—column B in the Sales Results worksheet—is numbered 1 through 10. However, the number of stores per district is not consistent. For example, the Pennsylvania district has only 3 stores whereas the New Jersey district has 5. If you just used the **VLOOKUP** function by itself, the New Jersey district would show the #N/A error for store counts 6 through 10 (range C9:C13). If the **VLOOKUP** function does not produce an error, the store number that is identified in the Sales Data worksheet is displayed in the cell. The following explains how the arguments of the **VLOOKUP** function are defined:

- **lookup_value:** CONCATENATE($G$2,B4) The **CONCATENATE** function is used to combine the district number in cell G2 with the value in the Store Count column in the Sales Results worksheet. The Store Count column is a numbered list that serves as a way to match the sequence that is produced by the IF function in column J of the Sales Data worksheet (see Figure 22). As a result, this **CONCATENATE** function is producing the same values as the **CONCATENATE** function in column A of the Sales Data worksheet. Notice that an absolute reference is placed on cell G2.
- **table_array:** 'SALES DATA'!$A$2:$J$500 This range begins with column A and extends over the imported data table in the Sales Data worksheet. Note that this range extends well beyond the last row of the table, which is row 81. This is done to add capacity to the project design and account for the possibility that the company opens more stores. If more stores are added to the imported data set, the table will increase.
- **col_index_num:** 6 The 6th column of the table array range is the Store column.
- **[range_lookup]:** FALSE The function will look for exact matches to the lookup value and will search the entire table array range.

- **Store Name (column D):** =IF(ISNUMBER(C4)=TRUE,VLOOKUP(C4,'SALES DATA'!$F$2:$J$500,2,FALSE),"") This **IF** function uses the **ISNUMBER** function to determine whether a number exists in the Store Number column (column C). If the **ISNUMBER** function is true, the **VLOOKUP** function will look for the store

>> **Quick Reference**

**Importing Data from an Access Database**

1. Activate a cell location in a worksheet where you would like to place the imported data.
2. Click the **From Access** icon in the **Data** tab of the Ribbon.
3. Select an Access database on your computer or network and click the **Open** button in the **Select Data Source** dialog box.
4. Select a table or query from the **Select Table** dialog box and click the **OK** button.
5. Select one of the three format options near the top of the **Import Data** dialog box.
6. Select or check the location for the data near the bottom of the **Import Data** dialog box and click the **OK** button.

number in column C and display the store name from column G in the Sales Data worksheet. Notice that because the lookup value is the store number, the table array range begins with column F in the Sales Data worksheet. If the **ISNUMBER** function is not true, the cell will be left blank.

- **Sales Last Week (column E):** =IF(ISNUMBER(C4)=TRUE,VLOOKUP(C4,‘SALES DATA’!$F$2:$J$500,3,FALSE),“”) This function is identical to the one used in the Store Name column; however, the column index number in the **VLOOKUP** function was changed to 3. This will display the sales results instead of the store name if there is a store number in column C.
- **Sales Last Week Last Year (column F):** =IF(ISNUMBER(C4)=TRUE,VLOOKUP(C4,‘SALES DATA’!$F$2:$J$500,4,FALSE),“”) This function is identical to the one used in the Store Name column; however, the column index number in the **VLOOKUP** function was changed to 4. This will display the sales results last year if there is a store number in column C.
- **Change in Sales (column G):** =IF(ISNUMBER(C4)=TRUE,E4-F4,“”) This function calculates the change in sales by subtracting the sales results last week last year (column F) from the sales results last week if there is a number in the Store Number column.

Figure 24 shows the Completed Sales Results worksheet. Notice that column A has been hidden, and **SUM** functions in row 14 are calculating the total sales results for the district. Once the data is refreshed, a business manager can use this worksheet to review the most current week of sales information by store and district.

Figure 24 | **Completed Sales Results Worksheet**

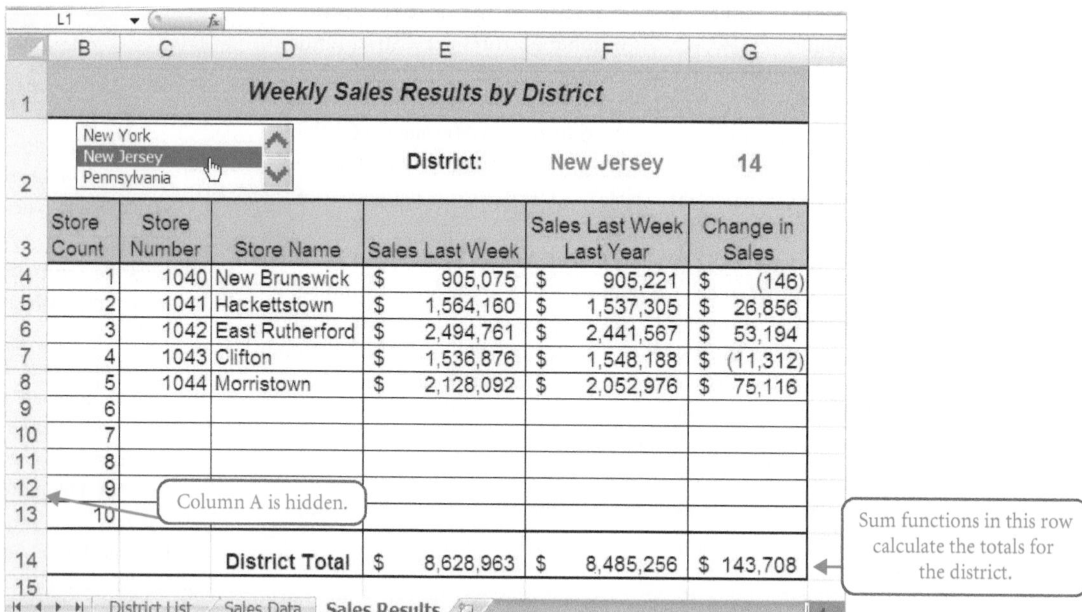

| | B | C | D | E | F | G |
|---|---|---|---|---|---|---|
| 1 | *Weekly Sales Results by District* | | | | | |
| 2 | New York / New Jersey / Pennsylvania | | | District: | New Jersey | 14 |
| 3 | Store Count | Store Number | Store Name | Sales Last Week | Sales Last Week Last Year | Change in Sales |
| 4 | 1 | 1040 | New Brunswick | $ 905,075 | $ 905,221 | $ (146) |
| 5 | 2 | 1041 | Hackettstown | $ 1,564,160 | $ 1,537,305 | $ 26,856 |
| 6 | 3 | 1042 | East Rutherford | $ 2,494,761 | $ 2,441,567 | $ 53,194 |
| 7 | 4 | 1043 | Clifton | $ 1,536,876 | $ 1,548,188 | $ (11,312) |
| 8 | 5 | 1044 | Morristown | $ 2,128,092 | $ 2,052,976 | $ 75,116 |
| 9 | 6 | | | | | |
| 10 | 7 | | | | | |
| 11 | 8 | | | | | |
| 12 | 9 | | | | | |
| 13 | 10 | | | | | |
| 14 | | | District Total | $ 8,628,963 | $ 8,485,256 | $ 143,708 |



## Importing Data from the Internet (Web Queries)

This segment will examine how you can connect to and import data from the Internet. The Internet is a valuable resource for business managers who monitor data that changes frequently throughout the day. For example, the Internet can be used to monitor specific stock prices or the current trend of market indices like the Dow or the Nasdaq throughout the day. A connection can be established between an Excel worksheet and a specific Internet site so that this data can be used in various calculations or analytical projects.

Figure 25 shows a worksheet that can be used to evaluate a hypothetical investment in Microsoft stock. Data will be imported directly from the Internet to show the current stock price statistics for Microsoft (symbol MSFT) in the range A8:B15. Then, formulas will be added to cells C4 and C5 to calculate any unrealized gains or losses.

Figure 25 | **Hypothetical Investment in Microsoft Stock**

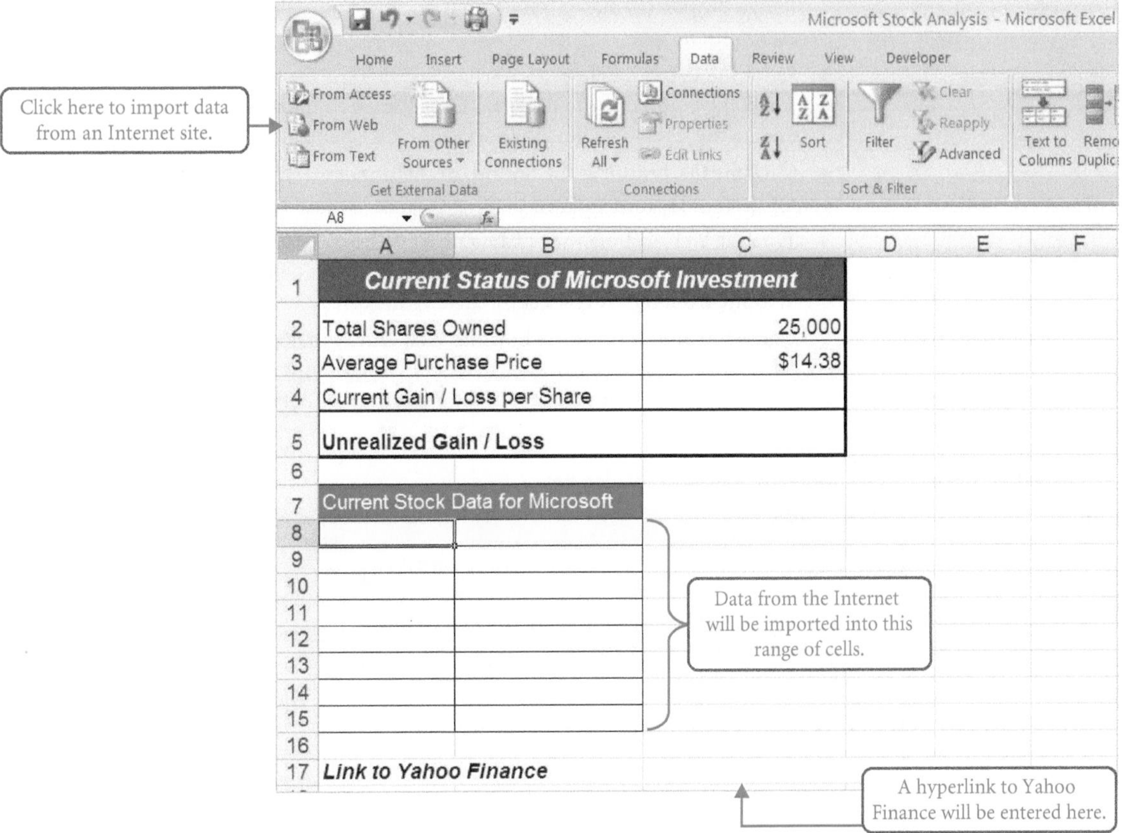


The following explains how stock data for Microsoft is imported from the Internet and placed into the range A8:B15 shown in Figure 25.

- Make sure your computer has a connection to the Internet.
- Activate cell A8 as shown in Figure 25.
- Click the **From Web** icon in the **Data** tab of Ribbon. This will open the **New Web Query** dialog box.
- Type the Web address **www.yahoo.com** and press the **Enter** key. This will place the Web address in the box at the top of the **Web Query** dialog box and then bring you to the Yahoo! Web site.
- Click the Finance link on the left side of the Yahoo! Web site (see Figure 26). The stock data for this example will be imported from Yahoo! FINANCE.

- Type the stock symbol MSFT in the Enter Symbol(s) input box on the left side of the Yahoo! FINANCE Web site, and then click the **GET QUOTES** button (see Figure 27). This will show current stock data for Microsoft.
- Select the table that contains the current stock price data as shown in Figure 28 and click the **Import** button at the bottom of the **Web Query** dialog box.
- Click the **Properties** button at the bottom left side of the **Import Data** dialog box.
- Select the **Refresh every** option and change the minutes to 1 in the **External Data Range Properties** dialog box (see Figure 30). This will update the stock price data every minute when the workbook is open.
- Select the **Refresh data** button when opening the file option and click the **OK** button at the bottom of the **External Data Range Properties** dialog box. This will update the stock data when the workbook is opened.
- Click the **OK** button at the bottom of the **Import Data** dialog box. This will import the stock data from the Yahoo! FINANCE Web site into the Excel worksheet.
- Type the Web address **`www.finance.yahoo.com/?u`** into cell C17. This will insert a hyperlink directly into the worksheet. This will enable you to open the Web site from the worksheet by clicking the cell.

Figures 26 and 27 illustrate how the **Web Query** dialog box is used to navigate to a Web site that contains data you wish to import into worksheet. For this example, data will be imported from the Yahoo! FINANCE Web site.

Figure 26 | **New Web Query Dialog Box**

Figure 27 | **Navigating a Web Site in the New Web Query Dialog Box**

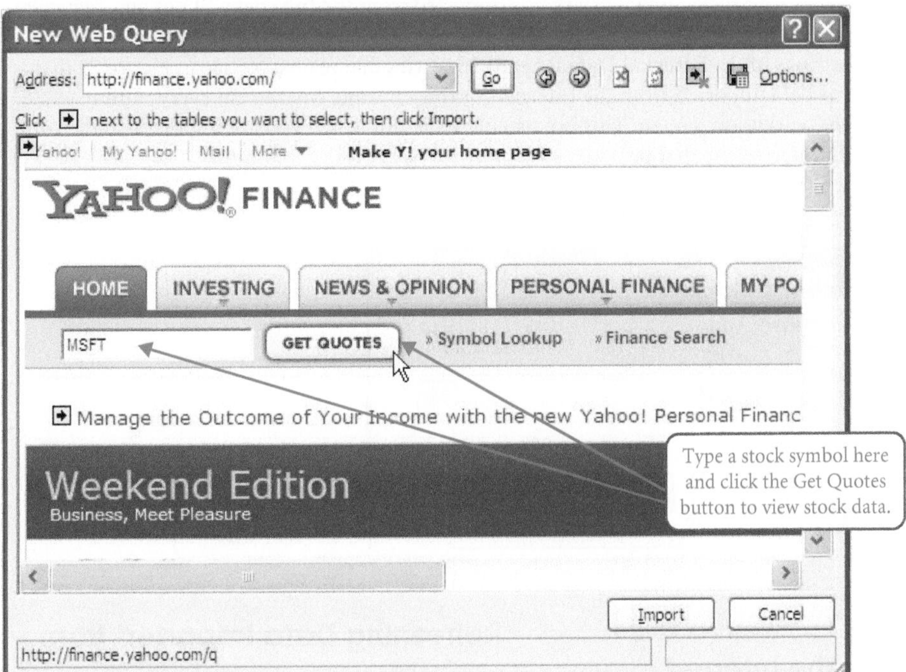


Figure 28 shows the current stock data for Microsoft in the Yahoo! FINANCE Web page. Notice the yellow boxes with black arrows. This indicates table positions on the Web site that can be selected and imported into a worksheet. If you place the cursor over any of the yellow boxes, an outline will appear indicating the data that is contained in the table. One or several tables can be selected and imported into a worksheet. Once a table is selected, the box will turn green with a checkmark.

Figure 28 | **Selecting a Table from a Web Site**

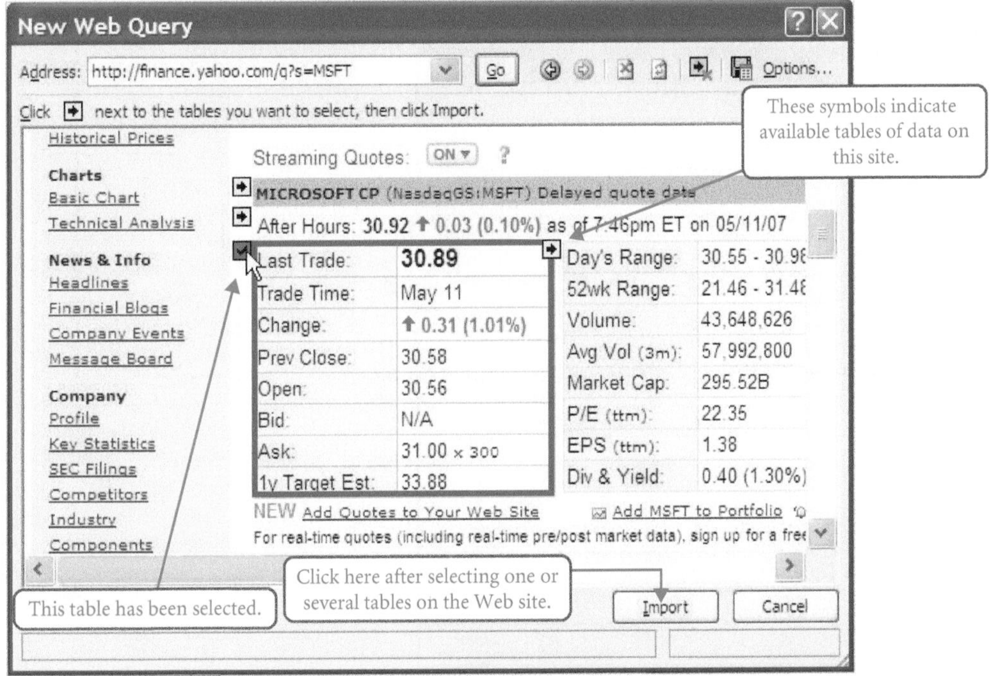

Figures 29 and 30 show the **Import Data** dialog box and the **External Data Range Properties** dialog box. Data that is imported from the Internet will not automatically update unless you click the **Refresh** icon in the **Data** tab of the Ribbon or adjust the settings in the **External Data Range Properties** dialog box. Notice in Figure 30 that the data imported from the Internet for this example will refresh every minute while the workbook is open. This is particularly helpful when you are importing data from an Internet site that provides streaming stock quotes.

Figure 29 | **Import Data Dialog Box**

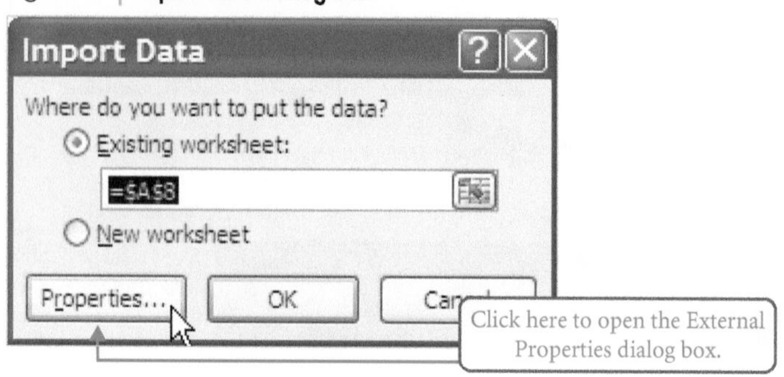


## COMMON MISTAKES | Refreshing Data Imported from the Internet

Data imported from the Internet will not automatically update unless you click the **Refresh** icon in the **Data** tab of the Ribbon or make the appropriate settings in the **External Data Range Properties** dialog box. This dialog box can be opened by clicking the Properties button in the **Import Data** dialog box. You can also click the **Properties** icon in the **Data** tab of the Ribbon after activating any cell in the table of data that has been imported from the Internet. The **Refresh every** option in the **External Data Range Properties** dialog box will automatically refresh the data imported from the Internet on a minute interval that you can specify. Your computer must have a connection to the Internet in order to refresh any data that has been imported.

Figure 30 | **External Data Range Properties Dialog Box**

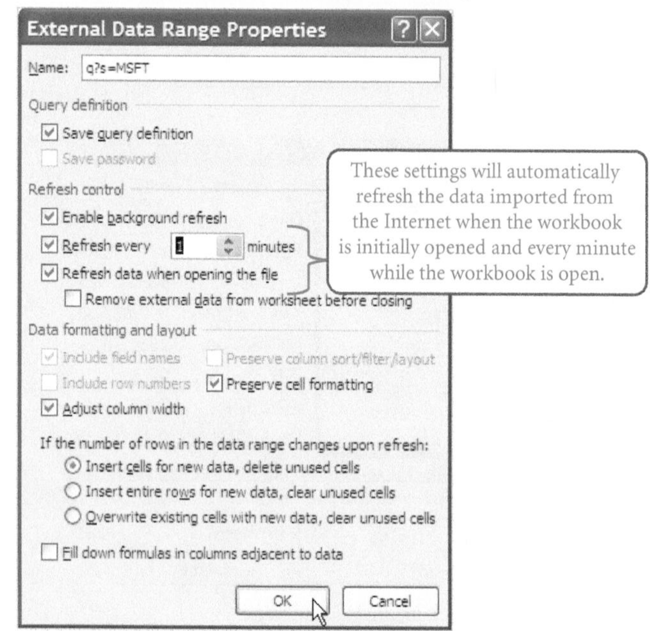

### Importing Data from the Internet

1. Connect your computer to the Internet.
2. Activate a cell location in a worksheet where you would like to place the imported data.
3. Click the **From Web** icon in the **Data** tab of the Ribbon.
4. Enter a Web address in the Address box at the top of the **New Web Query** dialog box and press the **Enter** key.
5. Navigate the Web site from the **New Web Query** dialog box to identify the data you would like to import.
6. Select a table or tables of data by clicking the yellow boxes with black arrows and click the **Import** button at the bottom of the **New Web Query** dialog box.
7. Select a location in the **Import Data** dialog box.
8. Click the Properties button in the **Import Data** dialog box and select one of the data refresh options in the **External Data Range Properties** dialog box if needed.
9. Click the **OK** button in the **External Data Range Properties** dialog box if needed.
10. Click the **OK** button in the **Import Data** dialog box.

Figure 31 shows the completed worksheet that contains stock data for Microsoft imported from the Internet. Formulas were entered into cells C4 and C5 to calculate the unrealized gain or loss on a per-share and total-investment basis. The formula in cell C4 is referencing cell B8, which contains data imported from the Internet. When this data is refreshed, the formula will recalculate the unrealized gain or loss. Notice the hyperlink that was typed into cell C17. When you type a Web address into a cell location, Excel automatically produces a hyperlink like the one shown in this figure. This will allow you to open the Internet site right from the worksheet as long as your computer has a connection to the Internet.

Figure 31 | **Completed Investment Worksheet for Microsoft Investment**

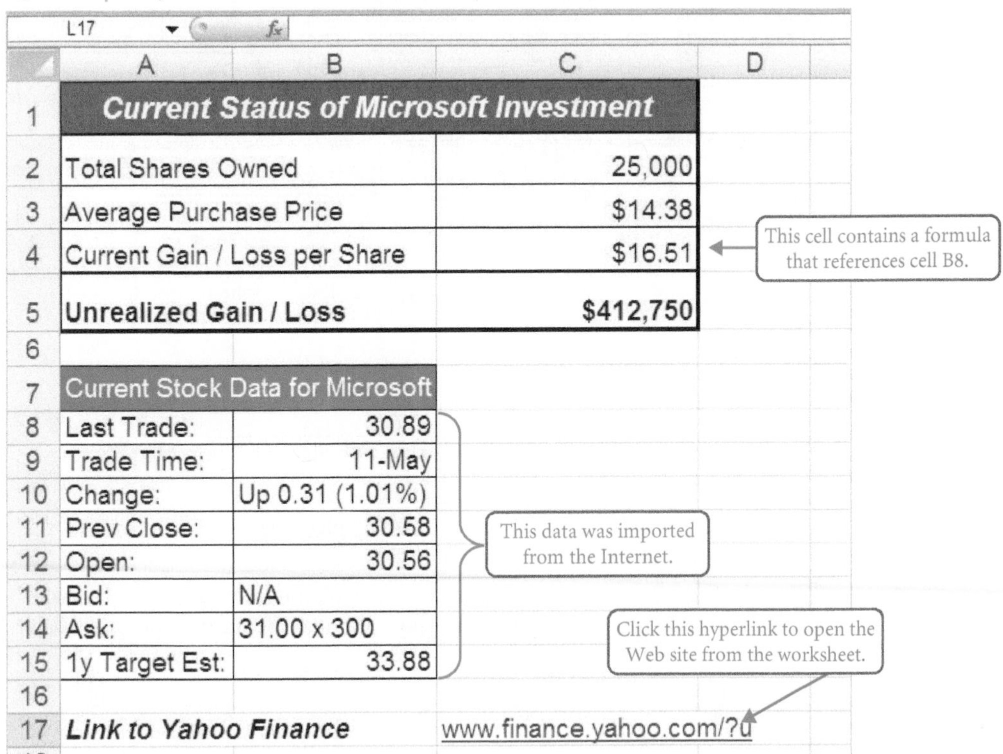


## Importing Text Files

The previous section of this chapter demonstrated how Excel can be used to open text files. However, once the text file is opened and saved as an Excel workbook, the data becomes static and does not change. This section demonstrated how connections can be established to an Access database or the Internet to refresh data that is imported automatically or on demand. This segment will illustrate how a connection can be established between Excel and text file.

Figure 32 shows an Excel workbook that might be used by a financial analyst to evaluate the current stock value of public companies. Notice that the last four columns of the Financial Status worksheet are blank. This is because the Current Price and Price Last Year will change every business day of the year. Therefore, the text file shown in Figure 1 will be imported into the Data worksheet, and **VLOOKUP** functions will be used to show the Current Price and Price Last Year for each company on the Financial Data worksheet. When the prices are changed in the text file, the data can be refreshed in the workbook instead of opening a new text file.

Figure 32 | **Stock Value Analysis Workbook**

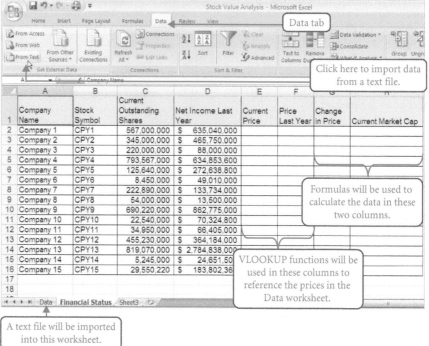

Data tab

Click here to import data from a text file.

| | A | B | C | D | E | F | G | H |
|---|---|---|---|---|---|---|---|---|
| 1 | Company Name | Stock Symbol | Current Outstanding Shares | Net Income Last Year | Current Price | Price Last Year | Change in Price | Current Market Cap |
| 2 | Company 1 | CPY1 | 567,000,000 | $ 635,040,000 | | | | |
| 3 | Company 2 | CPY2 | 345,000,000 | $ 465,750,000 | | | | |
| 4 | Company 3 | CPY3 | 220,000,000 | $ 88,000,000 | | | | |
| 5 | Company 4 | CPY4 | 793,567,000 | $ 634,853,600 | | | | |
| 6 | Company 5 | CPY5 | 125,640,000 | $ 272,638,800 | | | | |
| 7 | Company 6 | CPY6 | 8,450,000 | $ 49,010,000 | | | | |
| 8 | Company 7 | CPY7 | 222,890,000 | $ 133,734,000 | | | | |
| 9 | Company 8 | CPY8 | 54,000,000 | $ 13,500,000 | | | | |
| 10 | Company 9 | CPY9 | 690,220,000 | $ 862,775,000 | | | | |
| 11 | Company 10 | CPY10 | 22,540,000 | $ 70,324,800 | | | | |
| 12 | Company 11 | CPY11 | 34,950,000 | $ 66,405,000 | | | | |
| 13 | Company 12 | CPY12 | 455,230,000 | $ 364,184,000 | | | | |
| 14 | Company 13 | CPY13 | 819,070,000 | $ 2,784,838,00 | | | | |
| 15 | Company 14 | CPY14 | 5,245,000 | $ 24,651,50 | | | | |
| 16 | Company 15 | CPY15 | 29,550,220 | $ 183,802,36 | | | | |
| 17 | | | | | | | | |
| 18 | | | | | | | | |

Data | Financial Status | Sheet3

Formulas will be used to calculate the data in these two columns.

VLOOKUP functions will be used in these columns to reference the prices in the Data worksheet.

A text file will be imported into this worksheet.

The following explains how the text file shown in Figure 1 is imported into the Data worksheet shown in Figure 32:

- Activate cell A1 in the Data worksheet. This will place the data imported from the text file in the Data worksheet beginning with cell A1.
- Click the **From Text** icon in the **Data** tab of the Ribbon (see Figure 32). This will open the **Import Text File** dialog box, which is almost identical to the Open dialog box shown in Figure 2.
- Use the **Import Text File** dialog box to select a text file saved on your computer or network. The file type at the bottom of the dialog box must be set to Text Files.
- Click the **Import** button after selecting a text file. This will open the Text Import Wizard, as shown in Figures 3 through 5.
- Complete the three steps of the Text Import Wizard. If you are importing a fixed-width text file, remember to obtain a key. After you click the **Finish** button in step 3 of the Text Import Wizard, the **Import Data** dialog box will open (see Figure 29).
- Click the **Properties** button on the **Import Data** dialog box to adjust the data refresh settings in the **External Data Range Properties** dialog box. Deselect the **Prompt for file name on refresh** option by clicking the box to the left. Use this option if you expect the file name that contains the data you are importing to freqently change. For example, a new text file containing stock prices might be saved every day with the date in the file name. This would require you to select a new file in order to update the data in the worksheet. However, this example will assume that the file name will not change.
- Select the **Refresh data when opening the file** option in the **External Data Range Properties** dialog box.
- Select the **Overwrite exisiting cells with new data, clear unused cells** option in the **External Data Range Properties** dialog box. It is good practice to always select this option when importing data from any external data source into a worksheet, especially if you are importing data from other external sources on the same worksheet or using formulas in adjacent columns.

- Click the **OK** button on the **External Data Range Properties** dialog box and then on the **Import Data** dialog box. This will import the data from the text file into the Data worksheet.

Figure 33 shows the settings that were made in the **External Data Range Properties** dialog box.

Figure 33 | **Final Settings in the External Data Range Properties Dialog Box**

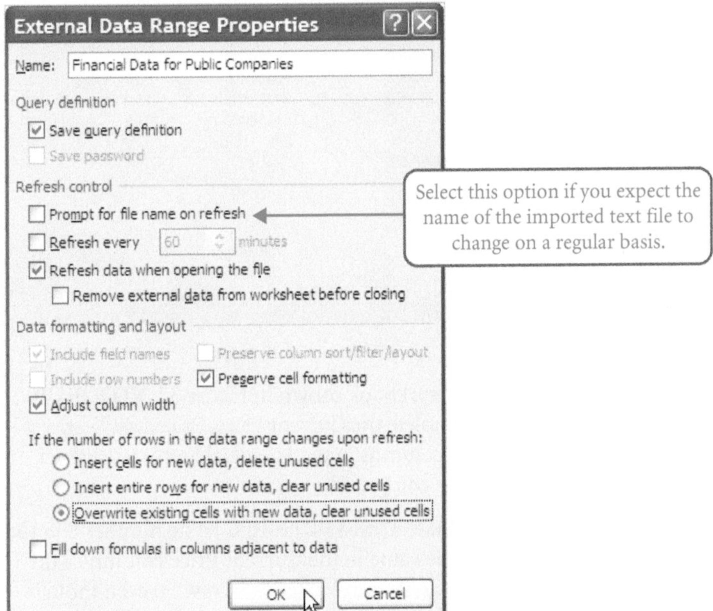


Figure 34 shows the appearance of the Data worksheet after importing the text file shown in Figure 1. Notice that the data is *not* imported into the worksheet in the form of a table as was the case when importing data from an Access database. Because of the settings in the **External Data Range Properties** dialog box (see Figure 33), any changes in the Financial Data for Public Companies text file will be automatically updated in the Data worksheet each time the workbook is opened. However, you must still click the **Refresh** icon in the **Data** tab of the Ribbon to see any updates in the text file after the workbook is opened.

Figure 34 | **Appearance of Imported Text File in Data Worksheet**

| | A | B | C | D | E | F |
|---|---|---|---|---|---|---|
| 1 | Company Name | Stock Symbol | Current Outstanding Shares | Net Income Last Year | Current Price | Price Last Year |
| 2 | Company 1 | CPY1 | 567000000 | 635040000 | 24.64 | 22.5 |
| 3 | Company 2 | CPY2 | 345000000 | 465750000 | 40.5 | 33.2 |
| 4 | Company 3 | CPY3 | 220000000 | 88000000 | 3.6 | 8.7 |
| 5 | Company 4 | CPY4 | 793567000 | 634853600 | 15.2 | 16.7 |
| 6 | Company 5 | CPY5 | 125640000 | 272638800 | 32.55 | 32.9 |
| 7 | Company 6 | CPY6 | 8450000 | 49010000 | 36.25 | 28.5 |
| 8 | Company 7 | CPY7 | 222890000 | 133734000 | 9.6 | 8.6 |
| 9 | Company 8 | CPY8 | 54000000 | 13500000 | 1.5 | 6.7 |
| 10 | Company 9 | CPY9 | 690220000 | 862775000 | 27.5 | 26.5 |
| 11 | Company 10 | CPY10 | 22540000 | 70324800 | 37.44 | 33.2 |
| 12 | Company 11 | CPY11 | 34950000 | 66405000 | 20.9 | 21.5 |
| 13 | Company 12 | CPY12 | 455230000 | 364184000 | 13.6 | 22.8 |
| 14 | Company 13 | CPY13 | 819070000 | 2784838000 | 61.2 | 60.7 |
| 15 | Company 14 | CPY14 | 5245000 | 24651500 | 32.9 | 26.5 |
| 16 | Company 15 | CPY15 | 29550220 | 183802368.4 | 55.98 | 54.9 |
| 17 | | | | | | |
| 18 | | | | | | |
| 19 | | | | | | |
| 20 | | | | | | |
| 21 | | | | | | |
| 22 | | | | | | |

Data | Financial Status | Sheet3

To complete the Stock Value Analysis workbook shown in Figure 32, **VLOOKUP** functions and formulas will be used to complete the Current Price, Price Last Year, Change in Price, and Current Market Cap columns in the Financial Status worksheet. The following explains how each column is completed:

- **Current Price:** =VLOOKUP(A2,Data!$A$2:$F$50,5,FALSE) The number 5 in the **col_index_num** argument will pull the value in the Current Price column in the Data worksheet. Notice that the table array range extends to row 50 even though the text file has only 16 rows. This is done in the event that additional companies are added to the text file.
- **Price Last Year:** =VLOOKUP(A2,Data!$A$2:$F$50,6,FALSE) The number 6 in the **col_index_num** argument will pull the value in the Price Last Year column in the Data worksheet.
- **Change in Price:** =E2-F2 This formula will show the dollar difference between the Current Price and the Price Last Year.
- **Current Market Cap:** =E2*C2 This formula will calculate the current market cap by multiplying the current price by the current shares outstanding.

Figure 35 shows the final setup of the Stock Value Analysis workbook. The cell references used in the **VLOOKUP** functions and formulas to complete columns E through H will automatically change when the imported data from the text file is refreshed in the Data worksheet.

**>> Quick Reference**

**Importing Text Files**

1. Click the **From Text** icon in the **Data** tab of the Ribbon.
2. Select a text file on your computer or network from the **Import Text File** dialog box and click the **Import** button.
3. Follow the steps of the Text Import Wizard.
4. Click the **Properties** button in the **Import Data** dialog box.
5. Set the refresh and layout options in the **External Data Range Properties** dialog box and click the **OK** button.
6. Select the desired location for the data and click the **OK** button in the **Import Data** dialog box.

Figure 35 | **Completed Stock Value Analysis Workbook**

Stock Value Analysis - Microsoft Excel

E2 =VLOOKUP(A2,Data!$A$2:$F$16,5,FALSE)

| | A | B | C | D | E | F | G | H |
|---|---|---|---|---|---|---|---|---|
| 1 | Company Name | Stock Symbol | Current Outstanding Shares | Net Income Last Year | Current Price | Price Last Year | Change in Price | Current Market Cap |
| 2 | Company 1 | CPY1 | 567,000,000 | $ 635,040,000 | $ 24.64 | $ 22.50 | $ 2.14 | $ 13,970,880,000 |
| 3 | Company 2 | CPY2 | 345,000,000 | $ 465,750,000 | $ 40.50 | $ 33.20 | $ 7.30 | $ 13,972,500,000 |
| 4 | Company 3 | CPY3 | 220,000,000 | $ 88,000,000 | $ 3.60 | $ 8.70 | $ (5.10) | $ 792,000,000 |
| 5 | Company 4 | CPY4 | 793,567,000 | $ 634,853,600 | $ 15.20 | $ 16.70 | $ (1.50) | $ 12,062,218,400 |
| 6 | Company 5 | CPY5 | 125,640,000 | $ 272,638,800 | $ 32.55 | $ 32.90 | $ (0.35) | $ 4,089,582,000 |
| 7 | Company 6 | CPY6 | 8,450,000 | $ 49,010,000 | $ 36.25 | $ 28.50 | $ 7.75 | $ 306,312,500 |
| 8 | Company 7 | CPY7 | 222,890,000 | $ 133,734,000 | $ 9.60 | $ 8.60 | $ 1.00 | $ 2,139,744,000 |
| 9 | Company 8 | CPY8 | 54,000,000 | $ 13,500,000 | $ 1.50 | $ 6.70 | $ (5.20) | $ 81,000,000 |
| 10 | Company 9 | CPY9 | 690,220,000 | $ 862,775,000 | $ 27.50 | $ 26.50 | $ 1.00 | $ 18,981,050,000 |
| 11 | Company 10 | CPY10 | 22,540,000 | $ 70,324,800 | $ 37.44 | $ 33.20 | $ 4.24 | $ 843,897,600 |
| 12 | Company 11 | CPY11 | 34,950,000 | $ 66,405,000 | $ 20.90 | $ 21.50 | $ (0.60) | $ 730,455,000 |
| 13 | Company 12 | CPY12 | 455,230,000 | $ 364,184,000 | $ 13.60 | $ 22.80 | $ (9.20) | $ 6,191,128,000 |
| 14 | Company 13 | CPY13 | 819,070,000 | $ 2,784,838,000 | $ 61.20 | $ 60.70 | $ 0.50 | $ 50,127,084,000 |
| 15 | Company 14 | CPY14 | 5,245,000 | $ 24,651,500 | $ 32.90 | $ 26.50 | $ 6.40 | $ 172,560,500 |
| 16 | Company 15 | CPY15 | 29,550,220 | $ 183,802,368 | $ 55.98 | $ 54.90 | $ 1.08 | $ 1,654,221,316 |
| 17 | | | | | | | | |
| 18 | | | | | | | | |

Data | Financial Status | Sheet3

Values in these columns will change when the imported text file in the Data worksheet is refreshed.

# >>Importing Data from Access

The purpose of this workshop is to demonstrate how data is imported from an Access Database. I will be demonstrating the tasks in this workshop in the following three videos: **Project Design, Importing Data from Access**, and **Using Formulas and Functions with Imported Data**. Open the Excel workbook named ib_e10_weeklysalesreview. Then, complete the tasks in this workshop and watch the related video for each section.

1. **List Box Setup (Video: Project Design)**
   a. Activate the List Box in the Sales Results worksheet. Then, open the **Format Control** dialog box by clicking the **Properties** icon in the **Developer** tab of the Ribbon.
   b. Define the Input range in the **Control** tab of the **Format Control** dialog box with the range C2:C21 in the District List worksheet. Then, set the Cell link input box to cell A2 in the Sales Results worksheet and click the **OK** button.
   c. Click cell F2, and then select the New Jersey district from the List Box.
   d. Enter the following **VLOOKUP** function into cell F2 in the Sales Results worksheet: **`=VLOOKUP(A2,'District List'!A2:C21,3,FALSE)`**.
   e. Enter the following **VLOOKUP** function into cell G2 in the Sales Results worksheet: **`=VLOOKUP(A2,'District List'!A2:C21,2,FALSE)`**.
   f. Save the workbook.

2. **Import Data from Access Query (Video: Importing Data from Access)**

   a. Open the Access database named ib_e10_storesalesdata.

   b. Open the Weekly Sales Results query in **Design View**. Then, run the query to view the record set.

   c. Close the query and then the database.

   d. Activate cell B1 in the Sales Data worksheet and click the **From Access** icon in the **Data** tab of the Ribbon.

   e. Locate and select the ib_e10_storesalesdata Access database from the **Select Data Source** dialog box and click the **Open** button.

   f. Select the Weekly Sales Results query in the **Select Table** dialog box and click the **OK** button.

   g. Click the **OK** button in the **Import Data** dialog box.

   h. Activate cell B1 and remove the **Filter** tool.

   i. Click the **Properties** icon in the **Data** tab of the Ribbon. Then, click the **Connection Properties** button in the **External Data Properties** dialog box.

   j. Select the **Refresh data when opening the file** option in the **Connection Properties** dialog box and click the **OK** button.

   k. Select the **Overwrite existing cells with new data, clear unused cells** option in the **External Data Properties** dialog box and click the **OK** button.

   l. Save the workbook.

3. **Add Functions (Video: Using Formulas and Functions with Imported Data)**

   a. Type the following column heading into cell J1 in the Sales Data worksheet: `Unique District/Store`. Then, click the **AutoCorrect Options** icon and select the **Undo Table AutoExpansion** option.

   b. Bold the column heading in cell J1, and then set the alignment to wrap text for the range A1:J1. Adjust column widths as needed.

   c. Type the number `1` in cell J2.

   d. Enter the following **IF** function into cell J3: `=IF(D3=D2,J2+1,1)`. Then, copy and paste the function into the range J3:J500.

   e. Type the following column heading into cell A1: `Unique District Sequence`. Bold this cell location and adjust the column width as needed.

   f. Enter the following function into cell A2: **`=IF(ISBLANK(B2)=TRUE,"",CONCATENATE(D2,J2))`**. Then, copy and paste the function into the range A3:A500.

   g. Hide column A in the Sales Results worksheet.

   h. Enter the following function into cell C4 in the Sales Results worksheet: **`=IF(ISERROR(VLOOKUP(CONCATENATE($G$2,B4),'Sales Data'!$A$2:$J$500,6,FALSE))=TRUE,"",VLOOKUP(CONCATENATE($G$2,B4),'Sales Data'!$A$2:$J$500,6,FALSE))`**. Then, copy the function and paste it into the range C5:C13.

   i. Enter the following function into cell D4: **`=IF(ISNUMBER(C4)=TRUE,VLOOKUP(C4,'Sales Data'!$F$2:$J$500,2,FALSE),"")`**. Then, copy the function and paste it into the range D5:D13.

   j. Enter the following function into cell E4: **`=IF(ISNUMBER(C4)=TRUE,VLOOKUP(C4,'Sales Data'!$F$2:$J$500,3,FALSE),"")`**. Then, copy the function and paste it into the range E5:E13.

k. Enter the following function into cell F4: **=IF(ISNUMBER(C4)=TRUE,VLOOKUP(C4,'Sales Data'!$F$2:$J$500,4,FALSE),"")**. Then, copy the function and paste it into the range F5:F13.

l. Enter the following function into cell G4: **=IF(ISNUMBER(C4)=TRUE,E4-F4,"")**. Then, copy the function and paste it into the range G5:G13.

m. View the sales data for few districts by making a selection from the List Box. Adjust the width of column G as needed.

n. Save and close the workbook.

# >> Importing Data from the Internet

**VIDEO WORKSHOP**

The purpose of this workshop is to demonstrate how data is imported from the Internet into an Excel worksheet. I will be demonstrating the tasks in this workshop in the video named **Web Queries**. Open the Excel file named ib_e10_microsoftstockanalysis and complete the tasks in this workshop.

**1. Importing Data from the Internet (Video: Web Queries)**

a. Activate cell A8 in the Stock Data worksheet.

b. Click the **From Web** icon in the **Data** tab of the Ribbon.

c. Type the Web address **www.yahoo.com** and press the **Enter** key.

d. Click the Finance link on the left side of the Web site in the **New Web Query** dialog box.

e. Click in the **Enter Symbol(s)** input box on the left side of the Web site and type the ticker symbol **MSFT**. Then, click the **GET QUOTES** button.

f. Scroll down on the right side of the **New Web Query** dialog box until the Last Trade price is visible. Then, click the yellow box with the black arrow next to the label **Last Trade**.

g. Click the **Import** button at the bottom of the **New Web Query** dialog box.

h. Click the **Properties** button at the bottom of the **Import Data** dialog box.

i. Select the **Refresh every** option in the **External Data Range Properties** dialog box and set the minutes to 1. Then, click the **OK** button.

j. Click the **OK** button at the bottom of the **Import Data** dialog box.

k. Enter a formula in cell C4 that subtracts the value in cell C3 from the value in cell B8.

l. Enter a formula in cell C6 that multiplies the value in cell C4 by the value in cell C2.

m. Type the following Web address into cell C17: **www.finance.yahoo.com/?u**.

n. Save and close the workbook.

VIDEO WORKSHOP

# >> Importing Text Files

The purpose of this workshop is to demonstrate how text files are imported into an Excel worksheet. I will be demonstrating the tasks in this workshop in the video named **Importing Text Files**. Open the Excel workbook named ib_e10_stockvalueanalysis and complete the tasks in this workshop.

1. **Importing Data (Video: Importing Text Files)**
   a. Activate cell A1 in the Data worksheet.
   b. Click the **From Text** icon in the **Data** tab of the Ribbon.
   c. Select the text file named ib_e10_finanicaldatadelimited and click the **Import** button at the bottom of the **Import Text File** dialog box. This is the same text file that was used in the first workshop of this chapter.
   d. Check that the **Delimited** option is selected in step 1 of the Text Import Wizard and click the **Next** button.
   e. Click the box next to the **Tab** option in step 2 of the Text Import Wizard to remove the check mark. Select the **Comma** option and click the **Next** button.
   f. Click the **Finish** button at the bottom of step 3 of the Text Import Wizard.
   g. Click the **Properties** button at the bottom of the **Import Data** dialog box.
   h. Deselect the **Prompt for file name on refresh** option and select the **Refresh data when opening the file** option.
   i. Select the **Overwrite existing cells with new data, clear unused cells** option, and then click the **OK** button at the bottom of the **External Data Range Properties** dialog box.
   j. Click the **OK** button at the bottom of the **Import Data** dialog box.

2. **Adding Calculations (Video: Importing Text Files)**
   a. Enter the following function into cell E2 in the Financial Status worksheet: `=VLOOKUP(A2,Data!$A$2:$F$50,5,FALSE)`. Then, copy the function and paste it into the range E3:E16.
   b. Enter the following function into cell F2: `=VLOOKUP(A2,Data!$A$2:$F$50,6,FALSE)`. Then, copy the function and paste it into the range F3:F16.
   c. Enter a formula in cell G2 that subtracts the price last year in cell F2 from the current price in cell E2. Then, copy this formula and paste it into the range G3:G16.
   d. Enter a formula in cell H2 that multiplies the current price in cell E2 by the current outstanding shares in cell C2. Then, copy this formula and paste it into the range H3:H16.
   e. Save and close the workbook.

## >> Tracking Investment Portfolios

The ability to access and analyze data on a frequent basis is a significant challenge for most business managers. What makes this challenge complex is that data by itself can rarely help business managers make critical decisions. For example, if you own stock in a public company, the current stock price is rarely enough information to decide if you should buy more shares or sell what you have. The buy-or-sell decision could depend on several other factors such as how much you paid for the stock, how many shares you own, or what other investments you have in your portfolio. As a result, data such as stock prices are usually one component of a broader analysis that is constructed by the business manager. Therefore, not only must the business manager overcome the challenge of introducing new data into a preexisting analytical project, but that data must somehow get placed into the project from an external source. This is why tools such as Excel and Access are so critical in the daily decision-making process for most business managers. External data such as stock prices can be imported into an Excel worksheet and used to manage buy-and-sell decisions that an investment manager must make every day.

**EXERCISE**

**Why Do I Need This?**

### Exercise

The purpose of this exercise is to use Excel to import data from an Access database and evaluate the stock portfolios for several investors of a hypothetical investment firm. On the basis of a customer's total unrealized gains or losses, a finance manager can decide if a customer should hold or sell a particular stock. Open the Excel file named ib_e10_portfolioanalysis and complete each task.

1. Activate cell B1 in the Customer List worksheet. The customers who are being serviced by this firm will be imported from a table contained in the ib_e10_invetmentportfolios Access database. It is necessary to import this data from the database because the customers who are being serviced by the firm could change on a daily basis.
2. Click the **From Access** icon in the **Data** tab of the Ribbon and select the ib_e10_investmentportfolios Access database. After clicking the **Open** button at the bottom of the **Select Data Source** dialog box, select the Client Names table and click the **OK** button in the **Select Table** dialog box.
3. Click the **Properties** button at the bottom of the **Import Data** dialog box. Then, select the option that will update the data from this table each time the file is opened, and click the **OK** button. This exercise assumes that the investment firm updates the Access database once a day with any new customers as well as stock and mutual fund prices at the close of the previous business day. Therefore, because the database is updated once a day, it is necessary to update any data that is imported into the Excel workbook once a day when the file is opened.
4. When the **Import Data** dialog box opens, check that the data is being imported into the form of a table and that the data is being placed in cell B1 of the Customer List worksheet. Then, click the **OK** button at the bottom of the dialog box.
5. Activate the Portfolio Analysis worksheet and open the **Format Control** dialog box for the List Box that appears between cells B2 and C2. Set the Input range for the List Box with the range B2:B501 in the Customer List worksheet. This range extends well past the last row of data that was imported from the Client Names table. However, this will add capacity to the design of the project. The firm can add up to 500 clients to its customer base and the new customers will automatically appear in the List Box. Set the Cell link for the List

Box to cell A2 on the Portfolio Analysis worksheet. After clicking the **OK** button on the **Format Control** dialog box, activate any cell location on the worksheet to activate the List Box, and the select Customer 1 from the List Box.

6. Enter a **VLOOKUP** function into cell D2 in the Portfolio Analysis worksheet that looks for the value in cell A2, which is the cell link value from the List Box, in column A in the Customer List worksheet. The function should then pull the Client Name in column B of the Customer List worksheet. Make sure that the **table_array** argument for the function includes column C in the Customer List worksheet and extends to row 501 to account for additional capacity that is built into the project design. The purpose of the function is to display the customer's name that was selected in the List Box in cell D2 in the Portfolio Analysis worksheet.

7. Enter a **VLOOKUP** into cell F2 in the Portfolio Analysis worksheet that is identical to the one that was created for item 6. However, the purpose of this function is to show the customer's account number in cell F2. Therefore, the column index number must be changed to 3.

8. Activate cell A1 in the Stock Detail worksheet and import the data contained in the Current Status by Stock query from the ib_e10_investmentportfolios Access database. Set the properties for this data so that it is refreshed every time the Excel file is opened. After the import is complete, format the values in the Total Cost and Current Value columns to Currency with 0 decimal places. The Portfolio Analysis worksheet is designed to show the finance manager a customer's portfolio summarized by sector. A sector is comprised of companies that operate in the same industry. However, it will be necessary to also examine details for specific stocks that have been purchased for various customers.

9. Activate cell B1 in the Sector Detail worksheet. Import the data contained in the Current Values by Sector query from the ib_e10_investmentportfolios Access database. This data should be refreshed every time the Excel file is opened.

10. Open the **External Data Properties** dialog box for the data that was imported from the Current Values by Sector query by clicking the **Properties** icon in the **Design** tab of the Ribbon. Remember that a cell location on the table must be activated in order to see the **Design** tab on the Ribbon. Select the **Overwrite existing cells with new data, clear unused cells** option in the **External Data Properties** dialog box and click the **OK** button. This setting is critical because functions will be added in column A, which is to the right and adjacent to this table.

11. Type the column heading `Unique Account/Sector` in cell A1 of the Sector Detail worksheet. Expand the width of column A so that the column heading is visible.

12. Enter a **CONCATENATE** function into cell A2 that combines the account number in cell B2 with the sector in cell C2. Copy and paste this function into the range A3:1501. The function is pasted well beyond the last row of data to add capacity to the design of this project. If more customers are added to the firm's client base, the number of records generated from the Current Values by Sector query will increase. This function will accommodate up to 1500 rows of data from this query.

13. Activate the Portfolio Analysis worksheet and hide Column A.

14. Enter the following function into cell C4 of the Portfolio Analysis worksheet:
```
=IF(ISERROR(VLOOKUP(CONCATENATE($F$2,B4),'Sector
Detail'!$A$2:$E$1501,4,FALSE))=TRUE,0,VLOOKUP(CONCATE-
NATE($F$2,B4),'Sector Detail'!$A$2:$E$1501,4,FALSE))
```

Then, copy the function and paste it into the range C5:C8. The purpose of this function is to show the customer's cost basis for each sector, which is in column D of the Sector Detail worksheet. However, we cannot assume that every customer is investing in every sector. Therefore, the function first determines if the **VLOOKUP** function produces an error. If the **VLOOKUP** function produces an error, it means a value could not be found in a particular sector for the customer who was selected from the List Box. As a result, the function will display a 0 for that sector, indicating that no investments exist. If the **VLOOKUP** function does not produce an error, the appropriate value column D will be displayed from in the Sector Detail worksheet. Notice that the **lookup_value** argument for the **VLOOKUP** function is defined with the **CONCATENATE** function, which combines the customer's account number with the sector name. This is identical to the values that were created in column A of the Sector Detail worksheet. In addition, notice that this function is pasted into row 8, which does not contain a sector description. This is another way of adding capacity to the project design. If the company decides to invest in a new sector, the sector name can be typed into cell B8 and the investments will automatically be incorporated into the portfolio analysis.

15. Enter the following function into cell D4 of the Portfolio Analysis worksheet: **=IF(ISERROR(VLOOKUP(CONCATENATE($F$2,B4),'Sector Detail'!$A$2:$E$1501,5,FALSE))=TRUE,0,VLOOKUP(CONCATE-NATE($F$2,B4),'Sector Detail'!$A$2:$E$1501,5,FALSE))** Then, copy the function and paste it into the range D5:D8. This function is identical to the one explained in item 14 except that the column index number in the **VLOOKUP** function was changed to 5. This is done to pull the current investment values from column E in the Sector Detail worksheet.

16. Enter a formula into cell E4 that subtracts the value in cell C4 from the value in cell D4. Then, copy the formula and paste it into the range E5:E8.

17. Enter a formula into cell F4 that calculates the percentage the current values for each sector represents to the total Current Value of the portfolio. Your formula should divide the current value for each sector by the total value in cell D9. Copy and paste your formula into the range F5:F8. Use absolute references to avoid errors when copying and pasting this formula.

18. Test the worksheet by viewing the portfolios of the first 5 customers.

19. You just found out that stock SY6 experienced a significant drop in price. Use the **Filter** tool for the data in the Stock Detail worksheet to show only those customers who own stock SY6. How many customers own this stock?

20. Go to the Portfolio Analysis worksheet and examine the investment portfolios of the customers you identified in item 19. Is the total Unrealized Gain/Loss (row 9) a negative number for all portfolios? Which customers are showing an unrealized loss for their entire portfolio? Explain why these customers are showing loss for their portfolio while other customers who purchased the same stock are not.

21. Save and close your workbook.

PROBLEM & EXERCISE

## >> What's Wrong with This Spreadsheet?

### Problem

You are working as a merchandise analyst in a retail corporation and a coworker sends you an Excel workbook that he created to track the sales of items sold in his department. He is importing data from the company's database system to analyze the sales of all active items in his department that have been marked down. He explains the following in his e-mail to you.

- I needed a way to get data from our database system into an Excel workbook. So I figured out how to import data from an Access database, which is connected to our main database system.
- I am using Excel to analyze the weeks of supply for all the active items that were marked down in department 10 as of last week. The number of items that are marked down changes from week to week, so I thought it would be nice to have this data come right into the worksheet from an Access database. By the way, that's why the IF function you see in cell H2 is pasted to row 101.
- I set this up last week and it worked great. However, when I opened the file this week, none of the items changed. The IT department assured me the database has been updated; however, I am certain we had fewer items marked down last week compared to 2 weeks ago. I can't understand why this data did not change.
- Also, I would like to use this worksheet in a report to the VP of Marketing; however, I want to get rid of all the blue shading on the worksheet as well as the arrows next to the column headings. Is this possible?

### Exercise

The Excel file your coworker attached to the e-mail is named ib_e10_itemanalysis. A connection has been established between this file and the Access database named ib_e10_itemsalesdata. You can open the Excel file while the DVD remains in your computer, or you should move both the Excel file and the Access database to the same folder on your computer or network, and then open the Excel file. When the file opens, enable the content by clicking the **Options** button in the Security Warning Message Bar, click the **Enable this content option**, and then click the **OK** button. Review the Excel file and consider the following points.

1. Look at the IF function in cell H2. Is the function accurately calculating the weeks of supply, which should be the current inventory divided by the unit sales last week? Why did your coworker use an **IF** function to do this calculation?
2. Your coworker mentioned that the items in the workbook should have changed. Based on the settings that were made during the initial import process, explain how the data in this workbook will be updated or refreshed.
3. Refresh the data in the workbook and examine the function that is calculating the weeks of supply in column H. Are all the functions in this column accurately calculating the weeks of supply?
4. Your coworker mentioned that he wanted to remove all the blue shading as well as the drop-down arrows next to each column heading. Is this possible?

What's wrong with this spreadsheet? Write a short answer for each of the points listed above, and then fix any errors you found. In addition, adjust the formatting based on your coworker's last point. Note, you may want to close the Excel file without saving it before making any changes. Then, reopen the Excel file, make your adjustments, and then refresh the data.

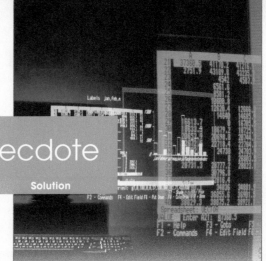

# Excel in **Practice** | Anecdote

## Solution

Even though the Vice President of merchandising had little experience using Excel, I was still able to provide a solution that provided him with accurate, up-to-date information that he could use easily. The combination of Excel's List Box feature along with the ability to create a connection to an Access database allowed me to create a very easy and accurate solution for his needs.

Getty Images, Inc.—Stone Allstock

## Assignment

The purpose of this assignment is to use Excel to create a solution similar to what was described in the anecdote. The Access database named ib_e10_divisioncategorysales contains data that is very similar to what was used to create the solution described. Your assignment is to use the data in this database so that a business manager could review the sales data by division and category. Use the following points to help complete this assignment:

1. The purpose of this assignment is to show the year-to-date sales results by division and category. The Sales Dollars Year to Date query in the ib_e10_divisioncategorysales Access database has been created for this assignment. It contains the sales year to date and the sales year to date last year for every category in the company. In addition, the query was constructed so that the data is sorted by Division Number and Category Number in ascending order. Therefore, all of the division numbers will be grouped together. Because this data will change on a weekly basis, you will need to create a connection to this database and import the data produced by the Sales Dollars Year to Date query.
2. Assume that the manager who will use this workbook has very little knowledge of Excel. Your goal is to set up the workbook so that a manager can simply select the Division Name to review the sales year to date for every category in the division selected.
3. The workbook should show the overall sales results for the division selected as well as the dollar change in sales for each category and for the overall division.
4. Assume that division numbers and names contained in the Division Names table in the ib_e10_divisioncategorysales Access database are permanent and will not change.
5. There are no more than 8 categories per division. In the worksheet you set up for the manager, there should not be any error symbols. The cells should either show the sales results by category for the division selected or remain blank.
6. Set up the workbook so that the data you import automatically refreshes each time the manager opens the file.
7. Use formatting techniques to make the worksheet you are setting up for the manager easy to read.
8. Once you set up the workbook, analyze the sales results for each division. Which division is showing the highest year-to-date increase in sales? Are the sales for every category in this division increasing? Which division is showing the highest year-to-date decrease in sales? Are sales for every category in this division decreasing?

## Questions for Discussion

1. How often do business managers analyze data for their business? Identify businesses for which managers would examine data on a frequent basis. How frequently is data available for the businesses you identified?

2. Does having access to data on a minute-by-minute basis improve your ability to make business decisions? Are there situations in which a business manager might prefer to wait a long period of time before making a decision even though data is available on frequent basis? Identify and explain at least one situation in which a business manager might wait before making a decision even though data is available on a continual basis.

# Review Questions

The following questions are related to the concepts addressed in this chapter. There are three types of questions: Short Answer, True or False, and Fill in the Blank. If your answer to a True or False question is False, write a short explanation as to why you think the statement is not true.

1. A file name that ends in a .csv is known as a ________ ________ text file.
2. True or False: Text files that contain data separated into columns are known as fixed-width text files. The columns are established by creating a specific fixed width between the last character of one column and the first character of another.
3. True or False: Once you open a text file in Excel, it automatically becomes an Excel worksheet, which means that any formatting enhancements or calculations can immediately be saved into the file.
4. If the Field Position on the key for a fixed-width file reads 15-30, a break line should be placed on what character number to mark the end of the column?
5. If the Field Position on the key for a fixed-width file reads 25-35, what is the Field Width?
6. You must obtain a ________ before opening a fixed-width file.
7. In the Text Import Wizard, how can you remove a break line once it has been added to the Data preview window?
8. True or False: When opening a fixed-width file, you will usually have to increase the width of each column in an Excel worksheet in order to see the column headings.
9. The ________ ________ icon in the ________ tab of the Ribbon is used to import data from an Access database.
10. True or False: When importing data from an Access database, the Select Table dialog box will show only the tables and queries that are contained in the database selected. No other objects will appear in this dialog box even if they exist in the database.
11. When you import data from an Access database, what properties adjustment should you make if you plan to use formulas in the columns adjacent to the imported data set? Why are these adjustments necessary?
12. Assume you are adding calculations in a column adjacent and to the right of a table that contains imported data. What can you do if you do not want that column to become part of the table?
13. True or False: When you import data from an Access database, the data in your Excel workbook will automatically be updated or refreshed every time you open the file.
14. To instantly update data imported from any external data source in an Excel workbook, you must click the ________ icon in either the ________ or the ________tabs of the Ribbon.
15. True or False: When creating a Web query, you can select one specific value to be imported into an Excel worksheet from an Internet site.
16. If you are importing data from the Internet that updates on a frequent basis, such as streaming stock quotes, what setting would you want to make in the External Data Range Properties dialog box?
17. A ________ will allow you to access an Internet site directly from your Excel worksheet.
18. True or False: When data is imported from a text file, the data will be in the form of a table and the Filter tool will automatically be applied.

# Skills Exam

The following exam is designed to test your ability to recognize and execute the Excel skills presented in this chapter. Read each question carefully and answer the questions in the order they are listed. You should be able to complete this exam in 60 minutes or less.

1. Open the file named ib_e10_chapter10skillsexam.
2. Use the key in the Fixed Width Key worksheet to open the fixed-width file named ib_e10_fixedwidthexam. After this text file is opened, copy the data and paste it into the Item Data worksheet beginning in cell A1.
3. Insert a row above row 1 in the Item Data worksheet and type the designated column headings for this data. Adjust the column widths so that the column headings and the data are visible and format the values in columns E and F to Currency with 2 decimal places. Then, close the ib_e10_fixedwidthexam text file.
4. Import the data in the comma-delimited file named ib_e10_delimitedexam into the Sales Data worksheet beginning with cell A1.
5. Adjust the External Data Range Properties for the data imported into the Sales Data worksheet so that a prompt does *not* appear when the data is refreshed.
6. Import the data from the Component Costs table in the Access database named ib_e10_examdatabase. The data should be imported into the Component Costs worksheet beginning in cell A1.
7. Set the Connection Properties for the Access table imported into the Component Costs worksheet so that the data is refreshed each time the Excel file opened.
8. Remove all formatting enhancements from the table in the Component Costs worksheet. Then, remove the Filter tool.
9. Import the data from the Component Order Quantities query in the ib_e10_examdatabase. The data should be imported into the Material Order Status worksheet beginning with cell A1.
10. Type the column heading **`Target Inventory`** in cell F1. Column F should *not* become part of the table. Then, add a formula into cell F2 that adds the value in cell E2 to cell B2. Copy and paste the formula into the range F3:F24.
11. Adjust the External Data Properties for the table in the Material Order Status worksheet so that the formulas that were added in number 10 do not get corrupted when the data is refreshed.
12. Save and close your file.

# Challenge Questions

The following questions are designed to test your ability to apply the Excel skills you have learned to complete a business objective. Use your knowledge of Excel as well as your creativity to answer these questions. For most questions, there are several possible ways to complete the objective.

1. Assume that you have $10,000 to create a small investment portfolio of stocks and mutual funds. Use Excel to create and track the current value of your investments. Your portfolio must contain at least 5 investments and can be any combination of stocks and mutual funds. Identify a resource on the Internet that can provide ticker symbols for each of your investments as well as current price information. Use Web queries to import the current price information into an Excel workbook so that you can automatically evaluate the status of your portfolio on a daily basis.

2. The Access database named ib_e10_challenge2 contains store sales data by month. Use the data in this database to create a workbook that can be used to analyze the sales by month for each store in this company. Your workbook should contain the following design elements:

   a. The data contained in the Sales Data by Month with Names query should be imported into your workbook. The data should automatically refresh each time the workbook is opened.

   b. The store names should appear in a List Box. When a store is selected, the store name and number should be displayed prominently on a worksheet.

   c. When a store is selected from the List Box, the sales results this year and last year should be displayed on the worksheet by month. The ib_e10_challenge2 database contains data up through the month of May. Set up your worksheet to show either sales values for the months January through May or blank cells. Your design should be able to show sales for future months when the database is updated.

   d. Show the change in sales this year versus last year on your worksheet as well as totals showing the year-to-date sales results for the store that is selected.

   e. Assume that this company might add more stores at a future point in time.

# Macros and VBA

## Goals

You may be familiar with several advanced functions and techniques in Excel. However, you may be in a situation in which more complex or specialized logic is required to compute the results of an analytical project or compile data for a report. In these situations you may need to use Visual Basic for Applications (VBA), which is the programming language used in Excel. This appendix demonstrates how to use VBA in Excel through two main objectives. The first is to review the Macro Recorder. The Macro Recorder is a simple tool for creating programs using the VBA language without having to type out commands. The second is to create a program by typing commands into the Visual Basic Editor.

## Excel | Skill Sets

**Macros**

- Recording a Macro
- Action Buttons
- Editing Action Buttons

**Visual Basic for Applications (VBA)**

- The Visual Basic Editor
- Adding a Procedure to a Module
- Declaring Variables
- Referencing and Assigning Values in Cell Locations
- IF Statements
- For Next Loops
- Running a Program
- Initiating VBA Code through User Events

Skill Set

# Macros

Excel macros provide a way to capture a series of procedures that you can execute automatically. A ***macro*** is a series of steps that are given a name and stored in an Excel workbook. Once a macro is created, the tasks it accomplishes can be run at any time. Macros are useful when you want to quickly run a series of commands, or when you create a workbook that will be used by others. Excel uses Visual Basic for Applications (VBA) as a programming language for storing the macros you create.

A common reason for creating macros is to set up functionality in a workbook that will be used by others. For example, you can store the steps to display a worksheet with a report, and then assign this macro to an action button. Anyone using the workbook will be able to click the button and display the report. A workbook with macros and action buttons is a custom application that meets a specific business requirement. This section will review how Excel macros are recorded and assigned to an action button. You will first learn how to display the **Developer** tab in Excel, which provides the tools you need to create and review macros. After you learn to record a macro using the Macro Recorder, you will use **Design Mode** to add buttons to Excel, and assign macros to these buttons. Figure 1 displays the Menu worksheet where you will add actions buttons to run the macros you will create.

Figure 1 | **The Menu and Category Sales Spreadsheets**

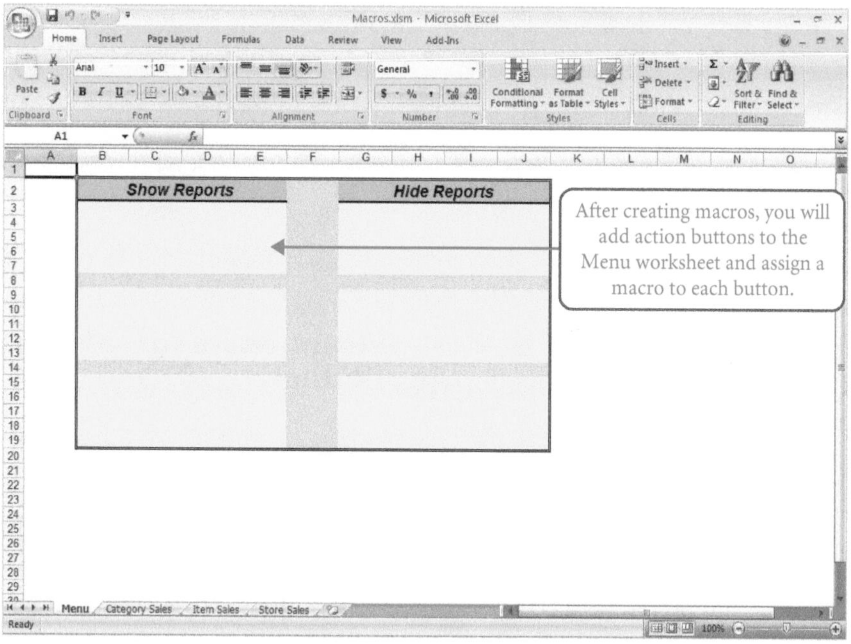

## Recording a Macro

The Excel ***Macro Recorder*** provides the simplest method for creating a macro. Before you create a macro, however, you need to display the **Developer** tab on the Ribbon. Here is how to display the **Developer** tab in the Ribbon:

- Click the **Microsoft Office Button** and then click Excel Options.
- In the **Top** options for working with Excel section, check the option to show the **Developer** tab in the Ribbon, as shown in Figure 2.

Figure 2 | **Displaying the Developer Tab in the Ribbon**

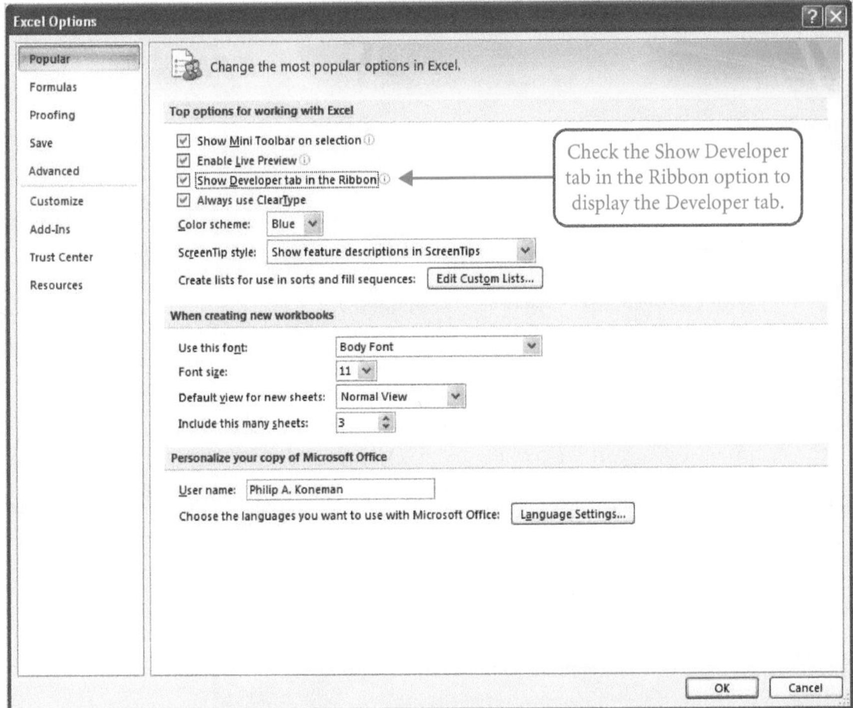


- Click the **OK** button.
- Now click the **Developer** tab to display the groups, command buttons, and tools for working with macros, as shown in Figure 3.

Figure 3 | **Groups, Tools, and Command Buttons Available in the Developer Tab**

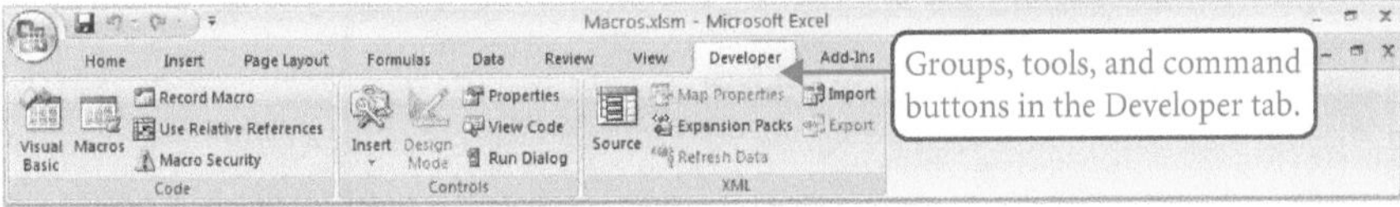


The Menu worksheet you will modify will contain six action buttons. Three of these buttons show a specific report, and three of the buttons hide the same reports. The procedures to show and hide the reports are very similar. Let us use the **CloseCategorySales** and **ShowCategorySales** macros as a way to learn how to create macros. Each macro performs a series of tasks. The first macro hides a worksheet, and the second macro displays the hidden sheet. The following is a brief description for each macro:

**CloseCategorySales**

- Hide the Category Sales worksheet.
- Set the Menu worksheet as the active sheet

**ShowCategorySales**

- Unhide the Category Sales worksheet.
- Set the Category Sales worksheet as the active sheet

  Here is how to capture these tasks in each macro:
- To start the macro recorder, click the **Record Macro** button in the **Developer** tab.

Figure 4 | **Recording a Macro**

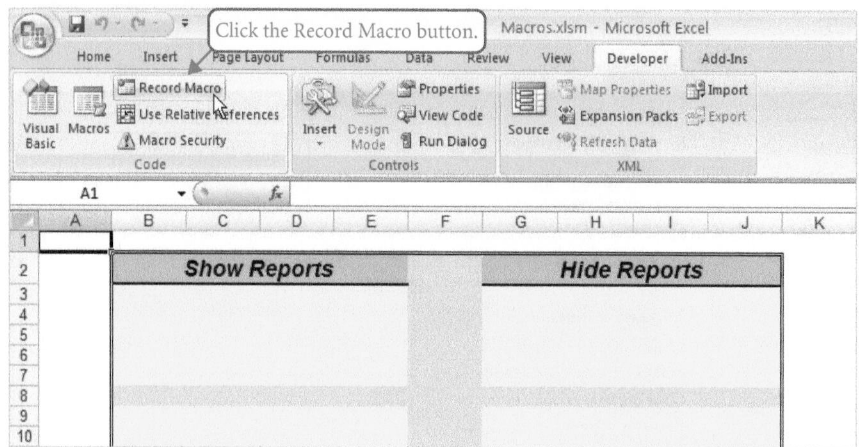


- Excel requires each macro to have a name. Name this macro **CloseCategorySales**. By default, Excel will store the macro in the current workbook.

Figure 5 | **Naming a Macro**

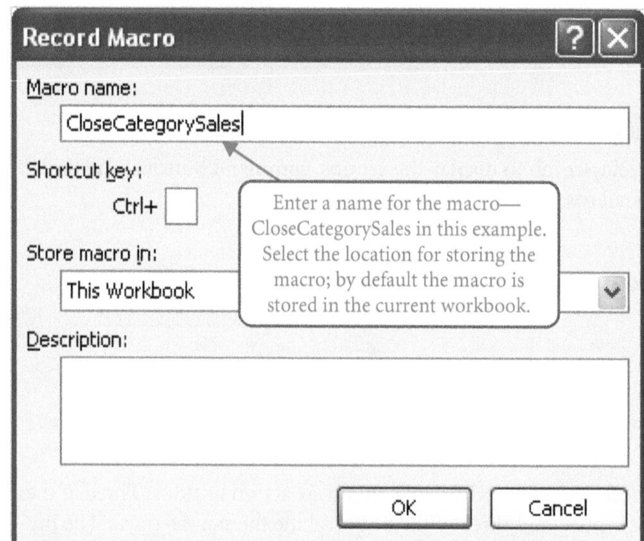


- Once you click **OK**, all the actions you complete are included in the macro, until you click the **Stop Recording** button. The actions we record here include the following:
  - Right-click the **Category Sales** worksheet tab and select **Hide** (see Figure 6).
  - Click the **Menu** worksheet tab (see Figure 7).

Figure 6 | **Hiding a Worksheet**

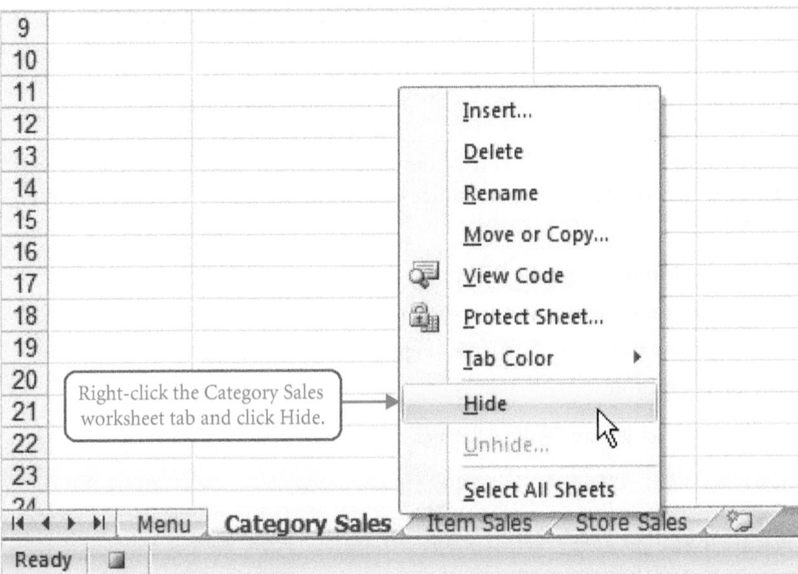


Figure 7 | **Activating a Worksheet**

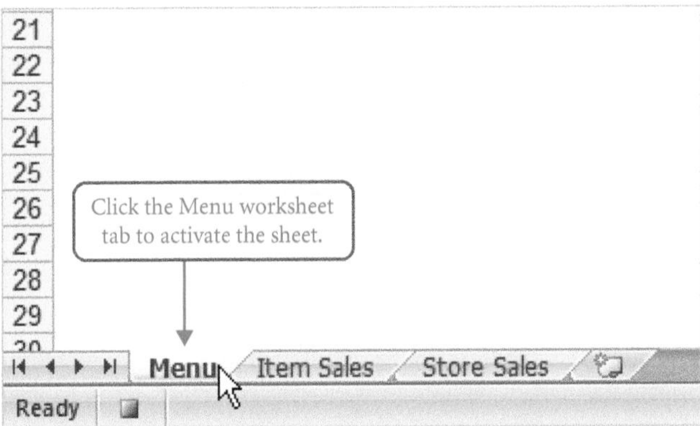


- Click the **Developer** tab, and then click the **Stop Recording** button (see Figure 8).

Figure 8 | **Stop Recording a Macro**

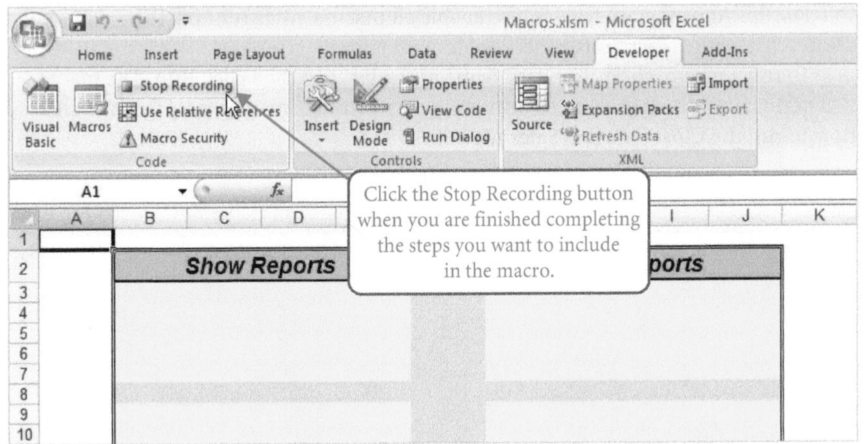

After you have created a macro, you can run the macro by clicking the **Macros** button on the **Developer** tab, or by simply pressing **Alt+F8**. Either method will display the **Macro** dialog box, which lists the macros in the current workbook, all open workbooks, or the filename you select in the drop-down list.

Because it is possible for macros to include malicious code, Excel allows you to manage your macro security settings. Thus, if you receive an Excel workbook as an e-mail attachment and you are not sure of the source, you can disable any macros so that potentially harmful viruses are not unleashed in your computer. To modify your macro settings:

- Click the **Developer** tab in the Ribbon.
- Click the **Macro Security** button in the **Code** group.
- Click the option to enable all macros (Figure 9).
- Click the **OK** button.

Figure 9 | **Trust Center (Macro Security) Settings**

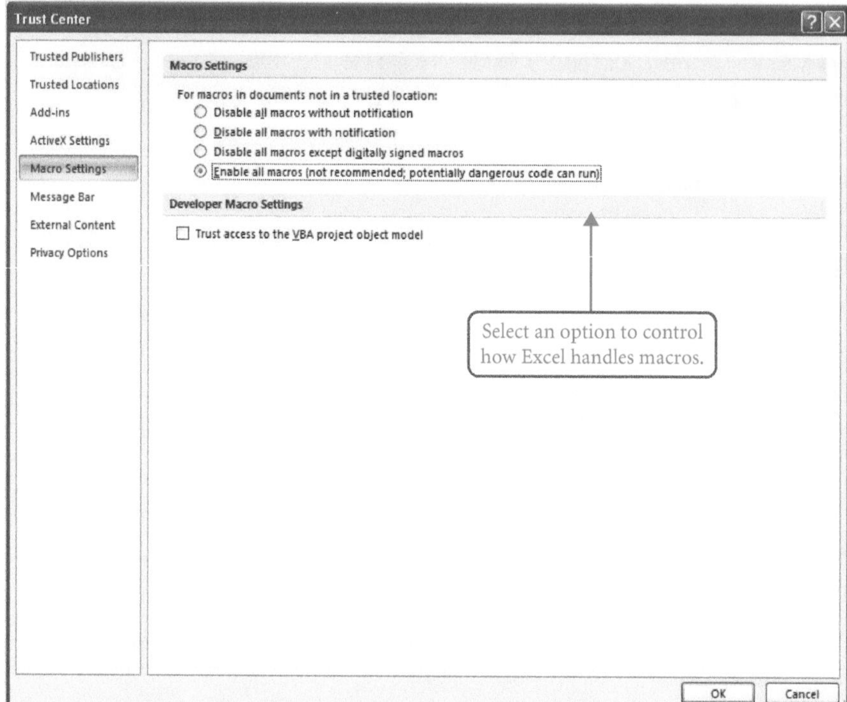


For this Appendix we will elect to enable all macros. After running the macros you create, change the Macro setting to disable all macros.

To run a macro, click the macro name in the list, and then click **Run**. The macro will perform all the steps you performed when the macro was created. Figure 10 shows how to run the **CloseCategorySales** macro.

**» Quick Reference**

**Recording and Running a Macro**

1. Display the **Developer** tab on the Ribbon if it is not visible.
2. In the **Developer** tab, click the **Record Macro** button.
3. Perform the steps you want to include in the macro.
4. Click the **Stop Recording** button in the **Developer** tab.
5. To run the macro, click the **Macros** button in the **Developer** tab, select the macro, and click **Run**.

Figure 10 | **Running a Macro**

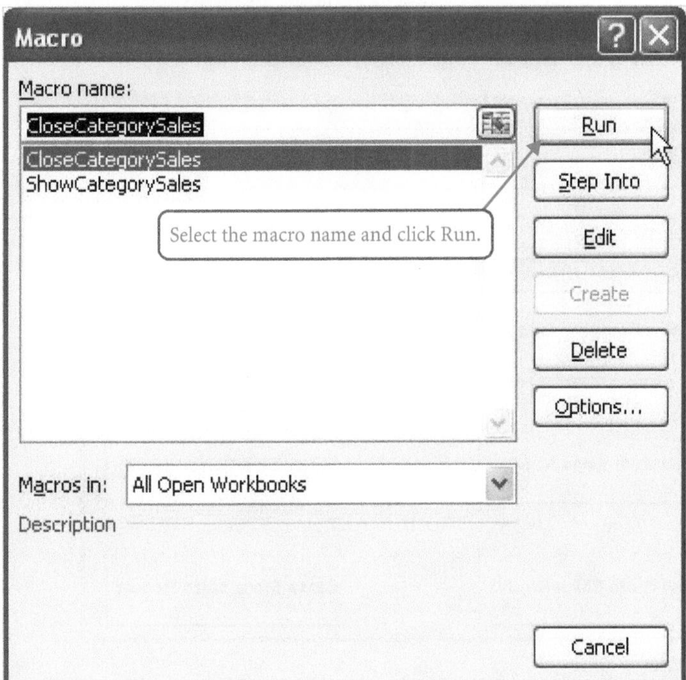


## COMMON MISTAKES | Macro Security

Before running a macro, you must configure your macro settings to allow macros to run. Use the **Macro Security** button in the **Code** group on the **Developer** tab to modify your macro security settings. If you elect to enable all macros, note that Microsoft recommends that you use this setting on a temporary basis only.

## COMMON MISTAKES | Excel Macros

When using the Macro Recorder to create macros, be careful in the steps you complete while recording the macro. Every task is included in the VBA code procedure. Therefore, carefully plan your steps *before* invoking the Macro Recorder.
If your macro contains extra code, you can edit is using the Visual Basic Editor, which you will learn to use later in this Appendix.

## Action Buttons

After you create macros in Excel, you can easily run individual macros using the **Macros** tool on the **Developer** tab. If you have a lot of macros, however, it becomes cumbersome to always use the **Macros** button to run your macros. In Excel you can assign a macro to a shortcut key, a keyboard shortcut, a menu, or an area on an object, button, or other control. An ***action button*** is a Visual Basic control that you can add to a worksheet; you can then assign a macro to the button so that when a user clicks the button, the macro runs. The Menu worksheet shown in Figure 11 contains six action buttons, each with an assigned macro. Clicking any button will run the macro that is assigned to it.

>> ***Quick Reference***

### Creating an Action Button

1. Click the **Developer** tab in the Ribbon.
2. Click the **Insert** drop-down list in the **Controls** group, and then click the **Button** button in the **Forms** group.
3. Drag a button control in the worksheet.
4. Select a macro from the list in the **Assign Macro** dialog box, and click the **OK** button.

Figure 11 | **Worksheet with an Action Button for Running a Macro**

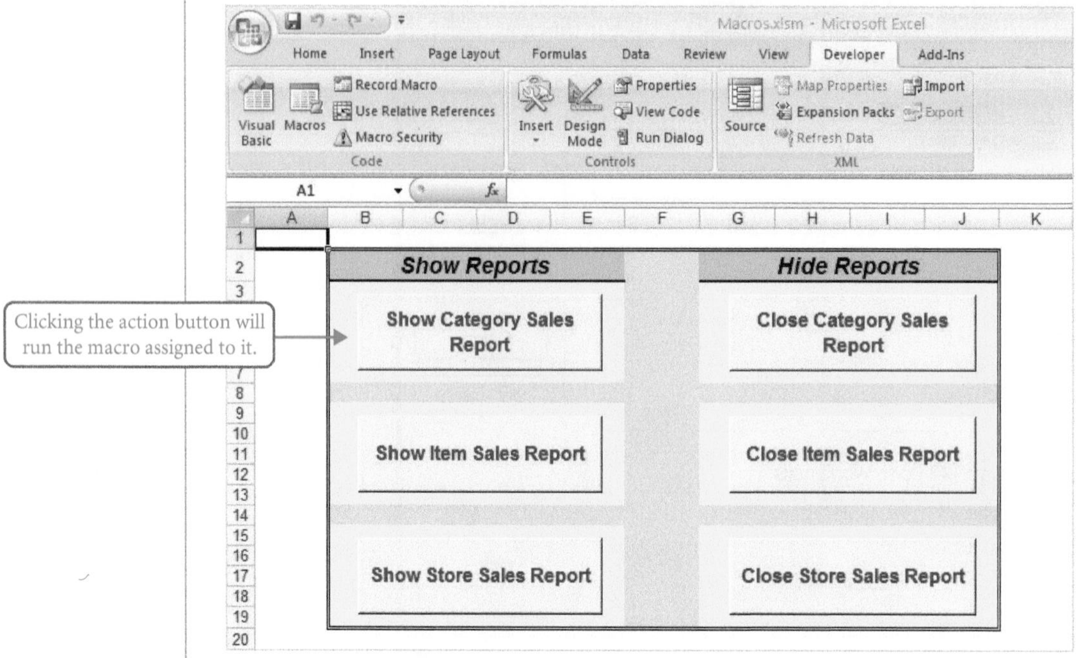

Clicking the action button will run the macro assigned to it.

An action button is one of many types of controls you can add to an Excel workbook. The **Developer** tab contains a **Controls** group with buttons for adding controls. Here is how to create an action button that runs a macro:

- Click the **Developer** tab in the Ribbon.
- Click the **Insert** drop-down list in the **Controls** group, then click the **Button (Form Control)** button in the **Form Controls** group, as shown in Figure 12.

Figure 12 | **Adding a Button to a Worksheet**

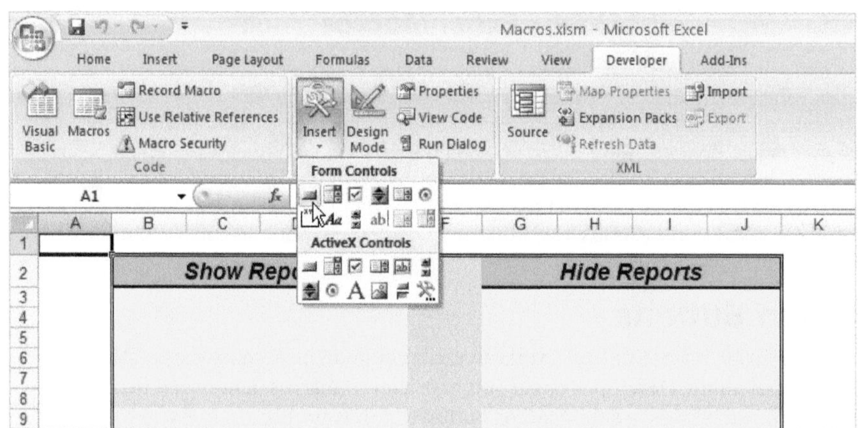


Click and drag the button to create it. When you release the **Left-mouse** button, you will be prompted to assign a macro to the button. Select the **ShowCategorySales** macro and click the **OK** button (see Figure 13).

Figure 13 | **Assigning a Macro to a Button**

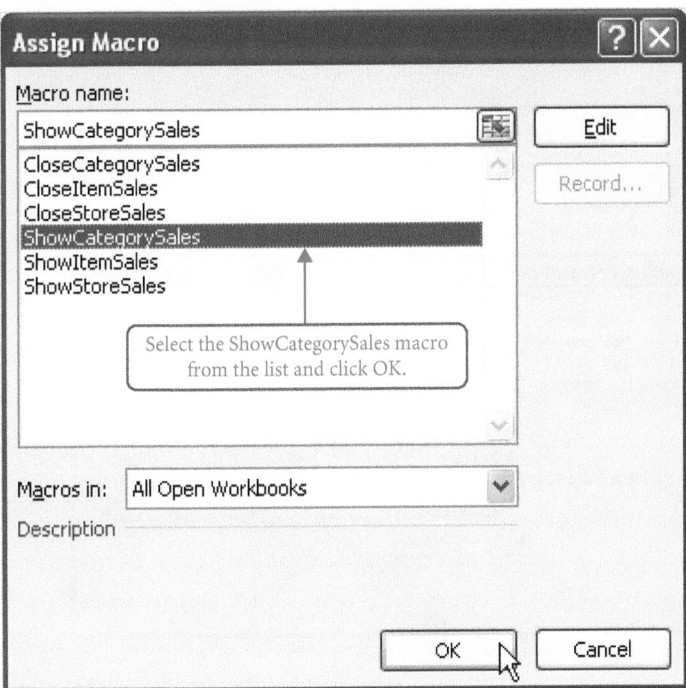


## Editing Action Buttons

When you add an action button to a worksheet, it is given a default name and text style. You can easily edit the text for the button. You can modify the button by right-clicking over the button and selecting an option from the menu. In our example, the button we added to the Menu worksheet contains the text Button 1 by default. We can use the **Edit Text** option to add a descriptive label to the button. For example, changing the text to Show Category Sales is more descriptive of the actions the macro assigned to the button will perform when the button is clicked. The button text should describe the action that occurs when the button is clicked. You can also change the format of the text for the button. Here is how to change and format the text for an action button:

- Right-click the button and then click **Edit Text**, as shown in Figure 14.

**>> Quick Reference**

**Formatting an Action Button**

1. Right-click the action button and click **Edit Text**.
2. Select the existing text, and type the new text.
3. Right-click the action button and click **Exit Edit Text**.
4. Right-click the action button and click **Format Control**.
5. Apply text formats and click the **OK** button.

Figure 14 | **Changing the Text for an Action Button**

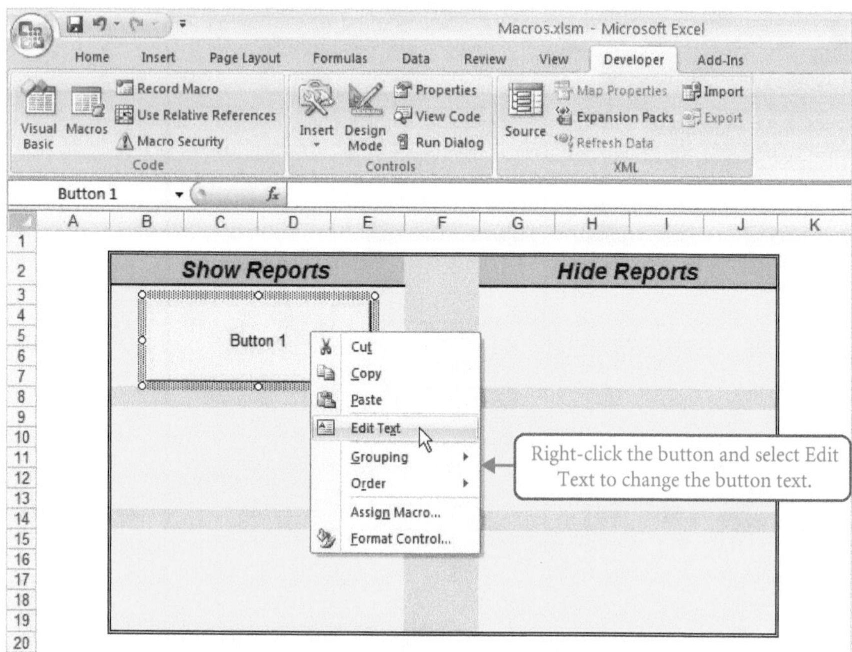


- Highlight the current caption (Button 1) and type **Show Category Sales Report.**
- Right-click the button and click **Exit Edit Text.**
- To change the text format, right-click the button and click **Format Control**, as shown in Figure 15.

Figure 15 | **Formatting the Text for an Action Button**

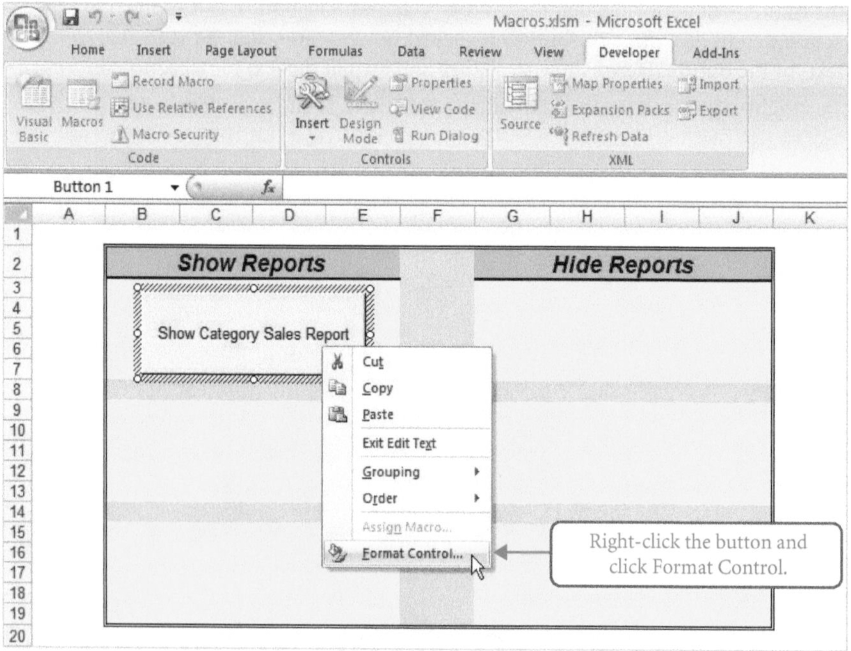

- Change the formats in the **Format Control** dialog box. In this example, the text is Arial, 14 point, Bold, Blue. Click **OK**, as shown in Figure 16.

Figure 16 | **Changing the Format for an Action Button**

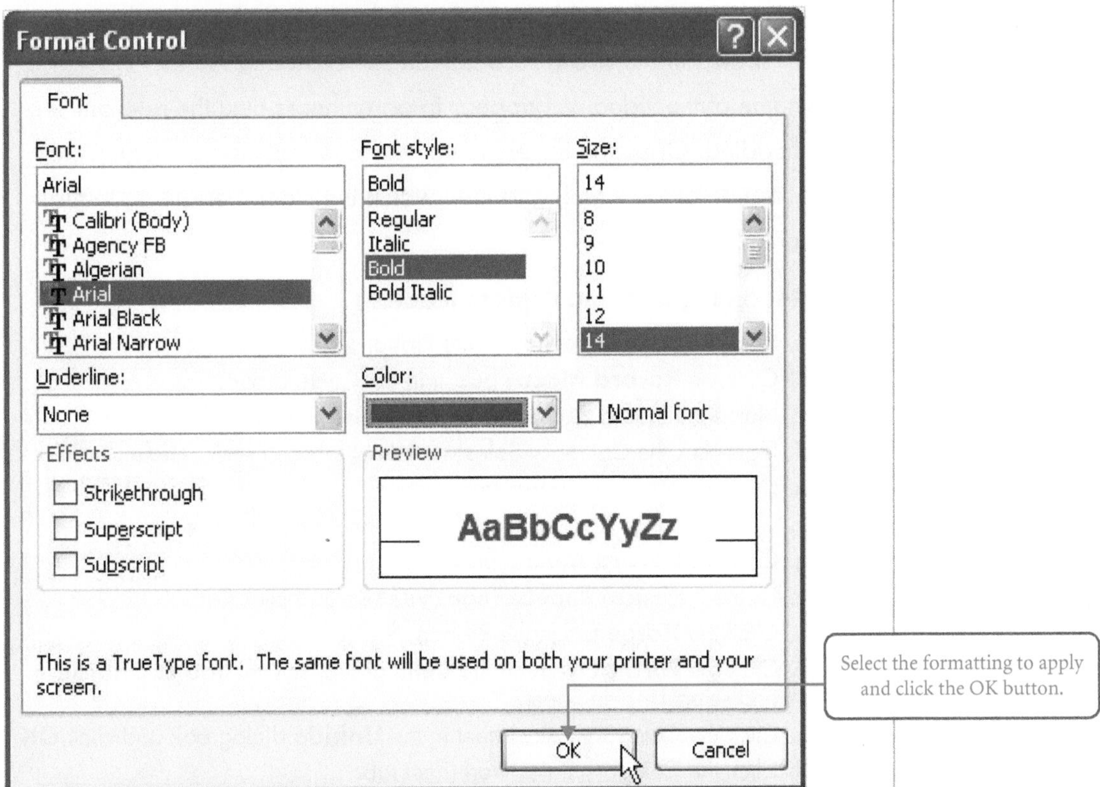

# Macros

The purpose of this workshop is to demonstrate how to create and use Macros. The Excel file that will be used in this workshop is identical to the one shown in Figure 1. You will see the tasks in this workshop demonstrated in the two videos named **Macros** and **Action Buttons**. The name of the video will appear in parentheses next the relevant section heading. Open the Excel file named ib_eapp_macros. Complete each section of tasks first, and then watch the video pertaining to that section.

1. **Recording a Macro (Video: Macros)**
   a. Click the **Developer** tab in the Ribbon.
   b. Click the **Record Macro** button in the **Code** group.
   c. Name the macro **`CloseCategorySales`** and click **OK**.
   d. Right-click the Category Sales worksheet tab and select **Hide**.
   e. Click the Menu worksheet tab.
   f. Click the **Stop Recording** button in the **Code** group.
   g. Click the **Record Macro** button.
   h. Name the macro **`ShowCategorySales`** and click **OK**.
   i. Click the **Home** tab in the Ribbon.
   j. Click the **Format** menu in the **Cells** group, select **Hide & Unhide**, and select Unhide Sheet.
   k. Click the Category Sales sheet in the **Unhide** dialog box and click **OK**.
   l. Click the Category Sales worksheet tab.
   m. Click the **Stop Recording** button in the **Code** group on the Developer tab of the Ribbon.
   n. Repeat steps b through f above to create a macro named **`CloseItemSales`**. This macro will hide the Item Sales worksheet.
   o. Repeat steps g through m above to create a macro named **`ShowItemSales`**. This macro will show the Item Sales worksheet. Make sure you click the Item Sales worksheet tab in letter l.
   p. Repeat steps b through f above to create a macro named **`CloseStoreSales`**. This macro will hide the Store Sales worksheet.
   q. Repeat steps g through m above to create a macro named **`ShowStoreSales`**. This macro will show the Store Sales worksheet. Make sure you click the Store Sales worksheet tab in letter l.

2. **Assigning Macros to Action Buttons (Video: Action Buttons)**
   a. Click the Menu worksheet tab.
   b. Click the **Developer** button in the Ribbon.
   c. Click the Insert drop-down list in the **Controls** group and select a Button in the Form Controls section.
   d. Create a button within the range B3:E7.
   e. Select the ShowCategorySales macro in the **Assign Macro** dialog box and click **OK**.

f. Click the button and remove the existing text. Then, type Show Category Sales on the button and click any cell on the worksheet to activate the button.
g. Select the existing text and type **Show Category Sales** as the new text.
h. Right-click the button and select click Format Control. Change the font size to 14, the font style to Bold, and the color to Blue. Click **OK**.
i. Create a button in the area of B9:E13 that runs the ShowItemSales macro. Change the text of the button to Show Item Sales and use the same formatting as in the Show Category Sales button.
j. Create a button in the area of B15:E19 that runs the ShowStoreSales macro. Change the text of the button to Show Store Sales and use the same formatting as in the Show Category Sales button.
k. Create a button in the area of G3:J7 that runs the CloseCategorySales macro. Change the text of the button to Close Category Sales and use the same formatting as in the Show Category Sales button.
l. Create a button in the area of G9:J13 that runs the CloseItemSales macro. Change the text of the button to Close Item Sales and use the same formatting as in the Show Category Sales button.
m. Create a button in the area of G15:J19 that runs the CloseStoreSales macro. Change the text of the button to Close Store Sales and use the same formatting as in the Show Category Sales button.
n. Save and close your file.

## >> Visual Basic for Applications (VBA)

Skill Set

In the previous section you learned how to create Excel macros and assign the macros to action buttons. When you create a macro, Excel stores the macro steps in a programming language called ***Visual Basic for Applications***, or VBA. When Excel creates the macro, it adds a code module to the workbook. This code module contains all of the program code required to run the macro. Because VBA is a programming language, you can modify the code statements to attach additional functionality to the workbook. So how do you view and modify the code statements? All VBA programming code is accessed using the ***Visual Basic Editor***. In this section you will learn how to open the Visual Basic Editor, and then apply your Excel skills to use VBA to produce and display an exception report.

The report your procedures will display lists sales exceptions, those inventory items from the Sales Data worksheet that exceed five weeks. Figure 17 displays the report worksheet with inventory items meeting this criterion.

Figure 17 | **Exception Report Results**

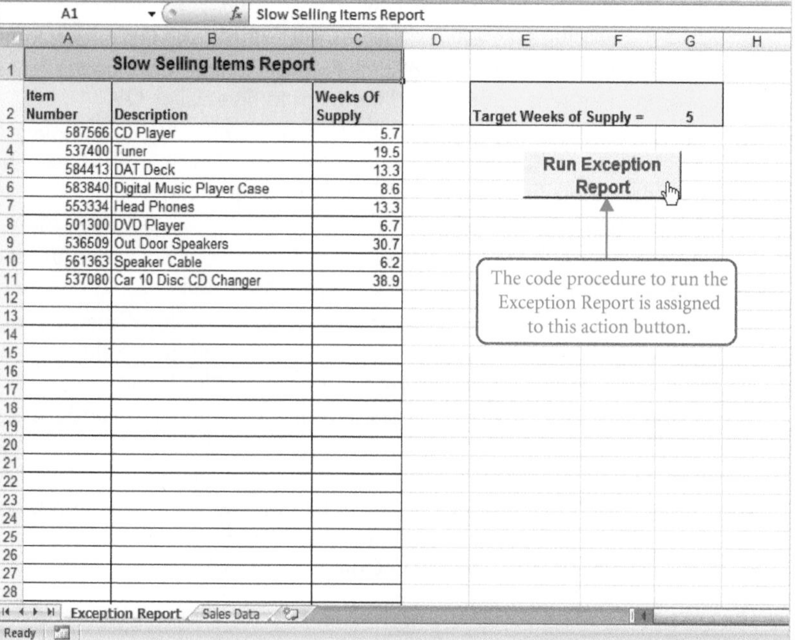


## The Visual Basic Editor

You can open the Visual Basic Editor in two ways: by clicking the **Visual Basic** button in the **Code** group of the **Developer** tab in the Ribbon, or by pressing **Alt+F11**. The Visual Basic Editor consists of two sections. The leftmost pane displays the objects and modules contained in any workbooks that are currently open. The right section is a text editor that displays the code for the object or module that is selected in the left pane. Figure 18 shows the macros you created previously as they appear in the Visual Basic Editor.

Figure 18 | **The Visual Basic Editor**

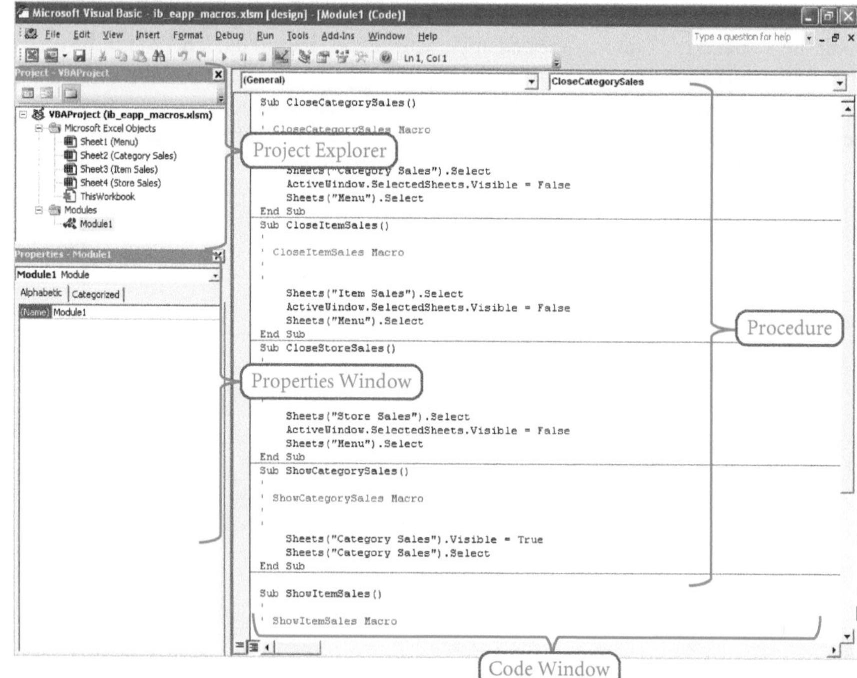

Let us review the components of the Visual Basic Editor. The left side of the editor displays two windows. The uppermost is the Project Explorer. This window displays the objects in the current worksheet. Objects include the workbook itself and any worksheets it contains. You can add code to any of the objects or to a code module. The lower left window is the Properties Window, which displays the properties of the selected object. You can use the Project Explorer to expand and collapse the list of objects displayed. The Project Explorer shown here displays the ib_eapp.macros workbook, Sheet1 through Sheet4, and Module1.

All VBA code is contained within a module. When you record a macro using the Macro Recorder, Excel creates a module (named Module1 by default) that contains the program code, which is displayed in the Code Window. The code for the macros you created is contained in Module1. You can also organize your code by incorporating additional modules into the project.

When you create or modify VBA code statements using the Visual Basic Editor, you are working in design time. When a procedure runs, Excel executes the statements in runtime.

To add a module to a workbook, launch the Visual Basic Editor, click the **Insert Menu**, and then click **Module**. The module will appear in the Project Explorer.

## Adding a Procedure to a Module

All VBA code is contained in procedures. VBA supports different kinds of procedures. The most basic kind of procedure is a sub procedure, which is a procedure that performs an action. The procedures you will create in this section are sub procedures.

All procedures are either public or private. A public procedure is available to any object in an application. A private procedure is available only to a specific object or module. Procedures are public by default, unless the procedure is associated with a specific event, such as clicking a button.

Sub procedures begin with a Sub statement, and conclude with End Sub. By default, sub procedures are public. You can add a procedure to a module by typing the Sub statement, naming the procedure, and ending the procedure with an End Sub statement. The code statements you create at design time define the actions that are executed when the procedure runs. You can add comments to your procedures to document the purpose of the statements; a VBA comment is any test preceded by an apostrophe character. As you type the code statements, any errors are highlighted in red. You will need to correct these before you can save the procedure. You can save a procedure by clicking the **Save** button on the Standard toolbar, or by clicking **File, Save.** Once you create a sub procedure, you can run the procedure by placing the insertion point within the procedure, then either clicking the **Run** button on the Visual Basic Editor Toolbar or pressing F5. To close the Editor, click the **Close** button in the upper right corner, or click **File, Close** and **Return to Microsoft Excel.**

Let us look at a simple example. Figure 19 shows the code statements for a sub procedure that uses the message box function to display a message on the screen. The figure also shows how the message box appears when the procedure runs.

> **Quick Reference**
>
> **Displaying the Visual Basic Editor and Adding Procedures**
>
> 1. Click the **Visual Basic** icon in the **Developer** tab of the Ribbon.
> 2. Click the **Insert** Menu, and then click **Module**.
> 3. To add a procedure, type Sub, the name of the procedure and press **ENTER**.
> 4. Type the Code Statements for the procedure.
> 5. Click the **Save** button to save the procedure.

Figure 19 | **A Simple Sub Procedure**

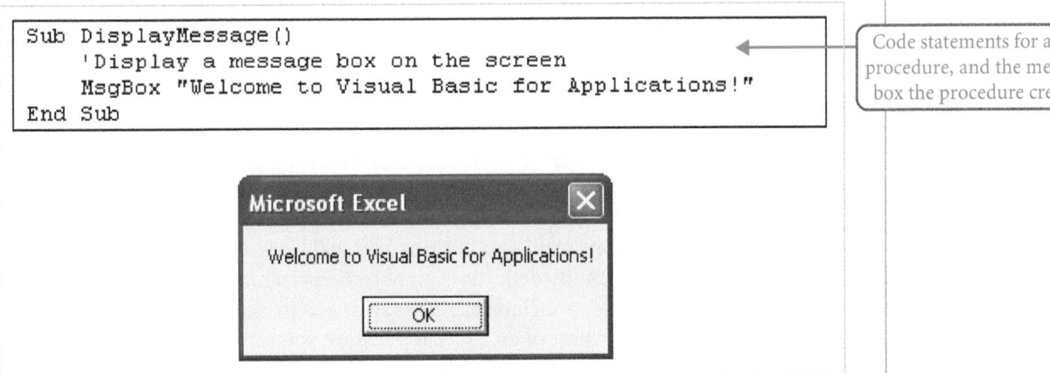

Sub DisplayMessage()
'Display a message box on the screen
MsgBox "Welcome to Visual Basic for Applications!"
End Sub
Microsoft Excel
Welcome to Visual Basic for Applications!
OK


Code statements for a sub procedure, and the message box the procedure creates

This is a very brief introduction to using the Visual Basic Editor. Now let us learn about the kind of code statements you will need for the Exception Report.

> **Quick Reference**
>
> **Declaring Variables and Assigning Values**
>
> 1. Click the **Visual Basic** icon in the **Developer** tab of the Ribbon.
> 2. Double-click the module that will contain the variable declaration.
> 3. Place the insertion point within a sub procedure that requires a variable.
> 4. Type the Dim statement, the variable name, and the data type.
> 5. Assign a value to the variable as needed.
> 6. Click the **Save** button to save the procedure.

## Declaring Variables

The Exception Report you will create requires three variables. Variables are basic elements in every programming language. A ***variable*** stores a value that can change and be retrieved while the application is running. Variables store values in memory, and the value can be changed at any time during program execution. Because variables are stored in memory, a value for a variable exists only while a program is running. A code statement can initialize the value of a variable in program code and then change the value as necessary.

A variable has a name, which is the word you use to refer to the value the variable contains. A variable also has a data type, which determines the kind of data the variable can store. Because each data type has different memory requirements, you can conserve computer memory and have your application run faster by carefully selecting the most appropriate data type for the kind of data your application needs to store. Some variables store text, and others store dates and numbers.

To declare a variable, type the ***Dim statement*** (Dim stands for *dimension*) and then enter the name and data type for the variable. You must use a letter as the first character for a variable name.

### COMMON MISTAKES | Naming Variables

Here are some guidelines for naming variables to help you avoid making common mistakes:

- You cannot use a space, period, exclamation mark, or the characters @, &, $, # in a variable name
- A variable name cannot exceed 255 characters in length.
- Most programmers prefer descriptive names that tell the purpose of a variable or constant and the kind of data it contains
- A standard or rule for naming variables or constants is to begin the name with the first three characters indicating the data type (in lower case), and the remainder specifying the variable's purpose (beginning with an upper-case letter).

In the Exception Report code statements, the Dim statement declares each variable. Once a variable is declared, you can assign a value by typing the variable name and assigning a value. Figure 20 displays the code statements that define the variables required to run the Exception Report.

Figure 20 | **Variable Declaration for the Exception Report Variables**

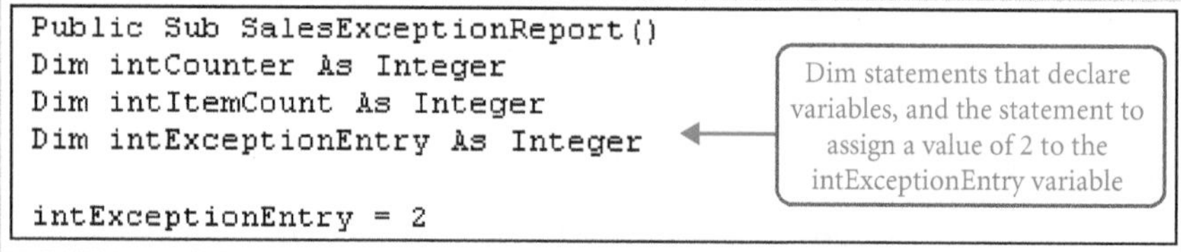

```
Public Sub SalesExceptionReport()
Dim intCounter As Integer
Dim intItemCount As Integer
Dim intExceptionEntry As Integer

intExceptionEntry = 2
```

Dim statements that declare variables, and the statement to assign a value of 2 to the intExceptionEntry variable

> **Quick Reference**
>
> **Referencing and Assigning Cell Values to a Variable**
>
> 1. Click the **Visual Basic** icon in the **Developer** tab of the Ribbon.
> 2. Double-click the module that contains the sub procedure that will reference the cell.
> 3. Place the insertion point within a sub procedure that requires a reference.
> 4. Type the code statement or statements.
> 5. Click the **Save** button to save the procedure.

## Referencing and Assigning Values in Cell Locations

When you develop custom Excel applications, you will work with numerous objects. Objects are central to VBA. By definition, an ***object*** represents an element of the host application. In Excel, objects include elements such as a worksheet, a cell, a range, or a chart, to name a few. Any part of an Excel application you can identify as a thing and therefore reference with a noun is an object. You can reference objects in code.

A common object is a cell. A cell belongs to a worksheet, which belongs to a workbook; each of these is an object, in an object hierarchy. When you reference objects in code, the elements in the hierarchy are separated by a period character. For example, here is a reference to cell A1 in Sheet1 of Book1:

```
Workbooks("Book1.xls").Worksheets("Sheet1").Range("A1")
```

You can reference a specific cell by listing all objects in the object hierarchy. Figure 21 shows code statements from the Exception Report that assigns the value in a cell to a variable.

Figure 21 | **Referencing Cells in Code**

```
intItemCount = Worksheets("Sales Data").Range("J2")
```

The Exception Report includes other code statements that reference specific cells. Make sure your statements include all objects in the object hierarchy.

## IF Statements

When you write procedures in VBA, your code conforms to a specific programming structure. A ***programming structure*** is the sequence in which the program statements are executed at run time. Programmers use programming structures to organize code. Program statements are organized in one of three ways: by using a sequence structure, a decision structure, or a repetition structure. All of the sub procedures you have seen up to this point use the sequence structure because the program statements are executed in sequence when the procedure is run. Sequence structures are the simplest programming structures.

A ***decision structure*** is a programming structure that makes a comparison between program statements. Based on the result of that comparison, the program executes statements in a certain order. Programmers use the ***If statement*** to create a simple decision structure. If the result of the comparison is true (or yes), one statement executes, but if the result of the comparison is false (or no), an alternative statement executes. Thus the result of the comparison determines which path the program takes. Figure 22 shows an IF statement that is contained in the code for the Exception Report.

>> **Quick Reference**

**Using the IF Statement**

1. Click the **Visual Basic** icon in the **Developer** tab of the Ribbon.
2. Double-click the module that contains the procedure that will contain the IF statement.
3. Type the IF keyword and the logical test, and then type the THEN keyword and press **Enter**.
4. Enter a statement for the result if the logical test evaluates to True.
5. Click the **Save** button to save the procedure.

Figure 22 | **If Statement in Code**

```
For intCounter = 1 To intItemCount
      If Worksheets("Sales Data").Cells(intCounter + 2, 6) >
         Worksheets("Exception Report").Range("G2") Then
intExceptionEntry = intExceptionEntry + 1
```

If statement that compares the value of two cells, and increments the intExceptionEntry variable by 1 if when the condition is True

The IF statement has a simple syntax:

- IF [Logical Test] Then
- Result if the logical test evaluates to True

This statement shown in Figure 22 is more complex than the previous examples. The IF statement is nested within a For Next loop, which you will learn about in the next segment. The loop compares each value for the weeks of supply for each inventory item listed in the **Sales Data** worksheet to the value in cell G2 of the **Exception Report** worksheet (this is the logical test). If the value of exceeds 5, the counter for the number of items listed in the Exception Report is increased by 1 (this is the result if the logical test evaluates to True).

## For Next Loops

Other program structures require an operation to be completed a specific number of times while a certain condition is true or until a condition is true. To handle these cases, programmers use repetition structures, also called loops. A ***repetition structure*** repeats the execution of a series of program statements. The ***For Next loop*** is an example of a repetition structure. The For Next statement requires a counter, which is an integer variable that determines the number of times the statement will repeat. Figure 23 displays the For Next loop that is contained in the code statements for the Exception Report.

Figure 23 | **For Next Loop in Code**

For Next loop with a nested If Then Else statement

```
For intCounter = 1 To intItemCount
If Worksheets("Sales Data").Cells(intCounter + 2, 6) >
Worksheets("Exception Report").Range("G2") Then
intExceptionEntry = intExceptionEntry + 1
Worksheets("Exception Report").Cells(intExceptionEntry, 1).Value =
Worksheets("Sales Data").Cells(intCounter + 2, 1)
Worksheets("Exception Report").Cells(intExceptionEntry, 2).Value =
Worksheets("Sales Data").Cells(intCounter + 2, 2)
Worksheets("Exception Report").Cells(intExceptionEntry, 3).Value =
Worksheets("Sales Data").Cells(intCounter + 2, 6)
Else: End If
Next intCounter
```

>> Quick Reference

**Using the For Next loop**

1. Click the **Visual Basic** icon in the **Developer** tab of the Ribbon.
2. Double-click the module that contains the sub procedure that will contain the loop.
3. Type the **For** keyword and set the counter for the loop.
4. Enter one or more statements that are processed within the loop.
5. Enter the **Next** keyword, followed with a reference to the counter variable.
6. Click the **Save** button to save the procedure.

This example is also more complex than the earlier examples, because as noted in the previous section, an IF Statement is nested within the loop. To be more precise, the nested statement is an If. . . Then. . . Else statement. This repetition structure executes the loop repeatedly until all inventory rows (specified by the **intItemCount** variable) are read. Nested within the loop is the If Then Else statement, which determines whether the **Weeks of Supply** value for the inventory item exceeds the value in cell G2 of the **Exception Report** worksheet. If the test evaluates to true (the **Weeks of Supply** entry exceeds 5), the **intExceptionEntry** variable is increased by 1, and data in columns 1, 2, and 6 for each row in the Sales Data worksheet are copied to columns 1, 2, and 3 of the **Exception Report** worksheet. If the value is less than 5, the Else statement ends the logical test, and the next iteration of the loop processes until all rows are evaluated. Review the code statements so you understand the logic for the loop.

## Running a Program

When you have finished entering procedures in the Visual Basic Editor, you can test them by placing the insertion point within a procedure, and clicking the **Run** button on the Standard Toolbar in the Visual Basic Editor. If there are any errors in your code, the editor will pause and highlight the line containing the error. You can correct the error and click the **Resume** button to finish running the procedure.

When you run a procedure from within the Visual Basic Editor, you typically do not see the results. You can click the Workbook icon on the Windows Taskbar to return to Excel and verify that the procedure is performing as expected.

>> Quick Reference

**Running a Procedure**

1. Click the **Visual Basic** icon in the **Developer** tab of the Ribbon.
2. Double-click the module that contains the procedure to run.
3. Place the insertion point inside a code procedure.
4. Click the **Run** button on the **Standard** toolbar in the editor.

## Initiating VBA Code through User Events

The procedures we have discussed up to this point provide examples of performing individual tasks such as displaying messages, declaring variables, and manipulating data in worksheet cells. When you begin using VBA to customize Excel workbooks, you might think of adding functionality to your workbook solutions. However, as VBA opens the door to great possibilities, and rather than thinking of your workbooks as mere documents, begin thinking of them as applications. Applications often require a beginning state, meaning that when the application launches, there is a consistent presentation of the workspace. For example, when you launch Excel, you are presented with a new workbook containing three worksheets, and the insertion point is placed in cell A1 of Sheet1. Opening and closing a workbook are user events, as are actions such as clicking command buttons. You can write VBA procedures that will place your workbook application in a predictable state when a user opens or closes the workbook.

The events that trigger specific procedures in the Exception Report are the Open event and the Close event. Figure 24 shows the statements contained in each procedure.

Figure 24 | **Code Statements Associated with the Open and Close Events**

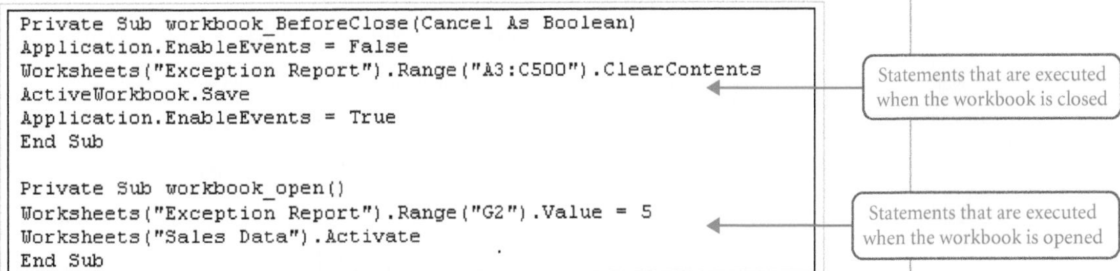

```
Private Sub workbook_BeforeClose(Cancel As Boolean)
Application.EnableEvents = False
Worksheets("Exception Report").Range("A3:C500").ClearContents
ActiveWorkbook.Save
Application.EnableEvents = True
End Sub

Private Sub workbook_open()
Worksheets("Exception Report").Range("G2").Value = 5
Worksheets("Sales Data").Activate
End Sub
```

Statements that are executed when the workbook is closed
Statements that are executed when the workbook is opened

Before the workbook closes, the Exception Report is cleared and the workbook is saved. When the workbook is opened, the exception value is set to 5, and the Sales Data worksheet is set as the active sheet.

Another example of user events are button clicks. In the first section of this Appendix you learned how to insert a button into a worksheet and assign a macro to the button. This provides an easy method for creating a menu page with buttons that run the macros you create.

There are two kinds of buttons available in the **Developer** tab in the Ribbon: a Button, which belongs to the **Form Controls** group, and a Command Button, which belongs to the **ActiveX Controls** group.

In general, the controls in the **Form Controls** group are more limited than ActiveX controls. You can change the format of Form Controls, assign macros, and edit the control text. There is no code you can access and modify that is associated with a Form Control. With ActiveX controls you can access all the properties and methods for the control, and the code. When you become more proficient using VBA, ActiveX controls will provide more capabilities for customizing your applications and launching events.

To run the Exception Report, you will add an action button to the worksheet and then assign the SalesExceptionReport procedure to the button. The procedure is listed in the **Assign Macro** dialog box, as shown in Figure 25.

Figure 25 | **Assigning the SalesExceptionReport Procedure to an Action Button**

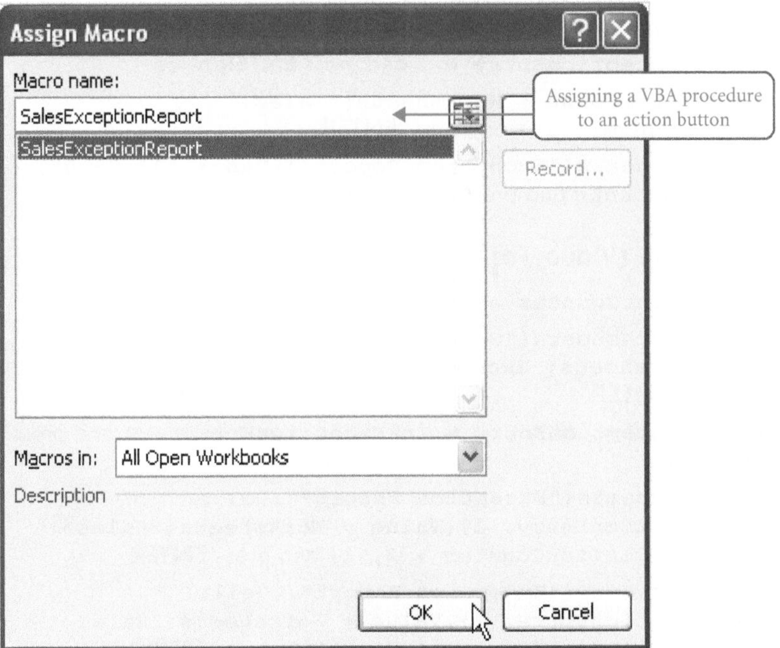

Assign Macro
Macro name:
SalesExceptionReport
SalesExceptionReport
Record...
Macros in:
All Open Workbooks
Description
OK
Cancel
Assigning a VBA procedure to an action button

**VIDEO WORKSHOP**

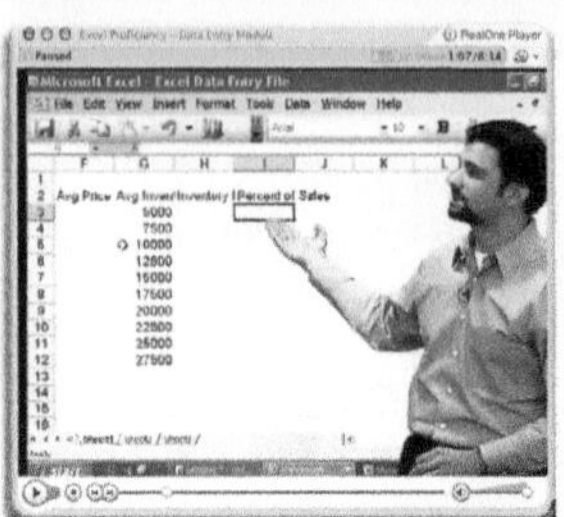

# VBA

The purpose of this workshop is to demonstrate the construction of an exception report using VBA code. You will see the tasks in this workshop demonstrated in the following six videos: **Visual Basic Editor**, **Adding a Procedure and Defining Variables**, **Content in Cell Locations**, **For Next Loops and IF Statements**, **Running a Program**, and **User Events**. The video related to each section will appear in parentheses next to the section heading. Open the Excel file named ib_eapp_vba. Complete the tasks for each section below first, and then watch the video pertaining to the section you completed.

**1. Starting a New Program (Video: Visual Basic Editor)**

a. Click the **Developer** tab in the Ribbon.
b. Click the **Visual Basic** button to launch the Visual Basic Editor.
c. Click the **Insert** menu and select Module.
d. Click the **Save** button on the Standard Toolbar to save the module.

**2. Subroutines and Defining Variables (Video: Adding a Procedure and Defining Variables)**

a. Click Module1 in the Visual Basic Editor if it is not currently selected.
b. Place the Insertion Point in the **Code** window.
c. Type `Public Sub SalesExceptionReport()` and press **ENTER**.
d. Type `Dim intCounter As Integer` and press **ENTER**.
e. Type `Dim intItemCount As Integer` and press **ENTER**.
f. Type `Dim intExceptionEntry As Integer` and press **ENTER** twice.

**3. Referencing Cell Locations (Video: Content in Cell Locations)**

a. Type `intExceptionEntry = 2` and press **ENTER** twice.
b. Type `intItemCount = Worksheets("Sales Data").Range("J2")` and press **ENTER**.
c. Type `Worksheets("Exception Report").Range("A3:C500") .ClearContents` and press **ENTER** twice.

**4. For Next Loop (Video: For Next Loops and IF Statements)**

a. Type `For intCounter = 1 to intItemCount` and press **ENTER**.
b. Type `If Worksheets("Sales Data").Cells(intCounter + 2, 6) > Worksheets("Exception Report").Range("G2") Then` and press **ENTER**.
c. Type `intExceptionEntry = intExceptionEntry + 1` and press **ENTER**.
d. Type `Worksheets("Exception Report").Cells (intExceptionEntry, 1).Value = Worksheets("Sales Data").Cells(intCounter + 2, 1)` and press **ENTER**.
e. Type `Worksheets("Exception Report").Cells (intExceptionEntry, 2).Value = Worksheets("Sales Data").Cells(intCounter + 2, 2)` and press **ENTER**.

f. Type **Worksheets("Exception Report").Cells(intExceptionEntry, 3).Value = Worksheets("Sales Data").Cells(intCounter + 2, 6)** and press **ENTER**.
g. Type **Else: End If** and press **ENTER**.
h. Type **Next intCounter** and press **ENTER**.
i. Click the **Save** button on the Standard Toolbar in the Visual Basic Editor to save your work.

5. **Running the Program (Video: Running a Program)**
   a. Place the Insertion Point inside the procedure you just created.
   b. Click the **Run** button on the Standard Toolbar in the Visual Basic Editor.
   c. Click the ib_eapp_vba.XLSM button on the Windows Taskbar to switch to Excel. Verify that the Exception Report returns nine inventory items, each with a Weeks of Supply value of 5 or more.

6. **User Events (Video: User Events)**
   a. Click the **Microsoft Visual Basic** button on the Windows Taskbar to display the Visual Basic Editor.
   b. Double-click the This Workbook object in the Project Explorer to open the **Code** window for the current workbook.
   c. With the Insertion Point at the top of the Code window, type **Private Sub Workbook_BeforeClose(Cancel As Boolean)** and press **ENTER** twice.
   d. Type **Application.EnableEvents = False** and press **ENTER**.
   e. Type **Worksheets("Exception Report").Range("A3:C500").ClearContents** and press **ENTER**.
   f. Type **ActiveWorkbook.Save** and press **ENTER**.
   g. Type **Application.EnableEvents = True**.
   h. Place the Insertion Point after the End Sub statement and press **ENTER**.
   i. Type **Private Sub Workbook_Open()** and press **ENTER**.
   j. Type **Worksheets("Exception Report").Range("G2").Value = 5** and press **ENTER**.
   k. Type **Worksheets("Sales Data").Activate**.
   l. Click the **Save** button on the Standard Toolbar in the Visual Basic Editor to save your work.
   m. Close the Visual Basic Editor.
   n. Click the Exception Report worksheet tab to make it the active sheet.
   o. Click the **Insert** icon in the **Controls** group on the **Developer** tab and add a Button from the **From Controls** group. Drag the button starting in cell E4.
   p. Assign the SalesExceptionReport macro to the button.
   q. Change the text of the button to **Run Exception Report**.
   r. Change the format of the text to Arial, Bold, 12, Blue.
   s. Save your workbook.
   t. Click the button to run the macro. Verify that nine inventory items exceeding 5 weeks of supply are added to the report.

# EXCEL Quick Reference Guide

### Absolute Reference

1. Identify a cell reference within a formula or function that requires an absolute reference or mixed reference.
2. Type a dollar sign in front of the column letter and row number of a cell reference to apply an absolute reference.
3. Type a dollar sign in front of the column letter or row number to apply a mixed reference.

### Accounting Format

1. Highlight a range of cells to be formatted.
2. Click the **Home** tab of the Ribbon.
3. Click the **Accounting Number Format** icon [$ ▾]. Click the down arrow next to this icon to change the currency symbol.
4. Click the **Increase** or **Decrease Decimal** icons and as needed.

### Adding and Removing Report Totals

1. Click anywhere in the PivotTable Report to activate the **PivotTable Tools** tabs on the Ribbon.
2. Click the **Options** icon in the **Options** tab of the Ribbon.
3. Click the **Totals & Filters** tab near the top of the dialog box.
4. Click the box next to the **Show grand totals for columns** or **Show grand totals for rows** to add or remove the check mark. When the check mark appears in the box, totals will be added to the PivotTable Report.
5. Click the **OK** button at the bottom of the **PivotTable Options** dialog box.

### Adding Annotations and Objects

1. Activate the chart.
2. Click the **Layout** tab of the **Chart Tools** area on the Ribbon.
3. Click the **Text Box** icon to add an annotation or the **Shapes** icon to add an object. If adding an object, select an option after clicking the **Shapes** icon.
4. Click and drag on the chart to place and set the desired size of the text box or object.
5. Format the text box or object by activating it and right clicking, or using the icons in the **Format** tab of the **Drawing Tools** area on the Ribbon.

### Adding Data to a PivotTable

1. Click anywhere in the PivotTable Report to open the PivotTable Field. List and activate the **PivotTable Tools** tabs of the Ribbon.
2. Click a field in the PivotTable Field List, and drag it over to one of the sections of the PivotTable Report. You can also click and drag a field to one of the sections in the lower area of the PivotTable Field List.

### Adding Formulas (Calculated Fields)

1. Click anywhere in the PivotTable Report to activate the **PivotTable Tools** tabs on the Ribbon.
2. Click the **Formulas** icon in the **Options** tab of the Ribbon.
3. Select the **Calculated Field** option.
4. Type a name for the calculated field at the top of the **Insert Calculated Field** dialog box.
5. Build a formula by double-clicking the fields in the field list and typing mathematical operators in the formula input box.
6. Click the **OK** button to add the calculated field to the PivotTable Field List.
7. Click and drag the calculated field from the PivotTable Field List into the Data section of the PivotTable Report.

### Add-Ins

1. Click the **Office** icon.
2. Click the **Excel Options** button.
3. Click the **Add-Ins** category on the left side of the **Excel Options** dialog box.
4. Set the **Manage** dropdown box to **Excel Add-Ins**.
5. Click the **Go** button.
6. Select the desired feature(s) in the **Add-Ins** dialog box and click the **OK** button.

### Adjusting Column Widths

1. Place the cursor between 2 columns.
2. Click and drag to desired width or double click to automatically set to the widest data point.

Or

1. Highlight at least one cell in the columns you want to change.
2. Click the **Home** tab of the Ribbon.
3. Click the **Format** icon.
4. Select **Column Width**.
5. Enter a desired width number in the **Column Width** dialog box.
6. Click the **OK** button.

### Adjusting Row Heights

1. Place the cursor between 2 rows.
2. Click and drag to desired height or double click to automatically set to the largest data point.

Or

1. Highlight at least one cell in the rows you want to change.
2. Click the **Home** tab of the Ribbon.
3. Click the **Format** icon.
4. Select **Row Height**.
5. Enter a desired height number in the **Row Height** dialog box.
6. Click the **OK** button.

### AND Function

1. Activate a cell location where the output of the function should appear.
2. Type an equal sign, the function name AND, and an open parenthesis.
3. Create at least one but no more than 30 logical tests. Separate each logical test with a comma. *All* tests must be true to produce a TRUE output.
4. Type a closing parenthesis.
5. Press the **Enter** key.

### Applying Filters

1. Click any cell containing data in a worksheet with several adjacent columns.
2. Click the **Filter** icon in the **Data** tab of the Ribbon.
3. Click the drop-down arrow next to any of the column headings and select a filter option.

### Applying Subtotals

1. Sort your data based on columns where subtotals will be applied.
2. Click any cell containing data in a worksheet with several adjacent columns.
3. Click the **Subtotal** icon in the **Data** tab of the Ribbon.
4. Select a column where a subtotal will be added in the first drop-down box of the **Subtotal** dialog box.
5. Select a mathematical function in the second drop-down box.
6. Select columns that contain data to be subtotaled in the third box.
7. If you are adding multiple subtotals to a worksheet, make sure the Replace Current Subtotals is not selected.
8. Click the **OK** button in the **Subtotal** dialog box.
9. Use the **+/−** buttons to show or hide details for a specific subtotal.

### Auto Fill

1. Enter sequential data into at least 2 adjacent cell locations.
2. Highlight all cell locations containing sequential data.
3. Drag the cursor over the **Auto Fill Handle**.
4. When the cursor changes from a white to a black plus sign, click and drag across or down to continue the sequence of data.

### AutoSum

1. Activate the cell where the output of the function should appear. The cell location should be below or to the right of a range of cells that will be used in the function.
2. Click the **Formulas** tab in the Ribbon.
3. Click the down arrow next to the **AutoSum** icon.
4. Select a function.
5. Press the **Enter** key.

### Basic Formulas

1. Activate the cell where formula output should appear.
2. Type an equal sign.
3. Type or click a cell location that contains a value that will be used to compute the formula output.
4. Type a math operator.
5. Type or click a second cell location that contains a value that will be used to compute the formula output.
6. Press the **Enter** key.

### Basic Functions

1. Activate a cell where the output of the function should appear.
2. Type an equal sign.
3. Type the name of the function or double click a function name from the function list.
4. Type an open parenthesis if you typed the function name manually.
5. Type a range or click and drag a range of cells (if you are using specific cells not in a continuous range, type or click each cell and separate with a comma).
6. Type a closing parenthesis.
7. Press the **Enter** key.

### Borders

1. Highlight a range of cells where lines should appear.
2. Click the **Home** tab of the Ribbon.
3. Click the down arrow in the **Borders** icon .
4. Select a line style and placement option.

Or

1. Highlight a range of cells where lines should appear.
2. Click the **Home** tab of the Ribbon.
3. Click the down arrow in the **Borders** icon and select the **More Borders** option.
4. Select a color and line style on the right side of the window.
5. Select the placement of the line using the locator box or placement icons.
6. Click the **OK** button.

### Cell Color

1. Highlight range of cells to be colored.
2. Click the **Home** tab of the Ribbon.
3. Click the down arrow of the **Fill Color** icon .
4. Select a color from the palette.

### Changing Field Settings

1. Click a field name in one of the sections of the PivotTable Report.
2. Click the **Field Settings** icon in the **Options** tab of the Ribbon.
3. Select a statistical function in the **Summarize by** tab in the **Value Field Settings** dialog box.
4. Click the **Number Format** button to open the **Number** tab of the **Format Cells** dialog box to format the values in a field.
5. Click the **OK** button in the **Format Cell** dialog box (if opened).
6. Click the **OK** button in the **Value Field Settings** dialog box.

### Changing the Font Setting for New Workbooks

1. Open a blank Excel workbook.
2. Click the **Office Button**.
3. Click the **Excel Options** button.
4. Click the **Popular** section on the left side of the **Excel Options** dialog box.
5. Select a font style and size in the **When creating new workbooks** section of the **Excel Options** dialog box.
6. Click the **OK** button at the bottom of the dialog box.

### Complex Formulas

1. Activate the cell where formula output should appear.
2. Type an equal sign.
3. Type or click cell locations or type numeric values if necessary.
4. Use parentheses and math operators where necessary.
5. Check that each opening parenthesis has a closing parenthesis.
6. Press the **Enter** key.

### CONCATENATE Function

1. Activate a cell.
2. Type an equal sign followed by the function name CONCATENATE and an open parenthesis.
3. Identify data that you wish to combine and enter it into each argument of the function, followed by commas. Remember to use quotation marks if you are typing words or text into an argument.
4. Type a closing parenthesis.
5. Press the **Enter** key.

### Conditional Formatting

1. Activate the cell location where the conditional format will be applied.
2. Click the **Conditional Formatting** icon in the **Styles** group on **Home** tab of the Ribbon.
3. Select the **New Rule** option near the bottom of the **Conditional Format** list.
4. Select the **Format only cells that contain** option in the top section of the **New Formatting Rule** dialog box if your criteria are based on the value in a cell location.
5. Set the first drop-down box to **Cell Value**.
6. Select a comparison operator in the second drop-down box.
7. Type a value in the third box or use the range finder to select a cell location on your worksheet.
8. Click the **Format** button to open the **Format Cells** dialog box.
9. Set the formatting options that will be applied to the cell activated in step 1 if the conditions defined in steps 6 and 7 are true.
10. Click the **OK** button on the **Format Cells** dialog box.
11. Click the **OK** button on the **New Formatting Rule** dialog box.
12. Click the **Conditional Formatting** icon and select the **Manage Rules** option to edit or add additional rules to the same cell location.

### Copy and Paste

1. Highlight a cell or range of cells to be copied.
2. Click the **Copy** icon in the Ribbon.
3. Highlight a cell or range of cells where copied data should appear.
4. Click the **Paste** icon in the Ribbon.

### Creating a New PivotChart

1. Click the drop-down arrow of the **PivotTable** icon in the Insert tab of the Ribbon, and select the **PivotChart** option.
2. Define the Table/Range in the **Create PivotTable with PivotChart** dialog box. If a range is provided, check it to ensure it contains all the data that is required for your PivotChart. To create a new range, click the range finder, highlight the range of cells that contain data for the PivotChart, and press the **Enter** key.
3. Select either New Worksheet or Existing Worksheet near the bottom of the **Create PivotTable with PivotChart** dialog box and then click the **OK** button.
4. Click and drag fields from the upper area of the PivotTable Field List into one of the sections in the lower area.
5. Make any formatting adjustments to the PivotChart using the same commands and techniques that would be used for any Excel chart.

### Creating a New PivotTable

1. Click the drop-down arrow of the **PivotTable** icon in the **Insert** tab of the Ribbon and then select the **PivotTable** option.
2. Define the Table/Range in the **Create PivotTable** dialog box. If a range is provided, check it to ensure it contains all the data that is required for your PivotTable. To create a new range, click the range finder, highlight the range of cells that contain data for the PivotTable, and press the **Enter** key.
3. Select either New Worksheet or Existing Worksheet near the bottom of the **Create PivotTable** dialog box.
4. Click the **OK** button at the bottom of the **Create PivotTable** dialog box.

### Creating Charts

1. Highlight a range of cells that contain values that will be used to define the X- and Y-axes of the chart.
2. Click the **Insert** tab on the Ribbon.
3. Click one of the **Chart Type** icons in the **Charts** group on the Ribbon.
4. Select a chart format option based on the needs of your project and the desired visual appearance.
5. Click the **Switch Row/Column** icon (in the **Design** tab) if the data on the X- and Y-axes needs to be reversed.
6. Click the **Move Chart** icon (in the **Design** tab) to move the chart to another existing worksheet or place the chart in a separate chart sheet.
7. Click the **Layout** tab in the **Chart Tools** section on the Ribbon and click the **Chart Title** and/or **Axis Titles** icons to add or adjust boxes for the chart title or axis titles.
8. After adding a title box to the chart, click it twice to type a new title or description.

### Data Analysis: Regression

1. Click the **Data Analysis** icon in the **Analysis** group on the **Data** tab of the Ribbon.
2. Select **Regression** from the **Data Analysis** dialog box and click the **OK** button.
3. Click the range finder next to the **Input Y Range** box and highlight the range of cells that contain data for the dependent variable on your worksheet.
4. Click the range finder next to the **Input X Range** box and highlight the range of cells that contain data for up to 16 independent variables on your worksheet.
5. If you highlighted column headings in steps 3 and 4, click the box next to the **Labels** option.
6. Select a placement option for the Regression output.
7. Select any of the **Residual** and/or **Normal Probability** chart options at the bottom of the **Regression** dialog box.
8. Click the **OK** button.
9. Apply formatting adjustments to the data output and/or charts as needed.

### Data Analysis Tools: Descriptive Statistics

1. Click the **Data Analysis** icon from the **Analysis** group on the **Data** tab of the Ribbon.
2. Select **Descriptive Statistics** from the **Data Analysis** dialog box and click the **OK** button.
3. Click the range finder next to the **Input Range** box and highlight the range of data you wish to analyze on your worksheet or type the range in the box.
4. Select either Columns or Rows based on the orientation of your data.
5. If you highlighted labels in step 3, click the box next to the **Labels in First Row** option.
6. Select an option designating where the output calculations will appear.
7. Select **Summary Statistics** to produce a comprehensive output of statistical calculations.
8. Select any or all of the three remaining output options if necessary.
9. Click the **OK** button.
10. Apply formatting adjustments to the output as needed.

### Data Analysis Tools: Histograms

1. Click the **Data Analysis** icon from the **Analysis** group on the **Data** tab of the Ribbon.
2. Select **Histogram** from the **Data Analysis** dialog box and click the **OK** button.
3. Click the range finder next to the **Input Range** box and highlight the range of data for which you wish to calculate the frequency on your worksheet.
4. Click the range finder next to the **Bin Range** box and highlight the range of data that contains values that will be used for grouping the frequency results.
5. If you highlighted labels in step 3 and 4, click the box next to the **Labels** option.
6. Select a placement option for the Histogram results.
7. Select any combination of output options. You must select at least one option.
8. Click the **OK** button.
9. Apply formatting adjustments to the data output and/or chart as needed.

### Data Tables

1. Create a formula that will be used to produce the results of the table. Your formula *must* use cell references.
2. Type one set of alternate values, which will be substituted into one of the cell locations referenced by the formula in step 1. These values must be typed in *a row* to the right and *adjacent to* the formula created in step 1.
3. Type a second set of alternate values, which will be substituted into a second cell location that is referenced by the formula created in step 1. These values must be typed in the *column* directly below and *adjacent to* the formula created in step 1.
4. Highlight a range of cells that begins with the formula created in step 1 and covers all of the values typed for steps 2 and 3.
5. Click the **What-If Analysis** icon in the **Data** tab of the Ribbon and select the **Data Table** option.
6. In the **Data Table** dialog box, define the Row Input Cell with a cell location that will be used to substitute the values you typed for step 2.
7. Define the Column Input Cell with a cell location that will be used to substitute the values typed for step 3.
8. Click the **OK** button on the **Data Table** dialog box.

### DATE Function

1. Activate a cell.
2. Type an equal sign, the function name DATE, and an open parenthesis.
3. Define the **year**, **month**, and **day** arguments using numbers, cell locations, formulas, or functions.
4. Type a closing parenthesis.
5. Press the **Enter** key.

### DAY Function

1. Activate a cell.
2. Type an equal sign and the function name DAY.
3. Type an open parenthesis.
4. Enter a cell location that contains a valid date Serial Number or type a valid date Serial Number.
5. Type a closing parenthesis. You can also type a date enclosed in quotations, i.e. "10/21/2006".
6. Press the **Enter** key.

### Deleting Columns or Rows

1. Activate one cell in the row or column you want to delete.
2. Click the **Home** tab in the Ribbon.
3. Click the down arrow in the **Delete** icon in the **Cells** group.
4. Select the **Delete Sheet Columns** or **Delete Sheet Rows** options.

### Deleting Worksheets

1. Activate the worksheet you want to delete by clicking the worksheet tab.
2. Click the **Home** tab of the Ribbon.
3. Click the down arrow in the **Delete** icon in the **Cells** group.
4. Click the **Delete Sheet** option.
5. Check the worksheet carefully to make sure it is okay to delete.
6. Click the **Delete** button at the bottom of the warning box.

### Editing Data

1. Activate cell containing data.
2. Click in the formula bar.
3. Type edits in the formula bar.
4. Press the **Enter** key.

Or

1. Double click a cell with data.
2. Type edits.
3. Press the **Enter** key.

### Filters

1. Click the down arrow next to a field added to the PivotTable Report.
2. Select a filter option or specific value by clicking a check box.
3. Click the **OK** button.
4. Click the filter symbol next to a field and select the **Clear Filter** option to remove a filter.

### Formatting a Data Series

1. Activate a data series by clicking an image (i.e., bar, marker, pie section) one time. Or click an image a second time to activate a series point.
2. Click the **Format** tab in the **Chart Tools** set of tabs.
3. Click the **Shape Fill** icon and select a color from the palette to change the data series or series point color.
4. Click the **Shape Outline** icon and select a color from the palette, one of the **Weight** options, or one of the **Dashes** options.

### Formatting Data

1. Highlight a range of cells to be formatted.
2. Click the **Home** tab of the Ribbon.
3. Click one of the icons in the **Font** group of the Ribbon or open the **Format Cells** dialog box by clicking the button in the lower-right corner of the **Font** group.
4. If using the **Format Cells** dialog box, click the **OK** button after making a selection.

### Formatting Numbers

1. Highlight a range of cells containing numbers to be formatted.
2. Click the **Home** tab of the Ribbon.
3. Click one of the icons in the **Number** group of the Ribbon or open the **Format Cells** dialog box by clicking the button in the lower-right corner of the **Number** group.
4. If using the **Format Cells** dialog box, click the **OK** button after making a selection.

## Formatting the Plot Area

1. Activate the plot area by clicking it once.
2. Click the **Format** tab in the **Chart Tools** set of tabs.
3. Click the **Shape Fill** icon and select a color from the palette to change the plot area color.
4. Click the **Shape Outline** icon and select a color from the palette, one of the **Weight** options, or one of the **Dashes** options.

## Formatting Titles and Legends

1. Activate the legend or title by clicking it once.
2. Select any of the format icons in the **Home** tab on the Ribbon and/or the icons in the **Format** tab of the **Chart Tools** area on the Ribbon.
3. To access more detailed formatting controls, click the **Format Selection** icon in the **Format** tab to open the **Format Legend** or **Format Title** dialog box.
4. To edit the wording of a title, click it twice and type any adjustments.
5. To move the legend or titles, click and drag it.
6. To change the size of the legend or titles, click and drag on one of the sizing handles.

## Formatting X- and Y-Axes Labels

1. Activate the X- or Y-axis by clicking once anywhere along the axis.
2. Select any of the format icons in the **Home** tab on the Ribbon and/or the icons in the **Format** tab of the **Chart Tools** area on the Ribbon.
3. To access more detailed formatting controls such the axis scale, tick marks, or label position, click the **Format Selection** icon in the **Format** tab to open the **Format Axis** dialog box.

## Freeze Panes

1. Activate a cell that is below the row and to the right of the column you wish to lock in place when scrolling (except cell A1).
2. Click the **View** tab in the Ribbon.
3. Click the **Freeze Panes** icon.
4. Select the **Freeze Panes** option (select the **Unfreeze Panes** option to remove any locked rows and columns).
5. Use the **Freeze Top Row** or **Freeze First Column** options to lock the first column or row.

## Future Value Function

1. Activate the cell where output should appear.
2. Type an equal sign.
3. Type the function name FV or double click **FV** from the function list.
4. Type an open parenthesis (if you double clicked the function from the function list, this will already be added).
5. Define the following arguments:

   **rate**: Interest Rate

   **nper**: Number of Periods or Amount of time

   **pmt**: Payments (must use a negative sign)

   **[pv]**: Present Value

   **[type]**: When payments are made (1 = beginning of year; 0 = end of year)
6. Close the parenthesis.
7. Press the **Enter** key.

## Goal Seek

1. Create a formula or function that uses cell references to produce a mathematical result.
2. Select the **Goal Seek** option from the **What-If Analysis** icon in the **Data** tab of the Ribbon.
3. Type a cell location into the **Set Cell** box or use the range finder to click a cell on your worksheet. This cell location should contain the formula or function you created in step 1.
4. Type a number in the **To Value** box that you want the formula or function you created in step 1 to produce.
5. Type a cell location into the **By Changing Cell** box or use the range finder to click a cell on your worksheet. The cell location in this box must be a cell that is referenced in the formula or function created in step 1.
6. Click the **OK** button on the **Goal Seek** dialog box.
7. Click the **OK** button on the **Goal Seek Status** dialog box.

### Hide Columns and Rows

1. Highlight at least one cell in each column or row you want to hide.
2. Click the **Home** tab of the Ribbon.
3. Click the **Format** icon.
4. Select the **Hide & Unhide** option.
5. Select one of the **Hide** options from the submenu.

### HLookup

1. Activate the cell where output should appear.
2. Type an equal sign, the function name HLookup, and an open parenthesis.
3. Define the following arguments:
   a. **lookup_value**: Cell location that contains the value to be searched in a second worksheet.
   b. **table_array**: Range in a second worksheet or workbook that contains both the lookup value and data for the output of the function (the first row in this range *must* contain the lookup value).
   c. **row_index_num**: Number of rows in the table array range counting from top to bottom that contains data for the output of the function (count the first row as 1).
   d. **range_lookup**: Type the word False to find the exact match to the lookup value. This argument will assume True and look for an approximate match for the lookup value if this argument is not defined.
4. Type a closing parenthesis and press the **Enter** key.
5. Use an absolute reference ($) on the range of the table array segment if copying and pasting the function to other cells. You may also need an absolute reference on the lookup value depending on your project.
6. Check the row index number after pasting to see if any adjustments are necessary.

### Horizontal and Vertical Alignment

1. Highlight a range of cells to be formatted.
2. Click the **Home** tab of the Ribbon.
3. Click one of the **Vertical Alignment** icons 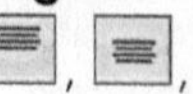,  to place data on the top, center, or bottom of a cell.
4. Click one of the **Horizontal Alignment** icons ,  to left justify, center, or right justify data in a cell.

### IF Functions and Nested IF Functions

1. Activate a cell where the output of the function should appear.
2. Type an equal sign, the function name `IF`, and an open parenthesis.
3. Create a test for the **logical_test** argument.
4. Define an output for the **[value_if_true]** argument (text outputs must be in quotation marks).
5. Define an output for the **[value_if_false]** argument or enter another **IF** function by typing the function name `IF` and an open parenthesis.
6. Type a closing parenthesis. If creating a nested **IF** function, type a closing parenthesis for each **IF** function that you started.
7. Press the **Enter** key.

### Importing Data from an Access Database

1. Activate a cell location in a worksheet where you would like to place the imported data.
2. Click the **From Access** icon in the **Data** tab of the Ribbon.
3. Select an Access database on your computer or network and click the **Open** button in the **Select Data Source** dialog box.
4. Select a table or query from the **Select Table** dialog box and click the **OK** button.
5. Select one of the three format options near the top of the **Import Data** dialog box.
6. Select or check the location for the data near the bottom of the **Import Data** dialog box and click the **OK** button.

### Importing Data from the Internet

1. Connect your computer to the Internet.
2. Activate a cell location in a worksheet where you would like to place the imported data.
3. Click the **From Web** icon in the **Data** tab of the Ribbon.
4. Enter a Web address in the Address box at the top of the **New Web Query** dialog box and press the **Enter** key.
5. Navigate the Web site from the **New Web Query** dialog box to identify the data you would like to import.
6. Select a table or tables of data by clicking the yellow boxes with black arrows and click the **Import** button at the bottom of the **New Web Query** dialog box.
7. Select a location in the **Import Data** dialog box.
8. Click the Properties button in the **Import Data** dialog box and select one of the data refresh options in the **External Data Range Properties** dialog box if needed.
9. Click the **OK** button in the **External Data Range Properties** dialog box if needed.
10. Click the **OK** button in the **Import Data** dialog box.

### Importing Text Files

1. Click the **From Text** icon in the **Data** tab of the Ribbon.
2. Select a text file on your computer or network from the **Import Text File** dialog box and click the **Import** button.
3. Follow the steps of the Text Import Wizard.
4. Click the **Properties** button in the **Import Data** dialog box.
5. Set the refresh and layout options in the **External Data Range Properties** dialog box and click the **OK** button.
6. Select the desired location for the data and click the **OK** button in the **Import Data** dialog box.

### Insert Columns or Rows

1. Activate a cell depending on where a blank column or row should be inserted. Rows are inserted above an active cell; columns are inserted to the left of an active cell.
2. Click the **Home** tab.
3. Click the down arrow in the **Insert** icon in the **Cells** group of the Ribbon.
4. Select **Insert Sheet Rows** or **Insert Sheet Columns**.

### Insert Function

1. Activate a cell where the output of a function should appear.
2. Click the **Formulas** tab in the Ribbon.
3. Select a function from one of the function category icons in the Function Library or click the **Insert Function** icon.
4. If using the **Insert Function** icon, select a function from the **Insert Function** dialog box and click the **OK** button.
5. Use the input boxes or range finders to define the arguments of the function in the **Function Arguments** dialog box.
6. Click **Help on this function** to see an expanded definition and instructions for building the function.
7. Click the **OK** button at the bottom of the **Function Arguments** dialog box.

### Inserting Worksheets

1. Click the **Insert Worksheet** tab at the bottom of the Excel screen.

### ISERROR Function

1. Activate a cell.
2. Type an equal sign.
3. Type the function name ISERROR and open parenthesis.
4. Type a cell location that contains a formula or function or type a formula or function.
5. Type a closing parenthesis.
6. Press the **Enter** key.

### ISNUMBER Function

1. Activate a cell.
2. Type an equal sign.
3. Type the function name ISNUMBER and open parenthesis.
4. Type a cell location.
5. Type a closing parenthesis.
6. Press the **Enter** key.

### ISTEXT Function

1. Activate a cell.
2. Type an equal sign.
3. Type the function name ISTEXT and an open parenthesis.
4. Type a cell location.
5. Type a closing parenthesis.
6. Press the **Enter** key.

### LEFT Function

1. Activate a cell.
2. Type an equal sign followed by the function name LEFT.
3. Type an open parenthesis and define the following two arguments:
   a. **text:** Cell location containing text data or typed text in quotation marks.
   b. **[num_chars]:** Number of characters the function will select from the text data in the **text** argument beginning from left to right.
4. Type a closing parenthesis and press the **Enter** key.

### LEN Function

1. Activate a cell.
2. Type an equal sign followed by the function name LEN.
3. Type an open parenthesis followed by a cell location containing text data, or type a text entry enclosed in quotation marks.
4. Type a closing parenthesis and press the **Enter** key.

### Linking Data between Workbooks

1. Open two workbooks.
2. Activate a cell location in the workbook where the data or output of a formula or functions should appear.
3. Type an equal sign, or type an equal sign and the beginning of a formula or function.
4. Click the name of the second workbook in the task bar.
5. Click a **Worksheet** tab that contains the data you wish to display or use in a formula or function.
6. Activate a cell location that contains the data you wish to display or use in a formula or function.
7. Press the **Enter** key, or complete the formula or function and then press the **Enter** key.

### Linking Data between Worksheets

1. Activate a cell location where the data or output of a formula or functions should appear.
2. Type an equal sign, or type an equal sign and the beginning of a formula or function.
3. Click a **Worksheet** tab that contains the data you wish to display in the first worksheet or use in a formula or function.
4. Activate a cell location that contains the data you wish to display or use in a formula or function.
5. Press the **Enter** key, or complete the formula or function and then press the **Enter** key.

### List Box

1. Click the **Insert** icon in the **Developer** tab of the Ribbon.
2. Click the **List Box** icon from the **Form Controls** options.
3. Click and drag the desired size of the List Box on your worksheet.
4. Click the **Properties** icon in the **Developer** tab of the Ribbon.
5. Click the **Control** tab at the top of the **Format Control** dialog box.
6. Click the range finder next to the **Input Range** box and then highlight a range of cells in one column that contains data displayed in the **List Box** window.
7. Click the range finder next to the **Cell Link** box and then activate a cell location that will be used to display the sequence number of the item selected in the List Box.
8. Choose a Selection Type.
9. Click the **OK** button in the **Format Control** dialog box.
10. Click any cell location on your worksheet to activate the List Box.

### Manually Defining a Column Chart

1. Activate a blank cell on a worksheet. A blank column or a blank row must appear between the data on a worksheet and the blank cell that is activated.
2. Select a chart type from the **Insert** tab on the Ribbon.
3. Select a chart format.
4. With the blank chart activated, click the **Select Data Source** icon in the **Design** tab on the Ribbon.
5. Click the **Add** button on the left side of the **Select Data Source** dialog box to add a data series.
6. Define the Series name in the **Edit Series** dialog box with one cell location or type a name in quotation marks.
7. Define the Series values with a range of cells.
8. Click the **OK** button to close the **Edit Series** dialog box.
9. Repeat steps 5–8 to add additional data series if needed.
10. Click the **Edit** button on the right side of the **Select Data Source** dialog box.
11. Use a range of cells to define the Axis Label Range. The descriptions in this cell range will be used for the X-axis labels.
12. Click the **OK** button on the **Axis Labels** dialog box.
13. Click the **OK** button on the **Select Data Source** dialog box.

### Merge Cells

1. Highlight a range of cells to be merged.
2. Click the **Home** tab of the Ribbon.
3. Click the down arrow of the **Merge & Center** icon and select an option.

### MID Function

1. Type an equal sign followed by the function name MID.
2. Type an open parenthesis and define the following three arguments:
   a. **text:** Cell location containing text data or typed text in quotation marks.
   b. **[start_num]:** Number of the first character that will be selected counting from left to right.
   c. **[num_chars]:** Number of characters that will be selected from the text data in the **text** argument beginning from the character number in the **[start_num]** argument from left to right.
3. Type a closing parenthesis and press the **Enter** key.

### MONTH Function

1. Activate a cell.
2. Type an equal sign and the function name MONTH.
3. Type an open parenthesis.
4. Enter a cell location that contains a valid date Serial Number or type a valid date Serial Number.
5. Type a closing parenthesis. You can also type a date enclosed in quotations, i.e. "10/21/2006".
6. Press the **Enter** key.

### Moving Data

1. Activate a cell or highlight a range of cells to be moved.
2. Move the cursor to the edge of the cell or range.
3. When the cursor changes to crossed arrows, click and drag.

### Moving Worksheets

1. Click and drag the worksheet tab.

### NPV Function

1. Activate cell where the output should appear.
2. Type an equal sign, the function name **NPV**, and an open parenthesis.
3. Define the following arguments:
   a. **rate**: The interest rate that is charged for a loan or a firm's cost to borrow money.
   b. **value1**: The initial investment for starting a new business or in an existing business. You must precede values or cell locations with a negative sign.
   c. **[value(n)]**: Cash generated by the end of the year for a new business or incremental cash generated by an existing business. Use a separate argument to add cash value for each year.
4. Type a closing parenthesis and press the **Enter** key.

### Opening Delimited Text Files in Excel

1. Click the **Office Button** and select the **Open** option.
2. Set the file type on the **Open** dialog box to Text Files.
3. Select a text file on your computer or network and click the **Open** button.
4. Select the **Delimited** option in step 1 of the Text Import Wizard.
5. Select a delimiter option in step 2 of the Text Import Wizard (i.e., select Comma for comma-delimited files, Tab for tab-delimited files, etc.).
6. If needed, make any format adjustments in step 3 of the Text Import Wizard.
7. Click the **Finish** button in step 3 of the Text Import Wizard.

### Opening Fixed-Width Files in Excel

1. Obtain a key that identifies the character position for each column in a fixed-width file.
2. Click the **Office Button** and select the **Open** command.
3. Set the file type on the **Open** dialog box to Text Files.
4. Select a fixed-width text file on your computer or network and click the **Open** button.
5. Select the **Fixed width** option in step 1 of the Text Import Wizard.
6. Set break lines in step 2 of the Text Import Wizard by clicking on the character numbers on the ruler.
7. Preview the arrangement of data in columns and make any necessary format adjustments in step 3 of the Text Import Wizard.
8. Click the **Finish** button in step 3 of the Text Import Wizard.

### OR Function

1. Activate a cell location where the output of the function should appear.
2. Type an equal sign, the function name OR, and an open parenthesis.
3. Create at least one but no more than 30 logical tests.
4. Separate each logical test with a comma. Only one test needs to be true to produce a TRUE output.
5. Type a closing parenthesis.
6. Press the **Enter** key.

### Paste Special

1. Copy a cell or range of cells.
2. Activate the cell where data is to be pasted.
3. Click the down arrow below the **Paste** icon to open the paste options list.
4. Select one of the paste options or select the **Paste Special** option to open the **Paste Special** dialog box.
5. If you are using the **Paste Special** dialog box, select an option and click the **OK** button.

### Pasting Charts into PowerPoint and Word

1. Activate a chart in an Excel file and click the **Copy** icon.
2. Open a PowerPoint file to a slide where the chart should appear. For a Word document, place the cursor where the chart should appear.
3. Click the **Home** tab in the Ribbon.
4. Click the down arrow below the **Paste** icon.
5. Select the **Paste Special** option to open the **Paste Special** dialog box.
6. Select the **Picture (Enhanced Metafile)** option and click the **OK** button in the **Paste Special** dialog box.
7. Adjust the size of the chart by clicking and dragging the sizing handles as needed.

### Payment Function

1. Activate a cell where output should appear.
2. Type an equal sign.
3. Type the function name PMT or double click **PMT** from the function list.
4. Type an open parenthesis (if you double clicked the function from the function list, this will already be added).
5. Define the following arguments:

   **rate**: Interest rate

   **nper**: Number of payments or period of time

   **pv**: Present value

   **[fv]**: Future value

   **[type]**: When payments are made (1 = beginning of year, 0 = end of year)
6. Close the parenthesis.
7. Press the **Enter** key.

### Printing Worksheets

1. Activate a worksheet to be printed.
2. Click the **Page Layout** tab of the Ribbon.
3. Make any necessary Page Setup adjustments by using the icons in the Ribbon or by opening the **Page Setup** dialog box.
4. Click the **Office Button**.
5. Click the side arrow next to the **Print** option and select **Print Preview** to view the document.
6. Click the **Print** icon in the **Print Preview** mode Ribbon.
7. Make any necessary settings in the **Print** dialog box.
8. Click the **OK** button in the **Print** dialog box.

### Renaming a Worksheet Tab

1. Double click the worksheet tab you wish to rename.
2. Type the new name.
3. Press the **Enter** key.

### Saving in Excel 97-2003 File Format

1. Open an existing Excel workbook or create a new one.
2. Click the **Office Button**.
3. Click the arrow to the right of the **Save As** option.
4. Click the **Excel 97-2003 Workbook** option on the right side of the **File** menu.
5. Select a location and type a file name in the **Save As** dialog box.

### Scatter Plot Charts

1. Activate a blank cell on a worksheet. A blank column or a blank row must appear between the data on a worksheet and the blank cell that is activated.
2. Click the **Scatter** icon in the **Insert** tab on the Ribbon.
3. Select a chart format.
4. With the blank chart activated, click the **Select Data Source button** icon in the **Design** tab on the Ribbon.
5. Click the **Add** button on the left side of the **Select Data Source** dialog box to add a data series.
6. Define the Series name in the **Edit Series** dialog box with one cell location or type a name in quotation marks.
7. Define the X Series values with a range of cells.
8. Define the Y Series values with a range of cells.
9. Click the **OK** button to close the **Edit Series** dialog box.
10. Repeat steps 5–9 to add additional data series if needed.
11. Click the **OK** button on the **Select Data Source** dialog box.

### Scenario Manager

1. Create a formula or function that uses cell references to produce a mathematical result.
2. Select the **Scenario Manager** option from the **What-If Analysis** icon in the **Data** tab of the Ribbon.
3. Click the **Add** button in the **Scenario Manager** dialog box.
4. Type a name for the scenario in the **Scenario Name** box.
5. Select cells that are referenced by the formula or function in step 1 by using the range finder, or type cells into the **Changing Cells** box, separating each cell location with a comma.
6. Click the **OK** button at the bottom of the **Edit Scenarios** dialog box.
7. Type values in the box next to each cell location that appears in the **Scenario Values** dialog box, then click the **OK** button.
8. Click the name of the Scenario you wish to apply to your worksheet in the **Scenario Manager** dialog box.
9. Click the **Show** button to apply the scenario selected in step 8 to your worksheet.
10. Click the **Close** button to close the Scenario Manager.

### Scroll Bar

1. Click the **Insert** icon in the **Developer** tab of the Ribbon.
2. Click the **Scroll Bar** icon from the **Form Controls** options.
3. Click and drag a vertical rectangle on your worksheet to define the size and placement of the Scroll Bar.
4. With the Scroll Bar - deactivated, click the **Properties** icon in the **Developer** tab of the Ribbon to open the **Format Control** dialog box.
5. Set the Current Value, Minimum Value, and Maximum Value based on the needs of your project (must be between 0 and 30,000).
6. Type a whole number in the **Incremental Change** box.
7. Type a whole number in the **Page Change** box.
8. Type the target cell location in the **Cell Link** box or use the range finder.
9. Click the **OK** button on the **Format Control** dialog box.
10. Click anywhere on your worksheet to activate the Scroll Bar.

### SEARCH Function

1. Activate a cell.
2. Type an equal sign followed by the function name SEARCH.
3. Type an open parenthesis and define the following three arguments:
   a. **find_text:** The character the function will search for in a text entry. Characters typed into this argument must be enclosed in quotation marks.
   b. **within_text:** The characters of the text data used to define this argument will be counted.
   c. **[start_num]:** Position in a text entry at which the function will begin searching for the character in the **find_text** argument. The function assumes 1 if not defined.
4. Type a closing parenthesis and press the **Enter** key.

### Show Formulas

1. Click the **Formulas** tab of the Ribbon.
2. Click the **Show Formulas** icon.
3. Click the **Show Formulas** icon again to display the formula outputs.

### Solver

1. Create a formula or function that uses cell references to produce a mathematical result.
2. Click the **Solver** icon in the **Analysis** group on the **Data** tab of the Ribbon to open the **Solver Parameters** dialog box.
3. Click the range finder next to the **Set Target Cell** box and highlight a cell location on your worksheet. This cell location should contain the formula or function you created in step 1.
4. Select one of the **Equal To** options based on the goals of your project. If you select the **Value Of** option, type a value in the box.
5. Click the range finder next to the **By Changing Cells** box and highlight cell locations that are directly or indirectly referenced by the formula you created in step 1.
6. Click the **Add** button in the **Solver Parameters** dialog box to enter any required constraints for your project.
7. Click the **Solve** button to calculate a solution.
8. Select either the **Keep Solver Solution** or **Restore Original Values** options in the **Solver Results** dialog box.
9. Click the **OK** button in the **Solver Results** dialog box.

### Sorting Data

1. Click a field in either the Row Fields or Column Fields section on the PivotTable Report.
2. Click the **Sort** icon in the **Options** tab of the Ribbon.
3. Select one of the sort options in the **Sort** dialog box.
4. If you selected the **Ascending or Descending** option in Step 3, click the down arrow next to the box below these options and then select a field that will be used to set the sort sequence.
5. Click the **OK** button.

## Sorting Data (Multiple Levels)

1. Highlight *all* the data on your worksheet that will be sorted.
2. Click the **Data** tab of the Ribbon.
3. Click the **Sort** icon in the Ribbon.
4. Click the **Options** button in the **Sort** dialog box and select the **Sort top to bottom** option if you are sorting a list of items.
5. Click the **OK** button in the **Sort Options** dialog box.
6. Select the **My data has headers** option if column headings are included in the range you highlighted for step 1.
7. Set the **Column**, **Sort On**, and **Order** options for the first sort level.
8. Add other sort levels as needed by clicking the **Add Level** button.
9. Click the **OK** button.

## Sorting Data (Single Level)

1. Activate a cell in the column you wish to use as the basis for sorting your data. The cell you activate must not be blank.
2. Make sure there are no blank columns separating data you wish to sort and the column containing the cell you activated in step 1.
3. Click the **Data** tab at the top of the Ribbon.
4. Click the **Z to A** (descending order) or **A to Z** (ascending order) icon in the **Sort & Filter** section of the Ribbon.

## SUMIF Functions

1. Activate the cell where output should appear.
2. Type an equal sign, the function name **SUMIF**, and an open parenthesis.
3. Define the following arguments:
   a. **range**: A range of cells that will be evaluated by data used to define the **criteria** argument.
   b. **criteria**: A logical test, cell location, value, and so on, that will be searched in the range used to define the **range** argument.
   c. **[sum_range]**: A range of cells containing values that will be summed if the data in the **criteria** argument is found in the range used to define the **range** argument. Define this argument only if the **range** argument does not contain the values that need to be summed.
4. Type a closing parenthesis and press the **Enter** key.

## TODAY Function

1. Activate a cell.
2. Type an equal sign.
3. Type the function name TODAY.
4. Type an open and then a closing parenthesis.
5. Press the **Enter** key.

## Trace Dependents

1. Activate a cell location that is referenced in a formula on a worksheet.
2. Click the **Formulas** tab on the Ribbon.
3. Click the **Trace Dependents** icon.
4. Use the **Remove Arrows** icon to remove the **Trace Dependents** arrow.

## Trace Precedents

1. Activate a cell location that contains a formula.
2. Click the **Formulas** tab on the Ribbon.
3. Click the **Trace Precedents** icon.
4. Use the **Remove Arrows** icon to remove the **Trace Precedents** arrow.

### Unhide Columns and Rows

1. Click and drag over to a cell on either side of the hidden column or row.
2. Click the **Home** tab of the Ribbon.
3. Click the **Format** icon.
4. Select the **Hide & Unhide** option.
5. Select one of the **Unhide** options from the submenu.

### Updating Workbook Links

1. Click the **Options** button in the Security Alert prompt.
2. Select the **Enable this content** option in the **Security Options** dialog box and click the **OK** button.

Or

1. Click the **Data** tab of the Ribbon.
2. Click the **Edit Links** icon.
3. Select the workbook link you wish to update from the **Edit Links** dialog box.
4. Click the **Update Values** button on the right side of the **Edit Links** dialog box.
5. Click the **Close** button at the bottom of the **Edit Links** dialog box.

### VLookup

1. Activate the cell where the output should appear.
2. Type an equal sign, the function name VLookup, and an open parenthesis.
3. Define the following arguments:
   a. **lookup_value**: Cell location that contains the value to be searched and matched in a second worksheet.
   b. **table_array**: Range in a second worksheet or workbook that contains both the lookup value and data for the output of the function (first column in the range *must* contain the lookup value).
   c. **col_index_num**: Number of columns in the table array range counting from left to right that contains data for the output of the function (count the first column as 1).
   d. **range_lookup**: Type the word False to find an exact match to the lookup value. This argument will assume True and look for an approximate match for the lookup value if this argument is not defined.
4. Type a closing parenthesis and press the **Enter** key.
5. Use an absolute reference ($) on the range used to define the **table_array** argument if pasting the function to other cells.

### Worksheet Tab Color

1. Click the worksheet tab where the color is to be changed.
2. Place the cursor over the worksheet tab.
3. Right click.
4. Select **Tab Color**.
5. Select a color from the color palette.

### Wrap Text

1. Highlight a range of cells to be formatted.
2. Click the **Home** tab of the Ribbon.
3. Click the **Wrap Text** icon .

### YEAR Function

1. Activate a cell.
2. Type an equal sign.
3. Type the function name YEAR.
4. Type an open parenthesis.
5. Enter a cell location that contains a valid date Serial Number or type a valid date Serial Number.
6. Type a closing parenthesis. You can also type a date enclosed in quotations, i.e. "10/21/2006".
7. Press the **Enter** key.

# Glossary

**Absolute Reference** The cell reference does not change when it is pasted to another cell location on a worksheet.

**Action Button** A Visual Basic control that you add to a worksheet and to which you assign a macro so that when a user clicks the button, the macro runs.

**Alignment** How data appears in a cell.

**Argument** The parts of a mathematical function that must be defined in order to produce a result.

**Ascending Order** Sorted in the order of lowest to highest.

**Auto Fill** Automatically completes a set of data points that are in sequential order, such as numbers, years, months, or days of the week.

**AutoFit Selection** This option automatically changes the width of a column to fit the width of the longest entered data.

**Basic Formula** Any equation that consists of two variables separated by a *mathematical operator* such as + (addition), – (subtraction), and so on.

**Borders** An Excel icon that provides several options for adding lines to a worksheet.

**Break Lines** Lines used in the Text Import Wizard to show where columns of data in a fixed-width text file begin and end.

**Break-Even Analysis** The process of determining how many units of product need to be sold to meet the costs of production.

**Cell** In Excel, the intersection of a row and a column.

**Cell Location** In Excel, the column letter followed by the row number.

**Cell Reference** A cell location that is used in a formula or function. Math calculations will use the value that is placed in this cell location to produce an output. This allows Excel to produce new mathematical outputs when one or more inputs are changed.

**Chart Legend** The reference area of a chart showing which color relates to each data series or category that is displayed in the chart plot area.

**Chart Sheet** A dedicated worksheet for a chart.

**Chart Tools** Tabs that are added to the right side of the Ribbon when a chart is created. The icons in these tabs are used to manage the chart appearance and data.

**Column Chart** Chart which displays data in vertical bars. Used mostly to compare data.

**Column Width** The width of a column which is adjusted to show text or numeric data that is entered into a cell.

**Comma-Delimited Text File** A file containing data that is separated into columns using the comma symbol. The comma is used to signal the end of one column and the beginning of another.

**Complex Formula** Any equation that consists of more than two variables and requires two or more mathematical operators.

**Data** Refers to any numbers or text items that will be analyzed or displayed on a spreadsheet.

**Data Entry** The most basic and fundamental Excel skill: typing information into a cell.

**Data Series** Refers to the image that appears on the chart, which is representing a category of values.

**Decision Structure** A programming structure that makes a comparison between program statements.

**Delimited Text File** A file containing data that is separated into columns. The method for separating or delimiting the file is usually a comma, space, or tab.

**Descending Order** Sorted in the order of highest to lowest.

**Dim Statement** The Dim (dimension) statement declares a variable.

**Embedded Chart** A chart that appears in an existing worksheet.

**Fill Color** A formatting technique used to change the color of the cells in a worksheet.

**Fixed Costs** Costs that do not change regardless of the number of units produced.

**Fixed-Width Text File** A file containing data that is not separated into columns. A key must be used to determine the character length for the beginning and end of a column.

**Footers** Used to display items such as the page number, file name, or worksheet tab name at the bottom of a printed document.

**For Next Statement** A repetition structure that repeats the execution of a series of program statements the number of times specified by a counter.

**Formatting** Excel commands used to enhance the visual appearance of a spreadsheet. Transforms the appearance of a basic spreadsheet into a professional-looking document and guides the reader's attention to the most critical information.

**Formula Auditing** Contains features that can be used for viewing and checking all formulas in a worksheet.

**Formula Bar** Used to change data after it has been typed into a cell location; always shows the contents of an active cell.

**Function** Used for specific types of mathematical, text, and date calculations.

**Future Value (FV)** Used to calculate the future value of an investment given a certain period of time, investment value, and interest rate.

**Gridlines** Horizontal and vertical lines that are visible on an Excel worksheet. Print settings are required for these lines to appear on a printed document. Also, the vertical and horizontal lines in the plot area of a chart.

**Headers** The area at the top of a printed document. Usually contains items such as the date, description of the document, or the file name.

**Histogram** The process of determining the frequency for a specific variable and presenting the data graphically in the form of a chart.

**HLookup** Is identical to the VLookup function; however, it looks horizontally across the first row of a range of cells to find a lookup value instead of vertically down a column.

**Horizontal Alignment** To center, left, or right justify data in a cell.

**Icon** Arranged in related groups and used to activate any Excel command.

**IF Statement** A statement used to create a decision structure by testing for one of two conditions. If the result of the test is true (or yes), one statement executes, but if the result of the test is false (or no), an alternative statement executes.

**Landscape** Printed orientation of a worksheet.

**Line Chart** Chart which displays data using lines and markers. Used for showing trends or comparing trends over time.

**Linking (Excel)** A cell reference which displays the contents of a cell in another worksheet or workbook. Often used when constructing spreadsheets for financial planning or accounting.

**Logical Function** A function that can be used to evaluate data and provide an output based on the results of a test.

**Logical Test** A test that uses comparison operators to evaluate the contents of a cell based on the contents of another cell location, a formula, constant, or text.

**Lookup Function** A function that looks for a value that exists in one worksheet in a second worksheet or workbook and returns another value based on settings that you define.

**Macro** A series of steps that are given a name and stored in an Excel workbook. Once a macro is created, the tasks it accomplishes can be run at any time.

**Macro Recorder** A tool in Excel that records each action you perform and stores these actions in a named macro.

**Margins** The space on the left, right, top, and bottom of a printed document.

**Mathematical Operator** Such as + (addition), – (subtraction), and so on.

**Merge Cells** Enables users to create one big cell out of several smaller cells; commonly used to center a title at the top of a spreadsheet.

**Mixed Reference** When a dollar sign appears before either the column letter or row number of a cell location.

**Object** An element in the host application. For Excel, examples of objects include a workbook, a worksheet, and a cell.

**Orientation** Either a *Portrait* or *Landscape* orientation for a document.

**Paste Special** Commands used to selectively paste contents that have been copied.

**Payment (PMT)** Function used to determine the payments of a mortgage or lease payments.

**Pie Chart** Used to show a percent-to-total comparison for various data categories.

**Plot Area** Area of a chart used to display a data series.

**Portrait** Printed orientation of a worksheet

**Present Value (PV)** Is used when a one-time investment is made to an account.

**Preview** Viewing a worksheet before printing.

**Print Area** Icon to use if you want to print only a portion of a worksheet.

**Print Titles** Duplicates the column headings or row headings of a worksheet on each page that is printed.

**Programming Structure** The sequence in which the program statements are executed at run time.

**Quick Access Toolbar** Contains a few commonly used icons, such as Save and Undo.

**Range** In Excel, a group of cells on a worksheet; noted by any two cell locations separated by a colon.

**3-D Reference** Using cell referencing to link data between two worksheets or workbooks.

**Refresh** To update data that has been imported into an Excel worksheet or used in a PivotTable or PivotChart. Items that need to be refreshed in order to see any change in data include Access databases, text files, and Web queries. Any data that is used in a PivotTable or PivotChart must be refreshed regardless of whether it is imported from an external data source or not.

**Regression** The process of determining the statistical significance of one variable explaining variations in a second variable when all other factors are held constant.

**Relative Referencing** Adjusts any cell references when a formula is copied and pasted to a new location on a worksheet.

**Repetition Structure** A programming structure that repeats the execution of a series of program statements.

**Ribbon** The area at the top of the screen in which Excel commands and features are contained.

**Row Height** Used to set a specific height for a row or group of rows.

**Scale** To manually reduce or enlarge the printed appearance of a worksheet.

**Security Alert** This prompt informs you that data is being linked to an external workbook and gives you the option of updating these links.

**Serial Number** A number that Microsoft assigns to a date. Each date has a unique serial number.

**Series Point** The method used to format the data series of a chart.

**Sizing Handle** Used to change the size of an object such as charts, chart components, text boxes, etc.

**Sorting** Used to rearrange data in a specific sequence or rank.

**Spreadsheet** A tool used to record numeric and text data for the purposes of making calculations, analyzing results, or tracking and storing information.

**Stack Column Chart** Shows the proportion or percentage that each category contributes to a total and can be used to show how this relationship changes over time.

**Status Bar** Area at the bottom of the Excel screen which shows items such as the Zoom slider and view icons.

**Tab** Located along the top of the Ribbon; opens a separate page of the Ribbon, which contains a different set of icons.

**Transposed** Data that has been reversed in its orientation on a worksheet (i.e. numbers in a column are displayed in a row). Also, the reversing of digits in a number.

**Variable** A declared element in program code that stores a value that can change and be retrieved while the application is running. Variables store values in memory, and the value can be changed any time during program execution.

**Variable Costs** Costs that increase when an additional unit of a product is produced.

**VBA** See Visual Basic for Applications.

**Vertical Alignment** To place data on the top, center, or bottom of a cell.

**Visual Basic Editor** The editor used by Microsoft Office 2007 to create or modify Visual Basic for Applications (VBA) code statements.

**Visual Basic for Applications (VBA)** A programming language included with Microsoft Office 2007 that stores the program code associated with macros.

**VLookup** A lookup function used mostly to display data from one worksheet or workbook into another.

**Web Query** The process of selecting tables of items from an Internet site to be imported into an Excel worksheet.

**What If Scenario** Used by business managers to understand how potential outcomes will affect the decisions they make.

**Workbook** The entire Excel file that contains a collection of worksheets.

**Worksheet** One page of an Excel file or workbook.

**Wrap Text** Automatically expands the row height and creates a second line to fit long entries.

**X-Axis** The bottom horizontal axis of a chart.

**Y-Axis** The vertical axis of a chart. Usually appears along the left side of a chart.

# Index

Page references followed by "f" indicate illustrated figures or photographs; followed by "t" indicates a table.